# Retail Management
## A Channels Approach

# Retail Management

## A Channels Approach

Roger A. Dickinson
*Rutgers University*

Wadsworth Publishing Company, Inc.
Belmont, California

Business Editor: Bruce Caldwell

Designer: Gary A. Head

Copy Editor: J. M. B. Edwards

Technical Illustrator: John Foster

ISBN 0-534-00318-4

L. C. Cat. Card No. 74-76122

Printed in the United States of America

2 3 4 5 6 7 8 9 10—78 77 76 75

*To Ruth, Robert, Roger,*
*Todd, and Bruce*

# Preface

There are several ways to present a course in retailing: (1) describe and analyze the institutions that deliver goods to the final consumer; (2) study the functions of retailing—for example, buying merchandise, pricing, advertising and display, services and personal selling, store location, and store design; (3) look at retailing as an economic activity; (4) focus on specific areas such as enterpreneurship and legal aspects of retailing.

Each of the above approaches has its advantages and limitations. To present the most comprehensive picture for students in their first retailing course, I have attempted to combine the approaches.

The book focuses on retail management throughout, with emphasis on the retailer's position in the distribution channel. The "channels" approach will (1) give students a better understanding of management functions by viewing retailers in their relationships with manufacturers, wholesalers, and consumers and (2) show the retailer as a persuasive force in the marketing chain whose success depends on the performance of the supplier as well as the consumer.

The book is designed for students of marketing who are going into retail management, marketing management, personal selling, sales management, advertising, and enterpreneurship. However, the book does not emphasize subjects easily taught in store training programs. Rather, the book is designed to give the student a competitive advantage in solving a variety of marketing and retailing problems. Several chapters (for example, Chapter 11, "Marginal Analysis," and Chapter 12, "Capital Budgeting") show how basic economic concepts and long-range financial planning are useful in retailing. The book does not presuppose,

however, that a student has had any previous training in economics or finance; the discussion is kept at an elementary level.

Many career opportunities exist in the retailing world, and this book attempts to encourage students to enter this challenging field. Many students tend to focus their career interests on employment possibilities in national and regional store chains. However, many opportunities are also available in smaller businesses, and a chapter on "Small Business and Enterpreneurship" is included for those interested in pursuing a career in this direction. The chapter on "Creativity" should interest those entering retailing businesses of all sizes. For those with an interest in the world of fashion, Chapter 17, "Fashion Management," should prove valuable.

Several pedagogical elements have been developed to aid readers: (1) chapter summaries and discussion questions bring out the main points of each chapter; (2) cases relate the content of the chapter to actual retailing practice, while discussion questions point up implications of the cases, and (3) references and suggested readings guide the student to more detailed knowledge of topics.

I wish to express my thanks to many individuals. In the academic world, Bert Duncan was an inspiration throughout. Marshall Howard created the chapter related to the legal environment. The framework for Part 3 was developed from the multistage approach of Alfred R. Oxenfeldt. Many of the chapters are enriched by the prolific work of Pete Bucklin, John Howard, Stanley Hollander, and Bill Cox. In addition, the comments of Bernard Codner, Stan Johnson, and James Donnelly were instrumental in altering the manuscript.

I also feel a debt to certain other writers of textbooks on retailing, including John Wingate, Dave Rachman, Don Thompson, Douglas Dalrymple, Bill Davidson, Al Doody, Rom Markin, and Ron Gist.

In the retailing world, I feel particularly indebted to Ken Kolker, Julie Seeherman, Hank Everett, Charlie Bernhaut, Joseph Nagy, and Robert Kahn.

I would also like to express my appreciation to J. M. B. Edwards for his extensive efforts in editing.

# Contents

# Part Three

# Part Four

# Part One

Part One communicates the dynamic nature of the retail world. Some of the institutions of retailing are described, and the importance and social implications of retailing are suggested. Retailing is then described as a system, and various theories of change are offered with regard to retail institutions over time. From here we consider two vital elements in the retail system: the supplier and the consumer. The supplier is of substantial concern to many retailers and often becomes a key partner with them in attracting consumers. Upon occasion, he may be more important in attracting consumers than the retailer. However, the retailer, in daily contact with the consumer, never has to be told of his or her importance. Indeed, few people in our society have to be told of the importance of their direct customers. Here, the retailer's approach to the consumer is distinguished from the marketer's and is analyzed in various respects. The efficiency and competitiveness of the retail world are also analyzed, and various criticisms of it are outlined. Entrepreneurship, small business, and franchising are considered in a retail context. Finally, the constraints of public policy on retailing are outlined from a legal perspective.

# 1

**Retailing affects** the lives of all of us. We buy in stores. We read the advertisements of various retailers. We pass a great many retail enterprises each day. Stores make up a key part of our cities and our society. It has even been suggested that before the twenty-first century is far advanced the average citizen may be born, raised, employed, wed, housed, and finally buried in a shopping center. This view may be a little extreme, but it is indeed quite likely that the shopping center will eventually become as much a place to live, go to school, or meet for cultural and religious activities as a place to shop.

The trend toward what might be called one-stop living is still a matter for speculation. But there is no doubt that retailing will powerfully affect the outcome, whatever it may be. For instance, any community that wants to plan its future environment will have to decide where to put its stores and what kinds of store to encourage. Older cities are decaying partly because many leading stores have followed their more affluent customers to the suburbs. Retail enterprises form a key dimension in the planning of most new cities. It is just possible that the future holds a place for a few tribes that will live entirely by hunting, fishing, or raising their own crops. But most people, wherever they live, will continue to depend on retailers for satisfying their increasingly complex needs and desires.

Retailing contributes to our society in many ways. By 1973, sales were running at a rate of over $500 billion a year. Table 1.1 shows the growth of retail sales for durable and nondurable goods over the two decades since 1950.

Dollar sales are just one measure of the retail sector's importance. After all, if an enterprise were to buy goods for $98 and sell them for $100, its dollar sales volume might be large but its total role in the economy might be quite unimportant. Hence the use of *value added* as an indicator of economic importance. Value added in retailing may be defined as the total amount received by retailers above the cost of the goods sold. By this measure, total value added by retail firms in 1973 can be estimated at about $125 billion, or some 10 percent of the entire *gross national product*.

# Retailing and Society

Table 1.1
Retail sales of durable and nondurable goods, 1951–72 ($ million)

|      | Durable | Nondurable | Total   |
|------|---------|------------|---------|
| 1951 | 54,579  | 102,069    | 156,548 |
| 1955 | 66,978  | 116,873    | 183,851 |
| 1959 | 71,608  | 143,805    | 215,413 |
| 1963 | 79,927  | 166,739    | 246,666 |
| 1967 | 100,173 | 213,636    | 313,809 |
| 1972 | 149,659 | 298,720    | 448,379 |

Source: For 1951–67, Statistical Abstract of the United States. 1970. p. 734; for 1972, Survey of Current Business. March, 1973, p. S-11. Prior to 1960, the data exclude Alaska and Hawaii. All figures are unadjusted, e.g., no allowance has been made for inflation.

Table 1.2
Employment in retailing, 1970

|                                         | Employees (millions) | Percent of work force |
|-----------------------------------------|----------------------|-----------------------|
| Food, bakery, and dairy stores          | 1.9                  | 2.5%                  |
| Eating and drinking places              | 2.3                  | 3.0%                  |
| General merchandise retailing           | 2.1                  | 2.7%                  |
| Motor vehicle retailing and service stations | 1.7             | 2.2%                  |
| Other retail trade                      | 4.2                  | 5.5%                  |
| Total                                   | 12.2                 | 15.9%                 |

Source: 1970 Census of Population, General and Economic Characteristics.

Retail firms are also a major source of employment. Definitions of retailing, as we shall see, vary a great deal, and employment figures from different sources may be difficult to reconcile. According to the *Survey of Current Business,* 11.8 million workers, representing about 16 percent of the labor force, were employed in retailing in 1972. The Census of Population for 1970 showed about 12.2 million employed in retailing (see Table 1.2). The figure has undoubtedly grown since then.

Retailing is not only a large employer but one of particular significance to the female population, and to both males and females between the ages of 16 and 24. The percentage of the retail *work force* that is female has risen steadily, from 29.2 percent in 1940 to 37 percent in 1950, 41.2 percent in 1960, and 45.8 percent in 1970. In 1970, women represented about 37.7 percent of the total work force and 36.2 percent of the nonretail work force. About one out of every five working females is employed in retailing, but only one in seven working males. Retail firms are also major employers of young people aged 16–24. One out of every four males in this age group works in retailing, and slightly more females work in retailing at this age than at other ages.

Dollars, of course, are not everything; having one's own small business still counts for a great deal. According to the *Statistical Abstract,* in 1967 about 74 percent of the retail establishments had less than four paid employees. In 1972, the number of retail establishments was estimated at 1,676,800. Indeed, the retail and service industries provide most of this country's small business opportunities.

Retailing helps keep alive the American tradition that it is each man's right to lose his shirt on a business once. Unfortunately, small retail enterprises seem to be on the decline. Since every year sees a drop both in the total number of stores and in the number per head of population, many small retailers are in trouble. This trend is discussed further in Chapter 6.

Another way to gauge the importance of retailing is by the size of the country's largest retail firms. Most have divisions that are household words in most parts of the country. The sales volume, assets, and net income of these firms are indicated in Table 1.3. Thus retailing is an interesting mixture of the very large and the very small.

## Perspectives on Retailing

It is generally agreed that most retailing involves stores. But not all stores belong to the retail sector. For example, cleaning stores and barber shops are classed with services by the U.S. Department of Commerce, although such stores sell merchandise upon occasion. Restaurants, on the other hand, are usually considered a part of retailing, although many of the things they do have at least a close relationship to the creation of services. In some ways restaurants might also be considered manufacturers.

If the distinction between goods and services is a hard one to apply, what about the distinction between stores and other commercial establishments? Laundromats, cleaning establishments, and so forth, would be stores under most definitions. But financial institutions such as banks have many of the characteristics of some retail operations, and might well be included. Even dentists, whose chief function is clearly to provide a service, also dispense gold, silver, and artificial teeth.

Another complicating factor is the highly local character of many retail enterprises. Generalizations about how retailers behave should always be taken with a grain of salt; there are many different types of retailer in many environments. The same caution applies to each of these types as commonly defined. For example, "the discount store" is a rather nebulous term often applied to stores quite different in size and character. Their main unifying feature is a preference for low prices, but occasionally they lack even that. All the same, the store remains the most logical starting point for the study of retailing.

### Store Retailing

Stores can be classified by type of product sold, as in Table 1.4. But the student should be very careful in interpreting such data. The retail scene is changing so rapidly that the Department of Commerce, which is the source of these classifications, has great difficulty in keeping the data comparable over time; many chain drugstores, for instance, sell large quantities of apparel and small appliances.

Another way of classifying the groups listed in Table 1.4 is by the percentage of the retail dollar each attracts. This is what has been done in Table 1.5, except that some of the groups have been combined. Even in this short period, certain trends are obvious—the decreasing percentage spent on food, for instance, and the fluctuating demand for automobiles.

Stores can also be classified by their percentage margin. High-margin stores are ones that offer a great deal of service and tend to sell a smaller amount of goods per dollar invested in inventory. Lower-margin stores tend to sell a lot of merchandise per dollar invested in inventory, but offer very few services. Food supermarkets and most discount stores might be considered low-margin units, while department stores are high-margin units.

Another useful way to group stores is by how they buy their merchandise; for example, stores that buy their merchandise centrally differ in numerous other ways from those that do not. Chain stores are an important element of retailing, and the competition between chain and nonchain units is an integral part of many kinds of retailing. It is also possible to classify retail firms in terms of the type of promotion they do and the amount of money they spend on it. Some firms promote heavily in newspapers; others rely more on radio or television. Some firms advertise a great deal and others hardly at all. The hard-sell approach of used car dealers is proverbial; florists and bookstores generally prefer a soft sell. Customer loyalty, type of clientele, corporate or noncorporate ownership—these and numerous other dimensions of retailing have also been used to classify stores.

### Nonstore Retailing

Most retailing—perhaps as much as 96 percent—is done by stores. However, this figure is misleading because some stores engage in nonstore retailing. Major department stores, for example, often sell via mail, solicit orders by phone, maintain vending machines, and sell in the home. When all this activity is taken into account, nonstore retailing adds up to as much as 10 percent of retail sales, or about $45 billion.

As important as nonstore retailing has become, it may be that we have seen nothing yet. Indeed, many observers feel that armchair buying, as they call it, will be the wave of the future. Much buying may be done by closed circuit television. The discount catalog showroom, discussed below, has been suggested as the beginning of such a movement, although presently the catalog showroom is a store.

Another form of potential retail business is

Table 1.3
The 15 largest retailing companies, 1973 (ranked by sales)

| Rank '72 | Rank '71 | Company | Sales[1] ($000) | Assets[2] ($000) | Rank | Net income[3] ($000) | Rank | Stockholders' equity[4] ($000) | Rank |
|---|---|---|---|---|---|---|---|---|---|
| 1 | 1 | Sears, Roebuck (Chicago) | 10,991,001 | 9,326,162 | 1 | 621,812 | 1 | 4,515,414 | 1 |
| 2 | 2 | Great Atlantic & Pacific Tea (New York) | 6,368,876 | 1,020,819 | 11 | (51,277) | 50 | 599,301 | 8 |
| 3 | 3 | Safeway Stores (Oakland) | 6,057,633 | 1,137,375 | 7 | 91,056 | 5 | 606,305 | 7 |
| 4 | 4 | J.C. Penney (New York) | 5,529,622 | 2,153,686 | 3 | 162,633 | 2 | 1,138,028 | 2 |
| 5 | 6 | S.S. Kresge (Troy, Mich.) | 3,875,183 | 1,383,439 | 5 | 114,674 | 3 | 779,726 | 6 |
| 6 | 5 | Kroger (Cincinnati) | 3,790,532 | 810,826 | 13 | 18,425‡ | 25 | 353,360 | 11 |
| 7 | 7 | Marcor (Chicago) | 3,369,321 | 2,522,949 | 2 | 72,672 | 7 | 957,214 | 3 |
| 8 | 8 | F.W. Woolworth (New York) | 3,148,108 | 1,719,865 | 4 | 79,165 | 6 | 891,331 | 4 |
| 9 | 9 | Federated Department Stores (Cincinnati) | 2,669,956 | 1,380,449 | 6 | 108,573 | 4 | 826,376 | 5 |
| 10 | 11 | Jewel Companies (Chicago) | 2,009,294 | 578,238 | 18 | 29,866 | 15 | 238,113 | 18 |
| 11 | 13 | Lucky Stores (Dublin, Calif.) | 1,988,376 | 401,447 | 24 | 30,500 | 14 | 154,882 | 28 |
| 12 | 10 | Food Fair Stores (Philadelphia) | 1,980,458 | 428,088 | 23 | (1,398)‡ | 48 | 134,506 | 33 |
| 13 | 12 | Acme Markets (Philadelphia) | 1,861,588 | 370,020 | 27 | 12,426 | 29 | 191,489 | 24 |
| 14 | 14 | Winn-Dixie Stores (Jacksonville) | 1,833,572 | 273,553 | 34 | 39,164 | 10 | 198,623 | 22 |
| 15 | 16 | W.T. Grant (New York) | 1,648,500 | 1,110,698 | 8 | 37,787 | 11 | 334,339 | 13 |

Source: The Fortune Directory, 1973.

[1] Net sales, including all operating revenues and including revenues from discontinued operations when they are published. For companies not on a calendar year, the 1972 figures are for any fiscal year ending no later than March 1, 1973. Sales of subsidiaries are included when they are consolidated.

[2] Total assets employed in business at year's end, less depreciation and depletion.

[3] After taxes and after special items when they are shown on the income statement. Figures in parentheses indicate net loss. A double asterisk (**) signifies a credit representing at least 10 percent of earnings shown. a double dagger (‡) a charge of at least 10 percent.

[4] Sum of capital stock, surplus, and retained earnings at the end of the fiscal year.

[5] Year-end, unless followed by a dagger (†), in which case average for the year.

growing at a substantial rate outside the traditional retail structure and is not technically a part of retailing because the customer is not the final user. This is the so-called nonconsumer business, which includes sales to the government and other institutions, whether nonprofit or commercial. Sales of this kind account for as much as 50 percent of the food, major appliance, and floor covering businesses. The initial purchasing for completely new cities will probably be nonconsumer business in this

Table 1.4
Retail sales for selected types of business, 1972

|  | $ billion |
|---|---|
| Passenger car, other auto dealers | 81.5 |
| Tire, battery, and accessory dealers | 7.1 |
| Furniture. home furnishing stores | 12.6 |
| Household appliance | 7.0 |
| Lumber, building materials | 16.0 |
| Hardware stores | 4.1 |
| Apparel group | 22.0 |
| Drug and proprietary | 14.5 |
| Eating and drinking | 33.9 |
| Food group | 95.0 |
| Gasoline | 31.0 |
| Department stores | 46.3 |
| Mail order (department store merchandise) | 5.0 |
| Variety stores | 7.8 |
| Liquor | 9.2 |

Source: Survey of Current Business. March, 1973, p. S-11.

Table 1.5
How America spends its retail dollars

|  | 1967 | 1968 | 1969 | 1970 | 1971 | 1972 |
|---|---|---|---|---|---|---|
| Total retail sales in billions | $310 | $342 | $363 | $376 | $409 | $448 |
| Furniture and appliances | 4.7% | 4.9% | 4.8% | 4.7% | 4.5% | 4.8% |
| Hardware and lumber | 4.0% | 4.2% | 4.1% | 4.1% | 4.3% | 6.0% |
| Automotive sales | 17.9% | 19.2% | 18.8% | 17.3% | 19.3% | 19.7% |
| Filling stations | 7.3% | 7.3% | 7.1% | 7.5% | 7.1% | 6.9% |
| Clothing | 5.4% | 5.6% | 5.5% | 5.3% | 5.1% | 4.9% |
| Food stores | 22.6% | 21.7% | 23.0% | 22.9% | 21.8% | 21.2% |
| Eating and drinking establishments | 7.7% | 7.5% | 7.4% | 7.9% | 7.6% | 7.5% |
| Pharmacies | 3.5% | 3.4% | 3.4% | 3.6% | 3.4% | 3.3% |
| All others | 26.9% | 26.2% | 25.9% | 26.7% | 26.9% | 26.7% |

Source: For 1967–71, 38th Annual Nielsen Review of Retail Drug Store Trends. p. 14; for 1972, Progressive Grocer, April, 1973, p. 96.

| Employees[5] | Rank | Net income as percent of: Sales % | Rank | Equity % | Rank | '72($) | '71($) | '62($) | Growth rate 1962–72[6] % | Rank | Combined return 1972[7] % | Rank | 1962–72 Average[7] % | Rank |
|---|---|---|---|---|---|---|---|---|---|---|---|---|---|---|
| 380,000† | 1 | 5.7 | 1 | 13.8 | 13 | 3.98 | 3.56 | 1.54 | 9.96 | 21 | 14.69 | 9 | 13.68 | 14 |
| 123,600 | 5 | | | | | (2.06) | 0.59 | 2.39 | – | | (18.68) | 29 | (3.51) | 41 |
| 105,613 | 7 | 1.5 | 26 | 15.0 | 8 | 3.55 | 3.14 | 1.53 | 8.78 | 23 | 24.32 | 6 | 10.33 | 25 |
| 175,000 | 3 | 2.9 | 11 | 14.3 | 11 | 2.86 | 2.46 | 1.10 | 10.03 | 20 | 25.17 | 5 | 17.99 | 8 |
| 112,000† | 6 | 3.0 | 10 | 14.7 | 10 | 1.00 | 0.85 | 0.09 | 27.23 | 2 | 47.14 | 1 | 47.15 | 1 |
| 52,119 | 12 | 0.5 | 41 | 5.2 | 42 | 1.37‡ | 2.41‡ | 1.62 | (1.66) | 41 | (30.86) | 40 | 3.53 | 33 |
| 128,224‡ | 4 | 2.2 | 15 | 7.6 | 36 | 2.17 | 1.64 | 0.75ˣ | 11.21 | 17 | (3.92) | 19 | 8.90 | 27 |
| 200,000† | 2 | 2.5 | 13 | 8.9 | 31 | 2.60 | 2.31 | 1.47‡ | 5.87 | 33 | (28.09) | 38 | 7.64 | 29 |
| 84,300† | 8 | 4.1 | 5 | 13.1 | 15 | 2.46 | 2.20 | 1.08 | 8.58 | 24 | 9.49 | 12 | 12.47 | 20 |
| 33,466 | 21 | 1.5 | 28 | 12.5 | 16 | 4.00 | 3.61 | 1.90 | 7.73 | 27 | (11.50) | 22 | 8.18 | 28 |
| 32,500 | 22 | 1.5 | 25 | 19.7 | 3 | 0.97 | 0.99 | 0.12 | 23.24 | 6 | (13.99) | 24 | 30.90 | 2 |
| 30,000 | 24 | | | | | (0.20)‡ | 1.52 | 1.54 | – | | (39.75) | 44 | (3.45) | 40 |
| 36,101 | 18 | 0.7 | 37 | 6.5 | 38 | 3.57 | 4.30 | 3.87ʸ | (0.80) | 39 | (39.66) | 43 | (2.70) | 39 |
| 34,050 | 20 | 2.1 | 17 | 19.7 | 2 | 2.97 | 2.60 | 1.38 | 7.97 | 26 | 28.14 | 4 | 12.79 | 16 |
| 75,000† | 9 | 2.3 | 14 | 11.3 | 20 | 2.70 | 2.51 | 0.72 | 14.13 | 14 | (4.98) | 20 | 19.93 | 6 |

[6] *Average annual growth rate, compounded. No figure is given if the company had a loss in either 1972 or 1962.*
[7] *Percentages shown are the returns received by the hypothetical investor described in footnote 8. The ten-year figures are annual averages, compounded. Where corporations were substantially reorganized—e.g., because of mergers—the predecessor companies used in calculating combined returns are the same as those cited in the footnotes dropped from the earnings-per-share figures.*
ˣ *Figure is for Montgomery Ward.*
ʸ *Figure is for American Stores.*

sense. Retailers do not appear well attuned to these new sources of income.

Apart from telephone selling, the three principal forms of nonstore retailing are vending, house-to-house selling, and mail order.

**Vending** Selling through coin-operated machines—known in the retail trade as vending—has grown steadily since the late twenties. In recent years the growth has been quite spectacular, from $3.8 billion in sales in 1965 to $6.9 billion in 1972. Part of this growth in dollar volume can be accounted for by higher cigarette prices, as well as higher taxes. Nevertheless, as Table 1.6 shows, Americans find it convenient to buy a wide variety of products from machines.

Vending, however, is not the great labor saver and expense reducer that it is often depicted to be. Vending machine operators, as Douglas J. Dalrymple and Donald L. Thompson point out, have an average labor expense of 10 percent. This is higher than the labor expenses for many small chains and is only slightly lower than the figure given by the Census

**Table 1.6a**
*Total retail sales through vendors, 1962 and 1968–72 ($ million)*

| 1962 | 1968 | 1969 | 1970 | 1971 | 1972 |
|---|---|---|---|---|---|
| $2,956.0 | $4,956.2 | $5,666.0 | $6,223.0 | $6,514.9 | $6,906.0 |

**Table 1.6b**
*Retail sales through vendors, 1972, by product*

| Product | Percent share | Volume ($ million) |
|---|---|---|
| Hot drinks | 7.7% | $533 |
| Cup cold drinks | 7.5% | $517 |
| Canned cold drinks | 9.3% | $641 |
| Bottle cold drinks | 9.7% | $668 |
| Packaged confections/snacks | 10.2% | $707 |
| Bulk vending | 2.6% | $176 |
| Milk | 2.3% | $155 |
| Ice cream | 0.6% | $42 |
| Pastries | 1.5% | $105 |
| Hot canned foods | 1.2% | $84 |
| All-purpose vendor foods | 4.6% | $320 |
| Cigarettes | 33.5% | $2,315 |
| Cigars | 0.3% | $22 |
| All other | 9.0% | $621 |
| Total | 100% | $6,906 |

Source: *Vend, May, 1973.*

of Business for all retail firms, which is 11.5 percent. In addition, the machines used by vendors depreciate rapidly, and the best locations for them usually command high rents.

**House-to-house selling**   Direct selling to consumers is a growing area of both marketing and retailing. The firms that regard themselves as mainly engaged in direct selling did about $4 billion in business in 1973! This figure was arrived at by adding together the sales figures of the larger direct sale firms such as Avon, Electrolux, Fuller Brush, and Grolier, and then adding in $1 billion or so for the many smaller firms. However, if one considers the various stores that, like Sears, also sell house to house, especially in the home improvement field, it is possible to reach an estimate as high as $10 billion for the total volume of annual direct sales. The largest firms in the $4 billion segment of the industry tend to be in cosmetics, education (particularly encyclopedias), home appliances, and cleaning agents. The industry claims to employ approximately 3 million people, most of whom work part-time. One firm is reported to employ half a million people in sales alone. Firms that sell directly to the consumer emphasize high margins with high quality. Much of the merchandise sold directly to the consumer is specially made for that purpose and cannot be found in stores.

House-to-house firms generally regard themselves as immune from shopping center competition, including the creation of new centers. By selling to consumers, manufacturers eliminate wholesale and retail channels, and thus control the selling effort all the way to the final user of the product. But most manufacturers continue to prefer the traditional retail channels. We shall see in Chapter 3 what this preference implies.

**Mail order**   A retail mail order establishment receives its orders by mail, and makes its deliveries by mail, parcel service, railway express, truck, freight, or any combination of these. In 1973 the total volume of mail order business could be conservatively estimated at about $4 billion. From 1960 to 1970, according to the *Wall Street Journal,* the number of catalog houses in the United States grew from 2,000 units to 5,000. The Census of Business reports that the dollar volume of mail order grew 30 percent between 1963 and 1967.

The first need of a mail order house is a good list of prospective customers. In recent years, lists of credit card holders have been sold for this purpose. Such lists furnish access to highly specialized markets.

The concept of mail order is far from new. It was in the early 1870s that Montgomery Ward established the first American company operating exclusively on a mail order plan. Sears followed in 1888. The initial growth of mail order business was fostered by the isolation of the farmer from the trading centers of the day, the great variety offered by the early mail order firms, their low prices, and — last but not least — improvements in the postal system. Today's mail order houses perform many functions. For instance, they can often obtain a large enough volume from unique offerings to justify selling an item that a local store could not possibly handle profitably. Customers can also be segmented far more closely than is possible for most retail stores: Penney's "large man" catalog is one example. The Book-of-the-Month Club is able to serve readers in areas where there are too few of them to support even a small book store. This is because, like many other mail order houses, it regards the total nation as its potential market. The savings obtained by mail order purchases are often eaten up by freight and postal charges. But the convenience of shopping by mail is of prime importance to many customers, especially affluent, highly educated ones with crowded schedules and complicated needs. It is interesting to speculate about the future of mail order. The proliferation of specialized clubs for readers, listeners, and viewers makes it a growing segment of the leisure industry.

### Some Key Developments

The institutions that make up the retail world have changed over the years to match the changing needs and desires of consumers. The trading posts, often called the first American retail institutions, were created to meet the needs of both settlers and Indians. The Yankee peddler carried his business into many geographic areas not previously covered by the trading posts; he even carried goods directly to the pioneers. The general store evolved to serve a more settled society; until the latter part of the nineteenth century it had no serious competitor. Today, it is hard to decide which elements in the retail scene are of most interest.

Automotive dealers control very large volume, but there are over four times as many restaurant proprietors. In terms of their social significance, perhaps consumer cooperatives deserve pride of place. This author has somewhat arbitrarily decided to discuss shopping centers and chain stores first, followed by franchising, supermarkets, department stores, discount stores, drugstores, and catalog showrooms. Merely to recite this list is to taste something of the variety and dynamism of today's retail scene.

### Shopping Centers

The shopping center is a growing element of retail trade that dramatically affects most of our lives. In 1972, according to a trade source, about 44 percent of all sales of shopping center kinds of item, or $123.5 billion, were done in shopping centers. *Business Week* reports that at the end of 1955 there were 1,000 centers; in 1964 the number advanced to 4,500, and to as many as 12,000 in 1971.

A shopping center has been defined by the Urban Land Institute as a group of commercial establishments planned, developed, owned, and managed as a unit related in location, size, and type of shop to the trade area that it services, and providing on-site parking in definite relationship to the types and sizes of store it contains. This definition applies mainly to the large, planned centers built since World War II in response to the growth of automobile traffic and shift of population to the suburbs. These centers are getting larger. Regional shopping centers used to be planned around one major department store; now there may be five or more, surrounded by parking lots that can accommodate anywhere from 3,000 to 9,000 cars. Large shopping centers—ones with 100 to 200 stores—may have 15 or 20 dress shops, 10 to 15 women's shoe stores, and so on, since their main attraction to the consumer appears to be fashion. More and more of them are featuring all-weather protection, which gives them a definite advantage over open-air centers of equal size.

Shopping centers are becoming integral parts of communities. In one of the *new towns*, a development may have 3,000 apartments set among 32 acres of parks, lakes, swimming pools, and other community facilities that complement a 1.5 million square foot shopping center. Facilities on this scale undoubtedly lead to customers with less store loyalty; there are just too many stores to choose from. Indeed, the promotional efforts of competing centers encourage loyalty to the individual center rather than the stores it contains. The logical consequence of such competition may well be the kind of "one-stop living" referred to earlier.

It is not generally realized that shopping centers charge different rents to different kinds of tenant. The large department store is a very powerful attraction and therefore pays a relatively low rent—perhaps as little as $1.00 per square foot, or even less when the store constructs its own building. The smaller tenant, who feeds off the traffic generated by the larger stores, may pay anything from $5.00 to $15.00 per square foot. In addition, each tenant usually pays a stipulated percentage for rent based upon gross retail sales. The percentage can be as low as one-quarter of one percent for a large department store or as high as 10 percent for small tenants. The advantages of size are obvious. Size, however, can be a liability if it is not combined with the right location. This aspect of shopping center development is discussed in Chapter 10.

### Chain Stores

A retail chain can be said to consist of two or more stores that are similar, are centrally owned, and in some degree are centrally managed. By this definition, most large American stores are parts of chains, though the Census of Business now puts the minimum number of stores in a chain at 11. In any case, the development is not a new one. The Great Atlantic and Pacific Company, today's A & P, is generally thought to have established the first chain, in 1859; it carried coffee, spices, and a few other food products. In 1879, F. W. Woolworth opened the first chain store outside the grocery field.

The concept soon caught on, but the major period of expansion for chain stores came after World War I, from 1918 to 1929. Over this period chains of two or more stores captured some 30 percent of all retail business, up from only 4 percent in 1919. From 1929 to 1948 there was a decrease in the number of chain units, but their percentage of retail business remained about the same. By 1967 that percentage had risen to almost 40, and there were more chain units. The trend has definitely been in favor of the larger chains; in 1964 chains of 11 or more units did over 26 percent of all retail business, and this progressed to 30.7 percent in 1972. The figures for the last few years indicate that the percentage of business done by chains appears to be remaining about the same. As Table 1.7 shows, the impact of these chains varies a good deal by product area.

### Franchising

The two keys to franchising are *constrained decision making* and the use of an *accepted format* for doing business. Constrained decision making means that the person to whom the franchise is granted — the franchisee — is limited in his discretion, either legally, in the form of a contract, or by some other means such as persuasion. What this means in practice is that the franchisee is given effective control over few aspects of the decisions affecting his end of the business, but is expected to become quite proficient in them. In essence, the small businessman who buys a franchise, whether he is selling a product such as fried chicken or automobiles, or providing a service, such as repairing mufflers or managing a motel, is told by the franchisor: "Do not think. Do not become a manager in the broad sense. We will do most things for you. Perform your functions well, and we will make a great deal of money together."

*Table 1.7*
*Multiunit sales as a percentage of all retail sales, by type of business, 1971*

| | |
|---|---|
| Tire, battery, and accessory dealers | 30.7% |
| Furniture and appliance group | 8.6% |
| Men's and boys' wear stores | 15.9% |
| Women's apparel, accessory stores | 25.9% |
| Shoe stores | 42.4% |
| Drug and proprietary | 34.2% |
| Eating and drinking | 8.7% |
| Food group | 51.5% |
| Department stores (excluding mail order sales) | 87.0% |
| Variety stores | 77.4% |

Source: Statistical Abstract of the United States, 1972, p. 740.

Large franchisors dominate franchising. The domination of the automobile manufacturers is obvious. Even in such recently established areas of franchising as fast foods (roadside hamburgers, fried chicken, etc.) or recreational services (bowling alleys are a leading example), 62 companies have 500 or more units each. Franchising permeates much of retailing. Gasoline service stations, soft drink bottling plants, motels, and, of course, the aforementioned fast food establishments are all operated under franchise. Retail sales in franchising were expected to reach about $142 billion in 1973, up from $130 billion in 1972. Thus about 30 percent of retail sales are accounted for by franchising (Figure 1.1). Further material on franchising will be found in Chapter 6.

### Supermarkets

Many of the characteristics of today's supermarkets were present in Henry Ford's company stores and in other types of retail outlet as early as 1919. However, the first real supermarket is generally thought to have appeared in about 1930. It is hard to give a more precise date because of lack of agreement on what a supermarket is. The Super Market Institute defines a supermarket as a "complete, departmentalized food store with a minimum sales volume of one million dollars a year and at least the grocery department fully self-service." Another trade source prefers to set the minimum sales volume at

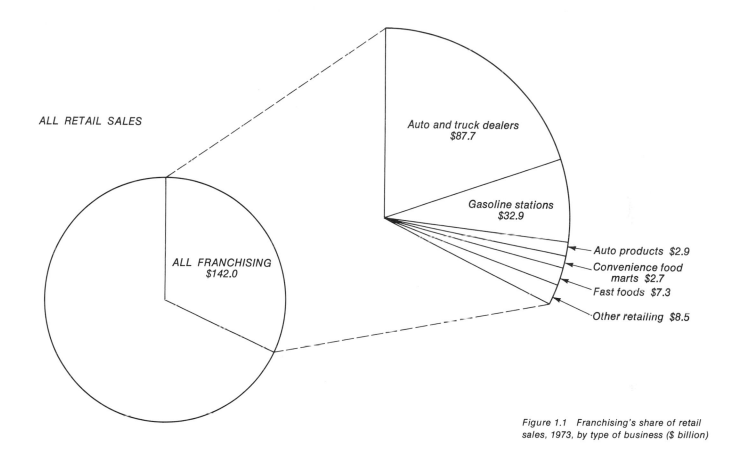

ALL RETAIL SALES

ALL FRANCHISING
$142.0

Auto and truck dealers
$87.7

Gasoline stations
$32.9

Auto products $2.9

Convenience food
marts $2.7

Fast foods $7.3

Other retailing $8.5

*Figure 1.1   Franchising's share of retail
sales, 1973, by type of business ($ billion)*

$150,000 a year. Supermarkets in the latter sense did over 77 percent of the food business in 1972. At the other end of the scale, the stores of one chain averaged over $9.5 million in sales for 1972–73. With only 38 percent of the stores, the supermarkets and superettes account for almost 90 percent of sales (Figure 1.2).

It is not easy to say exactly why supermarkets are so successful. They began by offering lower prices than the neighborhood grocery. Today, however, consumers in metropolitan areas generally have several supermarkets to choose from, and price is not always the decisive factor. Atmosphere seems to be important to many shoppers, as is the variety of

services offered under one roof. For these reasons, perhaps, the supermarkets now being built appear to be competing in size as much as anything.

### Department Stores

Any department store worthy of the name sells at least three categories of merchandise: furniture, home furnishings, and appliances; apparel for men, women, and children; and household linens and dry goods. Today the department store does more business in its suburban stores than downtown. Its high level of service usually requires a high margin—about 42 percent according to *The*

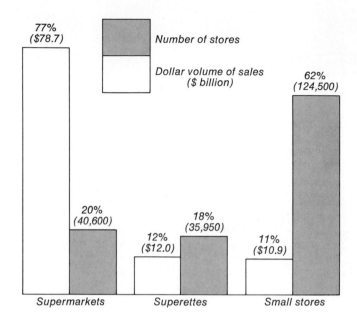

Figure 1.2   U.S. food retailing, 1972: dollar sales, by type of store (Source: Adapted from Progressive Grocer, April, 1973, p. 97. Convenience stores are contained in both the superette and the small-store categories, with about 70 percent in the former.)

*New York Times.* Besides service, department stores generally emphasize fashion. As their name implies, they have many departments, with managers in charge of each, and appeal to customers of all incomes (though the more regular the customer, the more affluent that person tends to be). They also cultivate different types of images. Some appeal to consumers of high income; others may stress youth, fashion consciousness, or the excellence of individual departments. Whatever their image, most department stores regard women as their main clientele.

Many customers travel a long way to get to department stores. A study presented in 1972 by the Westinghouse Broadcasting Company found that 64 percent of the customers of traditional department stores thought that it took 15 minutes or more to reach them. This is one reason why regional shopping centers bid aggressively to obtain leading department stores as "anchors."

The Census of Business has not yet found a useful way to distinguish between department stores and discount stores, and it is therefore necessary to consult trade sources. One of these, the *Discount Merchandiser*, puts the volume of traditional department store sales at about $17.5 billion for 1971.

### Discount Stores

The major growth of discount stores as we know them today has taken place since the end of World War II, although stores that sell at substantially lower prices than other stores have been with us much longer than that. Discount stores often carry the same kind of merchandise as traditional department stores, but they tend to have lower margins and correspondingly fewer services for the customer.

There is evidence that the discount stores are becoming more and more like department stores; for instance, they are carrying a larger assortment of merchandise. Low prices, however, remain the big draw, even though the low-price image has lost some of its attraction for the woman shopper. The rise of discount retailing has been a rapid one, from only $2 billion in sales in 1960 to over $33 billion in 1972.

### Drugstores

The independent drugstore has declined dramatically since World War II, especially in inner-city areas. Chain drugstores on the other hand, have thrived. From 1962 to 1971 the sales of such stores increased from $3.41 billion to $7.86 billion. In 1971, some 58 percent of their business consisted of prescriptions, proprietary drugs, toiletries, and cosmetics.

### Discount Catalog Showrooms

The main promotional tool of the discount catalog showroom is the catalog. The customer comes to the showroom, often writes up her own order, and then takes the merchandise with her; only about 5 percent of the merchandise is actually delivered. The catalog is centrally created, in the sense that a single catalog-creating firm may service many different catalog showrooms. Discount catalog showrooms sold $1.5 billion worth of goods in 1973, up from $1 billion in 1972. There is reason to believe that the volume will reach $3 billion by 1975.

The firms that started these showrooms were from the jewelry business, and many of them continue to sell more jewelry than any other category of merchandise. However, success inspires imitation, and other kinds of company, including supermarkets and trading stamp companies, have entered the fray. Discount catalog showrooms offer the following cost-cutting advantages:

1. There is far less shortage (i.e., loss from theft) than in other general merchandise stores.

2. Credit, which usually involves higher administrative costs, represents a far lower percentage of sales.

3. Delivery is a very small percentage of the business; often there is no delivery service at all.

4. Advertising expenditures (except on the catalog) are very low.

5. Since the catalog is the principal "salesman," selling does not cost much more than checking the customer out.

6. The showroom makes higher sales per square foot, and has less of its capital tied up in inventory, than a conventional store.

Because of all these features, it has been suggested that discount catalog showrooms are the prelude to shopping by closed circuit television. They may well be: one leading company, Best Products, was approaching $100 million in sales in 1973, and it was not unusual for companies in this field to increase their sales by 100 percent per year during the same period. Success like this will inspire imitation.

### The World of Retailing

Each of the perspectives on retailing discussed in this chapter has been found useful by some group of observers. But there is nothing sacred about any such perspective. Usually, it has been invented in order to solve or focus on a particular class of problem. For example, ownership would have significance as a perspective in the analysis of various legal problems. The same is true of looking at stores in terms of the products that they sell. For instance, closer analysis might indicate that discount food stores were closer in kind to discount drug stores than to regular-priced supermarkets. Similarly, a franchised gas station might be deemed closer to a franchised ice cream parlor than to a company-owned gas station. It just so happens that many observers, aided by the wealth of government data developed in this manner, have tended to think of stores in terms of the products they offer.

Classification by product is especially misleading during a period when the trend is toward *scrambled merchandising*. Food stores handle drugs; gas stations sell toys; certain drugstores come close to full-line discount houses; variety stores aggressively seek much higher price lines, and so forth. In short, the changing character of retail institutions over time makes any static classification system subject to question.

### Summary

1. Retailing is an important part of the lives of all of us, affecting where we live, work, and interact.

A. The volume of goods sold to final customers is running at a rate of over $500 billion. And it is growing dramatically year after year. The total amount received by retailers above the cost of the goods may be estimated at about $125 billion.

B. Retailing is a large employer: estimates range above 12 million people. It has particular relevance to the female labor force and to all workers between the ages of 16 and 24.

C. In 1972 it was estimated that there were 1,676,-800 retail enterprises. Probably about three out of four of them have less than four paid employees. The number of small retail businesses and the number of small retail businesses per member of the population have both been decreasing.

2. Most retail outlets are stores; but because retailing involves merchandise, many service establishments such as cleaning stores are not technically a part of retailing.

A. There are many ways to classify retail establishments: by the type of merchandise that is sold; by the percentage margin charged the final consumer; by the manner in which merchandise is purchased; by whether the store is part of a chain or not; and by whether or not the specific store or chain advertises the merchandise aggressively and if so at low or high prices.

B. Nonstore retailing includes such growth areas as telephone selling, mail order, vending, and in-home selling.

3. The world of retailing is always changing. Some of the more important developments are the following:

A. The shopping center is a dynamic force that affects nearly every aspect of our lives and accounts for about 44 percent of the merchandise of a shopping center type.

B. The chain store has grown dramatically over the years; chain stores of 11 or more units did over 30.7 percent of the retail business in 1972.

C. Franchising, which encompasses constrained decision making and the use of an accepted format for doing business, accounted for about $142 billion of retail sales in 1973.

D. Supermarkets have been growing in size and importance, to the point where in 1972 over 77 percent of the food business was done in them (by certain definitions of "supermarket").

E. The department store has been prospering by moving to the suburbs, to the point where far more business is done by the department store in the suburbs than in the inner city.

F. The discount store is difficult to define because of its changing nature over time. But its growth has been dramatic. The discount catalog store is a new kind of discount outlet that merits particular attention.

## Discussion Questions

1. Do you expect people to start living in shopping centers during your lifetime?

2. Why does retailing employ so many younger people? So many women?

3. Should banks appropriately be considered a part of retailing?

4. Why have food expenditures accounted for a smaller and smaller portion of the consumer's budget over the years?

5. Outline the various ways that one might classify stores.

6. What costs are involved in a vending machine operation? Are vending machines ever going to have low prices?

7. Why is ordering by telephone increasing rapidly?

8. What is the difference between a discount store and a department store?

9. Is mail order going to grow rapidly in the future? Why?

10. Will the discount catalog store grow as rapidly in the future as it has in the last two or three years?

## References

*Business Week,* September 4, 1971, p. 34.

Census of Population, 1970, *General and Economic Characteristics.*

Dalrymple, Douglas J., and Thompson, Donald L., *Retailing: An Economic View* (New York: Free Press, 1969).

*Discount Merchandiser,* June 1973, by telephone.

*Statistical Abstract of the United States,* 1971, p. 737.

*Survey of Current Business,* March 1973.

*Wall Street Journal,* December 18, 1970, p. 1.

Westinghouse Broadcasting Company, presentation to Retail Research Society, May 25, 1972.

## Further Reading

Dolan, J. R., *The Yankee Pedlars of Early America* (New York: Clarkson N. Potter, 1964).

Enis, Ben M., and Paul, Gordon W., "'Store Loyalty' as a Basis for Market Segmentation," *Journal of Retailing*, Fall, 1970, pp. 42–56.

*Franchising in the Economy, 1971–1973* (U.S. Department of Commerce, 1972).

Gillet, Peter L., "A Profile of Urban In-Home Shoppers," *Journal of Marketing*, July 1970.

Levy, Daniel S., "ABC's of Shopping Center Leases," in Larry Crandell, ed., *Corporate Real Estate Development and Management* (New York: President Publishing House, 1971).

*Monthly Retail Trade* (U.S. Department of Commerce).

Nystrom, Paul H., *Economics of Retailing, Retail Institutions, and Trends* (New York: Ronald Press, 1932).

Phillips, Charles F., and Duncan, Delbert J., *Marketing Principles and Methods* (Homewood, Ill.: Richard D. Irwin, 1968).

Ryans, John K., *et al.*, *New Dimensions in Retailing: A Decision Oriented Approach* (Belmont, Ca.: Wadsworth, 1970).

Spence, Homer E., *et al.*, "Perceived Risk in Mail-Order and Retail Store Buying," *Journal of Marketing Research*, August 1970, pp. 364–369.

Thompson, Donald N., *Franchising Operations and Antitrust* (Lexington, Mass.: Heath Lexington, 1971).

The following trade journals and magazines will also be found informative: *Advertising Age, Chain Store Age for Drug Executives, The Merchandiser, Progressive Grocer, Sales Management, Shopping Center World, Vend*.

## Case History: *Professor Cordova Looks at Discounting**

The discounting of general merchandise had always interested Professor Hyman Z. Cordova. Its

---

*\* Many of the facts in this case were taken from* Discount Store News, *December 11, 1972.*

growth had been spectacular. From 1962 to 1972 (according to *Discount Store News*, December 11, 1972), sales of full-line discount stores had increased from about $6 billion to over $28 billion.

The professor was aware of the fact that discounting had been part of the retailing scene for many years. Indeed, one source estimated that Klein's in 1932 had a turnover of 24 a year, a markup of 10 percent, and a cost of doing business of 7 percent of net sales. Professor Cordova knew that the original department stores had started out as discount stores. Having grown up in New York, he was acquainted with S. Klein, J. W. Mays, and Alexander's. These stores concentrated at first on soft goods with a low markup. Even in 1973, Alexander's was reported to have 85 percent of its merchandise devoted to what the industry terms soft goods. Furthermore, there were many small-appliance and stationery discount stores that developed in New York in the late thirties and had gone on to flourish.

But the rise of discount stores as we know them did not take place until after World War II. Their growth was so rapid that in 1972, according to one source, they accounted for 47 percent of all general merchandise sales. Professor Cordova was familiar with the various types of discount firms that existed in 1972, but he was not sure how each one had developed. He therefore assigned to his class the job of finding out. The class reports classified the way the discounters got into the business as follows:

*Large and small appliances* A substantial number of appliance stores that carried both large and small appliances became discount stores. The New York area appeared to spawn the founders of this movement, which included Korvette's, Master's, and Two Guys. All three still exist, but are only of regional significance. By the late 1940s, these stores were in high gear and sales were booming. At first, the department stores did not react to the discounters, so that they faced only light competition in their earlier years.

*Mill stores* A whole series of entrepreneurs took over various empty factories in New England and proceeded to flourish there. King's was formed in 1949 in an abandoned motorcycle factory in Springfield, Massachusetts. Arlan's started in a Massachusetts mill in 1948. Other chains such as Virginia Dare, Ann and Hope, and Mammoth Mart also used old mill buildings. Indeed, the availability of these buildings in a depressed New England aided the growth of many of the earlier discount chains.

**Government workers**  In the late 1940s, government workers in Los Angeles formed a company in order to purchase merchandise in a tight economy. The company was called Fedco. One hundred workers put $2 each into a kitty to buy items at wholesale, and only members could shop at the store. The concept grew; state, county, and city employees were attracted. Others copied the closed-door concept, but usually gave it up because of the limited customer appeal and began to admit the public. Fedco, however, stuck with the idea and built up a $50 million business with six stores in Los Angeles and San Diego.

**Drug chains**  A drug chain, Pay Less, opened a full-line discount store of 40,000 square feet in Oakland, California, in 1939. Since that time, this and other drug chains have opened similar stores and done very well with them. Long's is another such chain, also based in California.

These were the key elements of the discount revolution that surfaced in the 1940s. But many other types of retail firm took part in this revolution for various reasons and with varying success. The students classified the later entrants as follows:

**Variety chains**  Among the late entrants into the field were variety chains. Most managements seemed to be attracted to the field because their basic business was poor and getting worse. To many managements the discount business seemed a logical alternative growth area. Several chains, including Nichols, Kuhn Bros., Neisner Bros., and M. H. Fishman, tested discount stores in the late fifties. K Mart and Woolco started in 1962. The

growth of K Mart has been dramatic; by 1972 it had about 570 discount stores with a volume of over $3 billion. The chain is planning to add 90 new stores a year and is anticipating a volume of $10 billion by the end of the seventies. Woolco now has some 200 stores.

**Apparel specialty stores**  A substantial contribution to the growth of the discount industry was made by apparel specialty stores. Thus Zayre's, originally a spinoff from a women's apparel chain, grew from two stores in 1956 to nearly 220 in 1972. Other units opened by apparel specialty store chains were Shopper's Fair, Bradlee's, and Zody's. Many of these chains emphasized soft goods at first but over the years have striven for more of a balance with hard goods.

**Food stores**  The success of food stores with merchandise discount chains has been indifferent. In 1956 Grand Union launched the Grand Way discount chain, while several supermarket chains such as Stop & Shop and Food Fair have purchased discount chains with fewer units than themselves. In the Midwest, Cook United currently operates about 100 discount department stores.

**Conventional department stores**  As Professor Cordova already knew, department stores did not get into the discount business until late, although most realized the potential of the discount house very early. Interstate Department Stores launched a discount chain in 1959; Dayton-Hudson entered in 1968. Penney's took a step out of a test store in 1969 by setting up four Treasure Islands in Atlanta, while Federated opened two Gold Circle Stores in Columbus in 1968. Allied has been involved in discounting since 1961, through Allmart. Many other chains have been entering the competition.

**Leasees**  Owners that run departments or sections within stores are known as leasees. Some earlier discount stores were little more than a group of leasees brought together by a real estate operator. However, a number of leasees have since become operators of their own full-line discount chains. Some opened them from scratch; some took over the lease of a financially troubled store from leasors; some bought small chains. In 1960 Belscot, a men's wear leasee, launched a chain that has grown to 20.

**Franchisees** The key to the franchising of full-line discount houses is Gibson. This firm is reported to have grown from its beginning in 1958 to a volume of over $1.7 billion, which makes it the second largest discount chain. Gibson now has about 600 franchised units plus 24 or so company-owned units. In 1958 the firm controlled 34 wholesale houses in 10 states, but was losing money. In setting up its discount operation, then, the firm used its wholesale business to buy merchandise directly from manufacturers.

**Discount catalog showrooms** The students thought that discount catalog showrooms should be included because of their potential importance for the future, and because they were so similar to some of the earlier discount stores. The discount catalog showrooms were reported to be doing $1 billion in business in 1972 and were expected to be doing $3 billion by 1975. Most of them had started as jewelry operations but had just started to expand dramatically. In general, few discounters or general merchandisers tried to get into the business from scratch; almost all bought small chains of existing stores and then tried to expand.

Professor Cordova read the students' reports with interest and then treated them to the following observations:

1. *The keys to success in the discount industry had been effective management and luck.* Very few of the early innovators really came through. Most could not make the transition from the early years of rapid growth with limited competition to the years of limited growth with fierce competition from many types of outlet.

2. *Success was hard to come by even with good management.* The earlier firms had to make a se-

quence of important decisions, most of which probably had to be correct for the firm to flourish. And the decisions just were not correct. Professor Cordova was pondering whether even five correct decisions and one incorrect one might not doom a firm in a rapidly changing environment. Perhaps good management was not enough in the early years of a retail innovation; one might also have to have brilliant insight.

3. *The value of being first with a retail innovation might not be that great.* True, getting in early offered the chain great opportunities, but there were opportunities for mistakes as well as successes. Some of the firms that came in later did better, perhaps because the competitive environment was more stable later. Indeed, none of the early leaders of the late forties and early fifties was dominant today, although several were strongly in the battle. The professor tentatively concluded that the benefits of being first with a type of store were not as great as those of coming out first with a very different kind of new product. The changing competitive environment appeared to be far more difficult for leading firms to adapt to.

4. *Failure in the nondiscount field often led to success in discounting.* Many of the outstanding successes in discounting had gotten into the business because of the poor businesses that they were in. The variety chains were having trouble in their basic business; the leasees were having trouble; so was Gibson. Faced with threats to their markets, many entrepreneurs had switched management skills to the discount industry and done very well. Professor Cordova began to wonder what the discount business would have looked like if the variety and other businesses had remained profitable.

5. *A sound rule was to avoid getting into a retail business about which you knew nothing.* Many important decisions in the retail firm require a great knowledge of the specific kind of store. Thus department stores did not get into the discount business early, not because the executives generally felt that the future of the discount business was poor, but because these stores did not have executives who understood and could operate effectively in the discount business. Even today, retail chains with very competent executives in their specific retail field—

for example, many executives with M.B.A.'s from leading schools—are reluctant to go into a new form of retailing from scratch. Accordingly, these firms tend to buy out a small chain, thus acquiring executive talent with specific expertise.

And yet, Professor Cordova mused, some outstanding successes appeared to have been created just by effective management. Indeed, it could be argued that the top four discount companies in volume in 1973 were developed by retail executives with little if any previous experience in the full-line discount business. Apparently these individuals had enough managerial ability to make a go of their enterprises. Or perhaps this was just an exception.

### Discussion Questions

1. What is your position on each one of Professor Cordova's observations? Why?

2. Can you think of any promising area for discount operations that nobody has tried yet? What would be its chief risks and opportunities?

# Retail Systems

The changing nature of retailing can be estimated from some new forms and faces in the retail world. The Levitz Furniture Corporation, for instance, increased its dollar volume from $3 million in 1964 to over $325 million in 1973. In a short period of time, Hudson Oil Company, Martin Oil Company, and other independents expanded their businesses to the point where in 1972 (before the gas squeeze) they controlled almost one-third of the retail gas market. Convenience food outlets grew in number from 500 units in 1957 to over 13,000 units in 1970, 17,800 units in 1972, and an estimated 25,000 units in 1975.

Discount catalog showrooms are presently a dramatic growth area of retailing. In 1971, the volume of this industry was about $1 billion. By 1975, it is estimated that the volume will increase to about $3 billion. Best Products, a leader in discount catalog showrooms, increased its business from $20 million in 1970 to $52 million in 1972, and its six-month figures for 1973 were up nearly 100 percent over 1972.

Dramatic changes have also occurred in other segments of retailing. Wickes has grown in the homebuilding business to the point where in 1972 it did over $400 million in lumber and building supplies. The home center field is expected to grow over 15 percent in 1973 to about $3.5 billion. Fabric stores, too, have grown dramatically in recent years. Minnesota Fabrics' sales increased from $6.7 million in 1969 to over $27 million in 1972. Fashion specialty stores have also done well: Petrie grew from a volume of about $33 million in 1964 to over $168 million in 1973, and the firm's profits after taxes in 1973 were over $14 million.

Some firms have not done well. Small retail firms have not generally flourished. Stores depending heavily on the central business district have had their problems. Some older prestigious areas such as Fifth Avenue, New York, have not boomed. Department stores with poor images have not done well. Thus the excitement has not all been positive.

Retailing, then, is changing at an ever faster pace. But the complexity of the retail world, the shortcomings of most data on it, and the lack of appropriate techniques for data manipulation combine to obscure the nature of change in many cases. One way to try to overcome this is analysis. Problems are broken down into smaller parts. The parts are examined in a way not possible of the whole.

Analysis is often used as a technique of decision making, as in the following example. Suppose that a planning commission is interested in estimating the future of retail sales in a city's downtown sector. Projections have to be made for the next 5, 10, and 20 years. What factors will the commission have to consider? Obviously, they will want to know what will happen to the amount of office space and the number of office employees. What will be the populations in the different areas of the city and in the suburban community? Transportation, too, is a factor. Will there be more or fewer private automobiles? A new mass transit system? What will the parking facilities be like in the downtown area and in competing areas? Will the other cities and suburban areas have a higher or a lower sales tax? What federal and state programs will be instituted in that period of time that will affect retail sales in the downtown or competing areas? Given the answers to some of these questions, the reaction of local business may be estimated with a fair degree of probability. The commission needs to know if these firms will still be around in the relevant periods and, if so, how they will be doing. Here, estimates may be needed of business conditions in a dozen different markets for years ahead. Then there are social conditions to be considered. Will the city be perceived as safe enough in the years ahead to permit night-time shopping?

It will have been noted that while all these problems are difficult, even insoluble by present means, each appears more amenable to analysis than the main problem of what will happen to downtown retailing. The hope is that obtaining information about the parts—the factors connected with the problem—will make it possible to deal with the whole, which is the problem itself. The parts, however, are usually dependent to a greater or lesser degree on the other parts; for instance, the amount of crime in the community may depend on the amount of unemployment, which in turn depends on how the various local industries react to the business cycle. Such interaction among the parts may be a significant element of the problem. Exploring a part without considering or understanding its relationships to other important parts can lead to incorrect or highly misleading impressions.

## The Web of Relationships

The systems approach recognizes that, in any complex situation, many factors mutually affect one another, and that the situation cannot be analyzed correctly unless these interactions and their total effect are given their due. Some sceptics argue that this is too difficult; there are just too many factors at work. It is still true that there is more than one cause for most activities. Some causes are more important than others, and it may be useful to work out which ones these are. After all, if the activity being studied has many important causes, knowing something about each one of them is more likely to be helpful than knowing nothing about them.

There is a growing recognition in marketing and retailing that many problems, perhaps most of the important ones, cannot be effectively explored without considering the system or systems of which they form part. While many systems can be relevant to a given set of problems, several merit special attention with regard to retailing.

**Human system** Retailing is inescapably involved with people. Retail institutions create employment, distribute goods to consumers, influence the behavior and value systems of consumers, provide opportunities for social interaction, and much more. They influence many types of group—probably everyone to some degree. They also create new groups and group values.

**Power system** Retailing relates to the political system of which it is a significant part; indeed, it relates to the government in numerous dimensions. As retailers are brought under increasing pressure from consumer groups, they begin to appreciate the uses of political power. Retailing also has important connections with the legal system, which is part of the power system. These aspects of retailing are discussed in Chapters 3 and 7.

**Economic system** Retailing is of course intimately involved with the economic system in many ways. It plays a large part in the competitive struggle that makes the whole system go round. This is more thoroughly discussed in Chapter 5.

**Geographic system** Spatial patterns of retailing have evolved to profitably meet the needs of customers and suppliers. Some of these will be discussed separately toward the end of this chapter.

It is clear that the above systems are interrelated. Thus many problems in economics cannot be approached unless their human, geographic, and political aspects are also considered. Systems also have many characteristics just because they are systems. For example, some systems evolve, and the world is often described as a series of systems that are gradually evolving onto a higher level. The system in some sense has direction, or is thought to be so directed. Other systems remain in a state of equilibrium, or close to it. In economics, firms are often thought to interact in a manner that produces a long-term equilibrium. Yet others, as we shall see later in this chapter, have feedback mechanisms that make an equilibrium impossible.

### Systems within the Firm

Each major part of the retail organization is related to the other major parts in some way. For example, increasing the dollar value and physical quantity of the total merchandise stocked will affect many elements of the store. The finance department must find ways to pay for the merchandise if the cash is not readily available. Now that there is more merchandise, the protection department may want to change its procedures to try to prevent too large a percentage of it from being stolen. The receiving and marking departments may have to hire more people to handle the extra workload. The warehouse manager may have to allocate or obtain special space if the purchase is made at a time when there is no substantial unoccupied space. If sales increase due to the increased level of merchandise, the number of sales personnel may have to be increased and the accounts payable department will have to process more invoices.

Another good example of a single factor that may have widespread effects within a firm is its set of credit restrictions for customers. If these are altered, many changes may occur. One such case was reported by *Business Week* in 1971: a bank card program replaced a store credit system, so that interest was charged on accounts after 30 days instead of 60. As a result, it seems, 46 percent of the charge customers stopped doing business with the store. Clearly, changes in credit procedures can have either a positive or a negative effect on sales. Thus if the credit policies of a store toward minority groups are eased, the type of merchandise sold there will probably be different and the volume of sales will almost certainly be increased.

Because almost all decisions of one important segment of a retail organization will influence its other segments, top management stands to benefit from the systems approach. Large stores should develop their own data banks in order to provide usable information.

The logic of the systems approach is compelling, for firm and society alike. But few retailers have adopted it at the everyday, practical level. One reason for this is that the nature of the relationships in question has not been worked out. The kind of relationship a grocer needs to understand is what happens if he decreases the price of catsup. Will he sell more baked beans? If he advertises a special on catsup and a customer comes into the store in response to that advertisement, what is the value of this to his store? What will it cost him if he runs out of catsup? Although on first examination some of these problems appear easy to resolve, their ramifications can be extremely complicated.

**Change** No more important issue faces our society today than to find out how and why institutions change. Coupled with this is the still more perplexing issue of how they should change. The frustration of various groups seeking change can be attributed to the fact that they can see no way of changing institutions peaceably within a reasonable period. Perhaps they can't be changed peaceably; after all, the Declaration of Independence suggests that there is a necessity for periodic rebellion. However that may be, change is difficult for both individuals and institutions. Individuals can be helped by psychiatrists. But who will help corporations? In the last resort, a corporation is only a collection of individuals; its executives have most of the shortcomings attributed to other members of the population, plus a few perhaps that are indigenous to their profession. If they miscalculate the direction and rate of change in their corporation's environment, their competitors will benefit.

The reaction of any corporation to its changing environment tends to fall into one of the following three categories, adopted from the personality theory of Milton Rokeach:

1. *Natural change.* Change that takes place without substantially new procedures or actions on the part of the relevant managers can be defined as natural change. For example, retail sales information will usually cause the decision maker to alter the merchandise so that it reflects the changing desires of his customers. Styles, price lines, department space allocation, and so forth, can be changed in this manner. Alert managers will foster change of this nature without great effort.

2. *Planned change.* Major action in the face of anticipated environmental conditions is best defined as planned change. It usually takes place within the general existing business of the enterprise. Often, independent research — that is, research not part of the firm's day-to-day operations — is essential in making decisions of this kind. For example, the development of additional branch stores might be one example of planned change.

3. *Creative change.* Change of an entrepreneurial nature that goes beyond the present business of the organization deserves to be called creative change. Institutions are created where none of a similar type existed before, at least in that corporation. Creative change is extremely difficult to foster in a large corporation, and for that reason generally takes place outside the existing corporate struc-

ture. For a corporation, an example of creative change might be a discount store going into the franchise food business.

### Change among Firms

The above types of change concern the individual firm. However, there are broader patterns of change that involve many firms over a long period. Two of them will now be discussed.

*The wheel of retailing*    According to the theory known as the wheel of retailing, new types of retail institutions start with low retail prices, low costs, and few services to the consumer. They are initially successful, and other entrepreneurs are inspired to imitate them. As the newer firms succeed and grow, they compete more and more with other stores of the same type. Competition drives up costs. Each store must now look for ways to differentiate itself. Advertising in the various media is one way; among the others are increased merchandise assortments and encouragement of credit sales. In addition, as store volume increases, whether in one location or because other stores are added to the chain, there may be disadvantages that more than offset the positive aspects. Layers of management are often added, making the communications structure within the firm more intricate. Different types of demands are directed at the original managers, who may not be flexible enough to adapt. Older firms that have been hurt by the newcomers may launch successful counterattacks.

Let us suppose, however, that the newer firms and the type of merchandising they represent become more and more successful, until they become an accepted institution in society. The original entrepreneurs get older and change their operating perspectives, perhaps even their goals. The costs of running the various enterprises increase, which in turn sends up their prices. The firms are caught in a gradually increasing cost-and-price-spiral. At last the new firms come to resemble the very organizations they developed in reaction to. They are vulnerable to another attack by a low-priced operator.

The wheel-of-retailing concept fits the rise of some kinds of discount house quite well. The initial competition was against a common enemy, the department store. The discounters did indeed enter the market with very low prices. Many were instantly successful, as customers told others about the low prices in this unimposing retail structure. The department stores were slow to react, not believing that in a few years some observers would feel that their very existence was threatened by the new enterprises. Business was very easy to get for the early discounters. As other entrepreneurs saw the early, large volume successes and the large return on net worth, they too entered the discount business and succeeded at it. As they did so, not only did still more entrepreneurs enter the fray but existing discount stores added new outlets. Department stores started to compete more aggressively, although most did not meet prices head-on. In New York, some offered to come within 10 percent of the discount store prices. Department store buyers began to throw out merchandise lines that were handled by discount stores; they had decided that handling these lines was no longer profitable enough. Department stores thought about setting up separate retail units to compete with discount stores, but by and large did not do so, at least not effectively. The wheel-of-retailing concept suggests that the department stores could not compete effectively anyway, and apparently this was so, at least at the early stages. As the discount store advanced and the threat was clearly recognized by department stores, several did at last begin to meet discount store prices head-on, and met with such success that some of them continue it to this day. Necessary volume increases in business became harder and harder for the discount stores to obtain. Each one developed ways of differentiating its merchandising mix from other similar stores. One store allocated a larger percentage of its budget to advertising. Another felt that it might differentiate itself by adding consumer credit. Another gained a competitive advantage by adding blue shirts to its stock of white shirts. Others sought better locations, fixtures, or both, in place of their original bare existence in low-rent areas. Still others used various combinations of the foregoing. Since costs increased but sales volume did not increase sufficiently, prices had to be increased also.

If the wheel-of-retailing concept applies here, the discount store will become increasingly set in its ways—more like the department store, in fact, before the growth of discounting. This fosters a situation in which another set of entrepreneurs can create a new type of outlet in which price is the key dimension. And indeed today we have the growing discount catalog showroom, a great threat to discount stores.

The student should not infer that department stores have not done well. Many would suggest, however, that they have not done nearly as well as they should or would have done if they had developed the discount store innovation.

The wheel-of-retailing concept holds up quite well when applied to certain other areas in the retail industry. In the food industry, the supermarket developed as a low-margin competitor to the food chain, itself begun on low prices. As supermarkets grew in number, they raised their margins. Their status increased, but so did their expense. Indeed, a present-day development of some importance in the food industry is that of the discount food store, which has developed partially in reaction to the supermarkets' increasing margins. As one would expect, the leading supermarket chains have not fostered this innovation themselves.

Mail order also started as a low-priced institution. In the final quarter of the nineteenth century and later, around 1912, when parcel post made them direct competitors of country merchants, mail order outlets were condemned for price cutting. Today, mail order outlets have increased their margins substantially, and are no longer considered low-priced.

Some types of retail outlets, however, did not start with low mark-ups at all. Notable examples are vending, the department store branch movement, planned shopping centers, convenience foods, lumber and building supply centers, and fabric stores. These, for the most part, have been high-cost, high-price and high-convenience movements.

Furniture stores were involved in an interesting

battle in the early 1970s. It is recognized by both established furniture retailers and newcomers that the future volume of discount furniture stores is going to be very large. The established retailers have therefore been making substantial efforts to develop a strong foothold in the discount furniture business, partly through the purchase of firms but also through their existing retail network. Some of the discounters have done very well indeed: Levitz Furniture Corporation, for instance, increased its sales from a little over $3 million in 1964 to well over $325 million in 1973. However, it seems unlikely that most managements of large firms will adapt so well to this new market, even though its existence is no secret to them.

A great merit of the wheel-of-retailing concept is its emphasis on the need for a type of outlet to possess some competitive advantage if it is to have an impact on the market. It also stresses the creative role of the entrepreneur. The consumer is not an integral part of any change in retail methods until the new outlet has been created. He cannot usually vote for a particular type of retail outlet before it exists—not, that is, unless the outlet is created by consumer research, which is seldom the case. Of course, once the outlet has been created, the consumers can vote by purchasing from it.

However, the usefulness of the wheel-of-retailing concept as a managerial tool is open to question. To many people's way of thinking, pricing has become a less important marketing tool today than it was years ago; convenience, range of assortment, new services, and so forth have become just as important. Nor are future changes likely to be as heavily influenced by price. At the very least, other dimensions of the wheel will appear. Moreover, the time it takes to come full circle is too long to interest most managers, and the predictions it yields are too risky.

The newer types of retail outlet do not necessarily destroy the older ones. The department store may have destroyed the general store in some sense. But the department stores appear to have survived the onslaught of the discount houses by adopting some discount features themselves. Similarly, chain food stores have copied their younger competitors, the supermarkets. Most new firms feel the need to differentiate themselves from others of their type as competition increases, and this may force them to become more and more like the older firms, which have already gone through a competitive process. Old or new, each type of retail firm is continuously searching for answers that will increase its own profitability over the long term. Some firms go under because they cannot cope efficiently with changing conditions, but there are many ways of coping, and seemingly opposite ways can go on coexisting for years.

**The retail accordion**  The concept of the retail accordion is a way of looking at changes in a retail outlet's assortment. Why do some stores offer wider assortments than others, and what makes them expand or contract their assortments over time? Under the accordion concept, there are definite forces making for expansion or contraction.

Stanley C. Hollander has noted three phenomena that may induce a retail firm to narrow its assortment, that is, become more specialized. Many expanded merchandise mixtures have proved unsuccessful. Among the failures have been adding substantial variety to gas stations; selling haberdashery and women's wear through vending machines; and attempting to sell automobiles through department stores. Many stores have also dropped products. Some department stores actually dropped major appliances and some housewares in response to the challenge of the discount store in the 1950s. In many instances, even though conventional assortments continue to include a given line of merchandise, many specialized stores may enter the market to take a large share of it. Two outstanding examples here are greeting card and ski equipment stores.

Hollander has also noted five forces that promote contraction. First, many merchants really want to devote their attention to a limited group of offerings. Perhaps this gives them a greater sense of identification with trade groups; perhaps they just get more fun from dealing with only skis and related equipment. Second, the dealer may be subject to legal and other constraints. Among them may be fear of competitive retaliation by other types of outlet. For example, if a supermarket begins to carry newspapers, the luncheonette across the street may retaliate by carrying tooth paste and other pharmaceuticals. However, this factor does not usually loom large, since established outlets of different kinds rarely compete on equal terms in the same product area. For example, a drugstore's business might be hurt if a supermarket offers a line of pharmaceuticals, but the supermarket may not be hurt if the drugstore adds fresh tomatoes. Third, lack of capital and other factors such as the dearth of executive talent appear to limit the kind of merchandise expansion possible. Fourth, diversification of product line has the immediate effect of complicating the retailer's work with regard to buying invoices, taking inventory, and so forth. Fifth, the behavior of consumers is so complex that an entrepreneur can never be sure how the customer will feel about his efforts at diversification. Certain customers prefer a large assortment; others prefer one-stop shopping. To some, a long drive in a car to a shopping center may be welcome, to others unwelcome.

Several examples are offered by Hollander in defense of the accordion concept. A leading one is the drugstore, the specialized nature of which steadily decreased with the addition of other products. There was a particularly large increase in the 1880s and 1890s in the number of drugstores equipped with soda fountains. Since that time, drugstores have added lines of merchandise at varying rates, though there has been a substantial decline in the number of them operating soda fountains. In addition, large drugstores have been feeling competition from small discount drug operations with limited lines, and from the prescription-only type of outlet that is often located in medical buildings.

Several supporting examples can be offered from the food industry. Toward the turn of the century, soda fountains, lunch counters, and tea rooms were eliminated from food stores. Mail order firms and department stores retreated from the food business in the early 1900s. Convenience outlets for food have grown dramatically in recent years. Food stores have also had some trouble expanding their product lines into certain areas—soft goods, for example.

The concept of the retail accordion is a useful

reminder that no store can expand its assortment of merchandise indefinitely; there are limits to scrambled merchandising. Clearly, one-stop shopping has a large appeal for many customers. But so does the specialty store. The competitive advantages of specialty stores are continually changing, and the interaction between the forces for specialization and the forces for expansion create new opportunities and risks. However, rising incomes, expanding consumer demands, urbanization and suburbanization, and other factors will support highly specialized retail ventures. Indeed, it has been suggested that freestanding fashion specialty shops will be extremely important by 1980, as society seeks increased individualism.

***Other patterns in retailing*** Another observed pattern in retailing is termed the Ford effect. It has been suggested that, over a period of time, the relative number of stores that sell necessities will decline and the relative number of stores that sell luxury items will increase, and that these two factors will tend to cancel each other out, with a resulting constancy of stores relative to population. This theory was based on the apparent constancy of stores relative to population in 12 British towns between 1901 and 1931. Since the late 1960s, some observers have tried to relate the Ford effect to patterns of urban retailing in the United States, but without success.

The student should be cautioned that some patterns can be developed out of almost any data. This is why many scientists require a hypothesis to be stated before the data are collected. The real test of most patterns is their usefulness, especially in predicting the future. One obvious lesson, at least, can be learned from the preceding examples: trends often sow the seeds of their own destruction. Excesses in assortment, like other excesses, tend to create countervailing forces.

***Geographic systems*** The wheel of retailing and the retail accordion are systems that never reach or tend toward any equilibrium. This is not true of the three geographic systems to be considered briefly here. Geographic systems within retailing can be related to suppliers or consumers. Supplier relations often depend on geography. But most efforts have been directed toward understanding how retail establishments have adapted to the changing environment of their customers. For example, higher income levels and attendant factors such as more private automobiles produce bigger stores with larger trading areas and new location requirements.

The *rank size rule* refers to the arithmetic fact, observed many times throughout the world for highly developed countries with a high degree of urbanization, that the population of the second-largest city will be approximately one-half that of the largest city; the third-largest city one-third the population of the largest city, and so forth.

The relationship has been found to be

$$P_r = P_1/r^q$$

where $P_r =$ the population of the city of rank $r$
  $P_1 =$ the population of the largest city
  $q =$ the exponent that usually approaches unity.

Another geographic regularity for which there is good evidence is that population density decreases in direct proportion to distance from the center of a city. In other words, the poor live toward the center of the city on expensive land consuming little of it, and the rich live toward the periphery consuming much of it. Central place theory, which attempts to relate all retail activity in a geographic framework, is discussed in Chapter 10.

## Summary

1. There is growing recognition in marketing and retailing that many problems, perhaps most of the important ones, cannot be effectively explored without considering the system or systems of which they form a part.

A. Retailing is inescapably involved with people, and thus a human system is relevant.

B. Retailing relates to the government and its policies in many ways.

C. Retailing is intimately involved with the economic system, of which it is an integral part.

D. Retailing is part of a geographic system.

2. Each major part of a retail organization is related to each other major part in some way. And over time, retail organizations will adapt to their environments. Three types of change are identified.

A. Natural change takes place without substantially new procedures or actions on the part of the relevant manager.

B. Planned change occurs within the general existing business of the firm but is of a major nature.

C. Creative change goes beyond the present business of the organization and is often the kind that destroys other kinds of outlet.

3. There are also systems of change among firms.

A. The wheel of retailing is a theory that suggests that retail innovations start as low-priced outlets. Gradually, as competition increases, the costs of this new type increase. Eventually the new type of outlet becomes very successful and is ripe for picking by a new kind of retail outlet—at a low price—and the wheel goes on.

B. The retail accordion suggests that at given times there are forces within an industry that promote expansion and other forces that promote contraction. An overemphasis on expansion, as in some scrambled merchandising, will sow the seeds for increased specialization.

## Discussion Questions

1. Outline the advantages of the systems approach for the retail firm.

2. Trace the effects of a large advertising campaign on other parts of the retail firm.

3. Outline three ways that change can take place in a retail organization.

4. Outline the basic elements of the "wheel of retailing."

5. Is the discount catalog store the beginning of a new turn of the wheel of retailing?

6. How do you think a discount house would react to the threat posed by a discount catalog store?

7. Define the retail accordion.

8. List five examples of stores going into new lines within the same kind of outlet, for example the drugstore.

9. List five examples of stores discontinuing lines of merchandise.

10. What is the rank size rule? Does the relationship hold among the major cities in your state?

### References

*Business Week*, January 30, 1971, p. 62.

Hollander, Stanley C., "Notes on the Retail Accordion," *Journal of Retailing*, Summer, 1966.

Rokeach, Milton, *Beliefs, Attitudes, and Values.* (San Francisco: Jossey-Bass, 1968).

### Further Reading

Cooper, Philip D., "Will Success Produce Problems for the Convenience Store?" *Business Topics*, Winter, 1972.

Green, Paul E., and Tull, Donald S., *Research for Marketing Decisions* (Englewood Cliffs, N.J.: Prentice-Hall, 1970).

Grossman, Louis, *Department Store Merchandising in Changing Environments* (East Lansing, Mich.: Michigan State University Press, 1970).

Hall, Margaret, *et al.*, *Distributions in Great Britain and North America* (London: Oxford University Press, 1961).

Hollander, Stanley C., "The Wheel of Retailing," *Journal of Marketing*, July 1960, pp. 37–42.

———, "Competition and Evolution in Retailing," *Stores*, September 1960, pp. 11–20.

Simmons, James, *The Changing Pattern of Retail Location* (Chicago, Ill.: University of Chicago Press, 1964).

Young, Agnes Brooks, *Recurring Cycles of Fashion 1760–1937* (New York: Harper and Row, 1937).

### Case History: *What's Different about Levitz?*

In January 1972, a leading observer of retailing addressed the Retail Research Society. In the course of his comments he suggested that the coming years would see many more operations like Levitz, which was known at the time as the largest retail furniture operation in the country. It had grown from a volume of $3 million in 1963 to over $190 million in 1971. He went on to predict that the Levitz concept would spread to industries like appliances, toys, and sporting goods.

Clearly, growth like this was noticed by all interested in retailing. But what was to be learned from it? Indeed, it was difficult to specify exactly what was different about Levitz. Several members of the audience commented on this subject.

George Tatum, the director of research for a large discount chain, suggested that the key difference was that Levitz had established large, free-standing furniture stores, instead of putting their stores in shopping centers. Tatum admitted that there was nothing new about free-standing furniture units; on the contrary, they had been with us for many years. But Levitz was bigger, and their free-standing units were bigger.

Edgar Tyrome, merchandise manager for a leading department store, had a different viewpoint. Tyrome suggested that there was very little new about Levitz. The key to their success was the way they merchandised. The consumer had to walk through a very long section of the warehouse before he ever got to the selling floor. This long walk did several things. First, the customer was impressed with the magnitude of the operation. Second, he immediately knew that the store represented itself as something quite out of the ordinary. Third, the warehouse environment created the impression of good value and reasonable delivery time.

Charlie Long, research director of Olson's furniture chain, suggested that the key difference was that the customer could take the merchandise with him. While few customers did this with the bulky merchandise, delivery of it could be immediate. More important, however, the customer *felt* that the delivery could be immediate. Furthermore, the customer did in fact take a great amount of merchandise with him. This reduced breakage, the number of returns, and adjustment expenses, in addition to permitting more promotional flexibility (the firm could promote small items at a very low price).

Myron Kaufman, the advertising director of a supermarket, felt that the key to the success of Levitz was in the promotional advantages accruing to the firm. The chain could and did promote merchandise as a chain, rather than store by store. Thus numerous economies were presented in promotion, including the opportunities inherent in buying huge closeouts.

These were most of the possibilities offered by the researchers. Some of the line executives also saw great buying opportunities with the volume represented, even if promotion were limited.

After the presentation, three professors got together and reflected on the discussion. They were chiefly interested in the relevance of the Levitz success to the wheel of retailing and to the retail accordion. Levitz certainly had lower retail prices than most retail outlets. They were real price innovators who introduced many other types of innovation. The level of service was high in that there were credit services, delivery with a charge, and a great number of sales services. However, the reductions in cost from the remainder of the operation led many to label this new type of furniture store as the beginning of the wheel. If Levitz was a new element in the wheel of retailing, what could be expected of furniture retail stores in the future? They also speculated on the relevance of the Levitz success to the retail accordion. This appeared to be a clear effort at specialization. Was this perhaps why one expert had suggested that specialty stores would be the rage of the future?

### Discussion Questions

1. What do you think is different about Levitz?

2. Which concept is more relevant here, the wheel of retailing or the retail accordion? Why?

# 3

## The Supplier

The supplier is whoever sells goods to the retailer. As such, he plays a key role in the operations of the marketing channel. The channel's importance as a system has been increasing in recent years. Retailers therefore have a growing interest in the performance of the supplier and the supplier's supplier. For instance, the supplier often becomes a key partner with the retailer in attracting consumers. In so doing, he may greatly increase the effectiveness of the channel and give the retailer a competitive advantage.

### Passive and Active Retailing

The supplier's role may be illustrated, in part, by an example involving two different styles of retailing. Retailer A is starting a large, independent major appliance store that he estimates will do $10 million a year in sales. He has been thoroughly impressed by one interpretation of a marketing principle. According to this interpretation, one should please customers by giving them what they want so long as this can be done at a satisfactory profit. Indeed, he believes that satisfying one's customers is the key to large profits. In line with this thinking, he spends three weeks finding out the brand preferences of his potential customers in the geographic area he plans to serve. He decides to allocate the space for the different brands of washers, dryers, stoves, refrigerators and so forth on his selling floor according to the preferences indicated by the customers in the study. In addition, retailer A instructs his salesmen to find out the brand and feature preferences of each customer entering the store and to match these preferences as closely as possible with the merchandise on the selling floor. In such a store, the selling function breaks down into: (a) finding out what sort of major appliance the customer wants; (b) persuading him to buy that item, or its nearest equivalent, then and there. Special orders are encouraged because they are the only way to fill the consumer's varied needs and desires.

Retailer A feels that the customers in his trading area will be pleased with the extra efforts of the entire store on their behalf. He believes that they

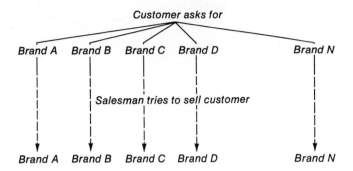

Figure 3.1

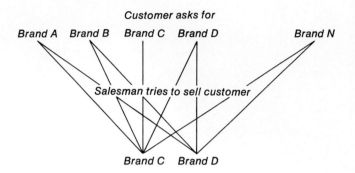

Figure 3.2

will come back again for other appliances and will also tell their friends about the store and its helpful policies. Figure 3.1 illustrates this retailer's philosophy.

Retailer B is also starting a large, independent major appliance store that he estimates will sell $10 million worth of appliances a year. However, his approach to the selling of appliances is different from retailer A's. Retailer B feels that there are three well-accepted brands in the appliance business and that he must carry one of them. He also feels that he needs a brand that offers a higher margin of profit than any of the three top brands. With these two brands and effective merchandising he feels that he can satisfy most customers. He evaluates the suppliers of the brands in terms of the extra concessions that each is willing to offer him. He finally selects two prime sources, one to supply a top brand and the other a secondary line. The salesmen hired by retailer B are told to evaluate the preferences and needs of each customer as he or she enters the store. The salesman is to judge through conversation if he can sell the profitable line with a probability of closing the sale of at least 50 percent. If the answer is yes, all sales efforts are to be bent in that direction. Of course, the salesman's compensation is higher on the more profitable line. However, if the probability of selling the top line appears to be higher, the salesman is told to sell that one. Thus the salesman has the job of selling one of the two lines to every customer

that comes into the store—and having the customer love him for it.

As a result of his policies, retailer B receives substantial concessions from his two suppliers in each of the following areas: price, merchandise held in reserve by the supplier without cost to the store, financing, advertising moneys, closeout models of appliances, special models, and several others. Retailer B feels that, with the advertising moneys and other goodies accruing to him in this way, he is assured of meeting his $10 million sales goal. Figure 3.2 illustrates this retailer's philosophy.

Both of these examples, of course, are artificial, and neither can be definitely established as superior (although in this author's view, retailer B has the greater profit potential). Deliberately left out of account were the social costs to the consumer of being sold appliances that may not be exactly what he wants, though they may be cheaper as a result. The examples do show, however, that the roles of retailers in the marketing channel may vary widely and that this has many ramifications for the supplier. Retailer A may be praised as the "buyer for the consumer" or deprecated as an "order taker," but whatever name he is given, retailer A is certainly worth little to any one supplier. Indeed, if all retailers were like A and if the total consumption of major appliances for the geographic area were not changed by his presence or absence, A's death would make little economic difference to any supplier. If the supplier wants to increase his business to A or to a group of A's, his best recourse is to appeal to the ultimate consumer through advertising, product performance, service, contests, or whatever. The retailers like A are just a passive element in the channel, and are so treated by most suppliers.

Retailer B is anything but passive. He is altering consumer attitudes and purchases to solve his own problem, namely, how to make a profit. When he succeeds in changing the behavior of customers in the way he wants, he becomes an economic power to be reckoned with. By a single decision he can transfer $5 or $6 million in business at retail prices to other supplier accounts. For that very reason, retailer B will receive extras of various types, perhaps quite legally under the Robinson-Patman act. Advertising by the supplier to the final consumer will do little good if the brand advertised is not carried in retailer B's store and if that is where the customer goes as a result of seeing an advertisement.

It is clear, then, that retailers in many industries must be dealt with as powerful and independent market forces. Many retailers are not passive instruments of the consumer, the wholesaler, or the manufacturer. Furthermore, the marketing concept requires that the marketer consider the changing retail sector as well as the changing consumer. For example, in the appliance situation the preference for a given brand may keep on increasing—perhaps because of superior advertising—but actual sales to consumers may decrease if the retailer does not handle the line. In short, suppliers must learn to deal with retailers.

## The Channel and the Retailer

The foregoing example dramatizes another key point: the manufacturer and the retailer are competitors for the profit dollars that accrue to the channel of which both are parts. While additional sales to the consumer may mean greater profits to both, often additional profits to one do come at the expense of the other. This conflict permeates most store-supplier negotiations.

The example also indicates that manufacturers, wholesalers, and retailers are also cooperators. Thus they cooperate in trying to increase consumer purchases, from which they will all presumably benefit. They also cooperate in order to survive in the battle with other channels of distribution. It should be emphasized that no member of the channel—manufacturer, wholesaler, or retailer—is self-sacrificing; each is acting in what he perceives as his own best interest, and will cooperate within the channel only for that reason. However, this is not as restricting a condition as it sounds; in fact, cooperation between supplier and retailer can take unlimited forms. Suppliers help retailers with inventory management and advertising, extend financial assistance to them, and cooperate in many forms of promotion. Conversely, retailers also aid suppliers in these activities. Cooperation within the channel is, in general, good business, and can achieve one or more of the following economies that make the total channel more profitable:

1. *Economies resulting from repositioning.* With cooperation, manufacturers, wholesalers, and retailers can arrange things in the channel in the way that suits all of them best. For example, the marking of products at retail (i.e., putting the prices on them) can be done in many instances more cheaply by the wholesaler or manufacturer than by the retailer—as much as 60 to 90 percent more cheaply, according to the January 1971 issue of *Stores*. Advertising in some instances may be done more effectively by persons or agencies working for the retailer.

2. *Scheduling economies.* If the marketing channel is a total cooperating unit, the different members of it can schedule their operations more precisely. For instance, a manufacturer selling his output to retail units that are cooperating in the total system need worry only about how much each of these units can sell. He need not worry about whether or not he will get any business from a particular retailer. For this reason, he may schedule with greater accuracy.

3. *Activities eliminated.* Cooperation within the channel can lead to the elimination of certain activities. For example, in integrated food channels personal selling is not necessary on a regular basis. In certain instances buyers can be replaced or given something more useful to do.

4. *Economies of scale.* Cooperating elements within a channel can seek the most efficient scale of activity for the entire channel, not just for the individual firm.

Survival usually requires minimal elements of cooperation in the sense that deadly competitors must abide by some rules, or neither may survive. All-out competition within the channel is not likely to produce sufficient cooperation to achieve the economies just outlined.

The most certain way to control all elements of the channel and to direct its activities is of course to own all of it. This can create integrated decision making at each level. The members of the channel can also be brought together through contractual arrangements such as franchising. Legal contracts can, however, be broken, and disagreements are not unusual. A degree of control less formal than that established under single ownership or contracts, but often effective, may be achieved by power, negotiation, cajolery, or mutually recognized dependence. For example, in the food industry the chain stores had a great competitive advantage over the large independent retail outlets. In order to compete, these independent firms had to develop integrated channels to gain some of the benefits of the large chain. The integration of the channel was a matter of survival.

The benefits of cooperation have led to a growth in channels that are coordinated in one of the above described ways. The growth of contractual channels has perhaps been most dramatic. The growth of the various vertical systems of integration has increased the amount of interchannel competition, leading some observers to suggest that, in the future, channel will primarily compete against channel rather than retailer against retailer.

## Supplier and Consumer

The supplier may be of critical importance to the retail members of his channel. There is a merchandising axiom that something well bought is half sold. In a store with many consumers passing through, merchandise that is well bought is almost completely sold—if "well bought" means particularly appealing to consumers in every possible way (price, style, fabric, silhouette, etc.). Consumers often prefer one brand of merchandise or one price line to another, and may have very strong feelings about a particular color, silhouette, or other feature or combination of features. This is a key reason why retail merchandising executives study consumer behavior. However, many supplier firms, both wholesalers and producers, are astute observers of the consumer scene and often build up a substantial following among consumers over a period of time.

Considerations of brand preference aside, a supplier's past success in attracting customers to his line is also important to the retailer because it usually indicates skill in the creation of a line. In the stock market a so-called analyst who has picked 10 winners is usually thought to be a good bet to produce another winner. So in many merchandise lines, a supplier who has consistently produced merchandise that has sold well is credited with the merchandise skill to produce another winning line. Naturally, a winning line is what every retailer would like to carry. Indeed, a supplier with skills in developing products that appeal to the final consumer can afford to be quite selective in choosing the retailers to whom he sells. In practice, most suppliers use some degree of selectivity, ranging all the way from almost complete exclusivity, for example one retailer in a city, to complete availability, as with cigarettes.

Suppliers often do not want to sell to all those who would buy from them for many reasons, including the following:

1. *Suppliers need substantial retailer support.* For this support the retailer typically demands concessions and often obtains them. Sometimes the concession, perhaps not directly requested, will be that the wholesaler or manufacturer will not sell to any competitive retailers. This type of distribution is often found in the men's wear, auto, and paint industries. The desirability and perhaps necessity of limiting the distribution may easily be seen if we imagine three Dodge dealers within a quarter mile

of each other. If one dealer spends a great deal of effort, time, and money in building up the reputation of the Dodge car, the other two would appear to be almost equal beneficiaries of his effort without any effort on their part at all. Indeed if any one of the three uses low price as a prime element of his merchandising mix, all are discouraged from alternative methods of appeal to customers because the resulting margins are not likely to be large enough.

2. *Suppliers may look to one type of store.* Unless the supplier obtains an unusually positive response to his offerings from consumers, a supplier of many types of merchandise cannot afford to sell to antagonistic types of retail outlets such as the discount store and the department store. A discount store, for instance, will not only compete with other stores for customers, it will often compete on the basis of price. In this way it may lower the entire structure of prices for a particular line of merchandise in a geographic area. For the most part, high-margin stores will not carry a line of this nature because there is no incentive for them to do so. Let us suppose, for example, that a handbag manufacturer is selling handbags to a large department store chain. The chain buys some handbags at $3 and sells them for $5. If the manufacturer sells the same item to a discount store in the same geographic area and that store prices the item at $4, then the department store has three general options:

1. Meet the price and decrease its margin 50 percent;

2. Keep the $5 price and look bad in the eyes of its customers;

3. Get rid of the line.

In most cases, the decision will be to get rid of the line. But because the manufacturer knows that this will probably be the decision, he does not usually sell the same item to a department store and a competitive discount store.

The following example illustrates how a supplier may use the support of a retail institution to battle the giants. In the television and high fidelity industry it became normal in the mid-1950s for the giants of the industry all sell to all the various types of store. The resulting competition among these outlets drove the margins for the retail outlets to a very low level. Then one relatively small manufacturer adopted a policy of selling directly to small stores and department stores offering fixed retail margins that were substantially higher than the ones then available. The department stores and the small stores vigorously supported the program so that over time another giant was made in the television industry. Indeed, this manufacturer used his institutional support to gain a very large share of the early high fidelity business. Selective distribution in the form of refusing to sell to discount stores was very effective in this given instance.

In addition, credit considerations, freight costs, selling costs, and many other factors may cause a supplier to refuse to sell to a retailer. It clearly does not pay to sell to a retailer who does not pay bills. It is also true that stores do not purchase from all suppliers who will enhance their volume. There are few appliance stores that could not increase volume to some degree by an increase in the number of brands handled, particularly if the increase were accomplished skillfully. Additional lines, however, usually cost something not only in terms of additional inventory, diluted sales effort, and so forth, but more importantly in terms of bargaining power. This was indicated in the example offered at the beginning of this chapter.

## Channel Approaches

Distribution channels, as Louis P. Bucklin has aptly said, are the sets of institutions that participate in the marketing activities undertaken to move goods or services from the point of production to the point of consumption. One simple approach suggests that the channel progress is as shown in Figure 3.3.

The retailer is the last link in what Bucklin has termed the commercial channel. The physical goods, the title to the goods, and communication on these and other matters all pass through the channel in some fashion. Clearly, they do not all pass through

raw materials supplier
↓
manufacturer
↓
wholesaler
↓
retailer
↓
consumer

*Figure 3.3*

by the same route; in fact, the channel often contains a large number of routes. Even if one focuses on a single aspect of the channel, such as the flow of the title to the goods, the channels of distribution are not always simple. Many deviations occur from the simple channel flow. Not only are elements added or omitted in given instances but elements lower down the chain sometimes sell to elements higher up, as when car dealers sell their wares to wholesalers for use in their own business. Furthermore, while both goods and title generally pass from the manufacturer to the retailer through various steps, the decision process often goes the other way, particularly as the size of the retail member of the channel increases. In other words, the large retailer or large wholesaler may decide what needs to be manufactured, or how a product should be sold.

The form and length of the channel, as E. Jerome McCarthy has pointed out, vary with many factors, including the product, the nature of the market, the width of the product line, the availability of the relevant middlemen, the product's stage of development, and the behavior of the consumer. For example, a product that is highly technical and requires special selling, service, and installation generally calls for direct contact between the manufacturer and the final link in the commercial chain. Also, perishable and bulky items tend to be distributed directly to that same link. Sales representatives that work on relatively small percentages are typical of industries where the manufacturing facilities are limited and the product lines narrow.

## Number of Resellers

Retailers are resellers of merchandise and in this sense are middlemen. So are wholesalers, who also resell merchandise. To some observers, the injection of middlemen into any transaction is inefficient, since they are thought to add to the cost of the transaction and so to the final price paid by the consumer.

In some senses this is true. The automobile dealer probably adds to the cost of cars, if indeed the customer has the alternative of buying the car direct from the factory. But most customers cannot buy direct from the factory, nor is there any prospect that they will ever be allowed to. They must therefore purchase from some dealer, whose added margin the customer must pay whether he wants to or not. He must also buy some of the dealer's services whether he wants them or not. This is an illustration of a general rule, namely, that a channel is designed to suit the interests of its stronger members, among whom the consumer rarely figures.

The small retailer's lot is not much better than that of the consumer. Even large retailers are caught in a myriad of channels upon occasion. For example, what can a large retailer do if he does not like the fact that he has to indirectly pay a 5 percent commission to a supplier's salesman or sales representative in the form of high prices? The salesman in a given instance may do little more than take up the buyer's time. A retailer may of course seek to do without the salesman or any salesmen, but this is far more easily said than done. A large retailer can request that a salesman not be sent, but this does not mean that the retailer will be offered the 5 percent or that the salesman who does not call on the retailer will not receive the 5 percent anyway.

A retailer may also seek to buy directly from a manufacturer and so bypass the sales representative, the wholesaler, the broker, or whoever the middleman happens to be. However, the policies of the supplying company may prohibit this, and the retailer may have to deal with the company's designated representatives. Naturally, these policies are not developed for the benefit of the retailer. If the retailer is large, he may devise all sorts of ways to get around the policies, but the battle on this front is continuous for many retailers.

The firm making the decision within the channel cannot really be blamed if it does not give prime consideration to the final consumer. A supplier uses a wholesaler, not to increase a product's retail price, but because it pays him to do so; the middlemen perform given activities more effectively. Actually, use of middlemen can make a product cheaper, since it has to be distributed anyway, and middlemen can often do this less expensively than the manufacturer or retailer.

### Low Cost

Lowest cost is not the critical aspect of most channels; for most companies, indeed, it is not even relevant. It is significant only if one assumes that all else remains the same. Firms within the channel are primarily interested in maximizing the difference between their total cost and their total revenues, and not in minimizing costs. While in certain instances minimizing costs will also maximize profits, this is unusual. For example, it would be relatively easy, in this author's opinion, for a prime manufacturer of television sets to lower the final retail price of his product, at least in the short run. This could be done by eliminating the retailers and wholesalers and replacing them with several huge discount warehouse operations dealing directly with the public. These outlets would permit a decrease in unit costs, and prices could be substantially reduced. However, the profits to our courageous manufacturer would appear to be much lower over the long term, and lower profits is not the name of the game. In short, lower costs are of interest only if profits can be increased thereby.

### The Push System

There are two basic philosophies that a manufacturer or wholesaler may entertain toward the forward members of the channel. One is called

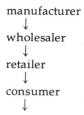

Figure 3.4

"push" and the other "pull." In a push distribution system the manufacturer "pushes" onto the next element in the channel the main responsibility of getting the goods to move farther down the channel. The element receiving these additional responsibilities is given an appropriate reward, usually in the form of extra margins, advertising moneys, and so forth. Figure 3.4 illustrates one form of push distribution.

A manufacturer of a new line of fishing reels might use a push system. Let us suppose that the manufacturer rejects the costly alternative of a heavy advertising budget for the new line. His reel is attractive and well-made, but customers will not immediately recognize it as superior. The manufacturer would have a difficult time even reaching the many retail outlets that sell fishing reels. He will therefore probably have to try to sell his reel to the large wholesalers, who in most instances already handle fishing equipment, including other brands of reels. When approached by the manufacturer, the wholesaler is going to ask the key question in most buyer-seller interactions, namely, "Why should I handle your line?" Since the wholesaler will usually carry several lines of reels, the manufacturer has to offer some advantages over the ones presently sold by the wholesaler. These advantages need not be in terms of price. They may be in terms of geographic exclusivity, additional features, dating on invoices, and many other things. In most instances, however, cost factors such as lower price will be involved. Although the wholesaler need not replace an existing line in deciding to add a new one, the least profitable line that he handles will often be a reference point that he uses in making that decision. A line that offers less profit potential than all the other lines carried by a multiline wholesaler is likely to be rejected unless it offers special marketing advantages. Usually, the manufacturer will have to offer some concessions just to become part of the existing channels.

However, merely getting into the channel, while costly, is not the only cost that has to be paid in a push distribution. So long as the manufacturer maintains his push policy, he must keep the forward members of his channel happy. The wholesaler has his problems, too. After purchasing the merchandise, he must undertake to sell it to other wholesalers or retailers, since these customers are not likely to be asking for it. Indeed, since the reel is not being advertised, they may not even know about it at first. The wholesaler must offer additional incentives to the retailer to get him to carry the line. The retailer may be equally ignorant—and equally skeptical. The retailer must spend extra time to sell the consumer. Neither the retailer nor the wholesaler is usually interested in purchasing goods that do not increase profit. The retailer is also going to have to be continuously satisfied with the line. Usually, there are many other suppliers waiting to replace it. Thus a wholesaler or manufacturer who adopts a push system of distribution will not be able to sell to both discount stores and department stores except under the most unusual conditions. The supplier with a push system develops a whole philosophy oriented around the reseller. This philosophy will permeate most aspects of the reseller's firm.

### The Pull System

A "pull" distribution system occurs when the manufacturer or wholesaler goes to the final consumer and seduces him directly by means of advertising, discount coupons, or anything else that creates a preferential attitude toward his product. A retailer will and indeed must be sensitive to the demands of his customers if those demands are not

manufacturer
↑
wholesaler
↑
retailer
↑
consumer

Figure 3.5

easily satisfied by the assortment he has to offer. This is particularly so if there is a high probability that many customers will visit the alternative outlets to obtain the desired merchandise and perhaps purchase everything there. In these instances the retailer has little choice: he must carry the merchandise they want. Figure 3.5 illustrates a pull strategy.

As an example, consider the food industry. Here, heavy advertising and promotion are normal, and heavy expenditures accompany the entrance of most new items into the market. Substantial advertising is usually necessary just to maintain the market position that a product has attained. The manufacturer will usually go to the wholesaler or retailer with his promotion plans before the item breaks in the advertising media. For many manufacturers the very revealing of the plan actually forces the wholesaler or retailer to handle the merchandise. While the seller tries to coat the pill as nicely as possible, often the retail store has little choice. The store is afraid of the actions of customers if they do not handle the merchandise of which they have heard so much. The manufacturer with a successful pull strategy can often sell to competing types of outlets, such as discounters and department stores. However, he must be aware of the activities of other pull manufacturers whose products can be substituted for his.

Just as the orientation of the push firm is to the reseller, that of the pull firm is to the consumer. In certain instances, this consumer orientation may be appropriately called an obsession.

Manufacturers and wholesalers will seldom be at

either pole of the push-pull dichotomy. Most will be somewhere in between. Even such pull manufacturers as Proctor and Gamble or General Foods make efforts to have their marketing policies appear palatable to the retail outlets to which they sell. As vague as the push-pull concepts are, they are useful in attacking certain types of problem. For example, if a manufacturer uses mainly a push type of distribution, he cannot afford to offend any level of the channel unless he feels that, if necessary, he can bypass that level completely.

### Control of the Channel

Who controls the marketing channel? Is it the retailer, the wholesaler, or the manufacturer? Control is not an easy concept to define, but complete control of the channel would appear to occur when one member of it determines what functions will be performed by all the other members, as well as how the total profits will be divided among them. The only choice the other members have is whether or not to exist in that channel or perhaps at all.

Complete control is probably as artificial a concept as perfect competition. Seldom does any member of a channel exercise or have the potential of complete control. At the very least, control of a channel should be divided into control by the retailer, control by another dominant member of the channel, and an area of balance between these two polar positions. However, control is influenced by many factors besides the market structure. The long- and short-range corporate goals of channel and potential channel members, their role expectations, the legal environment, the communication alternatives, the personalities of the participants—all are relevant.

If the key to economic control of a channel in which the participants are large is the relationship between the dollar profit that one participant (let us call him A) would lose by not dealing with the other participant (let us call him B), and the dollar profit that participant B would lose by not dealing with participant A, then we can conclude that the participant with the most to lose by not entering into the arrangement is the weaker of the two and the participant with the least to lose is the stronger. Let us call this the principle of relative loss.

Let us assume further that the supplier has more to gain under most conditions by selling to the retailer than the retailer has to gain by buying from the supplier. This is a reasonable assumption, since the manufacturers usually have (or think they will have) excess capacity, that is, the capacity to produce more than they are producing, and when they operate at full capacity it is only for a small part of the year. This is even truer of wholesalers. For manufacturers and wholesalers, then, no sale nearly always means no profit. Retailers, on the other hand, are sitting on a scarce resource whether they make a particular purchase or not. That resource is shelf space, the battle for which is so fierce that some suppliers even pay to have space reserved for them. Moreover, if a particular supplier does not sell to a particular retailer, the loss to the retailer is only relative, since there is always another supplier with other goods for a particular unit of space. In fact, it may be no loss at all, since in retailing most products can be replaced without great loss of profit by the retailer.

**The principle of relative loss applied**   We can now understand why suppliers (and marketing texts) put far more emphasis on developing a marketing mix than retailers put on developing a purchasing mix. Otherwise it would appear that a purchasing mix would be just as relevant as a marketing mix to the study of marketing. Sellers do, however, take a lot of trouble to make their products attractive to retailers. It is the seller who hires the sales force that, in most industries, goes out and calls on the buyer. This is an expensive process, and the seller has a great deal more to lose by not selling than the buyer has by not buying. Indeed the buyer usually sits back and waits for the various sellers to present values to him, because he does not feel that he has a great deal to lose by not having brand A as opposed to brand B. This is an example of what has already been defined as the principle of relative loss.

The principle also helps explain why retailers tend not to be sophisticated in such things as the development of new product models in the non-fashion area. Under most sets of conditions, they do not have a great deal to gain from such models. It is usually obvious enough which new products have outstanding sales potential. But most new products fall within a rather narrow range of differential profitability. This is not to say that it makes no difference which products the retailer chooses to sell. Indeed, later chapters will deal directly with this and related problems. It does suggest, however, that *from the retailer's point of view,* the difference in profits between old and new merchandise is not sufficient to justify the creation of costly models under most sets of conditions.

A further application of the principle is that unless the supplier makes great efforts, his natural state will be to be controlled by the large retailer. Thus part of the force for innovation in our society is the effort suppliers make in trying to avoid domination by retailers. In order to avoid this fate, suppliers have to keep developing new products and advertising them vigorously to consumers.

Negotiations between suppliers and buyers can also be viewed in terms of the principle. If a retailer is faced by a nonnegotiable set of alternatives from various supplying firms, it would appear reasonable for him to select the alternative that is going to maximize his profits, even if it is only going to leave him $1 better off than he would have been without the purchase. If, however, we drop the assumption of nonnegotiable alternatives, then it may be useful to compare the incremental profit that accrues to retailer and supplier respectively. Let us suppose that a given set of transactions will leave the retailer with a $1 increment in his profit while the same set of transactions leaves the supplying firm with an increment of $10,000. A retailer might not feel that this was a fair division and that part of the supplier's $10,000 should go to him. In order to get the extra profits, he might adopt many procedures. Some of these are discussed in Chapter 14.

Finally, the principle of relative loss suggests that the power relationships within the channel are influenced by supplier alternatives not selected by a given retailer. Thus it may pay a retailer to develop many supplier options which may lower the profit that he would lose by discontinuing a present supplier. In other words, if he dislikes one, he can always switch to another without much loss.

## Summary

1. In many industries the retailer is not the passive instrument of the supplier. He is an independent force that must be dealt with by other elements of the channel. As such, the retailer and the supplier are competitors as well as cooperators. There are certain economies to be obtained by the retailer and supplier getting together.

2. Suppliers are often of critical importance to the retailer and often have substantial expertise in attracting consumers. And suppliers do not sell to everyone because:

A. Certain suppliers need the support of certain retailers.

B. Certain suppliers may need the support of certain types of retailer, such as small stores and department stores.

3. There are a number of important channel concepts that should be understood by the retailers:

A. Middlemen such as retailers are used by manufacturers and wholesalers because it is in their best interests to do so. Often the costs of getting merchandise to the final consumer may be reduced by the interjection of a middleman.

B. The supplier is not interested in minimizing costs unless one assumes that everything else remains equal. He is interested in maximizing the difference between his costs and his revenues for a given level of risk and investment.

C. Under a push system of distribution, the supplier must induce the retailer to handle his goods by offering extra incentives. In this kind of channel, the supplier must always consider the interests of the retailer in establishing his policies because the retailer has the realistic alternative of throwing the line out.

D. Under a pull distribution system, the supplier forces the retailer to carry his line by actively wooing the final consumer. Suppliers who can effectively do this job have a stronger influence over retailer actions.

4. Large retailers will tend to dominate a channel unless the suppliers in the industry develop new products frequently and maintain a high reputation among consumers, probably through substantial advertising.

## Discussion Questions

1. In the example at the beginning of this chapter, which retailer, A or B, is likely to have the best chance of succeeding? On what assumptions do you base your conclusion?

2. Why isn't low cost the prime goal of a supplying firm?

3. How would you get a supplier to sell to you directly instead of through a wholesale intermediary?

4. What are the economies developed through an integrated channel?

5. Why are a supplier's past merchandising successes of interest to the retailer?

6. Why don't suppliers sell to any retailer who will buy their merchandise?

7. Why don't retailers buy from any suppliers who will increase sales?

8. What is a pull distribution system?

9. What is a push distribution system?

10. What is the principle of relative loss?

## References

Bucklin, Louis P., in Frederick D. Sturdivant *et al., Managerial Analysis in Marketing* (Glenview, Ill.: Scott, Foresman, 1970), p. 550.

McCarthy, E. Jerome, *Basic Marketing: A Managerial Approach* (Homewood, Ill.: Richard D. Irwin, 1968), Ch. 20.

## Further Reading

Craig, David R., and Gabler, Werner K., "The Competitive Struggle for Market Control," in J. E. Westing, ed., *Readings in Marketing* (Englewood Cliffs, N.J.: Prentice-Hall, 1963).

Dickinson, Roger, "The Retail Buyer and the Robinson-Patman Act," *California Management Review*, Spring, 1967, pp. 47–54.

## Case History: *John Tate Buys a Car*

John Tate was an aggressive individual with a medium income who lived in a small city in the Midwest. He had saved up enough money to buy a new car. In looking for a car, John could draw on 10 years' driving experience. He had also written to car manufacturers and received many of their catalogs. Not content with this, he had subscribed to several magazines on cars as well as *Consumer Reports*. John had been thrifty, so that he had the money to pay for a car through his savings.

After many months of thinking and exploring values with his friends and family, John decided on the make and model that he wanted. Since John had worked hard for his money, he did not want to throw it away. He found out the cost of the car from one of the magazines that he had examined. He then sent a check for this amount to the manufacturer, suggesting that he pick up the car. The manufacturer turned down John's request and recommended that he see the dealer in his area.

The car that John wanted cost $3,000, and had a list price of $4,000. The dealer offered it to John at $3,800. This disturbed John very much. He was giving a car dealer $800 for doing nothing. He also knew that the next closest dealer in that make was 80 miles away.

John began to ponder the whole deal. Why

should he give this money to the retail dealer? He knew which car he wanted before he came in the door. He thought the service of selling it to him was worth at most $30. As for the various warranties and their guarantees of service, John expected to be charged for most of this anyway.

Why, then, did car manufacturers keep retail dealers? Why did they not sell directly? Surely, much larger service outlets could be set up without local dealers. John even felt that if these larger outlets actually did anything for the customer they could make it on their own. John kept on thinking; the manufacturers were surely missing a bet here. Meanwhile, the consumers were asked to pay the bill for the fat dealers. And conscientious consumers were being asked to pay the bills for the lazy consumers who need substantial direction before the sale. It just didn't make any sense.

### Discussion Questions

1. Was John wrong? Are retail dealers of cars really necessary?

2. Should manufacturers consider a whole new system of automobile distribution? If so, what might such a system look like?

# 4

## The Consumer

American consumers are rich, but this does not seem to bring them happiness. A study described in *Psychology Today* indicates that the level of happiness reported by the U.S. population in 1970 was about the same as in the late 1940s, although real income had gone up 60 percent since then. On an international level, surveys of people living in economically developed countries suggest they often are no happier than people living in poorer, less developed countries. Facts of this kind have led many analysts to suggest that our society should strive more to increase the quality of life and less to increase economic growth.

Whether or not it adds to happiness, increased income certainly leads to great growth in retail sales. Some aspects of this rise in affluence can be inferred from Table 4.1. It can also be pointed out that while the population itself went up 45 percent from 1947 to 1973, the proportion owning cars went up 214 percent to over 96 million. Similarly, beef output in tonnage increased 45 percent between 1962 and 1972 and broiler output went up 68 percent in the same period. The population from 1962 to 1972 went up only

*Table 4.1*
*Cost-of-living index (1967-100) and average weekly earnings,*
*1947 and 1973*

| | Index | | Price |
|---|---|---|---|
| | 1947 | 1973 | Rise |
| All items | 66.9 | 129.8 | 94% |
| Food | 70.6 | 134.5 | 91% |
| Meat, poultry, fish | 76.3 | 152.7 | 100% |
| Dairy products | 73.2 | 121.5 | 66% |
| Fruits, vegetables | 67.2 | 136.8 | 104% |
| Durable goods | 80.3 | 120.2 | 50% |
| Apparel and upkeep | 78.2 | 124.8 | 60% |
| All services | 51.1 | 136.6 | 167% |
| Medical care | 48.1 | 135.8 | 182% |
| Weekly earnings | $45.58 | $140.23 | 208% |

Source: *Adapted from* Wall Street Journal, *May 7, 1973, p. 1, and based on U.S. Department of Labor consumer price index. "Weekly earnings" is the department's average for all nonsupervisory employees in the private economy.*

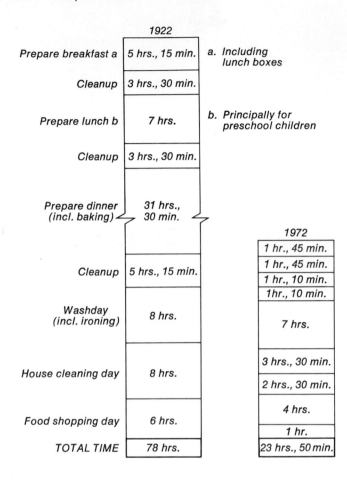

| 1922 | | a. Including lunch boxes |
|---|---|---|
| Prepare breakfast a | 5 hrs., 15 min. | |
| Cleanup | 3 hrs., 30 min. | |
| Prepare lunch b | 7 hrs. | b. Principally for preschool children |
| Cleanup | 3 hrs., 30 min. | |
| Prepare dinner (incl. baking) | 31 hrs., 30 min. | |

| 1972 |
|---|
| 1 hr., 45 min. |
| 1 hr., 45 min. |
| 1 hr., 10 min. |
| 1hr., 10 min. |

| 1922 | |
|---|---|
| Cleanup | 5 hrs., 15 min. |
| Washday (incl. ironing) | 8 hrs. |
| House cleaning day | 8 hrs. |
| Food shopping day | 6 hrs. |
| TOTAL TIME | 78 hrs. |

| 1972 |
|---|
| 7 hrs. |
| 3 hrs., 30 min. |
| 2 hrs., 30 min. |
| 4 hrs. |
| 1 hr. |
| 23 hrs., 50 min. |

Figure 4.1   One week's basic chores for a typical U.S. homemaker, 1922 and 1972 (Source: *Adapted from* Progressive Grocer, *April, 1973, p. 80.*)

12 percent. Thus the affluence of the American consumer is increasing dramatically.

Many other facets of our life are changing. Birth and fertility rates have dropped to their lowest levels in our history; even the absolute number of babies born in 1972 was the smallest in 27 years. Births have dropped off by so much that they indicate a fertility rate below the so-called *replacement rate.* However, because of the great number of women of child-bearing age, it would take 70 years at current rates

of birth for the nation to achieve zero population growth.

The consumer is also becoming more mobile. In one year, approximately 20 percent of the U.S. population change homes. The educational level is increasing dramatically. Consumer credit in March 1973 rose to $159.3 billion. Dramatic changes can be seen in the lifestyles of many social groups—women, for instance, as can be seen from Figure 4.1. In short, things are changing, and if one accepts the opinion of many experts, the *rate* of change is now increasing dramatically.

### The Consumer and the Retailer

Most stores will succeed or fail according to their ability to attract customers. So will most manufacturers and wholesalers succeed or fail according to their ability to attract customers. Whether retail stores handle any particular brand of merchandise is generally a function of whether or not they perceive it as profitable to handle. In the end, however, it is the reaction of the consumer to the retailer's merchandise that determines how profitable it is actually going to be. Clearly, the final customer or consumer is important to the retailer and to all other members of the marketing channel, since all depends in some way on the consumer buying the item.

Is the consumer king, then, as some say he is? Certainly, he can be made king, but whether such a king has any real power or is just a pawn of the court is another matter. Just because the consumer is first (or last, depending on one's viewpoint) in the chain of distribution, it does not follow that he is the most powerful member in the chain, nor is the retailer necessarily the second most powerful, the wholesaler third, and so forth. One thing, however, is obvious: in a market society each member of a channel must be concerned with all the other members, and particularly about the members further toward the consumer. Since the ultimate consumer is the last in line, he is of substantial interest to all the preceding members.

The importance of the consumer to the retailer

varies in a given instance according to a number of factors: the type of store; the assortment of products sold; the behavior of consumers; and so on. This makes it hard to generalize. In certain instances the owner of a store will have little knowledge of his customers except in the most obvious respects. In fact, he may depend wholly on his suppliers for consumer expertise. Sometimes, finding someone who will supply the merchandise that the consumer wants may be more important to the *storekeeper* than directly understanding consumer behavior. Brands such as Levi's pants, Hallmark greeting cards, RCA television, and others equally well accepted by the consumer may often be the foundation of a store's business. Obtaining a liquor license in an attractive area is practically a guarantee of economic success. Consumers, then, are just one consideration for most retailers, although clearly a very important one.

Because retailers see a lot of consumers, they have long understood most elements of the so-called marketing concept, which emphasized the importance of systematically focusing on the changing behavior of consumers. Wholesalers and manufacturers without retail operations may have trouble adapting to the marketing concept precisely because the consumer is not their immediate customer. Often they are separated from the consumer by more than one level of the channel. Because of his proximity to the final consumer, the retailer has often been considered the consumer's buying agent and the member of the marketing channel who knows more about consumers than anyone else. Many manufacturers and wholesalers prefer to hire marketing executives who have had retail experience because these executives are thought to have special insight into consumer behavior. The expertise of the retailer in this regard tends to be accepted in many merchandise areas, including most kinds of fashion, furniture, and some kinds of houseware. The extent to which a retailer is seen as an expert on consumer behavior seems to depend on his power within the channel—the more power, the more he has to say about the conditions of sale within the channel and the items handled by it. And the more the retailer influences these latter aspects, the more the wholesalers and manufacturers come to depend on his judgment of what the consumer wants.

## Approaches to the Consumer

There are many ways of looking at a purchase in a store. One might consider the decision-making process that the individual often goes through. One might also think in terms of the principal ingredients in the purchase; for example, under most conditions one needs a consumer, a store, and a product. In either case, it should be borne in mind that the store really does not know who the prime decision maker is. Retailers tend to think of the individual who says yes to the salesperson as the person making the decision to purchase. However, many individuals other than the purchaser can and often do influence this decision. For example, if a mother purchases a particular brand of cereal, she may have been influenced in that selection by her children, the father, friends, relatives, and so forth. A mother may frequent a store because one of the members of her family has a strong attachment for a brand carried only in that store. Or she may not purchase at another store because a family member objects to the only brand of ice cream carried by that store. Family members or friends may be asked to participate in the selection of both merchandise and store in which the purchase takes place. The father may influence the selection of a store or a type of store by requiring or not permitting the use of credit. Thus identification of the prime decision maker may be difficult. Indeed, it is not always clear that the individuals within a family understand who the key decision maker is.

Even if the retailer knew who the prime decision maker was, would he really know why the decision was made? Of particular importance to retailing is how the consumer perceives the relationship between product and store. Clearly, to some customers the store is an integral part of the product. Consider the following examples. The same cheese sandwich, with identical cheese and bread, may be purchased for $0.35 at one outlet and $1.50 at another. A car purchased from one Chevrolet dealer may not be perceived as the same as a car with identical equipment purchased from an unauthorized dealer or even from another Chevrolet dealer. Furniture from a leading department store may appear different from the very same pieces of wood and fabric selected in a discount house, even though these pieces of wood may have been put together in one plant on the same assembly line. The confusion becomes greater when the store sells its own private brand-name merchandise to customers, since the private brand may be displayed next to the name brand of the manufacturer who produced it for the store. Indeed, the store's only purpose in having a private brand may be to increase its own importance in the eyes of the consumer.

A related problem is whether retailers understand what it is they are trying to sell consumers. It is well known that a product is more than the sum of its physical characteristics, but how much more? Among the key variables are the atmosphere in which it is purchased; the terms of purchase, such as credit; the service reputation of the retailer; and the psychological satisfaction offered to the customer from things other than the product but related to it. Does any store really understand how it is varying these aspects of the merchandise mix to attract customers?

### Models of Consumer Behavior

An executive in a retail firm could approach consumer behavior in many ways. He could, as Alfred R. Oxenfeldt has pointed out, develop models to describe and/or explain the behavior of consumers. For example, he might assume that the consumer is a problem solver attempting to maximize his satisfaction. Or he might decide that, since a person learns over time, learning is the key to consumer behavior. Another executive might feel that the consumer is basically trying to reduce risk, and another that he relies mainly on impulse. Or is the consumer primarily a social animal who relies mainly on specific groups to establish values for

him? Perhaps the key to his behavior as a purchaser lies buried somewhere in his childhood. Each of the previous models has been deliberately oversimplified. But considering the extreme complexity and diversity of consumer behavior, such models may help an executive approach many problems more effectively than he could without them. Also, it may be possible to combine two or more of these models in such a manner as to provide useful answers to complex questions.

A second type of model, related to the maximizing of satisfaction mentioned above, assumes that each customer is trying his best with his limited resources to maximize his long-term economic and psychological benefits. Starting with certain assumptions about the values of consumers, the executive can predict how they will choose from among various merchandise mixes. In other words, the consumer selects whatever is in his best interest to select. Where the executive has difficulty making judgments about how a group of customers will choose, he may substitute judgments based on how he himself would behave in like circumstances. The assumption behind this approach is that people are much the same, with the same beliefs, values, attitudes, and so forth. Dubious though this assumption is, it does permit some allowance to be made for the consumer's point of view, something that is missing in many executives and their companies. This philosophy might be paraphrased as follows: The customer would like to have done to him as I would like done to me.

A third approach is to interview and otherwise study the consumer, with or without some theoretical model, but often just to obtain raw information. The logic of finding out what the customer wants is quite compelling. Customers have traditionally been thought of as carefully weighing their decisions in substantive terms, especially price. This may have been true when most people were more or less poor, but as our society becomes more and more affluent and the amount of discretionary income increases, there is obviously an increase in the variety of motivations and behavior entering into most decisions to purchase. It therefore appears very sound to find out what one's customers are doing; how they are thinking; what they are buying; how they perceive your stores; and so forth.

The executive might also want to concentrate on examining the internal customer records of his firm. What sort of people are the charge customers? Where do they live and work? What types of jobs do they have? What are their incomes and family situation? How (if the records are available) do they differ from the cash customers? This type of analysis can uncover a great deal of information that is of use in many types of decision.

Finally, it may be suggested that the identification of specific customers is not necessary because all that matters is whether more dollars' worth and units of merchandise are selling this year than last. If more people are buying what you are selling, and keep on buying more and more of it, why bother going to them and analyzing what they think? You know what they want. The key to this approach is determining what the customer wants and is going to want by analyzing what he has bought.

### Analyzing What Is Sold

A retailer tends to separate his decisions with regard to the consumer into two types. First, in selecting store locations and in selecting and creating an appropriate store image, the firm is concerned with potential consumer attitudes, the movement and composition of potential customers, the psychological characteristics of potential customers, and so forth. It gets this information as best it can. Second, it has to think about the merchandise. What types of merchandise should be carried? What price lines should be fostered in a given merchandise category? What items should be promoted? Most of these questions are answered by analyzing what merchandise is selling. Indeed, many retailers have developed complex systems to determine what items are selling and what they have in common. Nothing is given higher priority by most retail executives than finding out what is selling and

effectively using this information to sell more goods than would otherwise have been sold. Most retail executives, in fact, see the consumer world in terms of what has been selling in their own and others' stores.

If an experienced department store buyer were to go into a new department, one of the first things he would try to find out is what has been selling, in the last few hours, weeks, months—perhaps in the last year. Which items or classifications are selling best, which worst? Which are growing fastest or slowest? Which classifications offer the highest return per dollar invested in inventory, and which the highest profit per square or cubic or linear foot of shelf space? He might analyze the best-selling items in each classification to see what they have in common with respect to package size, shelf location, style, price line, fabric, or whatever. He might perform the same type of analysis after grouping all the items by supplier. In any case, his entire focus would be on what is selling and has sold in the relevant merchandise area.

### Unit and Classification Controls

Information about what is selling can be obtained in many ways, but unit and classification data provide the key. Most types of retail store develop rather inexpensive methods at either the store or the warehouse level to find out how individual items and classes of item are selling. The store has many ways of finding out how many of an item have sold over some given time period. For example, if a store knows that it had 12 dozen Brand X golf balls in stock at the beginning of the week and it received 24 dozen Brand X golf balls during the week, a stock count of Brand X golf balls at the beginning of the next week that showed 11 dozen in stock would indicate that 25 dozen had been sold, stolen, or misplaced during the week.

When combined with information related to merchandise on order, these controls provide one basis for ordering merchandise. Unit sales information can be obtained in many other ways. The salesperson may record the items sold at a particular cash register—for example, the one for major appliances. Or the salesperson may tear a ticket off the garment and the tickets may at some point be counted to indicate what has sold over the specific time period. Such counts can be very easily performed by computers, and today a computer system can offer information as to what is sold based on information fed to it automatically by the cash register or other device.

Thanks to his unit sales information, the decision maker will generally know that 12 of this, 18 of that, or 23 of something else sold over the time period in which he is interested. Thus if a customer buys an item in a store, he is in most instances voting in the store's decision process. He will therefore influence the item's future in that store as well as the way in which it is perceived by the store executives. If a consumer does not purchase an item, he is also voting, though in a less direct way.

The store executive may want to build up the unit sales information into something more meaningful. This something can take many forms. For instance, the item information may be broken down by size, so that the unit controls indicate that, say, 12 units of size eight of a particular shoe were sold during a week. The executive will also be interested in how many units were sold of that shoe in all sizes combined. Or he may want a breakdown of unit sales by price line. Thus it might be of some importance to him to know that the store sold 800 different types of shirt at $3.99, or 40 guns between $80.00 and $90.00, over some time period. If, of the 800 shirts sold at $3.99, some 200 were of a certain style, silhouette, color, or fabric, this might affect his thinking considerably. In short, a great deal of useful information can be obtained by combining unit sales with other relevant factors.

Merchandise will under almost all conditions be ordered by the unit. However, the key to most analyses of what is selling is the dollar sales by merchandise classification. If the price of one line is multiplied by unit sales, the result is the dollar sales of the item. If like items have been grouped together in some type of classification, the sum of the dollar sales for all items is the dollar sales of that classifica-

**Table 4.2**
Manual classification systems: hypothetical daily sales sheet for a sporting goods department

| | | | | | | Total |
|---|---|---|---|---|---|---|
| Guns and related | | | | | | |
| Fishing and related | | | | | | |
| Active sports and related[a] | | | | | | |
| Pool tables and related | | | | | | |
| Ping-Pong tables and related | | | | | | |
| Exercise equipment | | | | | | |
| Ski equipment and related | | | | | | |
| Bicycles and related | | | | | | |
| Golf and related | | | | | | |
| Tennis and related | | | | | | |
| Binoculars and related[b] | | | | | | |
| Miscellaneous | | | | | | |
| Total | | | | | | |

a. Excluding golf and tennis.
b. Including gun binoculars.

tion. Indeed, all the classifications in a store can be built up from the price and unit information. This type of buildup, however, is not usual. Classification data are generally obtained directly from dollar figures. At the simplest level, the salesperson may keep track of his dollar sales by registering the sale directly into a manual classification system. Thus the sporting goods department might develop a sheet somewhat like Table 4.2.

These sheets can be filled out daily by each salesperson as each sale is made. The store executive then has a breakdown of the dollar sales by classification at the end of each day. Much can be done with this. Sales can be analyzed in terms of any time period, and comparisons made with last year so that trends can be diagnosed and troublespots brought to light. Sales per unit of shelf or floor space and sales per dollar invested in inventory are only two of the useful indicators that can be calculated with these same dollar sales figures.

Most classification data can be obtained more simply and directly by using the register at the time of sale. Different keys or combinations of punches can represent different classifications and these keys can be linked to a computer system. Here, the number and type of statistical breakdown are limited only by the creativity and perception of the decision maker. However, the classifications need to be changed over time so that they reflect change in the types of item sold, the perceptions of the consumers, and so forth.

The unit and classification data within a retail organization are supplemented by information obtained from other sources, including the following:

1. *Unit sales and classification data from other stores.* The decision maker is not limited to unit classification data from his store or chain. In many instances, his store will be part of a regional organization or buying group. Substantial information may be obtained from these and other stores so that a decision maker may compare his performance with theirs. He may also corroborate his hunches by talking to other decision makers. Using data from other stores has the effect of increasing the sample size. This will usually make it a more reliable basis for generalization even though it does not meet the standards for probability sampling.

2. *Talk with the customer and salespeople.* One large store used to have a rule that its buyers had to actually sell to customers for at least an hour a day. While time pressures have made this type of approach to customers difficult to maintain, decision makers regard information obtained directly from customers and salespeople as an essential supplement to unit and classification data. The latter are, after all, based on what is past; even the most rapid

control systems usually are not completely up to date. Talking to customers is immediate. In addition, as previously suggested, the unit and dollar systems do not emphasize the whys of consumer purchase. At times the whys may enhance the interpretation of the unit data. For example, some merchandise may be out of stock, or if in stock not on display, and this may result in poor sales even though it is in great demand by customers. Discussions with customers and salespeople will give the decision maker a better understanding of the unit and dollar data.

In talking to customers the decision maker is seldom looking for deep reasons to explain their behavior. Rather, he wants answers for such questions as, For what obvious reasons is the $44.99 lightweight bicycle selling so well today? Perhaps a competitor advertised a similar bicycle in the newspaper. It may be that the $39.99 bicycle is not displayed, or has been mispriced at $49.99. It is even possible that the lightweight bicycle has been mispriced. Or a chess set at $6.99 may be selling in the adult games department because the stationery department advertised a similar set at $6.99. It may be that the washer at $189.99 is not selling because it does not have a porcelain top. The $129.99 electric dryer may be too wide for apartments in New York City. Certain classifications may do poorly because there are not enough salespeople. For the most part, this kind of information comes only at first hand.

3. *Supplier information.* Supplier firms are information centers for the dissemination of both correct and incorrect information to the retailer. In many instances, however, the supplier has little reason to mislead his customers. Suppliers obtain information from many customers, verbally and through orders. Indeed, many suppliers continually analyze their orders to discern patterns. Of course, they put their own profits first. But most of them also want their customers to prosper, and will not knowingly misinform them.

### Pros and Cons of Relying on Sales Data

There are many advantages in analyzing the merchandise that is sold. The data have a realism and a certainty that is missing in other types of data. The merchandise actually was sold or stolen; in either case somebody liked it enough to remove it from the shelves. The decision maker does not have to worry about all the uncertainties of conducting a sample survey of consumers, whether by mail or by interview. Another key advantage of relying on actual sales data is that they can be readily assembled at small incremental cost. Tearing off tickets to feed into a computer system and similar informational inputs of the salesperson at the point of sale can usually be accomplished by the existing staff as part of their jobs. Lost tickets, incorrect counts, and other typical problems of computer systems are a nuisance but can be handled in most instances by competent executives. The most significant advantage, however, is that present sales have proven in most stores to be an excellent predictor of future sales in both fashion and nonfashion merchandise categories. This is true even of such items as food.

However, there are also a number of disadvantages. First, the information generated by the system is necessarily limited by what the store has to offer. If the initial selections as to price, merchandise, display, and so forth are astute, then analysis of unit controls can presumably improve the merchandise mix. But if the initial selection is poor, much of the information generated by the control system may be misleading or worthless. A second limitation is that many small decisions based on such information can add up to one big mess. An example, in a nonretail context, may make this point clearer. In city X there are 10,000 cars for 2 million residents. Most of the residents therefore depend for their transportation on trains and buses. Economic conditions then so improve in our city that 1 million more residents can buy cars. Each weighs the advantages of the car against the utility of the money that he will have to pay for it, and each decides that the car represents the optimum use of his money. However, although each citizen is acting rationally within this framework of optimization, the quality of life within the city with all these extra cars may be substantially below what it was before. It can still be argued that each citizen would have

bought a car even if he had known that 999,999 others would also buy one, because he thinks he is better off in the mess with a car than without a car and with more money. However that may be, the city government has a real problem. Something like this goes on in many retail operations: a number of small units suboptimize in a way that produces one large mess, often a very unprofitable mess. For this reason, the unit controls tend to work best when gradual evolution is desirable. But when the need is for dramatic transformation, unit controls are less likely to offer an answer.

Another problem, already alluded to, is that the votes of customers who buy are easier to count than the votes of those who do not buy. In other words, if customers do not come into a store, or if they do not buy anything when they come in, there is no readily available record of their decision. It is true that the votes of the nonpurchasing customers may be discerned collectively in the form of declining sales within classifications and perhaps for the total store. If, however, dollar sales increase more in one part of a classification than anticipated, this may amply compensate for lost dollars in the other parts. Thus actual customers have a greater say in the future of a store than do potential customers. Similarly, output measured in terms of dollar sales tends to be fed into the categories and classifications that appear reasonable to the retail decision maker. Unless the executive is capable of changing the classifications to reflect changing conditions, the information so generated can be highly distorted and important trends can be missed. Long-range planning, in fact, requires more knowledge of the consumer than is offered by unit or dollar controls. What types of new store should we have? Do we attract the same type of customer now as we did a year ago? What is our largest class of potential customer? Information like this does not find its way to the cash register.

It must be admitted that unless interviews are made of both salespeople and customers little can be found out about why customers do anything. Why are customers buying at your store as opposed to other stores? Why do they buy only 80 percent of their weekly supermarket purchases from store A? Why do they buy more of your private brand than the national brand?

A final limitation of both unit and dollar controls is that retail executives often forget that these controls only reflect consumer behavior. The consumer is the most important element involved, and the controls are used only because it is so hard to assess consumer actions and attitudes directly. Despite all its limitations, however, the key to most effective merchandising is the analysis of unit and dollar systems. Indeed, entire courses in retail management have been devoted to developing more effective ways of finding out in an efficient, rapid, and meaningful manner just what is selling and what is not.

## Understanding the Consumer

So far we have concentrated on a firm's merchandising decisions for the good reason that many retail executives feel such decisions are the key to business success. But there are many other key decisions to be made in retailing. Indeed, a firm's image is composed of several dimensions, only some of which are directly related to its merchandise. Eleanor G. May, in a study of one full-line department store that was slightly above average in price, divided its image into seven aspects or dimensions:

Salespeople
Exciting—Modern
Advertising—General Appearance
Merchandise Variety
Price
Convenience
Delivery—Billing

In this evaluation, the consumer's perception of the store's nonmerchandising aspects takes on substantial importance, although the merchandise and nonmerchandise dimensions are clearly related. Each of these dimensions can be evaluated by consumer questionnaires, and the results can be used by progressive executives to aid in many decisions, including store location. When one approaches consumer behavior, the contributions of many academic disciplines become quite extensive. Economists, psychologists, sociologists, and anthropologists have all offered concepts of substantial interest to the observer of consumer behavior. For instance, C. Glenn Walters and Gordon W. Paul have listed the contributions of economics as follows:

(i) The more units of a specific product that a consumer uses, the less satisfaction he will derive from each additional unit that he consumes in a short space of time. This is known as the *law of diminishing utility.*

(ii) Consumers have unlimited wants and limited resources. They can therefore be expected to allocate their limited resources among products and services in such a manner that the satisfaction per dollar from the last unit of each product will be approximately equal. In other words, if a consumer has 50 cents, he should spend the 50 cents in the manner that offers him the greatest satisfaction.

(iii) The summation of individual choices of the various consumers equals the total demand for that product.

(iv) The quantity of a product produced by a firm may depend on the interaction of the marginal cost and the marginal revenue curves of that firm, derived from its total cost and the total revenue curves. This is discussed further in Chapter 11.

The behavioral sciences also offer many insights into consumer behavior. Psychologists, studying the individual interacting with his environment, have examined such relevant areas as motivation, learning, perception, and attitudes. Social psychologists have studied the experiences of individuals with regard to other individuals, groups, and cultures. Sociologists have emphasized the social pressures resulting from group membership. Anthropologists have studied different societies, our own included, emphasizing patterns inherited from the past that influence behavior today. All these disciplines will be drawn on throughout the remainder of this chapter.

### Individual Behavior

In the study of what merchandise is selling, the individual does not count for much unless a great many other individuals do the same thing. There are, however, a number of good reasons for studying the behavior of individual consumers, some of which will now be discussed.

If there are only small variations in the performance of consumers in a given buying situation, understanding a small number of them will be as good as understanding them all. Indeed, if there are no individual variations at all, or none worth noticing, one person can stand for the whole group. And even if the individual variations in some group are quite large, it may be necessary to study one or a few individuals before the relevant subgroups can be established or other useful hypotheses created. A further reason for the study of individual behavior is that if the behavior of individuals can be measured in comparable units, one can obtain group data by summing these units. Also, a random sample, if one can be obtained, will accurately reflect the behavior of the population from which it has been drawn. Moreover, all decisions are ultimately made by individuals even if subject to group values and pressures. The individual is the smallest decision unit and it is generally easier to obtain detailed information about his behavior than about the behavior of any of the many groups to which he belongs. Finally, it is the individual who must be satisfied by the store even though much of his satisfaction may relate to his group values.

### The Purchase Process

The act of purchase is the outcome of a series of events. One way to look at it is in terms of the conscious activity involved in the decision process. Purchase activity is of critical importance to many people and indeed a substantial number put in long hours improving their expertise as consumers. The tremendous growth in the circulation of *Consumer Reports* and other consumers' magazines bears witness to this fact. A first step in the process for some consumers might be to recognize the problem they are trying to solve, perhaps defining it explicitly. They might go on to specify and analyze alternative solutions. Finally, some sort of decision process could be used for choosing from among the designated alternatives. After the purchase the consumer may react to the purchase in various ways— for instance, by testing the actual value of his warranty. However, not many consumers are quite as systematic as this, even if they ought to be. Even if a consumer is conscientious, the time dimension, amount of thought, search effort, and so forth will vary with the product, previous use of the product, personality and attitudes of the individual, and numerous other factors.

Another way to look at the purchase process is in terms of the changes, both conscious and unconscious, that take place within some consumers before they purchase. For instance, it has been suggested that a customer goes through the following process, perhaps over a substantial period of time:

1. Awareness of the product's existence;
2. Knowledge of what the product has to offer;
3. Favorable attitude toward the product;
4. Preference for the product over other products;
5. Desire to buy the product;
6. Purchase of the product.

The purchase process can also be analyzed from the marketer's point of view. There are four basic steps: getting the attention of the potential prospect; developing his interest; creating in him a desire to own the product; and getting him to purchase. Propelling the customer through these stages becomes the task of the salesman or advertiser. The marketer in the above instances, unlike the consumer, nearly always goes through the same steps in the same order, and does so with conscious effort and attention to detail.

### Needs and Motives

Needs give rise to internal conditions that require relief. They may be physiological or psychological, innate or learned. Needs may conflict with each other in the sense that some take priority over others, and in the sense that, under certain circumstances, satisfying one may interfere with satisfying another. The consumer purchases items in order to satisfy his needs and perhaps to reduce his level of tension. According to most observers, if a consumer does not possess some kind of internal dissatisfaction, there will be no purchase.

While needs create conditions that require relief, motives give direction to relief-giving activities. A motive is whatever it is within a person that causes him to act, move, or behave in some goal-directed manner.

### Perception

Perception can be described as the process of becoming aware through any of one's senses. Clearly, consumer perception is subjective in that it exists in the mind of the individual. Perceptions also tend to be selective. Since an individual cannot respond to everything at once, if he looks at a store window, he will probably not see everything in it. Individuals also tend to have a more accurate and rapid perception of stimuli that fit in with their preconceived values and attitudes—a built-in perceptual bias, as it were.

An important influence on the study of perception has been Gestalt psychology. Roughly speaking, the Gestalt view is that perception cannot be explained in terms of its separate components, but only in terms of how the complete picture—*Gestalt* in German—appears to the individual. The following experiment is often cited by Gestalt psychologists: If two lights close to one another are turned on and off in alternating sequence at the appropriate rate, an observer will see, not two lights going on and off in succession, but a single light moving back and forth.

### Attitudes

An attitude might be defined as a relatively lasting set of beliefs organized around certain objects, events, or situations. It is, in Gordon Allport's classic phrase, "a state of mental and neural readiness." A consumer forms attitudes toward products and stores that influence his purchase behavior. The degree to which his attitudes and behavior are related is the subject of some research and considerable speculation. It can be argued that behavior change precedes attitude change in many instances rather than vice versa. The attitudes of consumers would be expected to vary in intensity and direction, and be more or less consistent with their other attitudes. It would also be expected that the key elements in a person's experience and background would have some effect on his attitudes as a consumer.

**Attitude change**   Retailers and marketers are of course especially interested in changing the consumer's attitudes in one direction, namely, in favor of their merchandise. Many things can cause attitude change. Among them are a change in the product or store, or at least a change in the customer's perceptions of them; a change in the strength of the customer's attitude; a change in the amount of information possessed by the consumer, particularly if he or she had a small amount of information before; a change in the importance of the product to the consumer; and a change in the content or quality of the communications to the customer.

Of particular interest here is the theory of cognitive dissonance, developed in the 1950s by Leon Festinger. Briefly, the theory states that an individual will tend to reduce any inconsistency among his cognitions. An inconsistency in his cognitions, or cognitive dissonance, occurs any time there is a discrepancy between what he knows or anticipates to be true and what he actually perceives. For instance, he may see someone he trusts committing a crime. The consumer may try to reduce his tension by removing the source of the dissonance. ("No, that can't be X—he wouldn't do a thing like that!") On the other hand, he may remove the dissonance by revising his opinions ("Obviously, X wasn't such a good guy after all"). This still leaves his basic value system intact ("Trustworthy people don't commit crimes"). Therefore, if a retailer tries to create change by inducing cognitive dissonance, he has a narrow line to walk. He must make the message close enough to the consumer's value system to be accepted, but dissonant enough to create the desired change.

### Learning

Learning may be defined as a durable change in behavior that results from experience. Some theories of learning suggest that we learn gradually over time, others that we learn immediately. Certainly, however, consumer behavior does change as the consumer purchases and uses merchandise. John A. Howard developed a theory that individuals change their behavior predictably over time as they interact with stores and products. As an individual tries a product or store and is satisfied, the probability of his trying the product in the future increases. In the beginning stage, called "extensive problem solving," the consumer actively seeks information from various sources (including, at times, friends); thinks about his purchase for some time; considers many alternatives; and his probability of purchase is low. As the consumer purchases the item and uses it, he learns. In stage two, "limited problem solving," the individual has narrowed his range of product alternatives, so that he need no longer consider them at such length; is subject to cues that trigger the purchase; and has a higher probability of purchase. At the final stage "automatic response behavior," the time from receipt of the cue by the consumer to the time of purchase is short; the type of cue that triggers the purchase may be different; and the probability of purchase is highest (see Figure 4.2).

Quite obviously, the usefulness of this learning model will vary with the product category and type of store. The purchase of safety pins cannot be thought of in the same manner as the purchase of a

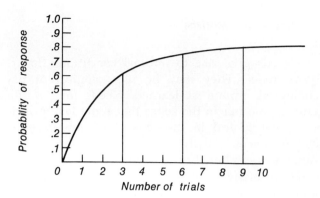

Figure 4.2    The learning curve for Brand A [Source: *John Howard*, Marketing Management: Analysis and Planning *(Homewood, Ill.: Richard D. Irwin, Inc., 1963), p. 36.*]

car. In addition, the amount of learning may depend on the number of trials that an individual has the opportunity to go through. For instance, since food is purchased frequently, one would expect learning of the stimulus-response type to be more important for this category of purchase than for a desk that may be replaced every ten years, if ever. A customer may purchase certain items from a department store quite frequently but may purchase from a major appliance store only once every five years. However, regardless of the relevance to a particular case of the model just described, it is clear that most consumers will change with experience.

Learning, as we have seen, is an individual process. But one can also divide customers into groups according to their position on the learning curve. Thus a store may think in terms of how many of its own or its competitors' customers are at the stage of extensive problem solving, limited problem solving, or automatic response behavior for a merchandise area or perhaps for a total store.

### Personality

Personality, in David C. McClelland's classic formulation, refers to the inner organization of the person. The components of a personality include all a person's physiological and psychological aspects. Thus personality encompasses not only a person's physical and emotional characteristics but also his or her attitudes, beliefs, traits, biases, and behavior patterns. It appears obvious that personality must affect consumer behavior in some way, but nobody knows exactly how. It may be that personality affects attitudes which in turn influence consumer behavior. Conversely, both attitudes and consumer behavior may influence personality. The evidence, however, is too mixed so far to be of much use to retail decision makers.

### Postpurchase Behavior

One of the advantages of the learning model is that it depicts purchasing as a continuous process in which the actual purchase may be a relatively unimportant event. For instance, the satisfaction that the customer derives from using the product may be the most important event for certain types of item. The *aftersale* would appear to be more important for the store than the manufacturer. A customer enters into many transactions with certain stores each year; in fact, he or she is interacting with stores continually. A store should therefore be quite conscious of the satisfaction customers derive from using its merchandise and services. Particularly important may be servicing appliances, but other services, such as fashion shows or demonstrations of cosmetic products, may be equally important.

### Influence of the Group on the Individual

Groups influence consumers in many ways. In one sense, the members of a group can offer information to other members that should improve their ability to make purchase decisions. Thus your friends and neighbors can probably tell you the type of grass seed that grows best in your area; which local store offers the best service on refrigerators, and where to buy good used furniture. Groups also

add a new dimension to the purpose of purchases, as consumers strive to conform to group values.

Different groups have different levels of importance. A basic group is the family. Indeed, the household is considered by many to be the basic unit of consumption. Most members of our society belong to at least two families during their lifetime. One of the more useful concepts related to the family is that of the life cycle. As an individual goes through life, his family obligations change. His purchase patterns will change accordingly. Thus families will change their expenditure patterns when they are just married; after they have purchased their first house; after the last children have gone to college; and so forth.

Individuals are influenced by the values and expectations of the groups with which they associate. The term "reference group" is used to designate a group to which individual consumers relate whether or not they actually belong to it. Such a group will exert substantial influence on the purchase behavior of many individuals. For example, if a man identifies with the members of the Yale Club, he will tend to adopt what he thinks are the values of that group and his purchases will reinforce the identification.

Culture is the distinctive life style of a large number of people, passed down from generation to generation. It helps to establish norms of behavior while enforcing group standards. Culture operates through social groups, reference groups, the family, and the individual to influence consumer behavior. A given culture may include numerous subcultures that can heavily influence purchase behavior. Thus E. Pell found that consumers of Jewish or French descent were more likely to purchase new products than consumers of German, Italian, or British descent.

### Groups and Segments

Groups were discussed in the previous section with regard to their influence on individual behavior. Another way to look at them is as cross-sections of the customer population. Both stores and

Table 4.3
Regular and nonregular customers of three types of department store,
by age of customer

|  | Traditional | | Nat. Chain | | Discount | |
|---|---|---|---|---|---|---|
|  | Reg. | Nearby nonreg. | Reg. | Nearby nonreg. | Reg. | Nearby nonreg. |
| Under 25 | 7% | 11% | 11% | 11% | 11% | 10% |
| 25–34 | 16% | 21% | 21% | 18% | 19% | 20% |
| 35–49 | 29% | 35% | 33% | 32% | 32% | 33% |
| 50–64 | 30% | 23% | 24% | 26% | 25% | 25% |
| 65 plus | 18% | 10% | 11% | 13% | 13% | 12% |
| Median age | 48 | 42 | 42 | 44 | 44 | 43 |

Source: *Presentation of the Westinghouse Broadcasting Company before the Retail Research Society, 1972.*

Table 4.4
Regular and nonregular customers of three types of department store,
by income of customer

|  | Traditional | | Nat. chain | | Discount | |
|---|---|---|---|---|---|---|
|  | Reg. | Nearby nonreg. | Reg. | Nearby nonreg. | Reg. | Nearby nonreg. |
| Under $10,000 | 38% | 41% | 46% | 38% | 48% | 38% |
| $10,000–14,999 | 34% | 35% | 34% | 35% | 33% | 35% |
| $15,000 plus | 28% | 24% | 20% | 27% | 20% | 27% |
| Median income ($ thousand) | 11.6 | 11.3 | 10.5 | 11.7 | 10.2 | 11.6 |

Source: *Presentation of the Westinghouse Broadcasting Company before the Retail Research Society, 1972.*

products can be created to appeal to homogeneous groups of customers. The individual need have no relevance to this approach except insofar as every group is composed of individuals.

A decision maker is interested in groups that make a difference in his decision making. While it is true that he or she will usually want to be sure that there is an actual difference between groups before creating a product or store to appeal to that group, the existence of a purely statistical difference is not meaningful. The manager is usually looking for big differences between groups. For example, a business executive will seldom care that only 59 percent of his white customers used the bus to get to his restaurant as opposed to 62 percent of his black customers. The fact that this difference might be statistically significant would not be a factor. A rule of thumb for most retailing is that if a statistical test is necessary to corroborate the existence of a difference, that difference will have no managerial significance.

It has been suggested by Oxenfeldt that there are four ways to group:

1. *Demographic.* Groups may be classified in terms of age, sex, height, weight, location, and so forth. Thus a store might be interested in the fact that no teenagers presently frequent its premises. Or perhaps a store might create advertising designed to attract a specific age group. Another store might be interested in the fact that 95 percent of its customers are men. Certain clothing stores appeal to individuals who wear certain sizes of dress. An

age breakdown for three different kinds of department store is given in Table 4.3.

2. *Socioeconomic.* One can classify customers by such factors as income and occupation. Thus airlines would be interested in individuals of certain occupations and not of others. Concepts such as social class might be of interest to furniture stores, department stores, and so forth. An income breakdown for three different kinds of department store is indicated in Table 4.4.

3. *Psychological.* Some marketing observers do not feel that demographic and socioeconomic classifications are the most meaningful. They suggest instead that as the society becomes more affluent and discretionary income increases dramatically, other aspects become more important. Such is the thrust of *psychographics* within marketing. One way to classify customers is along psychological dimensions ("aggressive" versus "submissive," etc.). A woman's apparel chain might well appeal primarily to customers who think young; it might even intimidate women into thinking young.

4. *Store-Specific.* This is a catchall category for consumer characteristics that relate to a given product or store but do not readily fit into any of the first three categories. For example, a wig store would naturally be interested in customers who wear wigs, and a fashion store in customers who buy early or late in the season. Another store might be interested in dividing consumers into buyers and nonbuyers.

The logic of dividing customers into groups is obvious. Executives have been taught to classify most of their lives. Therefore it is quite natural for them to accept and use concepts framed in group terms for their day-to-day decision making. One of the values of this *customer segmentation,* as it is known in marketing, is that it cautions against the use of averages for decision making where the variation about the *mean* is high. Thus a Ph.D. program in business at a university might have students with a mean age of 34. However, the group might well be composed of former executives over 50 and new B.A.s around 21. Another aspect of customer segmentation is that it forces the decision maker to focus on the needs and desires of the various groups. In this way, he will come to understand how the groups resemble each other and how they differ, as well as the changing nature of their various aspirations, desires, and characteristics. If he is wise, he will come to recognize the futility of trying to be all things to all people.

One of the purposes of classification analysis is to locate customers who have not been effectively cultivated by other firms but who can be profitably attracted by suitable merchandising mixes and marketing techniques. A company that can develop exceptionally attractive merchandise packages for specific groups of customers will often obtain higher prices and more isolation from competition. Nevertheless, many sophisticated companies apparently pay little heed to this type of marketing. Indeed many products are designed by sophisticated companies to appeal to rather obvious markets, such as women who own washing machines. Companies that are known to have specialized appeal to specific customer segments include Abercrombie and Fitch, Joseph Magnin, and the various 711 stores.

**Some classification systems** There are a number of commonly used classification systems that offer potential insights into consumer behavior. The validity and usefulness of these systems will vary from situation to situation, but all have the advantage of being related to the consumer in some direct way. For instance, marketing texts for many years have classified goods as convenience, shopping, or specialty, denoting three different attitudes of consumers toward them. The definitions in this classification system have varied greatly. Louis P. Bucklin suggests the following:

*Convenience Goods:* Those goods for which the consumer, before his need arises, possesses a preference map that indicates a willingness to purchase any of a number of known substitutes rather than to make the additional effort required to buy a particular item.

*Shopping Goods:* Those goods for which the consumer has not developed a complete preference map before the need arises, requiring him to undertake a search to construct such a map before purchase.

*Speciality Goods:* Those goods for which the consumer, before the need arises, possesses a preference map that indicates a willingness to expend the additional effort required to purchase the most preferred item rather than to buy a more readily accessible substitute. (Bucklin, 1967, p. 333)

A customer may also have a distinct preference map for stores. Here are Bucklin's definitions:

*Convenience Stores:* Those stores for which the consumer, before his need for some product arises, possesses a preference map that indicates a willingness to buy from the most accessible store.

*Shopping Stores:* Those stores for which the consumer has not developed a complete preference map relative to the product he wishes to buy, requiring him to undertake a search to construct such a map before purchase.

*Specialty Stores:* Those stores for which the consumer, before his need for some product arises, possesses a preference map that indicates a willingness to buy the item from a particular establishment even though it may not be the most accessible. (Bucklin, op. cit., p. 338)

The retail decision maker who uses this classification system may choose to take three steps:

(i) He can classify potential customers for some product or group of products in terms of the nine categories yielded by combining Bucklin's classification of goods with his classification of stores.

(ii) He can develop or consider strategies to appeal to these various market segments.

(iii) He can select the appropriate marketing strategies and segments.

Table 4.5
Customer-switching among selected stores

| No. of shoppers (000) | Total for 25 stores 12,773 | B. Altman 906 | Bloomingdale's 1,257 | Gimbels 2,220 | Korvettes 4,433 | Macy's 3,677 | Sears 3,940 |
|---|---|---|---|---|---|---|---|
| | | | Percent of shoppers | | | | |
| B. Altman's | 7.1 | 100.0 | 32.7 | 16.8 | 8.1 | 11.6 | 6.3 |
| Index | 100 | 1410 | 461 | 236 | 114 | 164 | 86 |
| Bloomingdale's | 9.8 | 45.3 | 100.0 | 21.5 | 12.9 | 15.5 | 9.4 |
| Index | 100 | 461 | 1016 | 219 | 131 | 157 | 96 |
| Gimbel's | 17.4 | 41.0 | 38.0 | 100.0 | 28.9 | 34.0 | 21.4 |
| Index | 100 | 236 | 218 | 575 | 166 | 196 | 123 |
| Korvettes | 34.7 | 39.5 | 45.5 | 57.8 | 100.0 | 55.5 | 50.3 |
| Index | 100 | 114 | 131 | 166 | 288 | 160 | 145 |
| Macy's | 28.8 | 47.1 | 45.2 | 56.3 | 46.0 | 100.0 | 35.2 |
| Index | 100 | 164 | 157 | 196 | 160 | 347 | 122 |
| Sears | 30.8 | 27.3 | 29.6 | 38.0 | 44.7 | 37.7 | 100.0 |
| Index | 100 | 88 | 96 | 123 | 145 | 122 | 324 |

Source: Sales Management. The Marketing Magazine. *January 22, 1973, p. 31. Copyright 1973. Reprinted by permission.*

### Loyalty

A great deal has been written about brand loyalty. Data on it are typically developed from *consumer panels.* These data indicate which and how many customers change from one brand to another during a given period. Store managements can find out through consumer panel data over time from which competitors its customers have come and to which competitors they go when they change loyalties. A management can estimate which are its closest competitors and how loyal its customers are compared to the customers of other stores. Alternatively, an analyst might ask a cross section of consumers where they last shopped or usually shop, and then ask them where else they have made purchases during the last two months or some other definite period. He might then develop a chart of the kind shown in Table 4.5. This approach to customers forces the store management to think of the customer in relation to the relevant competition. Many managements seem to feel that customers are in love with them. A loyalty analysis permits a store to see how loyal its customers are compared with those of other relevant retailers. It can also see to which outlets it is losing sales and perhaps the dollar volume of this loss. Loyalty analysis further suggests various advertising and merchandising strategies.

While little research has been done on store loyalty, a substantial amount has been done on brand loyalty. James E. Engel and his associates draw the following conclusions on the latter subject:

(i) Brand loyalty appears to increase with age.

(ii) Heavy users of a product appear to be more loyal than light users.

(iii) Brand loyalty appears to decrease as the time between purchases of the product increases.

(iv) The brand loyalty of an informal group leader appears to affect the behavior of other group members.

(v) Certain market structure variables, such as how extensively the brand is distributed at retail and what share of the market it can claim, affect brand loyalty.

A key factor in store loyalty is the mobility of population. About one-fifth of the population change their place of residence each year. For instance, according to the National Industrial Conference Board, between March 1969 and March 1970 some 36.5 million persons changed address. This varied dramatically with age. Over 40 percent of men and women aged 20–24 moved, compared with less than 15 percent of those 35–44, and less than 9 percent of those 65 or over. Most of the moves were not far: 60 percent chose new residences within the same county; 20 percent moved to residences in a different county but the same state; and 20 percent moved to a different state. Even a short move, however, necessarily involves changes in store loyalty.

### Amenability toward Change

Customers might also be grouped according to their amenability to change, as in the following classification attributed to Everett M. Rogers:

*Innovators.* These are individuals who actively seek change. For research purposes, the innovators are usually defined as customers who are the first to purchase a specific new product. Whether or not these are the same as the individuals who actually seek change is debatable, but it seems reasonable to assume that the earlier purchasers of major innovations in any product line would at least be amenable to change. Another common assumption is that innovators actively seek information related to change. For this reason, innovators are generally thought to be good customers for brands: their search for change is likely to make them loyal to no brand in particular. From the store's point of view, present customers who are both loyal to the store and seek change within it are ideal. A very different problem is presented by customers who satisfy their need for change by buying at a different store.

*Early adopters.* These are individuals who are readily amenable to change but do not seek it quite so actively as the innovators. Early adopters are thought to be less fickle and therefore more worthy of the marketer's attention.

*Early majority.* These are individuals who will change, but only after being subjected to pressures and inducements. The latter may be applied by other members of this group or by members of the two previous groups, viz., innovators and early adopters.

*Late majority and laggards.* These individuals actually resist change in varying degrees. They become very unattractive customers for new products but very profitable ones in many other respects; for instance, they not only will tend to purchase in the same store but also will purchase staple merchandise without promotional inducement.

Table 4.6 is a matrix that shows how these categories might be applied. It should be compared with Bucklin's classification system for goods and stores.

The student should not be misled into believing that there is a vast amount of evidence supporting

Table 4.6
*Classification system for rate of innovation among stores and product*

| | Innovator store | Early adopter store | Early majority store | Late majority store | Laggard store |
|---|---|---|---|---|---|
| Innovator product | | | | | |
| Early adopter product | | | | | |
| Early majority product | | | | | |
| Late majority product | | | | | |
| Laggard product | | | | | |

the above classifications or the descriptions of them given here. Rather, they provide a decision framework that may be used whenever applicable for the creation of hypotheses. Even if one were sure that these categories described real groups, the differences between these groups would have to be quite large to make any difference to a store manager. As suggested previously, differences of a few percentage points are not likely to make any such difference. In addition, the categories would have to refer to change with regard to several groupings of products. If each individual is highly innovative with regard to only one or two categories of merchandise, he would certainly be quite difficult to identify and perhaps not worth identifying. Also, the concepts of innovator and early adopter would be meaningful only if they could be utilized in a reasonable cost framework.

Many questions are raised by the above classification system. Is interaction between, say, early adopters and late majority more important in inducing change than interaction, say, among members of the late majority alone? Just what are the relevant groupings? Is an innovator for one product or store likely to be an innovator for many types of product or store? If these groups really exist, how can one identify them inexpensively? At the very least, however, the classification system would appear useful in framing an executive's view of the world. At best, it can lead to the identification of groups that the store will do well to cultivate by special merchandise mixes. It can also indicate the types of appeal that might be effective in catering to specific groups and in introducing new products.

***Opinion leadership***  An ambitious attempt was made in the 1950s by Elihu Katz and Paul F. Lazarsfeld to identify the sources of large-scale opinion change. Katz and Lazarsfeld found that a key dimension of opinion change was an indirect one: most people were influenced by what others told them they had heard, seen, or read. This process, known as "the two-step flow of communication," not only reaffirmed the importance of personal selling but suggested that some people were better than others at selling ideas. The question was, who were these people? They were certainly in a minority, and certainly influential. But how influential? Katz and Lazarsfeld called them "opinion leaders," and at first attributed to them a very wide spectrum of influence. Later research, however, showed that some people were opinion leaders in some areas and some in others—a discovery that disappointed advertisers very much, since they had been hoping to develop substantial market shares by the interactive process that would result from influencing a few thousand innovative families. The basic theory is sound, however, and probably deserves more exploration than it has been given in recent years.

***Consumerism***

Of more than passing interest to retailers is the movement for consumer welfare. Consumers are becoming more sophisticated with regard to evaluating purchase alternatives, and more vocal in expressing their collective interests. In addition the consumer is becoming more interested in the behavior of retailer. Organizations such as Consumer's Union have seen their enrollment multiply. Government organizations fostering the interests of con-

sumers have burgeoned in many areas of the country.

The idea of consumers getting together to try to get more value for their money is certainly not new, but the changing conditions of our society indicate an increasing role for the consumer in his efforts to obtain a larger share of the economic pie. The importance of the movement is obvious; its growth appears guaranteed, its direction a big question mark.

## Summary

1. Since the retailer has always sold directly to the consumer, he has never had to be told about the importance of the consumer.

2. There are many approaches that could be used with regard to the consumer.

   A. One could consider one or more of the simplified models of the consumer.

   B. A useful but simple model is to assume that the consumer is trying to maximize his economic and psychological satisfaction.

   C. One might interview and otherwise study the behavior of consumers.

   D. One might carefully study the store's internal nonmerchandise records.

   E. One might examine what is selling.

3. Of key importance in retailing is the analysis of what is selling.

   A. The store keeps track of the items that sell and those that do not sell. The desired items are reordered and otherwise merchandised.

   B. The executive tries to develop effective classification systems whereby he can understand the votes of customers in other than an item context. Classifications might be broken down by price line, product, color, silhouette, and so forth.

4. Often an executive will want to understand the consumer "better" than just through what is sold. This kind of information is generally useful but has

particular merit in developing store images and in the locating of stores.

A. The analysis of individual behavior may increase the understanding of the executive with regard to the consumer.

B. Further, there is an influence of the group on the individual.

C. Groups are often worth studying as a separate subject.

## Discussion Questions

1. What are unit controls?

2. What is classification analysis?

3. List the various kinds of information that can be used to supplement unit and dollar controls.

4. What are the limitations of a store relying solely on what is sold for information about the consumer?

5. How can the supplier help with consumers?

6. Outline the purchase process.

7. What are the prime reasons why stores interview customers?

8. List seven dimensions of department store image.

9. What is the relevance of learning for consumer behavior?

10. Why is postpurchase consumer behavior so important to the retailer?

## References

Bucklin, Louis P., "Retail Strategy and the Classification of Consumer Goods," in Philip R. Cateora and Lee Richardson (eds.), *Readings in Marketing* (New York: Appleton, 1967).

Engel, James E., *et al.*, *Consumer Behavior* (New York: Holt, 1968).

Festinger, Leon, *A Theory of Cognitive Dissonance* (Stanford, Calif.: Stanford University Press, 1958).

Katz, Elihu, and Lazarsfeld, Paul F., *Personal Influence: The Part Played by People in the Flow of Mass Communications* (Glencoe, Ill.: Free Press, 1955).

McClelland, David C., *Personality* (New York: William Sloan Association, 1951).

National Industrial Conference Board, *Road Maps of Industry, No. 1,666,* May 15, 1971.

Oxenfeldt, Alfred R., *Executive Action in Marketing* (Belmont, Calif.: Wadsworth, 1966).

Pell, E., "Consumer Innovators: A Unique Market for Newness," in S. A. Greyser (ed.), *Toward Science Marketing* (Chicago, Ill.: American Marketing Association, 1963).

*Psychology Today*, May 1973, p. 20.

Rogers, Everett M., and Shoemaker, Floyd, *Communication of Innovations* (New York: Free Press, 1971).

Walters, C. Glenn, and Paul, Gordon W., *Consumer Behavior: An Integrated Framework* (Homewood, Ill.: Irwin, 1970).

## Further Reading

Aronson, Elliot, "The Rationalizing Animal," *Psychology Today*, May 1973, pp. 46–52.

Enis, Ben M., and Paul, Gordon W., "'Store Loyalty' as a Basis for Market Segmentation," *Journal of Retailing*, Fall, 1970, pp. 42–56.

Howard, John A., and Ostland, Lyman E., *Buyer Behavior* (New York: Knopf, 1973).

Longman, Kenneth A., "Market Segmentation vs. Segmented Marketing," *TIMS Interfaces*, June 1971, pp. 38–40.

Palda, Kristian S., "The Hypothesis of a Hierarchy of Effects: A Partial Evaluation," *Journal of Marketing Research*, February 1966, pp. 13–24.

## Case History: *Consumer Research*

John Evans had a Ph.D. in marketing from a leading graduate school of business. Upon receiving it, he had gone to work in Evans Department Store, a growing, profitable organization with three stores and a volume of $60 million. The organization had been built up over the years by Louis Evans, John's father.

John had become an assistant buyer, then a buyer and a merchandise manager. He had worked pretty much within the established patterns of the store systems as they had been developed over the years. If the operating results of the areas to which John was assigned were accepted as a guide, John had done well.

In February, 1972, Louis Evans died. According to the wishes indicated in his will, John was installed as president and chief executive officer of the business.

One of the first questions that John considered was the business's lack of sophistication. Louis Evans had run the firm by what professors would call seat-of-the-pants decision making. However, old Louis had been first in his graduating class at Yale and would spend days deliberating over the pros and cons of the key decisions that he had to make. While John was sure that his business school professors were correct and that this was seat-of-the-pants decision making, he had not seen many ways during his years at the store in which the method of making these decisions could be improved. Meanwhile, the growth of the operation's sales and profits was reasonable.

John therefore decided to attack the area of the consumer. What could be more important to the future of the store than consumers? After all, he did have a Ph.D. in marketing, which necessarily involved heavy emphasis on consumer behavior. He reviewed what his father had done in this area. Louis Evans had the controller examine the credit records every two years by random sampling techniques. Credit customers in the three stores were analyzed with respect to where they lived, their incomes, family position, occupation, and so forth.

In addition, Louis had once paid a consultant to run a similar survey of cash customers. There did not seem to be any managerially significant differences between cash and credit customers, so Louis decided he would assume that the two types of customer were approximately the same. Furthermore, 60 percent of the Evans Stores' business was conducted for credit, so that the credit customers represented a significant portion of the overall business.

Louis Evans also utilized a very short, simple questionnaire that was filled out by customers at each of the three stores every two years. Initially, he had hired a statistician to insure that the survey results would be representative of all the customers. However, a check of the statistician's sample against a nonrandom sample designed by a store executive indicated that there was little difference in the results. Therefore, because the nonrandom design had cost one-fifth of what the randomized one had cost, nonrandom sampling was used in all subsequent surveys.

John Evans decided to follow the same inexpensive sampling procedure. Louis Evans had designed the following questionnaire:

Q. Please rank the Evans Department Stores along each of the following dimensions, considered separately (put an X in the column that comes closest to your impression):

7 6 5 4 3 2 1

Helpful Salespeople . . . . . . . .Unhelpful Salespeople

Pleasant Salespeople . . . . . . . .Unpleasant Salespeople

A Large Selection of Merchandise . . . . . . . . A Small Selection of Merchandise

Very High Prices . . . . . . . . .Low Prices

Poor Displays . . . . . . . . .Very Exciting Displays

Credit Easy to Obtain . . . . . . . . Credit Difficult to Obtain

Attractive Advertising. . . . . . . .Unattractive Advertising

Q. In addition, would you please mention:

Any Special Strengths of Evans _____

Any Special Weaknesses of Evans _____

The results of the questionnaire were distributed to the key executives, and action was taken where deemed appropriate.

The above "research" cost almost nothing, and indeed the information was only supplemental to the information generated by the firm's more sophisticated systems for determining what the customer was buying in the three stores. John knew that all retail operations emphasize what has been sold, and Evans Department Store was no exception.

John's problem was that he was not sure what to do to learn more about the customer. His education had made him familiar with many advanced research techniques. He also knew that many other industries were using sophisticated approaches to consumer behavior, but that retailing was not enthusiastic about their potential. He decided to seek the advice of two people, Morton Kondyke, the general merchandise manager, and George Rachander, his old professor.

Morton Kondyke was a man of some stature; as a retailer, he had an outstanding reputation. Kondyke asserted flatly that the reason why advanced consumer techniques did not permeate retailing was that they were of no value. While it was true that advanced consumer research techniques could yield new information, they simply did not yield enough to justify their incremental cost. Furthermore, the minds of retail executives had always been trained to analyze what items had been sold. Most retail executives were not even very good at that. Indeed, in certain key areas merchandise executives were not sure whether they should be concerned with unit sales of an item or the unit sales in relation to stock on hand. Morton Kondyke concluded that retailers in general and Evans in particular should spend their incremental research dollars on perfecting the analysis of what had been sold. In his opinion, a creative analysis or systems analysis of what had been sold would provide all the information generated by sophisticated consumer models, and at a very much lower cost. In defense of his position, he argued that many very sophisticated economists did not ask customers about the economy. Rather, they used what had happened to the economy as a basis for their projections. However, Morton Kondyke was for continuing the consumer research started by Louis Evans because this aided the store greatly in spotting problems and in opening new stores. He suggested that the store might consider analyzing these data by merchandise classification.

Professor Rachander, on the other hand, suggested that John read some of the more recent articles written in the various business and marketing journals. These articles stressed that perhaps various decisions could be aided by linear programming, multiple regression analysis, and so forth. However interesting the articles were, John could not find one example of these sophisticated techniques offering success beyond what could have been achieved by simpler techniques.

In earlier conversations, Professor Rachander had indicated that something might be done in the fashion area. If John could identify the consumers in his three geographic areas who were innovators, he might utilize some of the experimental techniques in finding what customers wanted four or five weeks ahead of the other stores. This would be a very important advantage.

Having received this conflicting advice from two people whom he deeply respected, John began to wonder if seat-of-the-pants decision making wasn't the wisest policy after all.

### Discussion Questions

1. If you were John, would you consider your education wasted? If not, how would you make use of it as president of Evans Department Store?

2. How would you persuade Morton Kondyke that some advanced research techniques might not be a waste of time? Which ones?

## 5

Are retail margins too high? Do retailers charge the poor more than the rich? Are retailers truly efficient, competitive, and ethical? This chapter raises these and other questions, mostly related to the economics of retailing.

## Economics and Retailing

### Why Retail Stores?

Except in a very primitive society, someone has to make goods available to the final consumer. However, this function does not have to be performed by stores. For that matter, there is no real need for the store as we know it to go on existing in the same form. It is therefore worth speculating on some of the reasons for having retail stores, and on some of the economic advantages that they offer.

Generally, a person trades one item for another because he expects to obtain greater satisfaction from the item he will get than the item he has. In most of our present society the item that the person has for trading is money in some form. The satisfaction he thinks he will derive from the ownership of the wanted item must therefore be greater than the satisfaction of keeping the money.

Stores offer many benefits, including transactional efficiency, location efficiency, and perceptual order.

#### Transactional Efficiency

The formula for the number of possible two-person combinations among the members of a group is

$$\frac{N(N-1)}{2}$$

where $N$ = the number of persons in the group.

Thus if five workers chose to exchange their wares with one another, each interacting with every other, it would be necessary to have (5 × 4) ÷ 2 = 10 transactions. But if there were a retail store with the goods of the five workmen in stock, only five transactions would be necessary. Similarly, if 10 individuals chose to exchange their wares without a retail store, there would be 45 different transactions. But in a retail store with all the goods in stock from the 10 craftsmen, there would be 10 transactions. The student may care to speculate on the level of transactional efficiency created by the average department store or supermarket. In short, retailing really does provide transactional efficiency, the more so as the complexity of society increases.

### Location Efficiency

If customers buy at a store in a central location rather than buying and selling with each other, then the store is providing them with location efficiency. The greater the number of individuals exchanging goods, the more numerous are the advantages in terms of savings in time, mileage, or both.

Figure 5.1 represents four individuals, $A$, $B$, $C$, and $D$, located the same distance from a central point so that together they form the corners of a square. If $X$ is the distance from the center of the square to any of its corners, then each side—for example, from $A$ to $B$—becomes equal to 1.414$X$. In order to go to each of the other points and then return to his corner, $A$ has to travel a distance of $4 \times 1.414X = 5.656X$. But this trip still leaves $B$ out of touch with $C$ and $D$, and $C$ out of touch with $D$. $B$ can travel to $C$ and $D$, transact business with each, and return to his corner via the diagonal, a total distance of $2(1.414X) + 2X$. In order to complete the mutual exchange, $C$ and $D$ must then travel a total of $2 \times 1.414X$. Thus $A$, $B$, $C$, and $D$, for lack of a retailer, have traveled $13.312X$ to satisfy their individual wants. Had there been a retailer located in the center of the square with a stock of what each one of them was looking for, they would have had to travel a total of only $4 \times 2X = 8X$. Had $A$ been a traveling salesman with such a stock, he would

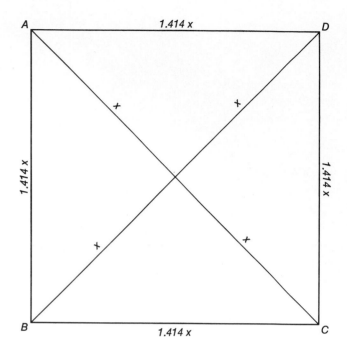

Figure 5.1  *Location efficiency in a four-person system*

have been the only one of the four who needed to travel, a further saving of $8X - 5.656X = 2.344X$.

### Perceptual Order

Retailing also helps the final consumer to see what kinds of merchandise are available at what price and quality levels. Thus if a customer needs food, she can go to the supermarket and find it displayed in a logical fashion. The problem of choice is simplified for her, and the entire process is or should be both psychologically and socially gratifying. It is interesting to speculate how the highly structural appearance of stores such as the supermarket affects the consumer's perception of the world and society.

Stores also create atmosphere; permit product comparisons; stock merchandise; offer credit and other services; and take risks from which the consumer stands to benefit. The result, more often that not, is to increase the satisfaction derived by consumers and decrease the costs of the retail system and the institutions that depend on it.

## Criticisms of Retailing

Retail stores have evolved over time to serve the ultimate consumer, on the one hand, and suppliers, on the other. Observers of retailing have often speculated about the effectiveness of the retail system. But what does "effectiveness" mean in such a context? It can be defined in terms of many kinds of values besides economic ones—moral, ethical, sociological, or psychological values, for example. Nor can retailing be criticized as if it existed in a vacuum; it is too closely bound up with marketing and with competitive systems in general. All this should be borne in mind when reviewing the following common criticisms of retailing.

1. *The retail system is inefficient.* The costs of distribution, as well as retailing margins, are frequently alleged to be higher than necessary. Among the inefficiencies mentioned are the large number of small independent retailers who make only half a living; the lack of automation and other labor-saving innovations in retail units of all sizes; the large number of stores in one geographic area that duplicate or seemingly duplicate each others' activities and yet run at substantially less than capacity (gas stations, for example); and seemingly high percentage margins in many types of retail store. Thus department stores with a volume of over $1 million had a store gross margin of 37.5 percent in 1970, up from 34.9 percent in 1963. Gross margins in self-service department stores increased from 26.4 in 1966 to 27.9 in 1970–71. Gross margins of food chains went from 22.2 percent in 1966–67 to 21.5 in 1971–72. Drug chains had a margin of 33.4 percent in 1971. Many critics find these margins unreasonably high. It is

also alleged that retailers actually foster inefficiencies by including in their prices the cost of numerous services such as delivery, credit, and so forth. Retail efficiency is covered in greater detail later in the chapter.

2. *Retailing is dishonest.* Some critics argue that the entire communications mix of retailing, primarily its advertising and personal selling, is dishonest. Most people have witnessed retail advertising that is completely false; almost all have witnessed retail advertising that is deliberately misleading. Furthermore, the spoken word, on which store and house-to-house salesmen depend so heavily, inspires less confidence than the written word, which is open to public scrutiny. It can also be argued that the increased mobility of customers and the apparent decrease in customer loyalty has removed the economic need for many types of merchants to be honest. We shall see in Chapter 7 that most dishonest retail activities are illegal, although law enforcement agencies seldom take vigorous action against them. Dishonesty in retailing is of particular concern to society because the retailer is the main contact for most individuals with the economic system, and in addition is a large employer of individuals in their first job.

3. *Retailers charge the poor higher prices.* Retailers are often accused of being directly and indirectly responsible for the fact that the poor often pay more for the same merchandise than do the wealthy. One example of this is the higher prices for various items in the inner-city areas. Actually, poor people pay more for many reasons, not all of them within the control of retailers. Among the reasons are:

(i) The costs of running an enterprise in the areas where poor people live tend to be high as a result of high insurance rates; high rates of theft; the high rate of default on loan payments by the poor person; and so forth.

(ii) The low-volume potential of stores located in the areas in which poor people live has been documented by a number of studies. These stores usually cater to potential customers in the immediate area of the store, and such areas tend not to offer a large-volume potential. In addition, many store owners in low-income areas regard running a store as an alternative to unemployment and are therefore willing to accept zero or almost zero profits. This makes the competitive position of more commercially oriented stores extremely difficult.

(iii) Consumers in low-income areas cannot get around as easily as those in more affluent areas. The result is a lot of high-priced, small stores. Stores in poor areas also tend not to compete with each other by lowering prices, because there is little response from consumers if they do. In addition, they are too small to benefit much from selling one item at a very low cost, since a customer attracted in this way is more likely to buy something at a regular price from a large assortment than from a small one. Another problem of many poor customers is that they must have credit. Students are often told of the very high interest rates that the poor must pay just because they are poor. This is just one part of the problem. The poor are also forced to pay much higher prices because often the inflated-price outlets are the only ones that will sell the merchandise to them on credit. In one nonretail example of which I am aware, a customer would have had to pay a 10 percent higher price just to get the credit. Differentials at retail can be much higher than this, as studies by the Federal Trade Commission and others have repeatedly shown.

(iv) Many credit programs favor the rich. It used to be that credit cost something, in the sense that a consumer had to pay more for credit. This is still typical in some situations. If, however, a consumer has a "straight" charge account or one of the bank cards, it is usual for no interest to be charged if the payment is made within a certain period of time, perhaps as much as 50 days or so from the date of purchase. Thus the well-to-do person gets the use of this money free, which is equivalent to a price reduction and costs the business both time and money. This cost, according to most interpretations of pricing, is borne by both the cash and the credit customers. The cash customer, however, gets no benefit from his share. In this sense the poor are actually subsidizing the well-to-do. Clearly, the entire credit system is weighted against those who are poor. Higher risks tend to pay higher interest than lower risks. Indeed the least expensive way of borrowing in the short term is usually *term loans* against security, and this option is completely foreclosed to poor people. For example, if an individual borrows $5,000 and this is backed up by $8,000 worth of marketable securities, the interest rate will be low.

(v) A rather good rule of thumb for a retailer is not to take advantage of a wealthy person. Such a person typically has a great many ways of retaliating. In contrast, it is often good business to take advantage of the poor.

They have difficulty fighting back. Legal aid societies, consumer action groups, and others are trying to change the costs to the various participants in this struggle.

Nothing here should be construed to suggest that entrepreneurs in lower-income areas are becoming fat at the expense of the consumers there. The reason that most if not all the larger American retail firms do not invest in the inner-city areas is that they do not see these areas as profitable to invest in. The lack of good opportunities for investment in such areas is known to all businessmen with experience of them. The FTC study already referred to uncovered evidence that stores in the inner-city low-income areas make a lower profit on net worth than other types of retail outlet. However, the various economic justifications for charging poor people higher prices offer little solace to the poor person living under this burden. And to many nonpoor, this additional burden on the poor is an unacceptable inequity of the market and the retail system.

4. *Retailing is the essence of crass materialism.* This criticism really breaks down into two dimensions. First, we Americans are thought to want too much. It is suggested that we are constantly being induced to acquire more and more material possessions, and that having acquired them, we feel no better off than before. Second, we are told, we want the wrong things. Retailers appeal to the lowest common denominator of taste because all that interests them is making a fast buck. Moreover, the argument runs, they also appeal to the lowest tastes, creating advertising, window displays, and so forth that cater to the worst in men and women to achieve greater profits. As a result, they not only fail to improve the quality of life in our society but actually hasten its moral decline.

5. *Retail stores are ugly.* Our present retail system creates stores that, however profitable to the owners or useful to customers, are eyesores to the community. Gas stations may be attractive to motorists out of gas, but are otherwise short on esthetic excitement, particularly if there are twelve stations in a row. The retail structure in the inner city has also been questioned by some observers on esthetic grounds.

6. *Retailing does not meet community needs.* For example, it has been alleged that many elderly citizens and minority group members do not receive proper medication because they lack access to drug stores.

There are many defenses that can be made for our retailing and marketing systems. These will not be presented at great length because the student has been exposed more to the positive features of the system than to the negative. However, the positive features should be briefly reviewed. A key defense is that our retailing system has helped build the most successful economic machine ever witnessed by mankind. The benefits, to many if not most observers, clearly outweigh the costs.

It can further be argued that the retail system is a product of our society and not the cause. Thus if appeals to greed are successful, it is only because people are greedy. If society were to raise its standards, the retail and marketing practices within it would improve. Accordingly, the reformer should start by improving society.

A third defense is that the parts of systems cannot be compared with any fairness. All systems will have some inequities and ostensible inefficiencies; the question is, will you buy system A with its strengths and weaknesses, or will you buy system B with its strengths and weaknesses, and so forth. You can not say that you will take system A without its weaknesses, since all complex systems will have some. In other words, you either buy a competitive market system or you do not. If you do, you also buy some of the inevitable inequities that result, although of course you may strive to limit their number and extent.

It is not the purpose of this chapter to evaluate any of these related arguments on their own merits; that would require a separate book. They can, however, be approached indirectly, via the key economic concepts of efficiency and competition.

## Efficiency

There are many ways of looking at efficiency. A decision maker is regarded as efficient if he achieves a given objective or set of objectives with the least cost. In this case, the objectives are given; the decision maker has only to look for the best means of achieving them. Usually, however, the objectives themselves are compared in terms of the efficiency that each will provide. This often involves comparing the outputs of activities that differ in kind as well as degree. Engineers measure efficiency in terms of the ratio of effective output to input. In order to do so, they have to express all outputs and inputs in quantitative terms. Such measures are not always available in other fields, which therefore tend to use other concepts of efficiency.

In marketing, in addition to the above approaches to efficiency, it has been suggested that exchange and innovative efficiency be considered. Exchange efficiency refers to the efficiency of the trading process itself in view of the fact that the organizational and informational dimensions of the market are not the same everywhere. Two dimensions of exchange efficiency are: *(1)* the stability of the market in terms of how often buyers and sellers can come together, complete their various exchanges, and anticipate market alternatives; and *(2)* the degree to which potential transactions are consummated. Another marketing concept is that of innovative efficiency. Are the products, institutions, and services offered by society, together with the attendant marketing activities, the best that could have come into being under the circumstances? The answer given to this question will be an estimate of the marketing system's innovative efficiency.

In the end, however, most discussions of marketing fall back on the engineer's concept of efficiency: the ratio of effective output to input. Clearly, a society will prefer economic activities whose output exceeds their input, so that there is a net gain in satisfaction for the society. Since resources are scarce, society would also like to allocate these resources in the best manner possible. This can be thought of arithmetically as the point at which no increase in satisfaction would result from changing the use of any resources.

As an element of the total economic system, the retail sector must take both partial credit and responsibility for the efficiency of that system. Indeed, in certain instances it may be possible to make the total system more efficient by alterations in the retail sector—shifting various activities from the manufacturer or wholesaler to the retailer, for instance. However, very little is known about such relationships.

The efficiency of the retail sector itself is clearly difficult to measure. There are at least four ways in which estimates can be made.

1. *Efficiency can be approached theoretically.* A model of some segment of the retail system can be developed. The outputs of this model can then be observed and compared with either the real world or the output of other models. Elements of the model can be changed, inputs varied, and so forth.

Small retailing is one area for which such an analysis has been carried out. It has often been suggested that most retailing is characterized by monopolistic competition. This means that there are many sellers trying to sell products that are not identical. Each of them is faced with a downward sloping demand curve, that is, as the price is lowered the quantity demanded increases. It can be demonstrated that, under certain conditions, such a market can continue to support many firms that operate inefficiently. In addition, if these firms are willing to operate unprofitably—as they may, if going out of business is simply an unacceptable alternative—they may stay in business indefinitely. Imagine, for instance, a neighborhood in which barber shops are prospering as never before. As a result, new barbers start moving into the area, until there is one barber shop in every five blocks instead of one in every six. As a result, there comes a point at which each shop begins to do less business. But its costs stay the same as before. So the barber is forced to charge higher prices—even though he is producing less, not more—or be faced with lower profits.

Paul A. Samuelson, from whom the foregoing analysis was adapted, concludes that grocery stores, taverns, undertakers, restaurants, nightclubs, and gas stations are typical retail trade examples of small businesses in an overcrowded, sick industry. These small firms are inefficient producers and do not sell their products or services cheaply. They tend to divide the business and charge high prices. Samuelson maintains that the resulting economic situation

may be worse than the situation under complete monopoly; not only are prices excessive, but valuable resources are wasted because each firm has too much idle capacity. The situation is bad in three ways: the retailers maintain losses, resources are wasted, and the prices charged the consumer are too high. The student should note that no empirical support is required for this type of conclusion; it is simply a deduction from a model of *imperfect competition,* which involves numerous sellers and easy entry to the market.

Another model that is often used for comparative purposes is that of *perfect competition.* Here there are assumed to be: *(1)* many buyers and sellers; *(2)* homogeneous products; *(3)* freedom of entry to and exit from the market; and *(4)* perfect knowledge possessed by all related to the market. Many economists have liked this model and have therefore assumed that deviations from it indicate a type of inefficiency. One of the more attractive features of pure or perfect competition is that it will lead to optimum allocation of resources if its assumptions are granted.

2. *Retailing can be compared to other sectors of the economy.* Such comparisons are most often made between retailing and either wholesaling or manufacturing. The comparison can be at one time or over time. For instance, a study by Harold Barger indicated that output per man-hour in the field of distribution has increased much less rapidly than in manufacturing or agriculture. Analyses of this type are handicapped by many factors, not the least of which are the differing characteristics of the various sectors. For example, the retail sector seems less amenable to automation than the manufacturing sector. Moreover, the activities and needs of the various sectors change over time. Thus certain parts of the retailing sector have taken on warehousing activities from wholesalers and manufacturers.

3. *Certain characteristics of retailing can be compared over time.* A high margin can be caused by many factors. Among them are an increase in the level of the service offered to or demanded by the consumer, and a change in the types of activity performed by the retailer. Analyses can also be made for such factors as the productivity of labor, capital,

Table 5.1
Selected measures of department store productivity, 1931–1970

| Year | Transactions per employee | Transactions per salesperson | Selling space as % of total space | Salespersons as % of total employees | Transactions per sq. ft. of total space | Transactions per sq. ft. of selling space |
|------|------|------|------|------|------|------|
| 1931 | 2,600 | NA | NA | NA | 6.9 | NA |
| 1940 | 3,019 | 7,850 | 43 | 39 | 8.5 | 19.8 |
| 1950 | 3,000 | 8,400 | 38 | 37 | 9.0 | 23.6 |
| 1960 | 3,728 | 8,220 | 49 | 45 | 8.1 | 16.6 |
| 1968 | 3,705 | 7,101 | 55 | 53 | 6.2 | 11.3 |
| 1969 | 3,567 | 7,035 | 57 | 51 | 6.4 | 10.6 |
| 1970 | 3,468 | 6,837 | 59 | 52 | 6.0 | 10.1 |

Source: Retailing Today. *January, 1972.*

and transaction size. For example, Dalrymple and Thompson have pointed out that in 1929 there was one food retailing employee for every 84 individuals in the population, while in 1963 there was one for every 250. Figures have even been developed to measure the productivity of department stores over time (Table 5.1). Figures such as the annual sales per full-time employee, weekly sales per square foot of sales area, and weekly sales per checkout are computed for the supermarket industry.

4. *Retail institutions of similar type can be compared with each other.* For example, hardware stores can be compared at one point in time. If a number of stores of the same type show wide variation in efficiency, for instance as measured by operating costs as a percentage of sales, then it is reasonable to conclude that a substantial portion of the industry is not efficient. For example, let us assume that there are four drug stores in the same town with the same price philosophy, hours, and so forth. If the operating costs of one store were 15 percent, of another 25 percent, of the third 35 percent, and of the fourth 40 percent, then clearly the retail drug industry in this town would not be operating at its most efficient level.

**Economies of scale** Relatedly, one might analyze economies of scale, that is, savings directly associated with the size of the retail unit. If a large number of stores are operating at a level that is not close to the most economic size, then it may be concluded that the industry is not near its most efficient level.

In retailing there are economies and diseconomies of scale associated with buying, selling, warehousing, store location, and many other activities. This is as true of entire firms as of individual stores. For example, where the economies of total size (i.e., of firms) are important and the economies of store size are not, an analyst would expect to find large chains of small stores.

The measures of the economies of scale are further complicated by the fact that as the size of stores increases, the level of consumer service will probably drop. In addition, because of the special characteristics of the proprietor stores with at most two employees, it might be desirable to consider these separately. David Schwartzman has suggested that the variation in sales per person in every type of store with one or two employees is explained by the low earnings of the employees and proprietors and not by any economies of scale. The economies of store size also appear to vary according to whether the stores are independent or part of a chain. Schwartzman found that the 1958 data support the hypothesis that the economies of scale at the store level are greater among chains than among independents.

One way to find out whether or not there are economies of store size is to look at the sales-payroll ratio as the number of employees of a store increases. If the ratio increases, then economies of store size probably exist. According to Schwartzman, substantial economies were present only in food stores. Sales per person as the number of employees increase is another such measure. Here the data suggest that in 1939 and 1958 there were large economies of scale in food stores and moderate ones in gas stations, apparel and accessory stores, and furniture, home furnishings, and equipment stores.

There also appear to be substantial economies of scale associated with the total size of the firm. Firms with larger assets, as Edna Douglas has pointed out, show substantially higher profits as a percentage of sales than do smaller firms, for every type of store. In addition, every type of store has increasing rates of profit with size, when size is determined by its equity.

Few conclusions can be offered as to whether large-scale retailing is efficient; a lot more research is needed on specific types of store. Small-scale retailing appears inefficient, but may be becoming less so as increasing numbers of small retailers are forced out of business. The spread of franchising in various forms may also be making small retailers more efficient.

### Competition

When many individuals acting independently are striving toward a goal, certain benefits are thought to accrue to society and possibly to those individuals as well. When in a market there are many buyers struggling against other buyers, all with about the same resources, to purchase from many sellers selling against other sellers, also with about the same resources, society is held to benefit. Economists have tended to emphasize horizontal competition, that is, competition at the same channel level. Retail firms do of course compete with each other but they may also compete with suppliers and consumers.

Part of the success of competition may be indicated by the zest with which most businessmen try to avoid it. Businessmen appear almost universally to favor aggressive, unregulated competition — in any industry but their own. Such competition is supposed to result in many related advantages, including:

*Lower prices*  Competitive activities among sellers often lead to lower prices and cut down sellers' profits. While it can be demonstrated that these results do not necessarily follow, in general such activities will lead to lower prices if the behavior they replace is noncompetitive. Competitive behavior is supposed to make prices more flexible as well as lower.

*Efficient allocation of resources*  Competitive forces allocate resources in what many consider a satisfactory manner without recourse to substantial centralized planning. Under perfect competition, according to most theorists, the resources would be distributed optimally. However, reality does not often come close to this ideal state of affairs. Accordingly, the competitive forces are considered to need at least some element of centralized planning in order to allocate resources in the best interests of society. Societies use different mixes of planning and the market, but even centralized, planned societies find they cannot do without competition altogether.

*Higher wages*  When firms compete for scarce resources such as labor, the price of the resource, in this case wages, will generally increase. Some observers have suggested that competition among firms is the main element that has increased wages over time.

*More innovation*  Competition tends to limit the profits that a firm can make on established products. In order to increase profits, or perhaps just to exist in a competitive environment, a firm needs to create new products, new kinds of assortment, and new services. Competition forces other firms to duplicate such innovations, within legal limits, and to undertake similarly innovative programs.

***Elimination of decadent enterprises*** Individual firms that are unable to compete are cast aside. Divisions of larger firms whose products fail to earn their way are generally disposed of by the parent firm in one way or another. Thus competition provides a mechanism both for pruning out the weaker brethren and for discontinuing unwanted activities. Such pruning is necessary if resources are to be efficiently allocated, in the sense referred to earlier.

***Consumer suffrage*** Competition as it has evolved in our society attaches substantial importance to the consumer and his activities. Therefore, in a very real sense, the consumer votes for the society in which he wants to live. He votes by buying a style of hat; he votes by giving money to a particular church; he votes by buying tickets to a sex movie. It might be that society would be better off if the consumer could not vote in any of these ways. But he can, and thereby participates to some degree in the system. The same is true of all modern societies, though clearly some are more responsive to consumers' needs and wants than others.

Incomplete though it is, this is an impressive list. But how much competition is desirable and whether the benefits of competition are worth the costs in specific situations are questions that are beyond the scope of this book. Some of the costs were introduced in the beginning of this chapter as criticisms of the retail system; others are described below.

It is of some interest to speculate on the competitiveness of retailing, even though people rarely agree on exactly what they mean by "competitive." For example, automobile manufacturing is quite often criticized for being noncompetitive, whereas automobile executives consider it competitive to a point approaching war. On the other hand, it cannot be denied that there are many fewer firms engaged in automobile manufacturing now than 30 years ago. Let us consider some of the various ways in which the competitiveness of the retail system might be assessed.

Of primary importance in this context is the *market structure*. Is the market characterized by pure competition, monopolistic competition, *oligopoly*, or monopoly? What percentage of total industry sales is associated with what percentage of firms in each industry? How easy is the market to enter? How many firms are competing in it? Analysis of these and other characteristics will indicate what sort of structure the market has. Many consider such an analysis essential to understanding the behavior of the units in the market. Structure is nearly always assumed to have a strong influence on behavior, although empirical evidence to support this is lacking. Retailing has generally been considered a form of monopolistic competition.

A second way that an analyst might assess the competitiveness of the retail system is to examine the *behavior of the firms*. How do firms conduct themselves with regard to such dimensions as setting prices and output levels, opening new outlets, and so forth? Evidence that most firms in a product category change price frequently up and down might indicate that retailing is truly competitive, even though price is not a major consideration for many types of retail outlet. So might evidence that shopping center owners are fair and open to all comers in the offering of choice sites (actually, most retailers seem to feel they are not).

A third way to assess the competitiveness of the retail sector is to *analyze its performance data*. For example, segments of retailing may be compared to each other and to other industries in terms of profitability, growth, product improvement, and so forth. If the profits in certain types of retailing are extremely high, this might be considered a sign that retailing is noncompetitive, and not effectively serving society. Naturally, any such performance data vary considerably from one part of retailing to another. For example, for years the discount store had a very high rate of return on investment as compared with the department store.

Finally, many analysts find it illuminating to *examine the restraints on retail competition*. Stanley C. Hollander has outlined five types of restraints:

1. Social pressures. The most potent and pervasive forces that control retail competition are custom, consumer

expectation, and social pressure. For example, bargaining is customary in automobile showrooms but not in candy stores.

2. Suppliers. Firms that sell merchandise or services often impose restrictions such as location on the ways in which retailers may compete. The greatest barrier of this kind is the right of the supplier to select the firms to which he may sell. This right is one aspect of the Colgate doctrine (for which see Chapter 7); it is the basis of much controlling of price at the retail level.

3. Labor. Labor has influenced such dimensions of retailing as store hours and wages. For example, food stores must consider the union's reaction to their being open for 24 hours.

4. Laws. Zoning ordinances, state and municipal licenses, taxes, and other legally imposed measures restrict entry to the market. At the federal level, the so-called price discrimination statutes impose restrictions on store-supplier negotiations. Retail price maintenance laws limit the price flexibility of the retail prices. Unfair practice statutes limit the type of competitive weapon that participants may use. Retailing and the law is the subject of Chapter 7.

5. Retailer imposed restraints. Retailers have developed numerous methods, legal and illegal, to mitigate the effects of competition. Among these are agreements on margins and price relationships, agreements on services to be performed, collusive pressure on suppliers, cost-and-price manuals, and persuasion of all types.

It is probably true, as Richard E. Lowe has contended, that the American economy is more competitive in conduct than in structure. And, generally speaking, those who favor strong antitrust policies tend to favor structural tests of competitiveness. Also, retailing is so diverse that it is difficult to generalize about it. At least, store-type studies would be essential before any meaningful conclusions could be drawn about any segment of retailing, and each geographic area would probably need separate treatment.

Whatever the net virtues of competition, American society has made it a guiding principle of its economic system. It is often argued that, at least at this point of time, the benefits of substantial competition exceed its costs. Some of these costs have already been dealt with under "criticisms of retailing." Some related criticisms are as follows:

*The American system allows economic considerations to dominate all others.* Historically, quality of life has been of minor importance.

*Under such a system, short-term considerations take precedence over long-term ones.* Indeed, for many products, unless there is a profitable short term there is no long term. Many small businesses cannot afford failures of any kind.

*Unbridled competition tends, without constraints such as religion, government control, and so forth, to make the lowest common denominator of behavior the moral norm.* This can be seen from the way in which businessmen often justify dishonest behavior on the grounds that their competitors do it, and they have to act in a similar manner in order to survive.

## Summary

1. Retail stores offer goods to the final consumer. There are certain advantages in having stores perform these services.

A. In transacting exchanges, stores offer substantial advantages over a barter society. The more complex the society, the greater these advantages are.

B. A store located in the center of a population area also offers substantial advantages.

C. The store organizes the goods in a manner that is convenient and usually logical for the consumer.

2. Various criticisms have been made of the retail system.

A. Retailing is often alleged to be inefficient in that the margins charged are thought to be high, and in many cases increasing.

B. Retailing is accused of being dishonest, particularly in the selling and advertising areas.

C. Retailers charge poor consumers more for the same merchandise than wealthy ones.

D. Retailing, it is said, is the essence of crass materialism.

E. Many stores are not only eyesores to the communities they serve, but often leave these communities short of vital goods.

3. There are many ways to evaluate retail efficiency.

A. Retail efficiency can be approached theoretically.

B. Retailing can be compared to other sectors of the economy, such as wholesaling and manufacturing.

C. Certain characteristics of retailing can be compared over time, for example the costs of labor and capital.

D. Retail firms can be compared with each other.

4. Competition is assumed to be a good thing, resulting in: lower prices; more efficient allocation of resources; higher wages; more innovation; fewer decadent enterprises; and more consumer suffrage.

## Discussion Questions

1. What is transactional efficiency?

2. Outline some key criticisms of the retail system.

3. Is our society too materialistic? Draw your supporting evidence from the retail field whether you answer yes or no.

4. Does society make retailing what it is, or vice versa?

5. Is the retail food industry efficient? Define what efficiency means in this case.

6. What are the principal ways of assessing the competitiveness of a component of the retail sector?

7. Are drug stores competitive?

8. List five constraints on competition.

9. What are some of the negative aspects of competition?

10. To judge from the retail field, are the social benefits of competition worth the costs?

## References

Barger, Harold, *Distribution's Place in the American Economy Since 1869* (Princeton, N.J.: Princeton University Press, 1955).

Dalrymple, Douglas J., and Thompson, Donald L., *Retailing: An Economic View* (New York: Free Press, 1969).

Douglas, Edna, "Size of Firm and the Structure of Costs in Retailing," *Journal of Business*, April 1962, pp. 158–190.

Gist, Ronald E., *Retailing: Concepts and Decisions* (New York: Wiley, 1968).

Hollander, Stanley C., *Restraints Upon Retail Competition* (East Lansing, Mich.: Michigan State University, 1965).

Lowe, Richard E., *The Economics of Anti-Trust, Competition and Monopoly* (Englewood Cliffs, N.J.: Prentice-Hall, 1968).

Samuelson, Paul A., *Economics: An Introductory Analysis* (New York: McGraw-Hill, 1967).

Schwartzman, David, *The Decline of Service in Retail Trade* (Pullman, Wash.: Washington State University Press, 1971).

## Further Reading

Bucklin, Louis P., *Competition and Evolution in the Distributive Trades* (Englewood Cliffs, N.J.: Prentice-Hall, 1972).

Federal Trade Commission Staff, "Consumer Credit and the Poor," in E. Epstein and D. Hampton (eds.), *Black Americans and White Business* (Encino, Calif.: Dickenson, 1971).

Heim, Peggy, "Merchandise Management Accounting: A Retailing Experiment in Explicit Marginal Calculation," *Quarterly Journal of Economics*, 1963, pp. 671–675.

Holden, Bob R., *The Structure of a Retail Market and the Market Behavior of Retail Units* (Englewood Cliffs, N.J.: Prentice-Hall, 1960).

*Operating Results of Self-Service Discount Stores, 1971–1972* (Ithaca, N.Y.: Mass Retailing Institute, 1971).

Preston, Lee E., *Markets and Marketing Organization: An Orientation* (Glenview, Ill.: Scott, Foresman, 1970).

Simon, Julian L., *Issues in the Economics of Advertising* (Urbana, Ill.: University of Illinois Press, 1970).

## Case History: *What's Your Poison?**

There are many people who believe that an increasing number of products sold in stores are harmful or even dangerous to health. This belief is constantly being reaffirmed by publications such as *Consumer Reports;* sometimes, as with cigarettes, it is backed by the authority of the federal government. Retailers justify their handling of such items with the argument that "since the customer is king we are only giving him what he wants." They frequently add: "Who are we to decide what other people should buy?"

However, every once in a while we hear of a retailer such as the sole owner of a small supermarket

---

* Based in part on a case by Charles Bernhaut, Supermarkets General Corp. and the Rutgers Graduate School of Business.

chain in California. He took a stand by refusing to sell cigarettes in his stores (by the way, he was reported to have *increased* overall sales after he put this policy into effect). On the other hand, he continued to sell not only beer but wine, which in California is permitted to be sold in food stores.

### Discussion Questions

1. Let us assume that excessive smoking and excessive drinking of wine or beer are equally harmful, and that you are a retailer who knows this. Would you be inconsistent if you refused to sell one but not the other? Are there other products you should refuse to sell? On what grounds?

2. Let us assume that the federal government has just legalized marijuana, and that it is being marketed by a number of major U.S. firms. You are the sole owner of a grocery chain and have long been well known in your community for your opposition to "dope." Nevertheless, your stores have always carried both cigarettes and alcohol, though you yourself neither smoke nor drink. Would you now sell the legalized marijuana? On what grounds would you base your decision?

# 6

## Small Business and Entrepreneurship

There were 1,657,600 retail establishments of all types in the United states in 1973. Of the retail establishments reported in the 1967 Census of Business about 65 percent had fewer than four employees. Thus, although all small business clearly is not retailing, most retail firms are small by almost any definition.

The small businessman is the classic example of the *entrepreneur*, or independent manager. However, many large retail enterprises have an entrepreneurial flavor and by certain definitions are related to entrepreneurship. For example, a department store may be considered a group of many small stores under one roof, and the manager of each one is in a sense an entrepreneur. From another perspective, small business need not be related to entrepreneurship at all. Indeed, as we shall see, small businesses operating under franchise may be anything but entrepreneurial in character.

Most discussions of small business fail to define what it is. Even the Small Business Administration varies its definition to suit specific purposes. However, one definition that seems appropriate to retailing sets the upper limit for a small business at $1 million in sales.

Entrepreneurship is just as elusive. To one group of observers, it is a particular way of thinking and behaving: an entrepreneur is a person with an entrepreneurial personality. Such a person, according to Professor David C. McClelland of Harvard University, seeks moderate risk; takes personal responsibility for the success or failure of his actions; likes to get feedback on the results of his efforts; relies on his personal experience to guide him in many decisions; and sets himself goals that are achievable. By these criteria, successful salesmen and academic administrators might both be considered entrepreneurs.

Others look not so much to the personality of the entrepreneur as to what he did. The real entrepreneurs, they argue, are those who started businesses where none existed before. Further, certain entrepreneurs not only start new businesses but through them destroy many older ones; the wheel of retailing may refer to such a process. Hopefully, as Joseph Schumpeter maintained, the net effect of this destruction is to make the institutions of society more efficient in satisfying the needs and desires of consumers. Most new enterprises, however, are not this innovative and follow the established patterns of doing business.

Others associate entrepreneurship with risk taking. The entrepreneur, in their view, is essentially the decision maker who is willing to take substantial risk, partly because he expects to benefit, but partly because he enjoys it. Many new enterprises, however, entail little risk. For example, in many types of gas station the franchisee for some firms may not be a large risk taker. A consulting firm with limited fixed expenses, and established by a well-recognized computer engineer, would be another example. Presumably, if the computer engineer is truly outstanding, he will be able to dissolve the firm and get another position without great financial loss. And yet, while he has his own firm, he is considered by some to be both a small businessman and an entrepreneur. He might be considered an entrepreneur not so much for his financial risk as for his total commitment to the existence of his own firm—perhaps by making his reputation depend on the firm's success. Many individuals may fear financial loss less than loss of prestige.

The rest of this chapter will not distinguish to any great extent among the definitions of either small business or entrepreneurship, except that entrepreneurship within large corporations is not considered. Some contributions of small business, some entrepreneurial perspectives, and franchising are now discussed.

### Contributions of Small Business

Americans have generally regarded small business with special fondness, as something characteristic of a good society. Part of this attachment can be traced back to what many consider the good old days, when small-town ways were still typical of American life. Indeed, most large corporations were small at some point in their development. In addition, over the years small business has contributed greatly to the development of the American economic and social machine, and commands respect for that very reason. The following are some of its major contributions:

1. *The small business is considered by many to be a prime agent of social change.* In retailing most large corporations have shown themselves to be incapable of exploiting the opportunities offered by change. It has previously been suggested that the discount house developed in spite of the department store. In the same way, the supermarket developed as an entrepreneurial endeavor despite the chain food stores. Franchising, too, was developed for the most part by individuals outside the large corporations. The same is true of the new type of discount catalog showroom such as Best Products; the home center industry such as Wickes; and the discount furniture operation such as Levitz. Clearly, the small business entrepreneur has been a most effective exploiter of opportunity and a dynamic force in many areas of retailing.

However, the fact that the entrepreneur has acted as a prime catalytic agent in the past does not necessarily mean that he will so act in the future. His role may very well be taken over by the many larger firms that have developed so-called new-product venture teams, as well as long-range planning departments with substantial authority. If, however, the corporate environment for any reason does not prove conducive to innovation, society will continue to depend almost wholly on the entrepreneur for new ideas in retailing.

2. *Small business, at least in certain instances, offers the individual the chance to control his own destiny.* This privilege, even if it is often more imaginary than real, is treasured by those who find the corporate environment a barrier to their personal development. Of particular importance are the opportunities that small business offers to certain disadvantaged groups. Some of these groups, such as the original Jewish immigrants to this country, have used small business to advance in a society not otherwise completely open to them. Today, small business may be essential to the development of the urban ghetto and the black minorities who live there. At any rate, small business is capable of providing, for both the individual and the community, a range of opportunities that may not be feasible with large business.

3. *Small business is a haven for individuals who cannot or will not pay the price of corporate success.*

Indeed, small business has been called the Western Frontier of the economic world. The firing of key individuals in large companies underlines the obvious: effective economic performance is only one criterion for the success of many executives, and often not a critical one. Political finesse is thought by many to play a much greater role in corporate advancement than other qualities. Certainly, not all top executives are outstandingly competent people. Small business is an obvious avenue for frustrated executives who are competent in their areas of expertise and are willing to attack the apparently more demanding—or at least different—requirements of running a small business. If there were no small business, they would have a much harder time adjusting to society.

4. *The existence of many large businesses may depend on small business.* Small businesses supply many items to large businesses, presumably because they can produce specific products or services more efficiently. Thus the existence of entrepreneurs may be necessary for the efficient operation of larger firms.

5. *Small business can serve certain aspects of consumer convenience more efficiently than large business.* For example, small retail stores can be made more accessible to some residential areas than large retail stores. Further, a small store can adapt more readily to the needs of a small group of potential customers and offer more personalized service.

6. *Small business represents an avenue of reward to certain types of exceptionally skilled executive.* For example, executives in the computer industry may start their own business after achieving some success in their corporate environment. The income of such an individual in his own small business is more directly related to his contribution to the firm and he has substantial tax deductions and allowances available to him.

7. *Small business is an employer for many who would otherwise be out of work.* Indeed, one of the reasons for the decrease in the number of small retail businesses in recent years would appear to be the increase in alternative sources of income for the relevant population. If a person can obtain a 40-hour-a-week job at $6,000 a year, he may prefer this to an entrepreneurial income of $5,000 a year

with 70 hours of work a week. Indeed, small business, particularly small retailing, permits the employment of many types of people who appear otherwise unemployable. For example, a man may be able to find useful employment in a small store for his wife and children. Whether such employment is socially desirable is another question.

8. *Small business facilitates new life styles.* Our society is offering more and more leisure time and producing more and more wealth to be shared by its members. Many are entering retirement at an early age. Job changes are becoming more and more frequent; many people now change jobs and even careers for reasons that have little to do with money. Such new life styles may have increasing importance in the future. It is small business that makes many of them possible. Thus an individual may plan to spend a certain number of years in the employ of a large corporation and a certain number of years in a small business. Transition from one life style to another may be aided by first cultivating the new life style as a hobby or even by training for it within a corporate environment.

Thus economically, socially, and psychologically the existence of small business would appear to be necessary for the future development of our society. Many recent graduates elect to work for large corporations such as General Motors or Hallmark because they know they will receive training in activities related to entrepreneurship.

### Entrepreneurship

As important as small business is, and as important as the entrepreneur may be in the formation and fostering of it, little is known about entrepreneurship.

A critical problem facing our society is that of creating more successful entrepreneurs. But what is success in this context? Mere survival in the entrepreneurial jungle is usually considered a substantial accomplishment, considering the large failure rate of small business. Indeed, Orvis Collins and David G. Moore have defined a successful entrepreneur as one who stays alive. Others define success in terms of high rates of return on sales and other accepted financial yardsticks. In any case, it seems that one precondition of success as an entrepreneur is willingness to fail, and ability to learn from it. Collins and Moore have even suggested a "school of driftmanship," so important do they consider failure in the education of entrepreneurs. The person who can get up off the floor and learn from whatever mistakes he has made is more likely to have the makings of a successful entrepreneur than someone who has never dared to make a mistake at all.

### Executives and Entrepreneurs

Another way to approach entrepreneurship is via the differences between the corporate executive and the entrepreneur. The following suggestions are not backed up by a wealth of empirical data, but represent the author's perception of the business world, reinforced occasionally by the literature.

The ability to deal with trouble, as Orvis F. Collins has pointed out, appears to be far more important to the small businessman than the ability to avoid it in the first place. It has been suggested that an entrepreneur may look for trouble because he enjoys encountering and mastering it. Also, a small firm has less control over its environment than a large one, as well as fewer resources to devote to the analysis of its future environment. Trouble is therefore very difficult for a small firm to avoid, and skill in dealing with trouble would appear to be a necessary component of the entrepreneurial world, probably more important than in the executive world. The entrepreneur also seems more receptive to innovation. This would fit in with the wheel-of-retailing concept.

While the entrepreneur has a high need for achievement, the corporate executive according to David E. Berlew, tends also to have a strong desire to influence other people. In fact, he really works at it, in contrast with the entrepreneur, who is more of a loner.

Small businessmen are usually more interested in obtaining information than they are in analyzing it. And indeed in many types of business it is more important merely to possess needed information than to analyze it in some sophisticated way. Large business has the personnel to analyze the information that it receives. But there are more layers of executives to go through and more motivational barriers to communication, so that the top management of large firms is less likely to have the right information.

Businessmen in general are "doers" rather than thinkers, and small businessmen tend to be even more action-oriented than the executives of larger corporations.

### Retail Small Business Failures

Anyone who has been connected with retail small business knows that the rate of failure is high. Moreover, this is a type of business in which not failing does not usually equal success by ordinary standards. A very large percentage of small retailers just manage to squeeze out a living.

The information with regard to small business failure is quite meager. A 1955 study by Betty Churchill indicated that more than three out of four individuals who start a retail business will be out of that business within five years. However, there are many factors other than low or negative profitability that might cause an owner to sell, transfer title, or close the operation. Two studies of franchising, one by U. B. Ozanne and Shelby D. Hunt, the other by E. Patrick McGuire, have not been able to pinpoint the failure rate of nonfranchised alternatives. However, all observers within the industry regard the failure rate of small enterprises as high. A failure rate of 75 percent in five years appears quite plausible.

The plight of the small businessman has helped foster an activity that attempts to combine the advantages of being large with the advantages of being small. This is franchising, which has been called the last stand of small business. Whether it is or not, it would appear that the areas of small business with the greatest potential at the present

Table 6.1
*Failure rate among franchised outlets, as reported by franchisors*

| Annual failure rate among companies' total outlets | Franchisors Reporting | | | | |
|---|---|---|---|---|---|
| | Total, all companies | Fast-food & beverage | Nonfood retailing | Personal services | Business products & services |
| Less than 1% ...................... | 51.3% | 59.6% | 48.9% | 53.4% | 34.5% |
| 1% to 4% ............................ | 23.3 | 17.5 | 33.3 | 20.7 | 24.1 |
| 5% to 9% ............................ | 10.1 | 12.3 | 8.9 | 5.2 | 17.2 |
| 10% to 14% ........................ | 5.8 | 0.0 | 4.4 | 8.6 | 13.8 |
| 15% or more ...................... | 2.6 | 0.0 | 2.2 | 1.7 | 10.3 |
| No estimate given ............... | 6.9 | 10.5 | 2.2 | 10.3 | 0.0 |
| Total ...................... | 100.0% | 100.0% | 100.0% | 100.0% | 100.0% |

*Note: Based on information reported by 189 franchise companies. Includes 57 franchisors of fast foods and beverages, 45 of nonfood consumer products, 58 of personal services, and 29 of business (or industrial) products and services. Column totals may not add to exactly 100.0% due to rounding. [Source: E. Patrick McGuire,* Franchised Distribution *(New York: The Conference Board, 1971), p. 99.]*

time, except for certain service enterprises not considered in this text, would be in franchising.

## Small Retailing and Franchising

Franchising usually involves a larger, somewhat more experienced entity, the franchisor, and a new, somewhat independent enterprise, the franchisee. If there is a contract, the franchise is usually for a specified time for specified fees, rates, or both, and the services to be performed by both parties are clearly spelled out. Typical examples of retail franchise operations are 711 Stores, International House of Pancakes, and Howard Johnson restaurants.

The major benefits to the businessman franchisee are a safer overall investment and also often the opportunity to earn more money than his nonfranchised counterpart. As suggested earlier, it is difficult to obtain reliable data that indicate how much safer a franchise is than going into other kinds of business. The problem is complicated by the fact that few government or other agencies segregate small business information by franchise and nonfranchise. A further difficulty relates to the definition of business failure. Dun and Bradstreet, as McGuire points out, treats a business cessation as a failure when there has been a recorded loss to any of the creditors. Some trade associations, such as the International Franchise Association and the American Petroleum

Institute, set a minimum level of creditor loss before the business is cited as a failure. Comparison is also hampered by the fact that the population from which franchisees are recruited would appear to be quite different from the general population, and even from the great mass of small businessmen. The franchisee typically must have some money, and perhaps other characteristics. In addition, many types of business are not involved in franchising. Some applicants for franchises are highly skilled; some need only be aggressive; and so forth. Thus comparisons between franchisees and other small businessmen are very difficult to make.

Three studies have offered figures on failures in franchising. Table 6.1 shows the National Industrial Conference Board's estimated failure rate, by selected types of franchisee. Ozanne and Hunt estimate that the failure rate for fast-food franchisees was higher than the 1.3 to 6.7 percent of total units per year suggested in their data. Finally, a study by the U.S. Department of Commerce, *Franchising in the Economy, 1971–73*, showed that less than 2 percent of the franchisee-owned units had terminated operations during 1971.

Table 6.2 offers the NICB data by size of franchisor: it will be noted that as the size of the franchisor becomes very large, the rate of failure among its outlets decreases. None of the above figures can be readily compared with figures for nonfranchisors. Nevertheless the figures do appear to corroborate what most observers would agree

Table 6.2
Failure rate among franchised outlets, by size of franchise company

| Annual failure rate among companies' total outlets | All franchisors | Franchisors reporting | | |
|---|---|---|---|---|
| | | Size of franchise company (gross annual income) | | |
| | | Under $2 million | $2 to $5 million | $5 million or more |
| Less than 1% ............................... | 51.3% | 47.3% | 40.0% | 66.7% |
| 1% to 4% ................................... | 22.8 | 19.6 | 36.7 | 24.4 |
| 5% to 9% ................................... | 10.4 | 14.3 | 10.0 | 0.0 |
| 10% to 14% ............................... | 5.7 | 8.0 | 6.7 | 0.0 |
| 15% or more ............................... | 3.1 | 3.6 | 0.0 | 4.4 |
| No estimate given ......................... | 6.7 | 7.1 | 6.7 | 4.4 |
| Total ............................... | 100.0% | 100.0% | 100.0% | 100.0% |

Note: Based on information provided by 187 franchisors. Includes 112 companies with gross income under $2 million; 30, $2 to $5 million; and 45, $5 million or more. Column totals may not add to exactly 100.0% due to rounding. [Source: E. Patrick McGuire, Franchised Distribution (New York: The Conference Board, 1971), p. 99.]

upon: it is safer for a businessman inexperienced in an endeavor in which he is starting to accept a quality, well-known franchise rather than go into business on his own.

### Advantages to the Entrepreneur

In order for franchising to have grown up as rapidly as it has, substantial advantages must be offered by the franchise relationship to both franchisor and franchisee. In many types of franchises the retail franchisee inherits substantial goodwill in addition to a preestablished general exterior and store plan that has been tested over time. Franchising, however, takes such varied forms that the student should beware of assuming all of it to be some particular manufacturer-retailer combination such as that between automobile manufacturers and dealers. There may be manufacturer-wholesaler combinations, as between most soft drink manufacturers and their bottlers, and wholesaler-retailer combinations, as so often appears in the food industry. There are also trademark franchises, which do not require any good or service to be produced or forwarded by the franchisor. Restaurant franchises and some associations of manufacturers, as in the mattress industry, typically operate in this fashion. Whatever the structure of the relationship, the franchisor typically offers advice that is of substantial value on many dimensions of the operation, including personnel selection, pricing, and so forth. Of particular interest, usually, are the following:

1. *Location.* The key to most new retail enterprises is their location. Many inefficient franchisees have prospered due to an attractive location, while many brilliant ones have not been able to overcome an initial error in that respect. The established franchisor has substantial advantages in locating a new store even if the nonfranchised competition is equally skilled in store location. One reason for this is that franchisors will know exactly in many instances, or in general terms in others, the types of customer to whom their franchises appeal, the distance these customers will travel to frequent the store, the general reasons they buy in the store, and so forth. This type of information is easily developed from analyses of present customers in the other outlets of the franchise. With this information, however precise or imprecise it may be, comparisons can readily be made between the proposed site and present locations. The obvious pitfalls will usually be avoided by this kind of analysis. In addition, most franchisors will have located many other outlets of this specific type, both for franchisees and for themselves, and will hopefully have become more proficient with each new opening.

Even a location expert is at an extreme disadvantage in locating the first of any type of store. A real methodological challenge to academicians is to find ways to locate new stores effectively without the aid of information generated from previous outlets. Most prospective entrepreneurs are not location experts and are often not even aware that location is important.

2. *Buying merchandise.* Buying merchandise is difficult even if the decision maker is knowledgeable. Large franchisors *are* knowledgeable, and most appear quite expert in buying. "Expert" is the key term here; buying intelligently without the benefit of previous knowledge of a merchandise area is extremely difficult, if not impossible. Thus if an entrepreneur were opening his first motel, where would he buy mattresses? If he were opening a hot dog stand, where would he buy the necessary machinery? Purchases such as these can be made without expert knowledge. But a novice will probably not be able to get the knowledge necessary to avoid a catastrophe, either in the selection of the equipment or in the price paid, or both. In addition to the purchase of merchandise and equipment, businessmen starting new ventures must often get involved with such complex issues as construction and real estate. Franchisors are often better equipped to deal with these issues than an individual is.

3. *Operational comparisons.* A franchisor can and usually does institute a system of comparisons that are highly useful to the decision maker. What does it mean if a store's delivery expense is running at 5 percent of sales? What does it mean if catsup purchases for a restaurant are running 2 percent of sales? These figures take on meaning primarily when compared to the figures for other outlets of a similar type. Of course, trade associations can often help in developing some kinds of comparison, but the comparisons offered by another outlet of the same chain are usually more direct and more meaningful.

4. *Establishing procedures and programs.* The opening of a new store is a complex event that can permanently affect its future. A chain that has opened many stores can do much to insure that its latest opening is a success. It can also provide a follow-up plan for the crucial first six months. Such a plan may be designed sequentially. Thus if business has not

reached $30,000 a month at the end of six months, the manager may be instructed to follow "policy 2D," or place "ad Z" in "media II." Whether formal or informal, decision alternatives can be developed without great cost after many openings.

5. *Problems.* The procedures just outlined are mainly designed to avoid large problems. However, unexpected large problems do occur and most franchisors have enough experts to solve them. For instance, without expertise it may be difficult to answer questions such as "What is wrong with my pizza?"

6. *Training.* An adequate training program for a chain of stores can usually be set up so long as there is sufficient funding. Employees can be trained in other outlets or at a common center. It is quite difficult, however, to set up training for the first outlet. Any serious attempt at training personnel, including executives, is usually dispensed with because there is no obvious way to obtain such training. Furthermore, such training as there is tends to be in other types of store, which may not be altogether relevant. Is training in a pizza parlor sufficient training for operating a pancake house? Perhaps, but most investors would prefer the executive to have been in a pancake house if he is opening a pancake house.

7. *Advertising and promotion.* One of the great economies of most chains is in advertising. A single retail unit advertising for itself on television or radio or in the newspapers will be paying to reach a rather high proportion of people who are never going to buy its merchandise anyway. A chain, however, can advertise in these highly effective media on behalf of all its outlets at once.

In addition to the preceding advantages, the franchisee is part of a vertically integrated channel. He benefits from the attendant advantages that accrue to the total channel of which the franchisee is one member, even though usually a nondominant member. The advantages of an integrated channel are discussed in Chapter 3. Meanwhile, it should be noted that the franchisee, because he lacks power, is not likely to get much of any additional profit accruing to the total channel. But he might benefit in that, if large profits exist in the channel, the franchisor may give up some of them in his own self-interest rather than let a part of his channel fail. This is one reason that franchisors can afford to spend a lot of time working with a franchisee who is not doing well.

### Disadvantages to the Entrepreneur

The above advantages of franchising are quite meaningful, but there are also some disadvantages, though they vary substantially from industry to industry, from franchisor to franchisor, and probably from one geographic area to another.

1. *Lower profits.* If all other things, including sales, are equal, the entrepreneur will make less money in a franchise than he would on his own. In most instances, of course, things would not remain the same, particularly sales. Nevertheless, the profits from franchises are often low and indeed can be kept low by the franchisor if he adjusts contracts yearly to insure that no extraordinary profits accrue to the franchisee. Yearly contracts are likely where the franchisee is, in most respects, an employee. The employer-employee relationship characterizes many low-fee franchises. However, as the franchise fee increases, the returns to the franchisee tend to increase also, and the latter begins to be treated with more consideration.

2. *Risk of deception.* The franchisee has to deal with many fast-dealing franchisors. Many franchisees have done extremely well with franchising. Many others have been taken advantage of by relatively unscrupulous franchisors. Still others have been essentially forced into signing rather technical legal provisions drawn up by the attorneys for the franchisor. The practical relationship between the franchisor and the franchisee is in no sense equal, except under very unusual circumstances, and it is probably misleading for the franchisor to represent it as a "partnership."

3. *Dependency.* The franchisee is a part of a system over which he has little control. He is often dependent on the actions of other franchisees whom he may not even know. If one Howard Johnson restaurant sells bad food, many others may suffer.

Generally all the franchisee can do is count on an effective franchisor organization.

4. *Loss of control.* The franchisee is only a shadow of an entrepreneur. Most of his activities are practically, if not legally, controlled. Thus the entrepreneur may lose some of the psychic benefit of being a successful small businessman.

### Advantages to the Franchisor

Naturally, there are advantages for the franchisor in setting up a franchise, otherwise he would not do it. The franchisor obtains his revenues from the sources shown in Figure 6.1. Some of the advantages of franchising for the franchisor are as follows:

1. *Owner on the premises.* Motivation is always a key problem in any business organization. Having an owner on the premises who is appropriately rewarded tends to solve most aspects of this problem.

2. *Lower capital outlay.* Expansion can be accomplished with less capital. Thus many young firms can expand more rapidly than might otherwise be the case. Perhaps at some point in time it may be profitable to buy back many of the franchises, but over some range of growth the lower capital requirements may be quite significant. A related advantage is that since the franchisee puts up much of the money for the new outlet, he also risks losing that money if things do not go well. Even if the franchisor bails the franchisee out of a poor location, there will generally be a cost to the franchisee. Therefore, the actual dollar risk is often lower to the franchisor.

3. *Local identification.* Developing a franchise organization permits a type of local identification not otherwise feasible. This is particularly important for firms that need community support if they are to be successful at all. Thus "George's Ford" has more community identification than does just plain "Ford" if Mr. George happens to be a well-known local figure.

4. *No unionization.* Historically, unionization has been feared by many companies. In certain circumstances franchising has been a mechanism to avoid such unionization. It will usually not pay a

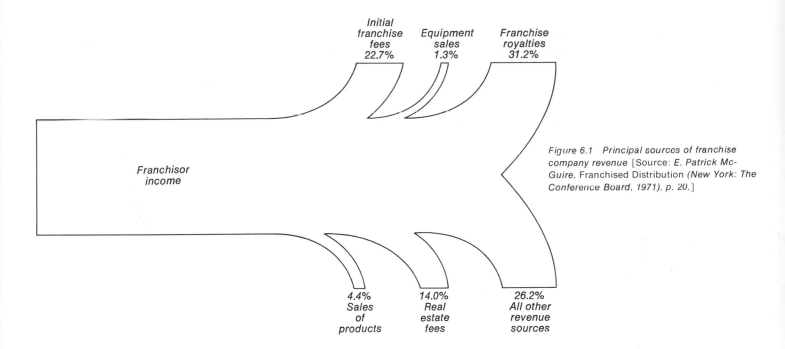

Figure 6.1 *Principal sources of franchise company revenue* [Source: *E. Patrick Mc-Guire*, Franchised Distribution *(New York: The Conference Board, 1971), p. 20.*]

union to try to organize four or five employees, while it might pay to try to organize 100 stores with four or five employees each.

5. *Avoidance of certain regulations.* Franchising permits the franchisee to avoid certain regulations, both directly and indirectly. For example, the price control program in 1972 exempted small businesses employing 60 or fewer persons.

6. *Permits certain questionable practices.* While the student should have had enough contact with automobile dealers to form his own opinion as to their general principles of doing business, this author feels that they have well earned their reputation. While the situation may not be correctable within a framework of competition and small business, the automobile dealer has certainly not led society in adopting ethical business practices. Society would not tolerate many of the sales, credit, and service practices of automobile dealers if the manufacturers could be held directly responsible for them. Because the dealers are small businessmen, however, there is little agitation on the part of society to correct whatever deficiencies exist. While the auto-

mobile industry is quite visible and therefore open to attack, many other examples could be offered of franchisees adopting profitable practices that are ethically or legally reprehensible, or both. The large firms are in most instances aware that their franchise systems create various immoralities, but they are generally not concerned so long as their expectation of long-range profits is not disturbed.

7. *Surtax advantage.* In our society there is a tax advantage that accrues to smaller firms. For example, in 1973, firms paid 22 percent on the first $25,000 of earnings. The maximum tax rate is 48 percent. If everything else remains equal, a franchisee and a franchisor pay lower taxes on a specific profit than a franchisor would alone.

### Disadvantages to Franchisor

Everything else remaining equal, the franchisor will still make less out of a franchise operation than a company operation. However, it is assumed by the franchisor that everything else will not remain equal. As the initial amount required by the franchisor increases, the percentage return required by the small businessman will tend to increase. Individuals who are not buying jobs will tend to demand a higher rate of return from their investment than individuals who are buying jobs. Very often, franchisees who can scrape up, say, $5,000 in fees are actually buying jobs for themselves and their families. However, if someone is worth not $5,000 but $500,000, he has many options, and will be able to weigh a franchise against other investment alternatives. In order to attract such an investor, then, the return on a franchise must be competitive, which is to say high.

Another disadvantage is that the franchisor has less control over his outlets even if he still has substantial influence. While he usually is not dealing with an equal, he is also not dealing with an employee even in the simplest franchise agreement. This loss of control is conducive to. many types of problems. In 1973 one observer suggested that three out of four legal decisions were going against the franchisor with regard to the franchisee.

## Summary

1. Americans have generally regarded small business with special fondness, and indeed it has made some dramatic contributions to American society over time. Some of its positive contributions are as follows:

A.  Small business has been a dynamic element for social change. The theory of the wheel of retailing relies heavily on the role of entrepreneurship and small business in creating change.

B.  Small business often offers the individual the chance to control his own destiny.

C.  Small business is a haven for individuals who cannot or will not pay the price of success in the corporate environment.

D. The efficiency of many large enterprises may depend on the contributions of many small enterprises.

E. Small business can serve certain aspects of consumer convenience more efficiently than large business.

F.  Small business represents an avenue of reward to certain types of exceptionally skilled executive.

G. Small business is an employer of last resort for many kinds of individuals who do not have present employment. Indeed, small business permits the employment of many types of people who would not otherwise be employable.

H. Small business facilitates certain kinds of life style in our society in which individuals change careers in a planned manner.

2. Entrepreneurs differ from corporate executives in several key respects. Entrepreneurs have particular ability to: (a) deal with trouble; (b) foster innovation; (c) obtain relevant market and other information; (d) get things done.

3. A key aspect of small retailing is franchising. The major benefit to the businessman-franchisee is a safer overall investment. Often, too, he has the opportunity to earn more money than his nonfranchised counterpart. Franchising presents the following advantages to the prospective entrepreneur:

A. The established franchisor has substantial advantages in locating a new store. The franchisor has at his disposal information regarding the type of customer to whom his franchises appeal; the distance the customers will travel to frequent the store; the general reasons they buy in the store; and so forth.

B. The franchisor is skilled at buying the necessary equipment and supplies.

C. The fact that most franchisors develop a large number of units within a chain makes possible operational comparisons that are meaningful to the decision maker.

D. The franchisor has usually opened many stores and therefore has developed procedures to meet various contingencies that might occur.

E. The franchisor has the technical wherewithal to solve many kinds of problem requiring particular expertise.

F. The franchisor has ability to train the prospective entrepreneur in outlets that are very similar to the kind that he will be using.

G. The fact that the small businessman is part of a chain means that he can participate in chain store advertising and promotion.

## Discussion Questions

1. List the contributions of small business to society.

2. Is small business or large going to be the key dynamic element in the society of the future?

3. How is an entrepreneur different from a corporate executive?

4. McClelland uses achievement motivation to predict the entrepreneurial potential of the individual. If an individual is high on achievement motivation, is he likely to succeed in his endeavor? What other characteristics would be required for success in a small business?

5. What are the chief causes of small business failure?

6. What is franchising?

7. List some advantages of franchising to the entrepreneur.

8. What are some of the costs of franchising to the franchisee, as compared to going into small business without a franchise?

9. What are some advantages of franchising to the franchisor?

10. What are some costs of franchising to the franchisor?

## References

Berlew, David E., in *First Annual Karl A. Bostroni Seminar in the Study of Enterprise* (Milwaukee, Wis.: Center for Venture Management, 1969).

Churchill, Betty, "Age and Life Expectancy of Business Firms," *Survey of Current Business*, December 1955.

Collins, Orvis F., in *First Annual Karl A. Bostroni Seminar in the Study of Enterprise* (Milwaukee, Wis.: Center for Venture Management, 1969).

Collins, Orvis F., and Moore, David G., *Enterprising Man* (East Lansing, Mich.: Michigan State University Press, 1964).

Collins, Orvis F., and Moore, David G., *The Organization Makers* (New York: Appleton, 1970).

Harris, T. George, "A Conversation With David C. McClelland," *Psychology Today*, January 1971.

McGuire, E. Patrick, *Franchised Distribution* (New York: Industrial Conference Board, 1971).

Ozanne, U. B., and Hunt, Shelby D., *The Economic Effects of Franchising* (Madison, Wis.: University of Wisconsin Press, 1971).

Schumpeter, Joseph, *The Theory of Economic Development* (Cambridge, Mass.: Harvard University Press, 1934).

## Further Reading

A development of the historical perspective of franchising will be found in: Thompson, Donald N., *Franchise Operations and Antitrust* (Lexington, Mass.: Heath Lexington, 1970), pp. 19–26.

An important government source is: *Franchising in the Economy, 1971–1972* (U.S. Department of Commerce, 1973).

## Case History: *Peter's Gas Club*

Peter Cranford owned and operated two large discount stores 60 miles south of a large midwestern city. Total volume of the two was $35 million. The stores were located about 10 miles apart. They had grown in volume over the years until their profits were small but positive.

Cranford had been considering establishing gasoline stations for a long time. His main interest in them was as volume builders for his discount house, but he also was interested in any profit contribution they could make to the major store operations. He began looking closely at different types of gasoline station. He was especially intrigued by the self-service units that were appearing in various sections of his area. Because he had always felt that direct observation was the one way to get to know an operation, he parked his car near a couple of these stations for two eight-hour stretches.

Over a period of time he observed that a great many women did frequent this kind of operation. Not only that, but many did not appear poor, nor did their automobiles appear old or shabby. Further, the customers got in and out of the station in a hurry, much faster than in a conventional station. His observations, plus what he knew of the labor situation, convinced Peter Cranford that he should open self-service gasoline stations next to both his operations.

His first concern was a source of supply for his gasoline. The source had to have three characteristics. First, the gasoline had to be inexpensive. Second, the gasoline had to be of top quality because Peter did not want to lose any discount store customers by selling them low-quality gasoline. Third, the supplier must supply him through thick and thin. If Peter adopted a low retail price, as he expected to, he did not want to lose a supplier because of the pressure that he knew would come from other stations and suppliers. Finally, one leading quality supplier did offer to sell to Peter at 31.5 cents a gallon delivered at the station, including all taxes. The supplier was willing to sign a long-term contract.

Now Peter's problem was how to sell the gasoline. If he sold it at 35.5 cents a gallon, the break-even point, even with self-service, would be very high. He figured that his fixed costs per station were $40,000 a year. Except for the gas, all expenses, including labor, appeared fixed once the lease was signed. The break-even point per station would be about 1 million gallons.

In playing with the arithmetic of the various prices, Peter Cranford hit on a new idea. He would try to start gas clubs, and then sell gasoline at 2 cents over his cost, or about 9 cents a gallon under the market. He would sell gas club tickets good for one year. These tickets would cost $5.00 per car and would permit the customer to purchase gas at 33.5 cents per gallon for one car. Peter thought that he could sell 5,000 of these tickets per station, which would give him $50,000 a year in fees alone. Thus only $15,000 of the fixed costs at each station would have to be covered by gasoline sales, and he would have a much lower break-even point. Peter felt that if the card idea succeeded he could open up many gas stations of the same type. The card revenue alone would more than pay the rent for the year.

Another dimension interested Peter Cranford: this appeared to be an ideal set up for a franchise. The franchisee could pay him one-quarter of a cent per gallon while actually running the gas station. If he worked sixteen hours a day, he would get double wages in addition to an entrepreneurial profit from the enterprise.

Peter Cranford was an entrepreneur interested in making a lot of money. Nevertheless, he pondered the social consequences of his actions. It staggered him when he thought of the savings that might accrue to customers if this type of gas station took off. The present retail price in town was 42.9 cents a gallon for regular gasoline of the same type he would be selling. This innovation might revolutionize the retailing of gasoline. He was also aware that in that case the regular gas station would go out of business. At this time the cost of regular gasoline to such stations was about 36.5 cents. There was no way many of them could compete, regardless of the support they might receive from their major suppliers.

### Discussion Questions

1. Will the card idea succeed? Give reasons for your answer.

2. Prepare a break-even analysis for a gas club station.

3. Should Peter Cranford have worried about the families of the entrepreneurs that he might put out of business?

4. Estimate the benefits to society of setting up a gas club station.

5. Would such a gas club help or hinder the federal government in its efforts to deal with the energy crisis?

# 7

Few if any aspects of American business life escape having to operate within the constraints of a public policy that is oriented toward the maintenance of competition. Competition, it has been said, is the life of trade, and retailing is no exception to this principle. A retailer is someone who buys merchandise and wares and resells them to the public. In his sales to the public he has to make his own policies with respect to pricing and any forms of promotion he may want to use. All of these activities are supposed to comply with certain "rules of the game" that have been established by society through the various arms and instrumentalities of government. This chapter describes some of the legal constraints imposed on the different areas of retail decision making.

## Retailing and the Constraints of Public Policy

### Trade Regulation Statutes

In the United States, the principal trade regulation statutes are the antitrust laws. They are designed to remove market inequalities—that is, inequalities among business rivals in access to the market—that may create unreasonable restraints of trade and even lead to truly monopolistic situations. The Sherman Act of 1890 was the first federal law in this category and it is still one of the most powerful. Growing economic concentration in some industries with a consequent fear of monopoly was an important contributing factor in the passage of this statute. It is written in very general language. Section 1 condemns "every contract, combination . . . or conspiracy, in restraint of trade," while Section 2 declares it to be illegal to monopolize or attempt to monopolize, or to combine or conspire to monopolize. These sections apply to both interstate and foreign commerce. Being worded in such broad terms, they have had to be interpreted by the courts so that they could

This chapter was contributed by Professor Marshall C. Howard of the University of Massachusetts.

be applied to actual market situations. In 1911, the Supreme Court decided that a "rule of reason" had to be applied in the use of the Sherman Act. Such a rule was needed because every time a sale was completed it could have been interpreted as having restrained trade, no other seller being any longer able to make that same sale. Thus only unreasonable restraints are now held to be illegal. Certain practices, however, such as collusive price fixing, have been determined by legal precedent to be illegal per se (a per se offense is one in which all that needs to be shown is the existence of the restraint). These practices are discussed below.

As supplements to the Sherman Act, two statutes were passed in 1914 with which the retailer should be especially familiar. The first was the Clayton Act, which attempts to pinpoint certain market practices then believed to be quite prevalent. The chief objection to them was that they often eventually led to situations in which smaller enterprises could be taken advantage of by larger suppliers or rival retailers. Section 2 of the act was designed to deal with situations in which suppliers charged different prices to different retailers, and Section 3 with situations in which suppliers forced firms to take certain other goods in order to get the goods they wanted (these are known as "tying agreements"). Section 7 was designed to regulate the merger or combination of firms. The last-named section was amended in 1950 to include the acquisition of assets as well as the acquisition of stock. None of these practices was condemned out of hand, but rather was declared to be illegal wherever the effect might be "to substantially lessen competition or tend to create a monopoly in any line of commerce." In this clause we have what has become known as the "doctrine of incipiency": actual injury to competition need not be shown provided that a reasonable probability of injury can be demonstrated. Thus application of the Clayton Act must rely on forecasts into the future as well as on market data generated in the past. An amendment to the Clayton Act which is of great import to the retailer is the Robinson-Patman Act of 1936. In an attempt to reach the problem of the large retailer who uses his massive buying power to demand and receive discounts in amounts that

other buyers are not receiving, Section 2 was amended in such a way as to make a very detailed statute. It has subsequently led to a considerable amount of confusion as to which buying practices are legal and which are not.

It should be noted that any retailer who can show he has been injured in his business or property by reason of anything forbidden in the Sherman or Clayton Acts can recover the damages threefold. Furthermore, wherever a party to a government antitrust suit has been found to violate the antitrust laws, this can be presented as prima facie evidence against him by any private party who is suing him. This helps explain why defendants in antitrust suits brought by the government often plead *nolo contendere*, "I do not wish to contend," in order to escape being found guilty, although they may suffer some penalty as a result.

The second major piece of business control legislation passed by Congress in 1914 was the Federal Trade Commission Act. This act established the important regulatory commission bearing that name. Section 5 declared that unfair methods of competition were illegal. Amended by the Wheeler-Lea Act in 1938, this statute now makes unlawful all "unfair methods of competition in commerce, and unfair or deceptive acts or practices in commerce." The 1914 statute was originally designed to supplement the existing antitrust laws, since the Federal Trade Commission (FTC), which was established as a body of experts to keep watch over trade and commerce, needed its own equivalent of the Sherman Act (the latter is subject only to the jurisdiction of the Antitrust Division of the Department of Justice, at least as far as government prosecution is concerned). Over the years, however, especially since the Wheeler-Lea Act, Section 5 has come to be used by the FTC to deal with problems of misrepresentation, including deceptive advertising and sales promotion. Indeed, Section 12 of the latter act specifically declared the false advertising of foods, drugs, therapeutic devices, and cosmetics to be an unfair or deceptive act or practice that violates Section 5 of the Federal Trade Commission Act. The commission has also been given the job of enforcing statutes that regulate the labeling of wool, fur, and textiles, in addition to its more general authority, under the Fair Packaging and Labeling Act of 1966, with respect to all products other than foods, drugs, therapeutic devices, cosmetics, and imported goods. All this legislation, as will be explained later in the chapter, involves the retailer directly or indirectly.

Finally, the retailer must comply with various state and local legislation and ordinances designed to control commerce and keep the competition fair. Some states have laws against conspiracies and restraints of trade, and some specifically refer to such practices as price fixing, sales below cost, price discrimination, tying contracts, and exclusive dealing. Some states have laws against bait-and-switch advertising and misleading pricing, and the same purpose is found in some community ordinances, which may even control the conditions of door-to-door selling.

### Areas of Regulation

#### Collusion

Getting together with one's competition to fix the price of goods and services is in itself illegal under federal antitrust laws. Section 1 of the Sherman Act and Section 5 of the Federal Trade Commission Act are both applicable to price fixing. The precedents are particularly clear on this point, as Chief Justice Warren pointed out in 1956. It matters not how the price is fixed; even collusively fixing a *lower* price is illegal. It is not just a matter of fixing the price directly; controlling the amount of a product that gets onto the market place is still in and of itself illegal. For the courts have recognized, in effect, the functional relationship between the price of a product and the quantity of it that will clear the market place. Many retailers may feel that the federal laws do not really apply to them, but the concept of interstate commerce has broad application: as long as supplies come from out of state, the courts will probably hold that interstate commerce is involved. Certainly, groups of gas station dealers attempting to fix prices through their local or state trade association have fallen afoul of the federal antitrust laws more than once. The fact is that any group action designed to eliminate competition can be considered per se illegal. It is illegal for competitors to divide up the market between them and agree to stay out of each others' way. It is also illegal for distributors or manufacturers to stage a group boycott of a retailer who cuts prices, no matter how much his behavior distresses them.

#### Resale Price Maintenance

Let us suppose, however, that a manufacturer or a distributor of a certain product decides on his own, not in collusion with other manufacturers or distributors, to boycott a retailer who is selling that product at a cut price. Should this be illegal? Perhaps the supplier feels that consumer acceptance of, and the goodwill inherent in, his branded products depends upon the maintenance of certain minimum retail prices. Perhaps he feels it will cheapen his product's image if it is used as a loss leader, that is, an item sold at, near, or even less than wholesale price in order to attract customers. Hasn't he a right to feel this way? The answer is that he has, and that he can probably refuse to deal with such a retailer. This is the so-called Colgate doctrine (*United States* v. *Colgate*, 1919). His action must be strictly unilateral, however. There can be no discussion of the retail price by the supplier with his other retailers, nor may he encourage wholesalers to refuse to do business with the price-cutting retailer. Such action would be viewed as a conspiracy in violation of the Sherman Act. In recent years, however, this ruling has been under increasing attack. A very interesting marketing question is what would happen to the retail structure if the Colgate doctrine were overturned.

State fair trade laws, where they exist, do permit the maintenance of a full-fledged program of resale price maintenance by a manufacturer or distributor of a branded product. State fair trade laws were passed during the 1930s by all but three of the states in an attempt to solve the problem of resale price maintenance as the retailers saw it. To the retailers, the problem was one of putting an end to price cutting, especially by stores of different types or of the same type but with different price policies. Loss-leader selling is a practice that small retailers feel nas favored the large retailer, who is in a better position to absorb the "loss" because he has a large assortment of goods. Actually, it is not always easy to distinguish between the ordinary variety of good, old-fashioned price competition and loss-leader selling. Some loss leaders are sold at wholesale (invoice) price. Others may be sold at even less than this, and are considered a promotional cost or expense to cover the sale of *all* items. It is undoubtedly true that most retailers, like most sellers, prefer to see stable and fairly high prices. Some types of retailer, such as retail druggists, have even been able through effective organization to pressure the manufacturers of branded goods into taking advantage of the enabling state fair trade legislation that the retailers themselves had pushed through the state legislature. The legal justification for the vertical price fixing of fair trade lies in the protection of the manufacturer's property as represented in the goodwill inherent in the brand name.

The state fair trade laws have been given an assist with respect to goods sold in interstate commerce by two pieces of federal enabling legislation. First, the Miller-Tydings Resale Price Maintenance Act of 1937 amended Section 1 of the Sherman Act to exempt this type of vertical price fixing from the antitrust laws. This same amendment was made applicable also to the Federal Trade Commission Act. Then, after the Supreme Court ruled that this federal legislation did not apply to the so-called nonsigner provisions of state laws, Section 5 of the Federal Trade Commission Act was amended by the McGuire-Keogh Fair Trade Enabling Act to exempt the nonsigner provision as well. This virtually gave federal sanction to retail price maintenance, since a nonsigner provision obliges all retailers to abide by the provisions of a fair trade resale price maintenance contract signed by *any one* of them. No federal fair trade law covering all 50 states, however, has ever been enacted, although several such bills have been proposed at one time or another.

The utilization of fair trade by a manufacturer or distributor places one positive constraint upon him: he cannot engage in retailing himself. The legal theory behind this prohibition is that if he did, he would be engaging in a horizontal price conspiracy with the retailers whom he has bound to resale price maintenance. Fair trade can thus be viewed as a force tending to place a restraint on forward vertical integration.

A prime reason why many manufacturers decide not to control the prices set by retailers under fair trade acts has been the cost of enforcing such a system. Enforcement rests with the fair trader; it is he who must sue the retailers if they cut prices. What is more, he must sue practically all such price cutters and get injunctions against them; he cannot single out one or a few for litigation, or he may be found to have discriminated. Merely to gather the evidence in such cases may cost far more than it is worth his while to pay.

The number of states maintaining effective fair trade acts has been steadily diminishing since the mid-1950s. Several states have repealed their fair trade acts in their entirety, while others have seen their acts emasculated by court decisions declaring the nonsigner provision to be unconstitutional. In early 1973 there were only 16 states with fair trade acts that included such a provision. Nineteen other states have fair trade acts without one. These latter acts are in effect sterile, for the fair trader cannot maintain price control over some retailers (the signers) if he does not have control over the other retailers (the nonsigners). The principal reason for the court's and society's withdrawal of full support for resale price maintenance is a recognition that it was spawned in the depression years of the 1930s in an attempt to place restrictions on price competition and so revitalize the economy. Fortunately, these conditions have not yet been repeated.

### Sales below Cost

Slightly more than half the states have what are known as "unfair practices acts." These are designed to prevent severe retail price cutting. They supplement fair trade laws in that they apply to all goods sold at retail and include both unbranded and branded goods. In general, they require that retail prices should cover costs (for this reason, they are sometimes known as sales-below-cost laws). "Costs" are usually defined in the statutes to cover invoice or replacement cost, whichever is lower, plus a low markup—for example, 6 percent—to cover overhead and other costs of operation. Some states have sales-below-cost laws that apply to specific products such as cigarettes, milk and dairy products, and gasoline.

State sales-below-cost laws do not make selling below cost illegal in itself. What is illegal, usually, is the intent or effect of injuring competitors and destroying competition. Intent and effect are difficult to prove, especially when most such statutes permit such selling when it is done in good faith to meet the price of a competitor. Moreover, when price cutting really gets under way and there is a retail price war, it is most difficult to discover who started it. As a result, litigation based on such statutes has been infrequent.

Selling below cost can also be an offense under Section 1 of the Sherman Act, if it unreasonably restrains trade, and under Section 2 if there is evidence of monopolizing or attempting to monopolize thereby. Section 3 of the Robinson-Patman Act, a criminal statute, provides that it is unlawful for any person to sell goods at unreasonably low prices for the purpose of destroying competition or eliminating a competitor. It has seldom been used.

### Buying and the Robinson-Patman Act

The 1936 Robinson-Patman Act amendment to Section 2 of the Clayton Act of 1914 was aimed directly at the buying practices of the large retailer. As passed in 1914, Section 2 declared price discrimination to be illegal wherever its effect might be to substantially lessen competition or tend toward a monopoly. It was aimed primarily against the price discrimination practiced by the large seller who discriminated in favor of certain customers (or perhaps in favor of a particular geographic region) in order to drive out his competitors. During the depression years of the 1930s, which saw many innovations in marketing as well as an increase in

chain-store selling, the issue of the big buyer came to the forefront. As a result, the Robinson-Patman Act was passed in order to close as many as possible of the avenues by which a big buyer, especially a large food chain, could exert its bargaining power successfully in negotiating with suppliers. Although the act is a very detailed one, its provisions are so tortuous that it is difficult to know when it is being properly complied with. Discounts, or simply negotiated prices, if challenged and deemed relevant to the act, have to be justified on at least one of four grounds:

1. Cost differences [Section 2(a)];

2. The competition is not substantially lessened by the discount or at least it does not "prevent competition with any person who either grants or knowingly receives the benefit of such discrimination, or with customers of either of them" [Section 2(a)];

3. The discount has been made in "good faith" in order to meet the equally low price of a competitor [Section 2(b)];

4. The discount has been made because of changing market conditions, such as perishability or obsolescence, that affect the marketability of the particular goods [Section 2 (a)].

It is in the attempt to justify a discount on any of these grounds that difficulties may be experienced. Cost justifications before the Federal Trade Commission, with the burden of proof upon the seller, have usually been unsuccessful. Just when competition is being substantially lessened is another question for which the answer is by no means clear-cut. And what constitutes "good faith" meeting of competition is subject to considerable difference of opinion.

Section 2(f) of the Robinson-Patman Act states that "it shall be unlawful for any person engaged in commerce, in the course of such commerce, knowingly to induce or receive a discrimination in price which is prohibited by this section." This, of course, is a direct reference to the buyer. But in many industries the buyer simply does not know what other buyers pay and has no way of finding out. Many if not most firms do not adhere rigidly to price lists, and numerous incalculable factors, such as special allowances, may affect the actual purchase price in a particular case. Further, at least some negotiation of prices is expected to occur, and when it does, few people would be naive enough to think that it could be conducted according to precise legal guidelines. What the Supreme Court appears to demand is that there be a reasonable awareness on the part of the buyer as to what he should be expected to know. Justice Frankfurter stated in 1953 that "trade experience in a particular situation can afford a sufficient degree of knowledge to provide a basis for prosecution." This may or may not be so, but the one thing that is clear is that there are no clear guidelines for the buyer to follow.

There are ways in which a large retailer can reduce the odds that he will be prosecuted under the Robinson-Patman Act. He might deal only with suppliers who deal only with very large accounts, so that the issue of discrimination against the small buyer is unlikely to arise. He might become the only account of a firm. He might insist on purchasing only merchandise that is thought to be different in grade and quality, since the Act refers only to differences in price "of commodities of like grade and quality." Such differences, however, cannot be attributed solely to a *private brand label,* for the Supreme Court ruled in 1966 that these alone do not create differences in "grade and quality."

**Brokerage payments**    Section 2(c) of the Robinson-Patman Act places a direct curb upon buying power. This section declares it unlawful to pay or receive a brokerage commission, or allowance in lieu thereof, to or from any party who is in any way affiliated with the buyer or seller, "except for services rendered." Although the words "except for services rendered" are indeed included in this section, they have, as noted below, been largely disregarded. A broker is an agent middleman whose prime function is to bring together buyers and sellers and negotiate transactions. He earns his living from commissions (brokerage) on the sales. Most brokers work for sellers. The purpose of Section 2(c) of the Robinson-Patman Act was to prevent large buyers, especially retail chains, from

claiming "dummy" brokerage fees from suppliers. Large buyers could use this as a mask to cover up price reductions secured in their favor that might otherwise have run afoul of the price discrimination section of the Clayton Act. Bypassing independent brokerage firms, these buyers were often able to secure the brokerage equivalent for themselves. A question was whether the large buyers received discounts that were greater than the value of the brokerage of the independent broker who was being bypassed. Thus the Robinson-Patman Act prohibits negotiation and bargaining by the retailer with his supplier over brokerage. This brokerage provision has also proven to be a drawback to those retailers who have formed cooperatives to save money through joint buying. Purchasing cooperatives or corporations whose stock has been held by what have been otherwise independent grocers has been found to be in violation of Section 2(c) of the Robinson-Patman Act because distribution of patronage dividends, corporate dividends, or advertising allowances has been held to constitute receipt of illegal brokerage.

Until the *Henry Broch* decision of the Supreme Court (*FTC* v. *Henry Broch & Co.,* 1960), the phrase "except for services rendered" was, in effect, of no consequence and the section therefore amounted to a flat prohibition of brokerage payments to a buyer by a seller. The reasoning was that only a broker could legally perform services for which brokerage might be paid. This ruling, however, was by no means unanimous, and certain later court decisions have suggested that the phrase "except for services rendered" may have some force after all. Certainly, the law of Section 2(c) is far from clearcut on these issues, and it may well be that, as Earl W. Kintner has argued, the business world will have to function in a legal limbo until they are clarified.

### Allowances and Services

The Robinson-Patman Act, in its efforts to prevent the large buyer from using his bargaining power to obtain disguised discounts from his supplier, includes Section 2(d). This section refers to the granting of allowances to buyers who provide services or facilities that aid in the processing, handling, sale, or offering for sale of the supplier's products. Among such services or facilities are local advertising and window and floor displays. Section 2(e) is similar in that it refers to services such as catalogs, demonstrations, display cabinets, and special packaging, that are granted by the supplier to the buyer to assist in the sale of the former's goods. An indirect form of price discrimination had been occurring: suppliers had been favoring some retailers and distributors over others, either by paying them for the above-mentioned services at more than their true cost, or by granting such services to one retailer and withholding them from competing retailers. Sections 2(d) and 2(e) attempted to correct the situation by requiring that both payments for services or facilities and the furnishing of services or facilities must be accomplished "on proportionally equal terms" to all competing customers.

While nothing in the act itself holds the buyer responsible either for inducing or for receiving the types of concession proscribed by Sections 2(d) and 2(e), nevertheless in 1968 a retailer was found guilty of violating Section 5 of the Federal Trade Commission Act for getting promotional allowances for himself that were not granted on comparable terms to his competitors. Thus it is of importance to the retailer to understand that in accepting such allowance he may be breaking the law. A retailer should also understand that a supplier who grants another retailer promotional allowances or services should hold out the same to him on proportionally equal terms — that is, unless the supplier can prove that he is thereby meeting the competition. But what does "proportionally equal terms" really mean? The Federal Trade Commission has found it necessary to issue extensive guidelines on this matter. No single formula is legally prescribed. The commission suggests, however, that payments or services be based upon the dollar volume or the quantity of goods purchased during a specified period. For example, in a cooperative promotional program the supplier may offer to pay a specified part, say 50 percent, of

the cost of local advertising up to an amount equal to a set percentage, say 5 percent, of the dollar value of purchases over a specified period of time. Whatever the program, however, the supplier is legally obliged to inform all customers of its availability. If a certain promotional program cannot be provided by or to all retailers because, say, some retailers are large and others are small, then the supplier should make room for whatever alternatives are functionally available. Thus, handbills for the small retailer may be equal to radio or television time for the larger retailer. In any case, the retailer should know his rights or his business may suffer.

The practices of suppliers on a "voluntary" basis have not always been on the highest ethical level. For instance, the Federal Trade Commission has found it necessary to issue a trade regulation rule for the men's and boys' tailored clothing industry stating that "the granting or furnishing, in whole or in part, of any advertising payment or promotional allowance, service or facility, by any seller of men's, youths' and boys' suits, coats, overcoats, topcoats, jackets, dress trousers and uniforms to a customer engaged in the resale of such products, will be presumed *not* to have been made available on proportionally equal terms to all the seller's customers competing in the resale of such products within the purview of Section 2(d) and (e) of the amended Clayton Act, unless such payments or allowances, services or facilities, have been made available pursuant to and in accordance with all the terms and conditions of a *written plan* supplied to all such competing customers." (Italics in original.) By the same token, however, a supplier who has advanced promotional funds to a retailer is expected to take reasonable precautions to see that the money is being used properly.

### Advertising and Representations

Advertising has come under regulatory control because of puffing, misrepresentation, and false advertising. Puffing is exaggerated praise or opinion of a product. It is a most common occurrence in advertising and is fully to be expected. After all, it is said that a man cannot be a good salesman unless he really believes in his product and conveys that feeling to the potential customer. Pushed a bit too far, however, puffing becomes misrepresentation, with the consumer being deceived. Finally, where the distortion is deliberate we have false or fraudulent advertising. Control over such departures from the truth is needed not only to protect the consumer but also to protect the scrupulous merchant who desists from such tactics.

At the federal level, the principal watchdog over misrepresentation and false advertising is the Federal Trade Commission, which can effectively use Section 5 of the Federal Trade Commission Act ("unfair or deceptive acts or practices") for the purpose. The general principle adhered to is that representations need have only the capacity or tendency to deceive in order to be found violative of this law. It need not be shown that a buyer has actually been deceived, or that a seller has intended to deceive a customer. Section 12 of the same statute specifically outlaws the false advertising of foods, drugs, devices, and cosmetics.

Misrepresentations can be with respect to many different aspects of a good or service. Misrepresenting the nature of a business, its commercial rating, and how long it has actually been in business are some of the aspects that may interest retail customers. The nature and effectiveness of a firm's products obviously interest a potential consumer. Are the products really "washable" or "unbreakable" or "harmless"? Other areas in which the FTC has found it necessary to intervene in behalf of the consumer with respect to specific representations have been the ingredients of a product, promotional contests, merchandise certificates won as prizes in contests, disparagement of competitors' products, endorsements and testimonials, exclusiveness and originality, free goods and offers, guarantees and warranties, manufacturing methods and processes, medicinal and therapeutic properties, new or rebuilt status, origin, and "passing off" products to the consumer as being something they really aren't. Section 5 of the Federal Trade Commission Act has been used against selling with the aid of lotteries, which is now clearly illegal in any form. This section can also require disclosure of information. Thus the FTC has

required sellers to disclose whether goods are imperfect or secondhand or of foreign origin. It has required firms to "correct" previous advertising by pointing out in future advertisements how the previous ones could have been misleading. In 1971 it adopted a program of requiring, where it felt advisable, substantiation of claims made as to a product's safety, performance, efficacy, quality, or comparative price.

Some undesirable advertising practices have been so common that the FTC has found it advisable to issue either guides or trade regulation rules. Guides represent the commission's actual interpretation of the laws administered by it, while trade regulation rules are drawn up by the commission, after full public hearings, to express its experiences and judgment in the area concerned. Where a trade regulation rule is relevant to the issue being adjudicated, the commission may rely upon the rule to resolve the issue.

The FTC guides against deceptive pricing provide a retailer with detailed legal guidelines on how to deal with such advertising practices as offering a "bargain" price that is supposed to be a reduction from the previous price. The basic question here is, When can the former price really be considered a genuine one? Was it offered for a very short time just in order to furnish a price comparison? Retail price comparisons with other similar items can also be subject to abuse. Are the prices really in the same market area, or is the comparison being made with goods that are not quite in the same category? Advertising the retail prices that have been established or suggested by manufacturers or other non-retail distributors—the so-called list price—can also be misleading, since a price reduction from a list price may not be a reduction in the true market price at all.

FTC guides have been issued to cover other practices in retail promotion and advertising. Bait-and-switch advertising is an alluring but insincere offer to sell a product or service when the advertiser does not really intend to sell the item. The "bait" ad brings the customer to the store; he is then induced to buy another, higher profit item (for further discussion of this practice, see Chapter 23). Both guarantees and warranties may suffer from inadequate disclosure of their conditions. Among the products advertised in a misleading way have been tires, shoes, mail order insurance, films and film processing, and pet food. Indeed, confusion over advertising in the dog and cat food industry has induced the commission to produce one of its lengthiest sets of guides. It also has guides for the following products or services: cigarettes, lipsticks, tile, fallout shelters, shell homes, radiation monitoring instruments, textile mill products, adhesives, debt collection, audience ratings, watches, beauty and barber equipment and supplies, ladies' handbags, and wigs and other hairpieces. More such guides are in the making.

Some of the rules adopted pertain to highly specialized advertising situations. How do you measure the true size of a sleeping bag? By the dimensions of the material going into the sleeping bag, or by the size of the finished product? Are all sewing machines really automatic? What is the difference between nonprismatic, partially prismatic, and prismatic binoculars? When are dry cell batteries truly "leakproof"? How do you measure the size of a tablecloth? By the dimensions of the material used, ("cut size"), or by the size of the finished product? What is the true leather content of a waist belt? There are FTC rules for all of these. Rules have also been promulgated to deal with deception (or failure to disclose) in advertising used motor oils; the size of viewable pictures shown by television receiving sets; the irritation to the skin resulting from washing or handling glass fiber curtains, draperies, and fabrics; the transistor count of radio receiving sets; the length of extension ladders; the lethal effects of inhaling quick-freeze aerosol spray products used for frosting cocktail glasses; and games of chance in the food retailing and gasoline industries. The trend is toward more protection of the consumer. For instance, the containers in which electric light bulbs are sold must show not only their wattage but their light output expressed in lumens and their average life expressed in hours. New trade regulation rules are continually being proposed, and retailers need to inform themselves about them.

### Consumer Credit

Special legislation was passed in 1968 to help protect consumers against the concealed high rates of interest they might have to pay for credit. This was the Consumer Credit Protection Act, better known as the Truth in Lending Act. The act requires creditors to make certain disclosures, notably the true annual rate of interest, to their customers, and sets standards for advertising credit terms. This enables the consumer to easily compare credit charges and to shop for credit as carefully as he does for merchandise. The duty of policing creditors under this act falls mainly upon the FTC, although other federal agencies cover certain credit areas. Since consumer credit is so widely used, the ramifications of this act are nearly endless (for further discussion, see Chapter 19).

### Labeling

Labeling requirement laws directly or indirectly affect retailing in many industries. The Wool Products Labeling Act of 1939, the Fur Products Labeling Act of 1951, and the Textile Fiber Products Identification Act of 1958 all require those who introduce these products into commerce to affix some kind of identifying tag or label on them. For example, the Wool Labeling Act requires the tag to indicate the percentage of that product composed of virgin wool, reprocessed wool, reused wool, and other fibers. One direct effect of this on the retailer is that he can substitute his own identification tag for that already on the garment. If he does so, however, he must be familiar with all of the labeling law requirements and accompanying record-keeping obligations. An indirect effect is that enforcement of these statutes is primarily through inspections, analyses, tests, and examinations. The FTC makes these inspections at the manufacturing, wholesaling, and retailing level. In the fiscal year 1968, the commission made 14,326 such inspections. A retailer should understand why federal inspectors are making such checks in his store.

The Fair Packaging and Labeling Act of 1966 can also have an effect on the retailer. A retailer as such is not subject to the law. But a vertically integrated firm retailing a consumer product that it manufactured, packaged, or labeled is subject to the law. Likewise, the law is directed at retailers purchasing consumer products under their own private labels. Such retailers must know the requirements of this law.

Several states, beginning with Massachusetts in 1971, have introduced unit-pricing laws. These laws require tags on the retail shelves of certain packaged categories of food and household items. The tags have to indicate the price per unit of whatever measure is customarily used. A consumer can thus compare prices, for example, on a pound-for-pound basis without having to calculate unit prices from combinations of fractional weights and multi-unit sales.

### Contractual Vertical Integration

Retailers may be quite dependent upon their suppliers as a result of the contractual arrangements that they have with them. The retailers may be independent businessmen, but by contractual agreement of one kind or another they may have relinquished some of their independence. This is known as contractual vertical integration. Various forms of it go under various names, depending partly on the arrangements and partly on the industry. In the gasoline industry, for instance, the so-called independent service station operator may well have signed real estate leases that make him a lessee dealer. A key element in contractual vertical integration is the franchising arrangement discussed in Chapter 6. Trademarks and trade names are also frequently the basis for franchises that limit the dealer's independence. Public policy has definitely been concerned with this type of retailer. The basic question is whether the retailer has contracted away too much of his power to make independent decisions. He is not capable of producing his own supplies, and his alternative sources of supply may be very limited. Indeed, there may not be a truly open market to which this retailer can turn in case he wishes to free himself from the influence of his supplier altogether. The policy issue is whether the retailer under such circumstances has voluntarily entered into such contractual agreements, or whether he has been coerced because he has no real choice in the matter. If the latter is the case, some violation

of the antitrust laws may be involved, since they are concerned with whether there exist unreasonable restraints of trade.

A 1969 staff report by the Federal Trade Commission paid special attention to several of the most common practices in franchising: exclusive buying, exclusive selling, territorial restrictions, customer restrictions, quality control, and termination restrictions. All these practices are to some degree restraints on trade and therefore potentially within the proscription of the antitrust laws. Even though what may appear to be reasonable business justification exists for each practice, at some point there are legal limits to what can be allowed. The report made it clear that, in the interests of competition, there was a real need to protect franchisees from the oppressive use of economic power by franchisors.

Exclusive dealing agreements require the retailer to deal only in the supplier's products. They are not illegal in themselves, but Section 3 of the Clayton Act makes them and other such tying arrangements illegal where the effect "may be to substantially lessen competition or tend to create a monopoly in any line of commerce." As we saw in Chapter 3, there may be many advantages for the retailer in dealing exclusively with one supplier. He does not have to shop around for supplies; they come automatically. In periods of shortage, he can more likely count on supplies. His inventory can be of lesser size than it would have been if he were handling more than one brand of goods. He can concentrate on promoting one branded line. And if technological "know-how" is involved, he can get most of that from the supplier too. On the other hand, there may be costs to the retailer in a system of exclusive dealing. Because he does not shop around, he may have to pay a higher price for the goods. He may be induced to handle certain products that he does not care to emphasize. A strike against his supplier can leave him without adequate supplies. And, from society's viewpoint, other suppliers will be excluded from making sales to this retail establishment.

The advantages and disadvantages to the competitive system have to be thoroughly analyzed in each situation. From a public policy point of view, there is one most important question: Has market power resulted in an exclusion of competitors from a substantial market? In the gasoline industry, for instance, exclusive dealing for all types of products at the retail level has been declared illegal because the major oil companies were using the practice and this added up to a "potential clog to competition." On the other hand, a court has ruled that in the farm machinery industry a manufacturer's desire to have his dealers devote the major part of their selling effort to his line did not violate the law, because there were alternative sources of supply available to dealers and, similarly, alternative dealers to whom the manufacturers could turn if they wanted to (*United States* v. *J. I. Case Company*, 1951).

A practice closely related to exclusive dealing is the tying arrangement. A supplier may have enough market power in one good (the "tying good") to require the retailer to purchase another good (the "tied good") along with it. For example, Automatic Canteen Company of America was tying in the sale of candy products with the lease of automatic vending machines. There were some 200,000 such vending machines in operation, and a court held that this constituted a very substantial interference with competition (*Automatic Canteen Company of America* v. *FTC*, 1952). The position of the law on tying contracts, under Section 3 of the Clayton Act, is that such contracts are illegal in and of themselves where either the seller enjoys a monopolistic position in the market for the tying product, or a not insubstantial volume of commerce in the tied product is restrained. That is, a detailed economic analysis of the effect on competition need not be shown if either of these positions can be demonstrated. Where the tying product is patented, some element of monopoly can be presumed.

Some franchisors of goods carrying the franchisor's trade name have attempted to compel their franchisees to buy all of their related supplies from the franchisor. For example, the Chicken Delight Corporation, a fast-food franchisor of fried chicken, had insisted that its franchisees purchase not only their chicken but also their wrapping papers, ready mixes, and condiments from the corporation (*Harvey Siegel and Elaine Siegel et al.* v. *Chicken Delight,*

*Inc.*, District Court of N. California, 1970). The argument to support this position is the maintenance of quality control of a trademarked product. Decisions in cases like these depend on the facts in the case. Perhaps wrapping papers and condiments from alternative sources of supply are equally satisfactory, whereas certain ready mixes may not be because they involve trade secrets or special recipes.

The granting of an exclusive sales territory to a franchised dealer has also been an issue of public policy. Such a grant is not illegal in itself. The Supreme Court has said that you have to examine "the economic and business stuff out of which these arrangements emerge" (*White Motor Co.* v. *United States*, 1963). If the manufacturer granted exclusive territories to given dealers because the dealers urged it, then the arrangement is no different from a horizontal conspiracy among competitors to divide up the markets among themselves and prevent competition. It is therefore a direct violation of the Sherman Act. On the other hand, if the manufacturer unilaterally decided that he wanted to encourage each dealer to promote his products intensively without worrying about competition from other dealers of the same products, then it can be argued that competition between brands is being fostered by restricting competition for a single brand. It may in fact be difficult for a manufacturer to get dealers to handle his products unless an exclusive territory is granted. This can be especially true where the product is new and untested by the consumer, or where product maintenance or guarantees are involved.

An issue frequently related to that of the grant of exclusive sales territories is that of customer restrictions, that is, limiting the type of customer the retailer may have. Thus a manufacturer may tell the retail dealer not to make sales to large institutional or government accounts. The defense for this practice is often that it takes more "know-how" to sell to such accounts than the relatively small dealer has. What the manufacturer actually may be doing, however, is reserving for himself some of the larger-volume and more profitable business. The dealers claim the manufacturers are "skimming the cream." The public policy view on this matter is that if the dealer has purchased the goods then the manufacturer no longer has dominion over them and cannot establish customer restrictions (*United States* v. *Arnold Schwinn and Co.*, 1967). The manufacturer can escape this legal restraint, however, by appointing the dealer as his agent, since as an agent he would not take title to the goods.

### Mergers

One way a retailer can insure himself a source of supplies is to merge with his supplier. In such a case, of course, the retailer loses his identity as an independent retailer and becomes part of a vertically integrated firm. On the other hand, the initiative for the merger could come from the supplier, who wishes to insure himself a steady customer. In either instance, public policy is concerned with this diminution in the number of firms. Section 7 of the Clayton Act condemns acquisitions, either of stock or of assets, where "the effect of such acquisition may be substantially to lessen competition, or tend to create a monopoly." This condemnation does not in itself prevent mergers among retailers, many of which have occurred; its real force hits the larger retailers in any given market.

The very first case under the 1950 amended Clayton Act to come before the Supreme Court involved vertical integration. This case involved the merger of the Brown Shoe Company, a firm primarily engaged in manufacturing shoes, with G. R. Kinney Corporation, a firm that operated some 400 retail shoe stores and owned or controlled through franchises or agreements some 1,230 retail outlets. The court found that the merger violated the law in that other manufacturers would be foreclosed from a substantial share of the markets for men's, women's, and children's shoes (*Brown Shoe Co., Inc.*, v. *United States*, 1962). Ordinarily, condemned mergers tend to involve industries characterized by oligopoly, that is, by few sellers selling relatively close substitute products. The shoe industry, however, was described as a "fragmented" industry, not dominated by very large firms. Brown Shoe Company was the fourth largest shoe manufacturer in the na-

tion, but it accounted for only about 4 percent of the national output of shoes. The court, nevertheless, saw a trend toward vertical integration in the shoe industry.

The lesson to be learned here is that a vertical merger involving retailing can be suspect under the Clayton Act even where the market structure does not exhibit a high degree of concentration. But the *Brown Shoe* case also violated the law against horizontal combination. In various communities of 10,000 population and over in which both Kinney and Brown Shoe had stores, the merger provided for combined market sales percentages ranging from 5 to 57 percent. Some of the higher percentages indicated too much market control.

Another case reaching the Supreme Court involved only retailing. The third and sixth largest retail grocery chains in the Los Angeles area merged to create the second largest. The court viewed this as part of a trend toward increasing concentration, and therefore to be condemned, even though the combined sales of the two firms equaled only 7.5 percent of the total of $2.5 billion of yearly retail grocery sales in the Los Angeles market (*United States* v. *Von's Grocery Company et al.*, 1966).

Two principal matters need to be properly defined before the legality of a merger can be resolved: what is the relevant line of commerce, that is, what products, specifically, are in competition with each other; and what is the relevant geographic market, that is, what are the physical boundaries within which the products are competing with each other? Until the relevant product and geographic markets are properly defined in economic terms, the competing firms and the effect on competition cannot be determined.

### Inflation Price Control

In certain periods, the retailer has been constrained in his decision making by a public policy oriented toward controlling inflation. In periods of inflation, competition appears to be inadequate to hold prices down to certain levels. Rapidly increasing costs force prices up, while the amount demanded at a given price level may be increasing faster than the amount supplied, with the same result. At the same time, an inflation psychology may be inducing prices to rise with regularity. Controls are then instituted by public demand.

During World War II and the Korean War a system of direct, item-by-item price control was utilized. Retailers were faced with price ceilings on the items they were selling. They became directly involved in a complex program of detailed regulations. Partly because of the inflation induced by the Vietnam War, but probably more because of an inflation psychology that appeared to be plaguing the economy, price controls were imposed in August 1971. Initiated by the president under standby authority granted by Congress in 1970, these controls were of a different character from the wartime ones. The economic stabilization program, as it was called, began with a 90-day freeze on prices, wages, and rents—Phase One. Phase Two, however, adopted what has been referred to as the "wholesale" approach: attention was focused upon the really large firms, with sales of $100 million or more per year. These had to get approval from the Price Commission before they could raise any price. Firms with sales of between $50–100 million could raise prices without commission approval so long as they followed certain rules and filed quarterly reports. Firms with less than $50 million sales and more than 60 employees were supposed to follow commission rules voluntarily, subject to a possible audit. Firms in certain industries that appeared to need it were given special attention even if they did not have 60 employees. These price controls were directed against only about one out of every 3,000 firms. Except for general price freezes, the great majority of retailers have not been directly controlled in the several phases of the program.

### Law and the Retailer

The so-called free enterprise competitive system is not entirely free for the retailer. He cannot make business decisions without taking into account the constraints of the legal framework of the competitive system within which he operates. A sound business reason may seem to fully justify a particular business decision, yet public policy constraints may still have to be reckoned with. It may seem profitable for a retailer to merge with his supplier, or to charge an especially low price for a good, but the law may not allow it.

Some uncertainty is introduced into retail decision making by this legal framework. The retailer can reduce this uncertainty to a minimum by familiarizing himself with the relevant laws and the precedents established under these laws. Not all uncertainty can be removed, however, for much of this body of law is written in general language that has to be interpreted. It may require a judicial proceeding to establish the applicability of a trade regulation law to a particular market situation.

### Summary

1. The principal trade regulation statutes in the United States are the antitrust laws:

A. The Sherman Act condemns contracts, combinations, or conspiracies in restraint of trade, and declares it to be illegal to monopolize or attempt to monopolize, or to combine or conspire to monopolize.

B. The Clayton Act attempts to deal with the problem of suppliers charging different prices to different retailers; to deal with agreements whereby suppliers force retail firms to take certain other goods in order to get wanted merchandise; and to regulate the merger and acquisition of firms.

C. The Federal Trade Commission Act established the Federal Trade Commission, designed to act as a body of experts to keep watch over trade and commerce. Section 5 declares that unfair methods of competition and unfair or deceptive acts or practices are illegal. This section has come to be used by the FTC to deal with problems of misrepresentation, including advertising and sales promotion.

2. Certain market practices merit the especial attention of the retailer:

A. Getting together with one's competitors to fix the price of goods or services is illegal in itself under federal antitrust laws.

B. A supplier may attempt to control retail prices through the use of fair trade in those states that still have the necessary statutes that permit a viable supplier fair trade program. A supplier may also (usually) be able to select the retailers to whom he desires to sell. In this way he may often be able to control the prices at which the merchandise will be sold at the retail level.

C. State sales-below-cost laws make selling below cost illegal if the intent or the effect is to injure competitors or destroy competition.

D. The Robinson-Patman Act, essentially an amendment to the Clayton Act, declares price discrimination to be illegal, unless certain conditions are met, where the effect is to substantially lessen competition or tend toward monopoly. Further, it is unlawful to pay or to receive a brokerage commission to or from any party who is in any way affiliated with the buyer or the seller. Services or facilities must be made available to competing customers on proportionally equal terms. The buyer for the retail store is not permitted to induce or receive concessions proscribed by the act.

E. The Federal Trade Commission keeps a close eye on possible misrepresentation and false advertising.

F. Certain laws have provided for labeling or packaging requirements for certain products introduced into commerce.

G. Often it is desirable from a business point of view for the supplier and the retailer to integrate their activities. Public policy, however, has been increasingly concerned with such practices as requiring the retailer to deal only in the goods of one supplier, of tying the sale of one good to another, and the use of exclusive sales territories.

H. Mergers and acquisitions are ways for the supplier and the retailer to combine their efforts. These actions are subject to judicial action by the federal government.

I. Inflation price control has become of increasing concern to society and its public policy makers, and should be of concern to the retailer.

### Discussion Questions

1. What does Section 5 of the Federal Trade Commission Act cover?

2. What were the two major pieces of business control legislation passed in 1914?

3. Which section of the Robinson-Patman Act most concerns the retailer?

4. Are sales below cost always illegal?

5. Why has fair trade legislation in the states been declining in importance?

6. What is the nonsigner clause?

7. What is puffing?

8. Under what conditions are exclusive sales territories illegal?

9. Why is the government so concerned with the merger of retail firms?

10. Are higher prices a proper concern of the government?

### References

Kintner, Earl W., *A Robinson-Patman Primer* (New York: Macmillan, 1970).

Warren, Earl, Chief Justice, summary statement in *United States v. McKesson & Robbins, Inc.,* 351 U.S. 305, 309–310 (1956).

## Further Reading

Dickinson, Roger, "The Retail Buyer and the Robinson-Patman Act," *California Management Review*, Spring, 1967, pp. 47–54.

Dirlam, Joel B., and Kahn, Alfred E., *Fair Competition: The Law and Economics of Antitrust Policy* (Ithaca, N.Y.: Cornell University Press, 1954).

Federal Trade Commission, *Annual Report*.

*Federal Trade Commission* v. *Procter & Gamble Co.,* 1967, U.S. Reports, vol. 386, 568–604.

*Harvard Law Review,* Note, "'Corrective Advertising' Orders of the Federal Trade Commission," December 1971, pp. 477–506.

Howard, Marshall C., *Legal Aspects of Marketing* (New York: McGraw-Hill, 1964).

———, "Government, the Retailer, and the Consumer," *Journal of Retailing*, Winter, 1972–73, pp. 48–62.

———, "Fair Trade Revisited," *California Management Review*, Fall, 1967, pp. 17–26.

Kintner, Earl W., *A Primer on the Law of Deceptive Practices* (New York: Macmillan, 1971).

Restrictive Trade Practices Commission, *Report on an Inquiry into Loss-Leader Selling* (Ottawa: Queen's Printer, 1955).

Stelzer, Irwin M., *Selected Antitrust Cases: Landmark Decisions* (Homewood, Ill.: Irwin, 1972).

Tarpey, Lawrence X., Sr., "Buyer Liability Under the Robinson-Patman Act: A Current Appraisal," *Journal of Marketing*, January 1972, pp. 38–42.

Walton, C. C., and Cleveland, F. W., Jr., *Corporations on Trial: The Electric Cases* (Belmont, Ca.: Wadsworth, 1964).

## Case History: *Nancy Driscoll Reads the Robinson-Patman Act*

Nancy Driscoll had just taken over as buyer of handbags for a ten-store chain of women's fashion outlets called Pageant Stores located in a large eastern metropolitan area. She had been the assistant buyer in the handbag department, and prior to that was department manager of one of the largest of the ten stores.

Nancy was superbly qualified for her job. She even had an M.B.A. from a leading business school. At school she had been exposed to the Robinson-Patman Act. Her impression at that time was that it was illegal for a buyer to solicit extra discounts from suppliers unless she was sure that other stores were also being offered the discount.

Since coming to Pageant Stores, Nancy had not heard much discussion of the Robinson-Patman Act. Miss Schultz, the buyer for whom she worked, did not discuss it. She knew that Miss Schultz bargained very aggressively, but she did not know how, if at all, her activities were altered by the Robinson-Patman Act. As assistant buyer this did not bother her. Now, however, she was the buyer. According to the way business was conducted at Pageant Stores, Nancy had all the responsibilities for negotiation.

Nancy decided that she would be conscientious in her efforts to find out about the law. A reasonable first step was to read it. She finally located a copy of the law in the back of a book. Section 2(a), she discovered, suggested that price discrimination by the supplier was illegal only if, in addition to other things, the effects of such discrimination were anticompetitive. Since Nancy's ten stores were small by comparison with, say, Sears, there appeared to be little she could do to be anticompetitive. Furthermore, Section 2(b) of the act permitted suppliers to meet competition in good faith. Nancy felt this would justify almost any action by a domestic supplier, since all the other suppliers were doing almost anything imaginable to get the business, particularly with the threat of imports. Nancy also found that Section 2(f), which was directed toward buyers, applied only to the prohibitions of Sections 2(a), which alluded only to price discrimination.

Thus Nancy felt assured that almost all her activities were legal.

Soon after her promotion Nancy ran into an

attorney friend of hers at a party. During their conversation, the attorney brought up the point that over the years the Federal Trade Commission had become more and more aggressive in its policing of buyers' activities. He stated that the courts had basically ignored the anticompetitive provisions of the act. Furthermore, while the act had only held buyers responsible for the price violations, the courts had held that buyers were indeed responsible for other aspects of negotiation such as advertising and services. Lastly, while the need to meet competition was a defense against violations, it was a very difficult defense for a buyer to use, mainly because much of the data on meeting competition was in the suppliers' hands.

Nancy was now confused. What should she do? She wanted to uphold the law, but what was it? She knew that bargaining was a key element in the handbag industry, and had tried to find out the practices of other buyers. But there was no way that she could find out what other buyers in her competitive area were paying for anything. As she thought her problem over, there appeared to be three general approaches that she might use.

First, she need not bargain at all. This procedure appeared safe legally, although the act implied that she could still be held liable because of its suggestion that it is unlawful "knowingly to induce or receive a discrimination in price which is prohibited by this section." One need not induce a discrimination; receiving the discrimination under certain conditions would be enough. There were other ways to be safe within the Robinson-Patman Act. For example, a buyer might deal with suppliers who qualified in the legal sense as dealing only in intrastate traffic. She might also deal only with suppliers who sold exclusively to large stores. Presumably, the problem would then not be as important. In-

deed, she might try to become the only account of a few firms, although Pageant was probably too small a chain for this. A clear alternative was to try to develop private brands. While these did not exclude one from the Robinson-Patman Act in and of themselves, goods of not like grade and quality are exempt from the provisions of the act.

Another alternative that occurred to her was to bargain vigorously but in a manner that was likely to be considered legal. But for this it was necessary to become fairly knowledgeable about the act. Nancy would have to find out such aspects of it as: (a) What did it mean for a supplier to meet competition? (b) Could a supplier meet an illegal price? (c) Where was the burden of proof? Putting the burden of proof on the government made it unlikely that any buyer would be caught. (d) What types of legal defense were permitted for the various kinds of discrimination? For example, the cost defense was permissible under several conditions.

A third alternative was to disregard the act in some intelligent manner. Most buyers did not understand it very well anyway; they lacked either the time, or the legal training, or both. Nancy thought most buyers bargained aggressively. But few were investigated. A buyer who chose to disregard the act need not be excessively stupid about negotiating. She would conduct herself with discretion.

### Discussion Questions

1. Which alternative would you have chosen if you had been in Nancy's position?

2. Do you think buyers should have legal training? If so, how much?

Part Two offers some tools that are necessary to solve many key retail problems. The problems of the retail manager are very different from, though related to, the problems of the marketing manager. Indeed, each field has a literature that clearly recognizes the substantial difference between the two activities. Chapter 8 discusses the retail method of inventory, a system created for retailers that offers much information not developed by conventional accounting methods. In particular, a retailer who uses this method knows the amount of merchandise that he is missing, if certain assumptions are granted. Further, the retailer is becoming more involved in research. He is involved in analyzing the prolific output of the newer point-of-purchase computer devices, as well as in continuing research on consumers. Part of this consumer analysis has to do with trading area analysis and the location of stores. The final two chapters of this section discuss the applications of marginal analysis and capital budgeting to retail decision making.

# Part Two

# 8

## The Retail Method

A retail executive might desire many types of information that are not given by unit and dollar controls. For instance, he might want profit statements on a regular basis, perhaps every month, or want to know the margin on the merchandise he just brought into the department. How much merchandise can he buy from suppliers for delivery to the store in the next three weeks and still meet his goals with regard to the level of inventory? How much merchandise does he have for sale? How much is disappearing, for whatever reason, and where from? What is the approximate cost value of his inventory (he may want to know this without the laborious task of taking an inventory)? Answers to all these questions will be of value both to the line executive in charge of everyday decision making and to the firm's top managers in their efforts to control the actions of subordinates.

Many large stores and a few small ones attempt to provide this needed information through use of the *retail method of accounting.* However, there are other systems, two of which will be discussed first.

### Cost Method of Inventory Valuation

To develop profit or gross margins figures within acceptable tolerances in the cost method, one must take a physical inventory—that is, count the merchandise systematically. The decision maker will not usually know what his dollar inventory is, either in total or by classification, except possibly as of the time of the last inventory taken. An inventory will therefore be necessary if a decision maker is to know exactly where he is and where he has been since the time of the last inventory. Since inventory calculations generally take some time, the information generated from the cost method of inventory valuation tends to focus on the past. Moreover, this system

The comments of Robert Kahn, Certified Management Consultant, were very helpful in the creation of this chapter.

answers none of the questions posed at the beginning of this chapter. There is no way, for instance,
to find out the dollar value of merchandise that is
"missing"; indeed, huge amounts of merchandise
may have been stolen without anyone's knowledge.
And yet this system is used in retailing more often
than any other, and is the basic method taught in
elementary accounting courses.

On the other hand, the cost method is relatively
simple to use and to understand. In addition, as will
be indicated later, it produces a lower inventory
evaluation than does the retail method, which
means that the firm can pay lower inventory taxes
(if it is taxed on that basis). In the opinion of many,
the cost method also fosters more flexible pricing
than the retail method. Indeed, the low-price
philosophy at the beginning of the wheel of retailing may be attributed partly to the use of the cost
system by most of these entrepreneurs. Moreover,
the decision maker may not need the additional information offered by the retail method, at least if he
is highly skilled and takes long-term factors into
account. Some of the advantages of the cost system
will become more apparent when the limitations of
the retail method are discussed later in the chapter.

### Direct Cost Method

When an item is purchased under the direct
cost system, the dollar cost of the item is added to
the book inventory for that particular classification
of merchandise. The cost dollar value of a sale to a
customer or of a merchandise return to a supplier is
deducted from the book value. All inventories are
kept at cost, and can be used to develop an extremely
accurate perpetual inventory. Physical inventories
are taken at cost from the codes that appear on the
item. In addition, since sales are recorded at both
cost and retail, the merchant is in a position to
calculate a daily gross margin.

This system is useful mainly in merchandise
areas where there are a relatively small number of
sales—jewelry, for example—because it becomes
unwieldy when the volume of daily transactions is

high. If a store uses sales registers, for instance, the
system cannot generally be used unless the registers
have been specially adapted for the cost and retail
recordings.

### Retail Method of Accounting

It is natural for retailers to think in terms of retail dollars. Sales, markdowns, and so forth are critical to the retailer and are usually thought of in this
way. One result is that dollar margins tend to be
expressed as a percentage of the retail price and
so appear smaller than they would if expressed as a
percentage of the cost.

Delbert J. Duncan and Charles F. Phillips have
described the steps involved in the retail method
as follows:

1. Charge incoming merchandise to the appropriate decision-making unit at both cost and retail prices. This unit
can be any size desired.

2. Accurately record increases in and subtractions from
stock.

3. Determine the *initial markup* and *cost percentages* on the
total merchandise handled. "Initial markup" is the difference between the cost and retail prices of the merchandise available for sale, divided by the retail price of
that merchandise, exclusive of markdowns and shortage
(see example on p. 109). The "cost percentage" of the total
merchandise handled is obtained by subtracting the initial
markup from 100 percent.

4. Calculate the retail value of the merchandise on hand
at the closing inventory.

5. Apply the cost percentage to the retail value of merchandise on hand at the closing inventory.

6. Periodically, take a physical inventory in retail dollars
to check the accuracy of the book inventory.

In considering the retail method it may be useful to follow Robert D. Entenberg and divide the
entire process into three parts: calculation of the
merchandise handled at both cost and retail, and of
the related markup and cost percentages (part I);

calculation of the total retail reductions that are to be deducted from the retail value of the merchandise available for sale to arrive at the ending inventory in retail dollars (part II); and development of the gross margin (part III).

The decision maker in a store that uses the retail method receives the information in Tables 8.1a-c as often as is thought desirable. There is a perpetual inventory kept in retail dollars and at computed cost. The retail method also permits the division of inventory, markups, markdowns, gross margins, and other factors by merchandise areas.

Table 8.1a
*Calculation of the merchandise handled at both cost and retail, and of the related markup and cost percentages*

|  | Cost | Retail |
|---|---|---|
| Opening inventory | $12,000 | $20,000 |
| Purchases during period | $12,000 | $20,000 |
| Transportation charges | $100 | |
| Transfer from other departments | $100 | $160 |
| Additional markups[a] less markup cancellations | | $60 |
| Transfers to other departments | ($50) | ($70) |
| Total purchases for the period | $12,150 | $20,150 |
| Merchandise available for sale | $24,150 | $40,150 |
| Markup percent | | |
| $\dfrac{\$40,150 - \$24,150}{\$40,150}$ | 39.8% | |
| Complement of markup, i.e. 1–39.8 equals the cost percent | 60.2 | |

a. If an item is marked up to a higher price after it comes into the department, this is an additional markup. The cancellation of such markups is subtracted to arrive at the net figure.

Table 8.1b
*Calculation of the total retail reductions and the ending retail inventory*

| | |
|---|---|
| Net sales | $20,000 |
| Markdowns, possibly including employee discounts, less markdown cancellations | $400 |
| Shrinkage or shortage[a] | $300 |
| Total deductions at retail | $20,700 |
| Ending inventory at retail | |
| $40,150 – $20,700 | $19,450[b] |

a. A percentage of sales usually based on prior history unless a physical inventory is taken.
b. This figure, the retail book value of the inventory, is reconciled at periodic intervals with the actual inventory.

Table 8.1c
*Development of the gross margin*

| The ending retail book value of the inventory multiplied by the cost percent equals the ending inventory at cost. In this case this is | |
|---|---|
| $19,450 × 60.2% | $11,709 |
| Cost of goods sold[a] | |
| $24,150 – $11,709 | $12,441 |
| Maintained dollar markup[b] | |
| $20,000 – $12,441 | $7,559 |
| Less workroom expense | $350 |
| Plus cash discounts | $1,000 |
| Gross margin | $8,209 |

a. Merchandise available for sale at cost minus the ending inventory at cost.
b. Net sales minus cost of goods sold.

Finally, it becomes possible to take inventory at convenient times because the perpetual aspects of the records permit easy reconciliations. Thus the decision maker using the retail method has a wealth of additional information. Some particular characteristics of the retail method are outlined in Appendix D. Open-to-buy, shortage, and markup are now singled out for special attention.

### Open-to-Buy

There is one key advantage of keeping a perpetual record of inventory: it is easy to calculate how much merchandise can be purchased to arrive at a desired final inventory, given the initial inventory orders and estimated level of sales, markdowns, and shortage. The amount so calculated is called "open-to-buy," and is generally considered in terms of retail dollars. Thus a buyer, if his planned sales and other factors are on target, can go into a market knowing that he can buy $23,000 worth of merchandise for delivery before January 15 if he is to approximate his planned inventory level.

The concept of open-to-buy is particularly useful to a firm that has a large number of buyers and must maintain careful control of the cash funds available to the company. Such firms can allocate to decision makers the open-to-buy in retail or cost dollars so that they can plan their purchases. The concept of open-to-buy is illustrated by the following example, in retail dollars:

Example: Calculation of open-to-buy, in retail dollars

| | |
|---|---:|
| Planned sales for period | $25,000 |
| Planned markdowns for period | $4,000 |
| Estimated shortage for period | $500 |
| Planned inventory at end of period | $200,000 |
| Total merchandise needed to arrive at ending inventory of $200,000 | $229,500 |
| Inventory at beginning of period | $112,700 |
| Merchandise on order to arrive during period | $50,000 |
| Total merchandise available | $162,700 |
| Open-to-buy for period | $66,800 |
| Total | $229,500 |

The individual decision maker can use open-to-buy as a useful tool with which to plan purchases. Top management can also use it as an instrument to control activities in a merchandise area. However, while the concept itself is clear, merchandise executives use it in many different ways. Some, for example, feel that a merchant should always be overbought—that is, have negative open-to-buy. This is thought to be an indication of a retailer's aggressiveness, concern for the business, and so forth. Others regard an overbought situation as a serious problem, but will let the individual decision maker work his way out of it over time, perhaps many months. In some instances, top management regards open-to-buy as an absolute constraint: thus if a men's sportswear buyer has too many coats, he will not be able to buy any more slacks. It is difficult to evaluate these and other approaches to open-to-buy by top management, since much depends on the ability of the decision maker doing the actual purchasing. If the latter knows exactly what he is doing, then the risks inherent in an overbought situation, when it occurs, are not large. The counterargument, of course, is that if he knew exactly what he was doing the condition would not occur at all. Much also depends on the number of customers who will, for example, buy a blue pen when the store is out of red

pens. Such substitutability of merchandise is difficult to estimate; it tends to vary with the nature of the merchandise, the time of year, and other factors.

Open-to-buy can be used at all levels of an organization, including the store level, for planning and control. A store that is overbought can take drastic steps to bring inventory into line. Stores have even been known to close their receiving docks for a period of time in order to bring inventory into line with their planned figures.

One of the more interesting problems within retailing is the relationship of open-to-buy and unit controls. If the retail decision maker correctly evaluates the unit sale of each item and places his orders accordingly, then there is no way that he can possibly get into inventory trouble. In this type of situation the open-to-buy can be developed completely from the unit control information; it has little or no independent role in decision making. This has led some retail managers to downgrade the importance of open-to-buy in merchandise areas where unit control of inventory can be maintained in great detail: keep control of your items, they believe, and the dollars will follow. In alternative situations, the decision maker may use both open-to-buy figures and unit controls to decide on the dollars that he will spend. The interaction between unit and dollar controls, which is highly complex, will be discussed further in Part Four.

Whatever his philosophy with regard to open-to-buy, the decision maker must make a realistic estimate of dollar sales in order to calculate it. Most stores rigidly relate this estimate to some conservative figure such as last year's sales. Thus a department will be limited to an estimated increase of 5 percent or so to insure that the planned sales figures are realistic. If a store does not do this, the final open-to-buy figures may be dependent on the whim of the estimator, who can cause severe inventory problems if he is overoptimistic. Thus, in the example just cited, if planned sales had been set at $50,000 instead of $25,000, the open-to-buy would have increased to $91,800. Similarly, if sales had been only $25,000 and all other aspects had remained the same, a buyer who brought in $91,800 worth of merchandise would have ended up with a stock of

$225,000 at the end of the period, or $25,000 over the desired level. This rather conservative method of estimating sales puts extra pressure on top management to be alert to any substantial increase in volume for a particular type of merchandise. If the merchandise is to go on selling in this way, more of it will have to be stocked.

### Shortage

It can be argued that if a decision maker prices optimally, then he need not worry about his initial markup or his maintained markup because, no matter what they happen to be, no improvement is possible. In other words, it is the price that matters, and since the prices of items can be made without recourse to some average called initial markup, the retail method is of little practical help. It can also be objected that open-to-buy figures are not essential to decision making because these, too, are the result of many item decisions that, if made in an optimal fashion, make open-to-buy almost irrelevant. The same may be said of the taking of dollar markdowns.

The users of the retail method argue, on the other hand, that if the method offered only the advantages mentioned by its critics, then indeed its benefits would not be greater than its costs. However, they continue, the method also provides a means of knowing and coping with the great and increasing amount of merchandise taken from the store. The difference between the book inventory created by the retail method and the physical inventory, usually expressed in retail dollars, is known as the *shortage* or *shrinkage,* and is usually expressed as a percentage of sales. The shortage is a composite of bookkeeping errors of various types—for example, incorrect recording of retail prices, or failure to record markdowns on broken or spoiled items—and the amount of merchandise stolen by employees and nonemployees.

Estimates of the amount stolen by employees and customers vary, but most observers agree that shortages are increasing, perhaps by as much as 20 percent a year. According to the National Retail Merchants Association, department stores with sales over $1 million a year reported a shortage of nearly 2 percent of sales in 1971, and shortages of well over 2 percent are no longer unheard of. One out of every 15 customers is a shoplifter, according to Saul D. Astor. While such figures would be expected to vary considerably with geographic area and type of store (both between and among types), shortages have become a serious problem for most retailers.

Shortage is perhaps the most feared of all retailing deficiencies. Executives at the department, division, and store level fear it because there are few acceptable excuses for a large shortage when one occurs, and nobody can tell how large it is going to be. Because of this, and because the retail method lends itself to such "games," many executives build what might be termed "kitties"—that is, overages that will at least partially offset the inevitable shortages. For example, a merchant may bring sale items into the books of the store at the sale price, say $9.99, but price the item on the selling floor at $14.99 until the sale is held. All sales at the $14.99 price level will offer a $5.00 offset against shortage unless the merchant takes a markup for this amount. In the same way, a supermarket may bring merchandise into a retail unit at the sale price and yet raise the price after the sale without taking a markup. Or a manager may take extra markdowns without changing any of the prices on the floor, thus creating an overage in the amount of the markdowns. It should be noted that none of these techniques changes the long-term profit level of the merchandise area. It is, however, easier to explain away a low initial or maintained markup by rugged competition, and so forth, than it is to explain why so much merchandise is missing. It should also be noted that top management can take steps to limit kitties if it wants too. More sophisticated computer systems will aid in closing the loopholes of the retail method because they take away much of the buyer's flexibility.

Top management is often plagued by a dilemma with regard to large shortages. If management reacts too drastically, lower-level executives will try, often successfully, to find ways of creating kitties and so perhaps conceal real organizational problems, such as a theft ring. On the other hand, a large shortage is an almost certain indication of inefficiency by the prime decision maker, his subordinates, or both. This dilemma appears to defy easy solutions.

Much can be done, however, to control shortage. The following checklist, compiled by Robert Kahn, details 56 causes of inventory shortage, as found under the retail method of inventory.

## Dishonesty

1. Shoplifting.
2. Employee theft of merchandise.
3. Intentional shortage in shipments from vendors.
4. Switching price tickets by customer.
5. Customer picks up merchandise off the counter and immediately returns for credit.
6. Employee sells merchandise to friend or accomplice for less than marked price.
7. Employee gives accomplice mark-down for soiled or damaged merchandise—but mark-down is not reported on the books.
8. Clerk pockets even change.
9. Charge sales check is destroyed.
10. Register is set back before the end of the day and charge (if on floor audit) tags and cash removed.
11. Payment of fraudulent or duplicate invoices when merchandise is not received.
12. Credit memos or cash refund issued when merchandise not returned.
13. Merchandise wrapped in with sold merchandise but not rung up or written up on sales check.
14. Buyer or other personnel approves for payment invoices for samples received in department—but samples then taken home.
15. Fitting room thefts—customer walks out with merchandise.
16. Clerk fraudulently classifies transaction as over-ring when customer actually received merchandise.
17. Customer claims over charge.
18. Customer claims shortage of merchandise which is replaced without mark-down.
19. Employee theft in transportation between stores.
20. Packages sent out as "Customers Own" or other authorized delivery of merchandise not properly sold.

21. Customer carries merchandise to another department for purpose of "matching with other merchandise" and leaves merchandise there.
22. Manipulation of physical inventory to conceal existing shortage.

## Errors in Selling Department

1. Wrong retail price placed on invoice.
2. Under count on number of items sold at mark-down prices (particularly occurs in recording advertising results).
3. Failure to record mark-down on merchandise (particularly arises on occasional mark-downs such as soiled, damaged, button missing, etc.).
4. Failure to record regular mark-down because forms are lacking—notation made on scratch paper and then lost.
5. Failure to take mark-down on exchanged merchandise returned as defective.
6. Failure to take mark-down on window damaged merchandise.
7. Error in addition on sales check (can produce either shortage or overage).
8. Error in entry on sales check or ringing up wrong price on cash register.
9. Lost charge sales check.
10. Guessing at the price of merchandise that has no price ticket.
11. On measured items, clerk gives customers extra merchandise "for good measure."
12. Department does not get back samples from display department, advertising, loan-out, etc.
13. Returned merchandise is not correctly re-marked at the sold price—frequently returned to stock at the current price, which is lower.
14. Improper recording of layaways.
15. Failure to void error rings (produces off-setting overage and cash shortage).
16. Returns made to manufacturer under procedure where recording held until credit memo received—and no credit memo issued.

## Errors in Handling Merchandise

1. Put wrong price on the merchandise—different from that shown on invoice. Frequently happens when ad-

vertised merchandise at reduced prices received during sale.

2. Not count incoming merchandise accurately.

3. Merchandise thrown out in containers (sometimes collusion between markers and people having access to the trash).

4. Utilize items in stock for internal usage without putting through to expense account.

5. Approve both original and duplicate invoice for payment.

6. Lost in transit between stores.

7. Failure to send claim forms to accounting office after merchandise is shipped.

8. In filling orders for customers (especially mail and telephone orders) send duplicate shipments.

9. Manufacturers' representatives pick up merchandise for replacement—and fail to replace.

10. When vendors agree to make allowances in merchandise for mark-downs taken on advertised sales—and as a result mark-downs are not received or credit memos issued—and vendor fails to bring in merchandise.

11. Last tag in pin machine is at old price and becomes first tag on the new item—at wrong price.

## Errors in Accounting

1. Inaccurate sales audit.

2. Errors in extending invoices, mark-downs, returns to vendors.

3. Errors in posting retail to the purchase journal (this is not a "double entry" entry in the bookkeeping system and must be subject to pre-listing).

4. Loss of mark-down forms, return to vendor forms, credit memos, etc. after merchandise is shipped. Sometimes arises when number control is not maintained.

5. Duplicate payments to vendors.

6. Failure to deduct claims.

7. Entries of items on the purchase journal without appropriate retail.

Another problem plaguing top management and sometimes lower decision makers as well is how much one can afford to allocate in terms of management time and energy or fees to outside consultants, to solving shortage problems. A shortage of $100,000 is in retail dollars; it will be substantially less in cost dollars except under the most unusual conditions. In addition, many accounting errors may be of a type that, while creating a smaller shortage, would only have decreased the initial markup and therefore have left final profit unchanged. Or perhaps one classification's shortage may be decreased and another increased by the same error. Similarly, errors made at different branches of the same store may cancel each other out. While management always likes to know of such errors, it may not find them worth correcting unless the findings can be turned into incremental profit in some way. In sum, as the moral values of American society deteriorate, it appears necessary for the merchant to be increasingly conscious of theft by customers and employees and to have ways of identifying it when it becomes a serious problem.

### Markup

The concept of markup is a key aspect of the retail method. However it is of interest to a decision maker whether he uses the retail method or not. Basically, markup is the amount by which the retail price of a merchandise item exceeds its cost price. *Initial markup* is the markup of the merchandise when it first arrives in the store, while *maintained markup* is its markup after adjustment for factors such as markdowns and shortage. Markup can be expressed as a percentage or in dollars. Thus an item that costs $6 and sells for $10 has a markup of 40 percent, the $4 margin divided by the retail price.

It is interesting to note the relationship between the gross margin of an item and a changing markup. If the markup of an item with a given cost increases from 30 to 40 percent, then the dollar margin increases about 56 percent. But if the markup of an item with a given cost increases from 40 to 50 percent, the dollar margin increases by 50 percent. For example, if an item costs $3.60, at a 40 percent markup the selling price is $6.00—a $2.40 margin. If the markup is 50 percent, the selling price becomes $7.20 for a margin of $3.60, or an increase of 50

Table 8.2
*Dollar margin increases corresponding to selected increases
in markup for an item costing $3.00*

| Markup[a] | Retail price | Dollar margin[b] | Approximate increase in dollar margin |
|---|---|---|---|
| 30% | $ 4.29 | $1.29 | — |
| 40% | $ 5.00 | $2.00 | 56% |
| 50% | $ 6.00 | $3.00 | 50% |
| 60% | $ 7.50 | $4.50 | 50% |
| 70% | $10.00 | $7.00 | 56% |

a. Dollar margin divided by retail price.
b. Retail price minus cost.

percent over the $2.40 margin. If the markup increases from 50 to 60 percent, the margin again increases by 50 percent. However, if the markup increases from 60 to 70 percent, the margin increases by about 56 percent. Table 8.2 shows an example with a $3.00 cost. A useful rule of thumb is that an increase in initial markup of 1 percent in the 30-to-70-percent range will result in an increase of about 5 percent in the gross margin of that item.

Markup is used by the retailer as a negotiation tool with suppliers; by the buyer's superiors as a control and planning device; and as a decision tool at both levels.

**Negotiation tool with suppliers** One use of markup is as a negotiation tool with actual and potential suppliers. The retailer can gain significant benefits by using markup effectively; and the supplier may benefit by understanding the retailer's use of it.

Markup may be used as a *commitment* on the part of top management or the manager of a specific merchandise classification. Thus the manager may bind himself to a specific markup policy—for example, he might only consider vendor offers with a minimum markup of 34 percent. He would set this minimum at a realistic level after considering the various industry practices and those of retail competitors, and the supplier would have to accept it if he hoped to sell any merchandise to the department. One direct selling organization is reported to have two policies in merchandising goods that it

does not produce. First the organization demands an 80 percent markup, that is, a cost of $2 for a retail price of $10. Second, the final retail price cannot be above the "regular" price charged in the market for the item. The combination of these two policies brings great pressure on suppliers to offer lower prices.

If a store dominates a given locality, a rigid markup used intelligently by the manager can provide another way to counteract the advantages held by a dominant supplier. The latter would normally enjoy great latitude in the setting of initial prices to the retailer. By establishing a rigid markup policy, the retailer withdraws part of this latitude. One could assume, therefore, that the retail store would obtain a larger part of any additional *joint profits* resulting from the buyer-seller relationship.

Since most department stores use markup and have similar expense structures and systems, their minimum markup requirements for a given merchandise classification tend to be much the same. Therefore, the minimum commitments of these stores tend to be in the same range; indeed, under certain circumstances they will have the effect of a minimum commitment for an industry. Obviously, suppliers will have to take account of this. Markup is also an effective tool in negotiating with suppliers for special merchandise—closeouts, for example. A decision maker may ask a supplier for a mattress with features that will create an exciting value for the consumer at a markup of 35 percent. This gives the supplier some latitude. However, it also puts pressure on him for low cost, because both buyer and supplier generally know the retail price line that a promotional item with specific features must have to generate excitement among customers. In addition, when the manager indicates that he expects a specific markup, he necessarily eliminates some price negotiation.

Markup also gives the manager an opportunity to introduce into the negotiating procedure a third party: "the store." He may do this by stating that "the store requires" suppliers to pay all the freight charges or that "the store requires" a minimum percentage on any promotion or item in a certain merchandise classification. Such an impersonal intervention by the third party does not require any specific knowledge of the merchandise. Since the supplier will not usually discuss the policies of the store with the store management, and since he will probably believe what the buyer says about store policy, two effects may occur. First, an effective commitment may be established, since the third party can not be reached easily to amend the policies laid down in its name. Second, the management may end up being perceived as the common enemy, thus giving buyer and supplier something they can both feel sorry about together, and get off a lot of hostility at the same time.

**Control and planning device** Markup is also a control and planning device of significant use to store management. By controlling the level of initial and/or maintained markup in a given merchandise area, the store management can strongly influence the behavior of managers in that area. Although management never states in so many words that the decision maker must secure lower prices by demanding a higher markup (and thus perhaps become involved in a violation of the Robinson-Patman Act), it can communicate its expectations clearly enough. If top management's requirements cannot be met by negotiating lower prices with suppliers, then the decision maker may try changing the mix of the items sold so as to include items of higher markup. If this does not work, then he may raise retail prices. His last resort is to create new products, preferably ones that will enable him to buy low and sell high.

It is interesting to note that while certain markup pressures may induce a buyer to violate the Robinson-Patman Act by obtaining illegal concessions on regular merchandise, *severe* markup pressure may force a buyer to create new products of unlike grade and quality that will put him entirely beyond the reach of the act! In general, pressure for increased markup tends to have the following effects:

1. It discourages an opportunistic approach to pricing that may be to the long-term detriment of the store's image and reputation. A low-price or a continuous-sale policy may prove satisfactory for the short term, or even for a few years. However, if the general reputation of the store is eroded because of low prices, it will be extremely difficult to restore its former status. Such pressure also makes it more difficult than it would be otherwise for a manager to use low price as a merchandise weapon in the battle for sales, at least without substantial analytical work to uncover the long-range advantages, if there are any.

2. It helps to prevent manager-supplier collaboration to raise the cost price of an item in order to develop funds to pay for advertising, and so encourages the supplier to make an independent contribution.

3. It may increase the accuracy of shortage figures by discouraging a buyer from artificially reducing his markup in order to make his shortages look smaller than they really are.

4. It helps to keep buyers honest—provided, of course, that it is applied continuously. Amounts the buyer will take for himself will be entirely outside the system, in that few of these transactions will ever be related to the store records. Continuous markup pressure, and perhaps the profit pressure generated by the frequent reports called for under the retail method, may induce buyers to deal with retailers more honestly than they might without such pressures.

**Decision tool** Managers sometimes use percentage markup multiplied by estimated sales to select from among the merchandise offered by suppliers. In situations where the cost structures of the alternatives are anywhere near equal, this may be a useful and accurate device. Even in situations where marginal systems are employed (see Chapter 11), markup multiplied by sales volume may still be preferred in some situations. This is not to suggest that retailers should be the slaves of arbitrary percentages, or that markup as a management tool does not have its limitations. Nor is it argued that markup should be nearly inflexible. Instead, markup should be thought of as one valuable retail tool among many.

## Summary

1. Many executives seek more than just sales information on a regular basis. Information as to margins and stocks by merchandise areas is extremely useful. In addition, ordinary financial statements do not offer precise estimates of the amount of merchandise that is stolen by customers or employees. The need for this kind of information has led to the adoption of the retail method of accounting by many firms.

A. In the retail method, firms stress dollars at retail. The merchandise coming in is charged to the appropriate decision unit at both cost and retail prices. A record is kept of increases and decreases from stock. The initial markup is developed along with its complement, the cost percentage. The retail value of the merchandise on hand can be calculated at any point in time. The cost percentage is applied to the retail value of the merchandise at hand to obtain the assumed cost. A physical inventory is taken to check the accuracy of the book inventory at specific intervals, usually every six months or every year.

B. There are many problems with the retail method. A key problem, discussed in Appendix D, is that much of the information is obtained by averages. Thus stock levels at cost and profits derived by the retail method are subject to bias. Another problem is that executives may become preoccupied with the various percentages— initial markup, for example. Fostering goals such as a high initial markup may be detrimental to profits.

2. An important output of the retail method is open-to-buy. Open-to-buy is the amount that a decision maker can purchase and yet arrive at his planned ending inventory figures, other things— such as level of sales and markdowns—being equal. Some firms regard open-to-buy as a rigid constraint to guide decision makers at all levels; thus, if a buyer of boys' wear has too many shirts, he cannot buy pants. Other firms regard open-to-buy as a flexible planning instrument.

3. Another important output of the retail method is the amount of merchandise that is stolen by employees and customers, assuming that the bookkeeping is correct. And this figure is becoming more and more important.

4. Markup may be useful as a negotiation tool with suppliers; as a control and planning device; and as a decision tool. It can be used effectively by decision makers but should not enslave them.

## Discussion Questions

1. Outline the advantages of the retail method of accounting.

2. Outline the disadvantages of the retail method.

3. Define "open-to-buy." If you were a merchandise manager for a fashion specialty store, how rigorously would you apply this constraint?

4. What is the relationship between open-to-buy and unit controls?

5. Many small store owners hide behind cars to see if customers or employees are stealing merchandise. If you owned a small store, how would you attempt to prevent shoplifting?

6. What is the value of markup to the retail decision maker?

7. List the main reasons for shortage and give examples of each type.

8. How is an additional $100,000 shortage going to affect the profits of a store?

9. Why is shortage so feared by retail executives?

10. List ten ways a retailer might prevent shortages.

## References

Astor, Saul D., "1 Customer in 15 is a Shoplifter," *Stores*, April 1971, p. 8.

Duncan, Delbert J., and Phillips, Charles F., *Retailing Principles and Methods* (Homewood, Ill.: Irwin, 1967), p. 677.

Entenberg, Robert D., *Effective Retail and Market Distribution* (New York: World, 1966), pp. 456–457.

Kahn, Robert, "A Checklist of Inventory Shortage Causes," *Retail Control*, March 1968, pp. 52–55.

## Further Reading

Corbman, Bernard P., and Kreiger, Murray, *Mathematics of Retail Merchandising* (New York: Ronald, 1972).

Dickinson, Roger, "Markup in Department Store Management," *Journal of Marketing*, January 1967, pp. 32–34.

McNair, Malcolm, and Hershum, Anita C., *The Retail Method and Life* (New York: McGraw-Hill, 1952).

## Case History: *Harry Spalding Views the Retail Method*

The discount stores run by Elegant, Inc., have been in business for 12 years. Dollar sales have gone from $3 million in 1959 to $30 million in 1971. While profits have been erratic, the three stores have been profitable in each year and in 1971 netted $300,000 after taxes. Harry Spalding was the founder of the firm and is presently its major stockholder.

The Elegant stores handle many types of merchandise. They have small appliance, television, and major appliance departments, as well as home building departments with a substantial commitment in plumbing supplies. Their automotive sections also do well. The stores carry many other types of goods, including sporting goods, toys, cameras, and fashion merchandise.

Presently there are 10 buyers in the store buying the various kinds of merchandise divided along what Harry Spalding feels are reasonable lines. Nevertheless, he believes that the decision makers in the firm are not getting enough of the information they need. For the past 12 years, the store has been on the cost system. Thus, the buyers do not get rapid in-formation on margins, stock positions, open-to-buy, and so forth. They do, however, get rapid feedback on the sales of items and the dollar sales of the merchandise areas that are their responsibility. While the store has done reasonably well with this system and the buyers have been indoctrinated with it, Harry is considering a change to the retail method.

Harry Spalding sees a lot of advantages in the retail method. His buyers and other executives would get reports on the initial markup and stock figures for their decision areas every two weeks. Therefore they should be able to quickly spot incorrect retail prices on a substantial amount of merchandise. They could spot trends in stocks and in initial and maintained markup by classification. Furthermore, Harry and his assistant will be able to see a variety of figures by merchandise area. This will enable them to offer advice and spot trouble before it exists. For example, inventory and markup figures will be available either every two weeks or every month, depending on the decision area. Another advantage of the retail method, Harry thinks, is that with it he will get a picture of the difference between the book inventory value and the actual physical inventory, and so get some idea of how much merchandise is missing. With the dramatically increasing (and well-publicized) theft rate, this factor was very important to him.

Elegant, Inc., would have introduced the retail method several years ago had it not been for the opposition of Kevin Wilson, the financial executive of the firm. Kevin maintained that the system as he saw it was not worth the additional $60,000 that he felt it would cost. In his opinion, most of the benefits that were envisioned with the retail method would just not be realized. Taking a deep breath, he explained his objections to the boss. True, it was nice to have additional information. But most of the information generated by the retail method was unnecessary. While it was true that one got such information as initial markup, maintained markup, gross margins, profit statements, and so forth, this information ended up as a composite of many other decisions. If one priced optimally, if one took markdowns intelligently, if one created assortments imaginatively and analytically, and if one utilized effective inventory techniques, the retail method could do little to improve decision making. True, it gave management more control, potentially at least. But with the right buyers this would not be important. In any case, more control could be a negative influence in the firm as well as a positive one. The major advantage of the retail method, according to Kevin Wilson, was that it would provide figures on how much was being stolen by employees and customers in each store. But he wasn't really sure that he would trust the figures anyway. He personally knew the controller of two stores in which the buyers fudged the books so badly that the stores showed overages. And there were many bookkeeping errors.

Kevin Wilson therefore concluded that the disadvantages of the retail method outweighed the advantages. He felt that in addition to the $60,000 it would take to maintain the system, there would probably be other costs: (a) The increased information would take up the buyer's time and would require two merchandise managers to control it.

Presently the buyers reported directly to Harry Spalding. But with the additional information generated by the retail method, they would need more supervision. (b) The figures generated by the retail method were not accurate, particularly in the beginning years. Thus profits would probably be overstated unless sufficient reserves were set up to compensate for the inaccuracies. (c) The firm had been built on an aggressive price image. He feared that the store would lose some of this. In his experience, stores under the retail method tended to charge indirect charges to the decision area on the basis of sales and thus charged higher prices.

## Discussion Questions

1. What is the validity of Kevin Wilson's objections?

2. Should Harry Spalding introduce the retail method into his firm?

# 9

## The Research Dimension

The Random House Dictionary defines research as "diligent and systematic inquiry or investigation into a subject in order to discover or revise facts, theories, applications, etc." Research in this broad sense has always been aggressively pursued by retailers, particularly large ones. Many years before the creation of formal research departments, executives were developing information on which to make decisions. Even today, they can obtain a great deal of information about the various dimensions of the market just by becoming heavily involved in it. Indeed, most research is directed forward in the channel. For retailers, the chief object of investigation, either directly or indirectly, is the consumer.

Two characteristics of retailing influence the type of research performed: the relative attractiveness of merchandise is easily determined at store level by testing; and the enterprise itself generates certain types of research information as a matter of routine.

### Tests

In most types of retail stores, experiments are a way of life. New merchandise is always being tested. In fact, testing new styles and items is the very soul of fashion merchandising. Here, the buyer takes in the styles that seem to him to have the highest potential and then examines the sales of each one closely. Such tests, and the decision maker's reaction to them, shape and reshape the whole fashion department. Merchandise is often being similarly tested in other kinds of setting: supermarkets, for instance, will test items over a period of time to see if enough people want to buy them. A supplier who has been valuable to the retailer in the past can usually arrange with him to test promising items. For the retailer, such tests are neither difficult nor costly.

Alert retailers are also continually testing methods of display, many times with the help of the supplier, but often without it. What types of item should be featured next to the registers? What types should be at the key spots in the aisles? How can the flow of traffic around the aisles be made more even? Should a product be displayed at eye level or at the bottom of a shelf or other fixture where there is more space for stocking it? How do the items displayed relate to each other from the customer's point of view? Any aggressive retail firm is constantly experimenting with these and many other problems.

Many retailers test items in advertisements in order to find out which ones should be featured in the future. In this way they find out how the interests of the customer are changing. For example, a merchant will tend to stop advertising an item that does not sell well either when advertised or when displayed on the floor. On the other hand, if it does sell well, he will not only advertise the item again but develop "take-offs" from it. Thus a merchandise area of a store—a department store, for example—might test for winning Christmas items at the beginning of November. The items that did particularly well would then be developed for the more important December period. For certain types of retail store, Christmas "mailers," may aid in selecting items for promotion during the remainder of the Christmas season.

Stores are also in a position to test the prices at which they should handle merchandise. One pricing procedure, discussed in Chapter 15, does emphasize the possibility of testing various price levels, from the higher ones downward, to arrive at a price. It would appear, however, that most of price testing is done through various kinds of advertisement. Thus supermarkets are very interested in pricing their products in advertisements to attract customers. Automobile dealers, too, emphasize prices that they think will attract a great number of customers. Price testing is feasible in these and similar situations because the retailer's advertisement gets an immediate response.

Other types of experiment can be profitably undertaken only by large retail firms. For example, if a firm has 1,700 stores, it can test the different store systems—use of salesmen, inventory procedures, and so forth—in just a few of them in the hope of making improvements that will be relevant in all 1,700. Even so, testing live systems is a major expense, and the firm may well find it cheaper (if

not just as effective) to run tests by means of *computer simulation.*

Except for very unusual cases, no retail testing situation is an experiment in any formal sense. Indeed, most retailers are not very interested in formal experiments and in general would trust the results of a formal procedure no more than those of the informal ones that they now use. Usually the data of interest to retailers can be obtained by any procedure that avoids the grosser kind of bias.

### Information Systems

A wealth of information on what has been sold in the store and in other stores is usually available at a very low cost. Retailers, as we have seen, get information from sales checks, from the stubs of merchandise tickets, from cash registers, from shipping invoices to stores, and so forth. Once an information system has been set up, extra information can usually be obtained from it at very low cost. Indeed the main problem of a retailer is to put the information into a usable form because the tendency is for the system to generate too much information, particularly if it is computerized.

Analysis of the internal records of retail organizations is in its infancy, but will be advanced substantially as more complete information systems are developed. Thus the retail method of accounting, unit and dollar control systems, charge accounts, and so forth develop much information that can be systematically evaluated by decision makers at all levels. The main purpose of all this is to create an information framework within which more effective decisions can be made. While only large stores can profit from the more elaborate information systems, all stores should carefully evaluate the information they are presently generating.

### The Organizational Perspective

Research within the larger retail firm is influenced by the firm's organizational philosophy.

Such philosophies appear to be of two distinct types, at least in retailing. One philosophy of retailing is that the lower-line manager should be responsible for the profits of his operation and must make the decisions related to it. Line executives in such an organization have a great deal to say about research within their departments. However, because the low-level decision makers here tend to evaluate research merely in terms of its possible contribution to short-range profits ("Will we sell enough extra socks?"), this philosophy tends to inhibit research that does not have immediate payoff. The other philosophy is to keep most research activities independent of lower-level management. In this case, top management determines what is important and what research will be undertaken. One purpose here is to keep the goals of lower management simple, so that the retail framework will be able to accommodate managers with a wide range of strengths and weaknesses. This approach is more amenable to research that does not have immediate payoff, mainly because top management usually looks at research from a longer-term perspective.

### Line Research

Most of the information developed from the constant experimentation described above relates to decisions made by the lower-level, but not necessarily low-paid, line merchandising executive. And indeed most of the research done by retail organizations has been done at this lower level, since it appears that lower-level managers need a great deal of information on which to base their decisions.

Perhaps the most basic of all information to the retailer is dollar sales. All retail outlets take care to find out their dollar sales, at least within a close range, if only to make out their annual tax report for the federal government. Total sales, however, is not a measure that offers great insights into a retail operation, and an alert merchandiser will look to some sort of classification analysis. Thus a furniture store manager will want to know the dollar sales of modern furniture compared with bedding, or of convertible sofas compared with traditional furniture. Such figures can be used over time to diagnose trends in consumer taste. The merchandiser can see how he is doing compared to last year or two years ago. He can compare his figures with those of other stores in the same district at one point in time or over the whole year. Perhaps other stores of the same type do 20 percent of their business in December and his do only 10 percent. This may indicate a potential for increased business. Tabulation of dollar sales by classification also helps him order merchandise for the coming season. Thus a merchant who knows how many sports shirts were sold last year has at least some information on which to base a forecast for the coming year. Moreover, it is probably true that an unintelligent retailer who has such information will do a better job of forecasting than a brilliant one who does not.

*Sales analysis*   There are many types of analysis that can be done with sales by classification. Two of the most obvious, and one that should be performed by stores of most types and sizes, are *sales per unit of space* and *sales per dollar invested in inventory.*

Many different units of space are in common use, including sales per square foot, sales per linear foot, and sales per cubic foot. There is no optimizing rule that says that sales per unit of space should be equal for each classification; the important thing is to make valid comparisons. However, if weekly sales in the slack section of a men's wear store are $10 per foot and the corresponding figure for the suit section is only $1, this is rather strong evidence that the space allocated to slacks should be increased relative to that allocated to suits.

Sales per dollar invested in inventory should also be calculated by firms of many types and sizes. Most firms take inventory periodically. Many are on the retail method, which, as we have seen, offers a perpetual inventory by desired classification. Again, there are no hard and fast rules. But it is not difficult to see that, if 90 percent of a store's inventory is in classifications that account for only 10 percent of the business, some executive action would be desirable. However, in almost every classification, certain key units will probably account for the bulk of sales.

Sales analysis may deal with classifications other than type of merchandise—price line, for instance. The merchant can break down his unit and dollar sales by $2.99, $3.99, $4.99, or any other interval, and see how sales vary by price. This will help him decide whether or not he has the right price lines or perhaps the right number of price lines. For example, one rule of thumb that would be accepted by most department store retailers is that if the highest price line in a classification produces the most volume, still higher price lines should be introduced. Many firms would like the price line that does best in unit and dollar terms to be in the middle price range of their selection. The decision maker can also relate dollar sales by price line to space, inventory level, or both. Tabulating sales by price line is an excellent way to get an economic picture of the store's customers. A store may also consciously change its price lines in order to attract a different class of customer.

A retailer might further examine dollar sales per supplier. The dollar figures may come from his own information system or they can be furnished by the suppliers themselves. In either case, such figures offer the retailer some idea of how one supplier is doing compared with the others. Some retailers have used supplier figures to direct department efforts. The figures take on additional meaning when compiled by unit of space and dollar of inventory over some fixed period of time. This type of analysis aids in the creation of standards against which to check the productivity of suppliers, who can then be taken to task if their performance does not approach demonstrably reasonable levels.

Another information-gathering device employed by retailers is the identification of best and worst sellers. Fashion systems, as we shall see, are often concerned with little else, but all types of retail decision maker benefit from this type of analysis on occasion. One example, though not from retailing, will show how. An appliance executive of a manufacturing firm was commiserating with a consultant about the fact that customers for appliances appeared to act irrationally. Many of their best appliances never seemed to sell, said the executive, and nobody could figure out why. The consultant asked the executive to have all the company's best sellers over the years put on one side of the room and all its worst sellers put on the other side. As the story goes, the reasoning behind the customers' choices was obvious: all the poor sellers required the user to bend over, while all the best sellers did not. Further research by the manufacturer uncovered various ways in which he could turn this fact to advantage. This type of research is done in retail firms quite often; decision makers are always looking for what the best selling items may have in common.

Not all types of internal research are related to sales; clearly, the name of the game is profit. However, dollar and unit sales can be good indicators of profits, and in fashion areas the margins are so high that most retail executives concentrate on sales almost exclusively. Nevertheless, for many types of retailing the analysis of factors related to margins, not sales, is the key to profits.

### Research as a Separate Activity

The previous section has emphasized research that is useful in a firm's day-to-day decision making and is closely related to its information system. Research in this sense is very important to retailers, probably more important than to non-retailers. But, as Robert F. Hartley has pointed out, research as a separate department, or as a statistically sophisticated endeavor for the individual decision maker, has seldom been of any significance in retailing. Indeed, according to Harold Clark and Harold Sloan, many years ago manufacturers spent fifty times as much as retailers on research done by a centralized research center.

Today, however, research in the latter sense has acquired new interest for top retail management. Rachman, for instance, has defined it as "the systematic collection of market information pertaining to the future strategy of the retail firm with the idea of reducing the risks involved in altering the three submixes of the store, namely the goods and services, physical distribution and communications mix, to the demands of the consumers."

Line research and centralized research may be compared in various ways. Clearly, most questions that are considered by the line executive working in his own department may also be considered by the centralized research unit. The latter has the advantage of seeing the same problems from the perspective of many departments but the disadvantage of not knowing them at first hand (the line executive can of course be very helpful here). A centralized unit is also likely to concern itself with other types of research relating to the whole store or chain of stores. Among the topics studied are store image, advertising effectiveness, and store location.

Centralized research will tend to differ from line research in at least the following related ways:

1. *Greater use of random sampling.* In probability sampling, every member of the universe has a known chance of being selected. Research based on random sampling avoids sample bias by giving the researcher a known range of error within which to operate. Thus if he follows the procedure correctly, the researcher can establish a *confidence interval* for the figures obtained. This enables him to say, for instance, that 95 percent of the time (or whatever confidence interval he desires) the true mean would fall between certain limits. An alternative procedure is just to pick whatever sample seems best. This is known as a *judgment sample;* its main disadvantage is that there is no way of knowing how much faith to put in the results. Nevertheless, most centralized research in retailing is presently conducted on a judgment basis. Much depends, therefore, on the acumen and experience of the decision maker who designates the sample and interprets the result.

2. *Use of formal questionnaires.* The reasons people give for the things they do are often quite different from the real reasons. Questionnaires are generally designed to uncover the former. Unfortunately, as everyone knows, the type of answer obtained very often depends on the way the question was put. Much, too, may depend on the method of interviewing, whether by mail, telephone, or face-to-face interview, and, if either of the last two methods are used, on the personality of the interviewer. Members of a central research unit do not often have formal training in questionnaire construction, but they generally develop facility with this type of instrument over time. However, this will generally happen only if they regard questionnaires as important, which is not always the case. Indeed, many retail firms contract out any research that involves extensive interviewing.

3. *Experimentation.* There are various degrees of experimentation possible at the retail level. It was suggested previously that much experimentation goes on at the retail level in the sense that new products, promotions, displays, advertising, and equipment are continually being tested. However, no effort is made to provide controlled conditions for these experiments; they are merely part of day-to-day decision making. At the other end of the continuum are controlled experiments such as David M. Gardner's study of price-quality relationships, cited at the end of this chapter. The store provides an excellent setting for experiments, and investigators have taken advantage of this. For instance, Leslie Schuller found that mannequins presented against a given scenic background were more noticed than the mannequins without this background, while William Applebaum and Richard F. Spears found that sales of fresh vegetables increased when they were prepackaged. However, the costs of this type of study tend to be high relative to the benefits, and there is nothing permanent about any of the findings. Accordingly, most decision makers feel they can do just as well with simpler tests.

4. *Use of more advanced techniques.* Centralized research departments can use various analytic techniques to avoid statistical and other biases and to get additional information from data. Among these techniques are *multivariate analysis* and various types of *mathematical model.*

5. *Secondary resources.* Line executives have access to some secondary resources in the form of trade publications, but members of the research department have access to many more, and are likely to be far more sophisticated in their use. Among the

more useful publications is the Census of Retail Trade, published at regular intervals by the U.S. Department of Commerce.

In sum, the more sophisticated methodology of the centralized research departments has allowed them to tackle many problems that cannot be approached effectively at the line level. Among these problems are store location, the evaluation of store images, and computer simulation of innovative systems.

### Research in the Supermarket

The supermarket will be used to illustrate some types of line research not previously discussed, and some types of research that might be undertaken by a centralized research department. Throughout this section, we shall be concerned with possible interrelationships between line and centralized research activity.

**Line research** Supermarket executives can use all the types of line research suggested earlier. In addition, however, they might be interested in the following:

1. *Pricing*. Customers, it is commonly thought, are attracted to a supermarket by its prices, among other things. Store managers may therefore be interested in other supermarkets' prices on a variety of goods. Perhaps they will be content to "eyeball" these prices, but as a method this is likely to be highly biased. A centralized research department could help here by compiling unbiased price lists that are inexpensively processed by computers or clerical personnel. Of even greater importance to a line executive might be the customers' perception of prices. A manager might talk to customers in order to get a vague picture; but customers' perceptions are not so easily accessible, and inexpensive questionnaires developed by the centralized research unit may offer more accurate data. An executive might also want to know how customers perceive price increases or decreases, and how they react to

the relevant competition. Here, too, centralized research can provide a more objective picture.

2. *Quality*. The line executive will usually carefully check his meat and produce to make sure that it is coming into the store in the condition envisaged at the time of the order; he may even set up a quality control procedure, such as examining every $n$th case that comes into the store. The perceptions of the customer are not so easy to examine. What key features does a customer look for in purchasing meat? How does your supermarket stand up to other stores on these key features, from the customer's point of view? The research department can answer these questions, and it may also be able to help in deciding how the produce should be packaged so as to be most attractive to the customer. There is also the interaction of price and quality. Should the produce items be priced in the department or at a central checkout? Various studies might be directed at finding out how the customer perceives value in your store and in other stores.

3. *Customer service*. The store manager might do quite a bit to foster customer service. He might periodically inspect the checkouts to see how effectively each is performing. Its effectiveness could be evaluated in terms of dollar output per unit of time, or the number of times each day that he saw more than three customers waiting in line at it. However, this would not tell him how the customer perceives waiting in supermarket lines. W. G. McClelland reported that customers who were in a checkout line less than three minutes might perceive this time to be as long as 40 minutes. If an executive knew in addition why the customer misjudged the time so badly, he might be able to do something about it, perhaps by setting up experiments to find out what makes a wait in line seem long or short. Analyses might be made to find out how and why the store runs out of stock, and how serious this problem is. But the manager would have difficulty evaluating the customers' perception of the store's being out of stock on a particular item.

4. *New products*. A typical supermarket might handle 8,000 items or more. There is a great deal of competition among suppliers to have their products selected, and supermarkets usually set up some

| (Extremely) | (Quite) | (Slightly) | (Neither) | (Slightly) | (Quite) | (Extremely) |
|---|---|---|---|---|---|---|
| Good | : | : | : | : | : | Bad |
| Convenient | : | : | : | : | : | Inconvenient |
| Large | : | : | : | : | : | Small |
| Friendly | : | : | : | : | : | Unfriendly |
| Neat | : | : | : | : | : | Disorderly |
| Fair | : | : | : | : | : | Unfair |
| Modern | : | : | : | : | : | Old-Fashioned |
| Active | : | : | : | : | : | Passive |
| Clean | : | : | : | : | : | Dirty |
| Reliable | : | : | : | : | : | Unreliable |
| Roomy | : | : | : | : | : | Crowded |
| Pleasing | : | : | : | : | : | Annoying |
| Low Prices | : | : | : | : | : | High Prices |

*Figure 9.1   Semantic differential for supermarkets (Source: R. Clifton Andersen and Richard A. Scott, "Supermarkets: Are They Really Alike?" Journal of Retailing, Fall, 1970, p. 17.)*

way of testing questionable new products. This poses some serious dilemmas for them. Should a test be made in three stores, six stores, or some other number? How can sampling bias be prevented if the research is undertaken by managers and employees? Can a procedure be set up to determine the "lemons" within ten days from the day the merchandise hits the floor? Would it work with the best sellers? The same type of procedure might be created for weeding out products that have ceased to sell.

5. *Advertising.* Stores may use coupons and similar devices to measure the short-term impact of advertising on store volume. But how is the image of the store changed by specific advertisements or advertising campaigns? What is an appropriate mix of price and image advertising in the newspapers, on TV, and so forth? Is the advertising too cluttered? Or not informative enough?

These are just a few of the ways that line executives can use research. Clearly, in nearly every case they would benefit from the advice and effort of a central research department. The best results are likely to be achieved by line and research personnel working together.

**Centralized research**   At the present time the most important function of centralized research departments in most supermarkets is to locate new stores. Centralized research can perform this function better than any other arm of the retail organiza-

tion, and the costs of building new stores are so high that the amount spent for research is a small part of the total. A procedure for selecting sites of stores is discussed in the next chapter.

Another important type of study conducted by centralized research departments establishes the image of a store and its merchandise in relation to the competition. In many stores, departments have very different images with consumers. Of particular interest here is the semantic differential, developed by Charles E. Osgood and others. A sample of this technique, applied to supermarkets, is shown in Figure 9.1.

Many other types of study can be performed by a supermarket's central research arm. Such an organization could accumulate panel data for the purposes of creating store switching matrices such as those already discussed (p. 56). Thus a decision maker would know to which stores his customers went when they decided not to buy at his any longer; where they bought the major portion of their food and other staple purchases; from which store customers could most easily be attracted to his; and so forth. Central research departments can also study such processes as the flow of customers in the aisles of the store and the flow of cars in the parking lot.

Of central importance to retail decision making, especially at high levels, is the long-term satisfaction of customers. The changing nature of the consumer and his environment is far more difficult to evaluate over the long term, but it must be a key object of research if the firm is to grow and prosper. Some ways of facing up to the realities of long-term change are discussed in Chapter 20, which deals with planning.

## Summary

1. Executives were developing information on which to make decisions many years before the creation of formal research departments. Two characteristics of the retail operation have heavily influenced most of the research at the retail level.

A. Tests are very simply and inexpensively performed. Alert retailers are constantly testing new items, methods of display, information systems, cash registers, traffic flows, and so forth. Testing in a nonscientific sense is a key element of all retailing.

B. Retailers develop a wealth of information about sales and customers, and this information is generally readily available as a by-product of the existing information systems.

2. The research a firm conducts is related to its organizational philosophy.

A. Firms that hold the department completely responsible for profits lean heavily on that department for research. Generally, little research is done. Few research projects of a formal nature will pay off quickly enough in terms of sales and profits to influence the lower-level line executive in charge of a department to conduct substantial research.

B. Many other firms try to pull many decisions away from the lower-line executive. The research decision in this case would be made by a higher authority, who usually can afford to take the longer-term perspective.

3. Most large firms, regardless of philosophy, do have centralized research departments. Centralized research differs from line research in the following respects:

A. Greater use of random sample;

B. Use of formal questionnaires;

C. Sophisticated experiments;

D. Use of more advanced statistical and mathematical techniques;

E. More effective use of secondary resources.

## Discussion Questions

1. What is research?

2. Outline the kinds of information that most stores generate without any particular research effort.

3. List six or seven types of test often performed by the retail manager.

4. In what ways does the organizational perspective of the firm influence its research?

5. In what respects does centralized research differ from line research?

6. Do large retail organizations do enough long-term research?

7. What are the advantages of a judgment sample?

8. Why would some executives prefer a probability sample?

9. List nine secondary sources that might be of use to a researcher employed by a supermarket chain.

## References

Applebaum, William, and Spears, Richard F., "Controlled Experimentation in Marketing Research," *Journal of Marketing*, January 1950, pp. 505–517.

Clark, Harold, and Sloan, Harold, *Classrooms in the Stores* (Sweet Springs, Mo.: Roxbury Press, 1962), p. 74.

Gardner, David M., "An Experimental Investigation of the Price/Quality Relationship," *Journal of Retailing*, Fall, 1970, pp. 25–41.

Hartley, Robert F., "Effective Expansion of Research by Large Retailers," *Journal of Retailing*, Winter, 1969–70, p. 36.

McClelland, W. G., *Studies in Retailing* (Oxford: Blackwell, 1963), pp. 47–48.

Osgood, Charles E., *et al.*, *The Measurement of Meaning* (Urbana, Ill.: University of Illinois Press, 1958).

Schuller, Leslie, "Scenic Background Increases Response to Dress Display," *Journal of Retailing*, Fall, 1962.

## Further Reading

Andersen, R. Clifton, and Scott, Richard A., "Supermarkets: Are They Really Alike?" *Journal of Retailing*, Fall, 1970.

Banks, Seymour, *Experimentation in Marketing* (New York: McGraw-Hill, 1965).

Brown, F. E., and Oxenfeldt, A. R., *Misperceptions of Economic Phenomena* (New York: Sperr and Douth, 1972).

Kunkeland, John H., and Berry, Leonard L., "A Behavior Concept of Retail Images," *Journal of Marketing*, October 1968.

Rachman, David J., *Retail Strategy and Structure: A Management Approach* (Englewood Cliffs, N.J.: Prentice-Hall, 1969).

# 10

## Store Location and Trading Area

Any group of retail decision makers trying to settle on the right location for a new store will find that the problem has many dimensions. In what geographic areas should they look for a location? Should they locate in a central city or somewhere else? If the former, what specific part of the center, or what specific piece of property, should they select? Should they hire someone to look for a location? If so', whom? Should they form their own shopping centers, or decide from among centers offered by professional shopping center creators? How can they become the first to be offered the more attractive real estate opportunities? Who are the best types of competitors to have in the same center or area? How many direct competitors of their type should the center or area have? Should they have a free-standing retail unit, one with two sides, or what? These are just some of the questions that they must answer.

Location analysis is closely bound up with trading area analysis (a store's trading area is the entire area from which it regularly draws customers). The following case history will give some idea of the difficulties involved.

Charles Jones was the store location expert for the Safemark Super Market chain. He was asked by the president of his firm to project volume for a possible supermarket at the intersection of U.S. Highways 12 and 13. Charlie did an intensive analysis of the store's estimated trading area. By using the most up-to-date techniques known to him, he was able to offer reasonably precise estimates to the president. Construction of the store was approved.

In the 18 months before the store opened, the following events took place. A major national chain got into financial trouble and radically changed its pricing policies, so that it started to average a 10 percent margin on packaged goods, down from 20 percent at the time of the study. Another large regional chain had decided to keep its stores open 24 hours a day every day in the week, including Sunday. A third chain had decided to give up trading stamps and establish a heavy discount policy, particularly with

The author wishes to express his thanks to Professor William Cox of Case Western Reserve University for his contributions to this chapter.

meats. Two small local chains threw in the towel and called it quits. Safemark changed policies dramatically over this period to meet these changing conditions. The margin on packaged goods was lowered to 14 percent from 18 percent, in an effort to keep a large segment of its volume from going to the major national chain already referred to, and hours in all stores were extended to midnight (formerly, they had closed at 9:00 P.M.). Customer services were curtailed dramatically to decrease costs, while the advertising budget was increased twofold and in-store coupons were increased fourfold. Charlie's original projections were now all out of date.

Charlie's problem is quite typical. It would appear that of all the decisions that most retailers must make, store location is the most complex and the most important. One observer of the retail scene has said that there are four Ls in store success: location, location, location, and location. Many an ineffective owner has been saved by the judicious or lucky choice of an attractive location, while many potentially effective ones are thwarted by locations that are inappropriate.

## Store Location and Purchasing Power

Stores are in the business of serving people and must change with them. Of critical importance to the retailer is where people live and work, since the retail structure will follow the population. In fact, nothing is more crucial to the future of a retail enterprise than populations in the community or region that constitutes its trading area.

A retailer is also particularly interested in what people who have money do. After all, his primary concern is with the dollars spent in his store, and this would appear to be related to what people have to spend on the type of merchandise carried in his store, not just to how many people live near it. Numerous studies have indicated that purchasing power is a more effective predictor of both retail dollar sales and the number of retail units in an

area than is its population alone. Income analysis, then, is a most useful tool for retail, though most authorities recognize the importance of other factors such as distance, population density, and changing retail technology.

A few examples will show just how much can be predicted about an area's retail structure on the basis of a comparatively few variables. B. J. L. Berry (1963) was able to explain 84 percent of the variation in the number of retail establishments in Chicago on the basis of population and median family income. Donald L. Thompson (1964) examined the 129 cities in the United States with more than 100,000 residents in 1960 and found that a purchasing power index, composed of population and income, explained more than 99 percent of the variation in these cities' retail sales. Ben-chieh Liu, in a study published in 1970, showed that variations in population and income explained more than 90 percent of the variation in total retail sales in 42 large SMSAs in the U.S. from 1952 to 1966. SMSA is defined below.

The above studies were concerned with large areas, but most retailers are concerned with much smaller ones. Thus Robert Ferber demonstrated that there was a close relationship between total retail sales and total income in 51 Illinois cities that ranged in population from 10,000 to 4 million in 1954. William Cox found in a study of 52 census tracts in Cleveland that when the census tracts were combined into larger neighborhood groups for purposes of analysis, the relationship between number of retail units and purchasing power tended to grow stronger. Clearly, purchasing power or the *proxy variable* of population should be carefully considered when one is deciding where to locate a store.

## Trading Areas

Individuals who live in California seldom shop in Maine. Clearly, most of the U.S. population is not relevant to the particular retail store or shopping center in a given community. It is therefore useful, when dealing with such a store or center, to think in terms of the population that is relevant to it. The area in which there is a realistic probability that the customers will in fact shop at the store or center over a reasonable period of time is known as its *trading area.*

### Reilly's Law

One way to think of trading areas is in terms of benefits and costs to the individual. Generally, the farther a store or center is from an individual in time, mileage, or convenience, the greater is the cost to the customer, although the customer's perception of this cost may vary with the purpose of the trip, his own state of mind, and so on. In most circumstances, the greater the number of stores in the area, the more attractive the particular center will be. It may be useful here to think of the population size of geographic areas as a force that attracts and space as a force that repels. This is often called the *gravity concept* of human interaction. The concept was formulated in general terms more than a century ago and was subsequently applied to the analysis of migration. The first to use it in retailing was W. J. Reilly, who suggested in the 1930s that two cities attract retail trade in style and fashion goods from intermediate areas in direct proportion to the size of their respective populations, and in inverse proportion to the square of the distances between them and these areas.

One modification of Reilly's original formula merits particular attention since it permits the decision maker to calculate the point between two competing cities where the trading influence of each is the same. If the same point is calculated for all competing cities, an estimate can be made of each city's general trading area. The modified formula, which was developed by P. D. Converse, is as follows, where A is the larger city:

$$D_b = \frac{D_{ab}}{1 + \sqrt{\dfrac{P_a}{P_b}}}$$

where $D_b$ = breaking point between city A and city B (i.e., the point at which a potential customer might shop at either) in miles from B

$D_{ab}$ = distance separating city A from city B

$P_a$ = population of city A

$P_b$ = population of city B

Reilly's law has been tested in various forms. Some observers have demonstrated the possibility of using it for estimating the trading areas of shopping centers. For example, the square-foot area for shopping goods can be put in place of population as the attracting force and the driving time of potential customers as the force that repels. However many criticisms have been made of this and all variations on Reilly's law, especially of the limited number of variables they contain.

### Huff's Model

An alternative model for analyzing the trading area of shopping centers was created in 1962 by David L. Huff. He suggested that a retail trading area could be portrayed in terms of *probability contours*—that is, delimiting areas in which there is the same probability of an occurrence. One such trading area is shown in Figure 10.1. Here the contours apply to the consumer and the probability of his traveling to the shopping center. As the distance from the center increases, the probability of the consumer shopping there decreases—but not at a uniform rate, otherwise the figure would resemble a target. For each relevant area, the probability of the customer shopping at the center can be multiplied by the number of individuals found living in that area to arrive at an expected number of customers. These figures can then be added to give an estimated total number of customers, which in turn can be used to calculate an estimate of total dollar volume. Allowance can also be made for the fact that different products have different drawing power: for instance, most people would drive farther to buy a new car than a new tube of toothpaste.

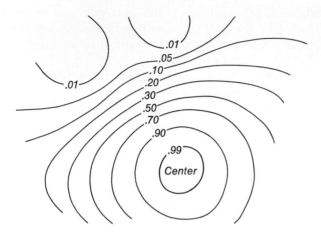

Figure 10.1   *Determining retail trade areas:*
*Huff's model* [Source: *Adapted from David L.*
*Huff*, Determination of Intra-urban Retail
Trade Areas *(Los Angeles: University of*
*California, Real Estate Research Program,*
*1962).*]

## Key Dimensions

Much can be done to analyze the trading area of
a store or set of stores once they are in operation.
For example, the license plates of the cars in the
parking lot can be traced, and the customers can be
interviewed in the store. A management can run
contests that not only appeal to most kinds of customer but require their names and addresses. For
certain types of retail outlet, credit records can give
a good idea of where customers come from.

The more difficult problem is to estimate the
trading area before the store or center is created. As
one would expect, most of the models developed in
recent years have aimed at precisely this. In addition to the size of the center and its distance in miles
or minutes from the consumer, numerous other factors are involved, among them the following:

1. *The competitive configuration.* Clearly, other
centers will influence the trading area for a given
center. Seldom will a customer go to another center
unless there is substantial incentive to do so.

2. *Total department store space in square feet.*
Many studies have indicated that consumers will
travel farther for certain types of merchandise, such
as fashion goods, than they will for other types,
such as groceries. A key fashion center for many
segments of the population is the department store.
Thomas Harrison has suggested that 50 to 60 percent
of the gross leasable space in what he terms super-
regional centers is department store space. Many
department stores not only compete but also complement each other, and that center in which they
exist has superior drawing power by virtue of their
joint presence. A center with four key department
stores is certainly well protected against competition from other centers.

3. *Total supermarket space in square feet.* People
would probably travel great distances for food if
they had to. But they do not have to. And while
food is important to most households, the differences between the readily accessible markets and
those quite a few miles away are not perceived as
important by the consumers, or at least not important enough to travel large distances. Thus the
trading area for most supermarkets is small: few
customers travel long distances. It follows that supermarket space in a large center is perceived as a negative in the total drawing power of that center.

4. *Total number of parking places.* The more parking spaces, the more attractive the center will be to
the consumers.

5. *Natural boundaries.* Natural boundaries such
as rivers and mountains influence the shape and
total drawing power of a center.

6. *Racial composition of the population.* Consumer
interests differ among races. Also, white consumers
are (in 1974) reluctant to travel to black areas to
shop, and black consumers tend to have less money.

7. *Configuration of the highways.* The center's
customers will tend to have easy access to it through
the main arteries. Thus for centers that are serviced
by one main road, one would anticipate an elongated
trading area following the road.

8. *Nature of the communication services.* Both the
circulation and the effectiveness of the local newspapers, television, and radio influence the trading
areas of the stores that advertise in them.

### Central Place Theory

A weakness of trading area analysis is that it is only indirectly concerned with relationships among trading areas. This weakness is remedied to some extent by central place theory, which has been described by Berry (1967) as relating to the location, size, nature, and spacing of clusters of economic activity. As such, it is the theoretical base for much urban geography, including the geography of the retail and service business.

Central place theory assumes that there is some dollar volume for a good below which firms dealing in it cannot operate profitably. This dollar volume is the point at which firms can only make what economists have defined as "normal profits," that is, the minimum scale or condition of entering a market with a good. This minimum scale is known as the *threshold sales level* for the provision of the good from a center. The notion of threshold level is basic to that of central place. Thus if a city is to be supplied with $n$ types of good, and if we rank the goods from 1 to $n$ in ascending order of their threshold requirements, the part of the city that supplies good $n$ will have the largest market area and will therefore be the *central place* for that good in that region.

Walter Christaller, the German economic geographer whose work in the 1930s laid the foundation of modern central place theory, suggested that in any region there will be a hierarchy of market centers, from the highest order of threshold to the lowest. In other words, each highest-order store location is a central place from which *all* other goods and services will be provided; the presence of good $n$ implies the presence of goods 1 to $n-1$. The lower a good's threshold, the more likely it is to be available in small market areas. Furthermore, there will be a spatial ordering of these centers, influenced by factors such as transportation routes; indeed, Christaller thought that there was a hierarchy of such routes, complementing the central place hierarchy of market centers.

Christaller developed his theory at a time when distance was more important as an isolator from competition than it is today. Furthermore, his research with regard to central cities did not foresee the huge metropolitan center that is characteristic of today. Berry has suggested that within the metropolitan area the articulation of the central place hierarchy has now been replaced by specialization; locations continue in their central place role, but others become resorts, dormitory suburbs, and so on. The economic structure over much of the contemporary United States is a set of interdependent metropolitan regions, each one specialized to a high degree instead of being subdivided into the progressively smaller regions called for by classic central place theory. Thus local specialization, rather than the repetition and uniformity of a central place system, becomes the key to understanding modern metropolitan forms. Within the city, the classic hierarchy is replaced by a pattern of business centers, ribbon developments, and specialized areas that depend on such factors as income and ethnicity. Such considerations have led Berry to assert that the only real security lies in the economies of further specialization.

Nevertheless, central place theory is relevant to modern retailing because it emphasizes the systemic nature of the relationships between population and retail outlets, on the one hand, and among the various retail outlets and centers, on the other. The consumers are the environment of the system: their demands are adapted to by the system of stores which, acting in their own interests, develop a hierarchy that satisfies the consumers' demands in a reasonably efficient manner.

### Rent

Economic rent may be defined as the amount by which sales exceed nonrent costs. Scott has suggested that the market rent, that is, the rent that is actually charged, will tend toward the economic rent over the long term. In any case, both sales and costs for a given location will vary with many factors, including the type of store, its reputation, and so forth. Presumably, landlords and tenants will be aware of the types of store that benefit most from a given location. Jewelers, for example, are able to pay

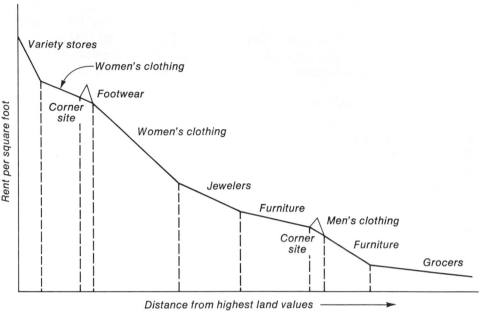

Variety stores

Women's clothing

Footwear

Corner
site

Women's clothing

Jewelers

Furniture

Men's clothing

Corner
site

Furniture

Grocers

Rent per square foot

Distance from highest land values ⟶

Figure 10.2  *Hypothetical rent gradient in one direction from the point of highest land values within a major unplanned shopping center* [Source: *Peter Scott,* Geography and Retailing *(Chicago, Ill.: Aldine Publishing Company, 1970).*]

higher rents on the average than furniture stores because they can more effectively exploit sites where pedestrian traffic is heaviest. Variety stores can normally outbid women's clothing stores, which in turn can outbid grocery stores. Each type of store can therefore be located on a *rent gradient.* Such a gradient can of course vary with many factors, including geographic area, but it should exhibit a downward progression of maximum rents as accessibility to the core decreases. The steepness of the slope will depend upon how the retailer's sales and costs are affected by changes in the ease with which consumers can get to the store. Figure 10.2 shows one way in which a rent gradient can be constructed.

In theory, rents should decrease at a uniform rate in proportion to their distance from a given center. This clearly does not happen. Some of the reasons are as follows:

1. *Special sites* may get advantages from certain aspects. For instance, in city centers certain kinds of business will derive particular advantage from corner sites, sunny sites, sites near lunch counters, and so on.

2. *Variations in lot size* in terms of frontage, total area, and so forth, affect different types of business differently. In seeking to maximize his profits, an entrepreneur will adjust not only for location but for these other factors as well. Thus shops selling goods of high value in relation to bulk can use smaller frontages than shops selling goods of low value in relation to bulk.

3. *Length of street,* and its general orientation, will affect the way stores are arranged along it. Scott has suggested that an ideal street for retail trade would be sufficiently long to accommodate most if not all of the stores at the top of the relevant rent gradient who are able to pay the rents. A longer street may deteriorate and gradually peter out.

4. *Side of street* can make a difference, if one side is more accessible to shoppers than the other.

5. *Retail affinity,* that is, the way certain retail stores appear to complement each other, may be more important than mere accessibility. Where such affinity exists, a different type of center is created. Such a center may have proximity to a given customer market, to the source of supply, or to outlets

similar in trade type. There have been many studies of retail affinity but seldom with conclusive results.

6. *Differences between stores*, especially differing efficiencies of managements and differing images, will create different sales and cost patterns even for stores of the same type. However, the rent gradient model suggests that these differences tend to be smaller than the differences between types of store.

## Store Location

The shopping center has already been discussed (p. 9). Before dealing with store location as such, two important related subjects should be considered: some theories of city growth; and the Standard Metropolitan Statistical Area.

### Theories of City Growth

There are numerous theories that attempt to explain the way the cities grew. Much is suggested by central place theory, at least as applied to European trading centers. In North America, however, additional perspectives are offered by three other theories.

The *concentric circle theory* suggests that, under many conditions, the American city has taken the form of five concentric circles. The first circle was the central business district, which gave way to a zone of transition that was ephemeral and in the immediate path of industrial and business expansion. Then came a zone of the homes of workingmen, a zone of middle-class dwellers, and, finally, a commuter's zone. Figure 10.3 offers a simplified version of this theory, which was developed by R. E. Park and others in the 1920s. Obviously, the theory is not applicable today—the automobile has seen to that— but many of our older cities apparently did develop in the above manner and reflect this today.

The *sector theory* suggests that over the years a city's high rent areas will move outward toward its outskirts in a path indicated by one or more sectors. In other words, if a given sector develops as a low-

KEY:

1. Central business district
2. Zone of transition
3. Zone of workingmen's homes
4. Zone of middle class dwellers
5. Commuters' zone

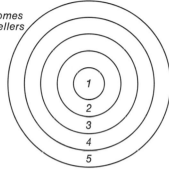

Figure 10.3 Community growth: the concentric circle theory [Source: Arthur M. Weimer, Homer Hoyt, and George F. Bloom, Real Estate, Sixth Edition. Copyright © 1972 The Ronald Press Company, New York.]

rent area, the remainder of the sector is likely to be occupied over a period of time by low-rent and low-price alternatives. Homer Hoyt has offered the following propositions as a basis for the sector theory.

A grouping occurs in the social order, primarily as a result of income and social position;

Low-priced housing is located near the business and industrial center, from which it fans out into the sector in question;

The main growth of cities in this country takes place by new building at the periphery rather than by rebuilding older areas;

High-priced residential areas will tend to develop along the fastest transportation lines;

Office buildings, banks, and stores will generally pull the high-priced residential neighborhoods in the same geographic direction.

The sector theory stresses the importance of transportation, income, and social class in the creation of residential neighborhoods and related activities. Many metropolitan areas and cities ap-

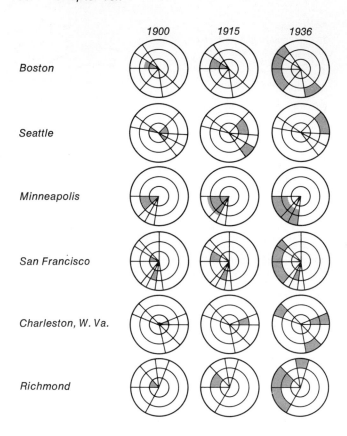

1900    1915    1936

Boston

Seattle

Minneapolis

San Francisco

Charleston, W. Va.

Richmond

*Figure 10.4   City growth: the sector theory, as applied to six American cities, 1900–36* [Source: Homer Hoyt, The Structure and Growth of Residential Neighborhoods in American Cities (Washington, D.C.: U.S. Federal Housing Administration, 1939), p. 100.] *Solid block sectors indicate fashionable residential areas.*

parently developed more or less according to the theory, and many of the factors specified in it are highly relevant to the development of today's cities. The sector theory is illustrated in Figure 10.4.

A third theory of city development is the *multiple nuclei theory*. This theory, pioneered by C. D. Harris and E. L. Ullman, suggests that a city develops around several nuclei rather than around a single center, and that the entire process reflects a combination of four factors:

Certain activities within the city require specialized facilities—for example, the retail district is related to the point of greatest accessibility.

Certain activities within the city benefit from being together.

Certain activities are detrimental to each other—for example, the street-loading activities of the wholesale district would be detrimental to the concentration of pedestrians, automobiles, and street cars in the retail district.

Certain activities within the city are not able to pay the high rents of the sites they would like to use—for example, wholesaling of large bulk items requires a great deal of space.

The multiple nuclei theory seems highly relevant to what is happening in many metropolitan areas: the dominance of the central business district is disappearing, and areas are developing many strong centers.

### Standard Metropolitan Statistical Areas

There are many ways to look at cities other than as political boundaries. One way is to treat the entire urban area as a single economic unit. The suburban areas that have grown so rapidly around our cities are clearly not economically independent of them. The Bureau of the Census has recognized this change over the years and has established a classification known as the Standard Metropolitan Statistical Area, or SMSA. This is defined by the bureau as a "county or group of contiguous counties . . . which contains at least one city of 50,000 inhabitants or more or 'twin cities' with a combined population of at least 50,000." Thus in addition to the city itself, certain suburban areas are included.

Two major subdivisions of the SMSA are the Central Business District (CBD) and the Major Retail Center (MRC). The CBD, according to the Census Bureau, is "an area of very high land valuation;

an area characterized by a high concentration of retail businesses, offices, theaters, hotels, and 'service' businesses, and an area of high traffic flow." However, CBD data must follow census tract lines in order to facilitate the gathering of data. CBDs vary greatly in character, size, and importance. For example, Revzan concludes that in 1963 the relative importance of the CBD in the city's total retail picture varied from a low of 7.3 percent of sales for Los Angeles to a high of 56.0 percent in Manhattan.

Major Retail Centers were first delineated by the Department of Commerce in the 1958 Census of Population, where they were defined as concentrations of retail stores, located inside an SMSA but outside the CBD, that include a major general merchandise store—usually a department store. MRCs include but are not limited to planned shopping centers.

There are other types of development within cities that offer substantial numbers of opportunities for certain kinds of stores. String developments, for instance, occur along the major transportation arteries of most cities: they tend to be along one street; or at the intersections of two or more principal thoroughfares. Also worth noting are neighborhood clusters of convenience outlets, and independent retail units that generate their own traffic.

### The Decision to Locate

There are many ways of approaching the decision to locate a store. Most times, a management will already have made a decision about the type of store in which it is interested. The decision as to type of location—only in new shopping centers of a certain size, perhaps—may also have been made. Or perhaps a firm will only consider locating in a Central Business District, or in a free-standing unit, or some combination of these. Other firms might regard the decision as essentially a passive one and evaluate each site on its individual merits as it is presented

to them. Despite this range of possibilities, there are certain basic considerations that few firms neglect. It is these that will be reviewed here.

A prime consideration in store location is the community. There are a great many different types of community in this large country. Some are growing rapidly; others are losing population. Some rely heavily on two or three industries, some on two or three firms. The future of these firms and industries can make a great deal of difference to the communities' retail firms; for instance, the future of the Boeing Aircraft Company will have to be weighed by any store considering locating in the Seattle area.

Another aspect of the community that should be weighed is the nature of the local competition. An important regional firm may be very aggressive and make entry into the market quite difficult. The type of consumer in a given community may also make a difference. Blue-collar workers tend to shop in different types of retail outlet than the very well-to-do. University students tend to have an interest in types of merchandise that would interest hardly anyone else.

Thus before the final decision to locate, certain assumptions should be made about the future and character of the total community in which the retail unit or units are going to have to survive. An analysis should be made of the area's key industries, the character of its population, the future growth of purchasing power, and so forth. Clearly, this analysis could be made at any point in the decision-making process, but it would appear that for most purposes it would best be made at the beginning.

**Narrowing the number of areas considered**    Having established the general area in which his firm will locate its store, the decision maker must still choose the actual site. However, he should first narrow down the number of areas to be investigated. Making the decision as to which neighborhood or shopping center to investigate before making an effort to evaluate sites in one of them may seem an obvious enough precaution. At times, however, this step will not be taken, and the site offered by a realtor or developer will be examined before any effort is made to evaluate the general area. Here, we are concerned with the various methods that a retailer might use in this narrowing-down process. These methods may be combined in various ways; the choice of combination is, in the end, a matter of personal judgment.

1. *Potential areas could be analyzed* to see how they conform to various rules of thumb. Thus prospective neighborhoods or shopping centers could be matched against data developed from neighborhoods and shopping centers of similar types. For example, a community with a minimum of $x$ families may have profitable food stores, drug stores, dry cleaners, beauty parlors, barber shops, and variety stores. A shopping center serving so many families probably has distinctive characteristics. This type of analysis can give an observer an insight into possible market voids, that is, openings in the retail structure in a given center or area.

2. *A specific model or group of models might be created* to develop some desired number of stores of a specific type for a particular area or shopping center. For instance, Cox has developed a model for planning the retail service requirements of an economically depressed inner-city neighborhood.

3. *An analysis of entries and exits* might be made for specific areas, by type of outlet over a period of time. Relationships might be developed between entries and exits, on the one hand, and successes and failures in specific types of stores, on the other. Vacancy rates might also be examined for their potential usefulness.

4. *A decision maker might contact potential consumers* in the relevant areas in order to find out how they perceive the retail structure. Of course, as Donald L. Thompson has pointed out, this would require less emphasis on published, "objective" data, and more on data obtained from surveys. But this could only add to our knowledge.

5. *The profitability of a new store can be estimated* by speaking to suppliers and consultants, and by taking counts of customers, in stores of the same type that already exist in the neighborhood or center where one plans to locate. It seems reasonable to assume that if models such as Cox's indicate that there should be four drug stores in a neighborhood area instead of two, or that a given shopping center should be able to support eight restaurants instead of four, then under most conditions some sort of excess profits are being made by the present entrepreneurs.

### Specific Sites

At some point the decision maker must decide on a specific site. This is true whether he is trying to locate a candy store or a huge shopping center. His decision may come after extensive search in a specific area or neighborhood for an appropriate structure or piece of land, or it may come in response to an inquiry from a realtor or developer as to whether the firm is interested in a particular site. In either case, site location analysis is designed to answer the question: Will the shopping center or the store in that location generate sufficient profit to justify the dollars that will have to be spent, considering the attendant risks? At this point it is essential to draw up a *pro forma* operating statement that includes such factors as expected sales, gross margin, estimated expense structure of the store (including rent), and so forth. Normally, most of these items are not difficult for the analyst to estimate, with the exception of dollar sales over the relevant years.

Most retail chains depend heavily on the *customer demographic profile*, that is, a classification of customers by age, sex, income, and so forth, so that one can tell roughly what proportion of customers in each category is likely to visit a store, and what the typical customer is like. Faced with the problems of store location, these chains tend to match customer profiles for their present store against profiles for stores of the same type at the proposed new site. Since the sales estimate is all-important, it certainly makes sense to be very interested in all facets of the customer. For example, a food store management will generally know where its customers live; the number of times per week that they visit the store; the dollar amount that they purchase on each trip (probably related to the distance from the store); their means of transportation; and all the demographic characteristics just referred to. Similar information can be developed for stores, gas stations, drug stores, or any other kind of retail outlet.

The sales estimate may be created by means of a formal mathematical model based on such factors as the number of cars that turn right at the next corner; or it may be more subjective in nature. Estimates prepared by this method tend to be reasonably accurate for a chain of stores.

Unfortunately, none of the procedures just described could be used in establishing the first unit of a possible chain, because little is known about the way in which customers will perceive the actual unit when it is in operation. Different supermarkets, for example, do not draw customers the same distance: supermarket A may draw 90 percent of its customers from a distance of two miles in area *x*, while supermarket B may draw 90 percent of its customers from a distance of one mile in the same area. Until several units have been opened, it is very difficult to know the type of appeal that your unit will have to large numbers of customers. Estimating the sales volume of the first unit with any degree of confidence is therefore a major problem. The Real Estate Research Corporation suggests that the following four factors be considered:

The number of households in the area.

The median income of those households.

The proportion of the typical household's income spent on the type of goods or services that will be sold by the store.

The percentage of the total business in the relevant goods and services that the new unit might be expected to capture.

The usefulness of this and other approaches to the location of the first store remains to be demonstrated. Clearly, however, there are great difficulties in estimating such a store's sales volume. Indeed, one of the great advantages of controlling a large number of retail outlets is the ability to predict the future sales of new units with reasonable accuracy and small cost.

## Summary

1. There are many dimensions to the problem of where to locate a retail store or chain of retail stores. In what general geographic area should it be? In the central city or the suburbs? In shopping centers or neighborhood areas? In regional shopping centers or smaller shopping centers?

2. Stores quite clearly follow consumers. But of more importance than the mere presence of the consumer is his purchasing power.

3. Stores are particularly interested in an area in which there is a reasonable probability that customers will purchase in a store. This is called the store's trading area. Some of the factors that influence the trading area for a regional shopping center are:

    A. the competitive configuration;

    B. the total department store space;

    C. the total supermarket space;

    D. the number of parking places;

    E. natural boundaries such as rivers, mountains, and so forth;

    F. racial composition;

    G. the configuration of the highways;

    H. the nature of the communications services.

4. Central place theory emphasizes the systemic nature of the relationships between population and retail outlets. Systems of stores relate so that customers of stores travel large distances for some merchandise and small distances for others. If we rank neighborhoods or cities according to the threshold requirement, the city that supplies the good of the highest order will have the largest market area.

5. There are several theories of city growth: the concentric circle, the sector theory, and the multiple

nuclei theory. All explain elements of how cities developed at the time of their rapid growth. Each offers some insight into the dynamic aspects of urban interaction.

6. The decision to locate a store is quite complex and can be approached in many ways. One perspective is offered.

## Discussion Questions

1. Why do stores follow consumers?

2. Will a consumer go farther to purchase fashion merchandise than nonfashion merchandise?

3. Is driving time always a negative to the consumer? What factors would tend to influence a consumer's perception of driving time?

4. How do race and low income influence the trading area of a store?

5. What is an SMSA? How might SMSA analysis be useful in locating a store?

6. What is a Major Retail Center?

7. What is economic rent?

8. What are the limitations of the rent gradient?

9. In what respects is Huff's model an advance on Reilly's law?

10. What factors influence the trading area for a large regional shopping center?

## References

Berry, Brian J. L., *Commercial Structure and Commercial Blight*, Department of Geography Research Paper No. 85 (Chicago, Ill.: University of Chicago, 1963).

———, *Geography of Market Centers and Retail Distribution* (Englewood Cliffs, N.J.: Prentice-Hall, 1967), p. 3.

Converse, P. D., "New Laws of Retail Gravitation," *Journal of Marketing*, October 1949, pp. 379–384.

Cox, William E., Jr., "A Commercial Structure Model for Depressed Neighborhoods," *Journal of Marketing*, July 1969, pp. 1–9. *While this model is not deemed useful for suburban areas, alternatives that are useful could certainly be developed.*

Ferber, Robert, "Variations in Retail Sales between Cities," *Journal of Marketing*, January 1958, pp. 295–303.

Harris, C. D., and Ullman, E. L., "The Nature of Cities," *Annals of the Academy of Political and Social Science*, November 1945, pp. 14–15.

Harrison, Thomas, "The Advent of the Super Regional Shopping Center," in John K. Ryans, Jr., *et al.* (eds.), *New Dimensions in Retailing* (Belmont, Ca.: Wadsworth, 1970), p. 318.

Hoyt, Homer, *The Structure and Growth of Residential Neighborhoods in American Cities* (Washington, D.C.: U.S. Federal Housing Administration, 1939).

Huff, David L., "Defining and Estimating a Trade Area," *Journal of Marketing*, July 1964.

Liu, Ben-chieh, "The Relationships among Population, Income and Retail Sales in SMSA's, 1952–56," *Quarterly Review of Economics and Business*, Spring, 1970, pp. 25–40.

Park, R. E., *et al.*, *The City* (Chicago, Ill.: University of Chicago Press, 1925).

Real Estate Research Corporation, *Retail Location Analysis Manual and Retailing in Low-Income Areas* (Chicago, Ill.: Economic Development Corporation, 1970).

Revzan, David A., *A Geography of Marketing: Integrative Statement* (Berkeley, Ca.: the author, 1968).

Thompson, Donald L., *Analysis of Retailing Potential in Metropolitan Areas* (Berkeley, Ca.: Institute of Business and Economic Research, University of California, 1964).

———, "Future Directions in Retail Area Research," *Economic Geography*, January 1966, pp. 1–18.

## Further Reading

Bucklin, Louis P., *Shopping Patterns in an Urban Area* (Berkeley, Ca.: Institute of Business and Economic Research, University of California, 1967).

Dalrymple, Douglas J., and Thompson, Donald L., *Retailing: An Economic View* (New York: Free Press, 1969).

Garrison, W. L., *et al.*, *Studies of Highway Development and Geographic Change* (Seattle, Wash.: University of Washington Press, 1959).

Goldstucker, J. L., "A Systems Framework for Retail Location," in John K. Ryans *et al.* (eds.), *New Dimensions in Retailing* (Belmont, Ca.: Wadsworth, 1970), pp. 322–339.

Huff, David L., "A Probabilistic Analysis of Consumer Spatial Behavior," in W. S. Decker (ed.), *Emerging Concepts in Marketing* (Chicago, Ill.: American Marketing Association, 1963), pp. 444–450.

Massy, William F., *et al.*, *A Model for Evaluating Retail Site Locations*, Research Paper No. 38 (Palo Alto, Ca.: Stanford Graduate School of Business, 1970).

Mertes, John, "A Retail Structural Theory for Site Analysis," *Journal of Retailing*, Summer 1964, pp. 19–30, 56.

Nelson, Richard L., *The Selection of Retail Locations* (New York: Dodge, 1958).

Scott, Peter, *Geography and Retailing* (Chicago, Ill.: Aldine, 1970).

## Case History:
### *Path-Rite's New Location**

Imagine that you have just received your degree in business administration and have accepted a position with Path-Rite Supermarkets, a leading chain food retailer in the New York metropolitan area. Your position is to head up a new department: market research. The president of Path-Rite has specifically charged you with developing a site selection strategy for the supermarkets.

In 1970, total U.S. grocery store sales were almost $95 billion. Of the country's 205,000 food stores, 39,000 were supermarkets; they accounted for $72 billion, or 77 percent of total food store sales. The trend, over the years, has been away from "mom and pop" stores and toward supermarkets. Supermarkets are divided into chains ($42 billion in 1970) and independents ($30 billion in 1970). Chain stores average 21.4% gross profit with net income (after taxes) of

---

* Based on a case by Charles Bernhaut, Supermarkets General Corp. and the Rutgers Graduate School of Business.

0.86 percent. The average new chain supermarket has 17,700 square feet of selling area. The supermarket industry is one of the most competitive in U.S. retailing. "Discounting" was first seen in it during the early 1960s, and has been a prime factor in changing the face of the industry.

Path-Rite Supermarkets (PRS) is one of the leading "discounters" in the country. It was formed 12 years ago by a merger of three independent supermarkets. Eight years ago, annual sales were less than $100 million. Today, the 98 supermarkets are doing $775 million. Their net profit is approximately 0.8 percent, while their gross profit is running at approximately 18 percent. PRS's new markets have over 30,000 square feet of selling area apiece; the overall store has approximately 43,000 square feet.

Historically, decisions in site selection have been made by John Allen, the vice-president for real estate, who has always shown an uncanny knack for recognizing a potentially successful supermarket site. His greatest successes, however, were made during a time when PRS was virtually the only supermarket "discounter" in the entire metropolitan area. Thus almost every location was an excellent one if it had sufficient population, which generally meant at least 70,000 people within the trading area. John Allen figured that a minimum of $10 was spent on each person's food per week and that 70,000 people would therefore mean $700,000 in potential food dollars. He figured that PRS would usually capture 25 percent of the potential grocery sales, or at least $180,000 per week.

PRS now has stores in all location types:

Regional malls (enclosed shopping centers with two or more department stores);

Discount centers (adjacent to such well-known discount stores as Grants, K Mart or Two Guys);

Strip centers (neighborhood shopping centers with several adjacent small stores such as cleaners and card shops);

Free-standing (standing alone without being part of a center).

The chain has followed a strict policy of giving "value," which it defines as attempting to offer the lowest prices consistent with reasonable quality. The stores have gotten larger and larger each year. Early stores ranged from 20,000 to 25,000 square feet and current stores from 40,000 to 45,000 square feet. Future stores are planned at 50,000 to 55,000 square feet. The stores offer the consumer "one-stop shopping" since in addition to grocery departments they have bakeries, delicatessens, and departments for liquor, flowers, health foods, drugs, and housewares. The chain sells more private brands than any other chain in the country and also has the country's highest volume per store.

The president has allocated a special budget of $25,000 that can be spent this quarter on developing the site-selection strategy for the supermarkets. He has been nervous over John Allen's approach to site selection. John could really pick a winner every time when PRS was the only discounter in the area. But with the competition copying PRS's approach, life has been getting much more difficult. Indeed, some of the recent new stores have not been doing nearly as well as projected. Your job, then, is to develop a "scientific" approach that will be more objective and hopefully more reliable than John Allen's shoot-from-the-hip approach.

You have now been on the job nearly two weeks. Suddenly, the president rushes into your office with a hot real estate submittal for a site in the proposed Willowbrook Shopping Center, to be built in Wayne at the intersection of Routes 46 and 23. The developer has prepared a complete research report and you already have a copy of it. In brief, the report says that:

The proposed center will have over 2 million square feet of retailing space, with 9,000 parking spaces;

The mall will be enclosed and all-weather conditioned;

Proposed are four major department stores and 200 small stores;

Within 10 minutes of driving time there are 300,000 people and within 20 minutes there are 1.15 million people;

The incomes of these people vary from low to upper-middle (average family income is $14,000);

There are excellent roads now and there will be excellent ones in the future; Route 80 has recently been completed;

The nearest comparable type of shopping development is in Paramus on Route 4, approximately 40 minutes away.

The developer plans two supermarkets for the Willowbrook Center. One will be part of the shopping center, on "Parcel A," and the other will be on a completely separate plot of land contiguous to the shopping center ("parcel B"). Parcel A will allow for 35,000 square feet of building with an entrance from the enclosed mall and a separate entrance from the parking lot. Parcel B is three acres (there are 43,280 square feet in an acre) and sits at the corner of Route 23 and the main entrance to the mall.

Now the president tells you that the developer has given PRS first crack at either supermarket location. He has 90 days in which to make a final decision, and he wants you to make sure that decision will be the correct one.

### Discussion Questions

1. How are you going to spend the next 90 days (assuming, that is, that you want to keep the job)?

2. What chance do you give yourself of coming up with the right decision? Do you think your decision has a better chance of being right than John Allen's?

# 11

*Marginal Analysis*

What is a firm's goal? To the stockholders, it appears reasonable for the firm to undertake only activities that are going to increase the value of the stock, or some combination of stock price and dividends. Indeed some consider maximizing returns to stockholders as management's only function. Others might suggest that a firm really maximizes returns to the board of directors: after all, the board controls the firm and does not usually have to pay any but the most perfunctory attention to the stockholders. Still others would argue that the firm's management is there to perpetuate itself and will make decisions accordingly. The employees also have a claim on the firm; someone who has put 40 years work into an organization most certainly has a stake in it. Finally, the consumers of what the firm produces or sells have a particular interest in its policies.

Thus firms have a multiplicity of goals. However, if we must single out one of them as *the* goal, it may be useful to suggest that, in general, a firm's goal is to maximize its long-term profits for a specific level of risk. This may offend certain members of society, especially those who believe that large profits are unethical. Also, many employees would like higher wages even if this means somewhat lower profits. But the board of directors, the stockholders, the firm's top management, employees worried about their pensions, and sundry others would appear to favor the goal of maximizing long-term profits while taking "reasonable" risks.

Stating that a firm is trying to maximize its long-term profits does not really tell anyone much about it. Where is the firm going? How is it going to get there? A student who decided that his goal was to maximize his happiness would still have to decide what he was going to do every day in order to achieve this. The same is true of any lower-level executive who decides that he wants to become president of a firm, even if his goal is more clearly defined. How much more numerous, then, are the decisions faced every day by top management in the pursuit of profit.

There are many ways in which management may narrow the scope of its daily alternatives. One way is to clearly identify the responsibilities of key managers. A level of management that knows it is in charge of improving the supermarket division, the drug division, or the men's clothing division can

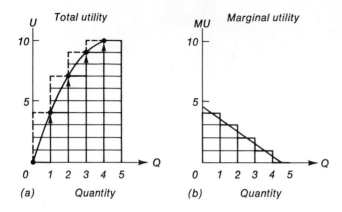

Figure 11.1   Total utility and marginal utility
[Source: *Paul A. Samuelson*, Economics: An Introductory Analysis *(New York: McGraw-Hill, 1967), p. 418.*]

his money. The second unit of that good to the same consumer at about the same point in time will probably increase the total utility to the consumer but the increment will be less than the first unit. Indeed, under most circumstances each extra unit of a given good will give less additional utility to the individual than the previous unit. The utility of the additional unit is here called the *marginal utility*. This aspect of utility is illustrated by Figure 11.1.

If a consumer is faced with a choice between two or more goods at the same price, his rule in general should be to select that item which offers him the greatest satisfaction. If the prices are different, the consumer might compare the utility of each good to its price. If the ratio of utility to price is the same in each case, the consumer will be indifferent—that is, he will conclude that he cannot better himself by selecting one good over the other. The choice can then be expressed arithmetically as follows:

$$\frac{\text{Incremental Utility Good 1}}{\text{Price Good 1}} = \frac{\text{Incremental Utility Good 2}}{\text{Price Good 2}}$$

Of course, this technique depends on various assumptions, one of which is that the utilities can be considered separately. But it has many practical applications in marketing and retailing. For example, imagine that a retail manager is trying to decide whether additional budget monies should be put into additional advertising ($X1$), additional salesmen ($X2$), or additional merchandising research ($X3$). The manager might estimate the incremental cost of a reasonable amount of each alternative (he will have to depend on his own subjective judgment of what is "reasonable"). If he can then estimate the incremental profit related to the cost of equally reasonable amounts of $X1$, $X2$, and $X3$, he should in general select that alternative with the highest ratio of profit to cost. In this example, it is assumed that the productivity of market research and personal selling does not change as the level of advertising increases, and so forth. It is also assumed that the ratios do not change over the relevant range: for example, if $400 worth of advertising is deemed a

at least focus its energies directly on that particular task. But other goal problems will remain. Shall management try to maximize short-term sales volume, or should it concentrate on short-term profits? Perhaps their share of the market in certain localities is what they should really worry about. Or perhaps it is the acceptance of their private brand over the short term, or the attitude of customers toward their store. Many of these goals are conflicting, at least at times. In case of conflict, the executive must make choices or be told what to do by others. He may well have to establish his own priorities.

Marginal analysis has substantial value in decision making. It can be used for long-term or short-term decisions, though its main application is to maximize short-term profits. This chapter outlines a variety of marginal concepts and indicates some of their limitations.

### Marginal Utility

If a consumer has one dollar to spend, he should spend it for that item or combination of items that will offer him the greatest utility or satisfaction for reasonable amount, the productivity of the first $100 is no greater than that of the last $100. In other words, a decision maker should select that factor or group of factors that will add most to the short-term profit of his firm.

But things are not as simple as this. Clearly, as the amount of advertising or other cost factor is increased, there comes a point at which the resulting profits begin to decrease. In other words, the ratio of profit to cost will change as the amount of advertising is varied. One way to handle this is indicated in the following example. Let us assume that we are the operators of a bicycle department in a large discount chain. We have received an incremental budget of $24,000 to promote our product in our geographic area. We feel that the three ways to increase the sale of our bicycles are increased advertising, increased personal selling, and merchandise research into the preferred styles of bicycle. We would like to undertake all three activities, but are not sure how much to spend on each. For simplicity we are assuming that the dollar profit from each bicycle is the same. After some analysis and a great deal of guessing, we estimate that increments of $3,000 spent on each activity will yield the following matrix:

|            | Advertising | Selling   | Merchandise Research |
|------------|-------------|-----------|----------------------|
| $ 3,000    | 300 bikes   | 250 bikes | 200 bikes            |
| $ 6,000    | 650         | 475       | 400                  |
| $ 9,000    | 875         | 700       | 600                  |
| $12,000    | 1050        | 850       | 800                  |

In other words, with $3,000 worth of additional advertising we anticipate selling 300 additional bikes and with $6,000 worth 650 − 350 more than with $3,000. With $3,000 more spent on selling, we anticipate selling 250 more bicycles, and so forth. The inputs for the ranges past $12,000 are not considered because it is assumed that each would continue declining in about the same fashion and therefore not be relevant.

If we assume that there is no relationship among our three activities and that our subjective estimates are correct, the maximum number of additional bicycles will be sold if our $24,000 budget is allo-

cated $9,000 to advertising, $9,000 to selling, and $6,000 to merchandise research. The key to the analysis is to think in terms of differences. Thus the difference between a $6,000 input into selling and a $9,000 input is 225 units. This is greater than the return from a $3,000 input into merchandising research, which is only 200 units.

### Marginal Cost and Marginal Revenue

Marginal cost and marginal revenue are central concepts in a firm's decision making, at least from a theoretical point of view. Marginal cost is the total cost of producing one extra unit more or less at a specific production level. There is no reason, as Paul Samuelson has pointed out, why the extra unit cannot be in denominations other than one, for example 100.

The following example indicates what marginal costs are:

| Output in hundreds | Total cost (Fixed cost = 25) | Marginal cost |
|--------------------|------------------------------|---------------|
| 0                  | 25                           | 0             |
| 1                  | 40                           | 15            |
| 2                  | 50                           | 10            |
| 3                  | 60                           | 10            |
| 4                  | 75                           | 15            |
| 5                  | 93                           | 18            |
| 6                  | 113                          | 20            |

Marginal revenue, on the other hand, is defined as the increment of total revenue, plus or minus, that results from increasing the production level by one unit.

| Output in hundreds | Price per hundred | Total revenue | Marginal revenue |
|--------------------|-------------------|---------------|------------------|
| 0                  | 50                | 0             | 0                |
| 1                  | 45                | 45            | 45               |
| 2                  | 40                | 80            | 35               |
| 3                  | 35                | 105           | 25               |
| 4                  | 30                | 120           | 15               |
| 5                  | 25                | 125           | 5                |
| 6                  | 20                | 120           | −5               |

It will be seen that the marginal revenue to 100 units exceeds the marginal cost by a substantial margin. Therefore it is more profitable to produce 100 units than zero units. Similarly, the marginal revenue exceeds the marginal costs up to 300 units and total profits are increasing, up to $45. From 300 to 400 units marginal revenue equals marginal cost, and the firm is indifferent between the two output levels. Past 400 units, however, marginal cost exceeds marginal revenue, and profits therefore decrease. At an output of 600 units, profits have been reduced to $10. Since we do not know the marginal cost and marginal revenue for output near 300 and 400 units, additional research might be suggested to pinpoint the specified desired level of output—that is, if the benefit of such research is greater than the cost.

There are numerous assumptions involved in the above analysis, including the following:

All other factors such as advertising are constant or irrelevant;

The range of outputs under consideration is the range that should be considered (here, the range from zero to 600 units of output);

The decision maker can estimate marginal revenues and marginal costs with complete certainty.

Some generalizations can be offered from the preceding analysis. First, no reference was made to fixed costs in developing the optimal price. The reason should be obvious: genuinely fixed costs are irrelevant over the range in which they are deemed fixed. Any variables that do not change with any decision are not relevant to that decision, and fixed costs, literally defined, cannot change. Nevertheless, it has historically been quite difficult for businessmen to accept the concept that fixed costs do not count. Since this is so, the same results are obtained by using profit figures—subtracting fixed costs from the contribution to overhead changes nothing. For example, in our bicycle illustration, nothing is changed if we assume fixed costs of $50, $100, or any other number of dollars. At some point, marginal analysis becomes a means of minimizing losses rather than maximizing profits, but fixed costs that are genuinely fixed are not relevant to the decision.

It should also be noted that marginal revenue

can be negative. As the price is decreased, the production level will increase under most conditions. The marginal revenue over any range of production levels can be obtained by analyzing two kinds of changes:

The loss in revenue from those customers who would have bought at the higher price but now will be able to purchase at the lower price;

The increase in the number of customers brought in by the attraction of the lower price.

For example, if a merchant were to price an item at $10, he might sell 100 units for a total revenue of $1,000. If he were to price the item at $9, he might sell 110 units, for a total revenue of $990—a net loss in revenue of $10. The $10 loss is composed of the loss of $1 a unit for 100 units and the increased sale of 10 units at $9 each.

The latter characteristic of marginal revenue has led to an activity called *skimming the demand curve.* Here, the decision maker tries to charge each segment of the curve the highest price that it will pay. In our example, he might try to sell 100 units at $10, or perhaps in small quantities at even higher prices. Then he might try in some manner to sell 10 units at $9. In our artificial example, this produces a revenue of $1,090. Fashion merchandisers often make efforts to skim the demand curve for certain types of merchandise. High prices are charged at the beginning of a season to customers who will pay the higher prices, and lower prices at the very end of the season. In the automobile industry, the manufacturers tend to reduce their prices to dealers as the year progresses, particularly in the form of specials, while dealers also reduce their margins over the year. This may lead to rather effective skimming of the demand curve. Other methods of pricing are discussed in Chapter 15.

### The Disadvantages of Marginal Analysis

The mathematics of marginalism must always be correct as long as its underlying assumptions are granted. It is, however, very difficult to make the necessary subjective estimates related to the demand curve. Also, many of the variable costs are not easily assigned to their appropriate decision areas, and many of the fixed costs, are not always as fixed as their designation might imply. Other shortcomings of marginalism will be discussed later. Meanwhile, the following will serve to dramatize a key aspect of marginalism as it applies to retail decision making. The lesson to be learned here is that marginalism is accurate only if all the important variables are considered, and if the decision maker can have confidence in his subjective estimates.

Let us suppose that a buyer for a high-quality department or specialty store has recently been graduated from business school, where he was thoroughly indoctrinated with the spirit of marginal analysis. He is trying to decide whether or not to lower the price of an item and advertise a special sale. He believes that there are only two price alternatives: one if there isn't any advertising and one if there is. He produces these figures:

| Price | Invoice plus other costs that buyer estimates vary with volume | Estimated Unit Sales | Cost of Advertising | Dollar Contribution to Overhead |
|---|---|---|---|---|
| 30 | 16 | 200 | – | 2,800 |
| 20 | 16 | 2,000 | 1,000 | 7,000 |

The arithmetic here is obvious: when the price is $30, each unit offers a $14 contribution to overhead, so that 200 units at $14 each contribute a total of $2,800. The contribution per unit at a retail price of $20 is $4, and the estimated unit sale is 2,000, so that the contribution to overhead is $8,000. If the advertising costs $1,000, then the dollar contribution will be $7,000.

The two alternatives may also be compared in terms of changes in costs and revenues. If we start at the $30 price, the increased revenues attached to this change are $40,000 (i.e., 2,000 × 20) − $6,000, (i.e., 200 × $30), or $34,000. The increased costs are 1,800 units (i.e., 2,000 − 200) × $16 (the cost of each extra unit), or $28,800, plus the $1,000 in advertising, which adds up to $29,800. The incremental revenues exceed the costs by $4,200, so that the lower price is

the better of the two alternatives offered. The student will note that this is the same difference in contributions (i.e., $7,000 − $2,800) as in our buyer's arithmetic, shown above.

If the buyer has confidence in his estimates, and there are no unusual factors to consider, then it would appear reasonable for him to select the lower price. If his estimates are substantiated by actual sales, the short-term profits of the enterprise will increase. Presumably the buyer will apply the same type of analysis to other situations. If he succeeds in these, too, other buyers in the store will probably emulate the new business school sensation and their profits may also increase; indeed, one would expect them to. It can be argued, however, that if a store management permits its buyers to use this type of approach indiscriminately, over a long period of time the image of the store will deteriorate. Thus the very asset that made the short-term profits possible may be destroyed. Many would go farther and suggest that such mass price actions by retail decision makers would certainly destroy the firm's image.

If the buyer or top management recognized the image problem, he might conclude that, since he is interested in the long term and the marginal analysis suggested is only short term, he should not bother with such calculations at all. Alternatively, he could try to estimate how much the store's image will deteriorate and make some allowance for it. Unfortunately, he is likely to have difficulty specifying whether the allowance for image should be 5 cents, 50 cents, $5, or $50 a unit. Obviously, such an estimate cannot be made with any degree of confidence, and the decision of which alternative to select will depend greatly on subjective factors.

It is clear that the decision maker must have some confidence in the subjective estimates of the important variables; the value of a variable cannot be assumed to be zero just because it cannot be easily estimated. Thus in the preceding example, the value of the store's image cannot be set at zero just because that assumption facilitates computation. All the important variables must be considered whether they can be quantified or not. Thus where time is important, time must be considered by the decision maker—that is, if he is to have confidence in the results.

### The Multistage Approach

One approach to the above dilemma, as Alfred R. Oxenfeldt has argued, might be termed the multistage approach. This approach first divides the decision into its important elements, then establishes priorities among them. There are several versions of the approach: here the more important elements in the decision become absolute constraints on future stages. Each stage is evaluated in terms of the previous constraints in the following manner:

1. *Selecting customer segments.* Management must begin by selecting the customer segments to which it feels it should appeal. These segments can be developed along many dimensions, whether demographic, socioeconomic, psychological, or other. For example, a specialty women's clothing store might be interested in appealing to customers who "think young," an automobile dealer to all customers within five miles with incomes over $15,000, or a department store to fashion-conscious customers with both taste and money. Appealing to several customer segments necessarily involves neglecting others: for instance, a restaurant designed to attract businessmen with substantial expense accounts will be too expensive for most families.

2. *Establishing store images.* Having identified its customers, the store must establish an image that will appeal to them. Thus our specialty clothing store must develop an image or a set of images that will appeal to customers who "think young," the automobile dealer may need a high service image, and the restaurant will have to have the high-prestige type of image that will appeal to businessmen taking clients out, and so forth.

3. *Establishing a merchandising mix.* Before the store is opened, its external appearance will be created with some estimate as to the effect on the desired customer segments. After it opens, the mix consists of such factors as price, assortment, atmosphere, and availability of credit. Each is given a role consistent with the images thought necessary to attract the desired customer segments. An automobile dealership might want to emphasize high service standards, reasonable but not low prices (since price alone would probably not bring customers to the store), a small but select sales force, and so forth. However, a dealership in a competitive environment trying to draw customers from 10 to 15 miles over an area of equal population density might have to give price, or perhaps credit, a dominant role. In other words, the role for the various elements of the merchandising mix accords with the image that the businessman feels he must have to attract the desired customer segments. For instance, the role of price in our restaurant would be not to repel customers but rather to attract them, since it is unlikely that low price would be much of an attraction to businessmen entertaining important clients. On the other hand, the restaurant would have to have an effectively created atmosphere.

4. *Setting up long-term policies.* The next step is to create long-term policies in light of the roles given to each element of the merchandising mix. Thus a supermarket chain might decide that it will open no new stores with less than 35,000 square feet of selling space. The policy of a candy store might be to add 10 cents a pound to the highest price of candy in the city. This would not only assure the highest prices in the city but would be consistent with the store's policy of having a high-quality image.

5. *Devising short-term strategies.* The retail environment is always changing, and a store's short-term strategies should change with it. For example, you might own a Hallmark card store. One half mile away a card store with Hallmark cards might have a sale at 30 percent off. Your reactions should accord with the decisions made for the previous steps in the multistage procedure.

6. *Setting an activity level.* The sixth and final step is to establish the level of the specific activity. In the restaurant example, the management might look at similar restaurants in other areas and copy their prices, if the *pro forma* operating statements of such restaurants indicate substantial profits. To speak more generally, in pricing, if the first five steps are not considered relevant to a specific situation, then the last step might consist of establishing a price at the point where the marginal cost equals the marginal revenue. Other methods will

be indicated in the chapters covering special activities, such as assortment, pricing, inventory, and advertising.

You may go through every one of these six steps and yet find the resultant profit estimate negative. An entrepreneur may simply not be able to make a living from the desired customer segments. If you have not started the enterprise, you can either adjust your various steps so that you feel you will make a final profit, or you can abandon the enterprise. In the former case, you may want to consider many different customer segments, images, and roles for the various controllable factors until some sort of profitable mix evolves. In the case of an ongoing store, the managers must constantly reevaluate the customer segments to which they are appealing, the images they offer, the roles for the various factors, and so forth. Thus the multistage approach forces decision makers to establish priorities.

The multistage approach has several important advantages. A key one is that it protects a firm's intangible assets, some of them, such as its image, among the most valuable that it has. Relatedly, the multistage approach permits substantial delegation of authority without jeopardizing the firm, since the earlier stages can be outlined by the firm's prime decision makers. The last stage is usually not the critical one, provided that all the previous stages have been dealt with thoroughly. Another advantage is that the multistage approach is actually rather a conservative one, financially speaking; problems such as image are handled without great risk to the firm.

The multistage approach is one answer to the shortcomings of marginalism. Instead of assuming that unquantifiable key variables have a value of zero, because this facilitates computation, it allows them to be absolute constraints on the decision-making process. Neither approach, however, offers anything like an optimal solution, and each requires substantial judgment in its use. Clearly, no progressive firm is going to insist on an unimpaired image if it has to forego huge profit opportunities as a result. Being conservative is an asset, but also a liability. In short, the student need not regard these approaches as mutually exclusive; they offer different, complementary perspectives on decision making.

## Retail Decision Making and Marginalism

The remainder of this chapter is concerned with marginal approaches to retail management. There are many uses for marginal analysis in retail decision making. The main requirement here is that the decision maker be held responsible for short-term profits. If the decision maker is held responsible for two, three, or more goals such as increased or high initial or maintained markup, increased sales, low shortage, and so forth in addition to profit, the use of marginal analysis is difficult since its focus is all on short-term profits. It is possible, as we have seen, to make a firm's higher management control many activities related to the lower levels. These higher-level managers may then create subgoals for the decision makers reporting to them. If they do, they may find that marginal analysis is an appropriate technique.

One way of relating marginal analysis to short-term profits is to hold the decision maker responsible only for contribution to overhead, which necessarily involves not holding him responsible for fixed costs. This has been called the *reservoir concept* in retailing and, as such, was used by some stores in the 1930s and probably before. One interpretation of the reservoir concept is that a store's merchandise area should be charged only for those costs that vary with volume, but should be charged with all costs that do vary with volume, whether it controls these costs or not. Noncontrollable costs may also vary with volume. For example, the costs of receiving will tend to be beyond the control of the merchandise area, but if the manager of the merchandise area doubles his shipments of merchandise to the store, this may raise the store's receiving costs.

One advantage of this concept is that a decision made through marginal analysis that maximizes

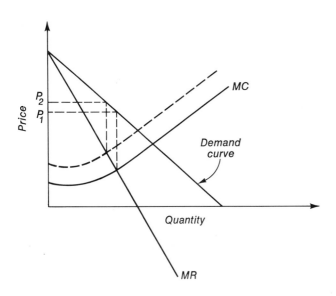

Figure 11.2

the short-term profit of the merchandise area will also maximize the short-term profits of the store.

If the store management allocates an overhead charge based on sales—let us say 7 percent of the sales of the merchandise area—the decision maker for the merchandise area can still use marginal analysis to increase his department's net profits. The percentage in question simply becomes an addition to the merchandise area's marginal costs. If the decision maker is pricing his merchandise by the marginal method, higher prices will result, as shown in Figure 11.2.

The manager who is charged overhead costs as a percentage of sales should adopt the higher price, $p2$. This is the intersection of the increased marginal cost curve (mc) and the marginal revenue curve (mr). However, from the store's perspective, the merchandise area should remain at the price of $p1$. Price $p2$ produces something less than the optimal for the store because costs that do not vary with volume are being considered. Thus in this instance there is a conflict between what is best for the total store and what is best for the individual merchandise area.

The reservoir model has not been accepted in many forms of retailing. It suffers from all the maladies of short-run profit optimization. Many firms have preferred to establish a great many other goals that, in their opinion, foster their long-term interests. Constraints such as increased initial and maintained markup, increased sales, net profits, low shortage, and so forth have often been imposed and have become goals in and of themselves. Another reason that the reservoir model has not taken hold in many forms of retailing is that firms often allocate variable costs to overhead costs simply because it pays them to do so. For example, marking (i.e., affixing prices) would be considered a variable cost by most stores. Some, however, might decide that the costs of getting a charge for this operation by merchandise area may not be worth their while. This is just one example of how fixed costs, far from being really fixed, are often directly related to volume.

Another disadvantage of the reservoir model is that marginal analysis is not particularly easy to comprehend, and that many lower-level managers are simply incapable of applying it. In addition, many sophisticated managers have difficulty buying the concept that fixed costs do not matter.

### Merchandise Management Accounting

The reservoir model can be used with or without the retail method discussed in Appendix D. So, too, can the application of marginalism that will now be discussed. As we have seen, many figures generated by the retail method are averages: this is true of initial markup, maintained markup, and in many instances initial inventory under the retail method. Some retail executives have become preoccupied with these statistics as ends in themselves: for instance, keeping the average markups high may become a goal to many. This type of thinking has lead to high retail prices and created a price umbrella under which the discount stores nicely fit. Since the discount stores did not have the retail method, they escaped this hangup—and proceeded to make inroads into the department store business.

The success of the discount stores forced the department stores to reassess their preoccupation with percentages based on the retail method. They therefore developed a method of applying marginal concepts to the item. This method, which became known as Merchandise Management Accounting (MMA), took many forms in different retail stores, mostly on a test basis, and many retail executives predicted a very bright future for it. Very few stores, however, eventually adopted MMA, and those that did have not been very successful with it. Nevertheless, it merits examination here because it is a very serious effort to apply marginal concepts at the level of the item, which is the level at which most merchandising decisions are made.

The main purpose of MMA is to furnish the decision maker with data on the profitability of various actions related to the item he is purchasing or may purchase. First, the buyer must examine the costs of an item or homogeneous group of items: all the various costs added together are the costs of the item. Given a retail price, one then has an estimate of the item's profitability. An example of this computation is offered in Figure 11.3. The profits at each price level are computed by multiplying the profit per item by the number of items expected to be sold.

**Deficiencies of MMA** Merchandise Management Accounting can be related to any decision area within the firm: its historical emphasis just happened to be on price because the key concern of its inventors was with the arbitrary high prices set in certain merchandise areas of department stores. Since MMA takes so many forms, its deficiencies, some of which will now be listed, are also various.

1. *Neglect of markup.* The inventors of MMA failed to grasp the full importance of markup, one of the maligned "arbitrary" concepts associated with the retail method. It is true that markup is potentially arbitrary. But, as we have seen, it does appear to have a definite place in retailing.

2. *Bias toward lower prices.* MMA is a very dangerous instrument to use in pricing. In addition to being purely mathematical, with all the risks that

involves, MMA does lead to lower prices under certain conditions without appearing to do so. Of course, lower prices are not necessarily a bad thing, but the executive should know that a system based on marginal principles may lead to lower prices in general unless steps are taken to prevent this. Although MMA is a neutral instrument that can indicate either higher or lower prices, the alternative instruments utilized by many types of stores are biased toward higher prices.

3. *Overestimation of marginal costs.* It is difficult to create any system that reflects small changes in costs among products. However, MMA is not as flexible as it could or should be. For instance, one breed of MMA treats selling costs as a standard cost, clearly some type of average. However, a minimum number of salespeople will generally be required to service the area, regardless of volume. In addition, at certain times of the day and week, salespeople will be very busy, while at other times they will have little to do. Thus most stores, regardless of the care with which they establish schedules, have few salespeople who are busy at all times, and many of these times are predictable. The marginal selling cost, therefore, varies with the day of the week and the time of day. Markdowns and advertising expenses are also problematic. MMA sets standards for both by means of averages. The net effect of using these standards is to overestimate the marginal costs. Retailers' expenses are largely fixed in the short run, and the marginal costs are not so large as they are usually represented by MMA.

4. *Failure to define profit.* The goal of MMA was always profit. There was none of the confusion of profit with other goals, such as increased sales, higher markup, and so forth, that characterizes much retail decision making. However, profit is an elusive goal unless clearly articulated. Should a decision maker maximize profits per unit of space, or per dollar invested in inventory? Is there some way he can maximize both? What about other criteria of profit? These problems have never really been resolved by the architects of MMA.

5. *Failure to set priorities.* MMA does not segregate important decisions from unimportant ones; all types of decision within the system are treated in

Department 46–00                    Item *Fur scarf*              Vendor *ABC Co.*

Category C                                                        Date  *2/27/57*

| | | | |
|---|---|---|---|
| Purchase price | $*100.00* | | |
| Discount | *8.00* | | |
| Invoice price | $ *92.00* | $*149.95* | Original retail |
| Less | | | Retail reductions: |
| Inward transportation (1.5%) | $ *1.38* | $ *11.14* | Markdowns (12%) |
| Item advertising | *.—* | *.64* | Shortages (0.7%) |
| Merchandise carrying charges (2%) | *1.84* | *1.38* | Discounts given (1.5%) |
| Receiving, checking, marketing, and transfer hauling | .20 | $ *13.16* | Total retail reductions |
| Delivery | .30 | | |
| Accounts receivable and credit | .03 | | |
| Departmental advertising (3%) | *2.76* | | |
| Buying (4.2%) | *3.86* | | |
| Merchandising (2.6%) | *2.39* | | |
| Selling (8.0%) | *7.36* | | |
| Sales audit | 0.01 | $*136.79* | Net sales |
| Accounts payable | 0.33 | *112.46* | Total costs |
| | | $ *24.33* | Contribution to overhead |

Figure 11.3  Buyer's worksheet for fur department, category C (Source: Malcolm P. McNair and Eleanor G. May, "Pricing for Profit," Harvard Business Review, May–June. 1957, p. 247.)

$$\text{Return on purchase outlay} = \frac{\$\ 24.33}{\$\ 92.00} = 26.4\ \%$$

Number of weeks in stock  *30*

approximately the same manner. The manager, however, can and should take the time to establish or corroborate the costs that are developed for the more important decisions. He cannot take the same time over the less important ones.

6. *Failure to allow for increases in "fixed costs."* MMA does not take cognizance of "fixed" costs that vary over time because of increased volume. Such costs, as we have seen, should really be considered marginal costs. Of course, the increase in cost does

not have to come in the period of the increased volume. Let us suppose that we are running an appliance store. We pay our salesmen 5 percent of the sales they make. Over the past year, this has worked out at $150 per week for each salesman. For various reasons, we now decide to contract with each salesman for a year's work at $150 per week. The new salaries become in some sense a fixed cost of the operation for that period. In addition, the marginal costs, at least according to some interpretations, are reduced by 5 percent of sales. If marginal costs are reduced while marginal revenue remains the same, the two will intersect at a lower price, which will presumably attract more customers, which will make the store more profitable if the existing salesmen can and will process this extra business. If more salesmen are eventually needed, the "fixed" costs will increase in discrete jumps as each one is hired. But it is unrealistic to consider each jump as a change in fixed costs; rather, it should be added to marginal costs. Otherwise a store could make a greater and greater contribution to overhead and yet lose more and more money.

7. *High cost.* MMA is often quite costly in relation to the potential benefits that might be expected from it. In certain instances several man-months have been necessary to install a system.

### The Need for Marginal Analysis

Most large retail organizations are taking advantage of today's computer technology to develop their own information systems. This trend, together with increasing reliance on mathematical techniques, will require the use of marginal systems directed to the level of the item. Such systems will not be confined to pricing or any other single use, but will offer information of relevance to many decision areas. Thus a decision maker can use marginal analysis to calculate the benefit or loss from any increase or decrease in cost. It will make little difference whether he is weighing additional advertising monies, the value of a supplier concession, the

value of another salesman or clerk, or the salary to offer a new employee; he will have to use marginal analysis if he desires to make the decision in an analytical framework. Many of these uses will be discussed in Part Three of this book.

A decision maker may also need marginal analysis in making comparisons between two alternatives. In certain instances he may find it enough to compare the alternatives by multiplying the markup of each by the relevant estimated sales and then subtracting the resulting products one from another. This method, however, does not always give the information as accurately as might be desired, since it assumes that the alternatives do not differ much in cost structure and markup. If greater accuracy is desired, marginal analysis may have to be used. For instance a decision maker may want to use it in comparing various vendor concessions; in comparing a given set of layouts or displays for an area of a store; in deciding which item to promote; in adding items to or subtracting them from a given merchandising line; and in comparing alternative uses for a given space.

At the item level, marginalism may be necessary to establish when merchandise should be reordered. A store might want to be in stock on high-profit items almost all the time, but might not be so interested in stocking very low-profit items. Seasonal factors are important here: at Christmas time, a store may be willing to take more of a risk on high-profit than on low-profit items. Marginal analysis at the item level can also refine many methods of pricing.

Many different types of system using marginal techniques could be created. It would appear, however, that any system that is going to be successful for most parts of retailing will have to develop a specific goal that is subject to other constraints developed by management.

### Summary

1. Presumably an individual does something because he feels that the benefits of the action exceed

the costs. Or, from another perspective, because he feels he gets more benefit per unit of input from the thing he does than from the thing he decides not to do, granting certain assumptions. Economists have always stressed that a firm should increase output until the marginal costs equal the marginal revenue. "Marginal cost" is defined as the total cost of producing one extra unit more or less at any production level $q$; it is developed by subtracting the total dollar costs of adjacent outputs. "Marginal revenue" is defined as the increment of total revenue, plus or minus, "that results from" increasing $q$ by one unit.

A. For a marginal equation to be accurate, all important factors must be considered and the decision maker must have some confidence that he can estimate or develop ways to estimate the value of each important factor. And marketing decisions have a great many factors—perhaps hundreds of them—that must be considered. Further, some key factors such as image attrition and reaction of competitors are extremely difficult to quantify. Thus while marginal analysis may be the beginning of analytical thought, it has great limitations.

2. One approach to the dilemma of marginal analysis is the multistage approach. Here, the executive first selects the customer segments to which he would like to appeal. Then he establishes a set of store images to appeal to the selected segments. In the third step, he creates a merchandising mix and indicates the roles for each element of it. The retailer can then establish long-term policies in light of the roles given to each element of the mix, the images of the firm, and the selected customer segments. In the fifth step, short-term strategies are developed in reaction to a changing environment. Sixth and last, the level of the specific activity is established.

3. A key experiment in marginal analysis has been merchandise management accounting (MMA). Here, the costs that vary with volume and the incremental revenues are analyzed in an effort to develop profitability at the level of the decision, mainly with regard to items and events. This is a short-term concept and has not been successful. It was developed as a reaction to the arbitrary use of markup in some types of store. Some of the deficiencies of MMA are:

A. Neglect of markup;

B. Bias toward higher price;

C. Overvaluation of marginal costs;

D. Failure to precisely define profit;

E. Failure to set priorities;

F. Failure to allow for increases in fixed costs;

G. Relatively high cost.

## Discussion Questions

1. Define marginal cost.

2. Define marginal revenue.

3. What is the relevance of fixed costs to decision making?

4. What would you do as a decision maker if fixed costs appeared to vary with volume?

5. Can marginal revenue be negative?

6. Why is marginalism primarily a short-term technique?

7. Is short-term profit the best goal for a retail firm?

8. Differentiate between the reservoir concept and merchandise management accounting.

9. Outline the advantages and disadvantages of the multistage approach.

10. What are the deficiencies of merchandise management accounting (MMA)?

## References

Oxenfeldt, Alfred R., "Multi-Stage Approach to Pricing," *Harvard Business Review*, July–August 1960, pp. 125–133.

Samuelson, Paul A., *Economics: An Introductory Analysis* (New York: McGraw-Hill, 1967), p. 439.

### Further Reading

Bell, Herman F., and Moscarello, Louis C., *Retail Merchandise Accounting* (New York: Ronald, 1961).

Clark, Carlos B., " 'Reservoir Concept' Is Keynote of Future Profits," *Retail Ledger,* December 1933.

Dean, Joel, *Managerial Economics* (Englewood Cliffs, N.J.: Prentice-Hall, 1951).

Dickinson, Roger A., "Marginalism in Retailing—the Lessons of a Failure," *Journal of Business,* July 1966, pp. 353–358.

———, *Buyer Decision Making* (Berkeley, Ca.: Institute for Business and Economic Research, University of California, 1967).

Heim, Peggy, "Merchandise Management Accounting: A Retailing Experiment in Explicit Marginal Calculation," *Quarterly Journal of Economics,* November 1963, pp. 671–675.

Jones, Robert I., "Objectives and Basic Principles of MMA," *Journal of Retailing,* Spring 1958.

*Journal of Retailing,* special issue on MMA, Spring 1958.

Wingate, John, and Friedlander, Joseph S., *Management of Retail Buying* (Englewood Cliffs, N.J.: Prentice-Hall, 1963).

### Case History:
### *Music Hath Charms . . .*

Marion Donnelly is about to open a card, candy, and gift shop. She has done most of the work, including creating the fixtures, when she is approached by the salesman for a company that pipes music all day into shops. The argument of the salesman is basically as follows: His company will pump music into her store 18 hours a day for $5 a month, plus a $200 installation charge. The salesman suggests that the following will be the benefits of the music.

1. The selections were scientifically selected so that tension will be created in a substantial segment of customers. The main way that the person can reduce this tension is to make a purchase.

2. Customers like to hear music and will tend to return to the outlet that offers music because individuals tend to return to places where they have had a pleasant experience.

3. The music will counteract many of the other sounds that are normally a part of business and disturbing to the mood of the prospective purchaser.

4. Employees like to hear music and indeed should work better when constantly exposed to it.

Marion is impressed by certain of the arguments. She asks the salesman to document the benefits in quantitative terms. The salesman cannot do this, but assures Marion that the company has many satisfied customers. He leaves her the telephone numbers of two in towns about 40 miles away. Marion calls the two recommendations. Both indicate that they are pleased with the service. She then asks them to quantify the benefits of the service they had purchased. This neither can do.

### *Discussion Questions*

1. What would you do if you were Marion?

2. What does the multistage approach have to do with this?

# 12

## Capital Budgeting

Capital budgeting is a many-sided activity that includes searching for new and more profitable investment alternatives; investigating market and other considerations in order to predict the business consequences of accepting a proposal or group of proposals; developing models for ascertaining the relative and absolute merits of such proposals; and auditing the results of one's selection. Historically, capital budgeting has emphasized decisions relating to plant and equipment and has been mainly the responsibility of the firm's finance department.

More and more observers are now suggesting that many decisions in marketing and retailing that do not relate to plant or equipment should be dealt with in a capital budgeting framework. In marketing, for example, such major expenses as advertising programs, the development of a sales force, entering a new geographic area, new product development, or the construction of new channels of distribution may have long-range implications that are critical for the firm's survival. Automobile firms, for example, benefit substantially from consumer advertising in years past. Indeed, almost any successful advertising campaign increases a firm's profits two years, five, even ten years after it has ended. Again, changing a firm's distribution channels is often costly, but if it is done effectively the firm may benefit from the change for many years. Thus the key elements of a firm's marketing mix will usually have a time dimension.

The same is true of the merchandising mix—the firm's inventory policy, for example. Thus if a store were to decide to advertise, "Don't say it doesn't exist until you have shopped Orange's Department Store," this may raise the level of short-term inventory required for a substantial period of time. Or a store may offer the customer $5 if it is out of stock on a certain item, which would presumably involve carrying a higher stock of it. Changing to an easier credit policy may have effects that will be felt for many years.

It is clear, then, that certain retailing and marketing decisions fit the two specified criteria for capital budgeting decisions—(a) that they are important, and (b) that they have impact over a period of years. Thus an argument can be made for bringing all important decisions under the control of capital budgeting. For example, in retailing the discounting of supplier bills is a competitor for the resources of the firm. Often a firm will take what is called anticipation. A baseball glove manufacturer might ship gloves to a retailer in November for payment in April. If a retailer pays in November, he will in almost all cases discount the bill to March. Payment of this kind of bill or the continuous payment of such bills competes for the resources of the firm.

It is appropriate, then, to ask that all increments in short-term assets increase the value of the firm, that is, return to it more than the relevant cost of capital. Or, to put it another way, it may pay a firm to decrease its commitment in short-term assets and increase its commitment in long-term assets. For example, rather than increasing the level of inventory in each of its twelve stores, it may be profitable to use the same financial resources to build a thirteenth store. Or while a firm may be able to use its resources to develop short-term alternatives that net returns of six percent on its capital, the stockholders may be able to generate alternatives that pay them 10 or 12 percent. These stockholders might well ask that the money be returned to them in some fashion so that they can invest in other enterprises rather than take a low rate of return on short- or long-term alternatives.

Such emphasis on maximizing the return from assets has led to a feeling in retailing that a decision maker ought to be maximizing the dollar contribution per dollar invested in inventory. The logic of this is compelling. How can an executive argue against selecting the alternative that offers the largest return from his resources? Clearly, if he has invested a hundred dollars in inventory, he will prefer a return of $35 to one of $30, other things being equal. This and other maximizing concepts are discussed later in the chapter.

There are two main reasons why a prospective merchant should familiarize himself with the basic principles of capital budgeting: in order to have them available as aids in selecting and implementing long-range decisions; and in order to enhance his performance as a merchant in certain short-term decisions.

It should further be recognized that most of these principles were developed with plant and equipment alternatives in mind and may not be relevant to other areas such as marketing. Two critical differences between marketing and plant alternatives are: (a) the cash flows from marketing changes are *nonfinite*, that is, the time at which the cash flows will stop is not known and could be very long; (b) cash flow projections for marketing or retailing alternatives are far more *variable*.

To illustrate the nonfinite aspects of marketing changes, let us suppose that a retail organization establishes a wholesale operation to sell to all types of retail stores, including its own. It would be difficult to establish a life span for such an operation. Certainly the payout will probably occur over a number of years, but how many? Five? Ten? Twenty? Most observers feel that a production improvement or the creation of a plant has a predictable finite life. The cash flow of marketing and retail alternatives are also very difficult to predict. For example, misses of 100 percent are not at all unusual for volume forecasts of a new product. For these reasons, it is far from obvious that the capital budgeting tools developed to aid financial management will have much value to retail management in general.

### Marginalism and Capital Budgeting

Many of the techniques of capital budgeting take net flows of cash over a number of years and discount this flow back to one point in time. Thus in the following example, the boxes represent net cash flow over time for an investment of $x$ in $A$ as compared with one of $x$ in $B$.

|  | 1975 | 1976 | 1977 | 1978 | 1979 |
|---|---|---|---|---|---|
| Alternative A | 5 | 4 | 3 | 2 | 1 |
| Alternative B | 1 | 2 | 3 | 4 | 5 |

Comparisons of alternatives at one point in time may then be made. These cash flows represent the total inflow and outflow of cash within each period of time. They are variable in the sense that fixed costs are not considered, only the flow of cash.

Capital budgeting has other features in common with marginalism. For instance, in order to be effective, capital budgeting should usually require the decision maker to adopt a profit-maximizing criterion that is subject to certain constraints. One of the commonest is that no investment be accepted by the firm that returns less than the cost of capital. Capital budgeting is also critical to some aspects of marginal analysis because in instances where time is important, capital budgeting must be used to establish the value of inputs for the use of marginal analysis. In addition figures may have to be formulated so that decision makers can be charged for the use of short-term assets, perhaps the cost of capital.

### Approaches to Capital Budgeting

Capital budgeting models are generally designed to permit comparability among investments that produce cash flows over several or many years. Most methods of capital budgeting divide net cash flows into periods, usually years. Often a discount rate for these cash flows is developed. The most frequently used discount rate is called the *cost of capital.* Cash flows with a rate above (or below) the cost of capital will raise (or lower) the value of the firm. Let us assume for the moment that we know how to compute the cost of capital (the method itself is discussed below). Let us also assume that our calculations can be made with certainty. Methods can be established to handle risk, but this is not essential to the purposes of this chapter.

The reader should be aware that none of the models that will be offered is universally applicable nor intended to be so; all make assumptions about the real world and are simplifications of that world. It is up to the decision maker in a given instance to decide which model or group of models is relevant to his needs.

### Payback

The payback period is the length of time required for a stream of net cash proceeds to equal the initial cash outlay for a particular investment or group of investments. Thus under certain conditions an investor will accept a proposal that pays him back in three years as opposed to one that pays him back in four. The implication is that under such conditions, the shorter the payback period the better. This is a technique that is frequently used by businessmen and just as frequently condemned in the academic world. It is illustrated for three alternatives in the following table:

| | Investment outlay | Year 1 Net cash | Year 2 Net cash | Year 3 Net cash |
|---|---|---|---|---|
| Alternative A | 10,000 | 10,000 | 5,000 | 0 |
| Alternative B | 10,000 | 8,000 | 8,000 | 8,000 |
| Alternative C | 10,000 | 0 | 10,000 | 20,000 |

For alternative A, the payback period is one year; for alternative B, one year and three months; for alternative C, two years. It is clear that the flows in year three do not influence any of the payback periods because by year three the end of the period has in each case been reached. Thus one of the method's limitations is that flows after the payback period are not considered. Also left out of consideration is the time value of money. Under most assumptions one dollar today is worth more than one dollar five years from today, if only because today's dollar can be invested over the next five years. The payback method does consider the time value in the sense that cash flows will count if they occur before the payback period, while earnings after the payback period will count for nothing. The method has other limitations, but since it is seldom regarded as a precise instrument these will not be explored here.

The payback method has advantages other than its simplicity. First, it is a conservative approach. If an investor does emphasize being paid back and indeed achieves little more than that, he has not lost money except in the sense that he might have made more in alternative endeavors. He is, however, still financially healthy. In addition, intelligent projections can often be made about the payback period, since it is generally limited to the nearer years. Further, many investors appear to have a different utility for the money after the payback point has been reached than before. In some sense, the investor is risking money before the payback period and perhaps not as much afterward — or if his risk is the same, at least his perception of it is different. A second advantage of the payback method is that it deals with a dimension that is of interest to nearly all sophisticated investors and is not readily measured by other techniques, namely, the payback period itself. It therefore complements other methods. For example, what investor would not be interested to know that in two years he will not only get all his money back on his investment but will have an excellent chance of making more money? Clearly this is not the only dimension in which he is interested, but it is an important one. Third, the limitations of the payback method are manifest to all sophisticated decision makers, which is certainly an advantage. For example, while in our illustration the payback period is shortest for alternative A, few decision makers would choose A because the figures under most sets of assumptions indicate that it would not be the best choice.

### Net Present Value

The approach known as *net present value* requires the establishment of a discount rate for the net cash flows in each period — usually, the cost of capital. Arithmetically, net present value *(NPV)* is expressed as follows:

$$NPV = \sum_{n=0}^{t} \frac{A_n}{(1+d)^n}$$

where  $d$ = discount rate
$A$ = net cash flow for the year
$t$ = time period in years
$n$ = number of years

If the discount rate is 10 percent, and if the flows for each year, over a four-year period, are $10,000, the present value of the alternative will be

$$NPV = \frac{\$10,000}{(1.10)} + \frac{\$10,000}{(1.10)^2} + \frac{\$10,000}{(1.10)^3} + \frac{\$10,000}{(1.10)^4} .$$

Some type of ranking of alternatives can be attained here by dividing the net cash inflows by the initial cash outlay.

It may be useful to examine some of the assumptions involved in the net present value approach, primarily because of the good reputation it enjoys among both academics and businessmen, but also because it is a good example of a model designed for use in the business community. The principal assumptions are as follows:

1. *Cash flows worth the same after cutoff point.* The net cash flows are reflected over the total life of the asset; or all flows for each alternative are equal past the cutoff point, perhaps 10 years; or the cost of capital is so large that the flow in far-off years, when discounted, becomes meaningless. Thus in our previous example, only four years were considered. In this example, if net cash flows are expected in years five, six, and so forth, then the net present value offered is incorrect by these amounts. If the cost of capital is low, for example 5 percent, the flow from years 10 to 20 can be quite significant in establishing value. But if the cost of capital is high, for example 25 percent, then the flows in year 20 or so will be insignificant. This assumption is critical, because marketing and retail alternatives do not usually exist for a known period of years. Furthermore, as projections are made farther and farther into the future, the reliability of the estimates decreases. Indeed, there is a temptation to assume that the value in far-off years is zero. But, as we saw in our discussion of marginal analysis, important variables may not be omitted just because the mathematical computations are simplified thereby. Thus in instances where flows past a cutoff point are going to be important, some mechanism must be found to take account of them.

2. *Cost of capital assumed constant.* In the particular version of the net present value technique specified here, the cost of capital is used as the discount rate for the net cash flows. The assumption is that the cost of capital remains constant over the life of the alternative. With the dramatic changes in

the interest rates over the past few years, a decision maker would certainly not expect a constant cost of capital, even though the assumption may not do great violence to his conclusions.

3. *Reinvestment at discount rate.* The cash inflows are reinvested at the *discount rate*, here the cost of capital. In some instances, a firm may have to reinvest incoming cash at less than this. Hopefully, the funds can be reinvested at something above the cost of capital. This assumption becomes particularly important when considering flows over differing time periods.

4. *Unimportance of earnings pattern.* Cash flow patterns over the time range considered are deemed unimportant. In addition, no emphasis is put on achieving any particular earnings pattern for the firm. For example, a board of directors might want to show a regular increase in earnings per share in the hope that investors will look more favorably on the stock and bid the price of it to higher levels. But the net present value technique, at least on this interpretation of it, cannot be adjusted to express such a preference.

5. *Future profits translate into stock prices.* Most methods of capital budgeting maximize profits to the stockholder in that they assume the stock market will translate all the company's profits, both long- and short-term, into appropriate stock market prices. As soon as this assumption is dropped, several awesome problems present themselves. One is that there may be a conflict between the stockholders' short-term and long-term interests. And indeed management may have to choose between short-term and long-term profits. For example, the stockholders of a company that went deeply into color television in the 1940s were unlikely to be rewarded in the short term; their reward probably did not come until the 1960s, and not all stockholders want to wait that long. Clearly, when top management considers the stockholder interest, it must decide which stockholders it means.

6. *All promising alternatives to be pursued.* Another assumption of the technique is that all alternatives appearing to offer a positive net present value should be pursued so long as the firm has the necessary resources. There is no easy way to handle this

problem: how long, after all, should one delay making a good investment? Perhaps a decision maker can work out some rule of thumb by which he waits for a certain period to see if a more attractive opportunity comes along.

7. *Concentration on profits.* Another assumption of most methods of capital budgeting is that profits are a main goal and that other factors—if considered at all—are constraints. A firm could have a goal of satisfactory sales growth subject to profit constraints; indeed several companies do have goals of this nature. And it cannot be proved that this type of goal is not in the best interest of the firm.

8. *Constant dollars.* A final assumption is generally that the net cash flows are in dollars of the same value. However, multiplying each net cash flow by the relevant price weight (perhaps a Consumer Price Index) easily solves this problem.

If the previous assumptions are justified, or nearly so, then the net present value technique should provide reasonable rankings of alternatives as well as a cutoff point for the investments considered.

### Internal Rate of Return

The discount rate that reduces the net cash flows associated with a project to a net present value of zero is known as the *internal rate of return*. This may be expressed mathematically as:

$$0 = \sum_{n=0}^{t} \frac{A_n}{(1 + d)^n}$$

The symbols are the same as those in the equation for net present value except that one solves for the rate, here *d*. Unlike net present value, however, this technique assumes that all the flows of cash that come in each year are reinvested at the rate of return. While there are certain inconsistencies in this approach, it has most of the limitations and advantages of net present value, which it otherwise resembles.

### Simulation

A fourth way of evaluating investment alternatives is to see how profits and other factors vary over time as investment mixes and other aspects are changed. This can be done by means of *simulation*. Simulations try to answer the question "what if?" and generally involve use of the computer. They can therefore be costly. They may also require some mathematical knowledge to construct, although managers should grasp the results with relative ease.

## Cost of Capital

At one time the cost of capital was not considered a crucial subject. For many years economists assumed that if a firm would earn more from an investment than the cost of borrowing the money in the markets, then the firm should invest. This seemed to make sense, because earnings are bound to increase if an investment returns more than the cost of the money borrowed to make it.

But as a firm borrows more and more, the interest rate it pays will also increase, at least under most assumptions. It will increase because investors will be more skeptical about the firm's ability to repay its debts. Indeed, at some point a firm may be forced to sell additional *equity*. And equity funding tends to cost more than a low rate of interest. Thus earnings that are only slightly better than the interest it is paying may actually hurt the value of the firm. Cost of capital is a rate introduced so that a firm will know when its value is decreasing. A cost of capital, as Myron J. Gordon has pointed out, has the property that an investment with a rate of return above (below) this rate will raise (lower) the value of the firm.

A decision maker might regard the cost of capital as the rate of return that he can get from other investments that he is not making. In other words, it makes some sense to think of the cost of capital as the rate of return from investments that would be accepted if the investment under consideration was not. Of course, this is vastly oversimplified.

It appears obvious that the cost of capital should also vary because different uses of funds often involve different degrees of risk. Thus a firm would probably not give up a certain flow of 8 percent if it could borrow the funds only for this purpose at 5 percent even if the overall cost of capital were deemed to be 10 percent. Not all the uses made of a company's funds involve the same level of risk.

So far we have considered mainly investment proposals in which time is considered important. But, as just suggested, if cash flows must create a rate of return above the cost of capital in order to increase the firm's value, it is clear that short-term decisions should offer a return above the cost of capital—that is, if all relevant long-term factors, including, for example, the image of the store, are considered. This generalization would probably be accepted by all observers. Its application, however, is quite difficult. In addition to all the problems associated with using marginalism, the decision maker has the problem of establishing the cost of capital.

It would also appear that the risk in many short-term decisions would be lower than the risk associated with most long-term decisions, and one would therefore expect a correspondingly lower cost of capital. It would appear to be less risky for a firm to increase its level of inventory under the direction of a knowledgeable manager than for it to invest in fixed equipment. But, as I have argued elsewhere, what the level of this cost of capital is, or how it is calculated, are other questions entirely.

One short-term approximation of a cost of capital that many retailers find useful is *imputed interest*. This is the paper charge percentage made by the firm to a merchandise area for inventory that it holds, even though the store may not have to go out and either borrow or offer securities to pay for the inventory. For example, five individuals might contribute $100,000 each to start a clothing store. Of the $500,000, some $300,000 might be allocated to inventory. Up to $300,000, then, no money need be borrowed. But interest might be imputed to the merchandise so that the decision maker knows that holding merchandise costs money. The imputed interest rate is usually higher than the rate that a large, well-financed store could obtain from debt financing in the open market.

### Maximizing Criteria

It is logical from the stockholders' point of view to pursue only those investments that increase the value of the firm, and to select the ones that offer the largest profit per unit of input. This is often thought of in terms of maximizing the return on investment, or ROI for short. As applied here, ROI is a short-term concept and suffers from all the maladies of short-run profit maximization.

A decision maker could try to optimize profit increments for any unit of input, for example per salesman. And indeed many retail organizations do develop figures on sales per salesman by merchandising area. They do not, however, regard this as an optimizing criterion in and of itself; it is just a tool that is used to complement other profit-maximizing criteria. In contrast, an optimizing criterion that does have some support among retailers is that one should maximize the profit per dollar invested in inventory. There appear to be several reasons why inventory was selected. First, it is a critical element in the merchandise mix of most types of store, and the largest short-term dollar expenditure over which the decision maker has some control. Second, in many small outlets the dollars that can be spent for inventory are fixed, or nearly so. Indeed, over the short-term inventory level may be just as rigid a barrier as the amount of space. Under such circumstances it becomes critical to maximize the limited number of dollars available for inventory. Third, it is not unusual for a piece of merchandise to stay on the shelf an average of three months. If accounts receivable are also considered, the time before the cash is returned from inventory may be quite long. The dollars of inventory are not returnable within a few days of the expenditure in most types of stores. However, the dollar amount of imputed interest is usually not large when compared to the dollar cost or retail price of the merchandise.

Again it should be stressed that merchants in many types of outlets have been computing sales-to-stock ratios for years, so that inventory management is in no sense new. These ratios have been used as tools for comparing the performance of many merchandise areas. But the concept of trying to maximize profits centered around inventory is relatively new, fostered by the increased information delivered by the computer. As an example of such inventory management, let us assume that there are two small merchandise areas A and B, over time X. The figures of each area are given in the following table:

|  | Area A | Area B |
|---|---|---|
| Gross margin | 10,000 | 10,000 |
| All expenses that vary with volume, excluding inventory costs | 4,000 | 4,000 |
| Rent | 2,000 | 2,000 |
| Contribution to overhead after rent | 4,000 | 4,000 |
| Inventory | 5,000 | 2,500 |
| Contribution per dollar invested inventory | .8 | 1.6 |

Other things being equal, area B has contributed the same amount with half the inventory commitment. Thus the profits generated from area B are worth more, under most assumptions, than those from area A because they were achieved with a smaller inventory investment. Indeed, if a firm only had $50,000, to invest in inventory, whether because of lack of credit or for some other reason, the profits generated from a whole series of area Bs would be far greater than from a series of area As. This is true not only of small firms; most firms would encourage their decision makers to stock more B-type merchandise.

A key problem of the contribution per dollar invested in inventory is the allocation of the rent factor. Dollar rent changes can balance the different value of space so that each inventory dollar is evaluated on an equal basis. However, it is highly difficult within a merchandise area to say that one part of the department space is worth $10 per square foot and another $20. And yet this must be done to fairly evaluate merchandise areas on contribution per dollar invested in inventory. Some areas—the main floor, say, as opposed to the eighth floor—are simply worth more to the store than others because they attract more customers.

A more useful approach is to maximize the contribution to overhead per unit of space, whether the unit is a square foot, a cubic foot, or something else. The rent problem is not solved, but it has at least been made tractable. Management must then either assess a rent factor, or ask itself the question, Is the difference in productivity per square foot the result of merchandise performance or difference in location? Or is it due to chance—or some other factor? Another reason for favoring this approach is that, for most merchandise areas in a retail store (or the entire store, for that matter), space is in a manner of speaking "more fixed" than inventory. Thus it is critical for a decision maker to get as much out of each unit of space as possible. The following illustrates how one space concept might be used:

|  | Area C | Area D |
|---|---|---|
| Gross margin | 35,000 | 35,000 |
| All expenses that vary with volume | 20,000 | 20,000 |
| Contribution to overhead | 15,000 | 15,000 |
| Number of square feet | 1,000 | 500 |
| Contribution per square feet | 15 | 30 |

Here, the productivity per square foot is greater in area D than in area C. This difference might be accounted for by the difference in the value of the respective space or other factors. But in contiguous spaces some reallocation of the merchandise effort is usually warranted to increase the amount of space devoted to merchandise in area D.

If the decision maker maximizes contribution per unit of space, the cost-of-capital question must be met directly, because he must be charged for using the inventory. In other words, he must be charged an imputed interest. Again, the dollar amount of this charge is not large when compared to the cost or the retail price of the merchandise.

It would appear to this author that as retailers get more used to computers, stores will prefer to maximize the contribution to overhead per unit of space rather than the contribution per dollar invested

in inventory. It should be emphasized, however, that many retail organizations already have adequate means of evaluating both their use of inventory and their use of space. Among these are the sales-to-stock ratios alluded to earlier. Many firms also regard sales per square foot as quite an effective indicator. It is impossible to say which of all these is the best: profit maximization, at least as discussed in this chapter, is a short-term goal and often of limited value in fostering a company's long-term success.

### Other Relevant Ratios

Stores often compare each others' performances, either in their own chain or in a common trade group. Most operating figures have more meaning when compared to figures of other similar operations. These comparisons can be made by industry, chain, store, or department. For example a chain might be interested in how well it used its assets compared to another chain. If its capital budgeting procedures have been effectively implemented over time, its net profits should be high when compared to its total assets. This simple ratio should offer the chain some idea of how it has done.

It may also be useful to think of this ratio as a combination of two other ratios:

$$\frac{\text{Net Sales}}{\text{Total Assets}} \times \frac{\text{Net Profit}}{\text{Net Sales}} = \frac{\text{Net Profit}}{\text{Total Assets}}$$

In other words, capital management may be thought of as Net Profit/Total Assets, being the result of the interaction between sales management (Net Sales/Total Assets) and margin management (Net Profit/Net Sales). Clearly, profitable combinations of these elements may be developed in several ways. The discount store, for instance, has historically developed extremely high sales when compared to assets. Its margins have been lower than those of department stores, but the interaction between the two ratios has given many discount houses rather attractive net profits in relation to their assets.

Some would suggest that the acid test for management is the volume of net profits that it can generate over the years compared to the firm's net worth. This ratio can be obtained as follows:

$$\frac{\text{Net Profits}}{\text{Total Assets}} \times \frac{\text{Total Assets}}{\text{Net Worth}} = \frac{\text{Net Profits}}{\text{Net Worth}}$$

Thus while it is important to develop substantial profits with regard to net worth, this ratio is also dependent on the ratio of total assets to net worth. This might be termed a leverage factor (the ratio of debt to equity) and depends on the capitalization of the firm. Thus if a firm borrows a great deal, the returns on the nonborrowed portion (the equity, or the amount owned by the stockholders) may be higher. The returns will be higher if the firm earns more than the interest from the investments generated from the debt funds.

## Summary

1. Time is an important aspect of many retail decisions. When a store is built, a return over many years is anticipated. When a training program is created for executives, the payoff will usually be in the long term. Advertising policies are relevant to the firm's long-term survival.

2. Capital budgeting is a many-sided activity that includes searching for profitable investment alternatives; predicting the profit consequences of accepting a proposal; developing methods of ascertaining the relative and absolute merits of each proposal; and auditing the results of the acceptable alternatives.

   A. Historically, capital budgeting has been thought of as relating to very long-term decisions. In recent years, however, observers have suggested that short-term assets such as inventory and accounts receivable often compete for resources with long-term alternatives such as new

stores. Thus capital budgeting techniques must be used to compare short-term and long-term alternatives.

3. Various approaches to capital budgeting are outlined, including the following:

   A. The payback is the time break-even point, i.e., the time period in which the firm gets its money back from a given investment alternative.

   B. The net present value technique discounts the net cash flow over a period of years back to one point in time.

   C. The internal rate of return is the discount rate that reduces the net cash flows over time associated with the project to zero.

   D. Simulation builds models of the process and then examines the effects of changes in inputs on the outputs.

   All of the above approaches have advantages and disadvantages. All are simplifications of a very complex environment.

4. The money that a firm uses costs something. If a firm borrows money, it will have to pay interest charges. In addition, as a firm borrows, its liabilities increase, and its value may therefore decrease. Thus most observers would put the cost of borrowing at something more than just the interest rate. Further, at some point in time the firm may have to go to the equity market. And the costs of equity are usually high when compared to the costs of interest.

   A. One way to look at the cost of capital is as the rate of return from investments that are not accepted at a given level of risk. The cost of capital should vary with the degree of uncertainty.

5. Two key maximizing criteria are discussed. A decision maker may choose to maximize contribution per unit of space. This makes sense if space is the most inflexible constraint. On the other hand, some managers might choose to maximize contribution per dollar invested in inventory.

   The student should be cautioned that this chapter just provides an introduction to capital budgeting, which is an extremely complex aspect of financial management. Further study is recommended in the finance department.

## Discussion Questions

1. What is capital budgeting?

2. Why should capital budgeting be considered in a course in retail management?

3. How do the short-term aspects of capital budgeting relate to the long-term ones?

4. What are some of the advantages of the payback method of capital budgeting?

5. Describe the limitations of the net present value technique of capital budgeting.

6. Indicate the relevance of marginalism to capital budgeting.

7. Define "cost of capital."

8. What are the advantages of maximizing contribution per unit of space?

9. What are the advantages of maximizing contribution per dollar invested in inventory?

## References

Dickinson, Roger A., "Department Stores Should Retain a 6 Percent Imputed Interest on Inventory," *Journal of Retailing,* Spring 1964, pp. 8–12, 61–62.

Gordon, Myron J., *The Investment, Financing, and Valuation of the Corporation* (Homewood, Ill.: Irwin, 1962), p. 218.

## Further Reading

Beckman, E., "Problems of Calculating the Return on Investment," *Journal of Retailing,* Summer 1968, pp. 3–16.

Bierman, Harold, Jr., and Smidt, Seymour, *The Capital Budget Decision* (New York: Macmillan, 1971).

Edwards, Ward, "Behavioral Decision Theory," *Annual Review of Psychology,* vol. 12 (Palo Alto, Ca.: Annual Review, Inc., 1961), pp. 478–480.

Howard, John, *Marketing Management Analysis and Planning* (Homewood, Ill.: Irwin, 1963).

Solomon, Ezra, *The Theory of Financial Management* (New York: Columbia University Press, 1963).

Van Horne, James C., *Financial Management and Policy* (Englewood Cliffs, N.J.: Prentice-Hall, 1968).

## Case History:
## George Hoffman's Dilemma

By 1956, the discount store revolution had gotten off the ground. The discounters' volume had increased dramatically, and many large department stores were apprehensive about their future. As a result of various pressures George Hoffman, president of a chain of department stores, had decided that he had to meet the discount stores' prices on the nose. This he did, and over a period of three years the volume of his major appliance operation tripled. His immediate problem was what to do with the major appliance department.

Louis Mason, the major appliance buyer, wanted to double the space that he had. He argued that he contributed a tremendous amount to overhead, and that if one used that as a criterion, he had one of the most profitable operations in the store. By 1958, his volume had increased to $3 million in the main store from the 1956 volume of $1 million. In 1958, he had contributed $210,000 to the store's overhead. After considering the 8 percent of sales that was charged as overhead to all merchandise areas, the appliance area had a loss of $30,000 for the operation.

Louis went on to argue that fixed costs were just an accounting device, anyway. They were not relevant to decisions. This he had learned many years ago in business school. Only costs that varied with the given activity should be considered. Second, the volume of the major appliance department had tripled over the last three years, so that his indirect expenses had jumped from $80,000 a year to $240,000. Louis doubted that he cost the store any more in 1958 than in 1956, and he was bringing in a lot of customers for whom he received no credit at all. Furthermore, he was bringing a lot of credit business to the store, and these customers were charged 1.5 percent a month. While Louis had read several reports indicating that the store lost money on credit, again it was not the average that was relevant to this decision but the contribution that his increased credit had brought to the store. And at 18 percent a year this had to be profitable.

The key to Louis Mason's argument was that his contribution to overhead per square foot was very high. The $210,000 contribution was accomplished in 2,000 square feet. This represented a contribution to overhead of over $100 per foot, the highest in that store. It appeared obvious to Mason that the space should be enlarged. He felt that the extra space would contribute $90 per foot, far more than alternative users of it would ever contribute.

By now George Hoffman was thoroughly confused. Obviously, this was a problem related to marginal analysis and capital budgeting, two subjects with which he regarded himself as reasonably familiar. And yet there were some aspects of the problem that bothered him:

1. *Fixed costs were not fixed.* These costs had been creeping upward. While some of the increases were not the result of increased volume, it was impossible to know which costs increased with volume increments of the merchandise areas and which would have increased anyway. Furthermore, most elements of the store did not really keep track of marginal costs. For example, marking the merchandise was clearly a marginal cost, but the costs of finding out what it cost clearly exceeded the benefits, at least for George Hoffman. Thus he did not completely trust the validity of the contribution figures that were offered to him.

2. *The contribution to overhead per dollar invested in inventory might be relevant.* This concept had always bothered him. Three years ago he had attended a top-level seminar at which several con-

sultants had argued that each store should maximize the contribution per dollar invested in inventory. While the concept was obvious on its face, George did not completely buy it. First, the number of dollars invested in inventory for his organization was not fixed. He could get out and borrow against inventory from banks. Or he could obtain greater trade credit. Indeed, in the major appliance department one could operate on negative inventory if one chose to. One could fill the orders from suppliers after the merchandise had been sold—at a substantial cost in contribution to overhead because the prices paid to the supplier were higher—but any return had to be infinite because of the negative stock commitment. So he pretty much decided to forget about the contribution per dollar invested in inventory, although he did note that the appliance department had had very high inventories over the years in relation to its contribution to overhead.

3. *Some factors could not be quantified.* It was impractical to quantify the grounds for his decision with any degree of certainty. How many appliance customers bought other merchandise because the appliance department had attractive prices? In the short term? In the long term?

But he still didn't know what to do about the major appliance department.

### Discussion Questions

1. Is there anything else that George Hoffman can find out at short notice in order to help him make the decision?

2. Would you have granted Louis Mason's request? Give your reasons.

# Part Three

Part Three discusses various elements of concern to and controlled by retail management. All the key elements of the retail firm that can be varied in the short term comprise what is here termed the *merchandising mix*. The retailer must combine the various elements of the mix in the most effective way possible in order to attract customers and suppliers. Certain factors are under the control of the retailer at one point in time and not another. For example, before the lease is signed, the site of the store is very much under the control of management, and afterwards it is not, or not entirely. Factors of this type are not here considered part of the merchandising mix.

The retail manager combines the various elements under his control in order to increase the firm's long-term profits. One way to think of the merchandising mix is as part of the multistage approach. In the multistage approach, the appropriate customer targets of the firm are selected. A set of images that will attract the selected segments to the store are then created. In the third stage, roles for each element of the merchandising mix are established. In the fourth, policies are created for each element of the mix, given the roles of the element, the set of images, and the selected customer targets. Finally, the specific element is set—for example, the specific price.

The management must consider the interaction of the elements of the mix when (a) creating the roles for each element; (b) establishing policies for each element; (c) creating the exact mix. The management is constantly relating one controllable element to the others in a continuous effort to maximize the appeal to the desired customer segments. The struggle to attain the key goals of the enterprise involves all the key elements of that enterprise. The multistage approach will be a recurring theme of Part Three.

## Classifying Elements of the Mix

It may be useful to break down the merchandise mix into parts, for example a goods and service mix, a communications mix, and a physical distribution mix. It should be recognized that any classification of elements of the merchandise mix is artificial because every part of the retail enterprise tends to be related to every other part. For example, salespeople communicate with customers, but also in many instances take care of merchandise, offer a variety of services to the customers, and so forth. Or the assortment of merchandise may communicate to the customer in approximately the same manner as store layout.

There are many purposes for which a decision maker might want to break down the various factors under his control. A meaningful allocation of the activities can be useful for both long- and short-range planning. A meaningful division of activities is useful in developing an organizational structure for the firm. What executives are responsible for what activities? A breakdown of the controllable activities can help a firm develop approaches to the competitive environment. A division of the activities can also help an executive form his perceptions of the firm and other retail firms. The activities of retail firms can be divided in many ways. Indeed, the division of the activities in a firm should vary with the purposes for which the classification is made.

There are many ways of dividing the activities of a retail firm in addition to a goods-and-service mix, a communications mix, and a physical distribution mix. A retail firm might divide its activities into (a) the merchandising package and (b) the service-and-facilitation package. In this particular division, the merchandise is thought to be the key to the profitable operation of the firm. And the individuals who control the merchandise tend to be the most important executives in the store. Such executives might be likened to product managers in a consumer product manufacturing firm. The merchandise package in this instance includes (a) selection of merchandise; (b) supervision of the quantities of merchandise that are bought; (c) control of the merchandise assortment that will be presented to the customers; (d) display of the merchandise; (e) layout of the fixtures to the extent that they are movable; (f) pricing the merchandise; (g) advertising the merchandise.

The second grouping of activities might be termed service and facilitating. None of these is considered critical to the success of the firm unless something is badly taken care of. If reasonably competent executives are in charge of these activities, the firm will be all right; excellence is not required, although naturally desired. The role of these activities is not deemed large in this particular arrangement of activities, which are (a) salespeople; (b) delivery; (c) credit; (d) complaints; (e) accounting; (f) other.

Another classification might be that of (a) buying; (b) selling; (c) facilitating. Under the buying would be (i) selection of the merchandise; (ii) supervision of the quantities of merchandise that are bought; (iii) control of the merchandise assortment that will be presented to the customers. Under selling would be (i) display of the merchandise; (ii) layout of the fixtures, to the extent that they are movable; (iii) pricing the merchandise; (iv) advertising the merchandise; (v) salespeople. Under facilitating would be (i) delivery; (ii) credit; (iii) complaints; (iv) accounting; (v) other.

It may also be useful to think in terms of the store as seen by the customer. Here, the most obvious breakdown would appear to be into (a) what the customer sees or does not see and (b) whether the activity is before or after the sale. Among the visible aspects to many customers before the sale are (i) merchandise assortment; (ii) displaying merchandise; (iii) pricing merchandise; (iv) layout of the fixtures; (v) advertising and promotion; (vi) salespeople; (vii) credit before purchase. Among the visible aspects after the sale are (i) delivery; (ii) performance of the item; (iii) the monthly bill. A great deal goes on in a store that the customer never sees—at least, until something goes wrong. Indeed a poor performance in a nonvisible area can make the area highly visible to all. Some of the nonvisible activities, whether before or after the sale, are (i) physical handling of the merchandise; (ii) accounts payable; (iii) customer complaints; (iv) housekeeping; (v) other.

Each of these ways of classifying activities may have relevance for the creation of particular merchandising mixes for particular firms. Each is a partial truth and represents an attempt by the decision maker to simplify his complex environment so that he may more effectively deal with it.

### Competitive Perspectives on the Mix

Managers design merchandising mixes in order to gain competitive advantages over other firms. Thus the actions or potential actions of other firms must be considered when adopting a merchandising mix. Here, two facets of the competitive struggle should be emphasized.

First, the total channel system may be involved in the competitive struggle. In instances where there is substantial coordination among the manufacturers, wholesalers, and retailers within a channel, the battle is really a channel battle. The store just happens to be the unit of one channel that is considered the front line.

Second, even in instances where substantial coordination among manufacturers, suppliers, and/or retailers is not present, the strength of the suppliers will influence the types of horizontal competition at the retail level. Strong suppliers make distinct efforts to mold the type of competition at the retail level so that it will foster their interests. For example, it may not be in their best interests to have price competition at the retail level. Under most interpretations of the law, a supplier is generally free to select the retailers to whom he wants to sell. Many suppliers do not select retailers who are going to use price as a main element of their merchandising mix. In addition, suppliers may strongly influence advertising competition by offering advertising moneys to the retailer. Thus the competitive struggle between stores is strongly influenced by the general situation of the stores' suppliers.

**Who is the competition?** Retail firms are more direct competitors of some stores than others. A direct competitor is a firm whose activities can take substantial sales from yours and/or vice versa. Certain departments of a large firm may compete with firm X while other departments of the same firm may not. Thus a discount house may find that its major appliance departments are in competition with local department stores in certain areas of the country but not in others. The two prime isolators from competition in retailing would appear to be geography and product difference, although in some sense all retailers compete for the same dollar.

*Perceived competition*    In studying retail competition, it is important to consider the perceptions of retailers. An executive looking at competition would be interested in such factors as the history of this type of competitor; the personalities of its executives; how it has interacted with his own firm in the recent past; its profitability; and so forth.

*Similar types*    Firms that offer approximately the same product lines by approximately the same merchandise methods in the same geographic area are said to be in direct competition. Thus supermarkets are thought to be competitors of supermarkets, department stores of department stores, discount stores of discount stores, and so forth. An alternative hypothesis could be offered that if the product categories are the same, for example ladies' wear or major appliances, the more similar the type of outlet, the less competitive will be the activities of the participants, or, at least, the less rivalrous the activity. Similar types of outlet have similar problems, and generally have established competitive responses to given problems that have been found acceptable by other stores of the same type in the same competitive environment. Department stores have often considered nearby discount stores as more important competitors than nearby department stores, particularly while the former were in their growth stage. In addition, historically similar types of stores have tended to band together to fight the enemy, be it the chain store, the mail-order store, the department store, the discount store, or the discount catalog store. Many substantial retail chains have developed by banding together to fight a common enemy. For example, several major appliance chains have developed in parts of the country to fight the competition of the large discount store and department store chain.

*Similar size*    Just as certain competitors feel a kinship to firms that offer approximately the same product lines by approximately the same merchandise methods, so others will feel a relationship with stores that are alike in other respects—size, for example, or the fact that both are franchises. Small stores have historically felt a common bond with other small stores and often a common hostility toward larger enterprises. The impact of this attitude on competitive behavior is difficult to assess.

*Competition not relevant*    Many stores emphasize their own unit and dollar sales. If these measures of sales increase satisfactorily, the store is assumed to be competitive. Specific competitors are only considered in time of difficulty, and then only until the problem is solved. This latter approach can be a conscious policy of sophisticated decision makers who suggest that the competitive picture in retailing is so difficult to assess that there is little merit in making the effort. Such a position by one firm may induce a similar attitude on the part of competitors, thus making competition nonviolent or at least nonpersonal. Supporters of this view of retail competition can point to the fact that when a large store in a metropolitan area fails, the volume seems to disappear or at least is not usually traceable to the surviving firms. Further, the survival of certain competitors may be essential or desirable to the survival of a given firm because the array of firms in a particular geographic area may offer more appeal to potential customers. This adds a dimension to retail competition that does not tend to exist with other elements of the channel of distribution. Managements often look for a competitive environment in which all stores thrive, with their own store hopefully thriving a little more than the others. In a shopping center, for example, each store's future is generally bound up with that of all the other stores.

*Competitive activity*    Any store's competitive activity centers around rivalry with other stores for the loyalty of consumers. As previously suggested, a store may vary many facets of its operation in order to try to obtain some type of competitive advantage. The actions that a firm may take differ in their competitive impact with respect to at least the following dimensions.

1. *Time.* Some mixes are designed to bring immediate sales results, while others have only long-term effects. Intangibles such as store image are of substantial importance to many types of retail firm. While it is difficult to assess the effect of given mixes on image, it is important for firms with effective images to take the steps necessary to protect them. Stores desirous of maintaining or attaining an effective image will usually have to limit many types of short-range, profitable alternatives.

2. *Reaction of competitors.* Some mixes of retailers will bring an immediate response from competitors. This is particularly true of a lower price on an item that the customers perceive as important. In contrast, a nonprice advertisement might bring no response at all. The response of competitors to a firm's mix will differ both in time and degree.

3. *Distinctiveness.* Some dimensions of mixes—low price, for example—are very easy to duplicate, while others, such as an effective advertising campaign, are not. Imported merchandise from a foreign country may be more difficult to duplicate than domestic merchandise, particularly if it has seasonal connotations.

4. *Ease with which put into effect.* Decreases in price are usually quite easily accomplished. A tradeup campaign designed to raise the price levels

in a store is quite difficult to develop. Indeed, improving the quality of the image of a store is very difficult and in certain situations impossible.

5. *Effect on the market.* In certain markets, particular alternatives such as low price may have lasting effects on the market. Thus a price war in gasoline, once started, is difficult to stop without direct collusion. In the same markets, other types of activity will not disturb the market to any degree nor have any degree of permanence.

# 13

## Assortment and Merchandise Selection

Assortment, as Charles G. Taylor has defined it, is the distribution of the merchandise on hand and on order according to classification, subclassification, style, color, pattern, size, and price. This is a very complicated matter. Consider the following example, taken from a men's shirt department:

. . . [if there were] three men's shirts to be carried in only three classifications, with only three brands in each, with only three price lines in each brand, with only three materials in each price, with three cuff and front types in each material, with three collar styles within each type, with three colors in each style, with nine collar sizes in each color, with three sleeve lengths in each collar size, and with only three units in each sleeve length, there would have to be a total stock of about 177,000 units (John W. Wingate in Taylor, *op. cit.*, p. 17).

A retailer will not usually be able to stock this number of units in one subclassification and must continuously trade one feature off against another —for example, color against fabric. In this way, he will hope to carry a combination of factors that will both appeal to the desired customer segments and be profitable for the store.

### Assortment: Some Perspectives

Assortment can be looked at in many ways. One way is from the overall perspective of the store or perhaps the chain. Robert D. Buzzell and his associates have presented evidence that assortment decisions that are relevant to one store in a chain may not in fact be relevant to the others. Nevertheless, a firm's top managers will usually try to coordinate the merchandise decisions of the various stores so that they will not hurt each other. For example, the decision of one restaurant manager to sell horsemeat steaks might well affect the image of other units in the chain. For the purposes of this discussion, however, the focus will be on one store and its departments.

It is important for a store to establish what overall functions its assortment will serve. Is the total assortment offered by the store going to be so large that customers will want to come a long way to survey it? If questions like this are not considered, a firm will lack good reasons for deciding where or even whether to build new stores, how large they should be, and what proportion of the space in each should be allocated to stock or selling.

The way in which the public perceives a store's assortment may be more important than the assortment itself. Thus a store or one of its departments may desire to create the illusion of a large assortment by mixing a few unusual items with the "meat of the line." A manager may also want to create the illusion of a large assortment without such means, since assortments can be so large that they repel customers instead of attracting them. A television store, for instance, might have 80 or so sets displayed but sell only seven of them in any quantity. It might therefore arrange its floor display so that the customer would be directed to the seven or so best-selling sets. This could be achieved by the configuration of sets, the quality of the antennas, the actions of the salespeople, or other means. In short, large assortments involve extra costs, and a store will do well to concentrate on the impression and avoid the costs.

Another problem is to decide which assortment classifications are relevant to customers' perceptions. One does not always know how the customer perceives additions of merchandise to a department: they may either increase or decrease her perception of the assortment width. For example, let us suppose that a buyer for a department store has added a boat department consisting of one boat to his sporting goods department. Adding this boat may increase the total space allocated to "water goods" to make it the largest for any competitive department store in the city. On the other hand, one or two boats may be a substantially lower number than is offered by competing marine dealers. Having just one boat may give the customer the impression that the store has other merchandise areas in which the selection is not competitive with alternative retail outlets. It will therefore be difficult to state conclusively in such a case that more customers have been influenced positively with regard to the assortment of the store than have been influenced negatively, or indeed how much they have been influenced at all.

Another way of examining assortment is in terms of the store's general appearance. A key role in creating the proper appearance is often given merchandise assortment, perhaps along with fixtures, layout, and display. There may be a certain "look" that is appropriate to a chain of stores and to which the merchandise assortments of each store are supposed to contribute. One store in a chain may also desire to achieve its own special look. A discount store will want to look something like a discount store and a candy store like a candy store. Stores have identity problems just like people. The total look of most stores is critical, and each merchandise area of a store may be called on to enhance the impression given by the whole. The latter impression will depend to a great extent on the initial selection of fixtures and layout, which should be consistent with the firm's overall merchandise objectives. The manager in charge of a given merchandise area is often at the mercy of the fixtures he inherits from his predecessor. A prime consideration of assortment is look. If you want to sell bicycles or mattresses, you had better look as if you are in the business of selling them—unless price is the dominant element in your merchandise mix, which would be very unusual.

Another perspective of assortment should be emphasized. So far this chapter has emphasized the customer and his perceptions of merchandise assortment. We have already seen that the supplier is the key to many successes in retailing. Thus many elements of the assortment must be considered in relation to the supplier. For example, consolidating suppliers often increases profits, sometimes because the remaining suppliers give extra concessions, but also because inventory commitments are lower.

### Space Allocation at the Classification Level

A key to developing an effective merchandise assortment is a well-designed classification system.

The National Retail Merchants Association has defined a classification as "an assortment of units or items of merchandise, which are reasonably substitutable for each other, regardless of who made the item, the material of which it is made, or the part of the store in which it is offered for sale." A classification is usually broken down into subclassifications. The challenge here is to classify and subclassify merchandise so as to isolate variables that are important to consumers. Does the consumer look first at price line, fabric, or style? The purpose of these and similar questions is to create a merchandise assortment organized in a way that will make sense to the customers.

After completing the task of classification and subclassification, the decision maker must allocate his space accordingly. Basically, there are two ways of thinking about this: estimates can be developed by working from the top down; or they can be developed from the item upward. The top-down estimates will be discussed first, although the two approaches are complementary and should be considered together.

**The top-down approach**   One procedure for estimating the amount of space for a given large subclassification is what might be termed the top-down or total store approach. The first step is to estimate the volume for the new store, something that can be done with considerable accuracy, as we have seen. Then trade figures are used to develop what percentage of the store's total dollar volume should fall in each major classification. By multiplying the store's total dollar volume by this percentage, the decision maker obtains an estimate of dollar volume for the classification. This dollar volume divided by the estimated sales per square foot (a figure that can be adapted from trade figures for the classification) yields an estimate of the square footage for the area.

For example, let us suppose that the trade figure for the amount of business likely to be done by the department of a women's specialty store is 11 percent. If the store's estimated total volume is $1 million, then, departmental volume can be estimated at $110,000. If the trade figure for sales by area is $75 per square foot, then one can estimate the amount of square feet by solving

$$\frac{\$110{,}000}{\$75}.$$

Of course, the resulting estimate may be changed for any one of many reasons.

Many chains of stores prefer to use data from their existing stores instead of trade figures, particularly if the more recent stores are doing well. Adjustments are then made for the physical character of the building and any other factors deemed relevant. Adjustments can also be made for known errors in the space allocation of present stores. For example, if the toy department in the most recently created store is doing much more volume than anticipated, and it is thought that increments in the space allotted to toys would add substantially to profits in the new store, such incremental adjustments should be made. Because it can make this kind of comparison, the chain has an advantage over a new single store when it comes to allocating space in a new unit. There is, of course, nothing to stop the single store from looking at the latest edition of many different stores and either choosing the best one to imitate or creating some structure that combines the best features of each. It must be remembered, however, that the building, the fixtures, the layout, and the allocation of space are only a few of the elements that go into creating a successful new store. Accordingly, mere imitation is not a very promising line to take.

**Item-up assortment models**   Assortments can also be developed by working from the item up to the level of the subclassification and classification. Indeed, for most types of retailing, the decision maker will at some point in time have to come down to the level of the item. Granted, it makes sense from some perspectives to increase the assortment for a given merchandise subclassification so long as the benefits from the increase are greater than the costs. However, such a policy is subject to all the negatives of marginal analysis discussed in Chapter 11. One rule of thumb that takes account of this principle is that the assortment of a subclassification should be rearranged until the profit contribution to overhead per unit of space is equal at the margin for all the relevant merchandise areas. For example, if the contribution of the last foot was $35 in the $3 price line and $55 in the $6 price line, the space for the $6 price line might be increased.

Such applications of marginalism can be extended. First, however, let us consider certain general principles that apply to merchandise assortments in many types of retail outlet.

1. *Key factors.* In many types of retailing, there are numerous key factors that the decision maker can vary in attempting to improve the assortment. One is brand; another is price line; still another is color—perhaps the most vital of all, as Taylor has suggested. In some merchandise areas, fabric may be the most important element. Thus if the decision is made to increase assortment, the merchant may have to decide which key factor to stress. Perhaps he should increase his range of colors for each brand and price line; perhaps he should keep his present color mix and increase the number of brands. In either case, he is responsible for ranking these factors or combinations of factors in the way that he feels customers will perceive them.

2. *Preference concentration.* A rule of merchandise assortments is that customers tend to have a distinct preference for a small part of any dimension of the assortment spectrum, for example a few colors. Seldom will colors sell at about the same rate. In one experiment, more sales resulted when stock was maintained on the eight colors that accounted for 90 percent of sales than when stock was maintained on 18 colors but the three best sellers were not in stock.

3. *Key selling price.* Some retailers believe that price lines should follow a bell-shaped curve: the largest assortments, they argue, are created in the medium price lines because the retailer feels that customers will buy more medium-priced items and

spend more on such items. Naturally, the concept of medium price will vary with the store's clientele. Certain stores may regard $3.99 as its key price line, while the equivalent figure at a higher-quality store might be $7.99 for the same type of merchandise. In both cases, a decision maker who believes in the bell-shaped curve will surround the key price lines with lower and higher ones. The customer will then "vote" for the price lines he desires. As previously suggested, a store may consciously try to attract certain types of customer by increasing or decreasing the amount of merchandise carried at certain prices. Clothing size also follows a pattern in which a few sizes will generally account for a much larger percentage of sales than all the others. The bell-shaped curve represents just one way of thinking about price lines. In contrast, as Donald L. Belden has pointed out, certain variety stores stress a "good, better, best" selection for which a reasonable sales pattern might be: good, 40 percent; better, 30 percent; best, 30 percent.

4. *Hot selling items.* No matter what the distribution of price lines, a few items will nearly always sell far better than other items of the same kind. This aspect of merchandising, which has been witnessed time and again in retailing, suggests two things about the creation of merchandise assortments. First, a great deal of effort must be expended to develop hot selling items ahead of the competition. Simply choosing such items for display will increase the dollar sales on the selling floor, but in a great many instances they will first have been aggressively advertised. Second, most of the items in any classification end up complementing its best-selling items. Indeed, the purpose of some items is not necessarily to sell, but to create an environment in which the best sellers can flourish. Table 13.1 illustrates a line —in this case, skin preparations—that is dominated by a few items.

5. *Law of threes.* Displaying too many items of equal attractiveness will only confuse the customer; there is such a thing as too much variety. Many leading retailers display only three lines of any item: good, better, and best. There is much logic in this law of threes, as it is sometimes known. However, it should not be forgotten that one of the purposes of

Table 13.1
*A line dominated by sales of a few items: the case of skin preparations
(hypothetical figures)*

| Annual dollar sales per SKU | Skin Preparations | | | |
| | SKUs carried | | Sales | |
| | No. | % | $ | % |
|---|---|---|---|---|
| $200 or more | 1 | 2.6 | 675.00 | 30.8 |
| $100 to 199 | 3 | 7.7 | 407.00 | 18.6 |
| $ 75 to  99 | 3 | 7.7 | 253.00 | 11.6 |
| $ 50 to  74 | 7 | 17.9 | 457.00 | 20.8 |
| $ 25 to  49 | 6 | 15.4 | 212.50 | 9.7 |
| $  1 to  24 | 19 | 48.7 | 185.50 | 8.5 |
| Total | 39 | 100.0 | 2190.00 | 100.0 |

Note: *Table does not include inventory figures. An SKU is a stockkeeping unit; see page 233.*

the merchandise assortment is to direct the customer's attention to a few exciting items that will look good in relation to the other merchandise.

**Marginalism revisited**   One application of marginal analysis here would be to select those items for an assortment that offer the largest incremental profit per unit of space over some period of time. Such incremental profit is known as *direct profit*; it is usually calculated per unit of space. A decision maker can decrease the space allocated to those items that offer a small direct profit per unit of space and replace them with others offering larger direct profits for the same unit over the same period. Likewise, he can increase the space allotted to the more profitable items. Thus the concept of direct profit per unit of selling space over time can be used to select new items, adjust merchandise areas, and establish assortment mixes. Nor are these all its uses.

There is some evidence that a profit-by-item approach of this type is of some practical use at least in the supermarket industry, where the major portion of the research has occurred. The study by Buzzell and his colleagues tends to support the hypothesis that: (*a*) if shelf space is shifted from an item with a relatively low direct profit per unit of space, then profits for the product group increase; (*b*) if an item with a low direct profit is eliminated and the space assigned to an item with a relatively high direct profit per cubic foot, then the total profits of the

product family also increase. This same study found a substantial variation in direct profit per unit of space for the same items among different stores in one chain.

The studies in the supermarket industry are interesting but not conclusive. Indeed, most of such before-and-after studies in the direct profit area cannot be conclusive because the observer does not know what type of management thinking the profit analysis by item is replacing. Some managements are highly competent; others are not. In the latter case it would appear that any reasonable rules would increase profits. The student should also bear in mind that profit analysis by item rests on the following assumptions, some of which will be familiar from Part Two:

1. *Relations between sales areas are held constant.* Some sales areas undoubtedly exert more attraction than others, and this has an effect on adjacent areas. But this type of analysis takes no account of such effects. Thus if many customers buy peas from a store because it has an outstanding selection of catsup but not vice versa, then the calculations will be off by this much if no allowance is made. In certain types of retailing, managements actually expect substantial relationships between areas. Indeed, merchants in today's department stores often feel that the dollar volume of the basement store influences the volume of the upstairs store. For instance, when there are large promotional sales in the basement, the upstairs store is thought to benefit. Merchants also feel that there is a substantial relationship between the sales volume of some departments, for example between toys and sporting goods, during the Christmas season if they are located near each other.

2. *The value of space is held constant throughout the store.* A second assumption of this technique is that space is worth the same for all elements of the store being compared. Clearly this is not always so. In supermarkets, for instance, certain traffic areas are better than others, while in department stores the first-floor traffic is certainly worth additional rent—at least compared to the eighth floor. Within a department, some areas are much better than others. The front of a department tends to make an impact quite different from the rear. However, this

assumption need not vitiate the use of a criterion that maximizes profit per unit of space.

3. *The costs of being out of stock are discounted.* Another problem with profitability calculations per unit of space in certain types of retail outlets is that the shelves are where the stock is kept. If the shelves are the key stock-keeping areas, a manager must be concerned with the costs of being out of stock. If he is truly interested in accurate profit calculations, he will not only make an estimate of the substitutability of other items for the items out of stock, but will calculate the damage done to the store's image for being out of stock on that particular item.

4. *The method pays for itself.* Finally, the benefits to be derived from item profitability analysis are supposed to be worth the incremental costs that will ensue.

Incremental analysis of this type is just one way of building from the bottom up, but whatever way is used, some bottom-up thought is necessary. At some point the item decisions have to be integrated so that the individual items are presented to the consumer in the framework of some type of attractive, meaningful whole.

### A Combination Approach

The top-down and bottom-up approaches can be combined to form the multistage approach, which has already been discussed at several points. The first four stages of this approach are (a) selecting the desired customer segments; (b) establishing the set of images; (c) offering roles for the various elements of the merchandise mix (including assortment); and (d) creating policies with respect to assortment. After these stages have been carried out, the following procedure is suggested:

1. *The classifications* are ordered according to the decision maker's estimate of the total dollar profit contribution of each. The exact order is not important, but the classifications with the largest contributions should be considered first.

2. *The required assortment look*—that is, the one that appeals to the right customer segments—is created. Thus in order to be in the movie camera

business, a store has to look to the customer as if it really is in that business. In other words, there must be a sufficiently impressive assortment of movie cameras on display even if the salespeople end up selling only one or two styles of camera. About the only case in which look is not important is when assortment is given almost no role in the firm's merchandising mix. Generally, a retail firm will have to give top consideration to the look achieved by its competitors.

3. *The number of price lines* should be considered in relation to the number of brands. Indeed, the number of price lines needed will often vary with the specific brands selected. Thus in some locations in the country, if General Electric or Frigidaire refrigerators are part of the assortment, it may be desirable to handle fewer price lines and brands than might be so if the store did not handle these brands.

4. *The number of suppliers* should be estimated. There is no easy way to do this effectively. When a large retailer is involved, an important consideration is the possible bargaining concessions. What will be the differences in concessions because a store has two suppliers instead of a higher number? In certain situations, other types of saving will also be important to the store. Among these are lower levels of inventory, more organized returns of merchandise to suppliers, lower ordering costs, fewer bad debts among suppliers, and so forth.

5. *Customer and supplier needs* should be systematically compared so that a compromise can be reached between them. It may be useful to think in incremental terms. What are the losses in consumer appeal from eliminating a specific brand? What are the benefits of the same action from the supplier's perspective? A trial-and-error approach, in which the decision maker estimates the impact of many combinations, may be adequate. Many formal techniques are available should the decision maker choose this approach. The key aspect here is to continuously search for a balance between consumer and supplier. Hopefully, the decision maker will develop some group of alternatives between which the differences are not large. One rule of thumb that he might choose to follow is to keep as many suppliers as the consumers seem to want unless one or

more of the suppliers has substantial concessions to offer.

6. *The optimum size of the merchandise classification* should then be derived from the bottom up. The executive already has the desired number of suppliers from the previous step. He has also done substantial analysis on price lines and brand (step 3). Some of the rules of assortment creation outlined earlier may also be useful to him; at this point he should include all factors that he perceives as relevant to the creation of the assortment. However, he may still need to consider certain factors individually. For instance, the space may turn out to be either smaller or larger than is needed for the assortment look specified in step 2. If it is smaller, he should increase the assortment by adding sizes, colors, or even styles, up to the minimum amount of space necessary to achieve the desired look. However, if the estimated square or cubic footage is more than the minimum look footage, the merchant should use the larger figure.

7. *Total space requirements* can then be derived as the executive goes on to the subclassification with the next largest direct profit possibilities, and so on, through the various subclassifications. Hopefully, when he adds up the space requirements of all the subclassifications he will find that they equal, or nearly equal, the size of the department as estimated by the total store techniques outlined earlier in the chapter. If they do not, then adjustments will have to be made either in the total size of the department or in the size of the individual subclassifications. Since a store, or at least certain types of store, can be looked at as a group of departments, just as a department can be looked at as a group of subclassifications, the total footage requirements for a store can be developed in this manner. The results can be compared with the results obtained from other techniques.

### Continuing Process

Much of the above suggests that determining assortment is a one-time operation, carried out only when starting a season, or when opening or building a new store. For many types of retailing, it is true, the key assortments are those established at the beginning of a season. After their creation, the customer is permitted to vote. For others, however, the assortments evolve continuously over time; there may be few or no seasons, and the lines may last for years except for occasional additions and subtractions. In such cases, adding or dropping items becomes very critical, and systematic procedures are often developed for it, as in the supermarket industry.

## Merchandise Selection

In most instances, and in most types of retailing, the selection of which merchandise to handle is directly related to which price lines, brands, fabrics, and so forth, the decision maker feels are needed. It may be difficult for a buyer or other decision maker to estimate the physical size or other aspects of his merchandise areas until he knows what the market has to offer. Thus merchandise selection is related to all elements of assortment creation. For our purposes, however, it is worth considering merchandise selection as a separate subject.

### Approaches to Merchandise Selection

There are many ways in which the merchandise selection process can be approached by the retail executive. Initially, perhaps, he should decide if his main interest is in suppliers, brands, items, or some combination of these. Retailers can have many kinds of relationship with suppliers. For instance, a retailer might go to a supplier and ask him to profitably fill a given floor space with merchandise that falls within specific price ranges. The retailer might then periodically check the contribution to the store's overhead that is generated by this particular supplier and decide whether the merchandise selections are meeting or exceeding profit objectives. These objectives might be created by analyzing alternative profitabilities per unit of space, per dollar invested in inventory, and so on. In certain types of retail outlet, for example supermarkets, *rack jobbers* may be given such an area to fill, and the retailer will often have little to do with how the area is run. On a larger scale, some discount stores have been created by dividing up the space in a whole store among various types of supplier. A discount store of this nature might be opened up by entrepreneurs with little capital and practically no merchandise expertise. However, the sales interrelationships among merchandise areas make this approach difficult to pursue, since customers do not tend to organize their perceptions of stores around suppliers of brands. Accordingly, this way of breaking down space has not generally been useful except under unusual circumstances.

**Leased departments**    One notable exception is the success that has been enjoyed by various types of leased department. In this instance a supplier supervises a whole department and, according to Robert D. Entenberg, offers the store an average of from 9 to 12 percent of sales—more, if credit services are extended. The primary strength of a leased department is that it is run by an organization with special merchandise know-how. In addition, the operator of leased departments may be very strong financially. Some of the merchandise areas in discount and department stores that have featured this type of arrangement are millinery, boy's wear, shoes, beauty salons, photographic studios, sewing machines, and automobile supplies. Discount firms have often relied heavily on leased departments during the earlier stages of their growth. But the economics of the arrangement seem to change in certain merchandise areas as the size and expertise of the discount store increase, and the store may finally take over many of the areas in which leases were offered. On the other hand, some supplying organizations that have concentrated on running departments in other stores have grown to be very large.

**Supplier's choice**    There are a great number of dependent relationships between suppliers and stores that do not involve measures as extreme as the complete allocation of a space to a supplier. Thus a supplier might offer to have a man sell vacuum cleaners in a store. Such a man would aid the store in various facets of its merchandising, but presumably would attempt to direct most sales to his employer's merchandise. Or a new buyer for a store might go to the present supplier of the department and say, in essence: "Send me what you think I ought to have from your organization up to $10,000 in cost. Let me know what you are sending, so that I can integrate your merchandise with that of other suppliers, or please come over yourself and help me integrate it." Suppliers will realize that the young buyer is interested in surviving, and that if he survives he will treat suppliers who take advantage of this type of relationship very toughly in the future. Thus suppliers who want a long-term relationship with the buyer will make sure that their best sellers are well represented in his store, and that their total line sells as well as can be planned.

**Supplier as consultant**    Some of the most sophisticated buyers also rely on the opinions of suppliers. A buyer will often select the suppliers with whom he wants to work, and then set about developing an assortment for his stores that integrates their various lines. Sophisticated buyers learn the types of decision with which suppliers can be trusted and those with which they cannot be trusted. For example, it would be fair to say that a fashion supplier has little reason to mislead the buyer, at least on the subject of which items will sell best, when he is showing him samples before the actual merchandise has been produced. Afterward, however, the supplier's perspective would be less objective, and in general, suppliers would appear to have a bias with regard to the price they charge the store. In some industries their word would never be trusted in answering a question like, "Is this the lowest price?"

There are of course many retail decision makers

who will buy precisely the merchandise they want without ever really using the supplier as consultant. Thus a buyer might be looking for 1,000 dresses of a certain style, fabric, and so forth, to retail for $3.99. Such a buyer will scout the market to find the best value that she can. A whole department can be built in this manner.

***Emotional-analytical*** Another way to look at merchandise selection is to concentrate on the subjective aspects of the selection process itself. One useful concept here is the emotional-analytical continuum. Emotional buyers are those who tend not to rely heavily on numbers. They may be aware of the sales statistics, but will give greater weight to their "feel" for the merchandise. Since this translates into a feel for the desires of potential customers, it is not such an emotional method as it might seem. Such "emotional" decision makers will generally possess great depth of knowledge about their merchandise. They will interact with customers on many occasions; they will talk extensively with suppliers and with other buyers. Armed with this information, they are in a good position to estimate the future desires of their customers. The method might be referred to as "seat-of-the-pants buying," but it is not necessarily unsophisticated; indeed it may produce highly profitable results.

The analytic approach, on the other hand, relies mainly on numbers. The analytical buyer studies the items that are sold, develops patterns from what has sold, looks for the common characteristics of what is selling. For example, a buyer might note the best-selling wheel size of a baby carriage, the type of spokes it has, and so forth. He might then ascertain the best-selling color and the best-selling material. Putting all these best-selling characteristics together, he might go to England to buy such a carriage from the carriage maker who supplies the Royal Family. It is entirely possible, however, that a carriage so developed would appeal to few. There is no assurance that a combination of best-selling parts will add up to a best-selling whole. Moreover, since the future need not mirror the past (particularly

a future that is six months or so off, the lead time for some types of import), there is no assurance that the analytical approach will in any sense be superior to the emotional one. It is an article of publishing lore that successful magazine editors operate by "feel"; the same may well be true of successful retail decision makers.

Both the emotional and analytical approaches entail risk when carried to extremes. The risk is diminished only as buyers develop skills in both areas. Thus as the buyer with substantial "feel" develops a facility for numbers, his performance will generally improve. So will that of the analytical buyer as he attains a greater feel for the market. Whatever the method used, merchandise selection is a focal point for the integration of the key elements in the merchandising mix.

### A Classification of Merchandise Selectors

The previous approaches to merchandise selection are all based on the assumption that the retail decision maker is always looking out for the store's best interests; his goals are assumed to be the store's goals. This is a little unrealistic. One need only be out in the business world a few years to understand that the personal goals of individual decision makers substantially influence their actions. That is why effective top managers try to develop methods that will bring the goals of the employee and the goals of the firm close together. In addition, employees at all levels have personal biases that may prevent them from dealing intelligently with their environment. The following typology of buyers in a segment of the department store field may shed some light on these biases as they affect decision making.

***Loyal buyers*** These are retail purchasers who purchase from the same supplier year after year for reasons other than that the supplier offers "the best deal." Such buyers can be broken down into (a) buyers "on the take"; (b) personally loyal buyers.

Buyers are on the take if they select suppliers primarily on the basis of the direct extras (i.e., bribes) offered to them personally. In some industries, if a buyer takes more than a small present at Christmas time and occasional entertainment at other times, he is considered on the take. Other industries may have different standards. In some instances, a great deal of money or other consideration may be involved. The student should not feel that in all industries the number of buyers in this category is small. Four independent observers in one industry suggested that 30 percent of the volume of that industry was accounted for by buyers who were on the take. Others have gone so far as to suggest that almost all the buyers in some particular organization are on the take in some manner. In contrast, some firms and industries appear almost completely without such buyers. A few retail managements apparently do not mind that some of their buyers are on the take so long as the profits of the profit center increase. Further, in industries under the influence of the Robinson-Patman Act, it can be argued that under certain conditions the buyer's takings could not be obtained by the store anyway.

Buyers may also be loyal to a particular supplier without any expectation of monetary gain. Some people apparently prefer to remain loyal. They have been dealing with Harry for a great many years, and they expect to go on dealing with him until someone gives them a whole lot of important reasons why they shouldn't. It can be argued that this type of loyalty is in the retailer's best interests, and indeed this is a very challenging question for anyone involved in purchasing. To what extent will loyalty be reciprocated by the supplier when it really counts? In my experience, such loyalty does not pay. When a deal from supplier A is far superior to one from supplier B and supplier B will not come close to meeting the offerings of supplier A, then under most conditions one should take the more attractive offering. Of course, one is not talking here of nickels and dimes. To be aggressive about nickels and dimes is probably short-sighted unless one happens to be in a nickel-and-dime business.

***Opportunistic buyers*** These are retail decision makers who make an appraisal of what suppliers can do for them personally. Suppliers who appear likely to help are put in an acceptable category, while those who cannot help are generally not purchased from unless the item or group of items is essential for the well-being of the department. There may be a large number of suppliers who are deemed acceptable. Perhaps a supplier can be of most help by placing or trying to place buyers in other stores (or in any type of supplier organization), and by trying to build the buyer's reputation in the industry in which he is trying to survive. A supplier may also build the buyer's reputation in his own store. Many suppliers are quite active in such placing and seducing of buyers. Within the preselected (but unwritten) list of acceptables, the buyer will select the suppliers who offer the most attractive mix for his store.

An argument can be made that an opportunistic buyer may do his store much good. Here is a man that, albeit for selfish reasons, regards the supplier's needs as paramount. He may even be said to practice a rudimentary version of what may be called the buyer-seller dyad approach. Here, both buyer and seller take great interest in each other's problems because in the long run it will be profitable to do so. Thus the "acceptable" supplier will realize that the buyer's future in the store is going to be related to the dollar sales and profit figures he can come up with. Thus things might work out well for all concerned, except for the poor suppliers who do not understand the name of the game with a given buyer.

***Best-deal buyers*** These are buyers who try to select both suppliers and merchandise from among existing market alternatives for the best interests of the store. Such a buyer does not directly try to influence a market with which he interacts; rather, he simply chooses one or more of the alternatives offered by the supplying firms. Often, however, if a buyer asks the obvious question, Why should I buy from you? the supplier will offer lower prices or make other adaptations without any further prodding. The best-deal approach to the market tends to be impersonal. Thus a key problem for the buyers who use it is how to obtain the benefits of personal relationships in the market place and yet retain their impersonality.

**Creative buyers**  These are buyers who make efforts to influence the markets in which they purchase by altering the suppliers' marketing mixes, including the way in which new products are developed. This buyer sees the market as being composed of an active buyer and seller. In the creative buyer's perspective, the initiative lies primarily with the buyer who is trying to change the offerings of the market so that it will more appropriately reflect the needs of his retail organization. Such buyers may get involved in the creation of a purchasing mix in the same way that marketers get involved in the creation of marketing mixes. They may therefore have to undertake some of the same type of thinking. A particular type of creative buyer is the one who is always pressuring his suppliers for additional advertising moneys; indeed, his decision to stock an item may well depend on how much money there is to advertise it. Such a policy can increase the profits of the store if the buyer does not obtain sufficient advertising funds from his own top management, and if the payoff from advertising is higher than that from the other alternatives.

**Chiseler**  Such a buyer is one who wants a lower price no matter what he is offered. If the supplier offers an item for $5.40, the chiseler will want it for $4.80. If the supplier offers it for $4.80, the chiseler will want $4.20—and so on. While humorous in some respects, chiseling is a practice that reveals much about retailers and consumers. Many people want to feel that they are buying better than others, if only so that they can feel that they are doing a better job than their counterparts in other firms. A lower price is a tangible sign of this superiority. As many buyers say, "Who needs a supplier who is not going to offer anything special?"

A problem of many buyers is how to obtain the benefits of being a chiseler without the disad-

vantage of being known as one. Aspects of this will be discussed in the next chapter. Some supplying firms try to give all their customers some type of extra but may end up giving them all about the same deal, at least when allowance is made for the quantities in which they buy. The result may even be legal under the Robinson-Patman Act.

**Nuts-and-bolts buyer**  This is the type of buyer who counts the threads in a sweatshirt. He is interested in offering top-quality merchandise, and he will select the merchandise that offers the best quality, particularly in terms of durability. As for the other elements in his marketing mix, he will be content if they are just satisfactory. It should be emphasized that most buyers are interested in the kind of quality that can be perceived by the customer at the time of the sale. Of course, interest in quality is not confined to this type of buyer. Few stores, for example, want to sell or feel that it is in their best interest to sell boys' pants that last two weeks. On the other hand, whether a man's sweatshirt lasts two years or fifteen years may be of little significance to the consumer, at least at the time of purchase. But the nuts-and-bolts buyer is not interested in the importance of that extra quality to the consumer or in whether the consumer will recognize eight years later where he purchased the shirt. Rather, his search for quality is a personal one.

The typology just outlined attempts to throw some light on some of the factors that buyers consider in their selection of suppliers and items. However, a buyer will not and cannot always be of the same type. For example, a buyer might prefer a creative role in which he can strongly influence the market with which he is interacting. If, however, there are only three suppliers in that market, and if all have inflexible marketing mixes, he has little choice but to become a best-deal buyer. Further, a buyer may be on the take with certain firms and yet deal aggressively and without personal benefit in other merchandise areas. The student should also be aware that this typology was developed for only one segment of the department store; other segments—and other institutions—may call for other typologies.

### Other Problems of Merchandise Selection

Today's computers can generate a vast amount of sales information with relative ease and at a low cost. The information is based in most instances on sales records at the retail and wholesale level. Thus a decision maker can soon tell which items are selling and who supplied them. Can the computer be used efficiently to select "winners" for the store or for suppliers before the merchandise appears on sale? All sorts of devices might be used for this purpose, but none has apparently proved of value. Presently, in various fashion systems, the computer is used to ascertain best and poor sellers once the item is in the store, but not before.

Another important facet of merchandising selection is the role of the committee. Merchandise selection in most forms of retailing is done by an individual, or perhaps an individual in a meeting with a superior. Supermarkets, however, have often used a committee system for purchasing certain types of merchandise, in particular, grocery products. A committee creates a whole set of interesting problems for the firm selling to retailers: for instance, the marketer may not know who the strong members of the committee are, or he may have access to the committee only through one member of the firm.

### Summary

1. The merchandise assortment can be thought of as the distribution of the merchandise on hand and on order according to classification, subclassification, style, color, pattern, size, and price. The kind of assortment that a retailer develops can be instrumental in attracting and maintaining a profitable customer clientele.

2. A key dimension of assortment is the allocation of space within a department and store. This problem can be attacked from the total store down, or it can be approached from the item up to homogeneous collections of merchandise, i.e., to subclassifications and classifications.

3. A multistage approach to assortment, merchandise selection, and supplier selection is clearly relevant in many retail buying situations. Merchandise and suppliers may be selected in the light of:

A. The customer segments to which a store is trying to appeal;

B. The set of images the store wishes to project;

C. The roles for the various elements of the merchandising mix, including the role for assortment, merchandise, brands, pricing, and so forth;

D. The policies and strategies designated with respect to assortment.

A model is presented that integrates the top-down and the bottom-up approaches to assortment.

4. In building from the bottom up, various rules of thumb are of some importance:

A. In many areas, 20 percent of the items account for 80 percent or so of the sales. Under certain assumptions the other 80 percent of the items may be declared unprofitable. If these 80 percent are not ordered, however, the 20 percent may do a much smaller business.

B. There are also key selling price lines. Many merchants, in fact, organize their departments around price lines—perhaps "good, better, best," perhaps a bell-shaped curve.

C. Hot selling items are of great importance to many merchandise areas.

D. There is such a thing as having so much variety that the customer is confused.

5. There are many ways to use suppliers, including:

A. Have the supplier run the department on a lease basis;

B. Use the supplier as a consultant;

C. Use the supplier as an independent provider of merchandise.

6. There are several approaches to the selection of merchandise, including:

A. The analytical approach that stresses numbers;

B. The emotional type that stresses the feel for the merchandise.

7. Another way to look at the assortment problem is to look at the characteristics of the individuals doing the buying. Often they may not even be trying to develop the best selection for the store. Among the types of buyer in one part of a department store there may be:

A. The *loyal buyer*, who remains loyal year after year for reasons other than that the supplier offers the best deal;

B. The *opportunistic buyer*, who selects from those suppliers who are likely to aid him personally;

C. The *best-deal buyer*, who selects suppliers and merchandise passively from existing market alternatives for the best interest of the store;

D. The *creative buyer*, who makes efforts to alter the marketing mixes of the suppliers with whom he deals;

E. The *chiseler*, who wants a lower price no matter what the initial offering price of the supplier;

F. The *nuts-and-bolts buyer*, who is preoccupied with the long-term durability of the merchandise.

## Discussion Questions

1. Too much variety in price line, style, fabric, or whatever can confuse the consumer. What are some of the ways that a merchant can decrease this confusion without reducing the number of items carried?

2. If a department store has three price lines in a small merchandise category and the unit sales of each for one week are as follows:

| | |
|---|---|
| $4.99 | 20 |
| $6.99 | 22 |
| $9.99 | 24 |

what merchandise decisions are likely to add to profits?

3. To what extent should a buyer rely, in each case, on the statements of a supplier who (a) is trying to sell to him; (b) is currently selling to him, but is showing a new item; (c) is trying to get more display space for merchandise already sold to the retailers?

4. In your opinion, should most buyers owe their prime loyalty to the store that pays their checks or to the market in which they purchase? Give your reasons.

5. Is the opportunistic buyer likely to be doing a good job for the store? Is he likely to get ahead faster or slower than the other types portrayed?

6. Outline the multistage approach to assortment. What are its chief advantages?

7. Why is it important for a decision maker to have a "feel" for the merchandise a buyer is selecting?

8. Outline an assortment procedure for estimating square footage from the top down.

9. Outline an assortment procedure for estimating square footage from the bottom up.

10. Why do 20 percent of the items of many classifications account for as much as or more than 80 percent of the business?

## References

Belden, Donald L., *The Role of the Buyer in Mass Merchandising* (New York: Chain Store Age Books, 1971), p. 80.

Buzzell, Robert D., *et al., Product Profitability Measurement and Merchandising Decisions* (Cambridge, Mass.: Harvard University Press, 1965).

Entenberg, Robert D., *Effective Retail and Market Distribution* (New York: World, 1966), p. 204.

Taylor, Charles G., *Merchandising Assortment Planning, The Key to Retailing Profit* (New York: National Retail Merchants' Association, 1970), p. 16.

## Further Reading

Baunol, William J., and Ide, Edward A., "Variety in Retailing," in F. Bass *et al.* (eds.), *Mathematical Models and Methods in Marketing* (Homewood, Ill.: Irwin, 1961).

Dalrymple, Douglas J., and Thompson, Donald L., *Retailing: An Economic View* (New York: Free Press, 1968). *Chapter 15 examines in detail the research on direct profit per unit.*

Davidson, William R., *et al.*, "Leased Departments as a Major Force in the Growth of Discount Store Retailing," *Journal of Marketing*, January 1970, pp. 39–46.

Dickinson, Roger A., *Buyer Decision Making* (Berkeley, Ca.: Institute of Business and Economic Research, University of California, 1967). *See especially Chapter 1.*

## Case History:
## *Creating an Assortment*

Laura Brandt was the sporting goods buyer for a large department store in the Midwest. For various reasons the store had decided to go into the ski wear business, a business that the store had not been in before. The store had allocated 1,000 square feet for this section from September to February.

Laura started thinking about what she had learned about developing assortments. Basically, she felt that the key to establishing any department was the creation of classification systems. The buyer had to make the decisions about how the area should be broken up by classifications from the perspective of the consumer. Thus she would probably break up the department into men's and women's ski pants, jackets, and so forth, and then go on from there.

As a beginning, Laura found out industry figures for the major classifications and prorated the square footage for each one by the relative volume figures. Since the margins in the various areas did not appear to differ significantly, she kept the space allocations for each classification developed by volume. She was aware of the limitations of the technique that she had used, but it was a start. After all,

she did not have last year's figures to guide her as she did in sporting goods.

Laura then started to review some of the principles of developing assortments for a given classification. One of these was that classifications do change over time. For example, the classifications of men's ties and shirts had changed radically over the years. Another principle, often violated, was the so-called law of three's, according to which a retailer should strive to offer the customer three alternatives, such as "good," "better," and "best." These options, Laura reflected, were supposed to reflect sufficient variety to convince the customer that the store was seriously in the business, and yet not offer so large a variety that she would become confused and go home without buying anything. The most direct application of this principle would appear to be with regard to price lines. Perhaps one ought to strive to develop three different price lines of men's ski pants. Even so, Laura was not completely sure that price line was more important to the customer than fabric, color, or other factors. If you started to think in terms of three choices in every dimension, you ended up with a very large commitment!

Even if one decided to have just three basic price lines in each major classification, without regard to color, fabric, and so forth, one would still have to make some value judgments about the relative importance of each line. Should one put most of one's inventory dollars in the lowest price line? Or should one perhaps expect that the price line volume would resemble a bell-shaped curve? Laura simply did not know, since the store had never had a ski wear department before, and she herself had never worked in such a department.

Other aspects of assortment creation also bothered Laura. One was that in most classifications one supplier appeared to dominate sales. For instance, in the cosmetics department of her store, a major supplier with not much more space than the other majors produced over 30 percent of the business. And there were 33 suppliers. The research director assured her that this pattern was typical for most classifications in the store; a key supplier tended to dominate the volume, for whatever reasons. This type of thinking led Laura to believe that maybe the way to stock her department was to try to find one key supplier or a key supplier in each classification and then build the assortment around him.

Not only did one or a few suppliers tend to dominate a department but a few items tended to dominate each of the supplier's lines. For example, one cosmetics item from firm X sold 137 units in a year, while another item from the same firm sold only 21. Since the inventory requirements for the better seller were only modestly greater than for the poor seller, the stock turn for the better seller was far higher. While these interesting facts were known by all, their practical ramifications were not so obvious. One usually tried to purchase merchandise that sold well and that had a high rate of sale in relation to stock. However, the sale of the better items might be dependent on the display of the poor sellers, so few specific laws could be offered.

Related to the above was the opinion of several buyers in the store that the key to assortment was the hot items; their motto was "Find the hot items in each classification, and the suppliers will follow." These buyers suggested that a buyer's job was to find the spectacular item or group of items. Then the whole classification could be merchandised around it. Thus the supplier with the key item or items would be dominant and so would the key item in that supplier's group of items.

A further problem of Laura's was that she felt the assortment would have to be varied over the season. In the beginning of the season, many of the retailers seemed to feature closeouts from last year. This was particularly important in the pre-season sales of October. December was a very im-portant month because of Christmas. Reduced-price sales were not too frequent then since the stores were trying to take advantage of the large traffic that would exist anyway. After December, however, stores featured clearances of all types. Thus while it was useful to think of some particular assortment pattern, different assortments would be relevant over different time periods.

Laura also knew that establishing an assortment was a continuing job. She might have to reposition her price lines as she found out what her competitors were doing with theirs. She expected to get a great deal of information as the season progressed, from the unit and dollar controls that had been established. In addition, she would get trade and vendor reports.

These were some of the considerations that Laura was mulling over. In addition, she was aware of the store's overall policy. It wanted to create an impression of having substantial variety, but also of being well stocked with the best-selling items. Laura felt that these policies meant that she was somewhat limited in her ability to optimize in the short term. She decided to do the best she could under the circumstances. Next year, after all, when she was faced with the same problem of setting up an assortment, she would have a year's experience in addition to all this season's records.

### Discussion Questions

1. How would you have gone about developing an assortment for Laura's ski wear area?

2. How would you have gone about developing an assortment for the same area one year later?

# 14

## Negotiation

Negotiation—real negotiation, not just casual inquiries—can be said to precede the selection of merchandise and even of suppliers. But the reverse can also be true, and in any case neither merchandise selection nor negotiation is a one-minute, one-hour, or one-day affair. The main reason, however, for dealing with negotiation at this point is the feeling of the author that retailers should generally not negotiate until they have something to negotiate about. An effective negotiator will generally know the concessions that he wants and will set a strategy to attain them. Without a strategy, he will waste a lot of time negotiating with suppliers in whom he has no real interest. A buyer who negotiates seriously with everyone runs the risk of being taken seriously by no one. He may even develop a reputation as a chiseler.

Negotiation in retailing might be defined as conscious effort on the part of the retailer to alter a supplier's marketing mix in a desired direction. Negotiation is therefore relevant only where the retailer thinks such alteration is possible. While supplier marketing mixes are flexible in most industries, the retailer may have to be strong financially in order to obtain concessions. Thus this chapter deals primarily with retailers who are large, at least in relation to their suppliers.

A buyer for a large retail organization may influence the market in which he purchases in ways other than through negotiation. It should be recognized that a retailer votes with his purchases just as a consumer votes with his. A buyer, then, is voting for a specific marketing mix by offering to purchase from one supplier instead of from the many others from which he might purchase. If many retail purchasers act in similar fashion, they will tend to change the offerings of the market in the direction they want. Of course, the suppliers may anticipate the retailers' actions. Sellers are continuously adjusting their marketing mix to be more attractive to the market segments that they are interested in cultivating.

A buyer may also induce concessions from suppliers without making any effort to do so. For example, he may simply ask the supplier the question, Why should I handle your line? This would appear to be a question that suppliers should ask themselves in creating a marketing mix. In any case, they will be asked the question by most re-sellers in the channel, particularly the retailers. During the discussions between supplier and retailer, it may become entirely clear to the supplier that there is no reason in the world why this given retailer should handle his line. The supplier then has the choice of either not selling to the specific retailer or developing a marketing program that has a chance of success with him. Thus the supplier may change his offerings without any inducement from the retailer.

One consequence of this is that the best-deal buyer may receive many concessions that he does not actively seek. The borderline between the best-deal buyer and the creative buyer, originally a clear one, becomes rather blurred, although the creative buyer is still the one who is actively seeking to change the market.

### Perspectives on Bargaining

No effort will be made here to distinguish between bargaining and negotiation. People generally have some sort of model in their minds when they think of either. Perhaps most think of negotiations as occurring primarily between labor and management, or even between husband and wife. In labor negotiations most assume that the areas of disagreement have to be resolved and that the two parties must get together. An automobile plant cannot usually function without laborers, and laborers need some place to work. Similarly, husband and wife will usually try to resolve their differences, since their marriage is a joint investment in every sense of the word. There are some retail situations in which this concept of bargaining is relevant, but really quite few. Even in instances where it is clearly in both parties' interest to get together, each will usually survive quite well without the other. In addition, the parties may agree that they will interact only up to a certain point, as when a retailer commits himself to buy up to $25,000 of merchandise from supplier X, but not the $100,000 that supplier

X originally wanted him to buy. Thus the selection of suppliers need not be thought of as a go, no-go decision; rather, the buyer asks himself, What dollar volume shall we do?

In any given situation, the types of negotiation that are possible are strongly influenced by the perceived strengths of the participants. In a good number of instances the retailer is simply not permitted to negotiate at all: the supplier is so much stronger economically that no meaningful negotiation can take place. A retail manager should recognize such instances and not go to any lengths to obtain concessions unless he can spare the time and do no harm to retailer-supplier relations. Even in a situation of this kind, a profit-conscious supplier will generally listen to suggestions that improve channel efficiency and therefore (probably) channel profits.

In many instances neither retailer nor supplier is dominant. Thus neither party can really take the other party for granted, and real negotiation is necessary. In many instances, however, the large retail firm will dominate the supplier by virtue of its indifference or near-indifference to which supplier it selects. A large department store buyer interacting in a market with many small suppliers may be in a very strong position with respect to any one supplier.

### Philosophy toward Suppliers

There are many different philosophies that purchasers have toward suppliers. The two polar positions are of particular interest. One is that a purchasing agent for a firm, particularly a large firm, should not be too rough on suppliers. Proponents of this view suggest that in the long term: "We really want our suppliers to be partners. We want suppliers who are very interested in us and our long-term success. Elementary psychology—the psychology of the Golden Rule—suggests that you increase the probability of others acting positively toward you if you act positively toward them. Interaction between supplier and store should be based on mutual trust, a mutuality of problems, and—most of all—mutual profitability." Thus a buyer should make no effort to extort the last penny from a supplier; this is felt to be penny wise and pound foolish. Suppliers, so the argument goes, are always in a position to help certain stores more than others, for example by introducing or delivering new products sooner. Developed to its logical extremes, this view would suggest that there should be no negotiating at all.

A second philosophy of negotiation, at the other end of the continuum, regards the marketplace as a battleground in which no holds are barred. Suppliers are the enemy and are to be dealt with accordingly. Favors are not to be returned; long-term relationships are to be avoided unless on a contractual basis. The long term is an aggregation of smaller decisions: if one maximizes the buck in the short term, the long term will take care of itself.

Obviously most firms fall somewhat between these two polar positions. In determining where he should position his firm on this continuum, a decision maker needs to answer many questions. For example, of what importance is the success of the supplier to his company? What are the chances of a big merchandise shortage in this industry? Should extra concessions be demanded of the supplier regardless of how they will affect either his or the channel's profits?

### Negotiation Ratios

One way to look at the negotiation process for two firms that know they are going to get together is in terms of developing a relationship that will maximize their joint profits. It is not so much that each cares about the profitability of the other, at least not in any altruistic sense. Rather, it is that if the two parties combine to maximize their joint profits, there will be more profits to divide. Thus one approach to negotiation would be that each firm should consider the effects of any change in the relationship on the profits of *both* firms. The negotiation ratio is one way of examining such effects.

A negotiation ratio is here defined as the estimated additional net benefits to the store as a result of a change in the supplier's marketing mix, divided by the estimated additional net costs to the supplier of making these changes. It may be expressed as follows:

$$\frac{\text{Additional Benefits to the Store}}{\text{Additional Costs to the Supplier}}$$

These benefits and costs are derived by relating the relevant revenue and cost changes for both retailer and supplier. For example, if a retailer uses supplier money to place an advertisement in the newspaper, the retailer must pay for the merchandise and other costs related to the sale of additional merchandise. The retailer will get the retail price for each unit sold to his customers and the advertising moneys from the supplier. The supplier is paying for the cost of the advertisement in the newspaper; the supplier benefits by the profit from the sale of the additional merchandise to the store and the profit from the sale of merchandise to other retail accounts because of the advertisement.

In most instances, the cost increase to the supplier as a result of giving in to the retailer's demands (e.g., for advertising moneys) will exceed the increases in revenue that he will gain from this action. Otherwise, the supplier should have incorporated the increased costs into his marketing mix. Thus the term "cost" is used here to refer to the impact on the supplier.

A retailer may choose to formalize his negotiation ratios by developing figures for all the costs and benefits to each party. However, the concept of a negotiation ratio may be useful even when it is applied informally. A bargainer may well ask himself what substantial benefits he can get that will cost the other fellow little. This will have the effect of increasing the dollar profits within a given channel, provided that the value of the concessions to the retailer really is greater than their cost to the supplier. Interpersonal relationships such as marriage can also be looked at in this way: for instance, the husband may decide that helping his wife with the Saturday morning shopping will cost him little and be deeply appreciated by her. If both parties to a marriage were to act in this fashion, both marriage and society would be better for it (and no arithmetical calculations would be necessary). Some observers would liken a retailer-supplier relationship to a marriage.

The logic of the negotiation ratio may be seen in the following example. The benefits to a store of $200 worth of advertising in the local newspapers may well be only $150. The net cost to the supplier of the same advertising, considering his profits from the extra units that will be sold to the store that places the advertisement and from the extra units that will be sold to other stores in the area may be $37.50, calculated as follows:

| | |
|---|---:|
| Cost of advertising to supplier | $200.00 |
| Profit contribution from extra sales to store | − 120.00 |
| Profit contribution from extra sales to other stores in area | − 42.50 |
| Net cost to supplier | $ 37.50 |

Thus for this specific amount of advertising, there is a negotiation ratio of 4:1. A given amount of sales services offered by the supplier—perhaps the presence of the account salesman on the selling floor two nights a week—is estimated to offer $300 worth of benefit to the store. The net additional cost to the supplier in this case is estimated at $150, a sum that allows for the salesman's salary and the profits from the extra units sold by him. The negotiation ratio is therefore 2:1. If both supplier and store understand the logic by which these ratios are created, then ways can be found to increase the profits of one or both parties.

The negotiation ratio can also be used as a means of getting the greatest benefit for a given supplier cost. Thus if for some reason a store feels that it is "entitled" to from $100 to $125 in concessions at supplier cost, it will be better off taking the advertising at a cost of $37.50 to the supplier and then perhaps negotiating a salesman for one night a week on the floor, perhaps for a benefit of $150. The total benefit to the store would in such a case be $300—$150 from the advertising and $150 from the salesman. Or perhaps the store should negotiate more advertising, if its management thinks this will bring greater benefits.

The buyer is generally interested in the supplier's profits only to the extent that they will help to boost his own, whether in the short or long term. If, however, the negotiation process can produce a more effective channel system, then the joint profits of the channel participants will have been increased more than they would otherwise. It may be that the retailer can get most if not all of the additional joint profits, plus whatever else he can "steal" from a supplier. It is also true that the supplier is generally interested in the store's profits only to the extent that they encourage the maintenance and expansion of his relationship with it. In a bargaining relationship it is generally desirable for a vendor to offer a store concessions that are of relatively small cost to himself but of substantial benefit to the store. This type of thinking can enable vendors to create effective marketing mixes.

So far we have concentrated mainly on the store receiving extra concessions from the supplier. And indeed most stores will negotiate for something extra while making efforts not to give up the concessions they already enjoy. The negotiation ratio, however, can just as well be used to exchange concessions. In the above example, the supplier might presently be using a salesman on the floor one night a week at a cost to him of $75. It would, however, be in the best interest of the store to get some of this money directed into advertising. All the same, as the reader should note, the negotiation ratio for sales service is still 2:1, so that profits in the channel are still increased when this service is used. In fact, any negotiation ratio in excess of 1 will increase the additional profits of the two entities in the negotiation. Under given sets of conditions, then, the retailer is better off paying a higher purchase price for the merchandise than giving up any concession that offers a negotiation ratio substantially in excess of 1. Indeed, if negotiation were to proceed with the purpose of allocating activities between the two bargaining parties in an optimal manner, presumably all the negotiation ratios would approach 1. This might occur, for instance, in situations where channel efficiency is deemed critical by a channel leader; or where two firms are enamored of the concept of the buyer-seller dyad.

It must be admitted that under most conditions the relationship between buyer and seller will not be completely open. Both parties are usually in favor of increased channel efficiency, but the appropriate division of activities or profits between them will be far from obvious. Thus the buyer will tend to approach the problem not so much with a view to equalizing the negotiation ratios but with a view to following a *negotiating path*. This means that the retailer negotiates for concessions in order of the negotiation ratios, starting from the highest ratio and proceeding until he reaches the total level of cost that the supplier will surrender. Thus a retailer would start at a ratio of 4.0, go to 3.0, 2.5, and so forth. Both the negotiation ratio and the resultant negotiation path allow for the effects of changes in the supplier's marketing mix on the store's profits as well as on the supplier's own costs.

Among the assumptions implied in the creation and use of the ratios, the following are crucial:

1. *The supplier is acting in his own best interests.* Therefore the supplier should be primarily concerned with minimizing the net dollar costs of the concessions to him; other factors such as the number of concessions are immaterial. Thus if in our previous example the supplier had offered the store a choice between advertising moneys and sales service, obviously the store should have taken the sales service, since it offered more benefits ($300 as opposed to $150).

2. *The relationship is linear over the range of the variable being considered.* Thus if $1,000 in advertising is thought to be a reasonable concession in a given instance, the advertising dollars between $900 and $1,000 are deemed to be just as productive (and no more productive) than the dollars between $0 and $100. In instances where this assumption does violence to the facts—and there should be few such instances—the buyer can break up the amount representing a "reasonable concession" into as many segments as may be thought necessary. A retailer might then calculate the negotiation ratio for the first $500 of advertising, the second $500, and so forth.

3. *The concessions are independent of one another.* Obviously, the elements that create the specific negotiation ratios are not always independent of the elements that create the other negotiation ratios, although the relationship may not be a very strong one. After the retailer has obtained one concession from a supplier, the other negotiation ratios may change. Thus if a buyer obtains a lower cost for an item, the contribution to the retailer's overhead for each unit sold will be correspondingly greater. In addition, the second or third concession obtained by a buyer may alter the value of the negotiation ratio for the first concession. However, the amount of change in the negotiation ratios due to such interrelationships will not usually be large. Therefore, the assumption that the negotiation ratios are in fact independent may be justified; it depends on the degree of precision desired. In some instances it may be useful to group several concessions because of their interdependence.

Two other characteristics of negotiation ratios deserve mention. First, many concessions will be of the type that, as one adds more of a factor, for example advertising, a smaller and smaller negotiation ratio results. This is simply an illustration of the law of diminishing returns, but relates to both the numerator and denominator of the negotiation ratio. Second, the negotiation ratios will generally be invariant to the level of sales within the range being considered by the buyer. In other words, it makes little difference in calculating the ratios whether the buyer estimates that the sales of an item will be 2,000 units or 3,000 units without the concession. He is far more interested in the negotiation process as to what will happen as a result of the concession.

### Types of Concession

The retail decision maker may negotiate for many different kinds of concession. Indeed, there is probably no limit to the number of kinds or combinations of kinds that can be developed by a dynamic retailer and supplier. The following are among the ones most frequently used.

**Additional features**  Often an item will be considerably more attractive as a result of the addition of one or more features. Thus the value of a bicycle may be enhanced by the addition of whitewall tires. Such extra features may be part of a model that is not given to competitive retailers and may therefore create a degree of market exclusivity.

**Market exclusivity**  Many merchandise lines are of almost no value without either some retail price protection or some limitation on the type and number of competitors that the store faces. For example, a men's shirt line that is sold in discount stores at an initial markup of 30 percent is of no interest to a department store or a men's furnishings store.

**Lower cost**  A lower cost is always of interest to the retailer. It may be of particular interest to buyers in merchandise classifications where the retail profit margins are under pressure. For example, in major appliance areas claims there is considerable pressure for lower prices.

**Closeouts**  A relatively prosaic offer from a supplier may be enhanced considerably by a substantial amount of closeout merchandise. It makes little difference whether the merchandise is old and has been closed out in some legitimate fashion, or whether it was produced specifically for the purpose of being closed out.

**Advertising**  Suppliers often offer or are induced to offer moneys to support the advertisements of retailers. These monies are most easily negotiated when the supplier has something to gain from their being spent in this way. For instance, the store might be able to do some of the supplier's advertising for him, at lower cost, or help him sell mer-

chandise to other retail accounts. For example, if a supplier were already using ad X in newspaper Y, it might be reasonable to have an adapted ad X put in by retailer Z in newspaper Y. Indeed, the retailer will usually be able to obtain a lower price from the newspaper for this advertising than the supplier.

**Guaranteed sales**  A guaranteed sale is generally an arrangement by which the supplier agrees, before the order is received from the retailer, to take back merchandise that the store is unable to sell —usually within a period mutually agreed upon by the seller and the buyer. A guaranteed sale may make sense to both negotiating parties when the supplier (a) can increase the sales of the merchandise classification in the store; (b) will make fewer errors in merchandise selection than the buyer; or (c) has the distribution system to handle errors in merchandising decisions more efficiently than the single store or chain. In most guaranteed sales, some of the decisions normally made by the retailer pass to the supplier.

For example, ice skates sell at different weeks in different parts of the country because some geographic areas encounter cold weather sooner and longer than others. A supplier might offer a guaranteed sale to a store in the colder climate on the assumption that he can dispose of the next returned skates in the warmer climate, where they will go on sale later.

**Service**  Additional services may be offered by the suppliers in many ways. Most often the extras offered are those that are not essential to the transfer of the merchandise. One example would be the taking of stock counts of the supplier merchandise in each of the stores; another might be selling with the retail salespeople in various stores at specific times.

**Backup stock**  Backup stock is merchandise held in reserve by the supplier for a specific store without any obligation on the store's part to take it. A buyer may therefore be able to purchase in small quanti-

Table 14.1
Calculation of expected value

| | Cost to retailer | Dollar profit payoff to vendor | Subjective estimate of getting the order with the given price proposal | Expected value |
|---|---|---|---|---|
| Alternative 1:38% | 6.20 | $10,000 | .4 | $4,000 |
| Alternative 2:40% | 6.00 | 6,000 | .5 | $3,000 |
| Alternative 3:42% | 5.80 | 3,000 | .9 | $2,700 |

Note: *The dollar payoff of not selling is considered to be zero. The expected value is obtained by the following equation:*

$(p_1 \times v_1) + (p_2 \times v_2)$ *equals the expected value of an alternative where*
$p_1$ *is the probability of selling the retailer with the given alternative*
$v_1$ *is the dollar payoff in selling to the retailer with the given alternative*
$p_2$ *is the probability of not selling to the retailer with the given alternative*
$v_2$ *is the dollar payoff of not selling to the retailer.*
*Since $v_2$ is assumed to be 0 in this example, the expected value breaks down to $(p_1 \times v_1)$.*

ties and still be in stock, even in seasonal merchandise. In many supplier operations it costs little to offer backup stock, particularly if few retailers ask for it. In effect, a supplier may be offering little more than an option on a production run. Of course, if all his customers seek this type of commitment, then he will have to establish priorities.

## One Negotiating Procedure

There is one procedure that can be useful in a variety of negotiating situations. However, there are several other aspects of negotiation that should be discussed first.

### Competitive Bidding v. Negotiated Prices

The main stronghold of competitive bidding appears to be the contract divisions of the various government agencies, which are bound by law to require it; in retailing or indeed in purchasing for large manufacturing firms it is seldom used.

One way of examining competitive bidding is to ask how suppliers make up competitive bid prices. Let us assume that a supplier is trying to sell an item to just one retailer, and that he is using an *expected value approach*. The item has a known re-

tail price of $10. The supplier has a choice of only three different billing prices to offer to the retailer. He will offer the retailer one of the following initial markups: 38 percent, 40 percent, or 42 percent. In order to develop his expected profit, the supplier must establish a dollar payoff for each markup level, together with the probability of obtaining the order at that level. The whole procedure is illustrated in Table 14.1. While it is not suggested that suppliers quantify in this fashion, they do think in terms of payoffs and probabilities.

In this artificial example, the supplier will select the highest price, $6.20, because this offers him the highest expected profit. It is interesting to note that if the retailer had suggested to the supplier before he received the bid that he would consider only offerings at a markup of 42 percent, the supplier (if he believed what he heard) would have had to change his subjective probability estimates accordingly. In fact, he would have had only one choice — to offer alternative 3.

It should further be noted that if the buyer states to a supplier that he will definitely purchase this merchandise at a markup of 42 percent, and if the supplier believes this statement, all doubt about not selling the account is removed and the expected value of the third alternative is thereby increased to $3,000. By such means, retailers can increase the expected value of an alternative to the supplier.

The above example indicates clearly that competitive bidding offers no assurance of the lowest price. Depending on his perceptions of the probabilities and the payoffs, the supplier may select high as well as low prices. In addition, it is clear that negotiation offers many options that are not present in competitive bidding. For example negotiation permits the supplier to adjust and readjust his view of the payoff probabilities. It also seems likely for other reasons that large retailers will generally do better to negotiate, or at least combine some type of competitive bidding with negotiation. Among these reasons are:

1. *Competitive bidding is limited in outlook.* It is difficult to consider all the various facets of the possible concessions in competitive bidding, since it tends to emphasize such factors as price. This may not be desirable at all.

2. *Competitive bidding discourages innovations.* Retailing emphasizes the differences in the suppliers' products; it does not encourage them to present the same old thing again and again. Competitive bidding, on the other hand, often starts with specifications, one purpose of which is to introduce comparability between the suppliers' offerings.

3. *Competitive bidding is too impersonal.* Few retailers desire arm's-length transactions with suppliers either economically or psychologically. The very essence of certain merchandise areas is involvement with suppliers. Certainly, the systems approach to the channel suggests involvement of buyer and seller in the mutual solution of problems rather than the impersonal interaction of competitive bidding.

4. *Competitive bidding lowers perceived payoffs.* Suppliers often perceive the payoff of negotiated transactions as higher because they usually lack a precise ending date. In contrast, if a contract let out for competitive bid comes in every six months, the life of the winning offer may also be set at six months. But if the deal is negotiated, there need be no time limit.

### Preliminary Negotiation Period

In negotiation, as we have seen, a great deal depends on each party's perceptions and the re-tailer's ability to alter them. It is difficult to see how the retailer can induce such alterations unless the supplier believes him. Mutual trust between retailer and supplier is generally built up over time. Thomas C. Schelling suggests that:

. . . trust is often achieved simply by the continuity of the relation between parties and the recognition by each that what he might gain by cheating in a given instance is outweighed by the value of the tradition of trust that makes possible a long sequence of future agreement (Schelling, 1963, pp. 134–135).

The importance of mutual trust may be indicated by the following example. Let us suppose that we are a new supplier and produce an item similar to that produced by 12 other firms in the country. In order to get a position in the distribution system, we decide to price the item 10 cents a unit below competition, or $3 a unit. We hop on a plane and visit 30 leading accounts in the country whom we do not presently sell and have never met before. How many of these stores will be sold at this price? The answer is, few if any. All the supplier will probably achieve is that other suppliers will be given a chance by their respective retail customers to meet the price, and will do so. Thus there is no incentive for a firm in this kind of situation to come in at the lower price. As the parties develop trust over time, perhaps through interaction on a variety of matters, the supplier will develop some confidence that he will not be treated in this fashion. The supplier's offer has a greater chance of success in this atmosphere, and the retailer's offers may well be accepted if he has built up a reputation of trust over the years.

### Overvaluing Long Odds

Experiments have shown that people tend to see events with a low probability of occurrence as happening more frequently than they do, and events with a high probability as happening less frequently than they do. Thus if a buyer assumes that a seller will overvalue long odds under certain conditions, then it may pay him to create situations in which the vendor is presented with long odds as an alternative. For instance, a newspaper advertisement that results in a huge volume of sales may be a low-probability event that the seller might overvalue. The seller might also overvalue his chances of selling to a store that had never bought anything from him. Consumers, too, may overvalue long odds. If a consumer purchases more hair tonic because he expects to have greater success with girls (something that hair tonic rarely achieves), he may purchase other products for similarly improbable reasons.

The reader should be warned that all sellers—and, for that matter, all buyers—will not have the same attitude toward risk-taking. More people, however, appear to overvalue long shots. Further, as Nathan Kogan and Michael Wallach have amply documented, an individual's attitude toward risk may be affected by personality characteristics such as avoidance of failure and a concern for image maintenance. Such personal elements may indeed be very important in negotiation. Various experiments have indicated that a person may act against his own self-interest, especially if he succeeds in harming the interests of others in the process. Thus a retailer should be aware that personal elements may be of substantial importance in negotiation.

### Successful Negotiation: An Outline

Any goal may usually be attained in a large number of ways. Accordingly, the method of negotiation to be outlined here is certainly not the only one available, and may very well not be the best. However, it is a method that many individuals will be capable of applying in instances where the retail organization is large and powerful. The steps are as follows:

1. *Establish a purchasing mix* for a given merchandise subclassification. Firms create marketing mixes, hopefully in full knowledge of what they are doing. Retail decision makers should create pur-

chasing mixes for merchandise subclassifications. These purchasing mixes should include consideration of the subclassification's needs. The decision maker should go through the various elements that create the profit, and select the ones that appear to be of greatest importance. These should be selected independently of brand, unless brand is one of the subclassification's primary needs. Among such elements are the various concessions discussed in this chapter. In addition, he might want to budget reasonable amounts for the elements that create profits.

2. *Search the market* for what is needed. Armed with the purchasing mix, the store's buyer should explore the market. He would have to do this anyway, but it helps to explore the market with some definite ideas in mind. Sometimes it may be useful to let the firms that can solve the problem bid, perhaps competitively, to fill the merchandise void. The more important the merchandise classifications, the more time the decision maker can afford to use in search.

3. *Select a list* of relevant suppliers. The present list of suppliers should be augmented by candidates that meet the standards of the subclassification and possibly fill the designated voids. The list is created by making certain assumptions about what the marketing mix of the supplier will be after negotiation, but up to this point almost no negotiation has occurred. In other words, the retailer should make estimates of the concessions that he feels might be offered by each supplier.

4. *Select the supplier* that you want to do business with most, given the estimates of the possible concessions.

5. *Sell the selected supplier* on a reasonable deal by making him a firm offer to purchase. By removing all doubt in this way, you, the buyer, can obtain the expected value increment suggested in Table 14.1.

6. *Proceed down the list* of suppliers, if a desirable deal cannot be arranged with the preferred one, until you have the deal you want. Of course, if the preferred supplier accepts, the negotiations are over unless you happen to need more than one supplier.

## Negotiation and Game Theory

A game can be defined as a situation in which the participants are attempting to attain some goal or goals in which their success or failure depends not only upon their own decisions but upon those of all the others. According to this rather broad definition, almost all business situations are games. This section does not adhere to any rigid definition of a game, but offers some concepts, developed mostly by those associated with game theory, that may be of value to a negotiator in retailing.

### Commitment

The word "commitment" is here used in the sense of pledging oneself or the store to a given action. By limiting his own alternatives, the retail decision maker may alter the range of alternatives open to the supplier. To be successful, as we have seen, such a commitment must be believed by the supplier.

A commitment may be used in several different ways. For example, a buyer may impose a commitment on himself by stating to the supplier that he deals only with vendors who offer a 38 percent markup. Because the commitment is self-imposed, the buyer can always be approached by the vendor and the subject can be discussed and negotiated. However, such a personal commitment by the buyer may also be considered coercive by the vendor and make amicable relations difficult. The buyer's commitment, however, does not have to be his own: either his immediate superior or top management can participate in a commitment with the buyer or act on its own. A buyer could state to a vendor that he is committed to his merchandise manager for the raising of $12,000 in genuine, vendor-paid advertising moneys for a Christmas mailer. If either the merchandise manager or store policy do not permit paying the supplier more for his merchandise in order to develop these moneys, the buyer will have to get the money by direct negotiation. If the supplier believes him, he will probably recognize that failure to offer at least some advertising money

will mean no order if another vendor is able to step in with both advertising money and goods. In addition, the buyer is probably powerless at this point in time to change the commitment. This is, therefore, a commitment of a more binding nature than one offered by the buyer, because the buyer cannot withdraw the commitment of a higher authority.

A third type of commitment is that actually imposed on the buyer by his superiors, either the merchandise manager or top management. For instance, the buyer may not be permitted to select vendors who sell to discount houses in merchandise classifications where other alternatives are possible. This then becomes a most binding commitment against which a specific vendor would have no practical recourse whatsoever. However, such a commitment may not be official because of the possible legal ramifications. Thus the arbitrariness and inflexibility of a commitment may be useful to a buyer in certain situations. The student should be cautioned that vendors may also utilize commitments, but in this chapter only the advantages to the buyer are considered.

### Simple Splitting

Differences between bargainers, as M. M. Flood has shown, are often resolved by simple splitting (i.e., by dividing in half). This type of resolution may occur because there is some ethical norm in our culture to divide the rewards, because neither side will admit defeat, because of the natural attractions of mathematical simplicity, because splitting is the prominent solution, or some combination of the above.

The retailer may utilize simple splitting in at least two ways. First, he can create a situation where splitting or some other simple mathematical formula will be to his advantage. This principle is used quite frequently in business and is most obviously reflected in the practice of raising the initial asked price or lowering the initial offered price in anticipation of some sort of (probably uncomplicated) reduction or split. There are, it should be noted, both advantages and disadvantages in making unrealistic initial demands. In addition, a buyer may create alternative break points, so that a split can be avoided when it would be to his disadvantage. If he seeks a specific concession, he can introduce one or several points under his asking price. This then may prevent the split from being as obvious or prominent. For example, if the asking price for an item is $80 and the bid price is $76, $78 might be considered a logical final price. However, a buyer who is set on paying $77 may inform the seller that he has already refused several offers to sell for $78.

### Third Party

A third party has value in many situations. In the present context, the third party will usually be the merchandise manager, the buyer's superior. For most bargaining purposes, a third party must be used sparingly. If one is used too often, the supplier may adjust his bargaining strategy in anticipation. In addition, constant use of a merchandise manager as a third party may decrease the buyer's importance in the eyes of both the supplier and the market, which could negatively affect the buyer's performance in many ways.

The merchandise manager, when introduced into the bargaining situation, may use all the techniques open to the buyer. He may also corroborate any commitment made by the buyer to a vendor. In addition, he may try to act in the role of a mediator instead of as the buyer's superior. Thus he can state to the vendor that he makes it a policy never to interfere with the selections of his buyers—but that he would like to preserve the store's relationship with this specific vendor. He may also be capable of introducing attractive solutions that either the vendor or the buyer might have difficulty in introducing himself.

A third party may serve another significant function: if he is hated by both buyer and seller, the latter may get on together much better than they would have otherwise. Thus a buyer may refer to his superior, or to "the store," or perhaps to another group not related to the store or business at all, as an object that both he and the vendor can appropriately hate and commiserate about. There can be few suppliers who have not heard from at least a few buyers about those ____ ____s upstairs and their unreasonable demands. The presence of a hated third party, if he is one of the buyer's superiors, makes the commitments by management more believable to the vendor because they appear that much more binding on the buyer. In addition, it also makes it possible for management's commitments to be enforced without breaking up the buyer-vendor relationship. Even a commitment that is self-imposed may be more effectively presented as a commitment imposed on the buyer by management. The moral choice is the retailer's.

### Opportunity Profits

It is often argued that a store should select the supplier who offers the highest contribution to overhead per unit of space, per dollar of inventory, or whatever. Suppose, however, that the store makes $10 more than it would have made by interacting with some other supplier, while the supplier makes $10,000 more. From the retailer's perspective, this might not be considered an equitable split of the *opportunity profits*. The retailer might therefore employ some type of strategy to induce a recalcitrant supplier to disgorge some of his extra profits. For instance, the store might try taking a $10 loss by doing without the supplier altogether. This might impress on the supplier the desirability of sharing his gains, perhaps 50-50.

### Summary

1. A retailer can adopt many different approaches to the negotiation process. It may be useful to think of the suppliers as members of a team, each member's health being of interest to every other. Or one might look at negotiation and the supplier relationship as a battleground from which no holds are barred. Most

negotiation takes place under conditions somewhere between these two extremes.

2. In general, retailers should not negotiate until they have something about which to negotiate. Thus a buyer should have a pretty good idea of which suppliers he wants to use before he tries to obtain concessions. Not only is it usually a waste of time to negotiate with firms that are not potential suppliers, but the decision maker runs the risk of developing the reputation of being a chiseler if he is bargaining at every turn.

3. There are two keys to effective bargaining.

A. The first key is *cost benefit analysis,* in which a decision maker must know the benefits to the store of various kinds and degrees of concessions and the costs of these concessions to the supplier. Under most conditions, the supplier would prefer to offer a concession of low cost to himself, while the retailer prefers concessions that offer large benefit to himself. The decision maker for either the retailer or the supplier can formalize the benefits in terms of the *negotiation ratio,* which is:

$$\frac{\text{Added Benefits to the Store}}{\text{Added Costs to the Supplier}}$$

Negotiation ratios can be ordered from high to low to represent a *negotiation path.* This would tell the retail decision maker to bargain, e.g., for advertising instead of additional features, backup stock, or whatever.

B. The second key is to sell the desired concessions to the relevant suppliers. A retailer should generally offer his business to the supplier in such a manner that the supplier believes that if he accedes to the requests of the retailer, he will get the business. In such situations the supplier will value the retailer's potential business more highly.

4. Many kinds of concessions are possible, including:

A. Additional features;

B. Market exclusivity;

C. Lower cost;

D. Closeouts;

E. Advertising;

F. Guaranteed sales;

G. Service;

H. Backup stock.

5. Observations about negotiation are offered.

A. Competitive bidding is not generally used in retailing, nor ought it to be. To the extent that competitive bidding is used, it generally precedes negotiation.

B. Negotiation generally requires a period of preliminary negotiation during which a degree of mutual trust is built up.

C. Participants tend to overvalue long odds in that they believe the long shot has a greater chance of winning than it actually has.

6. The relevance of game theory to the negotiation process is discussed.

A. By limiting his own alternatives, the retail decision maker may alter the range of alternatives open to the supplier.

B. The participants may split the difference on given issues.

C. A third party can be used to aid in the process.

D. Stores may seek an "appropriate" division of the opportunity profits.

### Discussion Questions

1. What kind of philosophy should a large supermarket hold with regard to suppliers?

2. If you were the purchasing agent for a large retailer, would you actually calculate negotiation ratios and negotiation paths?

3. What are the main assumptions involved in the creation and use of negotiation ratios?

4. Explain the difference between backup stock and guaranteed sales as a concession.

5. Why is competitive bidding not used extensively in retailing?

6. How can third parties be useful in negotiations?

7. Why do bargainers often split the difference?

8. Should negotiations be carefully planned?

### References

Flood, M. M., "Some Experimental Games," *Management Science*, vol. 5, 1958, pp. 5–26.

Kogan, Nathan, and Wallach, Michael, *Risk Taking* (New York: Holt, Rinehart, and Winston, 1964), pp. 188–214.

Schelling, Thomas C., *The Strategy of Conflict* (Cambridge, Mass.: Harvard University Press, 1963).

### Further Reading

Dickinson, Roger A., "Game Theory and the Department Store Buyer," *Journal of Retailing*, Winter 1966–67, pp. 14–24.

Fouraker, L., and Siegel, S., *Bargaining Behavior* (New York: McGraw-Hill, 1963).

Iklé, Fred C., and Leites, Nathan, "Political Negotiation as a Process of Modifying Utilities," *Journal of Conflict Resolution*, vol. 6, 1962, pp. 19–28.

Joseph, M., and Willis, R., "An Experimental Analysis to Two Party Bargaining," *Behavioral Science*, vol. 7, 1963.

Stone, Jeremy J., "An Experiment in Bargaining Games," *Econometrica*, vol. 36, 1958, pp. 294–296.

### Case History: The Name of the Game

John Kraft had just been made buyer of sporting goods for Triple D, a chain of three discount stores. The stores were of small size and averaging $2 million each in sales annually. The sporting goods component of the business was substantial. Each store averaged $250,000 for the year. The stores carried the usual sporting goods such as equipment for baseball, football, hunting, fishing, and so forth. In each of these categories Triple D was a major factor in the market.

John was skilled in sporting goods, having been assistant to an experienced sporting goods buyer in another firm several years ago. He undertook an analysis of each of his classifications with an eye to increasing profits. The fishing area particularly bothered him. He dealt with one wholesaler for the overwhelming majority of his merchandise in this area, and the wholesaler had assigned one salesman for all three Triple D stores. It was the salesman's job to count the merchandise in each store, see that reasonable amounts of merchandise were ordered, make sure the displays were attractive, and so forth. A vendor analysis of the sporting goods area turned up the fact that John bought $75,000 worth of merchandise at cost from this supplier last year for all stores. He fully expected to buy at least that amount this year. The fishing classification appeared profitable and the deal with Folger Wholesale was about as good as he could obtain. He was convinced of this because he had tried to get a better deal from five other wholesalers but could not.

In his profit analysis John had calculated the benefit of Folger's salesman to the Triple D stores. The salesman was nice and cooperative and, considering all factors, John thought he was worth about $1,000. John felt that with $1,000 he could pay one of his own salesmen to work overtime to take the counts and perform the other aspects of the job. Since John also dealt with the principals of Folger Wholesale, the relationship could be maintained without the salesman. John knew that Folger's was paying Marty Hansen, the salesman, 5 percent of the sales of Triple D, or about $3,750 including expenses. Thus John felt that there was a waste of $2,750 here. John's problem was how to get this money for the store.

John had considered several alternatives. One would be to go directly to Henry Folger, president of Folger Wholesale, and state the problem to him. There was nothing wrong with the salesman, but the stores would be substantially more profitable with the money that would be saved by doing without him. Perhaps he could be used on Folger's other accounts. If John did not want to appear greedy, he could always come to Henry Folger with the story that his boss had become exceedingly aggressive about increasing margins. Perhaps, after all, this was the only way to do it.

John also considered presenting the problem to Marty Hansen. Perhaps a way could be found to make him worth more to Triple D. For instance, he could sell on the floor Wednesday and Friday nights in one or more of the Triple D stores and so, with this and other contributions, become actually worth $3,750.

A third alternative would be to try sheer bluff. John could go to Henry Folger and tell him that the store simply must have an additional five percent. In the course of the discussion, cost reduction might be mentioned as an alternative. An obvious way to achieve the reduction would be to eliminate the selling services. The salesman might have to be disposed of, at least for this account. John would try to have old Folger suggest this himself.

A fourth alternative open to John was to do nothing. After all, each of the preceding methods might create enemies. And John had just started in his new position. In addition, John knew from his experience in the sporting goods industry that a good reputation in the market would not only help him in his present position but also if he were to be fired or wanted promotion outside the store. If survival wasn't the name of the game, what was? Accordingly, if he wanted Marty Hansen's goodwill —not to mention the goodwill of Henry Folger, a very influential man—John perhaps had better do nothing. His predecessor had done nothing, and he had been placed very well in the industry.

### Discussion Questions

1. If you were John, what would you do?

2. *Is* survival the name of the game? In your answer, consider what would happen to retailing if everyone in it behaved as you propose to do.

## 15

## Pricing

For certain retail outlets, pricing is of major concern. Supermarkets, automobile dealerships, and tire outlets are among the many merchandise areas in which the retailer often relies on price in his efforts to differentiate himself from his competition. In other outlets, such as department stores, price is less important as a differentiating factor, often because retailers and suppliers regard it as so important to the customer that they permit few variations in it.

One characteristic of price is that it is very easily duplicated by competitors, at least competitors of about the same size. Accordingly, if store X reduces its price on an item, the price will soon be matched by competing outlets. This is not true of such features as an advertising program, a physical store, or an assortment program. These are not only more difficult to duplicate but, in most instances, are not worth duplicating, because the benefits to the duplicator would probably not be great and might even be negative. Copying a competitor's advertising, for instance, is not likely to be a successful policy.

Another characteristic of price is that where the price of an item is considered of critical importance to retailers, any major decrease in price by any retailer in the immediate area will be met by the competition. Moreover, while competitors will meet decreases in price, they will often not copy price increases. Therefore prices are difficult for retailers to raise in such markets.

Another important characteristic of price is, of course, that price times quantity sold equals revenue. Thus the influence of price on a firm's revenue (and therefore on its profits) is clearly perceived by most executives.

### Long Term v. Short Term

The significance of the long-term aspects of pricing can be illustrated in terms of the wheel of retailing. A retailer that raises price in order to increase short-term profits often runs the risk of creating an umbrella for new entrants to the market. Thus a supermarket manager may feel that he can get an extra 2 cents a bottle for brand X of catsup. He may be right in the short run; he may even have just done a study finding that only a handful of customers really know what prices they are paying for catsup anyway. A policy of increasing prices in this fashion might work for many years and indeed has worked in several industries and for specific firms within industries. The wheel of retailing suggests that when an industry embarks on this path, or a strong firm within an industry leads an industry into such a path, at some point in time a low-price innovator or group of innovators is going to enter the field and change the competitive structure rather radically. Long-time participants in the industry who have gotten used to the higher prices may not be able to adapt to the new competitors and may even fail. These new entrants are weak in the beginning, but there is little reason to expect them to remain weak.

It does not follow from this that prices should never be raised in the short term. However, decision makers must be aware of the long-term significance of their actions, and short-term actions may often be detrimental to the long-term interests of the firm. This, presumably, is why many firms develop long-term price policies that do not permit short-term variations. Thus a firm could have a policy of not changing prices over a period of a month unless the costs of suppliers change substantially during that period. The firm could even advertise and promote this policy on the assumption that the benefits from it in a given situation might outweigh those of trying to take advantage of short-term retail price changes. Thus short-term methods of maximizing prices may not be relevant to some firms.

### Pricing Perspectives

Pricing is of concern to a retailer from three perspectives, each of which may be essential to his success:

1. He must develop a merchandising mix for his customers—a mix that includes price.

2. He is himself the object of the marketing mixes of his suppliers and potential suppliers.

3. He may desire to create a purchasing mix in order to interact with his supplier.

Pricing has been of greater importance in the study of economics than in the study of marketing or retailing. This can be traced to many factors, not the least of which is that economics, which is older than either, was developed at a time when price was more important to the firm than it is today. In addition, economics as a formal discipline grew out of a more academic environment than either retailing or marketing. Finally, prices are more easily quantified by analysts than any other element of a marketing or merchandising mix and thus permit many more academic exercises. Prices have therefore become central to such areas of economics as the theory of resource allocation.

The importance of pricing to a particular firm and to some extent to a type of store will depend primarily upon the role that pricing plays in its merchandising mix. The multistage approach suggests that this role would be established after a firm has selected its customer targets and decided on an appropriate brand or store image. In many retail firms, price has a relatively small role in that the firm has little price flexibility. For example, a men's furnishing store often may not vary the price of its men's shirts. In a few firms the role of pricing is extremely important: discount supermarkets, for example, may rely on price to bring customers in. Having established a role for pricing, a firm utilizing the multistage approach would then go on to create both long-term price policies and short-term price strategies before actually setting the price.

#### Dimensions of Creating Prices for Customers

In creating prices for customers, retailers have to worry about many other questions besides what to put on the price tag. For example, should a charge be made for delivery and return of merchandise? Perhaps there should be such charges in certain merchandise areas, such as furniture, but not in others, such as men's shirts. Should different customers be charged different prices? Appliance and auto dealers are notorious for doing so. How should special types of merchandise such as fashion goods vary in price over time? Should supermarkets offer more price specials in the middle days of the week, to fill up unused capacity, or at the end of the week, when more shopping tends to be done? What is the effect of the prices of some merchandise, for example *loss leaders*, on the sale of other merchandise? This topic is discussed below. At what time and by how much should slow-selling merchandise be marked down? In fashion merchandise areas, should decision makers take a two-or-three-dollar markdown on a $10 dress early in the season, or a five-or-six-dollar markdown at the end of it? Should a store develop a penalty charge schedule for charge customers who do not pay within 30 days, 60 days, or some other period? What competitors, if any, should the store meet in price? Should the prices of these competitors be met on the selling floor, so that all customers will benefit, or should they be met selectively, for customers who complain? If the prices are met selectively, should this be on the spot at the time of the complaint, or should the store require a shopping of the item to verify the lower price? Should a store limit the number of sales units that a single customer may purchase? If so, how — by coupons, or some other means?

### Supplier Pricing: Store Perspective

Several types of questions arise when a retailer interacts with suppliers, including:

1. *What is the relative importance of price in the store's purchasing mix?* "Relative" here means relative to other possible concessions from the supplier. Should the store bargain for a lower price, or are other concessions from the supplier more important (this was discussed in the previous chapter)?

2. *Should a store accept fair trade or other* retail price maintenance *procedures fostered by suppliers?*

3. *Should a store pay bills with terms on time?* A bill "with terms" is one that is discounted if it is paid early, usually within a specified period. The terms are commonly expressed as a number that combines discount and period. Thus 2/10 terms mean that one discounts the bills by 2 percent if one pays the bill within 10 days, usually of the date of the invoice. There are many other possibilities: 2/10 EOM, which means that a 2 percent discount may be taken if the bill is paid by the tenth of the month after the month of the invoice. High interest rates may also make it worthwhile for a store to pay suppliers late and then battle over the terms.

4. *Should a store take anticipation?* To take anticipation is to discount the bills of suppliers if the store pays them substantially before the due date. For example, a baseball glove manufacturer might offer stores the privilege of paying in April for goods delivered in November. But some stores might not find it convenient to segregate bills of this nature for special handling in the future; they might prefer to pay the bill now and discount the bill to the time when it is due. If the store does take anticipation, it still has to decide at what rate. Should it be at the cost of capital alluded to in Chapter 12? At a short-term or long-term rate of interest for large corporations?

### Supplier Pricing

The pricing perspective of the supplier is of importance to most stores, particularly if there is scope for bargaining. Thus a retail decision maker should become familiar with supplier pricing problems and procedures. Alfred R. Oxenfeldt suggests that, when suppliers sell to retailers, the supplier may consider the following:

1. Should a supplier price all items separately or as a product line?

2. Should a supplier charge different prices to different types of customer?

3. Should a supplier offer lower prices to larger stores than to smaller stores? This has the legal connotations discussed in Chapter 7.

4. Should closeouts be offered to outlets that will not lower the retail price severely but will take the lower price as extra margin? The supplier might well prefer this, since retail outlets stuck with the old merchandise would not be hurt so much.

5. Should a supplier vary price systematically over time? Perhaps over a period of a year, as in the automobile business, or over weeks or months, as in ladies' fashion. Discount policy is still more complex.

6. Should a supplier offer discounts for cash? If so, how rigidly should he enforce the terms? For example, if a supplier offering 2/10 terms is paid less 2/10 as late as 14 days after the date of the invoice, should he accept the check? If he does, should he forget the difference, or should he bargain later on?

7. Should a supplier foster a stable retail price level, among various types of retailers? If so, over what period?

8. Should a supplier limit the output on some items that are not deemed profitable below what the stores would purchase? For example, a television manufacturer has limited the number of private brand sets it will sell to an account.

9. Should a supplier offer different prices to different customers of the same type? For example, he might offer discount house A a price $X$ and discount house B, which is the same size, a price of $X - 10$.

## Price Differences at Retail

For certain types of product, at least, there is considerable variation in price among retail outlets selling the same items. For instance, Louis Bucklin (1970) noted differences in prices among supermarkets ranging from 13 percent for bread to 90 percent for fresh peas. Substantial differences may also be noted in the gasoline industry. Thus S. H. Clark and his associates found that differences in gas prices before federal and state taxes ranged in one area from 12.2 cents per gallon to 22.9 cents per gallon. For other types of item and brand there is little or no price variation among outlets. For example, a given brand of men's shirt will very likely be the same price in all the stores in a given geographic area.

Of course, a single outlet will vary its prices over time; indeed, some variations, such as weekly supermarket "specials" or the end-of-season reductions of fashion stores, occur on a regular basis. But we are concerned here with the great number of factors that create price differences among the same kinds of retail outlet. They include the following:

1. *Differential role of price.* A key factor is that price performs different functions for different firms. Thus, one supermarket may rely on price to bring customers into the store while another may rely on variety or location or some combination of other factors. Price in the latter instances may be only passive, that is, designed merely not to repel customers.

2. *Perception of the competition.* As suggested previously, some executives see themselves as competing specifically against other firms that they regard as their own firm's prime enemies. Such executives often attach great importance to meeting their prime competitors' prices. Other executives, in contrast, may regard competition as more of an impersonal force. They create a merchandise mix to get "their share of the business," and abstain from direct attacks against specific competitors. An executive with this perception might be more willing to let another firm have a price advantage in some limited area.

3. *Size of market area.* Price differences among retail outlets of the same kind would also appear to be related to differences in the sizes of the geographic market areas that they serve. It might be expected that as the size of a metropolitan area increased, the price for a given item would become lower, other factors remaining the same. One reason for this is that most of the large retail centers are also wholesale centers. Therefore, the cost of freight to the nearby store in the large city is usually lower. And indeed, certain firms have a policy of paying freight to specific large cities (a policy that, incidentally, presents substantial problems when the major city store has numerous branch stores surrounding the city). In addition, very large cities are usually sales centers for the various suppliers. Thus, many more of the customers in the city can be serviced by the sales organization at small incremental sales cost. Another factor conducive to lower costs for the retailer is that the buyers

Table 15.1
Relative discounts from list prices for selected products in five
major American cities (average product discount = 100)

| | Mean discount for all products | Auto-mobiles | Carpet-ing | Major appliances |
|---|---|---|---|---|
| New York | 120.8 | 119.6 | 123.3 | 114.2 |
| Chicago | 132.3 | 130.9 | 203.3 | 107.3 |
| Detroit | 98.2 | 126.8 | 86.7 | 93.8 |
| San Francisco | 68.1 | 30.9 | 73.3 | 90.4 |
| Boston | 81.9 | 90.7 | 20.0 | 94.6 |

Source: *Adapted from A. F. Jung, "Price Variations Among Discount Houses and Other Retailers,"* Journal of Retailing, *Spring 1961, pp. 13–16.*

for the retail organization are usually located in large cities and are much closer to the firms' principals. This is particularly so in cities like New York and Chicago. One hypothesis would be that the closer the buyer is to the supplier, the more likely he is to gain price and other concessions. Another might be that the number of potential consumers for a given outlet in a large center will tend to be greater than in the smaller center. Thus a low-price offering of one store should draw more customers in a larger market area than in a smaller one. This increased *price sensitivity* also acts as an incentive to suppliers to grant retailers price concessions in the larger markets. While the amount of hard data on the relationship between market size and price is not large, the little that there is tends to support the hypothesis that the bigger the market, the lower the price. Thus the data in Table 15.1 indicate that the mean discount across the four products studied is greatest in New York and Chicago.

4. *Consumer search activity*. Data also show that consumers are more inclined to search aggressively for high-price products than for less expensive ones. In another study by Bucklin (1966), the proportion of women who made more than one store visit before purchasing a specific product increased from 38.8 percent for articles priced from $5 to $14 to 64.4 percent for articles priced at $100 or more. It would be anticipated that the greater the search activity by the consumer the more similar would be the retail prices.

5. *Economies of scale*. There are *economies of scale* associated with the physical size of the par-

ticular store and there are economies of scale associated with the volume of goods that it or its parent organization purchases. It should be noted that the latter can be created either by a few very large stores or by a great many smaller ones. In general, chain stores have done best in merchandise areas in which the size of each store tends to be large—for example, general merchandise, variety, low-price department stores, food, and drugs. Some of these economies are passed on to the consumer, not because there is any moral feeling on the part of management that prices should be lower, but because it often pays stores with low cost merchandise or operations to offer lower prices. At the very least, low costs permit the sale of merchandise at lower prices. Thus, in the food industry larger units do tend to charge lower retail prices than do smaller units. Indeed, in this industry a firm generally has to have competitive prices if it is going to draw from a substantial trading area. Large buying power may also be conducive to aggressive *private brand* programs that may result in lower prices to the consumer in certain merchandise categories.

6. *Negotiation*. A further cause of differences in price among retail outlets of the same type is the manner in which consumer and retailer interact. Some retailers, as we have seen, individually negotiate prices with customers. In such instances there is little reason to assume that each customer strikes exactly the same bargain; an automobile dealer, for instance, will negotiate prices with many customers and often arrange different deals with each. One factor a dealer might consider in setting price is the probability of getting the same order from that customer at a higher price. Appliance dealers, too, often charge different prices to different customers and indeed often reward their salesmen with higher commissions on higher profit margins. Thus, a certain amount of price variability within the firm is only natural if it negotiates with the consumer. In all likelihood if price varies within firms in an industry, the price variation among those firms will be substantial.

7. *Type of store*. Prices also vary with the type of outlet that sells the merchandise. A classic and still topical example is the variation between dis-

count and department stores. For many items the typical department store was and is higher priced than the discount store; one observer suggests that its markup is as much as 7 percent higher. A study by one chain indicated that prices in its discount catalog showrooms were 15 to 17 percent lower than prices for the same merchandise in the *same* chain's discount stores. Gas stations charge lower prices for certain toys than do toy stores. Supermarkets in general charge lower prices for toothpaste than do neighborhood drug stores. In short, as the concept of the wheel of retailing suggests, certain types of retailers do and perhaps must charge higher prices than others offering the same merchandise.

### Short-term Pricing Concepts

Marginal analysis, with all its limitations, offers a useful approach to the mathematics of pricing. Thus a brief review of both marginal revenue and marginal cost should be undertaken at this point.

Marginal revenue curve is derived from the demand curve. A demand curve simply offers the relationships between price and quantity of units sold. Thus one can construct a demand curve from the data in Table 15.2. The marginal revenue is the revenue that is added by an advance from $q$ to $q + 1$. So long as total revenue increases whenever $q$ increases, the marginal revenue is increasing. Marginal cost is the added cost from $q$ to $q$ plus 1. Its derivation from the total cost curve is shown in Table 15.3.

The decision maker is supposed to price at the point where marginal cost equals marginal revenue. Given various assumptions, so long as marginal revenue exceeds marginal cost it pays to increase the

Table 15.2
Derivation of marginal revenue with unit increases in sales and unit decreases in price

| Units sold | Price | Total revenue | Marginal revenue |
|---|---|---|---|
| 8 | $12 | $ 96 | |
| 9 | $11 | $ 99 | $ 3 |
| 10 | $10 | $100 | $ 1 |
| 11 | $ 9 | $ 99 | $−1 |

Table 15.3
Derivation of marginal cost with unit increases in production and total cost

| Units produced | Total cost | Marginal cost |
|---|---|---|
| 8 | $53 | |
| 9 | $54 | $1 |
| 10 | $55 | $1 |
| 11 | $56 | $1 |

quantity and as a result lower the price. It pays to lower the price because each increment in quantity is bringing in more revenue than cost. However, if the decision maker proceeds past the point where marginal cost equals marginal revenue, the extra costs will exceed the extra revenues for the additional unit of quantity, and profits will decrease. The logic of this is compelling. As we saw in Chapter 11, the usefulness of this type of analysis is often questionable, but it does provide a starting point.

Another arithmetical concept is of some interest to the firm, despite its limited practical use. This is the concept of *elasticity*. The portion of the demand curve where a decrease in price leads to an increase in total revenue is held to be "elastic." Conversely, a demand curve is held to be "inelastic" over the points where an increase in price leads to an increase in total revenue. Thus elasticity may be expressed as:

$$\frac{\text{Percentage Change in Quantity}}{\text{Related Percentage Change in Price}}$$

If the marginal revenue is positive, the elasticity is more than one and the demand curve at that point is considered elastic.

Since costs are not considered, a firm can make few value judgments about price starting from the notion of elasticity alone, unless the decision maker is willing to assume that marginal costs are close to zero over the relevant range. In most forms of retailing, marginal costs are high because the merchandise cost is a high percentage of the selling price. Therefore, except under the most unusual conditions, a retail manager has little interest in whether his demand curve is elastic or inelastic. For almost all decisions, he may assume that it is elastic.

It is probably most useful to think in terms of elasticities when discussing whole industries. Gasoline prices are a well-known example: the amount of gasoline demanded by all consumers is not thought to be responsive to small changes in price. For this reason the industry demand curve for gasoline in a given geographic area is usually designated as inelastic over the relevant price range. The demand curve for a gasoline station, on the other hand, is deemed to be elastic so long as other stations do not meet the decrease in price.

However, the concept of elasticity does highlight one key question for the retail manager: What will be the amount of change in revenue for the firm if the price is raised or lowered from the present price by some moderate amount? Thus only price differences within a small range of the demand curve are relevant. For example, a supermarket manager might ask himself the question: What would happen if I raised the price of my poorest sellers by 3 percent and lowered the price of my best sellers by 2 percent?

For certain types of decision, it may be useful to assume that the amount paid to the supplier is the only cost that varies with increased volume and thus becomes the marginal cost. At the very least, the manager under most circumstances does not want to lower price when the cost of the merchandise is greater than the incremental revenue that can be attributed to the lower price. Since many observers feel that costs other than merchandise are fixed or close to fixed in many types of retailing in the short run, it may be useful to think of marginal cost and marginal revenue in this way. One might want to call this a *price change ratio* and express it thus:

$$\frac{\text{Change in Revenue from the Price Change}}{\text{Cost of Additional Merchandise}}$$

As for price increases, the revenue would presumably decrease and the change in merchandise cost would be negative. If the revenue decreased less than the decrease in merchandise cost, then a price increase might be considered.

## Ways to Price

Sooner or later, a retail price must be set. In the multistage approach to pricing the actual setting of the price is the sixth step. Marginal analysis typically establishes price in one step and includes efforts to quantify all the relevant variables. For many neither a multistage approach nor marginal analysis has much to say about pricing itself, which can be done in numerous ways. This section deals with some of them.

### Cost Plus Pricing

There are two distinct types of cost plus pricing: cost plus a fixed dollar or percentage margin; and cost plus a varying dollar or percentage margin. Giving each item the same initial percentage markup, for example 40 percent, is one way to achieve cost plus a fixed margin.

Various observers have suggested that the same initial percentage markup occurs over and over again in retail outlets because that is what retail decision makers want. In this author's opinion, however, it is more a reflection of one retailer's inability to control retail prices. Suppliers often exercise such control indirectly by only selling to accounts that will maintain the desired price. In addition, the retail price line "set" by the supplier is created in the knowledge of how consumers will react at that level. Knowing the price line, the supplier offers the retailer the minimum markup that is consistent with a high probability that he will obtain the order. This often creates an illusion of a fixed markup. But if sales do not meet his expectations, the supplier may lower his price, either to increase the support of the retailer or to create a new retail price line.

For example, let us suppose that a marketing manager is trying to establish the price to the consumer for an item. He checks with four knowledgeable merchandisers in his firm. They suggest that the retail should be $5 if the item is to sell well in the relevant markets. The marketing manager, who knows the retailers well, is aware that the minimum retail markup on which they will work in this department at the $5 retail price is 40 percent, or a $3 cost. If a retailer does not want to charge $5, and if he only operates on dollar price lines (i.e., prices at multiples of a dollar) in the relevant merchandise categories, he might have to switch to $4 or even $6, or markups of 25 and 50 percent, respectively. Markups in between are of course not possible within a dollar price line framework. In addition, such retailers would assume that other retailers would price the item at $5. Thus the marketing manager's four knowledgeable merchandisers may well be correct: $5 may be the "golden" price of acceptance. Thus a so-called fixed markup may not be simply a consequence of rather inflexible pricing methods at the retail level.

Cost plus a fixed percentage is an incomplete method at best, since it takes no account of variations in demand. In most circumstances it is of doubtful value, though a rigid markup policy may sometimes offer advantages from the point of view of game theory.

Cost plus a varying margin, on the other hand, presumably reflects differences in the amount demanded at different price levels. Seldom, however, will the interactions between demand and supply factors be clearly articulated in this method. Cost plus a varying margin is difficult to evaluate because all merchandise lines that do not have a fixed margin necessarily have a varying margin, regardless of how the price was obtained. Nevertheless, to the extent that prices by this method are set without consideration of the relevant demand factors, the likelihood of effective pricing is small. To the extent that the method does this, it may be justifiably criticized.

### Skimming the Demand Curve

If a retailer chooses a price of $15 from the following two alternatives:

| Price ($) | Estimated Quantity Demanded |
|---|---|
| 20 | 200 |
| 15 | 300 |

then 200 individuals will receive a five-dollar surplus inasmuch as, while they are prepared to pay $20, the price is only $15. A retailer might try to obtain these economic surpluses by charging $20 for two weeks and $15 thereafter, in the hope that the 200 will buy at the higher price and the other 100 at the lower price. This might be a useful technique in pricing certain types of fashion merchandise. On the other hand, a retailer might try to package the two products differently, so that some of the buyers willing to pay $20 might buy the "deluxe" package. In both instances the retailer is in effect skimming the demand curve. While this can take many forms, its purpose is always the same: to charge identified segments of the market as much as they are willing to pay, thereby minimizing the surplus to the consumer and maximizing the revenue to the store.

Clearly, effective use of this method requires some knowledge of the makeup of the relevant demand curve. At times, certain manufacturers and wholesalers will skim the curve by "using" different retail institutions over time. For example, the item may initially be sold to the department store at a high cost price that includes substantial advertising moneys. Thus the cost to the department store might be $6 and the retail price $10. There is enough supplier profit so that the supplier agrees to pay all the expenses of the retail advertising. As will be suggested in the chapter on advertising, the store may make money even if nothing is sold. The department store will usually sell some—possibly many—of the items to its customers, but whether it does or not, it will have established a retail value for the item. This is often more important to the supplier. As the excitement related to the item diminishes, the supplier will sell to other outlets in addition to the department store. If the value of the item has been established, so that a discount price will act as an incentive, fewer advertising moneys are necessary and the cost price to the retailer may be lower. In addition, the later purchasing outlets will often use a lower percentage markup. Such combination creates a substantially lower retail price that may appeal to customers that are highly interested in price. Some department stores will resist being used to establish the price as in the above example because it may negatively affect their image, while others may insist on more initial advertising moneys to compensate for them being "used" in this manner.

A good example of skimming the demand curve is the automobile industry, which appears to skim the curve over the model year both from manufacturer to retail dealer and from retail dealer to consumer. The result is a complex, flexible price that varies over the model year as demand changes.

### Blind Item Pricing

In order to skim the demand curve, one needs to identify the different kinds of customer. The next two methods of pricing are ways of estimating parts of a demand curve for a new product. Blind items are those that cannot be readily compared by consumers in other retail outlets: for example, an exclusive import. In blind item pricing, the decision maker establishes the price at the highest level at which it seems at all likely to sell well. He may estimate this initial price level directly, or he may ask others, such as his own sales people. The unit sales of the blind item are then watched carefully. If its sales are up to expectations the price is left where it is. But if it does not sell well, the price is lowered to the next relevant price line. This process is continued until a price level is found where the item sells satisfactorily. Defining "satisfactorily" is a matter for the decision maker. He may stop at a given level because if he were to try the next lower one, to see if it were more profitable, he would probably have trouble raising the price again if he turned out to be wrong. Of course, if he *knew* that the price level was more profitable, he would certainly adopt the lower price. But if this were the case, he would have little reason to use blind item pricing, because he would already know all the relevant parts of his demand curve. Finally, if a satisfactory price is not reached within

a "satisfactory" profit range, the item is discontinued.

The following is a (fictitious) example of blind item pricing. Let us suppose that an executive for a ladies' clothing store chain went abroad to buy some umbrellas. In Italy she found some very exciting patterns that the manufacturer offered to her exclusively in her geographic area. She bought 1,000 of these umbrellas at a cost of $2 FOB her store, i.e., the manufacturer said he would pay the freight to the store (foreign merchandise is not usually shipped in this way, but it makes the example clearer). She took a sample of the umbrellas back to the States and asked the salespeople in several of her stores: What is the highest price that you can get for this item and have some probability of it becoming a good seller? Their answers averaged out at $14, so this became the initial price. All one thousand of the umbrellas went on display in all the stores on May 1. By June 1, however, there were still 800 units in stock, i.e., only 200 units had been sold, stolen, or otherwise disposed of. This information was furnished to the executive by a computer printout. The executive did not consider 200 units per month a satisfactory rate of sale. However, she decided to keep the price at $14 for the time being. At the end of the season she had a huge clearance sale of the overstocked Italian umbrellas at $7. Since the quality image of the item was by now firmly established, the sale was very successful.

Blind item pricing as described here is biased toward higher prices. The student should not infer, however, that all blind items are priced at so high a percentage margin. Clearly, a margin of $12 on an item that cost $2 is unusual. When it occurs, it is not to be dismissed out of hand by the retailer as "profiteering"; high prices are desirable in many circumstances, and may even be essential for the survival of the firm.

### Differential Pricing

One of the commonest forms of pricing in retailing and marketing firms is differential pricing. Once again, the key variable is the decision maker's knowledge of the market. Skimming the demand curve assumes that the decision maker has enough knowledge of his curve to divide it into meaningful segments. Blind item pricing assumes that he knows very little about his demand curve and therefore sets out to empirically develop one or more points on it. Differential pricing estimates a point on the demand curve for an item by looking at points on the demand curves for similar items. It is assumed that the decision maker knows points on several such demand curves. Thus he may know that item X is priced at $15 and that 240 units have sold in the last two weeks. He may then ask: What is the difference between item X and item Y in the eyes of the consumer? If item X, to which item Y is being compared, is selling satisfactorily at $15, and if item Y is priced so that the difference between it and item X in price will seem reasonable in the eyes of the customer, item Y will probably sell well, too. It will be seen that differential pricing emphasizes the customer and his perception of the manifest differences within or between brands. Here, if one adds to or deletes a feature from an item, the question is how much is it worth to the customer. The benchmark is the price paid by the customer for a known product with a known sales rate and price.

It follows that in differential pricing, cost is not considered except as a constraint. Thus a difference between products that cost the store an extra $50 but are only worth an extra $2 to the customer is not apt to be very profitable to the firm. Furthermore, if an item cost an extra $2, but the customers perceived the incremental value of the difference to be $50, then, if one were using differential pricing, one would price the item $50 higher. This might even be true if the cost of the extra feature is negative. Thus a decrease in cost of $2 might actually bring a $50 increase in the price of an item. One example of a negative cost bringing extra revenues might be certain automatic transmissions on cars.

Differential pricing can also be used between brands. This has particular relevance to a retail firm in pricing its own brands. If a manufacturer's item is priced at $1, what difference does the customer perceive between this item and the new item, considering the fact that the new item will have the retailer's name on it? In most instances, a private brand must be priced lower than the national brand just because it *is* a private brand. The reputation of the national brand is typically worth something to the customer. However, a store with a loyal following may be able to claim special merits for its private brand and so charge a higher price.

### Price Lining

Most of the preceding has suggested that a retailer develops his prices one item at a time. We have also seen that the price is just one element of the total merchandising package to be presented to the consumer. However, it is just as true that a price for one item is just one element of the total package of prices. Thus a merchant must be concerned with how the prices of various items interrelate.

For a given merchandise classification one can build up an assortment by grouping together various brands and items. Thus one can make an effort to blend the various brands and prices selected by the decision maker into some type of whole that will be meaningful to the customers. In developing an assortment, the decision maker might choose to focus on the price lines, which might then be constructed on various bases—the store's present price lines, its expectations for the coming season, any relevant theories of price lines, and so forth. One such theory suggests that in a given merchandise area, the quantity of merchandise should be distributed among price lines according to a bell-shaped curve. Thus a store might have only small representation on the lowest and highest price lines; the largest amount of dollars and the largest assortment would be in the middle. The bell-shaped curve is of course only one reference point for the decision maker, and is continually supplemented by other information. Another theory of price lines suggests that each item alternative should offer three distinct options, such as good, better, best. Both theories were discussed in Chapter 13.

A store may even define its place in the competitive environment by consciously making allowances for the way in which the customers perceive its price lines. For example, a store management might determine that the best-selling price line of store X is $4.99 and of store Y is $5.99. It might then decide to stock mainly items selling at $6.99. In this way it would be molding an image of itself in the minds of customers. Alternatively, a store can let price lines "just happen," and develop them only after analyzing unit and dollar sales. Thus the managers will constantly be adapting to the votes cast by the consumer for the various price lines.

Merchants in many types of store buy to price lines and consider brands only secondarily. The decision maker searches the market for the desired price lines in the desired quantities. Suppliers are aware that many retailers buy this way, and they create merchandise accordingly.

### Price Leadership

In many retail markets, prices among various retail outlets show considerable interdependence. Such has historically been the case with the pricing of gasoline at the retail level. Each station of a similar type—e.g., all stations selling the same major brand—will generally keep approximately the same prices as others in its immediate trading area because each operator feels that the other stations will meet any substantially lower price. It is generally therefore in everyone's self-interest to maintain a high retail price, because the total amount demanded by all customers does not increase substantially when prices are lowered. Almost any member of a market in which there is great price interdependence may initiate a price decrease, and the others will follow. The same is not true of price increases, since firms tend to follow some firms more than others. Those that regularly lead the market in increasing prices are considered *price leaders*. Leadership of this sort may accrue to a firm for many reasons, including acknowledged expertise in the market, a large share of the market, and a desire on its part to be the leader.

Price leadership may take numerous forms in retailing. In many types of retailing new items are a way of life and are coming out all the time. A single firm may assume the lead in giving a price to an item

for which there is no established price, and other firms carrying the item may follow suit. For example, a fashion good that costs $3.60 might be priced by the first firm to carry the item in a geographic area at $6.99. Others might follow this leadership and also price the item at $6.99 instead of what some might consider the more obvious price of $5.99. Another form of price leadership might rest on a whole series of actions, as when a store or set of stores establishes the policy that it will not knowingly be undersold by any other stores in the area. Such a policy may require quite a few store-paid shoppers to enforce; a department store, for instance, would have to employ shoppers to stop at discount stores, small stores, supermarkets, and so forth. Once the first store in a given area had set up this system, any other store of the same type could have such a policy, if it chose, simply by having a few shoppers watch the prices of the first store. Thus the first store would become a price leader—at a price.

The supplier may also act as the catalytic agent in raising price, especially when there is great price interdependence among retail outlets. Thus under the Colgate Doctrine (Chapter 7), firms are usually permitted to select the retailers to whom they would like to sell. In certain fashion industries, as well as furniture and others, this means that the supplier will choose to sell outlets of similar types. These are industries that tend to feature the push type of distribution considered in Chapter 3. In a push distribution, a supplying firm cannot afford to antagonize any group of resellers. Thus these suppliers tend to select the most attractive reseller segment. Consider a supplier in a fashion industry in which a 40 percent markup is typical. If he raises billing prices from $3.60 to $4.20, all the retailers know without being spoken to that they are supposed to raise the price from $5.99 to $6.99.

### Other Aspects of Pricing

Some key subjects related to retail pricing are now discussed briefly.

### Price-Quality Relationship

A very important question for some retailers is: Is there a relationship in the customer's mind between price and quality? Does a high price for an item connote high quality in the mind of the consumer? Apparently, if a consumer does not have other cues by which to establish value, she will look to the price. Thus under certain conditions it is possible for a firm to sell more units of a product at a higher price than at a lower price.

### Market Basket Pricing

In certain types of retail outlet — those in which customers typically purchase a number of different items — it is probably useful for a retail manager to think in terms of the profits yielded by a customer's total purchases during a single shopping trip to the store. A store that looks at pricing in this manner does not mind offering some items at a very low price, perhaps below invoice cost, if the customers so attracted also purchase enough high-margin merchandise. Loss-leader promotions in supermarkets are usually defended by alluding to the market basket. Of course, loss leaders aid the large business because it has more items for the customer to buy.

### Creativity and Pricing

An item can often be put on sale for a higher price, and nevertheless sell better, if it has been altered to make it more attractive to the customers the retailer is trying to reach. Selling more items at a higher price is not inconsistent with the assumption of a negatively sloped demand curve, which in any case has nothing sacred about it. The demand curve assumes that all other factors, including product, remain the same. When the physical product is changed in a meaningful way, a new demand curve is called for.

### Odd Prices

It is usual in some forms of retailing to price at a level just below the next largest unit of currency. Thus one finds that prices often are 29 cents, $1.99, $5.95, or perhaps $1,999.00. It has been suggested that this type of pricing may have been fostered by merchants to require the sales clerk to give change to the customer and thus ring up the sale on the register. Most, however, defend the practice on the grounds that odd price endings sound less expensive than even ones. In recent years, discount houses have adopted other endings such as 88 cents. These are supposed to appear even cheaper than the 95- and 99-cent endings that have always been associated with the higher-priced department stores. Odd endings, in addition to their effect on customers, can be used to communicate something to the store's decision makers. For example, all regular prices might end in 88 cents, all first markdowns in 77 cents, all second markdowns in 66 cents, and so forth. One could further differentiate high-markup and low-markup items by the various endings. For example, markups between 40 and 50 percent might end in 9, and so forth. All this can be made easier by computers.

As might be anticipated, if many consumers feel that $9.99 is a lot less than $10.00, others will feel that an even price is characteristic of a quality store. Accordingly, stores that seek to develop a quality image may foster even price endings. Such a store might sell a diamond ring at $2,000.00, a shirt at $10.00, and so forth. Managements have to use their judgment in this matter, since the studies undertaken offer little conclusive evidence in either direction. In addition, it may be that consumer attitudes toward odd endings change markedly over time, and also depend on the nature of the local competition. There are, then, no simple rules for using these endings.

### Markup and Cost

It has been hypothesized that in the supermarket industry, the percentage markup varies inversely with the cost of the item: the higher the dollar cost, the lower the percentage margin. Whether this is so or not—and there is some evidence to confirm it—percentage markups in many other types of retail outlet will increase as the price increases, at least within a given brand. This is true of cars, most furniture, and many other items. The phenomenon is probably due to such factors as the heavy price competition in the low-cost end of most merchandise lines; the effective use of personal selling at the retail level; the preoccupation of many types of retail outlet with percentage markup; and the relatively low unit sales at the top of most merchandise lines. Thus low unit sales may mean that the margin for the item has to be high to create an acceptable profit per unit of space.

## Social Aspects of Pricing

Nothing has been said in this chapter so far about fair prices. To most observers of marketing in this country the question has little meaning: the decision maker simply makes prices that he hopes will maximize the firm's long-term profit. Business is business and fair prices are irrelevant, because there are no generally accepted standards of fairness. Besides, competition is supposed to be good for society. Thus if a retail organization buys an item for $2 and sells it for $14, this is good business if it sells enough units to make a juicy profit. Recently, however, many individuals and organizations have begun to question the fairness of certain prices, particularly in the inner-city communities. Why, for example, should poor people pay more than the well-to-do for the same or worse merchandise? Even if businessmen are not concerned with the moral implications of charging high prices, they may have to be concerned with the possible effects on their businesses. The businessman of the future is going to have to reckon with the community in which he lives. The community is finding ways of dealing with merchants that flout its interests too conspicuously. Soon there may be some type of social accounting system that will impose a modicum of social con-

science on all retailers. A further threat that society can hold over retailers is price control. Since August 1971, retailers have had to take this threat quite seriously.

## Summary

1. Pricing is such a potentially destructive form of competition that firms of the same type generally prefer not to use it as a competitive weapon. A key reason for this is that pricing is usually the easiest element of the merchandise mix to copy. Thus many types of outlet do not have great price flexibility, and in this sense retail pricing for those outlets is not important.

2. Pricing has both short- and long-term significance to the firm. The long-term significance is dramatized by the wheel of retailing described earlier. A firm can make a series of decisions that increase short-term profits. If prices are gradually increased over time, under certain conditions low-priced firms can enter the market profitably. And these firms can grow into strong competitors.

3. Pricing is of major concern to the retailer from three perspectives:

   A. The retailer must develop a price for his customers.

   B. The retailer is the object of the marketing mixes of suppliers and potential suppliers.

   C. The retailer may want to create a purchasing mix to interact with suppliers.

4. There are a great number of factors that create differences in price among retailers:

   A. Different role of price for different firms;

   B. Different perception of competition by the market participants;

   C. Size of the market area;

   D. Consumer search activity;

   E. Economies of scale;

   F. Negotiation between consumers and retailers.

5. There are many short-term pricing methods that might be used, including:

    A. *Skimming the demand curve,* by which groups of customers are charged as much as they will pay;

    B. *Blind item pricing,* by which the retailer empirically estimates elements of the demand curve;

    C. *Differential pricing,* in which the decision maker makes reference to a point on the demand curve of another item.

6. Price lining deserves special mention in retail pricing. Firms can develop and change an image by adjusting its price lines.

7. Other aspects of pricing are discussed.

    A. In price leadership, firms follow others down in price but may only follow a price leader upward.

    B. Customers tend to feel that, if they do not have other cues, the higher the price the better the quality.

    C. Firms that sell many items to a customer may think in terms of price and profitability of the entire basket (so-called market basket pricing).

    D. Changing a physical item means that a new demand curve is relevant and that one may be able to profit by charging more money even if the cost is the same or less.

    E. Odd endings such as .77 cents are often used in retailing.

8. The imposition of price controls has dramatized a relatively neglected subject, the social aspects of pricing. Society is beginning to suggest that retailers consider such things as fairness in pricing.

## Discussion Questions

1. Outline the advantages of the multistage approach.

2. Differentiate among skimming the demand curve, differential pricing, and blind item pricing.

3. Describe two types of cost plus pricing.

4. Describe market basket pricing.

5. What is price elasticity?

6. What is price leadership?

7. What are some long-term considerations in pricing?

8. How can a retailer use price lines to change his image?

9. Devise a price ending system that would serve at least three useful functions.

## References

Bucklin, Louis P., "Testing Propensities to Shop," *Journal of Marketing*, January 1966.

Bucklin, Louis P., in Frederick D. Sturdivant *et al.* (eds.), *Managerial Analysis in Marketing* (Glenview, Ill.: Scott, Foresman, 1970).

Clark, S. H., *et al., An Analysis of Competition and Price Behavior in the British Petroleum Industry* (Menlo Park, Ca.: Stanford Research Institute, 1964).

Oxenfeldt, Alfred R., *Pricing for Marketing Executives* (Belmont, Ca.: Wadsworth, 1961).

## Further Reading

Belden, Donald L., *The Role of the Buyer in Mass Merchandising* (New York: Chain Store Age Books, 1971).

Dalrymple, Douglas, J., and Thompson, Donald L., *Retailing: An Economic View* (New York: Free Press, 1969).

Holton, Richard, "A Simplified Approach to Capital Budgeting," *California Management Review*, Spring, 1961.

Kaplan, A.D.H., *et al., Pricing in Big Business* (Washington, D.C.: Brookings Institution, 1958).

Nelson, Paul E., and Preston, Lee E., *Price Merchandising and Food Retailing: A Case Study* (Berkeley, Ca.: Institute of Business and Economic Research, University of California, 1966).

Sturdivant, Frederick D., *et al., Managerial Analysis in Marketing* (Glenview, Ill.: Scott, Foresman, 1970).

## Case History: *Fair Trade and the Colgate Doctrine*

Jane Harrison was a student at Eastgate College and an avid consumerist. One day she excitedly brought an article to her retailing class. The article, published in April 1973, suggested that fair trade was losing ground rapidly. The Massachusetts Supreme Court had just unanimously ruled to set aside the state fair trade law. Now only 16 of the 50 states enforced fair trade. The article went on to suggest that the Senate Judiciary Subcommittee on Antitrust and Monopoly was going to consider recommending the repeal of federal regulations enabling state fair trade statutes. Jane was enthusiastic about the fact that the "free" marketplace was about to become the only price control over goods in areas where prices had formerly been fixed. She related her opinions to the class, which was being taught by Professor Samuel Eisenbahn.

The professor had always been against fair trade. In response to Jane's question, however, he suggested that in his experience fair trade had not been of great significance; indeed, it had been of smaller and smaller significance as time went on. In his opinion, the main advantage of fair trade from the manufacturer's point of view was that it permitted him to sell retail outlets with varying costs and margin requirements. For example, he told his students, let us suppose that a bottle of aspirin had a list price of $1 with a 40 percent margin, which would mean that it cost 60 cents. A small drugstore might feel that it did not want to go below a retail price of $1. However, a supermarket chain might want to sell it for 80 cents, as might a discount and department store chain that carried drugs. The drugstore might very well get rid of this aspirin rather than meet the competition. But if the price were maintained at $1, all these different outlets might carry it. Stores are far more prone to accept a higher-than-desirable margin than to accept a lower-than-desirable one. Thus fair trade often permitted a manufacturer to sell to various kinds of outlet, although the margins that he offered were not always as high as some of them would have liked.

It was true that fair trade if effectively maintained by the manufacturer also severely limited price advertising at the retail level. However, continued Professor Eisenbahn, fair trade had had a much smaller effect on maintaining retail prices than the Colgate Doctrine. By the Colgate Doctrine a supplier could, under most sets of conditions, actually select the firms to whom he sold. By and large, suppliers in the building, furniture, and clothing industries, to name only a few, could not afford to sell to antagonistic types of outlet like department stores and discount stores. Thus firms were forced in general to stick with compatible outlets — for example, department stores and small stores. There was, then, no great risk that prices would be cut because it was in no one's best interest to cut them. It was not so much, he hastened to explain, that retail organizations prohibited the supplier from selling to other organizations by actually threatening them, although this did happen. It was that the perceived profits of the higher-margin stores with the relevant brand would be greatly affected by sales to a low-margin operator such as a discount store. Thus the brand in question would be thrown out. Since both the retailer and the manufacturer knew this would happen, the manufacturer simply would not sell to low-margin outlets. The effect on suppliers was great.

In conclusion, Professor Eisenbahn suggested that observers of retailing were increasingly questioning the Colgate Doctrine. He also pointed out that practically no analysis had been done by retailers or marketers on what would happen if the Colgate Doctrine were overthrown. What would happen, for instance, if anyone or any organization with a certified check could buy from General Motors at the same price as a dealer? Or if a discount store could buy directly from any manufacturer in the country? What kind of a market would we have then?

## Discussion Questions

1. Is Professor Eisenbahn right about the importance of the Colgate Doctrine as compared with fair trade?

2. Would completely free trade, i.e., trade unregulated by law, necessarily result in lower prices for consumers? Describe the circumstances under which it might or might not do so, assuming that the laws governing contract and fraud remained in force.

## 16

## Inventory Management

Inventory permeates the entire retail decision process. But it is of chief concern to the decision maker after the suppliers have been chosen, the merchandise assortments created, and the negotiations finished. To a great extent, the purpose of inventory management is to carry out the intentions of the manager who made the initial arrangement with the supplier. Clearly, someone must order and reorder the merchandise as needed or desired. If this is to be done effectively, the merchandiser must keep track of the merchandise in the stores. He must know how fast or slowly each item is selling now: he must forecast how the items will sell in the future. The *inventory system* is designed to keep track of unit sales. It is therefore the central focus of the store's merchandise information system. The outputs of the inventory system strongly influence the store's future assortments, its choice of suppliers, the negotiations with them, the price lines it carries, its price markdowns, and so forth.

Most stores and merchandise subclassifications can take in only a limited amount of merchandise during any one period of time; the limits are set by the physical size of the store or department and the money available. In the retail method of accounting this restriction is formally introduced in the form of open-to-buy. As will be remembered from Chapter 8, open-to-buy is the amount of merchandise, usually expressed in retail dollars, that the specific merchandise area can bring in over some time interval to achieve the dollar level of inventory that is desired at the end of the period, granting certain assumptions.

### Various Inventory Pressures

The amount of inventory in a store is of substantial importance to its top management. Since total inventory is only the sum of the inventories of each merchandise area, top management is usually heavily involved in planning inventory levels for these areas. And top management will usually watch the inventory levels to make sure that they do not get out of hand. One distress signal for a merchandise area is a stock that is sharply out of the line with projections.

Top management also fears inventory shortages and obsolescence. The dollar value of inventory in some merchandise areas such as fashion can deteriorate very rapidly if the customer no longer wants it. It is useful to consider the pressures that a merchant faces for keeping either a small or a large amount of merchandise, because the inventory decision is always a compromise between these conflicting forces.

The following factors induce a merchant to carry a small amount of merchandise:

1. *Inventory costs money.* The merchant must consider the cost of the inventory that he handles. Even if the firm has the money to pay for the inventory, interest or other potential sources of income are being foregone. Thus retail firms generally impute interest to a decision area as a way of making sure that the decision maker understands how much increased inventory costs (and, indeed, inventory can cost a great deal). For many firms, the most important cost associated with a higher level of inventory is that of lost opportunities for investment, whether short- or long-term. For example, a series of increased short-term commitments for alternatives such as inventory might prevent a firm from undertaking other, longer-term alternatives, such as the opening of new stores.

2. *Loss of value.* The merchant who purchases in large quantities runs the risk that the cost price of the merchandise will drop, whether because of style obsolescence, changes in market conditions, or the seasonal evolution of a product. We are not dealing here with drops of a mere 2 or 3 percent: end-of-season differentials of 50 percent are not uncommon in many merchandise areas.

3. *Freshness.* The more frequently the merchandise is delivered by the supplier, the fresher it is likely to appear or taste. Fresh merchandise tends to be easier to sell, and enhances the image of the firm.

4. *Risk of theft.* The smaller the amount of inventory on hand, the less merchandise is likely to be stolen. The amount of theft should increase with increased inventory because more merchandise will usually be exposed to more employees of the firm, if not to more consumers. Also, it is easier for a manager to control a smaller amount of merchandise throughout the store system.

5. *Adaptability.* A smaller level of stock permits the retailer to be more adaptable. Consumers' wants and needs are always changing; suppliers, too, are continually faced with changing opportunities. If the retailer is locked into a merchandise situation in which the merchandise is not selling, he often cannot take advantage of exciting merchandise opportunities. For instance, an analysis of his unit controls may indicate that three new styles would sell very well. If he is heavy on nonselling inventory, he may not be able to buy more of the potential sellers.

6. *Overhead.* Storage, insurance, and related costs generally increase as the level of inventory rises.

There are also pressures on a merchant to carry large quantities of inventory. They include the following:

1. *Advantages of large orders.* Quantity discounts, special purchases, special models, and aggressive buying generally require larger initial purchases or commitments. A retailer who is desirous of creating new products cannot do so by placing orders for three units at $10 each. If the retailer is going to be a potent force in the market, he is probably going to have to place initial commitments that seem large to the supplier. This means that while the supplier may hold much stock in his warehouse, the retailer's inventory commitment will have to be large.

2. *Risk of nondelivery.* Suppliers may run out of best-selling merchandise and be unable to process orders for it within the desired period. Especially when the goods have been purchased from foreign countries, it is not usually possible to reorder them at short notice. Many retailers strive to develop the necessary information rapidly enough so that reorders can be placed ahead of other retail firms, and the probability of delivery increased. But the risk of nondelivery is always there unless the retailer owns the merchandise.

3. *Savings to supplier.* Various supplier costs should be reduced by larger retail orders. If the store's own efficiency is not reduced, larger orders will often increase the efficiency of the entire channel. Indeed, at certain times a retailer may be able to take a railroad car of merchandise and so bypass one step in the physical distribution process. Dynamic buyers interacting with suppliers that have malleable marketing mixes should be capable of getting substantial concessions in instances where the supplier's own efficiency would be increased by granting them.

4. *Lower ordering costs.* Fewer merchandise orders per unit of time will usually mean lower ordering costs for both store and supplier. Ordering costs include the costs of processing the merchandise through the accounting, marking, receiving, warehouse, and other departments.

5. *Fewer lost sales.* There should be fewer lost sales of an item in which the stock position is higher, provided that

the larger inventory is handled as skillfully as the smaller inventory. There should be fewer orders from the supplier and correspondingly fewer opportunities to be out of stock.

6. *Less frequent counts.* A larger level of inventory requires less frequent physical counts of merchandise, if physical counts are necessary for the purpose of reordering.

7. *Future price increases.* Supplier prices may increase over the period of time.

## The Ideal Inventory System

There is no ideal inventory system for solving problems as complex as those in retailing. Every mathematical model must make simplifying assumptions that set it apart from reality. The most that can be hoped for is a model that works well under real-world conditions or at least works better than the present system. Searching for the optimal model is an exercise in futility, for the following reasons (among the many that could be cited):

1. There are many problems relating to the cost of capital that appear unanswered, at least at this point in time. Is it possible to designate a cost of capital that can be applied to inventory for a given firm? Would this cost be the same for inventory used to increase an existing store's level of stock as for the inventory level of a new store before the decision to build the store has been made? Is the cost of capital for bricks in a new building the same as for the minimum inventory level required to open the new store? Similarly, can an acceptable cost be developed for equity capital, and can a retail decision maker balance it against the cost of debt capital, on the one hand, and the cost of capital for retained earnings, on the other? In this author's opinion, most of the above questions have not been satisfactorily resolved, nor does their resolution appear close. It is therefore impossible to *precisely* designate the costs to the store of bringing in additional inventory or of maintaining a given inventory level. These problems need not overwhelm the retailer so long as he understands the limitations of his mathematical model.

2. It is not at all clear what cost a retailer should attribute to being out of stock on an item. The student should realize that many merchants will run out of stock on certain items deliberately, especially if they are unprofitable items stocked largely for promotional purposes. For example, retailers might sell one pound of Brand X coffee at 99 cents when the cost at wholesale is $1.00. Thus they may want to be in stock for only part of the day. These merchants believe that there is a positive benefit in being out of stock on special merchandise. There may even be a positive payout for being out of stock on regular merchandise. Thus if a store runs out of $2 blue pens with a markup of 40 percent, and if all the customers that ask for the $2 pens end up buying $3 ones with the same markup, it might be said that in the short term the department is better off being out of stock.

Other factors should be considered in estimating the costs of being out of stock. Will many customers think that if the store is out of stock on blue pens, it is probably out of stock on $49.99 mattresses, and so not bother to visit the bedding department? More importantly, perhaps, will the customer change his impression of the total store—at least with regards to its various assortments? Will she talk to other customers about her sad experience? Or, conversely, will she be happier with the $3 pen than she would have been with the $2 one, and tell all her friends about its and the store's merits? The complexity of these problems is obvious, and most sophisticated inventory programs disregard them— necessarily so, it appears, for the present.

3. The effect of the level of inventory on the level of sales is still largely unknown. Many systems of inventory assume that the relationship is a direct one. Others assume that there is no relationship, so long as the level of inventory remains above zero. Deductively, there would appear to be some relationship between sales and level of stock for most types of items; there is even some empirical confirmation of this for certain kinds of merchandise. The retailer would expect sales to decrease if many of his shelves are almost bare. Similarly, sales may decrease on an item if it is nearly out of stock. Probably most merchants would concede that for most types of inventory there is some relationship between the sales and the level of inventory that

appears for the item on the shelves. But what relationship? This subject is considered in greater detail in connection with fashion merchandising, the subject of the next chapter.

## Types of Inventory

It is often useful to consider the inventory problems of similar types of merchandise. One classification, developed by Spencer B. Smith, groups together items that are staples, fashion items, big-ticket items such as major appliances and furniture, small-ticket items such as nuts and screws, and one-time purchases such as toys for Christmas. Here, we shall be dealing mainly with two groups, staple and fashion—staple in this chapter, fashion in the next. Of course, the distinction between staple and fashion is not always clear; many if not most merchandise areas consist of elements of both types.

Fashion and staple systems have several characteristics in common. First, they generally emphasize items and units rather than dollars. Moreover, they both tend to be based on exception reporting, that is, an item is brought to the attention of the decision maker only when its performance exceeds a certain range, positively or negatively. Mathematical elegance is of relatively little importance to either group.

Nevertheless, staple systems are treated quite differently from fashion systems. It is true that staple systems are characterized by their consistent demand pattern, but this consistency is obvious only when compared to the demand pattern for fashion merchandise. Actually, most staple merchandise does not have a consistent sales pattern at all, and substantial changes in demand occur within staple merchandise classifications from week to week, year to year, and season to season. Even if merchandise is not affected positively by various seasons, it may be affected negatively in that the interest in seasonal merchandise will decrease the interest in nonseasonal merchandise.

### Logic of Staple Systems

Staple stock systems are generally designed to indicate when to order the merchandise and how much to order. Ideally, the order is placed when the inventory level on hand will just last until the new merchandise comes in from the supplying firm. For example, let us assume that it takes nine selling days for the merchandise to get from the supplier to the retail selling floor. If one of the items sells each day, then in nine days nine units will be sold. When the stock reaches nine, then, we order the merchandise knowing that this stock will last exactly nine days and that when the old stock is gone, the new stock will be in.

All this, of course, assumes that we have a known sales rate, which could happen only in a deterministic world. Once we drop this assumption, the problem changes. We can find out what the average rate of sale for our item is. In the above example, it could be one unit a day. However, it is likely, indeed probable, that we would have sold some number other than nine over the nine-day period. Perhaps we would have sold eight or seven units, in which case we would still have stock. However, we *might* also have sold 10, 11, 12, or even more units over the same period. If we had used our deterministic reorder point and had reordered when the stock was at nine units—we would have been out of stock on the item for all customers after the ninth unit had been sold—until the new merchandise came in.

Given (a) the specific number of days for the merchandise to get from the supplier to the store, typically called *lead time*, and (b) the sales data for the item; then a distribution can be constructed as shown in Figure 16.1. Knowing the distribution of the sales, the decision maker may be able to select the number of extra units to add to our deterministic reorder point. In this way he may achieve the desired probability of remaining in stock on that item from the time the merchandise is ordered until it gets on the floor. This extra stock is called the *buffer* or *safety* stock, because it provides a buffer for extra safety against being out of stock. If the decision maker only wants to take a one in 20 chance of being

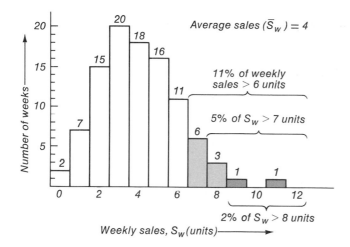

Figure 16.1 *Distribution of weekly retail sales of one item for 100 weeks* [Source: *Joseph Buchan and Ernest Koenigsberg*, Scientific Inventory Management (*Englewood Cliffs, N.J.: Prentice-Hall, Inc.,* © *1963), p. 8. By permission of the publisher.*]

out of stock on that item for each reorder, then he selects the safety stock that will offer him this chance. Given the situation in Figure 16.1, and assuming a lead time of one week, the decision maker would order when the stock level reached seven if he wanted the one in 20 chance. Only for 2 percent of the weeks will the sales be greater than eight units. The decision maker can decrease the probabilities of being out of stock by raising the in-stock position at which the order is placed, for example from seven to eight.

A key assumption of the above technique is that the lead time from the time of the order until the time that the merchandise comes onto the selling floor remains constant. This assumption is rarely justified, since the retail decision maker can usually speed the delivery time from the supplier should he choose to. He can also usually speed the merchandise through the various in-store steps, such as receiving and marking. In addition, the supplier's behavior might be quite unpredictable unless carefully monitored by the retailer. Thus any system based on the assumption of a constant lead time is apt to produce substantial error.

A further problem in establishing the best reorder point is that a retailer usually orders in groups of items from a given supplier, not just one item at a time. Seldom will all these items reach a reorder point simultaneously. Thus the stock level at which the order is placed is often a compromise between the reorder points of many different types of item. Furthermore, some of the items ordered will be in stock at the supplier's and some will not. Some can be ordered only in units of twelve; others can be ordered individually. Thus the problems of combining items into one purchase order are not simple.

### Two Basic Staple Systems

So far we have considered the stock level at which the order should be placed. A decision maker must also order some particular quantity of each item. He must therefore weigh the advantages of carrying a large stock of an item or group of items against the advantages of carrying a small stock. The quantity that is ordered is often directly related to the method of determining when to order. This is made clearer by the two systems now outlined.

The staple systems that have evolved over time to meet the retailer's needs are of two basic types: the *reorder point system* and the *fixed replenishment system*. Under the reorder point system, the merchandise is ordered when the units in stock reach a predesignated level, the order point. This is obtained in the same way as in our initial example. In other words, it is equal to the anticipated unit sales for the time between the order and the receipt of the merchandise on the selling floor, plus some additional safety stock to take account for the variability of this sales estimate.

To use the reorder point system, one must usually develop an economic order quantity. This is based on the minimum total variable costs of the inventory. The classic model of the economic order quantity regards inventory costs as being made up of two parts: (*a*) the costs of ordering; (*b*) the carrying costs. The costs of ordering are all the costs related to placing an order—costs that are assumed to be independent of the size of the order. The carrying costs are the extra costs attached to increasing the level of inventory. Some costs fit one of these two molds; others do not. It is further assumed that consumer demand is uniform throughout the period under analysis. Thus the total variable costs can be expressed as follows, on an annual basis:

$$\text{Total Annual Costs} = \text{Cost of Ordering} + \text{Carrying Costs}$$
$$= \frac{Co(S)}{Q} + \frac{Cu(IQ)}{2}$$

where   $Q$ = amount of each order, in units
$Co$ = cost of placing an order
$Cu$ = unit cost of the item
$I$ = carrying cost, in percent per year
$S$ = annual sales, in units.

The minimum of these costs is the economic order quantity. It is derived by taking the first derivative of the above equation with respect to $Q$, and setting the result equal to zero. The resulting formula is:

$$Q = \sqrt{\frac{2Co(S)}{Cu(I)}}$$

where the designations are as above.

There are many other ways of creating an economic order quantity. For example, one might establish such a quantity in weeks—let us say eight weeks—from a given supplier with regard to a specific group of items. The retailer might make a subjective estimate of sales for the next eight weeks, or he might examine last year's unit controls to see how the item or a similar item sold last year over the specific eight-week period. An economic order quantity that is created in terms of weeks can be said to alter as the sales of the item alter over the year. The amount of safety stock might also be set by examining how sales of the units vary with the time of year. Under certain conditions, this procedure would offer more exact safety stock levels. In the safety stock figures created from the frequency distribution in Figure 16.1, it is assumed that each seven-day period is equally likely to produce any of the levels of sales in the frequency table. No allowance is made for the fact that, for reasons known to the company before the weeks occur, more merchandise will be sold in certain weeks than others. The Christmas period is special in many merchandise areas. To the extent that the poor or outstanding sales periods can be identified beforehand, and will recur, more effective safety stock levels may be designated. Thus there are many ways that the reorder point system can be adapted to meet the needs of the situation.

The reorder point system is not used extensively in retailing. One of its great drawbacks has been that in order to utilize a reorder point, a perpetual inventory must be kept. This has been unusual. For many years, perpetual controls, which are kept by adding or subtracting from an inventory rather than by actual count or visual inspection, were not common. They were used primarily in merchandise areas that were highly volatile in sales, irregular in terms of reorder pattern, strongly seasonal, and required rapid liquidation of stock when the sales appeal was spent. Today, however, more and more departments are turning to perpetual controls because the various computer systems are making it more economical to capture sales information in this manner. In addition manual systems are made less desirable by rising wage rates and an increasingly less efficient labor force. Most ordering is done by groups of items, and it is difficult to establish a common reorder point for a substantial number of different items.

The key advantage of the reorder point system as described here is that it emphasizes costs and their minimization. And, if everything else remains equal, the lower the costs the higher the profits. In addition, a system that has established reorder points is nearly always a carefully thought out system, and is therefore apt to give satisfactory results.

A second basic system, used more frequently

in retailing than the one just described, keeps the time between reorders constant, for example by ordering merchandise every three or four weeks. Regular inventory counts taken by store or supplier personnel may be part of its information system, and the orders may be developed from these. Computer systems can be adapted to register sales by unit. At the designated times, inventory is ordered up to the desired level, often called a *replenishment level*. For example, if there are six units in stock at the time of the reorder and the replenishment level is 16, then 10 units of the item would be ordered. One view of the replenishment level is as follows:

$$Replenishment\ Level = B + Sd(L + R)$$

where  $B$ = buffer stock, in units
$Sd$ = average daily sales, in units per day
$L$ = lead time, in days
$R$ = time between review days.

The replenishment system is relatively simple, but a replenishment level is usually established only after substantial analysis. Replenishment is not a concept that directly considers either the costs of placing an order or the costs that vary with level of inventory.

There are many ways of adapting to the replenishment system. For example, an economic order quantity can be built into the system at the time the order is placed, or a minimum quantity for the ordering of an item can be established.

### Selected Inventory Models

**Important items**  One of the more important principles in retailing is that a relatively small number of items within an assortment account for a large percentage of the business. A figure often mentioned is that, for a given store or merchandise classification, 20 percent of the items will generally do about 80 percent of the business. Whatever the figure, it is generally accepted that for all types of outlet the best sellers will account for a very large proportion of the volume. This does not mean that a store should eliminate the 80 percent of the items that do not sell well. Indeed, the 20 percent that constitute the best sellers may need the support, visual and otherwise of the majority. However, the decision maker may want to treat the two groups of items in a different manner for inventory purposes. The more important the item, generally the more resources one can assign to effectively manage it in inventory. For example the safety stock level for the more important items may be put at a higher level. Or an entirely different system might be created for the more important items, perhaps by means of a perpetual inventory of some type. A decision maker is justified in spending more of the firm's resources on effective inventory management of an item if by so doing he increases its profitability. He might also be justified in setting up special systems for departments with particular inventory problems. For example, in a department store, the drug or stationery department would appear to warrant a more sophisticated inventory system than the sporting goods department.

**Staple inventory demand patterns**  Forecasting is an integral part of most staple inventory systems. In forecasting it is important to know the demand characteristics of the item or items with which one is dealing. Is the demand for it highly seasonal? Is the demand growing at a rapid pace? at a slow pace? or declining? Four models have been found to be particularly useful in forecasting demand at the retail level.

1. *Horizontal or constant.* The horizontal or constant model is one in which the data are represented by a horizontal line such as the one in Figure 16.2. The amounts demanded appear to be randomly distributed about the average, and do not show any indication of rising or falling over a relatively long period of time. A great many items can be usefully represented by such a model.

2. *Trend.* In the trend model, the data are distributed around an average line but the average itself increases (or

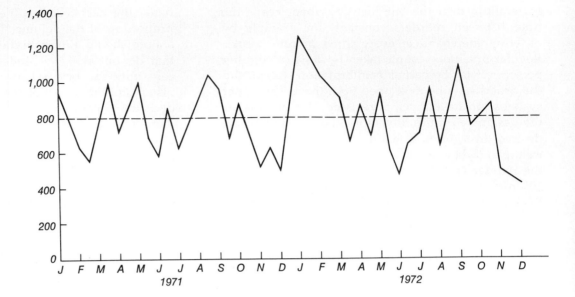

Figure 16.2

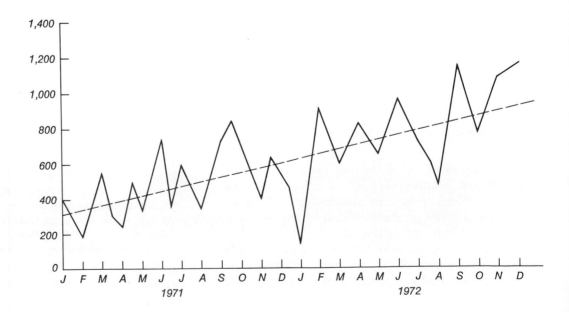

Figure 16.3   A trend model

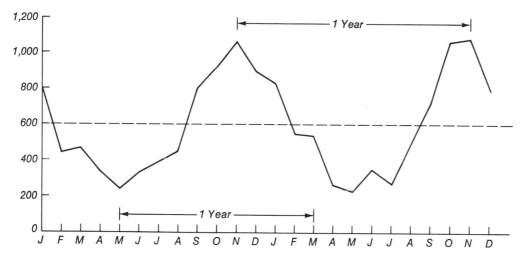

*Figure 16.4   A seasonal model without trend*

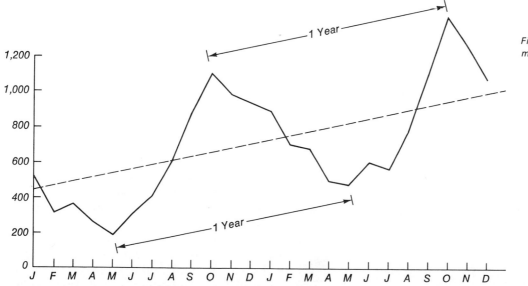

*Figure 16.5   A seasonal model with trend*

Table 16.1
Calculation of a four-period moving average

| Period | Demand in units | Total of last 4 periods | 4-period moving average |
|---|---|---|---|
| 1 | 54 | | |
| 2 | 52 | | |
| 3 | 46 | | |
| 4 | 48 | 200 | 50 |
| 5 | 50 | 196 | 49 |
| 6 | 54 | 198 | 49.5 |
| 7 | 54 | 206 | 51.5 |
| 8 | 46 | 204 | 51 |

decreases) over a substantial period of time. A trend model is shown in Figure 16.3.

3. *Seasonal model without trend.* Here, the trend is cyclical in nature in that it follows the same basic pattern from year to year. There are peaks and valleys in the time series graph that occur at about the same time of the year, each year. Despite the seasonal effect, annual sales do not tend to increase or decrease and hence are "without trend." A seasonal model of this type is illustrated in Figure 16.4.

4. *Seasonal with trend.* When the seasonal swings are accompanied by a trend, the data are cyclical in pattern, in that there are recurrent peaks and valleys at about the same time each year, but there is a consistent increase or decrease in the sales of the item over a long period of time. Such a time series is shown in Figure 16.5.

**Forecasting aids**    Short-term data are often subject to influences of many types. There may be sharp swings in sales from day to day or week to week. Averaging data from the past reduces the impact of such short-term variations. On the other hand, data on sales from a few years back may not be relevant to the future. Many inventory systems try to effect a compromise between the uncertain swings of short-term data and the irrelevancy of old data; for instance, the forecasts may be based on a limited number of past observations, perhaps seven months.

A *moving average* is one way to develop an average based on a constant number of past observations. Thus a twelve-month moving average would be based on (a) the current amount demanded and (b) the relevant months preceding the current period. The greater the number of observations, the

less the influence of any one period. Table 16.1 illustrates the calculation of a four-period moving average.

**Convenient statistical distributions**    Expected sales of an item seldom equal actual sales over any time period. There are usually deviations from expectations, often rather large ones. In some systems, it is the role of the safety stock to reduce the number of days that a store is out of stock for this reason. For some systems, the time frame is the lead time, which is assumed to be constant. When developing safety stocks for lead times, it is often useful to be aware of certain statistical distributions. It is possible in a given merchandise area to develop a *frequency distribution* for each item. A frequency distribution is an ordered arrangement of data, from the lowest value to the highest value, that indicates the relative occurrence of various values.

To compute such a distribution for each item can be a tedious process. Therefore the decision maker often searches for distributions that more or less reflect variations in the sales of the item. This can save him from making a complete set of computations. One distribution often used in retailing is the Poisson distribution. This is a distribution that is humped to the left of the average. It is known when its mean is known; one of its characteristics is that its *variance* is equal to its mean. A good working rule for the Poisson distribution, as applied to retailing, is that only about 2 percent of individual sales will exceed average sales plus twice the square root of this average. The Poisson distribution is illustrated in Figure 16.1.

The exponential distribution also fits a great many retail situations. The form of this distribution is illustrated in Figure 16.6, below. The complete distribution of the exponential distribution is also known when its mean is known, since the mean equals the *standard deviation*.

Finally, the normal distribution—the familiar beehive-shaped curve—will often fit sales distributions at the factory level, where Poisson and exponential distributions seldom apply. There is no convenient relationship between the standard devia-

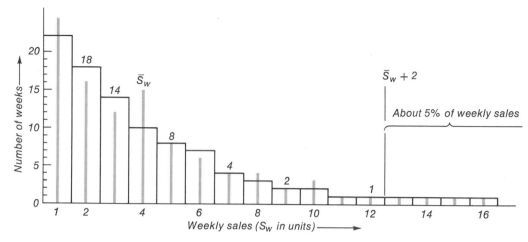

Figure 16.6   *A sales distribution that is approximately exponential* [*Source: Joseph Buchan and Ernest Koenigsberg,* Scientific Inventory Management *(Englewood Cliffs, N.J.: Prentice-Hall, Inc.,* © *1963), p. 11. By permission of the publisher.*]

tion and the average here, but once these are known, the distribution can be completely described. The normal distribution is illustrated in Figure 16.7.

### Other Key Inventory Factors

Another factor to consider in creating an inventory system is the likelihood of the supplier being out of stock. Most of the inventory systems discussed so far are based on the assumption that the supplier will be in stock on all relevant items. It would certainly be most unusual for a key men's shirt factory to be out of stock on such items as blue shirts in the *belly sizes*. However, there are many types of items that suppliers do run out of, and indeed should plan to run out of in approximately the same manner as the retailer who uses safety stocks. In addition, the supplier is exposed to such hazards as strikes, losses in transit, damaged goods, and so forth. The supplier's problems must therefore be considered in creating an inventory system for a retail store.

We have also seen that the lead time does not remain constant, but can be changed by numerous supplier and retailer considerations. It is possible and indeed often desirable for a decision maker to simulate what would happen given varying lead

times and the varying sales that go with them. Such a simulation can be performed on the computer, or it can be run over time within the merchandise classification in question. Many tests related to inventory can be run at almost no cost by a sophisticated decision maker, even over long periods of time.

A key aspect of inventory management that tends to be overlooked is that getting accurate data into the system is often the largest part of the problem. Many a computer inventory system at the retail level has been junked because the information fed into the system has not been accurate. Perhaps the system depended on tickets torn off by salespeople. As many as 20 percent of these tickets might have been lost, misplaced, or maliciously thrown out. At Christmas time, when a great number of employees are new, a system that depends on salespeople may have no value at all in certain merchandise classifications. Of what value is a perpetual inventory system when the input is off by 20 percent or so? Thus the quality of the data is of the utmost importance and cannot *usually* be taken for granted.

Relatedly, the systems creator should realize that a retail store's chief purpose is not to keep accurate inventory systems or beautiful records. Rather, its purpose is to sell merchandise in such a manner that the total enterprise prospers and grows. Inventory

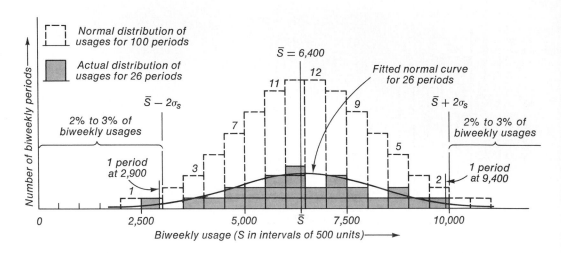

*Figure 16.7 An actual usage distribution that is approximately normal* [Source: *Joseph Buchan and Ernest Koenigsberg, Scientific Inventory Management (Englewood Cliffs, N.J.: Prentice-Hall, Inc.,* © *1963), p. 12. By permission of the publisher.*]

management must contribute to this goal and not detract from it. But inventory systems, while important, seldom determine an enterprise's future by themselves. Thus a manager must also worry about how long it takes a salesperson to process an order that has to be used in the inventory system. Often a balance must be struck between long, angry customer lines and getting information for the inventory system. Most aggressive retailers satisfy the customers first, changing the system to adapt to the customer and not vice versa.

### Rules of Thumb

It should be clear by now that the world of inventory management is rather a confusing one. Here, then, are some rules of thumb for the line decision maker who wishes either to create informal systems of his own or to evaluate existing systems.

1. *The presumption should be in favor of smaller inventories.* This applies, of course, once the selection of merchandise has been made and the deal with the supplier arranged. In other words, the merchant should keep his level of stock on a given item as low as is consistent with the image of the store and other key factors. In the overwhelming majority of cases, far more trouble is generated by being overstocked than by being understocked. Therefore, particularly when an inventory system is not very sophisticated,

the presumption should be in favor of low inventories.

2. *If a store is never out of stock on items, the level of inventory is too high.* An examination of the Poisson, exponential, or normal distribution indicates that to achieve a situation where the merchandise is always in stock is very costly. Thus almost all inventory systems should yield something less than always being in stock.

3. If a decision maker is ordering very frequently from a supplier, he should check into what this is costing in terms of the costs of ordering, freight charges, quantity prices from the supplier, lost sales, and so forth.

4. *When stock space is expanded, buyers will buy merchandise to fill it.* This rule, discussed in the March 1973 issue of *Retailing Today*, offers great caution to those supervising inventories.

### The Computer and Staple Inventory

Most sophisticated staple systems are related to the computer in one way or another, since the computer permits a far higher degree of sophistication than would otherwise be the case. In almost all computer systems, the line executive has to understand most of what is going on, and may have to intervene to overrule or change the system in some respect.

David McConaughy suggests that the computer has been particularly helpful in improving control over inventories in branch stores; in identifying item movement; and in planning inventory requirements. Whatever its role in tomorrow's staple systems, that role will certainly increase.

One byproduct of this trend has been the term SKU, or individual stockkeeping unit. This is the lowest denominator of inventory.

### Overall Inventory Considerations

So far in this chapter, we have imagined ourselves as building up inventories from the individual item. We have made the necessary arrangements with the supplier to purchase the item, then we have set up an inventory system to keep the item in stock. In establishing the various inventory systems, however, we have made no allowance for open-to-buy. Indeed, open-to-buy can be regarded as an output of the system. A merchandise area must have enough open-to-buy to permit the system to have the desired level of *stock outs*, given that the item should be stocked in the first place. Indeed, from many perspectives the open-to-buy should be built up from the item and be an output of many item decisions. Thus the sum of the various stock requirements for the individual items becomes the inventory requirement of the subclassification, and so on for the classification, the department, and the division.

Open-to-buy can be created from total department stock figures as well as from the item up. For example, management can impose merchandise limitations so that a merchant must choose between item A and item B. Or it can suggest that a higher or lower level of stock outs may be desirable in a given instance. Thus inventory systems, while focusing for the most part on the item, do have aspects that concern top management.

### Summary

1. Inventory is of primary concern to the decision maker after the suppliers have been chosen, the mer-chandise assortment created, and the negotiations finished.

2. There are substantial pressures for small inventories because:

A. Inventory costs money.

B. Inventory often loses value over time.

C. Inventory may not remain fresh.

D. Large inventories are conducive to increased theft.

E. Large inventories limit the ability of the decision maker to put his money into exciting alternatives.

F. Storage, insurance and other costs increase with larger inventories.

3. There are substantial pressures for large inventories because:

A. Aggressive buying requires large orders.

B. Small inventories are conducive to being out of stock.

C. Large orders are efficient for most members of the channel of distribution.

D. Ordering costs are smaller for large and less frequent orders.

E. Large orders, if effectively handled, should lead to fewer lost sales on the relevant items.

F. Large inventories may mean fewer inventory counts for the purposes of ordering.

G. Large inventories are a hedge against price increases.

4. The merchant must constantly balance the costs of increasing the inventory with the costs of handling smaller amounts. This is a difficult art because there is no ideal inventory system.

5. For many kinds of retail store, it pays to break the merchandise down into groupings with similar characteristics. One observer designed separate systems for staples, fashion, big tickets such as major appliances and furniture, small tickets such as nuts and screws, and one-time purchases such as toys for Christmas. This chapter emphasizes staple merchandise.

6. Staple inventory systems are designed to indicate when to order the merchandise and how much

of it to order. Two basic types of systems have evolved over time to meet the needs of the retailer:

A. The *reorder point system*, in which the economic order quantity is ordered when the units in stock reach a predesignated level;

B. A *replenishment system*, in which the time between orders is kept constant—for example, every three weeks.

7. Selected inventory models:

A. In many systems, it pays to distinguish between important and unimportant items. The 20 percent of the items that are responsible for 80 percent of the sales may require a more extensive staple system.

B. There are differing demand patterns among items, such as: a constant demand; a demand with trend; a seasonal model without trend; and a seasonal model with trend.

C. There are statistical distributions that aid in forecasting. In addition to the normal distribution there are the exponential and Poisson distributions.

8. Some rules of thumb related to inventory may prove useful.

A. The presumption should be in favor of smaller inventories once the selection of merchandise has been made and the deal arranged with the supplier.

B. If the store is never out of stock on items, the level of inventory is too high.

C. If orders are being placed very frequently with the supplier, the costs of this procedure should be examined very closely.

D. When stock space is expanded, buyers will buy merchandise to fill it.

## Discussion Questions

1. What is lead time in a staple inventory system? List some ways by which the retail decision maker can vary lead time.

2. What is a safety stock?

3. Compare and contrast two basic types of staple inventory systems.

4. What are the distinguishing characteristics of the exponential, the normal, and the Poisson distributions?

5. What are some of the costs of having too much inventory?

6. What are some of the costs of having too little inventory?

7. List several ways in which important items might be treated differently from less important items.

8. Why is there no ideal inventory system?

9. What is a moving average?

## References

McConaughy, David, "An Appraisal of Computers in Department Store Inventory Control," *Journal of Retailing*, Spring, 1970.

Smith, Spencer B., "Automated Inventory Management for Staples," *Journal of Retailing*, Spring, 1971.

## Further Reading

Brown, Robert G., *Statistical Forecasting for Inventory Control* (New York: McGraw-Hill, 1959).

———, *Decision Rules for Inventory Management* (New York: Holt, Rinehart, and Winston, 1967).

Buchan, Joseph, and Koenigsberg, Ernest, *Scientific Inventory Management* (Englewood Cliffs, N.J.: Prentice-Hall, 1963).

International Business Machines Corporation, *Retail Impact—Inventory Management Programmed Control Techniques, Operation Description* (White Plains, N.Y.: latest edition).

Taylor, Charles G., *Merchandise Assortment Planning* (New York: National Retail Merchants Association, 1970).

## Case History: *Buying Advertising Money: The Case for Loads*

Mary Spalding was a student in the Graduate School of Business of Midwest State University. In the winter months her school had an intercession period during which students were sent out to various corporations and other institutions to work for a period of six weeks. This period was thought to benefit the students by making them more aware of what the real world was like, exposing them to a specific company, and so forth. The corporation got a look at the student as a potential employee but also put her to work on some sort of project for which her background might qualify her.

Mary was retained by the Garfunkle department store chain in a large midwestern city. Hiram Garfunkle, the chain's president, was interested in getting Mary's impression of loads. He explained to Mary that a store loaded merchandise when the cost price of the merchandise was increased artificially. In one example, the merchandiser or the store might increase the amount paid to the supplier from $5 to $6.

Garfunkle's used loads in two instances. First, when goods were imported into the store, the store increased their paper cost to the department by 10 percent. This had the effect of increasing the cost of the merchandise to the decision unit. And if the immediate decision maker and his superiors paid any attention to keeping the initial and maintained markup of the department high, then this increase in the cost would foster higher prices in the stores. Hiram Garfunkle felt these higher prices were needed to cover the additional costs created by handling imports. For example, there was substantial spoilage in imports, while reorders were very difficult and often impossible. Occasionally, the wrong merchandise was shipped. While there was recourse against the manufacturer, this did not help the lost business that was bound to occur. Also, imported merchandise tended to be treated differently with regard to merchandise returns to suppliers. Merchants tended to gather and send back all the merchandise of domestic manufacturers. Any doubt about whose was the responsibility for a defect was resolved in favor of the store. The returns of imported merchandise were all handled by the store unless the quality got completely out of hand. Most of the quality control was accomplished by not ordering again from a manufacturer that did not supply merchandise to reasonable standards. Thus in Hiram Garfunkle's opinion these additional costs of imports required that the price to the consumer be higher. He therefore charged the department a percentage of the cost reflected on the invoice. Once every quarter, this money was refunded to the department through a special account. Thus the net profit of the buyer was not influenced by the loading action but the initial and maintained markup were.

The store also used advertising loads, which were fostered by the department manager or buyer of a merchandise area. The buyer went to the supplier and suggested that the supplier increase his price to the store and accumulate the extra dollars per unit in some sort of fund. This fund could be used by the buyer at any time that he chose. In essence, this kind of loading permitted the buyer to go to the advertising vice-president with the information that he had $1,000 in supplier-paid moneys. Could he get into the *Daily Forward* with his exciting promotion? Since the store made a substantial amount of money on the supplier advertising, the buyer was very likely to have the vice-president accept his offer. Hiram Garfunkle had always questioned this practice. But he really did not know what to do about it because the buyers could proceed for the most part without making any explicit arrangements with the suppliers. He had compromised to the point where he permitted advertising loads provided that:

1. Under no conditions could a buyer load merchandise that ended up having less than the initial markup for his merchandise area. For example, if the initial markup, all items considered, was 42 percent, the advertised merchandise after loading had to offer more than 42 percent. The net effect of the rule, then, was to make sure that the initial markup of the department was not lowered materially by the promotion of loaded goods.

2. Under no conditions could a buyer, just for the sake of buying advertising money, buy more merchandise than he would have bought otherwise. Hiram felt that nothing could get the buyers into greater trouble than to buy merchandise in excess with this sole purpose in mind.

Many buyers had lost their jobs over the years by not effectively managing inventory. Buying advertising money was one way in which a buyer could get into great trouble reasonably fast at Garfunkle's.

Hiram Garfunkle asked Mary to consider the two kinds of load and come up with recommendations for the store. He suggested that she see at least two buyers and the controller to get their opinions on whether or not loads were helpful in increasing the store's profits.

The first person Mary contacted was George Wilson, the buyer of handbags. George did not feel that it made a great deal of difference whether he loaded imports or not. His decisions would not change materially anyway. He figured all the costs of the merchandise in setting his price. Clearly, as his costs increased, except under the most unusual conditions, he raised his prices. Imported goods by any standards cost more. Indeed, George went to Europe once a year to buy goods, and this cost the department substantially more than a local buying trip. Thus George did not care what the store did about loads. He did believe that a few of the less sophisticated buyers might be influenced, but not himself.

With regard to advertising loads, George felt that the store could do little. The buyer was always bargaining with one supplier or another. When a buyer chose to bargain for price, he was often giving up bargaining for other things. The same was true of advertising. A buyer could bargain for advertising and in most instances would get it. But he would necessarily forego other things, such as the price he wanted. To George this was the same thing as loading. And the buyer in this instance never knew what was loading and what was not loading. True, there was no direct load arrangement in this case, but the difference to George was not great. George did not load specifically but would be hard pressed to prove it, because he received substantial advertising moneys.

Mary then visited Laura Blondell, the buyer of women's suits. Laura was very much in favor of loads. She and her merchandise manager planned continually with regard to initial markup. Indeed, her manager and top management held her accountable for initial and maintained markup. And she felt that these were useful concepts to her. Naturally, she also felt one should evaluate imports and domestic manufacturers differently, otherwise the markup figures would be highly misleading. As for advertising loads, she did not use them and did not care what the store did with them.

Mary then visited Louis Kaufman, the controller. Louis turned out to be very much in favor of import loads. After all, these buyers were not very bright anyway; they needed to be controlled, and this was one method of controlling them. He pointed to the extreme difficulty he had had in getting qualified trainees in the store. Often the store had to take individuals with poor educational backgrounds. How could such people keep track of all the costs, develop optimal pricing patterns, and so forth? He felt that by altering the cost structure the store insured that the buyers would price the imported merchandise high. On the other hand, he was very sensitive about advertising loads. In fact, he did not see that they had any place in the store at all. Who were they fooling anyway? It was only an internal mechanism. The buyers did overbuy to get advertising money despite the ruling of Mr. Garfunkle, particularly if business was lagging. Just two years ago a buyer had to be fired for developing too large an inventory, a lapse that Louis Kaufman attributed to loads.

Finally, Mary visited Charlene Johnson, the advertising manager, and asked her about advertising loads. Generally, she felt they were useful. They promoted both higher-margined merchandise and supplier-paid advertising. Because the store bought the space at far less than it charged the supplier, it made a lot of money on this. Doing away with advertising loads would really hurt the store.

### Discussion Questions

1. Are Hiram Garfunkle's rules about advertising loads good or bad for the store?

2. What would you have recommended to him about import loads?

# 17

## Fashion Management

Fashion might be regarded as whatever happens to be the prevailing custom—the latest in dress, manners, and so forth. It permeates much of our life, and is an element in many products that would not normally be associated with fashion. Fashion is usually considered as innovation in form but not substance. There is something meaningful to being in fashion, and something that is in fashion will at some time be out of fashion. Thus fashion emphasizes the nonfunctional aspects of value. Some observers differentiate between fashions and fads, reserving fashion for the longer-term innovations. In this chapter no such distinction is made.

Fashion merchandise areas are different from other areas in several ways:

1. An item that is in fashion will sell very well just for that reason. But as soon as it is out of fashion, it will not sell well; it may even become unsalable. Thus fashion merchants watch the best-selling items and features very carefully for signs of changing customer desires.

2. There is a great difference in sales between a merchandise area or store that is perceived by the customer as fashionable and one that is perceived as unfashionable. Thus merchandisers are continually trying to develop the right fashion image with customers.

3. Because of the great sales potential of individual items that are thought fashionable, a search is always going on for them. One aspect of this search for winners is the continual testing of new items. This testing need not be "scientific" and indeed usually is not. But to a decision maker experienced in fashion merchandise it can reveal much.

4. Fashion merchants make many mistakes. Indeed, mistakes are a necessary part of fashion merchandising and an average markdown percentage of 15 percent of sales for a year is not unknown.

5. Fashion merchandisers tend to have more factors to worry about than merchandisers in other areas. For example, in a dress they must be concerned with: What season is it? Is the dress to be worn for afternoon, casual, day, or formal wear? What type of silhouette does it have? What type of neck, sleeve, and skirt? What is the fabric or fabric type? What colors and sizes are available?

6. Creation of merchandise and assortments in fashion merchandising have to be based less on past performance and more on projections into the season ahead.

Certain types of store are known to be fashion leaders, particularly department and specialty stores. Likewise, certain departments within those stores—women's dresses and sportswear, for instance—are particularly concerned with fashion. Despite all these differences, however, the same basic retail operations still apply. Fashion merchandisers must still create assortments; price merchandise; negotiate with suppliers; feel constrained by open-to-buy restrictions; and indeed do most of the things that other merchandisers do. Thus many of the early chapters are just as relevant to fashion as to other areas of retail management. Indeed, some of the material on consumer behavior and product innovation would appear to be even more relevant, as we shall now see.

## Consumer Behavior Revisited

Many observers have suggested that some consumers are more amenable to change than others. Indeed, certain consumers are thought to seek change avidly, while others have little interest in changing. Besides the innovators and laggards, there are, as we have seen, the early adopters, the early majority, and the late majority. One index of a consumer's thirst for change would appear to be the extent of her interest in fashion. In support of the above, Charles W. King has found a difference between the early and the late buyer of fashion.

Not only are certain individuals more amenable to change than others; some of them may act specifically as diffusers of fashion information within a society. Thus diffusion long studied by social anthropologists, should also be of great interest to fashion merchandisers. One theory, often called the *trickle down theory*, suggests that fashions begin in the upper classes and are then passed down through the various social classes by the appropriate retail stores. As soon as the merchandise or style becomes accepted by the lower classes, the upper classes, in their eagerness to remain uncontaminated by everything lower class, seek new fashions and styles. Thus wearing certain styles of clothing at one point in time can indicate membership in a social class or other reference group.

The trickle down theory is based on the concept of intergroup diffusion. Many observers feel that this type of diffusion is not as important to fashion now as it used to be, and that today any group can start a fad or a fashion trend. Buyers from stores that have most of their customers among the masses now attend international fashion shows. Thus Rom J. Markin suggests that clothing for young people—for example, the *mod look* and other fashion innovations of the 1960s—were diffused through a similar group of persons having similar orientations and life styles. It seems that nowadays any group with large buying power can start a fashion cycle, and that any store with substantial elements of their target audience in a given group can act as the catalytic agent for that group's fashion behavior. For this reason, many of today's leading fashion designers derive most of their income from designing mass-market items for large retail outlets.

It can be argued that many new fashions originate from within the group, not from any "trickling down" of influences from one group to another. However, it seems likely that both processes are at work diffusing fashions in today's society. Some key questions here are: How does one group communicate with another? and, How do members of one group communicate with each other? Clearly, television and newspapers are prominent among the means by which fashion news is communicated. Imitation of one person by another is also significant in many instances. Of some importance may be the concept of opinion leadership (p. 58). Fashions may be adopted early by certain members of a group and then diffused throughout it. According to King, there is evidence that the early adopters of fashion are more socially oriented than the later purchasers.

Consumers seem to react to fashion in much the same way as they react to other new products. Indeed fashion usually represents a deluge of such products. A new product goes through a life cycle, and so does a fashion item. Robert D. Entenberg has located four stages in the fashion cycle:

1. Creation, adaptation, initiation;
2. Acceptance and popularization;
3. Large-scale production;
4. Decline.

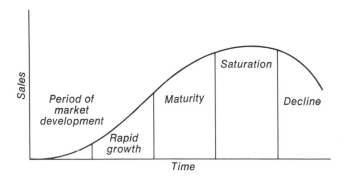

Figure 17.1a  *The theoretical normal life cycle of a fashion or other new product*

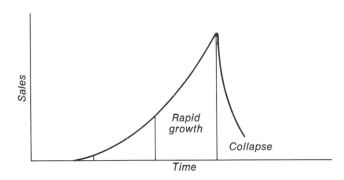

Figure 17.1b  *Usual trajectory of a fad*

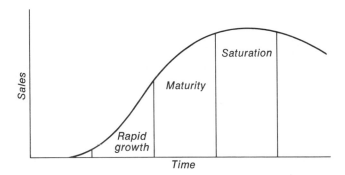

Figure 17.1c  *Apparent life cycle pattern of some new products for which the market seemed to be waiting* (Source: Chester R. Wasson, "How Predictable Are Fashion and Other Product Life Cycles?" Journal of Marketing, *July, 1968, pp. 36–43. Reprinted with permission of the American Marketing Association.)*

Another model has been offered by Chester R. Wasson, who compares the growth patterns of fads, fashions, and other new products (Figures 17.1 a-c).

## Fashion Perspectives

It would appear useful to look briefly at fashion from the perspective of various groups, in particular economists, consumers, suppliers, and retailers.

## Economists

For the most part, economists have avoided fashion. This is only natural: economists tend to prefer dealing with substantive values, and are uneasy in a world that dramatizes the nonsubstantive. There are many good economic reasons for questioning the existence of fashion. In many instances, it appears highly wasteful. Thus the concept of yearly style changes for the automobile industry has been attacked by many as a wasteful practice. Radical changes in style for industries such as men's wear would add dramatically to most men's clothing budgets without improving their clothes in any practical sense. The trend towards men's cosmetics can scarcely be thought of as having substantive value. The woman who owns 38 pairs of shoes may have something above a practical minimum. The list of types of item that we seek as individuals or are induced to seek by marketers, and that are not essential to our physical well-being, is extremely large and apparently becoming larger every day. Of course, society's definition of physical well-being changes over the years, and one generation's luxury item may be the next generation's "essential."

It is natural to expect that the constantly changing nonsubstantive aspects of new products would raise the prices charged for them. The change would be expected to add to production costs, for example in automobiles. Moreover, the consumer's fashion interests, assiduously fostered by manufacturers, create a greater demand for variety. Fashion manufacturers strive for product differentiation in order to avoid some of the consequences of pure or perfect competition outlined by economists, namely, low profits. Since most manufacturers strive to differentiate their products, the risk of not selling the merchandise is high. It follows that the percentage profit on the sales that are consummated will be higher with fashion than with similar merchandise put on sale at a lower risk. Thus it would appear that, on balance, the fashion demands of the consumer create higher prices.

Although the overall price of goods related to fashion would appear to be raised by the fashion element, there is substantial price discrimination between different customer segments, particularly the very early customers and the very late ones. Customers who are willing to wait until the end of a season, or at any rate until the later phases of the fashion cycle, would appear to purchase attractive values—perhaps more attractive than would be possible under a system without fashion. Retailers take large markdowns in fashion areas, and so do suppliers. Mistakes—fashion items that the public simply did not buy—are seldom held by the better-managed manufacturers or retailers. Instead, the merchandisers dispose of such goods at prices the market will take. These prices are often very low; legitimate retail price reductions of 70 percent are not unusual. Thus a customer who does not have to have exactly the current fashion may benefit handsomely under the present system.

Economists might also be interested in the influence of fashion on the level of consumer expenditures given a specific level of personal disposable income. While a high level of consumption under given conditions may be either good or bad, it is probable that under most conditions an increased interest in fashion will increase the level of consumption. A person who "has" to be dressed just so, or who "has" to have the latest-style car or house, would probably spend a larger proportion of his income on clothing, transportation, and lodging than less fashion-minded individuals, given a certain level of personal disposable income.

It can be further argued that the consumer's interest in fashion is the key incentive to productive and industrious behavior for many individuals in our society. "Keeping up with the Jones's" may well be a prime motivator in the behavior of Americans. It is quite conceivable that staying in fashion is a necessary pillar of our economic edifice. Human wants, it is often said, are limitless, and fashion is the supreme illustration of this truth.

### Consumers

It is interesting to contemplate the influence of fashion on the retail structure, in particular its influence on large regional shopping centers and downtown shopping areas. Many studies have indicated that consumers will travel greater distances to purchase fashion merchandise than merchandise of any other type. It is this fact that permits the profitable establishment of these huge centers, each with one or more strong department stores as its base.

On the other hand, in our market society the consumer is never given the opportunity of voting for no fashion at all. Fashion is here and is aggressively merchandised by those who expect to profit from it. Within this economic framework, consumers obviously like the newest fashions because they buy so many of them. The value to the consumer of a given piece of merchandise must exceed the value of the dollars that she gives to the retailer, or there would be no purchase. Therefore, in some sense, the existence of fashion must increase the customer's utility.

The importance of fashion for certain product areas undoubtedly puts a lot of pressure on individual consumers. Some of them react to this form of competition by trying to make an art of shopping. But for whose benefit is this art displayed—if it is displayed at all? Undoubtedly, many women do purchase items of clothing with the idea of differentiating themselves from others and perhaps of besting them in some way. But a substantial number of others probably purchase fashion in order to withdraw from the competition, that is they do not want to be conspicuously out of fashion. Or they may want to buy a fashion that is "correct" in relation to some reference group, but offers some scope for individuality—perhaps because it conforms with some ideal image they have of themselves. Certain stores exist to serve this very purpose.

Fashion merchandise also provides a wide range of opportunities for self-expression. This is most obvious in the case of clothing. By her selection of fashion a person can indicate her acceptance or rejection of society in general, of various social roles, and of other people. It is fashion that enables her to proclaim her reference group or groups, her social or aesthetic preferences, and many other things. In general, far more hostility can be manifested in clothing without provoking severe reactions from observers than can be in words. A teenager can in most instances say a lot more with the selection of his clothes than verbally and still remain on speaking terms with his parents. Thus the psychological and sociological implications of fashion are considerable.

### Suppliers

Suppliers, as we have seen, expect to benefit economically from consumers' interest in fashion. More interest in fashion generally means that industry sales will increase, because a consumer must buy a larger variety of merchandise and buy more frequently in order to stay with the fashion. Thus in recent years the men's wear industry has been aggressively trying to induce men to become more fashion-conscious. A substantial interest in fashion by the final consumer means that the supplier can differentiate his product on this dimension from his competitor's product. Under such circumstances, fashion rather than price becomes the main area of competition. Furthermore, the supplier can develop his own expertise to counteract the strong positions of the major retailers with which he deals. If most men's shirts were about the same, then price would almost necessarily become the major selling point.

### Retailers

Some types of retail outlet are more closely associated with fashion merchandise than others. Among these are the department and specialty store, which try to develop a reputation for being fashionable so that customers will automatically look to them for this kind of merchandise.

Another advantage of having a reputation for fashion merchandising is that it attracts key suppliers. That is why suppliers of fashion merchandise seek out department stores. Indeed, they will generally not be able to sell to outlets that do not sell at the same price as department stores or higher, because if they do, department stores will usually drop the line. Thus, partly because of its reputation for fashion, the department store and other fashion outlets are to a great extent isolated from the competition offered by outlets such as discount stores.

### Fashion Systems

It is quite costly for a store to maintain a fashion image: A substantial assortment of merchandise must be displayed and periodically refurbished. Nevertheless, stores seldom regard themselves as creators of fashion. Rather, they aggressively seek information about what is selling, from their own and others' stock, and adapt their selections accordingly. At the purchasing level, executives need to know little of the why's of fashion—the length of fashion cycles, reasons for the recurrence of cycles, and other topics dear to social scientists. They have little reason to distinguish between a fashion and a fad. The basic principle of fashion at the retail level is that a fashion that starts selling well today will continue to sell well for a substantial number of weeks unless factors such as the end of a season intervene. This is true of the item itself as well as such features of it as color, silhouette, and fabric. A related principle is that those items that sell poorly are very likely, indeed almost certain, to continue as poor sellers in the near future. Thus the key to dealing with fashion merchandise effectively is to set up a merchandise information system.

Fashion systems may have three main purposes:

1. *To spot the best-selling items.* A system that does this enables retailers to reorder the item in sufficient quantities for the needs of the time period under consideration. Thus the items promoted in the various media will be selected from among the best-sellers and be in stock. Usually, the displays in the department will be organized to feature the styles that the customer is known to want. A decision maker will therefore pay attention to the reordering of merchandise when he can receive it while it is still selling well. Thus a firm, in order to make successful reorders, may either have to be reasonably close to suppliers, or else have a great deal of merchandise shipped by special handling, perhaps by air freight.

2. *To spot the poor sellers as rapidly as possible.* Thus informed, the merchandise area can de-emphasize these styles and minimize their impact on the departmental profits. It is usually thought the earlier that markdowns are taken the better, because the moneys received can be reinvested in the better sellers. Moreover, the amount of markdown need not be as large as it will have to be later. Often, poor sellers can be returned to the supplier, usually in exchange for the best sellers. Naturally, the retailer will find it easier and more profitable to return goods if he can get the information about poor sellers faster than the other retailers, so that supplier still considers the poor seller saleable, and still has the best sellers in stock.

3. *To buy into the trend.* By combining information on the items that are selling best with the information on the items that are selling worst, the decision maker may develop a picture that permits him to buy into the trend in its incipient stages. This may be a particularly useful tactic if he is too far away from the market to reorder effectively, or if he has to release a catalog promotion some considerable period in advance. Or perhaps the new style bought to anticipate a trend may be more exciting to the customer than more of the existing style. And buying to trends may offer the retailer a way of getting a head start on the competition, since competitive stores will often be testing many of the same styles, and may reorder them.

### Creating a System

Fashion systems typically require the division of various units of merchandise into relatively homogeneous classifications. Such classifications, perhaps including not only such aspects as price line and fabric but comparison of unit sales, sales-to-stock ratios, or both, are thought to have more meaning. Thus a comparison of the unit sales or sale rates of two men's sweaters of a similar type at $3.99 is thought to have more meaning than such comparisons of a $3.99 sweater with a $19.99 sweater.

Of particular importance in many types of fashion analysis is the *sales-to-stock* ratio, which relates unit or dollar sales of a style to the unit or dollar quantities of the style that have been in stock. For example, a store might have sold 12 units of two styles of women's $9.99 blouses. If, however, the store had 70 units of one and only 12 units of the other displayed from time X, the sale of the 12 units would not be regarded in the same light. In fashion areas most of the styles are put on the selling floor and there is little stock in the storeroom. Thus the number of pieces handled stands in almost direct relationship to the amount of selling floor space that is occupied. For items in the same price range, a sales-to-stock ratio is therefore very close to sales per square foot.

Two facets of sales-to-stock ratios have particular interest for creators of fashion systems:

1. *Inventory level and unit sales.* If a store sold 24 units this week of a style in which it had 96 units in stock on the selling floor at the beginning of the week, would it have sold twice as many units during the same period if twice as many had been on the selling floor? A study of inventory management conducted by IBM indicates that styles do sell in proportion to the level of stock, within the range that a merchant thinks is reasonable to introduce the item. This finding goes against the assumptions underlying the staple inventory systems outlined in the previous chapter. Instead, the view that an item's sales increase as the amount of it displayed increases is defended on the ground that display is an important influencer of sales. The more stock on the selling floor, so the argument goes, the greater the

Table 17.1
Constant sales-to-stock ratio (SASR) over style life

| | (1) On hand beginning of week | (2) Expected unit sales | (3) Expected SASR |
|---|---|---|---|
| Style 1, week 1 | 80 | 20 | .25 |
| Style 1, week 2 | 60 | 15 | .25 |
| Style 1, week 3 | 45 | 11.25 | .25 |

Note: Column 3 = column 2 ÷ column 1.

Table 17.2
Constant weekly unit sale over style life

| | (1) On hand beginning of week | (2) Expected unit sales | (3) Expected SASR for week |
|---|---|---|---|
| Style 1, Week 1 | 80 | 10 | .125 |
| Style 1, Week 2 | 70 | 10 | .143 |
| Style 1, Week 3 | 60 | 10 | .167 |

Note: Column 3 = column 2 ÷ column 1.

impact on the consumer and the more likely that the requested size will be in stock.

2. *Short-term and long-term variations in sales-to-stock ratio.* What is the pattern and variation of the sales-to-stock ratio over the lifetime of a style? Can a best seller or a poor seller be recognized in the first week of a season, the first two weeks, or when? What degree of variation should be expected in the sales-to-stock ratio from week to week or from day to day? A style could possibly sell 100 units out of a stock of 400 units in the first week, and only 20 out of 300 units in the second. If, however, the sales-to-stock ratios remain about the same for some reasonable period of time, perhaps eight weeks or so for all elements of a classification, then the selection of best and worst sellers may be made with some certainty on the strength of rather sparse data.

Two well-known systems illustrate elements of the above problems. The first assumes that sales-to-stock ratios remain constant over time, and that the ratio of a particular style can be readily compared to that of its group after a sufficient number of units have been sold. The sales-to-stock ratio (SASR) may be created in a great variety of ways. For tables 17.1–2, the formula is:

$$\text{SASR} = \frac{\text{Sum of Unit Sales for All Periods}}{\text{Sum of the Beginning on Hand for All Periods}}$$

If the sales-to-stock ratios remain constant each day except for random influences, or if the assumption of a constant ratio does not do great violence to reality, styles within a group may be compared even if they are brought onto the selling floor in different weeks and on different days. Thus in the example in

table 17.1, the expected SASR is constant for each week. As the merchandise on hand decreases, the expected unit sales also decrease, so that the SASR remains the same. If the stock in any period were increased, the sales would be expected to increase in a linear fashion so long as (a) the amount of stock brought in was a reasonable one in relation to the department's needs, and (b) all the merchandise brought in was displayed.

Note that if the assumptions of such a system are justified, best sellers and poor sellers alike will become obvious. Group sales-to-stock ratios can be compared with individual ones. The items with higher SASR's are the best sellers. Thus in table 17.1, if the group SASR were .10, then an SASR of .25 would be considered outstanding. For one day, random influences could create such a difference. However, if the difference were to persist over days or perhaps weeks, the item with the higher SASR would be tabbed a best seller.

The second system assumes a constant weekly unit sale over the life of the style. This figure is developed from the initial level of the stock on hand, so naturally the sales-to-stock ratio increases from week to week. The length of life for each style in a homogeneous group is assumed to be equal, so that the expected SASR's of all styles are equal for a given week, for example week four of their style life. This method suggests that if a buyer purchases 80 units of a style for a classification or group with an eight-week style life, he will sell 10 per week, as shown in table 17.2. In this case, a comparison among SASR's at one point in time has little value because the SASR's are changing from week to week. What can be done, however, is to develop an expected sales pattern for a homogeneous group over

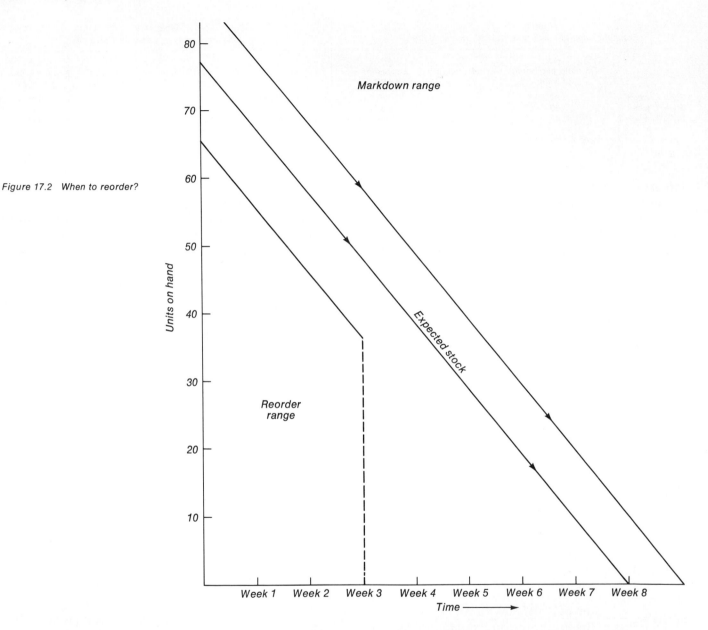

*Figure 17.2   When to reorder?*

the assumed *style life*. The style that deviates substantially from this pattern can be designated as a "best seller" or a "poor seller," according to whether the difference is positive or negative.

One system based on a constant number of unit sales per week is illustrated in Figure 17.2. In this particular system, the decision maker has made the value judgment that the item has to break out of its current sales pattern by the third week or he will not reorder and will look for more attractive styles. In week one, 17 units will have to be sold by the end of the week for a reorder to be indicated. By the end of week two, the figure is 30 items, and by the end of week three, 43 items. Thus ever larger absolute deviations are required by the system as the weeks pass. The reader should note that the reorder and markdown lines were arbitrarily selected; in most instances, they should be matched to departmental needs.

In addition, the markdown line indicates a markdown at any time that actual sales are less than expected sales by a constant amount. Poor sellers cannot enter the markdown area until they have been on the floor at least one week. This system reflects the feeling of most fashion observers that while it is important to recognize poor sellers early, it is even more important to do the same for best sellers.

In the procedures outlined in Tables 17.1–2 and Figure 17.2, sales in each week are related to the initial stock received. However, the relationship between sales and stock in the two systems is quite different. This is so despite the fact that in both instances sales increase directly with stock. And yet neither needs to be correct in the sense that it must accurately reflect reality. Each is designed to provide a way by which effective comparisons can be made among the various styles in a homogeneous classification. Which procedure approaches the designated goals of a given manager, in a given subclassification, in a given department, in a given store, in a given chain of stores, in a specific season, and perhaps at a given time, can in most instances be determined empirically—although apparently this effort is seldom made. Limited data from one study conducted by this author suggest that, under appropriate conditions, either approach may be useful. The final decision is one for store managements and computer manufacturers.

## Models of Short-term Fashion Management

Most retailers make assumptions about fashion processes. Seldom, however, are these assumptions made explicit. Indeed, one of the more useful aspects of computer programs is that systems designers are forced to examine their own basic premises.

The following models make no real effort to reflect the dynamics of fashion. Rather, they are designed for the consideration of decision makers before they create their own detailed systems. Nevertheless, line fashion executives should find them helpful in reevaluating their own assumptions.

### No-Change, Sequential Sampling

This model assumes that the population of customers to whom a retailer wants to appeal remains about the same over at least the major portion of the style life or season. Each day's sales are assumed to offer additional information about this population's desires. Therefore, the statistical procedures of *sequential sampling* can be applied.

### Predictable Change

Quite obviously, specific customers do change their desires with time. In addition, the composition of the customer population may be different at the beginning and end of the season. In the latter instance, if the early purchasers influence the later purchasers to select about the same merchandise, or if common outside factors influence the later group to do so, then the assumptions of the no-change model should be useful. Customers may, however, vary over the season in a manner that makes the assumption of no change untenable. Indeed, many retailers presently make changes in their stock over a season in order to appeal to varying customers. Some of these changes are:

1. The season's initial merchandise selections tend to be sprinkled with many test styles. Accordingly, the earlier the consumer makes her choice, the more variety she has to choose from.

2. The display of the department does not direct the consumer to the best-selling items to as great a degree in the early stages of a season because the merchant does not yet know what those items are. As the season advances, the alternatives open to the consumer become more limited; she is directed by the displays to consider mainly the best sellers, the stock of which has now been increased. Meanwhile, the poor sellers have either been marked down or are not being reordered. This reduction in variety appeals mainly to customers who want a limited

choice, and to those who know little about fashion but want accepted merchandise.

3. Styles that are making fashion news are brought in early by the retailer to appeal to the fashion-conscious consumer even if they are not expected to sell particularly well. Fashion-conscious consumers may ask to see nationally advertised merchandise even if they are not likely to purchase it. If it is not in stock, they will be disappointed at the store's lack of fashion leadership.

4. Some managers bring in "classic" (i.e., more conservative) merchandise as the season progresses in order to appeal to those less fashion-conscious customers who tend to purchase later in the season. This classic merchandise has appealed over many years to a substantial group of customers.

5. The ratio of markdown merchandise to regular-priced merchandise increases. The later in the season that a consumer waits, the greater will be the selection of marked-down merchandise, and the markdowns will originate from both retailers and suppliers.

### Rapid-Change Model

Another possible approach to fashion recognizes that since there will be substantial change during the season anyhow, the decision maker should recognize that it is coming and try to work with it. He need not understand or even be able to identify the factors inducing the change, as long as he can discern patterns that help to show what customers want. This model assumes the consumer market is changing so rapidly that the use of such statistical techniques as random sampling or forecasting is precluded. The decision maker will be required to make rapid decisions on the basis of very limited information. A buyer with this picture of the world will emphasize immediate information and rapid adaptation to it.

### Expected-Value Approach

A fourth possible approach might be termed the expected-value approach. Clearly, a new fashion style in a store can be considered a new product. A buyer might establish mutually exclusive and exhaustive prior probabilities for selling different quantities of a style for different specific stock-on-hand levels. These estimates can be based on his own subjective estimates, or he may take previous sales data (whether from the same or an earlier season) into account. By making profit-and-loss estimates for each style according to whether he expects it to sell at full price or marked down, he can forecast the payoff for each inventory level of that style. This enables him to select those styles and quantities with the highest expected value per unit of space or per dollar invested in inventory. For this reason, the procedure is here called the *expected-value approach.*

### Expected-Value (Time Considerations) Approach

In the expected-value approach, the decision maker chooses the alternatives that offer the most profit per unit of space or per dollar invested. Thus the choice is go or no go. A retailer might, however, choose to wait for additional information on his styles—or at least he might want to calculate the advantages of waiting. Perhaps a more attractive purchase alternative will come along in a week or so; perhaps the information system will soon indicate that a certain style has a more impressive pattern; perhaps other merchandise will be closed out. A theoretical model is available to compare the expected values of buying now with the expected values of waiting for additional information. Here, it will be called the expected-value (time considerations) approach.

### Trend Analysis

The previous models have all emphasized the ordering, reordering, and marking down of individual styles. Many observers suggest, however, that the key to fashion merchandising is neither selecting the best-selling styles presently on the selling floor nor identifying the poor sellers, but recognizing, evaluating, and estimating trends. These observers would attribute the failure of many complex computer fashion systems to the fact they are really measuring the wrong things very accurately. The alternative, they argue, is to use unit information to develop information for trend analysis. In this view, individual styles become secondary to information about changing patterns in the customer's attitudes toward silhouette, color, fabric, and so forth. Of course, when a store is not in a position for geographic or other reasons to effectively deal with reorders, then it must emphasize trend. Even if it can deal with reorders, it must make value judgments as to how they will be used. Here, trend analysis can help to make a more appealing mix for the store's customers.

All of the above models are incomplete. Indeed, some look as if they would be unworkable under many sets of conditions. But all offer some insight into the complex area of fashion management. Both the no-change and the predictable-change models emphasize the familiar retailing phenomenon, that styles that sell well at the beginning of the season tend to sell well throughout the season, or at least over a reasonable period of time. The rapid-change model dramatizes the futility of assuming that the world is orderly when it is not. Perhaps the past is not the appropriate reference point for the future. The expected-value approach offers a methodology for formally introducing the subjective profit estimates of buyers into the decision-making process and makes some allowance for markdown risk. The expected-value (time considerations) approach evaluates the costs and benefits of waiting for more information. Finally, trend analysis cautions against overemphasis of individual style, and offers a dimension that can complement an individual unit system. It is up to the individual decision maker to evaluate which model or mix of models is relevant to a particular set of situations.

### Markdowns

A markdown is a reduction in the retail price of merchandise on hand. As such, it is an integral part of fashion management. The more fashion items one tests, the more will probably have to be marked down. The continuous search for winning items, as well as the effort to diagnose fashion trends, make slow-selling items an integral part of the system. In years when a retailer has a higher batting average—i.e., spots more winners—he probably need not take as many markdowns as when he has a low one. Thus in fashion departments the markdowns can be extremely high—over 15 percent of sales in some instances.

The principal reason for marking down merchandise is that it is not selling up to expectation, or at least not at a fast enough rate to dispose of itself in a reasonable period of time. However, there are many other reasons. Merchandise may be marked down in order to meet the lower price of another store. Special markdown merchandise may be created for sales events. Or a decision maker might want to get extra sales at various times of the day. In that case, he will have the store's public address system announce something like, "Listen shoppers, for the next ten minutes all our $12.49 toys will be one-third off in price." Merchandise may be marked down for specific types of sale table—an "opportunity corner" that supposedly attracts customers. Markdowns might also be taken because the merchant felt that he would make higher profits at the lower selling price than at the initial one. Thus markdowns are related to many aspects of merchandising and will be used in various ways to achieve the goals of the enterprise.

Nevertheless, the main justification for markdowns is that they get rid of merchandise that is not selling well. A characteristic of a good merchant is that he gets rid of his mistakes. He does not nurse poor-selling items to make sure that he gets his full dollar value from them. He gets rid of them, to a supplier, to a noncompetitive store to whom he sells, or to the customer by a price reduction. While in most cases he does not have to get rid of his "bombs" right away, there is no substitute for getting rid of what does not sell. All retailers make mistakes, but it is the poor merchants who hold onto them. And lowering the retail price is often necessary. A manager should not feature poor sellers in key displays just in order to get rid of them. Nor should he advertise poor sellers. The price is lowered, and this action costs something in almost all cases. But the costs are far less than the costs of keeping the merchandise. It would be hard to overemphasize this point. A retailer must keep his stocks in merchandise that is selling. The motto is, Get out of what is not selling and put the moneys into stock that is.

Because markdowns can be an important factor in influencing profits, retailers often regard them as an area for special consideration and subject to special controls. In a department store, for instance, the person in charge of the department is typically given a markdown budget to live within. Also of considerable importance to fashion merchants is the timing of the markdown. A good general rule for fashion merchants is that the style should be marked down as soon as the manager is sure that it will not sell well. It is important to realize that probably the largest cost of not getting rid of a poor seller is the space that it continues to occupy and the dollars that it ties up. It is also true that the longer one waits to take a markdown, the larger it will generally have to be. This latter cost, while legitimate, is small, for the most part, compared to the cost of not having the department look right, of not having the incoming customers effectively directed to the best-selling items by organized displays, and—perhaps most important—of not having enough of the leading sellers in stock. One important executive in a large fashion store recently suggested to me that there is almost no way of getting too many of the best-selling items. A severe limit on the display and promotion of the best sellers is the number of poor sellers that are in the department. Thus, under most conditions, it behooves merchants to get rid of these as soon as possible by any reasonable means. Some stores try to group their markdowns in a certain period of the month, so that they can obtain maximum advantage from these poor sellers in the form of extra sales, perhaps as end-of-the-month specials.

Another factor of substantial importance to fashion merchandisers is the number of dollars that the poor-selling style should be marked down. The problem appears easy to solve if the goal is to have the level of stock for a given style reach zero by the end of the season. The price of the style is then put at a point at which the decision maker feels it will sell out in the required number of weeks. With the right kind of information system, the inventory figures can be monitored to see that the desired sales rate is being obtained at this lower price. If the sales rate is lower than anticipated, additional price reductions can be made. The problem of the dollar amount of the markdown becomes more difficult if the decision maker feels that the department should get out of such merchandise extremely rapidly in order to free dollars and space for the best sellers. In the latter instance, a value judgment must be made about the time period for selling the merchandise at different price levels.

### Auxiliary Fashion Model

Toward the end of a season, a retailer may often have to decide whether to buy an item or group of items at low closeout prices. He may even order merchandise in the early part of the season in small enough quantities to permit the purchase of closeout merchandise from the middle of the season on. This type of merchandise may offer the following advantages:

1. Very high markups can be offered during the latter part of the regular selling season. Thus if an item sells for $10 with an initial cost of $6, purchasing a huge amount of this item at a 30 percent discount from the cost price offers an initial retail markup of 58 percent so long as the price remains $10.

2. Closeouts at the end of the season can be offered to customers at substantial discounts and still be profitable to the store. In the above example, 50 percent discounts from the retail price can be offered at a 16 percent markup, while 30 percent discounts from the same price can be offered at 40 percent markup.

3. Preseason opening sales may be designed for the next season to get rid of the remainder of the merchandise, or

the merchandise can be remarked at $10 with the 58 percent markup already alluded to.

A retailer will have increased costs if he goes in for this type of purchase—storage, imputed interest charges (i.e., the cost of capital), any additional markdown risks, shortage costs, market risks, opportunity costs, and so forth. The benefits will have to be weighed against the negatives.

## Fashion Cycles

One of the more interesting aspects of fashion as a process is that it is often considered to go in cycles. Fashions tend to be in style, then go out of style, and after a period of time, the style comes back. A famous study by Agnes Brooks Young suggests that fashions in women's dress styles recur periodically. This type of cyclical behavior has been corroborated by J. Carman. Rita A. Perna has commented that revivals of style may occur from time to time, but the fashions of former days never come back in their entirety. Some manufacturers of dresses keep many of their old styles because they feel they will be useful when the particular fashion comes back again. The cyclical recurrence of fashion is a part of many industries, including automobiles and Yo-Yo's.

## Summary

1. Merchandise with an important fashion element is treated differently by retail stores than is other merchandise. Nevertheless most of the aspects of retail management discussed so far are also relevant to fashion.

2. The fashion perspectives of economists, consumers, suppliers, and retailers are outlined.

3. Most fashion systems have two key purposes:

A. Managers would like to identify the best sellers as soon as possible. Thus the decision maker can try to rearrange his department to reflect the interests of the consumer; reorder merchandise before the supplier runs out; decide on item newspaper advertising; and so forth.

B. Decision makers would like to know what the poor sellers are. If this information is known in the first few weeks of the season, perhaps the merchandise can be exchanged for better-selling merchandise.

4. Many fashion systems rely on sales-to-stock ratios to evaluate the performance of items. Generally, the decision maker assumes that the more of a given style he brings in, the more he will sell. By dividing the sales by the stock, he can compare the performance of one style against the performance of other styles of about the same type. This method of comparison is defended on the grounds that, in a fashion department, the more of a given style that is brought in, the more of it will be put on display. Indeed, for most merchandise areas, almost all the fashion goods are on display. Thus the sales-to-stock ratios offer some measure of the productivity of the space.

5. Various models of short-term fashion management are offered.

A. One might assume that each sale of merchandise is a vote cast from a large static universe. Therefore one learns more and more about the universe as votes come in from customers.

B. Since change does occur during the season, one might make efforts to predict the change.

C. Another approach suggests that change is so rapid that history is of relatively little value.

D. The expected-value approach suggests that items be treated according to the expected profit from the item, including anticipated markdowns.

E. The expected-value (time considerations) approach suggests that time brings additional information. The decision maker must weigh the costs of waiting against the possibility that a better opportunity may come along later.

F. The trend approach emphasizes changes in fashion over time that can be recognized.

6. Markdowns are an integral part of fashion merchandising. The general rule for markdowns is to take them as soon as possible. The earlier the markdown is taken the smaller it will have to be to move the merchandise rapidly. But more importantly, the dollars received from the sale of the markdown merchandise can be reinvested in the merchandise that is selling.

7. There are many opportunities for special purchases offered to buyers who have sufficient open-to-buy to avail themselves of the opportunities, particularly as the season develops.

8. Fashion cycles often repeat themselves over time.

## Discussion Questions

1. Could your retail class start a fashion?

2. Wouldn't the consumer be better off without fashion? Just think of what fashion costs.

3. What is the value of fashion to the retailer?

4. Why are sales-to-stock ratios important in fashion?

5. Outline two approaches to sales-to-stock ratios.

6. A key assumption of fashion retailing is that a style that starts selling well today will continue to sell well for a predictable period of time. Is it true?

7. What are the main purposes of setting up fashion systems?

8. Why should markdowns be taken early in the season?

9. Do fashions repeat?

## References

Carman, James, "The Fate of Fashion Cycles in Our Modern Society," *Proceedings of the American Marketing Association*, September 1966, pp. 722–737.

Entenberg, Robert D., *Effective Retail and Market Distribution* (New York: World, 1966), p, 284.

International Business Machines Corporation, *Retail Impact—Inventory Management Program and Control Techniques, Application and Description* (White Plains, N.Y.: IBM, 1967), p. 76.

King, Charles W., "The Innovator in the Fashion Adoption Process," in *Reflections on Progress in Marketing* (Chicago, Ill.: American Marketing Association, 1964).

Markin, Rom J., Jr., *Retailing Management* (New York: Macmillan, 1971), p. 343.

Perna, Rita A., "Analyzing Fashion Trends," in Jeanette A. Jarnow and Beatrice Judelle (eds.), *Inside the Fashion Business* (New York: Wiley, 1966).

Wasson, Chester R., "How Predictable Are Fashion and Other Product Life Cycles?" *Journal of Marketing*, 1968, pp. 36–43.

Young, Agnes Brooks, *Recurring Cycles of Fashion, 1760–1937* (New York: Harper and Row, 1937).

## Further Reading

Daniels, Alfred H., "Fashion Merchandising," *Harvard Business Review*, May 1951.

Deming, W. Edwards, *Sample Design in Business Research* (New York: Wiley, 1960).

Dickinson, Roger A., "Are Present Computer Fashion Approaches Useful?" *Retail Overview*, Winter, 1970, pp. 46–52.

# 18

## Retail Advertising

"The advertising of practically every one of our giant retailers—department stores, food chains, variety chains, drug chains—is horrible. It is a depressing witch's brew of uniform banality." Such is E. B. Weiss's opinion of retail advertising—a rather common opinion among advertising men who are not directly employed by retailers. Retail advertising is in this deplorable condition, Weiss suggests, because:

The cooperative allowances offered to retailers by suppliers create many management problems;

Top retail management lacks interest in the retail advertising function;

Stores do not allocate sufficient talent to the advertising function;

Few advertising agencies have the required organization to effectively handle a store's day-to-day advertising.

These observations would tend to suggest that all is not well in the way that retailers present themselves to their potential customers, regardless of the medium used. Many retailers would tend to agree. They would decry their advertising's obvious reliance on price, its uniformity, and many other features. Many have experimented with various forms of nonprice advertising; many have tried to be innovative. But few have been successful. Nevertheless, retail advertising over the years has probably been close to its optimum, if only because few if any retail institutions have been capable of escaping the rather mundane formats that emphasize price, merchandise, or both. Many very sophisticated retailers have tried to escape them. But depressing as retail advertising is to the creative professional, it appears in general to be considered by customers in a favorable light—more favorably, in fact, than most other forms of advertising. Indeed, a study by James Ferguson indicates that more newspaper executives believe retail advertising has a positive effect on circulation than believe it has a negative effect.

Retailers are interested in advertising from many perspectives. For most of them, the main thing is that advertising is an integral part of their merchandising mix. Retailers must compete with other retailers for customers, and advertising must contribute its part. Increasingly, however, retailers are also having to compete with the national and regional brands of suppliers. Many retailers, as we shall see, have extensive private brand programs. The management of one supermarket chain has even claimed that in most categories it sells more private brand merchandise than national brand. The implication is that it would prefer selling all private brand if possible. In this battle of the brands, retailers of many types are developing a substantial stake. Retail executives will have to become highly skilled in the ways of national advertisers if they are going to compete effectively with them on either the regional or the national level.

From another viewpoint, retailers in many industries—food, for example—are constantly bombarded with propaganda about the large impact that the upcoming supplier advertising campaign is supposedly going to have. Dealers who are not stocking the merchandise that is being promoted are asked to take in substantial quantities of it in preparation for the onslaught of the consumers who will be attracted by the campaign. Dealers who are presently stocking it are asked to order in large quantities so that the store's customers will not be disappointed. Thus the field of supplier advertising is of interest to the retailer not only because he so often competes with the national advertiser, but because he must, in his own self-interest, learn to estimate the probable impact of various types and forms of supplier advertising.

Finally, suppliers usually advertise to retailers in the trade publications. This type of supplier advertising appears to have little significance for most large retailers because buyers for large organizations buy narrowly defined merchandise lines, for example hosiery, and can keep well-informed with regard to events in the market. Buyers for smaller stores, on the other hand, may buy for many merchandise areas, and may therefore need the help of trade magazines.

### Nonretail and Retail Advertising

There are many differences between retail and nonretail advertising. Four are of particular relevance:

1. *The nonretailer brand products can usually be purchased in many other stores.* Therefore retailers are not generally interested in the long-term future of the supplier's brand. They are just trying to get the customer to buy items in their stores.

2. *Much retail advertising is special-price advertising.* One way to create excitement at the retail level is to give the customer the impression—which is usually a correct one—that the price for an item has been reduced. Many such reductions can be combined into an "event" such as a gigantic special purchase, closeout, clearance, national holiday, store anniversary, assistant buyer's sale, and so forth. It is very difficult for a supplier to conduct an effective advertising program on this basis, and indeed few try.

3. *Retailers do not extensively work through advertising agencies.* One reason is that retail advertising is thought to be so different from national advertising that the expertise of advertising agencies is thought for the most part not to be relevant. Further, retail advertising is thought to demand less creative brilliance than national advertising. Also, the fact that items are constantly changing at the retail level means that communication between the creative branch and the line executive is more difficult than at other levels—that of manufacturing, for instance.

4. *Retailers are less interested than suppliers in new products.* Of course, it is important for the retailer to offer the customer the impression that he, the retailer, has an interest in new products; the whole fashion area rests on dedication to the new. However, retailers do not have a great stake in any one new product under most sets of circumstances. And indeed the individual retailer usually has less to gain by being innovative with respect to products than does the supplier. Even the retail giants have seldom been innovative within their private brand

programs. The thrust for innovation has tended to come from the suppliers.

It is interesting to note that retail advertising escapes much of the criticism aimed at national advertising in our society. Retail advertising may be mundane, but it is generally informative. Such advertising offers much information about prices, new styles and products, shopping hours, and where certain types of item may be purchased. Many consumers seek the information offered in retail advertising.

## Roles of Advertising

It is useful to think of advertising in terms of the multistage approach. Here, the first step is to designate the relevant customer targets. Then the store establishes an image or set of images in relation to these targets, and a merchandising mix for the firm is developed in which each element of that mix is given a role or group of roles. Thus the role for advertising in the merchandising mix of the store is quite complex. This complexity is indicated by the following example of a manufacturer's advertising campaign.

Three months ago a copy requisition was issued in the XYZ Company's advertising agency which read:

| | |
|---|---|
| *Client:* | XYZ Company |
| *Product:* | Wife-Saver |
| *Medium:* | Daily Newspaper display |
| *Size:* | Full page |
| *Copy:* | Announcement ad |

This called for a consumer advertisement to announce an entirely new type of product that would take a great deal of the remaining drudgery out of housework. In the advertising plan, the goal defined for the campaign, of which this was the first advertisement, had been stated as: "Persuade 500,000 housewives to visit 12,000 XYZ dealers for a demonstration of the Wife-Saver, in twenty-six weeks."

Today is A-Day and this announcement advertisement is appearing in newspapers all over the United States. Let's see how this message might be received by a few of the readers of the New York Times who perceive the advertisement at home, while commuting, or at their place of work.

A housewife, who was previously aware of XYZ products thinks: "This seems just what I want. I believe I will go to Brown's Appliance Store for a demonstration when I go downtown on Thursday." This response was consonant with the defined goal for this advertising. But there were other entirely different responses, as we shall see.

Mr. Brown of Brown's Appliance Store reads the ad on the train and it reminds him to put in a window display of the Wife-Saver today.

A recently-married housewife, who has never heard of the XYZ Company, becomes aware of the brand for the first time.

An investor reads of the Wife-Saver and thinks: "That ought to increase XYZ's earnings." He calls his broker and places an order for 100 shares of XYZ common even though it is up two points from yesterday's close.

A housewife who now has two other XYZ appliances in her home calls Macy's and orders a Wife-Saver to be sent out and charged to her account.

A prospective dealer whom XYZ's salesmen have been calling for years, without success, is impressed by the Wife-Saver announcement and finally decides to take on the XYZ line.

A young engineer who has been thinking about looking for a job with a more progressive company is favorably impressed with the design of the Wife-Saver which is illustrated in the announcement ad. He calls the XYZ employment department for an interview.

The purchasing agent for a large hotel chain reads the ad and says to his secretary: "Ask a salesman from XYZ to call." He has an idea that this innovation might reduce their operating costs.

A securities analyst who is writing a report on the XYZ Company, reads the advertisement and it confirms his belief that XYZ represents a sound "growth situation." His report is just a little more bullish than it otherwise would have been.

An employee of XYZ, who is having breakfast with his wife, sees the advertisement and says: "Boy. Look at that ad. I'll bet this new Wife-Saver really increases production. And if it does, I'm in line for a promotion. XYZ is really a good outfit to work for."

And even the senior loan officer of XYZ's principal bank reads the Wife-Saver advertisement and thinks: "The way XYZ's earnings have been climbing with their successful new product introductions we can probably increase their line of credit." He makes a note to discuss this at the next Loan Committee meeting (Campbell, 1963, pp. 1–3).

Thus an advertisement may have value in many ways. It may therefore be useful to distinguish the various goals of retail advertising as follows.

### Image Development

A firm may be interested in changing or re-establishing its key images with its customers; for example, it may have a reputation for variety, service, or low prices. Retailers may try to communicate interest in the community or indicate the types of customer that shop at the store. Upon occasion, they may even designate a percentage of their advertising budget specifically for longer-term purposes. Seldom, however, will they devote a large portion of their advertising to image building or changing. Indeed, perhaps the major criticism to be made of retail advertising is that it does not put sufficient emphasis on the longer-term aspects of firm development.

Image building, however, is very difficult. Indeed, it would be difficult to point to any retail advertising campaigns that have effectively altered a store's image. And changing the image of a manufacturing firm is no easy task either. Probably because of this difficulty, retail firms often try to foster the desired images within the context of merchandise advertising.

### Short-term Profit

Many retailers, such as department and specialty stores, will try to make a profit from the actual merchandise presented in the advertisement. Such merchandise is characterized by high margins and good value to the consumer. The value is necessary to create enough excitement to sell a large number of units. Hopefully, the number sold, together with sales of related merchandise, will make the advertising profitable, or nearly so. The high margin of the merchandise is often contributed to by lower, negotiated prices from the supplier. The merchandise is usually sold by mail and telephone as well as in the store because the high margin makes it possible to sell the merchandise profitably in this manner.

### Extraordinary Values

Many stores offer very attractive values in their advertising with only small consideration for profit. The main purpose of this advertising is to create excitement in the store. The small or negative contribution to overhead from the advertised merchandise is a secondary consideration because the main profit, as we shall see, is to be made in other ways. The management expects that some of the customers that come into the store as a result of the advertisement will buy other merchandise in the department, perhaps because the advertised merchandise is not exactly right for their needs. Further, when the customer is in the store, she may purchase other, unrelated merchandise at "reasonable" margins. Finally, the retailer feels that offering extraordinary value backed up by other factors such as service will help win new customers and help maintain old ones. Customers are naturally interested in trading at stores that offer them good value, so that stores are very interested in conveying this impression to the consumer. And once a customer likes the store, she may come back again, and again, and again. A store that offers substantial discounts from its former prices runs the risk of alienating customers who buy regularly. A store that sells $50 lamps for $10 may scare customers away from buying its regular merchandise. What customer wants to buy a $50 lamp that may be $10 tomorrow?

On the whole, supermarket advertising does not emphasize profits on the items advertised. Clearance-type advertisements in furniture, major appliance, and other types of store often do not stress profits on the items advertised. Discount stores depended almost entirely on advertising of this type during their early stages. Sales increments from this type of advertising would tend to be measured more in terms of increments in total department or store sales.

| Item A | Item B | Item C | Item D |
| Item E | Item F | Item G | Item H |
| Item I | Item J | Item K | Item L |
| Item M | Item N | Item O | Item P |

Figure 18.1

### Supplier Advertising

Many stores try to gain substantial profits from retail advertising irrespective of sales. Suppliers often contribute moneys to retail advertising. This cooperative advertising, together with the price concessions that the retailer may obtain from various media, makes it possible for retail firms to show a profit on certain advertisements even if no merchandise is sold. And the amount of money involved need not be small. According to the *New York Times* total cooperative advertising in 1973 stood at $2 billion. Edward C. Crimmins states that as much as 30 percent of all department store advertising has been thought to be paid for by cooperative advertising. Supermarket profits have often been aided substantially by cooperative advertising programs. These and other aspects of cooperative advertising are discussed below.

### An Example

Figure 18.1, which represents an advertisement, shows how the four roles of advertising just discussed can be, and often are, combined in the same format. It will be seen that 16 items are being advertised. How have they been selected? Suppose that the main purpose of the advertisement is to make clear to the customer the fact that the store carries a large assortment. In that case, all 16 items could be related to golfing equipment. In fact all 16 might be golf clubs—perhaps even all putters. Eight of the items might be clubs immediately recognized by the golfing customer as being very low-priced. The leading items of Wilson, Spalding, and MacGregor might be used. The low price for these items might serve to reinforce the value image that the store is trying to foster with its customers. The creator of the advertisement might also try to generate incremental profits from the other eight items, possibly store brands that cannot be compared in price with items at other outlets. If the customers recognize eight of the items as good value, without contrary information, they may assume that the other eight are good value as well. The store may take advantage of this to try to make a high margin on them (of course, high-margin items may offer good value). In addition, those advertised items that are thought by customers to be great values may induce many of them to come into the store and shop. Hopefully, many other items will be bought in this way besides the advertised ones. Some customers may be so impressed with the values offered in the store's advertisement or (when they visit it) by its total merchandise mix, that they become regular customers. A few of the 16 items may qualify for supplier advertising moneys. Indeed, it is possible that the money from a few items may pay for the entire advertisement.

As we saw in the Wife-Saver example, advertising has many other possible roles. A retail firm might attempt to change the attitude of the store's salespeople by advertising to consumers. For example, one company advertised that its gas station attendants would approach customers in less than 10 seconds. Presumably this type of advertising will actually improve the performance of participating dealers. One supermarket advertised the expertise of its butchers in the hope of improving their performance. Similarly, automobile manufacturers may advertise the quality of their dealer service in the hope that it will get better. Thus retail advertising can have many objectives.

### Using the Media

Newspapers have long been the retailer's favorite medium. A breakdown of advertising expenditures by medium for mass merchandisers such as Sears is shown in Figure 18.2, and an age profile of media use in Table 18.1. A retailer should be aware of some of the characteristics of the important media, since each has its advantages and disadvantages.

#### Newspapers

People usually read newspapers at their leisure. However, few things are duller than yesterday's news, and newspapers do not stay around people's homes as long as magazines. Accordingly, the reaction sought by a retailer for his newspaper advertising is both an immediate and a purposeful one. There is every indication that he gets it. A joint study by the Kroger Grocery chain and *Progressive Grocer,* made in 1966, indicated that 86 percent of the housewives in the country not only read grocery ads in their newspapers but use them extensively in deciding which items they will buy. Among the other advantages of newspapers, the following are often cited:

They are amenable to complex presentations that might be lost in other media;

They are particularly geared to offer news, so that advertisements that can be put into a news format may do well in newspapers (price and style are two dimensions of news that appear frequently in print);

They are taken about 85 percent by subscription;

They offer flexibility as to the size of the advertisement;

They offer special sections, such as a women's section;

They permit flexibility as to the day of the week;

They are chiefly local in character;

Newspaper advertising can be created very rapidly to respond to changed conditions.

Among the disadvantages of newspapers are the following:

**Table 18.1**
*Heavy media users, 1972, by age and medium*

|  | Heavy users of: | | |
|---|---|---|---|
|  | News-papers | TV | Radio |
| *Under 35* | 15.8% | 32.0% | 24.0% |
| *35–49* | 29.8% | 25.1% | 32.3% |
| *50 plus* | 54.4% | 42.9% | 43.7% |
| *Median age* | 52.0 | 45.8 | 47.0 |

Source: *Presentation of the Westinghouse Broadcasting Company before the Retail Research Society, 1972.*

The inability of a newspaper advertisement to capture the reader's attention unless it is particularly exciting (many newspaper advertisements hardly make any impression at all);

The lack of movement and sound in a newspaper advertisement largely robs it of "mood," i.e., the kind of emotional appeal so effectively presented on radio and television;

Color reproduction in newspapers is usually worse than in any other mass medium.

#### Television

Television is definitely becoming more important to retailers, partly because they are competing more and more with national and regional supplier brands. Among the advantages of television are:

It is a medium that reaches almost everyone;

It combines sight and sound, and so excels at creating various types of mood;

Because television pictures move, they can be used to demonstrate almost anything;

It has more effective color than newspapers;

The television audience, intent on the programs that commercials interrupt, is largely captive, so that the advertisement is not likely to be skipped, as it might be in a newspaper (though it appears that some viewers are able to "tune out" the undesired ones).

Among the disadvantages of television are the following:

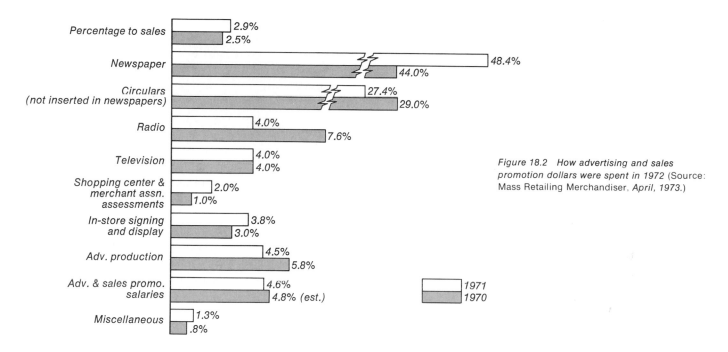

Figure 18.2  *How advertising and sales promotion dollars were spent in 1972* (Source: Mass Retailing Merchandiser, *April, 1973.*)

It is known as a medium with low involvement on the part of the viewer;

Minutes cannot be added to a television schedule in the same way as pages to a newspaper, since the total amount of advertising is regulated by the Federal Communications Commission.

The advertising disappears as soon as it is over, leaving the viewer without a list of merchandise to ponder or bring with him to the store;

The price discounts in television tend to favor the large consumer goods manufacturer advertising many products in many markets;

The price of television time is considered high relative to that of other media;

The message must be kept particularly simple because time is short and television is not a medium that favors complexity.

### Radio

Radio has been used frequently by retailers over the years. Among its advantages are:

It can easily create moods through sound;

Its listeners are loyal, i.e., they do not change stations as often as television viewers, and so are more likely to be hit many times by the same commercial (an important advantage for certain advertisers);

Its listeners often relate to the specific disc jockey, newscaster, or other "radio personality";

The audience for many radio stations is more highly segmented than that of television, thus often presenting a homogeneous target for the advertiser;

It is amenable to "dogmatic," advertising, that is, advertising in which the commercial proposition is merely stated, without special claims or emotional overtones (in radio, dogmatic messages often take the form of singing commercials, which rely on repetition for much of their effect).

It provides an audience of which a high proportion consists of males, especially males in cars;

It is considered inexpensive compared to television, that is, a sponsor can purchase many more advertisements on a radio station than he can typically purchase on television for the same money, and the cost per thousand persons reached will be very much lower.

Among the disadvantages of radio are the following:

It does not offer television's visual impact, and therefore lacks one of the two dimensions that, as various studies have shown, enable individuals to learn more rapidly (the other dimension, of course, is sound);

Its messages have no permanency, and therefore cannot be mulled over by the consumer at his leisure;

It is not conducive to complex thought because the medium imposes limitations of sound and time;

It covers too large a geographic area for most retailers—indeed, a small retailer will find that most of the people who hear his message have no reasonable access to the store.

### Magazines

Retailers have not used magazines heavily in the past. As they become more and more involved with the promotion of their own brands, one would expect them to use magazines more frequently. Among the advantages of magazines are the following:

Since the color in magazines is generally thought to be the best in any of the media, magazines are frequently used in advertising for which color is of substantial significance, as in creating emotional appeals;

Magazines may appeal to very specific groups of people —campers, for instance, or mothers of infant children;

Magazine advertisements are considered by some groups to be less annoying, more informative, and less offensive than advertisements received through the other media discussed here;

Readers can go through magazines at their own pace, and then pass them on (it is estimated that 30 million people used to see and look into *Life,* while the paid circulation was about 8 million);

High reader involvement.

Among the disadvantages of magazines are the following:

It is difficult to know precisely when magazines will be read and when the impact of the advertising in them will be felt (it is even hard to find out precisely when the magazine is delivered to the homes of subscribers);

Magazines are only visual, and thus lack the artifices of sound;

The long lead time between the creation of the advertisement and its publication makes it difficult for the retailer to alter his merchandise plans to meet changed conditions;

Although sales are characteristic of retailing, it is difficult for most stores to announce them successfully in magazines;

Magazines usually offer substantial waste circulation, because few retailers will be represented throughout the entire area reached by a magazine.

### Direct Mail

Certain types of retail outlet rely considerably on direct mail. Mailing lists of diverse types can be obtained commercially and may be of value to those who know how to use them. It is possible to obtain lists of doctors, owners of recent-model cars, expectant mothers, individuals who have moved recently, and so forth. Of particular importance to many types of retailers is the store's own charge list, but other kinds of list are increasing in importance. Some of the advantages of direct mail are as follows:

Both message and merchandise can be keyed directly to the relevant target audiences (the merchandise need not be in the store at all);

Target groups can be hit one or two at a time, a procedure that both lessens the retailer's risk and gives him a chance to improve his salesmanship;

It is often easy to compute the short-term benefits of direct mail and compare them to the costs;

Direct mail advertising may be used to increase customer loyalty, as when charge account customers are offered special markdowns or services.

Some of the disadvantages of direct mail advertising are as follows:

The recipient, unless he is one of the store's charge customers, is not usually eager to receive sale announcements or other commercial messages in the form of "junk mail."

Messages sent by direct mail have to make their impact rapidly, since it is unlikely that the recipient will sit back and contemplate their artistic merits or succumb to their influence through repeated exposure.

There is no sound or motion.

### Setting the Dollar Advertising Budget

If a retailer could not only specify the goals of his advertising but determine how much it contributed to achieving these goals, then he might relate the costs of the advertising to its benefits. In general, he would presumably continue to advertise for as long as long-term benefits of the advertising exceeded its long-term costs.

However, retailers do not usually articulate all their advertising goals in this way. Instead, they tend to want everything at once: short-term profits, long-term profits, a better image, highly motivated line managers, supplier moneys—the list could be extended. Retailers are in favor of any alternative that contributes substantially to any of these goals, provided that none of the other goals is impaired. And very few advertisements meet all the criteria. For instance, most forms of retail advertising seldom demonstrably increase short-term profits, even when designed to do just that. The remaining costs of the advertising must therefore be justified or perhaps rationalized in terms of other benefits.

Thus retail advertising is in a confused state. Retailers know that advertising has contributed to the growth of many firms over the years, but they are generally not quite sure how this was done. They know that their competitors spend many dollars on advertising: they know of many individual advertisements that have proven profitable, for them and for themselves. Given the environment of the firm, top management makes the value judgment that the firm must advertise. The conflict, or perhaps the tradeoff, between some of the advertising goals

does not present top management with great problems; consistency among the goals may appear desirable but is not high on their list of priorities. They are willing to live with this ambiguity and perhaps even thrive on it. They tend to select their advertising in a manner that seems to them to be consistent with the diverse goals of the enterprise, and to contribute the greatest amount to its short-term profits given that they are going to advertise a specific amount. By "short-term" they mean something like three days after the advertisement. Managements are aware that this approach is not an optimizing one, but they do not know of a better way. Thus while most types of store will make some calculations related to the profitability of a given advertisement or advertising campaign, these efforts are generally not major. All stores are reluctant to take such calculations at their face value, and apparently justifiably so.

If the important effects of retail advertising cannot be evaluated with any precision, then the problem of creating advertising budgets becomes insolvable by any precise means. And indeed that is exactly the case for most forms of retailing. Retailers appear to use the percentage of estimated sales in designating the amount of moneys to be allocated to the advertising function. Perhaps they are right: the percentage of sales, while analytically offensive to almost everyone, seems a reasonable guide given the great complexity of the problem, and according to Kenneth A. Longman is favored in nonretail firms.

The percentage-of-sale technique is offensive to observers for many reasons, but especially because the level of sales is established before the amount of the advertising budget is set. Clearly, advertising is supposed to increase sales. Establishing the budget for advertising after sales have been established is therefore putting the cart before the horse. Thus the technique does not explicitly consider the differences in the short- or long-term profits to be anticipated from advertising budgets of different levels. Indeed, it has nothing to say about what the goals of advertising are, much less about the costs and benefits of attaining any such goals. No substantial research need be done to develop an advertising budget by this means. In short, percentage-of-sales is primarily a subjective, seat-of-the-pants mode of decision making.

Nevertheless, there are some key advantages to using the percentage-of-sales approach. One is that it does not pretend to sophistication. There is an advantage in knowing what you do not know, and the sophisticated executive who uses this approach realizes that it has no analytic base. Another advantage is that comparison with one's competitors' advertising budget is made much easier. Executives will usually know what percentage of sales their competition is devoting to advertising, and can adapt their own budgets accordingly. But the greatest advantage or perhaps argument in favor of percentage-of-sales is that in many situations, the other methods are worse. Establishing an advertising budget in order to achieve specific goals requires a clear conception of exactly what the enterprise is trying to communicate. In the case of retailing, this would seem to involve mostly short-term considerations. Furthermore, if a dollar value and cost can be designated for the specified communication objectives, marginal analysis can be used, with all that that implies, both negatively and positively. As Longman suggests, the test market approach has not proved satisfactory for supplying firms under most conditions, and there would appear to be no reason to suppose that it would work better in a retailing context. It is interesting to note that, according to Longman, percentage-of-sales is the most frequently used method at the supplier level.

Robert Kahn suggests that the magic sales percentage figure varies for different types of retailing: for some businesses it is 1 percent, for others it is 4 percent. Kahn adds that he has never seen a planned retail advertising figure for other than a unit percentage of sales, or its half, i.e., 1, $1\frac{1}{2}$, 2, $2\frac{1}{2}$ percent. He asserts that it is never policy to have alternative planned advertising budgets.

In addition to marginal analysis and the percentage-of-sales method, a firm might use an objective-task approach; an all-you-can-afford approach; competitive parity; last year's dollar amount; or a combination of these and other approaches. These names are self-explanatory except possibly for the objective-task approach, which might be thought of as a careful definition of communication objectives coupled with explicit calculation of the relevant costs.

### Allocating the Advertising Budget

Once the magic percentage-of-sales estimate has been made, the moneys budgeted for advertising must be allocated. The modes of allocation are numerous: among merchandise areas; among types of mass media; among specific media; over the month; over the day of the week; between advertising in which the merchandise will provide the main impact and advertising in which it will not; and so forth. In general, retailers will and probably should allocate additional advertising moneys to those merchandise areas in which they feel that the greatest incremental sales and/or profits will be developed. Those in charge of merchandise areas will often be asked to present detailed plans and sales projections for key events before they can be allocated their share of the advertising budget. Top management then make their selections among various groups of merchandise areas. Without additional evidence, retailers will generally assume that the indirect benefits from each department's extra sales are the same. Thus the choice among merchandise areas is generally made by the short-term optimizing criterion of where the extra short-term sales and profit dollar is. In most instances, short-term incremental revenues will still be below incremental costs, but an effort is usually made to minimize this difference by selecting those sales events with the greatest short-term impact. The motto is: If you're going to hold a sale, make it a memorable one.

In allocating the advertising moneys among merchandise units, simple considerations of profit and sales may be tempered by any of the following:

1. The store may be divided into various administrative units—hard goods and soft goods, for example. It may be reasonable for top management to assume that each of these units has some hot areas that can use the advertising moneys. Under

this assumption, the advertising budget increment is simply divided among the parties in charge on some basis such as present lineage. Similarly, if the individual in charge of hard goods has four merchandise managers reporting to him, he, too, may assume that each has some hot areas of this kind. In addition, he may prefer not to show favoritism in the allocation of funds. Past this point, that is, at the level of the department or merchandise area, substantial discrimination is generally called for: departments or areas that show results tend to get more, and so forth. Because of this, managers sometimes "cook" their sales figures to make it look as if their areas benefit more from the store's advertising than they really do.

2. Some managers may regard not being given any money for advertising as a slur against the operation that they run. Therefore stores may not want to risk losing a key line executive by starving him for incremental advertising moneys. Such executives, if they are aggressive enough, may make the psychic costs of not giving them moneys very high. Indeed, they may conduct campaigns resembling psychological warfare to gain the extra advertising moneys that they feel their areas deserve.

3. Another key consideration is that of supplier moneys. This takes us into the topic of cooperative advertising, which is discussed in the next section.

A preliminary estimate of the store advertising budget for any month may be developed by applying the planned advertising percentage to the planned sales for the month. Typically, stores will not be able to advertise all that they would like to in December, because there is a limited supply of newspaper space. In this case, either the total budget can be decreased or the moneys can be reallocated to the remainder of the year. One frequently applied advertising rule is that the dollars allocated to retail advertising should peak for the store and the relevant merchandise classification just before the major selling season. The assumption appears to be that the incremental sales response for the total season will be largest at this point in time.

How advertising moneys are allocated by day of the week for a particular type of store is dictated by numerous factors: customers' shopping habits, the characteristics of the media, the behavior of other retailers, the goals of the specific advertising, and so forth. For example, a newspaper supermarket section that is supported by a substantial number of supermarkets may force other supermarkets to advertise on that day.

### Cooperative Advertising

Cooperative advertising is a $2 billion business, and a very important aspect of retailer-supplier relations. A 1966 study by the Association of National Advertisers of 138 supplier companies with consumer products found that more than 65 percent engaged in cooperative advertising, and that the median amount of their total advertising budgets spent in this way fell between 12 and 14 percent. Cooperative advertising occurs under the overall advertising of the store but with the product and brand of a given manufacturer. Thus both national and regional brands play a key role in cooperative advertising. Cooperative advertising is used in many countries and has been in operation in the United States since about the turn of the century. It is called "cooperative" because both the retailer and the supplier generally pay something toward the cost of the advertising. Today it is extensively used in supermarkets, department stores, appliance stores, drug chains, tire outlets, floor-covering dealers, shoe stores, jewelry stores, and discount operations. Most other forms of retailing also use it from time to time. About three-quarters of all cooperative advertising is in newspapers.

Crimmins offers some interesting insights into how cooperative advertising developed in a few industries. In the packaged goods field, manufacturers developed the practice of offering special price discounts to retailers whose business they particularly wanted. This practice was made difficult by the Clayton Act of 1914, after which many companies decided to use promotional advertising for the same end. The Robinson-Patman amendment to the Clayton Act in 1936 made it potentially illegal to offer advertising concessions in a discriminatory manner. Many companies then developed cooperative advertising plans. However, because of the history of the industry, these plans usually required a minimum of performance on the part of the retail firm. In many segments of the apparel industry, cooperative plans arose to move merchandise off the shelves of existing retail outlets. The retailer was expected to buy advertising for the moneys he received, and very often he had to share the cost of the advertising as well.

At one time in the toiletry industry, manufacturers placed national advertising in newspapers themselves. But, as we will see later in this chapter, the retailer can usually place such advertising at a lower rate than the supplier. Manufacturers in the toiletry industry developed cooperative advertising programs that gave the full national rate to the retailer for placing the advertisement, allowing the retailer to pocket the difference. Presumably some retailers will stock more of the manufacturer's merchandise under these conditions. In any case, under this arrangement there is a definite relationship between the amount of merchandise ordered from the supplier and the amount of advertising moneys offered. In the cosmetic industry, on the other hand, although manufacturers had not historically placed their own advertising in newspapers, they wanted to offer some inducement for the retailers to do this on their behalf. The manufacturers therefore offered to pay most of the local rate, typically lower than the national rate, as an inducement to advertise.

In thinking of cooperative advertising, it may be useful to regard some of it as being induced by retailers, usually very large ones. Cooperative advertising of this type has often been close to a price discount. The suppliers are forced to give such "discounts," and to design their marketing plans so as to gain the favor of these large retailers. Other types of cooperative advertising program—the ones in the toiletry and cosmetics industries, for example—have been created to solve certain problems of the suppliers, who have (among others) the following reasons for favoring such arrangements:

1. *Lower rates.* Suppliers can take advantage of the fact that the retailer will tend to get lower rates in newspapers than will nonretailers.

2. *More control.* Suppliers can time special promotions to both the retailer and final consumer. Generally, the manufacturer has more control over cooperative advertising than he does over retailer-sponsored advertising. With cooperative advertising, he can integrate various facets of the channel where necessary or desirable.

3. *Better communication.* Cooperative advertising will usually carry beyond the next member in the channel, if the next member is a nonretailer. Thus if a manufacturer sells to a wholesaler, a cooperative advertising program designed for the retailer may force more communication than might otherwise have occurred.

4. *Testing new products.* Generally, if a present supplier will pay for the advertising, the retailer will advertise any new items that he wants. This may be well worth paying for on a test market basis.

5. *Acceptance of low markup.* For many reasons historical and otherwise, some merchandise such as sugar and coffee is sold at low markup. Some brands are also typically sold at low markup in certain classifications. A cooperative advertising allowance induces the retailer to promote a brand or subclassification that he might not have promoted otherwise. And this cooperative advertising may be a much greater inducement to advertise and push the merchandise than a lower price might be, because the lower price would probably not be sufficient to make the merchandise profitable enough in the retailer's eyes to warrant promotion.

Cooperative advertising also has many disadvantages for the supplier. Often it is not well used. In 1973 it was estimated that $1 billion of cooperative advertising moneys were not used, mostly by the smaller stores. Also, the supplier has difficulty in controlling cooperative advertising. He may not know what rates the retailer pays to the media; he usually cannot control the type of space that the retailer gives to him in a given medium. Page 280 in a newspaper may not be as good as page two, and Saturday may not be as good a day as Sunday or Wednesday. He often cannot make sure that the advertisement was really run. In any case, he loses much control over its content. Thus cooperative advertising is a headache as well as an opportunity for the supplier.

## Control of the Press

In 1973 advertising by retailers in newspapers was about 75 percent of the amount spent on newspaper advertising by retailers and national advertisers combined. Since newspapers could not exist without advertising, their success or failure often depends on retailers. In a society in which power of any kind is eagerly sought after and as eagerly scrutinized, this immediately brings up the question of the retailers' influence on the newspapers' content and policies. The question is particularly important in a society in which the press is represented as "free," and in which the effective working of democratic processes may well depend on its remaining so.

Various representations have been made about how the power structure influences the press, and about how retailers, in particular, influence the coverage of local news. Some newspapers apparently distort weather reports so that shoppers will not be dissuaded from shopping downtown. Advertisements are occasionally printed as regular copy. Various retail events are given coverage that their news value alone might not justify. Lawsuits against retail outlets have not tended to get prime space. The names of retailers are often omitted from news stories that would place them in an unfavorable light. In addition, newspapers have not been known generally as champions of such causes an increased sales taxes to be imposed on retailers.

It is difficult to tell how badly the public's trust in newspapers is being abused. Retailers do, however, need effective newspapers. Of 1,511 newspaper cities in 1972, according to the *New York Times,* only 37 had two or more competing dailies. Thus the power works two ways. And the growth in a newspaper's circulation can positively influence the sales of at least some of the retail outlets associated with it. In addition, if a newspaper wants to keep on growing, it probably needs to appear free of bias. However, there are no hard data on how much bias actually exists, and the influence retailers may have over the press is therefore left for the reader to judge from his or her own experience.

## National and Local Rates

American newspapers have historically charged "national" advertisers a higher rate than "retail" advertisers. The difference between the two rates may be quite large. In the mid-1950s, according to James M. Ferguson, it was about 34 percent for papers with a circulation over 50,000, and 72 percent for papers with a circulation over 300,000. From 1930 to 1960, the differential increased steadily, but may have declined somewhat in recent years.

The reasons offered for this discrepancy are many and varied but the following are among the most plausible:

1. *Sensitivity to lower rates.* The reason most often featured in the literature is that the retailers' dollar advertising budgets are more sensitive to low-price newspaper inducements than are the budgets of national advertisers. The dollar budgets of mail order retailers would appear the most sensitive to a reduction in rates, because a mail order house will generally know exactly how many units each advertisement produces, and a lower cost for an advertisement will lower the point at which a promotion breaks even. Because the short-term merchandise return from a retail advertisement, i.e., the reaction in the first three days or so, is also relatively easy to judge, stores, too, may increase their advertising budgets if newspapers offer them better rates.

2. *Competition between local newspapers.* While the total dollars spent for retail advertising might not increase substantially as a result of lower newspaper space rates, one newspaper might get substantially more retail advertising than another by offering lower rates. Large retailers do negotiate their own arrangements, and can usually switch any

extra business to other newspapers. Large cities would presumably have greater discrepancies between retail and national rates because they would tend to have more newspapers. Proponents of such a theory might anticipate a continuous narrowing of the differential between national and retail rates as the number of newspaper competitors in the individual cities decreased.

3. *Bigger circulation.* Retail advertising, according to some observers, has a positive effect on circulation. We have already seen how more newspaper executives believe that retail advertising has a positive than a negative effect on circulation, although half believe that an increase in advertising has either no effect or a negative one. Thus newspapers in many areas of the country have to have a supermarket section on one or two days of the week or run the risk of offending customers. Newspapers, in our society, really need certain types of retail advertising in order to be accepted as newspapers.

4. *Geographic proximity.* The key might lie in the mechanism of buying space in newspapers. Large retailers tend to buy directly from the newspaper. Since they deal so extensively with the newspaper, they can often negotiate to accommodate its needs. For example, a retailer might take certain undesirable space, e.g., Saturday's, and use this for cooperative advertising. Personal interaction between newspaper and retailer is made easier by the proximity of the two. Indeed, proximity generally makes for better arrangements, even if transportation costs are not considered, since both buyer and seller get to know more about each other's needs.

5. *Stability of economic relationships.* Retailers have historically been the basic supporters of newspapers. The newspapers have had confidence that retailers will be back the next year, and that negotiations conducted with only one year in view in fact represent a commitment that will last for many years with only small periodic adjustments. Raising prices would threaten the stability of the relationship. Moreover, when the time comes to raise prices, it is more difficult to raise them for old customers than for new ones, particularly if the old customer has other choices.

## Observations about Advertising

There are many generalizations that can be offered about retail advertising. Some apply to one facet of retailing and not to the others. Some may apply primarily to national advertising. Some may be unfounded. It is useful, however, to outline at least a sample of them. The reader can infer their relevance to his or her particular areas of interest.

1. *There is a very large difference between advertising successful items and advertising unsuccessful ones.* Sometimes an expensive advertisement will draw no customers at all. Other advertisements will draw very extensively; indeed, if an item or event has all the ingredients the customer wants, the reaction can be overwhelming.

2. *Retail decision makers will generally advertise the best-selling items.* Effective decision makers do not get rid of the worst sellers by putting them in advertisements. Poor sellers may show up in notices of clearance sales, but here the item is not the focus of the copy so much as the event. Moreover, the fact that an item sells well on the selling floor does not mean that it can be effectively promoted. The key question is, Can the best-selling item, with all its features, be effectively represented in the newspapers or some other mass medium? However, an item that sells well on the selling floor should in most instances be considered for a promotion.

3. *Quality of readership can be more important in a mass medium than quantity.* The cost of the advertising per purchaser of a newspaper can be quite misleading. Some newspapers with very large circulations have gone out of business—the *New York Mirror*, for instance. A newspaper must have readers who not only look at but act on its advertisements or it will generally not flourish, regardless of how many people buy it.

4. *There is substantial communication among stores in different geographic areas about items to be advertised.* This is true of chains of stores, of members of buying groups, and between friends. Thus an item can have national distribution almost immediately if it is successful in one of the stores belonging to

a given communication system. All that is needed is one very successful advertisement. Not only is there a communication system among certain stores, so that each is apprised of the others' successful items, but one communication system will tend to keep tabs on competing communication links. Thus the two main competitors in town will not usually be in the same communication system, but the management of one will certainly look at the other store's advertising and check store traffic in the other store in instances where an item appears to have potential. In addition, certain stores in leading cities have won a reputation as introducers of new items. The advertisements of these stores are watched very closely by stores all over the nation.

5. *Strong emotional appeals are usually best carried by sound-using media such as television and radio.* The sense of hearing, as we have seen, tends to be more responsive to emotional appeals than the sense of sight. Apparently people are more moved by music than by the visual arts.

6. *The copy for most advertisements should be kept simple.* In most instances, according to the best authorities, the words used in an advertisement should be of a type familiar to the person for whom the advertisement is intended. Moreover, the message should be limited to a few points, since that is all most people can retain.

7. *Nothing does as well as the first advertisement.* Under most conditions, repeated advertisements over the same medium within a short period of time will not do as well as the first advertisement. In other words, two advertisements have less than twice the effect of a single advertisement in the same medium. Virtually all published mail order data plus the experience of the author support this finding. Victor Schwab has estimated that a second full page for an advertisement will pull 70 to 75 percent as much as the original ad if inserted within 30 to 90 days. The third ad, however, will pull only 45 to 50 percent of the first. The main exception to this rule appears to be the Christmas season. For some merchandise areas, the number of shoppers apparently increases at a greater rate than the attraction of the item decreases. The result is an in-

crease in sales for a given advertisement as time progresses. Indeed, one approach to Christmas merchandising would have the decision maker test various items around November 1. As the results come in, promotional winning items are selected. These items are then reordered in bulk and promoted aggressively as Christmas nears.

## Summary

1. Retailers are interested in advertising from many perspectives.

    A. As an integral part of the merchandise mix;

    B. As a competitor with the advertising of national brands;

    C. As an evaluator of the advertising of suppliers to consumers;

    D. As a user of trade advertising directed to them.

2. Retail advertising is different in many respects from supplier advertising.

    A. The supplier-advertised item can usually be purchased in many stores.

    B. Much retail advertising relates to price.

    C. Retailers do not extensively work through advertising agencies.

    D. Retailers are less interested in new products than suppliers.

3. Advertising has many roles and functions, including:

    A. Image development;

    B. Short-term profit;

    C. Extraordinary values;

    D. Supplier advertising, by which the store obtains cooperative advertising moneys;

    E. Some combination of the above or of alternative goals.

4. Not all the mass media are attractive to retailers to the same degree or for the same reasons.

A. Newspapers have long been the favorite medium of retailers. Newspaper advertising must be exciting to be read, i.e., the advertisement must be news. Style and price are the two prime ways of making advertisements newsworthy. Many consumers feel that retail advertising enhances the value of the newspaper.

B. Television is becoming more important to retailers partly because retail brands are competing more and more with supplier brands. The television audience is captive in a sense that the radio and print audiences are not. Television effectively combines sight and sound.

C. Radio has been used by retailers over the years. It is particularly effective in creating mood and is often used for highly repetitive, assertive kinds of advertisements, such as jingles.

D. Magazines are not used extensively in retailing but probably will be used increasingly. They are extremely effective in producing color, and have readerships that are involved with their contents and policies.

E. Direct mail is important when directed to such targets as loyal charge customer lists.

5. There are no satisfactory ways to set a retail advertising budget. If a store were to rely on short-term profits as the only goal, a marginal procedure would be feasible. But short-term profits are not the only goal. So most firms, for better or worse, end up using a percentage of sales as the starting point.

6. A firm must also allocate the advertising moneys among the various merchandise areas, the various days of the week, and so forth.

7. Cooperative advertising is a $2 billion business. Retailers generally obtain lower advertising rates in newspapers than do suppliers. This and other reasons are conducive to the retailer and supplier combining moneys and efforts to develop an effective combined advertising program. There are advantages and limitations to this kind of advertising.

### Discussion Questions

1. The consumer appears to like retail advertising. Why?

2. How would you improve the aesthetic quality of retail advertising?

3. In what ways is retail advertising different from supplier advertising?

4. List four goals of retail advertising.

5. What are the advantages and disadvantages of newspaper advertising? of television advertising?

6. If you were the chief executive of a large supermarket, how would you set your advertising budget?

7. Why should a retailer be interested in the advertising of the supplier?

8. Give at least three possible explanations of why retailers get cooperative allowances from suppliers. Do you accept any of these? Give your reasons.

9. Retailers are heavy advertisers in newspapers. Do you believe that retailers control the press? On what evidence (or lack of evidence) do you base your belief?

### References

Campbell, Roy H., *Measuring the Sales and Profit Results of Advertising: A Managerial Approach* (New York: Association of National Advertisers, 1969).

Crimmins, Edward C., *A Management Guide to Cooperative Advertising* (New York: Association of National Advertisers, 1970).

Ferguson, James M., *The Advertising Rate Structure in the Daily Newspaper Industry* (Englewood Cliffs, N.J.: Prentice-Hall, 1963).

Kahn, Robert, in *Retailing Today,* September 1970.

Longman, Kenneth A., *Advertising* (New York: Harcourt Brace Jovanovich, 1971).

Schwab, Victor O., "Successful Mail Order Advertising," in Roger Barton (ed.), *Advertising Handbook* (Englewood Cliffs, N.J.: Prentice-Hall, 1950).

Weiss, E. B., in *Advertising Age*, May 31, 1965, p. 61.

### Further Reading

Greyser, Stephen A., and Reece, Bonnie B., "Business Looks Hard at Advertising," *Harvard Business Review*, May–June, 1971.

Kriegbaum, Hillier, *Pressures on the Press* (New York: Crowell, 1972).

Shryer, William A., *Analytical Advertising* (Detroit, Mich.: Business Service Corporation, 1921).

Simon, Julian L., *Issues in the Economics of Advertising* (Urbana, Ill.: University of Illinois Press, 1970).

Whitney, John O., "Better Results From Retail Advertising," *Harvard Business Review*, May–June, 1970.

### Case History: *The Wisdom of John Wanamaker*

Michael Farnsworth was president of General Department Stores. He had recently read a book of quotations and had come across a statement attributed to John Wanamaker. In essence, the quotation was that Wanamaker was sure half his advertising was a waste and that he spent a great deal of time trying to determine which half. Farnsworth had also come across a quotation, attributed to Wrigley, to the effect that once one got a plane off the ground, one did not test various elements to find out what made it work. One might find out, all right, but by then it would be too late.

General Stores had grown over the years. However, there had never been a complete review of the firm's advertising expenditures. An advertising committee created by the president had maintained a budget at about three percent of sales. In some years the budget was not used up because of the difficulty in getting adequate newspaper space around Christmas. In other years a little more was spent to meet particular competitive activities of other stores. The initial budget was not held to religiously but adapted to the competitive environment as it evolved. The president kept a close eye on the store's volume figures, and if an area looked in need of additional advertising, he gave it more money. And as merchandise areas developed individual hot items, additional advertising revenues were allocated.

These quotations had bothered Michael Farnsworth. He decided to call a meeting of his key executives to get their feeling on how much money the stores should spend on advertising and how these funds should be allocated among merchandise areas, on the one hand, and the different advertising media, on the other.

All the executives agreed that the store had to spend at least one percent of sales on advertising or go out of business. The customers had to be convinced that General was still in business and had representative merchandise offerings. No one could say why the minimum was one percent rather than two or three; it just seemed like a reasonable figure. The question was, How much above this figure should General go?

Michael Farnsworth first asked the opinion of Henry Jones, his tough-minded controller. Henry suggested that the answer was easy: each advertisement had to pay for itself. After all, General's advertising over the years had been merchandise advertising. Each department should be held to contribution to overhead. And if the decision maker were held to this goal, he should be allowed to make his own advertising decisions. If the decisions were that bad, he should be fired and replaced by someone who could make effective decisions. It was the merchandise area heads, Henry continued, who should add up the requests of the individual merchandise areas. The advertising budget would then be more or less a summation of these requests. The decision makers would not be acting blindly, since they would be instructed in marginal analysis. Each buyer would ask himself: Does the advertising pay or not for my area of concern? If the summation of the various areas was under one percent, then some method of allocating advertising up to one percent would be devised. But he felt that the requests of the areas would in fact add up to about three percent of sales.

Adrian Keller, formerly president of and now consultant to the company, basically agreed with the controller except that he argued that, in his experience, few advertisements paid for themselves completely. And after all there were substantial benefits of advertising other than the short and immediate returns to the department. There were sales generated in the other parts of the store as a result of the customers coming in; some customers were even introduced to the store for the first time. The increasing number of mobile customers made advertising to new customers of continuing importance. In addition, there were image dimensions to the advertising. Adrian suggested that each department receive a credit of 25 percent of its space charges for the benefit that this advertising was to the total store. Beyond that he was willing to accept the merchandise areas' requests for space and time. If allocation were necessary, the areas that could prove their claim to the largest incremental margin return from the dollars spent should get the money.

Paul Campbell, the advertising vice-president, had a different perspective. He suggested that what had made General work over the years was the effective image it had built up with its customers. And advertising had not really done its share. In his experience as vice-president of an advertising agency on Madison Avenue, most of the really important advertising campaigns had been image-changing campaigns. Thus the key role for advertising at General should be to favorably influence the attitudes of its customers. Historically, advertising at General had been only merchandise advertising. Paul suggested that this was wrong. The company should first decide what image it wanted, and then go out and develop this image. To the extent that merchandise was needed in this context, it should be used. But if merchandise was not necessary, it should not be used. The merchandise was just an element in image creation; it should not be the whole thing.

Irving Everett, vice-president in charge of hard goods, could not buy the "image forever" approach. Irving felt that of course the firm's image was important, and of course he wanted to improve it. But the image was a constraint, and not the purpose of the advertising. It was merchandising that made the store exciting and merchandise that was the key differentiating feature of the store. Let the merchandise areas create the advertising and be charged 100 or some other percent for it, but let them make sure at the same time that the advertisements conformed to an image-enhancing format. And each merchandise manager should make sure that the merchandise being promoted conformed to the desired store image.

Louis Small, vice-president in charge of soft goods, believed neither in a firm budget nor in the firm allocation of that budget to merchandise areas. Louis thought that the key to all budgets was the reaction to circumstances, mainly to competition. True, one needed a budget. And one might as well start with last year's figure or with some percentage of sales as with any other. One should, however, carefully monitor the sales results and the competition's advertising. Sales should be watched to see if any areas were in trouble. Troubled areas should be examined to see what was wrong. To the extent that advertising could correct the trouble, it should be utilized. Hot items should be promoted when appropriate. And customers and potential customers should be interviewed every six months to see if and how the image of the store had been altered. Again, since image was important, appropriate action should be taken where relevant.

Margaret Cohen, the general merchandise manager, held a slightly different view. She suggested that, basically, buyers and merchandise managers were responsible not just for net profits or contribution to overhead but for the growth of the store and its image. The store tended to use the volume of the merchandise areas as an indication of how the future growth criteria of the department were being met. And the initial and maintained markup were carefully monitored as separate entities to make sure that the volume was not obtained at the cost of the store's image. The promotion of goods at low markups was thought to damage this image, particularly if the merchandise promoted was not a famous brand. Therefore, one could not develop a budget or allocate that budget according to just one criterion, and at that a criterion that few observers would accept, namely, short-term contribution or profits. While everyone would like ways to make the advertising budget scientific and relate this to one goal, perpetual hankering after this ideal was mental masturbation. Three goals—sales growth, high markup, and short-term profit—had to be kept in mind all the time. One simply had to do the best that one could; advertising was an art, not a science.

Margaret concluded that last year's budget should be used as a base, while last year's advertising budget should be adjusted for exceptional performance the year before. The managers of each area should use the money in the best way they knew, recognizing that these three goals applied to most of the areas.

Michael Farnsworth was more confused than ever after the meeting. He had expected more unanimity among people who had been in merchandising so long.

## Discussion Questions

1. How would you suggest that Michael Farnsworth set the firm's advertising budget?

2. How should he allocate that budget among the various merchandise areas?

# 19

Sales promotion can mean almost anything. This chapter discusses certain elements of retailing that, while important, have not been adequately covered in the preceding chapters. The elements in question are the retailer's use of private brand, credit, trading stamps, public relations, and point-of-purchase material, all of which can be critical in enhancing sales. Each can help to attract the desired customer segments. Each can complement the other elements of the merchandising mix and so create a more attractive package for the consumer.

## Sales Promotion

### Private Brand

In 1960, according to Donald L. Belden, 10 large variety chains did an average of 15 percent of their dollar volume in private brands. By 1965 the volume of private brand had increased to 20 percent, and by 1970 to 32.8 percent. Further growth is anticipated. In the department store field, private brand has also experienced substantial growth. In food, where national manufacturers are very strong, a source quoted in the *National Observer* feels that sales of private brands have increased from 11 to 16 percent of supermarket sales during the period 1967–73. Within the food industry, bakery products, dairy products, frozen juices, and frozen vegetables appear particularly amenable to private-brand selling. In other types of retailing similar trends have been noted. A key exception is the retail gasoline business, where the independent share of the market decreased from 33 percent in 1971 to 25 percent in 1973.

Distinctions between private and national brands are not always obvious. Observers tend to identify as private those brands that are neither national nor strong regional brands. National or regional brands tend to be associated with large manufacturers, who usually spend great sums of money in advertising them to the final consumer. Brands that are neither national nor regional may also be usefully grouped under two heads: those that receive substantial promotional support from the retailer, and those that receive little promotional support of any kind. Many observers suggest that retailer-promoted brands are closer to those of national brand manufacturers than they are to private brands that have little identity because of small promotional support. However, no clear distinction is made in this chapter between types of private brand, although the student should bear in mind that grounds for such distinctions do exist.

It should be further noted that many manufacturers' brands are really controlled by retailers. The manufacturers may need the large stores in order to exist, and the retailers may have the option of creating private brand with this supplier. However, it may be in the best interests of both the large retailer and the manufacturer to maintain a quasi-national brand status for the latter's goods. In this fashion the manufacturer may be able to use the large retailers to sell other wholesalers and retailers.

Clearly, retailers use private brands because they anticipate higher long-term profits with them than without them. While true, this observation does not offer much insight into the private brand situation. Firms might also use the short-term criterion of maximizing gross margin dollar per unit of space. And some apparently do. A study of food brands cited by Dalrymple and Thompson indicates that while the percentage margin for the private brands was higher than it was for the national brands, the sales per *facing* for private brands were lower. As a result, the dollars of gross margin developed in the study were about the same for each. While short- or long-term profit guides may be useful in interpreting a store's private-brand behavior, it might be interested in private brands for many reasons, some of them related to short-term profits and others not. Among them are the following:

1. *A private brand will often take a store beyond the scope of the Robinson-Patman Act.* Clearly, a private brand that is of like grade and quality is not excluded under the Act. However, large retailers often find it a rather small jump from private brand of like grade and quality to private brand not of like grade and quality, as Frederick M. Rowe has pointed out. Thus a buyer for a large store can create products that require separate and different molds,

and this will probably bring the retailer beyond the control of the Act. The advantages of this from the bargaining perspective of the retailer are obvious.

2. *A private brand can appeal to specific customer segments.* In a given situation, almost any customer may be appealed to. Since private brands are almost always priced lower than comparable national brands, customers interested in good value at every price level are always prospective purchasers of them. Further, it has been established that highly educated individuals tend to purchase more private-brand items than those with less education. This is one factor that augurs well for the future of private brands. Private brands also have appeal to those interested in a cheap price on cheap goods; in fact, they tend to have greater representation in the very low price lines. Finally, private brands may also appeal to customers that have a desire for risk. A customer who samples a great many private brands will almost surely be exposed to a greater variation in quality than one who buys the same number of nationally advertised brands. This would tend to be true whether one or a great many different private brands were sampled. Thus a marketer might well expect a risk-reducer to be drawn to national brands. On the other hand, someone who enjoys taking risks may prefer to find out what the private brands have to offer.

3. *A private brand that performs well is conducive to repeat sales.* If you offer the customer great value, she will generally be interested in trying the item again—particularly if it is the type of item that she purchases frequently. Thus stores meticulously build up private brand programs because the customer must return to their outlet in order to "know" that she is getting the same item. In addition, if one customer tells another of her great satisfaction with a store's private brands, the store will probably gain new customers.

4. *Particular stores may be capable of trading off their image for style, quality, and so forth.* Over time, a store may have built up a steady clientele through its private programs and other merchandise endeavors. These customers may look to the store for merchandise leadership. The store may "take advantage of" this customer viewpoint by putting its name on some items. The value of the items may

even be enhanced in the minds of many customers by this action if the store has been quite selective in the items that it has put its name on in the past. Thus the store will receive a higher margin, possibly even a higher absolute price, and the customer may receive more utility.

5. *Private-brand merchandise may be required to fill certain promotional voids.* In certain types of store, one of the major roles of advertising is to bring customers into the store. Stores have found over the years that one attraction for the customer is low price. A full-sized bicycle advertised at $19.99 will generally draw many customers to the store regardless of what country it was made in. A full-sized table tennis table at $14.99 will draw customers regardless of where it was made. Not that everyone that comes into the store will buy these items. But price is a substantial promotional inducement to many customers, and merchandise at the very low end of the quality spectrum (which may be reasonable quality) can be useful to many types of store in their efforts to obtain promotional mileage. A related consideration is that in certain states the prices of certain goods are price-maintained. Thus a management might have to develop its own private brand in order to introduce price flexibility in its advertising. For example, a discount store might develop its own private-brand liquor program for this reason.

6. *A private brand gives firms greater control over the quality of the item.* In general it is true that quality standards for the national brand are higher than the standards for a comparable regional or local brand. In specific instances, however, the standards for the private brand may be higher than the standards for the national brand—and the private-brand standards are usually under the control of the retailer. The national manufacturer may be forced by competitive pressures within the channel to lower his quality standards. The store, however, is subject to different pressures and may deem it worthwhile in given instances to have higher standards. Judging from some of the ratings offered by *Consumer Reports*, a leading retailer quite frequently has a better performance record for a specific private-brand item than its supplier when selling a similar one under his own brand name. One cause might be that the retailer has higher specifications.

7. *A private brand program creates an appearance of variety.* Private brands would appear to be particularly well suited to create variety in the low-priced ranges. It would be a mistake to assume that all items within a store are designed to be profitable in and of themselves. Some items, as we saw in Chapter 13, just add to the overall impact of the assortment that is presented to the customer, and the addition of certain items may make it easier to sell other items. If a retailer expects to sell 10,000 units of an item on his selling floor, it may be worth his while to take in 24 or 36 units of one or two other items in order to make the prime items sell better. Similarly, a private brand program offers the retailer a degree of price flexibility over time that he often cannot get in dealing with a national brand supplier. For example, a retailer might bring in the 24 or 36 items mentioned above at very high margins. The addition of these items may not only make the other items on the selling floor appear better value but also set the stage for big clearance events, clearance catalogs, and so on. And these clearance events can take place with the goods at high margins after the markdown. The tire business, for instance, has always seemed to this author to operate along these lines.

8. *A private brand acts as a brake on the price behavior of national brand suppliers.* One consideration in the relationship between supplier and store is the number and kind of alternatives open to the store. In many industries, the supplier is presented with the continuing threat that a particular store will increase the merchandise support it gives to its private brands. In industries where the price and other dimensions of the supplier marketing mix are highly malleable, the threat may bring quite advantageous results for the retailer. Even in areas where the key dimensions of the supplier's marketing mix are rigid, the threat that the retailer may give increased support to his private brand might induce the supplier to do such things as create a package that is more to the retailer's liking.

The above are just some of the reasons why retailers are interested in fostering private brands. A similarly diverse list might be created of reasons why suppliers seek private brand business. Clearly, no suppliers would do so unless he perceived it to be in his best interests. Some manufacturers, indeed, do not have brands of their own and only manufacture wholesaler or retailer-controlled brands.

### Social Benefits of Private Brands

The overall impact of the private brand on our complex economic machine is difficult to assess. It would appear to have contributed in at least the following areas.

**Price level** Private brands do generally offer the consumer a lower-priced alternative to the national ones. It is not that private brands are better for society than national brands. It is just that if the national brands of most products are going to sell at price *x*, then, under most conditions, the private-brand counterparts will have to sell at something less than *x*. In other words, there has to be differential pricing with the national brand as the base. If there were no national brands, the price of the private brands might be above *x*. The merits of having only private brands are highly debatable.

In many instances, the price that the retailer pays to the supplier of private brands, particularly in an industry with substantial excess capacity (which means most industries), is going to be based substantially on the costs of the supplier. Thus the profits to the supplier of private-brand merchandise would appear to be limited. However, the profits to the retailer on brands that he controls are not limited by this kind of factor. What does tend to limit them is the retail price of the national brand, together with the prices of *horizontal competition*.

**Stimulus to new products** Private brands tend to thrive after a product has been established for a while. As a nationally branded product progresses

through what might be termed its life cycle, it becomes more and more susceptible to competition from private brands. The profits of the product gradually decline as the various private brands are introduced and as the manufacturers of the product under its national label produce more and more of it as a private brand. The changing competitive environment forces the profits of the product down to a level where, at some point in time, the manufacturer will be making only a slight amount over his cost. Manufacturers seeking higher profits are forced to innovate by substantially improving the product; indeed they must innovate continually in order to maintain their competitive advantage. Thus the existence of private brands is conducive to a high rate of innovation among manufacturers who seek higher profits than private brands can offer.

**Institutional variety** The existence of private brands offers the consumer not only a greater variety of both prices and brands but also, in all likelihood, a greater variety of retail institutions. For instance, Sears would probably not have progressed in the manner that it has if it had not relied heavily on its own brand. Many other examples could be offered of private brands that have contributed substantially to the development of the retail firms sponsoring them. The result for society appears to be a greater variety of retail institutions for the consumer to choose from.

**Vertical channel competition** Most competition contains elements of cooperation—and vice versa. In the case of retailing, it can be said that the various members of the channels of distribution interact both cooperatively and competitively whether they use private brands or not. It would appear, however, that the existence of private brands in a channel that already fosters a national brand adds a new dimension to this competition. Thus private brands add complexity to our already complex channels of distribution.

**Small manufacturers**   Many factories have break-even points at high levels of output. It might be very difficult—and very risky—for a small manufacturer to compete with a national brand. If one or two large retail accounts will accept its product as their brand, the small firm may be past the break-even point. Thus many manufacturers who could not otherwise do so are given a chance to compete with the larger manufacturer in a highly competitive market.

### Credit

Credit scheduled to be repaid in two or more installments has grown at a rate of about 9 percent annually since the early 1920s. In the first 10 years after World War II, its growth rate approximated 19 percent annually. This type of credit includes automobile loans, repair and modernization loans, personal loans, and other consumer-goods paper. It includes both revolving charge accounts and budget accounts paid in equal periodic installments, but excludes single-payment loans and charge accounts. Further details are given in Table 19.1.

The growth of credit has been substantial whether considered in absolute terms or as a percentage of *personal disposable income*. From 1947 to 1972, total consumer credit increased from about 5 percent of personal disposable income to about 20 percent. The ratio of outstanding installment credit to personal disposable income increased from 1.4 percent in 1945 to 15 percent in 1972. Clearly, credit is important to the retailer (supplier credit, while important, is not considered here). Approximately two-thirds of all retail sales according to Dennis W. Richardson, are made on a credit basis. He further estimates that three-quarters of all American families hold credit cards or have charge accounts. About one-half of all Ward's sales are on credit.

Of the retail sales related to credit in 1970, excluding automobiles, groceries, and liquor, about 60 percent were made on what have come to be called *revolving charge accounts*. With an account of this kind, the customer generally will pay in full

Table 19.1
Consumer credit, 1940–72 ($ million)

|      | Total   | Installment | Noninstallment |
|------|---------|-------------|----------------|
| 1940 | 8,338   | 5,515       | 2,824          |
| 1950 | 21,471  | 14,703      | 6,768          |
| 1960 | 56,141  | 42,968      | 13,173         |
| 1970 | 127,163 | 102,064     | 25,099         |
| 1972 | 157,564 | 127,332     | 30,232         |

Source: Federal Reserve Bulletin, *April, 1973, p. A-54.*

within 30 days of the billing date without any service charge. Any balance after that is assessed a service charge on a monthly basis. A second type of retail credit is the *charge account*. Here, the customer is allowed to run up an account for which he is periodically billed, often without interest charged. A third type of consumer credit is the *installment purchase plan*. Approximately two-thirds of all automobiles are sold on an installment basis.

Credit is an integral part of the merchandising mix of many enterprises and is assigned many roles, including the following:

1. *Credit is supposed to increase the quantity of merchandise sold at a given price.* It may induce some customers to purchase the merchandise earlier than they might have otherwise. Or it may help to induce some customers to buy the merchandise in one store rather than in another. Most stores use credit because they expect to sell more merchandise at a given price level with credit that without credit.

2. *Credit may permit and at times require a retailer to charge higher prices for the merchandise.* To most enterprises, as we shall see, credit is a cost, that is, running a credit operation costs something above the interest returned. These increased costs may require the retailer to charge higher prices for his merchandise. From another perspective credit may offer the retailer the opportunity of making more money by increasing his prices. It is probably true that credit at the present time does increase prices for those outlets that offer credit. There is no reason, however, why a given retailer would have to raise prices when he instituted credit. His additional business might more than make up for the credit costs.

3. *Credit can aid the retailer to trade the customer up to a higher price line*, usually one with a better

quality. Thus a customer who has credit as an option may be willing to buy an $8 shirt instead of a $5 shirt.

4. *Store credit programs are designed in the hope that the customer will make a higher share of his purchases in that store.* Stores would like customers to develop the habit of using their particular credit card.

5. *Credit is a way to enhance a relationship with customers.* The monthly statement can be used to show some interest in the customer and to involve him in the store.

6. *The charge list provides the store with a selected list of customers.* Most of them will be highly receptive to merchandise events of all types.

7. *The charge list provides an inexpensive way of finding out what some of their customers are like.* The management can even get information on such sensitive topics as income. This might otherwise be quite difficult to obtain.

Since credit is such an important element in the appeal of so many different enterprises, few of them will want to worry whether it is profitable in some overall sense. The option of discontinuing credit is usually not present. Nevertheless, many legislative bodies have taken an interest in retail credit. They believe that when stores often charge an average of 18 percent interest on most accounts profits must be there somehow. States such as Washington and Wisconsin have even limited the amount of interest that can be charged to 12 percent. In response to what might be termed this movement to alter the interest-rate structure of retail credit, various department stores have reiterated their position that credit for them is a losing proposition. And indeed if the advantages of credit as a selling tool are not considered, the loss attributable to the credit operation in a store is apt to be quite high. Part of this loss comes from charge accounts that bring no interest. One study sponsored by the National Retail Merchants' Association in 1969 indicated that the net cost to department stores of granting credit averaged 2.55 percent of credit sales. The study found that all three methods of granting credit—the 30-day charge account, the revolving account, and installment sales—were unprofitable, although costs for the long-term installment sales were almost equal to service income. For the small stores in the study, not one of the three types of accounts yielded revenues that exceeded 65 percent of the costs of offering credit.

### Bank Credit Cards

It is obvious from the preceding that the benefits of creating an effective credit program are large for most retail outlets, and that, in most types of retailing, the large retail outlet has a great advantage over the small one. This was a key consideration in the development of the first bank credit card in 1952. Small merchants in the neighborhood of New York City felt that they could compete with the suburban branches of the New York City department stores with respect to price and quality, but that they could not afford to carry charge accounts. The Franklin National Bank set up a program that went a long way toward answering this need. Since that time giant credit programs such as Bankamericard and Master Charge have been established to serve the small and medium-sized merchant, the consumer, and, of course, the banks. Credit outstanding on bank plans amounted to over $5 billion at the end of 1972.

The large, traditional retailers, on the other hand, have viewed the development of bank cards as more of a threat. They do not wish to use these various cards because they will lose some of the advantages that are associated with a private credit system. However, they do fear that at some point in time the customer will resent having 12 or 15 credit cards in her wallet or bag. Thus large retailers are gradually adopting bank credit cards.

### Social Aspects of Credit

We seem to be progressing toward what is often termed the cashless society. This trend may well continue unless there is direct intervention by the various legislatures to prevent it. While speculation on this topic is hazardous at best, because of its extreme complexity and pervasiveness, it would appear that the following generalizations about credit are worth entertaining. The negative aspects of credit will be considered before the positive ones.

1. *It is through credit that the poor, who are not usually allowed credit on reasonable terms, often subsidize the rich.* Many merchants used to sell merchandise at a lower price for cash. This practice appears to be on its way out. The overwhelming majority of merchants charge the cash and credit customers the same price, at least to the point where interest is due. Since the credit operations of most retail firms appear to operate at a loss (and certainly when bank cards are accepted), costs are higher for the credit customer than for the cash customer. It would appear that these added costs increase the price, and that this higher price is paid by both cash and credit customers.

2. *Those who purchase for credit often pay less.* If a consumer uses a major bank card and pays within the stipulated time from the billing date (which may be 30 days or more after purchase), he generally pays no interest at all, often for more than 60 days. The credit customer can obtain interest from other sources over this period, so the price for him nets out to less than for the cash customer.

3. *Credit severely hampers individuals trying to get out of poverty or near-poverty.* In a society that emphasizes materialism to as great a degree as ours, it is very difficult for an individual to keep money in a savings institution when it could be used as a down payment on such things as furniture, appliances, and television. The poor person often makes a purchase from a small retailer to whom he pays a very high interest rate that has been tacked on to an extraordinarily high price. This bind is very difficult to get out of. Remember, interest at the normal "low" 18 percent is not exactly the rich man's delight. Even this "low" interest rate can keep a person in poverty for quite a time. A consumer has to be relatively frugal, very wealthy, highly disciplined, or some combination of these, to get to the point where he can utilize credit to his advantage. The fact is that when one has to buy on credit, one will often buy at an institution that will offer this credit to you at reasonable psychological and related costs. Further, the easier an institution is with credit to consumers, the greater will be its bad debt loss. The greater the

bad debt loss, other things being equal, the higher the price the merchant must charge to exist. Therefore poor credit risks tend to gravitate toward institutions with higher prices.

4. *Credit induces people to buy more than they would purchase otherwise.* This may have positive or negative ramifications for society. But many lives are lost on the sea of credit. Some customers overbuy, and then cannot meet their obligations.

There are clearly many advantages to having substantial credit in our society. Indeed, if many purchasers did not consider credit to be in their self-interest, credit would not have grown in the manner that it has.

1. *Credit permits the consumer to enjoy a certain standard of living before he actually reaches that standard.* This is true for consumers of any age. For example, were it not for mortgages, many young people would not be able to purchase houses until they were considerably older, perhaps after their children had grown up. A University of Michigan study shows that 73 percent of all households of which the head is under 35 — twice the proportion of those with heads over 55 — still have unsatisfied consumption needs. Thus credit influences the life styles of many individuals with respect to many types of goods.

2. *Credit is very convenient.* Bills can be paid at one time of the month, payments can often be delayed for a month or so, and large amounts of cash need not be carried on one's person.

3. *An increasing amount of credit will increase what economists call the consumption function.* At every level of personal disposable income for the total economy, a higher level of consumption would be expected with increasing credit. Some economists believe that a higher level of consumption for a given level of personal disposable income is usually a good thing, and may be conducive to increased employment in a society with a substantial number of unemployed. The opposite view is that large amounts of credit may be a burden for many customers, causing them to overreact when times look bad by substantially decreasing consumption, and so add to the volatility of the business cycle.

4. *Credit is a weapon in the hands of the consumer to make sure that the retailer lives up to his agreement.*

At present, retailers in many states assign their receivables to other, usually financial institutions. Thus the consumer may not have recourse against the retailer. In general, however, the consumer does have recourse if the item does not perform well, since he can simply stop payments until the retailer does something. In addition, if a person is a good credit customer, this means something to the store's management; they will not just ignore him. And it is far easier for a credit customer to demonstrate his importance to a large store than it is for a cash customer or one with a bank or other nonstore card, because the records of dollars purchased are readily available in almost all instances.

5. *Credit decreases the rewards of holding up or otherwise stealing from stores.* This is one of the benefits of the cashless society toward which we are moving. Already, certain stores will refuse to accept cash, mainly for this reason. A great number of small retailers fear for their lives, and would presumably welcome a higher percentage of credit sales.

## Trading Stamps

Trading stamps have been with us for many years. According to Harold W. Fox, trading stamps were first used in England about 1880 and in the United States from the 1890s onward. After the turn of the century they spread across Europe and the United States. They enjoyed a surge of popularity until World War I and a strong tide of enthusiasm after 1951. In the early 1970s, however, their popularity began to decrease.

Trading stamps have not changed a great deal since the early period except that they were originally offered as a discount for cash. They are one of many nonprice methods of promoting the sales of merchandise. Stamps may be used by the retailer as a substitute for other promotional alternatives or they may be regarded as an increased cost designed to gain additional business. In a way, they are a retail price concession, because they are directly convertible into other merchandise. Customers, however, do not usually know the stamps' precise value, and competitors do not tend to regard stamp competition in the same light as price competition. Stamps, therefore, occupy a place of their own in the retailer's promotional kit.

Analysts have often pondered the relationship between stamps and retail prices in stores carrying the stamps. From a theoretical point of view, there can be no answer to this question. Under given conditions, the introduction of stamps may lead to higher prices, lower prices, or no change in prices at all. If every store in a given competitive area offered stamps, the prices of the merchandise in this area would generally be expected to increase to reflect each unit's higher costs. This assumes, correctly so for most markets, that revenues for all units will not increase sufficiently to cover the increased costs that are bound to occur. Seldom, however, do all retailers in a given area carry stamps. Often the stamps are a substitute for alternative promotional activities — games, for example. If they are, the presence of stamps would not be expected to have any substantial impact on the level of prices; indeed, one promotion might just replace another. Various studies have been conducted to find out what happens to retail prices when stamps are added or dropped. The results have not been conclusive.

If a store is considering adding stamps to its promotional kit, two questions may be pertinent:

If the stamps are an added expense to the store, will the added benefits of the stamps in the long term be greater than the expense (cash outlay, inconveniences to the customer, extra time of the salesperson and so on)?;

If the stamps are replacing an alternative promotional tool, are they more effective in achieving corporate objectives than the tool they are replacing? Stamps, after all, are just one element of a store's promotional kit, and must be considered in conjunction with any other inducements that it might use. The added dollar sales or increased margins that it will obtain from the addition of stamps will depend on many factors: how its customers see the stamps, what the local competition is like, how competing stores adjust their prices, and so forth.

One of the more interesting aspects of trading stamps is that the customers' perception of them changes over time. From 1968 to 1972, the volume of business done by the trading stamp companies declined from over $900 million to close to $600 million. In 1972, according to *Progressive Grocer*, 20 percent of the local and regional supermarket chains used trading stamps, down from 30 percent in 1968. In 1960 three-quarters of all supermarkets used stamps. There is little reason to feel that the attitude of customers toward stamps will be the same a year from today as it is today. Certainly, their attitude toward stamps has changed substantially in most parts of the country over the last five years, and managers should take note of the changes in consumer attitude from time to time.

Throughout the history of trading stamps, opponents have been quick to foretell their demise from any signs of consumer apathy. The following quotation from 1904 illustrates this point.

During the past year there has been a great change of opinion regarding Trading Stamps, not only among merchants but among customers as well, and today the better class of dealers who have not stopped using Trading Stamps are preparing to do so, while the more intelligent housekeepers instead of seeking places where stamps are given, as they did a year ago, are now bestowing their custom where this petty imposition is not practiced by the shopkeeper (Anti-Stamper Association, 1904, p. 1).

### Social Aspects of Stamps

Trading stamps have been severely criticized over the years. Many have suggested that they are just one big pain. Their presence adds to the already lengthy waiting time at some retailers' checkout stands. They are difficult to keep track of in the shopping bags, the car, the wallet, everywhere. Although they are not worth much in dollars, many individuals feel guilty about throwing them away—the only reason why they save them. Once she has collected enough books of them, the consumer often has to travel substantial distances to the stamp redemption center, only to find that the item she desires is not in stock.

On another level, stamps can be criticized on the grounds that they are often considered a substitute for price competition. Stamps are one technique that a store can use to differentiate itself in the eyes of its customers. Many feel that competition of this type is something less than socially desirable. Most critics would prefer to see the competition take place on the basis of price alone. Whether price competition is greater with or without stamps, however, is a difficult question to answer and one that depends on many factors.

There are several ready arguments in favor of stamps: they are closer to price than are most other types of promotional inducement; they can readily be converted into merchandise; everyone wins. And the winnings are not insignificant. For instance, Harvey L. Vredenburg and Howard Frisinger found a spread in retail value per book of from $2.47 in the purchase of small appliances to $4.38 for lamps. A retail value of $3.00 per book might be used as a reference point, though stamp companies vary. At one time, the cost of such a book to the retailer was $2.68.

Another argument that can be made in favor of trading stamps is that they give the saver a feeling of substantial conscientiousness with respect to the family funds. It takes quite an effort to keep track of stamps, and many consumers pride themselves on being able to do it. Relatedly, and perhaps because of the additional effort, many stamp savers may feel that this is money that they have earned. They can therefore redeem the stamps for any merchandise they like without feeling guilty.

### Public Relations

Firms are very interested in their public relations. Other than paid advertising, the most important form of this is generally the free publicity given them by the local newspaper, television, and radio. This free publicity may relate to such community activities of the firm as children's fishing contests, ice-skating contests, fund-raising drives for charities, and so on. It may also relate to merchandise events, and perhaps fashion news. Consumers are often fashion-conscious, and any publicity connected with fashion is of substantial importance to certain types of retail outlet. These stores go to great lengths to project themselves onto the fashion pages of the newspaper.

In a society that pays as much deference as ours to economic power, it is only to be expected that the stores with the heaviest advertising commitment in a newspaper will get the most coverage in the relevant section of it—provided, of course, that they can supply the newspaper with appropriate matter for publication. And this is clearly so. Steven A. Shaw, for instance, has noted that there is a direct relationship between the size of the retailer's advertising expenditures in a newspaper and the amount of free publicity he gets in it.

### Point of Purchase

A key element of sales promotion for many types of retail outlet is point-of-purchase material. This can be defined as devices or structures that are used in, on, at, or adjacent to any point of sale. Point-of-purchase displays are generally devised by suppliers to increase the sale of their products at the retail level. They are often used with other sales aids such as coupons and premiums to help create excitement about the product. This business has grown dramatically, until today point-of-purchase displays represent a $2 billion industry.

The impact of point-of-purchase ("p-o-p") material on the sale of merchandise has been proven many times. According to a trade source:

When Kimberly-Clark introduced a new Kleenex facial tissue, researchers varied merchandising approaches in the following ways: (1) displays with full p-o-p highlighting the new item (2) displays with no p-o-p except a price sign (3) non-highlighted shelf location. The two kinds of displays were the same size and positioned in similar in-store locations in test stores. The results: Displays using p-o-p produced sales 81% greater than displays without manufacturer p-o-p, and 232 percent higher than the store's

sales where the product was on the shelf only (Grocery Manufacturers of New York, n.d.).

Retailers should familiarize themselves with the opportunities present in point of purchase. While much of the initiative is taken by suppliers, retailers are important beneficiaries, and should make sure that their stores use the better displays effectively.

### Summary

1. Sales promotion can mean almost anything at the retail level. This chapter discusses some elements that are designed to increase sales but have not been given much coverage up to this point in the text.

2. Private brand can be defined in many ways, but in this text we are using it mainly with regard to retailer brands. And retailer brands are becoming more and more important in food, toiletries, drugs, department stores; and many other areas.

3. Some of the advantages of retailer brands are as follows:

A. A private brand will often bring the store beyond the scope of the Robinson-Patman Act in the sense that a private brand is more likely to be "not like grade and quality."

B. A private brand can appeal to specific customer segments.

C. A private brand that performs well is conducive to repeat sales for the retailer.

D. Certain retail labels in such things as garments may enhance the value of the merchandise to the customer.

E. Private brand may fill certain promotional voids.

F. A retailer has greater control over the quality of the private brand.

G. Private brand may permit the store to have increased variety, including additional price lines.

H. Private brands act as a constraint on the prices and other activities of national brand suppliers.

4. Private brands have social benefits. For example:

A. Private brands provide a lower-priced alternative to national brands.

B. Private brands act as a stimulus to new products because suppliers prefer to get out of the low-profit private brand alternative.

C. Private brand has stimulated certain kinds of retail outlet, such as Sears.

D. Private brand is another element in the competition among channel members.

E. Private brand often aids small manufacturers.

5. Credit has grown dramatically by any standards. From 1947 to 1972, total consumer credit increased from about 5 percent of personal disposable income to about 20 percent. Credit is an integral part of the merchandising mix of most retail firms and performs many functions, for example:

A. Credit increases the quantity of merchandise sold, particularly in seasons such as Christmas.

B. Credit may permit a higher price.

C. Credit can help a retailer to trade a customer up to a higher price level.

D. Credit can increase the share of a customer's expenditures in the store.

E. Credit may enhance the customer's relationship with the store.

F. Credit customers are an excellent target for promotions via mailings.

6. Bank credit cards are important to the small store in its efforts to compete with larger enterprises, which often have their own credit networks.

7. Credit has numerous social connotations. For example:

A. The poor often subsidize the rich.

B. Those who purchase for credit often pay less.

C. Credit hampers individuals trying to get out of poverty.

D. Credit induces people to buy more than they would have otherwise.

8. Trading stamps have been an important but decreasing element of the promotional mix of many retail stores. The future of these stamps is very difficult to evaluate.

9. Many firms make extensive efforts to obtain free publicity in the media. The effectiveness of these efforts appears to vary with the amount of advertising placed by the firm in question.

10. Point of purchase is dynamic and growing. Sales and profits can obviously be increased by effective use of point-of-purchase materials.

## Discussion Questions

1. Are private brands going to continue to grow? If they are going to continue to grow, what can a manufacturer do to counter this influence?

2. Why do stores offer private brands?

3. What are the benefits of private brand to the consumer?

4. Store managements argue that the costs of credit systems exceed the revenues obtained through interest. Why, then, do they continue credit programs?

5. Are bank credit cards going to replace major retail credit cards?

6. What are the advantages and disadvantages of credit?

7. Consumer advocates have tended to condemn trading stamps. Is this condemnation justified?

8. Why has the point-of-purchase industry grown so rapidly in the last few years?

9. Should the consumer be continually stimulated to buy more merchandise by various sales promotion activities?

## References

Anti-Stamper Association, *Story of the Trading Stamp Swindle* (New York: the Association, n.d.).

Belden, Donald L., *The Role of the Buyer in Mass Merchandising* (New York: Labhar-Friedman, 1971).

Dalrymple, Douglas J., and Thompson, Donald L., *Retailing: An Economic View* (New York: Free Press, 1969).

Fox, Harold W., *The Economics of Trading Stamps* (Washington, D.C.: Public Affairs Press, 1968).

Grocery Manufacturers of New York, "The Value of In-Store Support" (New York: the Association, n.d.).

*National Observer*, April 7, 1973, p. 9.

*Progressive Grocer*, April 1973, p. 99.

Richardson, Dennis W., *Evolution of an Electronic Funds-Transfer System* (Cambridge, Mass.: MIT Press, 1970).

Rowe, Frederick M., "Current Developments in Robinson-Patman Law," *Business Lawyer*, January 1966.

Shaw, Steven A., "Store Press Publicists and Their Work on Women's Pages," *Journal of Retailing*, Winter, 1956–57.

Vredenburg, Harvey L., and Frisinger, H. Howard, in Fox, Harold W., *op. cit.*

## Further Reading

Brown, F. E., "Price Movements Following the Discontinuance of Trading Stamps," *Journal of Retailing*, Fall, 1967, pp. 1–16.

Herndon, Booton, *Satisfaction Guaranteed* (New York: McGraw-Hill, 1972).

Poissant, William G., "An Analysis of the Bank Card, Part I," *Akron Business and Economic Review*, Winter, 1971, pp. 29–36.

Rachman, David, "Games of Chance in Grocery Supermarkets and Their Impact Upon Small Business," in *Retail Management Strategy* (Englewood Cliffs, N.J.: Prentice-Hall, 1970), pp. 301–309.

Stern, Louis, "The New World of Private Brands," *California Management Review*, Spring, 1966, pp. 43–50.

Wheatley, John J., and Gordon, Guy G., "Regulating the Price of Consumer Credit," *Journal of Marketing*, October 1971.

## Case History: *To Test or Not to Test?*

Dorf's was a large supermarket chain that serviced 10 large metropolitan areas in five states. The firm had exceptionally large stores that were very well accepted by the consumers. One aspect of Dorf's was its strong private brand program. Indeed, over 30 percent of the packaged goods it sold were private brand, a very large percentage. The firm's management prided itself on having the largest sales per square foot in its geographic area and the largest percentage of private brands in packaged goods.

Professor Nick Spalding was a stockholder of Dorf's and an avid user of private brands. The professor felt that, while the variation in quality of private brands was certainly larger than the variation in the quality of accepted national brands, in general it paid for a consumer to invest in private brands. Being a stockholder, he developed an interest in the private brands of Dorf's. As he made his own purchases, he was surprised at the poor quality of some items. Being familiar, however, with the aggressive nature of the management and the success of their private brand program, the professor felt sure that, in this day and age, Dorf's knew what the customers thought of each important private brand. Certainly, Dorf's must have conducted taste tests of its private brands among its customers. Thus the professor convinced himself that his personal reactions were unimportant.

One day Professor Spalding was talking to the research director of Dorf's, Paul Simel. He presented the situation to Simel and asked him what kind of testing procedures the store used. Simel had to admit that the store had never done any consumer tasting tests. He outlined the procedure that was used to check on the quality of the firm's private brands.

The quality reference for Dorf's was the relevant major brand. Where economically feasible, an effort was made to duplicate the national brand. Professional testers were used to establish the initial taste specifications and to make sure that the manufacturer did indeed produce what was desired. In reality, the firm seldom could duplicate the national brand because many key suppliers would not sell to them. And duplicating such quality products was not easy. Further, there was always the haunting question of price. Quality cost money, and often Dorf's had to compromise a little on quality in order to sell the item profitably. No consumer questionnaires were used to evaluate specific private brands of peas, for instance. The store did use questionnaires to evaluate the acceptance of its entire private brand program with consumers. The acceptance was the highest in the business.

It was no wonder, then, that the management of Dorf's was basically satisfied with its private brand program. After all, they were really the envy of the industry. Furthermore, did not the fact that customers kept on buying the private brand indicate that the program was successful?

The professor was disturbed by what he heard. Admittedly, the major brand reference made sense. While the best-selling major brand might not have the most accepted taste for the customers of Dorf's, certainly the taste was reasonably well accepted. Furthermore, if customers really thought that the private brand was the same as the dominant major brand in all categories, sales would increase for all the private brands in the store. And if professional tasters told him that the products were the same, probably no tasting research with consumers was necessary.

But a great number of private brands in the store did not approach the quality of the national brands. And it was for such items that the supermarket said it used professional tasters. The professor was disturbed at this. What did the professional tasters taste? Could a taster say that customers would perceive an obvious substitute as similar to the reference brand? The professor doubted that. But what really bothered him was that this aspect was readily and inexpensively testable.

Furthermore, if the management decided to go to a private brand that was not close in quality to the major brand, maybe one should no longer use the dominant major brand as the reference. Indeed, if one was going to develop a product that would be significantly inferior in quality, possibly one should

go in a different direction from the major. The reference group here might more appropriately be other private brands.

The more Professor Spalding thought about it, the more he decided that there was no excuse for not having in-store taste tests, or home-use tests, or consumer surveys of users of important private-brand items. Any of these would have offered new insights into private brands and their appeal to consumers. The professor expressed his views to Paul Simel. He did not claim that there would assuredly be great findings from research of this kind. He honestly did not know. He did state, however, that one of the things that could ruin the company over time was a deterioration of its private brand image. This deterioration need not be a falling off in the physical quality of the merchandise. It might be an increase in the appeal of the private brands of other supermarkets that catered to the taste levels of Dorf's customers more effectively. At worst, a research program directed to private brands would be an insurance policy that would cost the company a mere $10,000 or so a year.

Paul Simel bought the idea. He really did not feel that such a testing program would revolutionize the company. But he had found before that once he started research into a new area, new opportunities for increasing profits would always turn up. Further, he could test the idea for a few months to see if it had merit.

Paul Simel brought the idea to his superior, Marvin Krump, the firm's executive vice-president. Marvin simply would not buy the idea. He felt that he could not justify spending $10,000 on such a project. He had been receiving lots of flack from consumerists lately, and was trying to raise $10,000 from his budget to make sure that the firm's products met basic safety standards. And there were other projects that would have to take priority over testing private brands with consumers. It was very difficult, he argued, to justify money for this when Dorf's had what was generally recognized as the best private brand program in the industry. Constant feedback could already be had by analyzing what was selling. Thus if no one bought Dorf's orange soda, they could see this on their sales sheets and change accordingly. Paul Simel withdrew his request with the best grace he could muster and retired to his office to think the matter over. Maybe he was working for the wrong firm.

## Discussion Questions

1. Was Professor Spalding correct?

2. If you were Paul Simel, what would you do?

# 20

## Long-Range Planning

Wisdom, according to Russell Ackoff, has four aspects: the ability to see the longer-term consequences of one's current actions; the willingness to sacrifice short-term gains for long-term advantages; the ability to control factors that are in fact controllable; and the ability to predict but not worry unduly about what is not controllable. In short, the essence of wisdom is concern for the future.

Certainly, retailers have always been concerned with the future. Most of their concern, however, has been manifested over the next six-month period or other short interval in the form of a merchandise budget or plan. Such a plan usually involves: (a) the specific statement of objectives; (b) a written plan of how to get there. Merchandise budgets usually have to include estimates of such factors as sales, inventory, purchases, and gross margin. Often they also take into account such things as stock turnover by merchandise area, various expense estimates, profit projections, and budgets for advertising and promotion. The merchandise budget should not only indicate definite courses of action where needed but also provide a series of yardsticks by which decision makers can see if individual budget figures are being met. The six-month plans can be broken down into whatever shorter periods are deemed desirable, so that projected figures can be compared with actual ones, every two weeks, once a month, or whatever the period is.

The merchandising budget is a short-term planning instrument. It can be created haphazardly or after great thought. There is also a need in most retail organizations for longer-term plans. A store must decide if it is going to open new stores of the same type. Are the store's price lines about right, or should some effort be made over the next year or two to trade them up? Decisions of this type concern what might be termed an intermediate time frame, since they focus neither on the shorter-term merchandise plans nor on plans for the longest desirable range of management's interest in the future. Over the very long term a firm might be interested in such subjects as: Will stores be as important in the future as they are today? Will the word "store" even mean the same in the year 2000 as it does now? What fundamental changes are likely to occur in society over time and how can the firm take advantage of them? For instance, will the trend toward individualism foster a trend toward specialty stores and away from large department stores? How are the customer segments to which the firm presently appeals going to change over the short, intermediate, and long term? Should the firm attempt to appeal to very different customer segments over time? What business is it in? Should it change or redefine its business so that it can more effectively adapt to the changes that are likely to occur?

One definition of long-range planning might be the conscious altering of the firm's direction in order to take advantage of the opportunities that are likely to be presented by a changing environment in the light of the firm's objectives. Thus for the long term to have much significance it must be given some priority over the short term, otherwise there is a risk that it will be viewed as a series of short-term maximizations. And there is little reason to believe that a series of short-term maximizations will in any sense approach an effective policy for the long term. At times the requirements of the long term require a little less attractive—and in some instances a far less attractive—prospect for the short term. The multistage approach to decision making that we reviewed earlier is one device for giving the long term priority over the short term. Often, explicit trade-offs have to be made by top management between short- and long-term payoffs.

### Environment of Planning

In short term it is usually reasonable to assume that the social environment in which a decision will be made will not change dramatically. Thus short-term plans can usually be made without worrying about noneconomic factors, however important. However, as the planning period lengthens, basic environmental changes are more likely. While such change is generally beyond the control of the individual firm or industry, it can often be not only planned for but taken advantage of. In addition, there is some reason to believe that the rate of change in our society is increasing, so that change may be even more important to the firm of the future than the firm of the past.

One rather fundamental decision that retailers should be considering is the type of society in which they will be participating over the years. Recently, some of our culture's value systems have been severely challenged. It therefore behooves the retail executive to be aware of possible fundamental changes in cultural attitudes. The following is a list of some areas in which, according to Warren Bennis, the new culture may well become quite different from the old.

1. *Personal over property rights.* Many young people have made clear their feeling that the old culture puts too large an emphasis on property values as opposed to human values. For instance, should an individual be shot while escaping from a nonviolent robbery?

2. *Human development over technological development.* In the old culture, human beings are developed primarily in order to make the world safe for machines. The focus is on the machine and the ability of humans to adapt to it. Young people are suggesting that society should place the main emphasis on the development of the whole individual, and make machines the servants of man, and not the reason for his existence.

3. *Cooperation over competition.* Many of the young are stressing the advantages of cooperation and are questioning the basic need for the threat, imaginary or real, inherent in a world guided by competitive hands. Do the benefits of a highly competitive society outweigh the costs?

4. *Ends over means.* A perennial topic of discussion in thoughtful circles is whether the ends justify the means. Members of the old culture put substantial emphasis on the means. The members of the newer culture are putting more emphasis on the ends: if the ends are worthwhile, they think, the means can be justified somehow.

5. *Openness over secrecy.* There is an openness about the youth of today that many feel was not characteristic of the youth of the past. And indeed many feel that the whole society as represented by the old culture put a substantial emphasis on secrecy: many power relationships are to be taken for granted, many deep feelings not expressed.

6. *Less formal over formal.* Many of the younger groups are openly scornful of the older generation's formality. The older culture demanded a type of deference that was related to social class: one had better respect those in the classes above you. Their worth as human beings was irrelevant. So long as they belonged to the right social class and exhibited its symbols, deference was expected.

7. *Gratification over striving.* The younger culture strives more for immediate self-gratification; there is much less that they are willing to postpone. The value of striving as a goal unto itself is questioned. For many in the older culture, on the other hand, striving is the name of the game.

8. *Truth over loyalty.* The old culture puts little emphasis on what might be termed the truth; indeed, hypocrisy appears to be an integral part of it. However, it does emphasize loyalty to the various values that it cherishes. In contrast, the younger culture emphasizes truth and scorns the older culture's love of appearances.

It is not the purpose of this presentation to indicate which set of values is superior. Executives, however, will sooner or later be faced with the task of deciding to what extent various social groups are departing from traditional norms and how this will affect his business. How can he redirect the enterprise to take advantage of these changes? It may be that the new culture's values are shared by only a small percentage of the young. If, however, they are commonly held or becoming commonly held, it appears obvious that retail institutions over the years will have to modify themselves accordingly. The same applies to some firms' business practices — their advertising, for instance.

The new values may be those of a minority, but their influence on various other, perhaps larger groups within society is of some significance. It has been hypothesized that the old culture both envies and fears the younger one. Three dimensions of this envy and fear are: (a) the community of feeling that tends to be associated with the young; (b) the power that accrues to an individual who is not caught up in the materialistic world; (c) the dedication that appears to be part of the youth movement. All three are closely related to the problem of where society is headed. Are we moving toward a post-industrial society in which science and technology will rule our lives? Or are we going to have a person-centered society in which learning will be an end in and of itself, and in which human potentiality will no longer be a commodity to be bought and sold but a value to be cherished. We may require a society composed of many minisocieties, each requir-

ing goods and services. The number of alternative institutions that might be developed is very large.

Nathan Glazer has dared to predict what Americans are likely to be like over the next seven or eight years. Like other such predictions, these should be treated with caution; American social scientists did not predict the civil rights revolution of the 1960s, the student revolution of the 1960s, or this country's substantial involvement in the Southeast Asian war. Nevertheless, the following had some plausibility in the early 1970s.

1. It will no longer be possible to say what Americans are like because there will be an enormous diversity in their life styles, values, attitudes, and behavior.

2. A good part of these diverse elements will form a very large minority consisting of people very hostile to our government, society, and economy. Large numbers of people will not identify themselves with the nation at all. These people will react against every authority whether in business, university, or government.

3. Much of this diversity and criticism will be institutionalized. Some avant-garde magazines and newspapers already have circulations up to 100,000.

4. There will be a remarkable tolerance of variety in language, behavior, value, and style in American society. In this whirlpool of diversity, mass-market conditions will continue to disintegrate. The supermarket will be challenged by the health food store; the clothing industry will be challenged by a continuous stream of do-it-yourself innovations; the mass media may be challenged by innumerable small-scale alternatives representing the new range of diversity.

Glazer may be too alarmist in his predictions, but there is no doubt that profound social changes lie ahead.

## Modes of Planning

Although planning is achieved in a great many ways, it may be useful here to consider Alfred R. Oxenfeldt's approach to the long-range planning process.

### A Systematic Approach

1. *Establish goals.* State the objectives of the firm as explicitly as possible and make sure they are understood and accepted. Shorter-term goals should be created for the relevant period of the plan. If possible, operational definitions of each goal, together with a specification of the measures to be used in evaluating the firm's progress toward them, should be specified. Possible conflicts among goals should be examined and provisions made for eliminating or minimizing them should they occur.

2. *Conduct self-appraisal.* Assess the firm's strengths and weaknesses as realistically as possible. Retailers are in a battle to obtain competitive advantages over other firms, primarily other retailers. It is desirable to enter such battles with as many advantages and as few liabilities as possible. A firm should take stock of both before choosing the battleground.

3. *Make forecasts.* Forecast future developments in the relevant dimensions. It is generally desirable to invest in areas where the market will grow substantially. Hopefully, there will be substantial market voids that the firm can fill. An analysis of future economic conditions, including technological change in the industry, will aid in determining if there is a niche for a given firm.

4. *Identify alternatives.* The most promising of the feasible alternatives should be identified. Here, the entire area of creativity is relevant, as the firm strives to develop an attractive range of choice.

5. *Select alternatives.* The firm should select the alternative or group of alternatives that appears most promising. The various methods of capital budgeting, including computer simulation, will be useful in this phase of planning.

6. *Establish a program.* The necessary strategies and tactics, with specific deadlines for implementing the alternatives chosen at stage 5, should be combined to make an effective program.

7. *Establish a review procedure.* The program should constantly be reviewed and, if necessary, changed to meet changing conditions.

### Intuitive v. Systematic Planning

Academicians tend to label any executive decision making that they cannot understand as intuitive. It makes no difference to them if the executive spent 24 hours mulling over a relatively unimportant decision. In fact, they tend to use the term "intuitive" as a euphemism for "inadequate" or "irrational." There is, however, a defense for both intuitive decision making and intuitive planning—a defense that is perhaps best conducted in terms of the artificial contrast between intuitive and systematic thinking processes. In either case, the following presentation, which is based on a paper by Robert Mainer, is concerned with the long term.

**Systematic planning** A distinguishing characteristic of systematic planning is that it tends to be explicit; the individual and the organization know exactly what is going on and when. Systematic planning is a subject for specific consideration and occupies a substantial amount of time for many in the organization. It also tends to be research-based; there is a deliberate and systematic collection of information. In fact, this type of planning usually requires a consciously created information system that will offer those doing the planning at least a modicum of information on which to base their decisions, and will tell them what they still need to find out. In short, the entire organization tends to be heavily involved, and the plan is the culmination of inputs from many people. Indeed, it has often been suggested that the process of systematic planning is more beneficial than its product, especially since it involves executives in the planning process. It has therefore been suggested that effective planning cannot be done to or for an organization, but only by the firm's responsible managers. In any case, whatever the value of a formal plan, it is usually the output of systematic planning. Such a plan tends to support its various conclusions in substantial detail.

Systematic planning is also conducive to delegation of authority. Indeed, a formal plan is often an instrument of delegation, since it enables the firm's objectives to be more readily understood by others and so, presumably, to be translated into policies, procedures, and schedules. Finally, systematic planning in detail facilitates control, in that performance can more easily be measured against the specified objectives.

*Intuitive planning* A distinguishing feature of intuitive planning is that it tends to be implicit, that is, it is going on all the time, at least in the heads of top managers. However, no separate time is usually set aside for planning; in fact, the planning is usually combined with many other activities.

Intuitive planning tends to be leadership-based. Strong leaders tend to rely heavily on their own planning and less on other people's. Needless to say, such planning easily obtains top management support, while the staff is left to infer the firm's objectives and what top management wants done about them. Conflicting goals are seldom resolved in this way. However, many top managers feel that it is not in their best interests to explicitly formalize many of their goals, whether personal or corporate goals. Indeed, while a world of conflicting objectives is a threat to many executives, others thrive in such an environment.

Planning of the intuitive type tends to be the product of a few people, usually top managers and their staff. Because so few are involved, the plan tends to take on more importance than the process that created it. In spite of this, the plan is seldom a detailed one; rather, it is in the form of generalities. One advantage of intuitive planning is that it has a faster *reaction time*, because only the leadership is responsible for it.

To sum up: professional planners are all in favor of systematic planning: they believe its benefits far outweigh its costs. But intuitive planning also has advantages that it may be costly to forego. Systematic planning could be adapted to include at least some of those advantages, particularly the rapid reaction time.

### Key Aspects of Planning

*Lower-level plans and the overall plan* Planners are often forced to wonder if they should create the firm's lower-level merchandise plans before proceeding to its overall plan. On the one hand, they cannot create realistic lower-level plans unless they have some idea of where, in general, the firm thinks it is heading. On the other hand, they cannot create the firm's overall plans unless they know what its particular divisions can and cannot do. This is in some sense a chicken-and-egg problem. One possible solution is to develop both sets of plans at once, so that they can evolve together over time as each interacts with the other.

*Timing of constraints* We have already seen that the firm should assess its strengths and weaknesses before it proceeds further with the planning process. However, this kind of procedure, since it comes early in the planning process, may overemphasize the present with its attendant constraints. It may encourage management to think small when it should be thinking big, and to suggest small changes instead of the big ones it really needs. For this reason, some people believe that present conditions and the constraints they impose should be ruled out of account until a later stage. This permits a fresher approach to problems. The planner can work backward from an unpractical theoretical position toward reality rather than vice versa. For example, should the continued existence of stores be taken for granted in a retail firm's long-range planning just because it has $2 billion invested in stores? Rather than start with stores as a given it may be useful to introduce reality *after* deciding where, ideally, the firm would like to be. The constraints of reality may turn out not to be such large constraints after all.

*Involvement of key line executives* Planners generally like, if they can, to involve key line executives in the planning function. Indeed, from many perspectives the chief executive and the board of directors must eventually take responsibility for long-range planning. Although the role of the top managers in the planning process can vary a great deal, planning will generally not work well if it runs counter to the style of top management. Thus one of the planner's jobs is to develop a plan that agrees with the style that the senior executives have developed over their executive careers.

***Creativity and planning***  Many observers of the planning process have suggested that planning of a formal nature tends to stifle individual creativity within the firm. The overall process is so mechanized and often goes into so much detail that it is impossible to be creative without deviating from the plan. Loss of creativity is generally not considered a desired result; on the contrary, planning as a process should increase the creativity of its various participants, both line and staff. This, then, is yet another thing that planners should take into account.

***Company balance***  Any overall planning model that really does what it should will tend to change the balance of power within the company. Certain key line executives will be given authority over the model, and as a result their authority will often be enhanced. Indeed, the advance of computerization in retail firms has increased the prestige of the executives (usually the controllers) in charge of the computers. Therefore, planning and the attendant models that are likely to be developed are not neutral instruments, but represent a threat to the power of some executives as well as an opportunity to many others.

***Planning and the individual***  The student who gives intelligent approval to the idea of corporate planning does not often have a written plan for the next few years of his life or over the long term. This, of course, can be defended on many grounds; the student suffers from no barriers to communication with himself; the personal costs of evaluating events in terms of his written plan may be great; the environment of any individual is too unpredictable and

uncontrollable for planning to have much personal value. Whatever the rationalization, however, the student should weigh the pro's and con's of incorporating a formal planning process into his life.

### Failures in Planning

Planning is supposed to aid in the development of a firm's long-run health. It is therefore involved with the future. Nevertheless, it is useful to examine past mistakes that might be attributed to planning. Mistakes, as one might expect, tend to be examined less thoroughly than successes. However, analyzing mistakes can be a very useful procedure. After analyzing a series of marketing failures, Thomas Berg offered the following observations as to the causes of failure, most of which could be attributed directly to ineffective, faulty, or nonexistent planning.

1. *Confusing tactics with strategy.* Strategic considerations must be assigned higher priorities than tactical or operational ones, because it is strategic considerations that are difficult to reverse. For example, a policy of increasing the firm's inventory level is easier to reverse than the actual creation of new stores. In general, it may be useful to think of strategic planning as concerned with the longest and tactical planning with the shortest period worth considering. In addition, the more functions of an organization's activities that are affected by a plan, the more strategic it is. Strategic planning is therefore broad in scope. Further, strategic planning is concerned with both formulating goals and establishing the means of attaining them, while tactical planning emphasizes the means of attaining goals specified by a higher level in the organization.

This is another way of looking at the multistage approach to decision making emphasized in Part 3. It is often useful for management to emphasize that long-term considerations take precedence over short-term ones. In this approach, selecting the target customers is basic. The appropriate set of images is then selected, and a role assigned to each element of the merchandising mix. How are the building and fixtures supposed to attract customers? What is the role of advertising, pricing, assortment, inventory, and so forth? Policies can then be created for the specific merchandise areas. Throughout the multistage approach, it will be noted, longer-term considerations take precedence over short-term ones.

2. *Failing to define a firm's business.* For the last decade, observers of marketing have been stressing that each firm should know the business that it is in. Is it in the clothing business? Or is it really in the franchise business—or, for that matter, the retail business? If so, is the firm in the business of servicing given target customers? Such questions are not easy to answer. It seems clear, however, that a progressive firm must at least tackle the issues involved. In the final analysis, a firm is going to have to provide goods and services that are wanted by a sufficient number of customers to maintain its profitability. The top management of the firm should keep this in mind, and be quite knowledgeable about who the target customers are.

3. *Underestimating the number of parties concerned.* Many parties are concerned with a firm's merchandising decisions. For example, in pricing, a firm must be concerned with the government because of the various laws that relate to pricing, with the supplying firm because of its possible reaction to this or that price, with its own managers, because of their possible reactions, and with numerous competitors, potential competitors, consumers, and consumer action groups. For other types of decision, the reactions of the firm's employees, labor unions, stockholders, and so forth, may be just as relevant.

4. *Underestimating the dangers of a frontal assault.* Berg maintains that although military strategy has long extolled the virtue of the indirect approach, marketers have yet to learn this lesson. "Rather than exploit lines of least resistance, many marketers still misfire by engaging the enemy on his own terms, instead of exploiting his weaknesses, avoiding decisive engagement when that seems prudent, outflanking him, or using other forms of indirect marketing maneuver." For example, consider the history of one direct frontal assault. A leading discount store moved directly across the street from a major depart-

ment store in a large eastern city. This was a direct assault on that store's business. Within hours of the opening of the discount store, the department store met almost all its prices. However, because this department store had to meet the prices, other department stores in the area were forced into a far more competitive posture. In addition, the policies of the department store were quite successful in combating the discount store and became the pattern for other department stores meeting similar competition. The discount store's policies apparently changed after this adventure, but it was too late: many irreversible competing forces had been created by the direct frontal assault.

5. *Faulty communications.* When stores were small, it was rather easy for the top managers to keep in close touch with their employees, customers, suppliers, and others. As the volume and the number of stores increased, however, entirely new organizational concepts had to be created in order to meet the needs of the situation. When people are organized into logical subgroupings, various layers of management are created. The more numerous the layers of management, the greater the barriers to communication with the firm's lower-level decision makers, its supplying firms, and its customers. While information systems are being established to bridge these gaps, effective communications are a continuing problem.

6. *Off-target merchandising.* Planning errors often arise when management fails to zero in on the designated customer targets. Marketing management courses generally stress that a firm has difficulty being all things to all people. If it tries to appeal to the so-called average customer, it runs the risk of appealing to no one. Other firms may effectively appeal to smaller customer segments and, segment by segment, take the whole market away from a firm that has no target customers. This is not to say that there are no firms that successfully market to most customer segments, but this is thought to be unusual.

In retailing, it is management's interpretation of unit and classification controls that brings the store's merchandise into line with the desires of the customer segments who are presently buying there. Thus the customers, through their purchases, vote for the type of store that they want. Segmentation of this type is largely unplanned. However, stores often plan segmentation by income group. Thus some stores are thought of as appealing to low-income groups, others to customers of a broad middle-income range, and still others to individuals with a high income. Occasionally, stores stress a youth appeal.

The methods that a firm uses to differentiate itself can vary greatly. It should be emphasized that a firm need not think in terms of satisfying one homogeneous group of customers. However, few of its policies will be attractive to all the target groups, and some will appeal to only a few of them. The more target groups a firm has, the more difficult it will be to assess the impact of a given policy or strategy on each, and to devise policies that will attract or at least not repel most of the groups.

7. *Underbalancing the merchandising mix.* Novices in management tend to look for single causes. Seldom, however, is one element of the merchandising mix the single cause of the failure. Most of a firm's merchandise decisions are systemic in nature, that is, all key elements of the business tend to influence all other key elements. Such interaction is critical and must be appreciated. For example, many individuals feel that price is the main cause for the success of a discount store, it if does succeed. However, there are few if any discount stores left in competition where price has not been combined with one, two, or more other elements of the merchandising mix to create an effective package of services to the customer. Assortment and price, in an effective display environment with a good location, appear to be a minimum mix for a discount store in most geographic areas. And the other elements of the merchandising mix must be given at least some attention or the package may be ruined.

8. *Inflexibility in planning and execution.* Planning should be flexible, innovative, and imaginative. In many cases, however, the written document takes on quasi-religious significance within the firm. Controls must be established to make sure that the plan continues to be relevant and useful. Unforeseen events may have made most of the elements of the plan no longer relevant.

### Trends in Planning

From a very modest start, formal, long-range planning has developed into a substantial endeavor in many corporations. More firms are developing systematic, long-term planning procedures and relying less on what has previously been called intuition. Indeed, it would appear that opportunities and necessity for planning effectively are increasing as society changes. Further, the penalties of not planning to meet the changing needs, desires, and aspirations of the consumer would appear to be increasing as well. Many firms are having to plan extensively, if only to keep up with their present competitors.

With the growing importance of the long-range planning function has come greater participation of top management in it. Part of this is related to top management's increasing interaction with the computer. Top management is coming to agree more and more with planning analysts that the participation of top management in the planning effort is essential.

Relatedly, more and more firms are developing sophisticated mathematical models in order to deal with planning in both its overall aspects and its smaller direct applications. For example, overall systems can be developed that may offer answers to such questions as, What will happen to the firm's profits in five years if credit policies are changed? On the other hand, solutions are being sought for many smaller decision areas—inventory analysis, for example. Clearly, computers have a growing part to play in the planning activities of retail firms.

### Summary

1. Planning is a continuous process in most effective retail operations. In some sense, executives are plan-

ning every day to meet the emergencies of next day or next week. Formal planning at the retail level tends to take place at longer intervals, perhaps six months, in the form of the merchandise budget. Retailers have seldom distinguished themselves in long-term planning.

2. The environment of retail decision making is changing. Some of our youth are questioning the older generation's approach to such problems as:

    A. Property rights;

    B. Human development;

    C. Competition;

    D. Ends versus means;

    E. Secrecy;

    F. Formality;

    G. Gratification;

    H. Loyalty.

3. One approach to planning is as follows:

    A. Establish goals;

    B. Conduct self-appraisal;

    C. Make forecasts;

    D. Identify alternatives;

    E. Select alternatives;

    F. Establish a program;

    G. Establish review procedures.

4. Systematic planning has certain advantages over intuitive planning. However, systematic planning also tends to have disadvantages that should be understood.

5. Some key aspects of planning are:

    A. The relationship of the low-level plan to the overall plan for the enterprise;

    B. The timing of the imposing of constraints on the plan;

    C. Involvement of key line executives;

    D. Creativity of planning;

    E. Planning will tend to upset the balance of executives within the company.

6. Some failures in planning can be attributed to:

    A. Confusing tactics with strategy;

    B. Failing to define a firm's business;

    C. Underestimating the number of parties concerned;

    D. Underestimating the dangers of a frontal assault;

    E. Faulty communications;

    F. Off-target merchandising;

    G. Underbalancing the merchandising mix;

    H. Inflexibility in planning and execution.

## Discussion Questions

1. Outline one approach to planning.

2. What are Americans likely to be like over the next seven or eight years, and how could this affect retailing?

3. Some observers suggest that the planning process is more important to a company than the final plan. Do you agree?

4. What are some of the older generation's values that the younger generation is questioning?

5. Compare and contrast intuitive and systematic planning.

6. What should be the relationship of the lower-level plan to the overall plan?

7. Why is involving the line executives in the planning process so important?

8. Will stores be as important in the future as they are today?

9. List six failures of planning.

## References

Ackoff, Russell L., *A Concept of Corporate Planning* (New York: Wiley-Interscience, 1970), p. 1.

Bennis, Warren, "Corporate Planning in the Context of Human Values," presentation at the International Planning Conference, November 12, 1970.

Berg, Thomas L., *Mismarketing* (Garden City, N.Y.: Doubleday, 1970).

Glazer, Nathan, "Is There an American Character? A Perspective for the 70s," presentation at the 1972 Annual Meeting of the American Association of Advertising Agencies.

Mainer, Robert, presentation at the International Planning Conference, November 12, 1970.

Oxenfeldt, Alfred R., *Executive Action in Marketing* (Belmont, Ca.: Wadsworth, 1966).

## Further Reading

Duncan, Delbert J., and Phillips, Charles F., *Retailing Principles and Methods* (Homewood, Ill.: Irwin, 1967).

Oxenfeldt, Alfred R., *Pricing for Marketing Executives* (Belmont, Ca.: Wadsworth, 1961).

Weiss, E. B., "The Retail Store Won't Last Forever," *Marketing Insights*, November 18, 1968, pp. 12–13.

People are involved in all facets of retailing. People are in charge of the receiving dock; marking the merchandise; writing copy for the various advertisements; buying, displaying, and pricing the merchandise; selling the merchandise; stocking the merchandise; answering phones; and so forth. The supplier's salesmen call on the purchasing agents of the retail stores. Customers are people. Thus the management and understanding of people are critical to the success of the retail operation. Indeed, it is difficult to get ahead in most forms of retailing without constantly interacting with people.

While people are important to all corporations, many observers feel they are more important in retailing because:

For most kinds of retailing, people are the largest nonmerchandise expense;

The performance of the salespeople and certain other employees of the retail firm is a key element in differentiating a firm from its competition;

The pay for nonexecutive retail personnel is not high;

Employment in many parts of retailing is highly seasonal;

A great many employees are part-time.

This part is concerned with people inasmuch as it discusses creativity, personnel, and personal selling.

# Part Four

# 21

*Creativity*

The executive world is populated with individuals who do many things. Some of them are troubleshooters who spend much of their time trying to spot trouble before it occurs; others are primarily decision makers who weigh ramifications of the alternatives open to them. Still others, even some company vice presidents, implement the policies and decisions of executives above them. However, it is the executive as decision maker who has been played up by American business schools, which thereby neglect many other executive functions. Thus in many executive positions, developing alternatives from which to choose is a more important function than evaluating them once they have been chosen. Indeed, formulating a sufficiently ingenious alternative may make the right choice obvious. One reason why business schools have not tended to emphasize the development of alternatives is that this process is considered by many difficult if not impossible to teach. The capacity to develop new alternatives is what many people would call creativity, or a large part of creativity.

In recent years the academic world, at least, has been paying increased attention to creativity as a phenomenon that can be studied and understood. According to J. P. Guilford (1970), the percentage of titles of psychological publications devoted to creativity increased by a multiple of over 10 from 1955 to 1969. This growth in interest has undoubtedly been related to the increasing frustration of many who are trying to induce change in our society; to the truly urgent nature of the world's human problems; to the dehumanization of society that seems to accompany each technological advance, especially in the use of computers; and so forth. Perhaps the most important reason is the increasing frustration of many in society with the educational process.

Almost all observers of retailing would agree that creativity is of vital importance to the success of many types of retail store. They would also agree that it is an indispensable quality for merchandising executives performing a variety of functions. There would be far less agreement, however, as to what creativity is, how much of it is essential or desirable for merchandise executives to have, to what extent it can be developed, or how top store management can select creative individuals. Indeed, creativity in the world of merchandising may mean little more than successful merchandising, and many successful merchandisers are fast duplicators rather than originators. Opportunities for creativity in many merchandise areas are often missed because retailers are not even conscious that the opportunities exist.

There is general agreement in retailing on at least one aspect of creativity: in retailing, it cannot consist of art for art's sake. The store employee does not have the free rein that the creative artist may have; instead, his creativity should be directed at increasing the firm's sales and profits. Accordingly, creativity will be defined here as the development of new or original ideas that have economic value to the retailer.

It should not be inferred from this that there is only one kind of creative ability; Guilford, for instance, identified 24 more or less independent abilities conducive to creative thinking. It would seem that most individuals have uneven amounts of such abilities, and that a large percentage of the population would be above average in at least some of them. This view of creativity is optimistic because it assumes that nearly everybody has some creative ability, together with the potential to improve it.

Another way to look at creativity is as the rearranging of what we know in order to find out what we do not know—in this case, for the purpose of increasing the firm's sales and profits. The advantage of looking at creativity in this manner is that there are many ways of rearranging what we know, and some of them require little talent or ability. In fact, all sorts of aids can be devised to rearrange our perspective on things. This, too, is an optimistic view of creativity in that almost anyone can devise systematic ways of rearranging what he already knows. Any individual of average ability would appear to be able to raise his level of creativity, whatever it may be. It is also heartening that, according to most studies, changes in creative performance can be assessed and exercises developed to make the improvements permanent. Also implied in this definition is that all the techniques used to foster creativity in the individual may be about the same regardless of which aspect of retail (or nonretail) decision making is the object of improvement.

Since the development of alternatives is an integral part of problem solving, any executive should be able to benefit from increasing his creativity. An executive may look for creative solutions to employee problems. There appear, however, to be three prime activities in which creativity will be important for a merchandise executive:

In changing the physical products offered to the store (this would include all facets of new product creation at the retail level);

In trying to alter the marketing mix of a supplier to both supplier and the store's mutual benefit;

In developing ways to display merchandise to the final consumer.

### The Importance of Altering the Physical Product

A substantial number of advantages may accrue to the retailer if he alters the physical products offered in the market. For many firms and departments these advantages more than offset both the time costs and the cost of larger inventories. One advantage is that such action may bring a buyer beyond the scope of the Robinson-Patman Act. For example, as Frederick M. Rowe has stated, the FTC has ruled that bathtubs and other equipment of slightly different mold, design, and features are not "of like grade and quality." Goods that are determined not to be of like grade and quality are clearly beyond the scope of the act.

A second advantage is that a manager may be able to cater more exactly to the needs and desires of his customers. For example, the price of an additional gallon of water used in a washing machine may vary from zero to significant amounts depending on the part of the country. Thus, the feature of a water saver on a washing machine cannot be expected to have substantial utility to all consumers. In areas where additional water costs a small amount, a merchandiser might well be better off substituting other features. Porcelain coating on a washing machine will generally make the washer easier to clean. This feature, however, may not be of great importance to consumers in all areas of the country, or to groups within a given area. If the price of the product is kept constant, one would expect that a store would sell more of a product specifically tailored to the needs and desires of its customer segments.

Why, then, does the manufacturer not differentiate the product in the above manner on his own? Some manufacturers do just that. But everything else being equal, a manufacturer will generally benefit more from increased standardization of product. The retailer, however, is closer to his customers than anyone else, and usually has a wealth of data about them that the manufacturer does not have. Often, then, he is in a far better position to design products that will suit his customers' exact needs.

A third advantage, related to the second, is that the retail manager might be able to charge a higher price for an item specifically designed for his customers. And since the item is different, it may well be possible to charge a higher price for it and sell a greater quantity at the same time. A retailer may also obtain a higher price for an item if he has created it to be sold exclusively by his store in a given geographic area, because the customer can no longer compare the item in other competitive stores. Thus the very fact of a difference may have value to the store even if the changes have no real economic value to the customer. Even a professional merchandiser would find it hard to recognize a difference of $10 retail on a $200 retail item. Customers, then, will certainly have difficulty discerning a $25 difference on the same item without the advantage of being able to compare it directly in other retail outlets.

A fourth advantage is that the buyer may be able to obtain a lower cost from the supplier. This may be partly due to the fact that once the Robinson-Patman Act is seen to be irrelevant, the manager is free (subject to any restrictions of other laws) to obtain an arrangement consistent with his bargaining power. Another factor that may induce a lower cost price is that marginal concepts, which can be dramatized to the supplier, will lead to lower prices if the alternative supplier procedures are biased toward higher prices. The advantages for a supplier in accepting an arrangement at a small increment over his *out-of-pocket costs* may be dramatized if the alternative is clearly indicated as no purchase. A lower cost may also be obtained because if the buyer definitely offers to buy an item with certain characteristics at a specific price, the alternative of his not purchasing at the designated price is no longer present. If the supplier uses an expected-value approach to pricing, the value to the supplier of the retail offer is therefore raised (see page 197).

Finally, many managers obtain satisfaction from being creative, and changing the physical aspects of the product is one outlet for creativity. The development of new merchandise is interesting and exciting to many people. Accordingly, a position with these possibilities is more appealing to certain prospective executives and others who are considering entering the retail field.

### The Advantages and Disadvantages Evaluated

The merchant must decide if it is profitable for him to consider creating his own merchandise in a specific classification or situation. In most instances, he may estimate the profit differential by calculating the markup and volume for a probable or existing situation and then comparing it with a projected markup and volume. Thus, by multiplying the initial markup by the volume for both alternatives, and then subtracting one product from the other, the merchant will have a rough estimate of the profit differential. In developing these rough estimates the buyer must include an allocation for the cost of this time—usually in terms of *opportunity costs*. When these rule-of-thumb methods yield no obvious solution, the merchant may turn to the more refined techniques of marginal analysis.

Unfortunately, the above measures relate only to the short term, and are limited to the specific merchandise area. Certain stores do develop long-term policies that encourage the use of merchandise that is different from that handled in other stores. Such policies may be implemented, at least in part by selecting merchandise that is not sold in competitive stores. It may be more profitable, however, for the store to change the products of suppliers to its own liking. The store's private brand policies may follow this pattern, since it is easier for many types of stores to implement a private brand policy with physically different items than with items that are physically the same.

## Stages of Creativity

The payoff for creativity in retailing appears high. It may therefore be useful for a decision maker to learn more about creativity. What happens when someone creates? What exactly is the creative process? Unfortunately, these types of question defy ready solution in the present state of research. But serious investigators have postulated many different stages in the creative process that are interrelated and complex. It is widely held, however, that the creative process has four recognizable phases: preparation, incubation, illumination, and verification. For the purposes of this discussion, the first stage, preparation, will be separated into two. Clearly, the five stages are related, though in given instances stages will be bypassed, intermixed, and so forth.

**Stage one: identification and formulation**  Creativity is intimately involved with the solution of problems. Indeed, the reason for studying creativity in a survey course in retail management is that it leads to more effective decisions, primarily by fostering a divergent thinking process. In retailing, as in other fields, the first step is to identify and formulate the problem or set of problems. It is difficult, although clearly not impossible, to solve problems without knowing exactly what they are. For example, one problem may be how to get additional concessions from suppliers, which may in turn depend on what type of new product the store can create.

**Stage two: preparation**  Both during and after identifying the problem, various preparations should be made. The creator should generally learn a great deal about the problem he is trying to solve

and all the possible ways of solving it. It is one of the paradoxes of creativity that in order to think originally we must familiarize ourselves with the ideas of others. Thus if a decision maker is trying to get concessions from suppliers, he should become thoroughly familiar with the structure of the industry, its practices, ethics, personalities, and so forth. Thus knowledge and hard work seem to be prerequisites for the effective development of divergent thought. But while knowledge is a necessary condition for divergent thought, it is in no sense a sufficient condition. And indeed most of the devices that are used to make an individual more creative are really ways of making the familiar strange. These are discussed later in the chapter. In the present example, insights into obtaining concessions might be obtained by looking at how they are obtained by buyers in other departments, industries, or countries. Checklists might be developed to impose new ways of thinking about the problem.

**Stage three: incubation**  Most observers defend the role of the nonconscious in creativity. Guilford (1967) goes so far as to say there is no doubt that the phenomenon of incubation exists and that some creators use it effectively. According to John W. Haefele, the existence of a period of incubation is everywhere acknowledged, and there is a large body of evidence to suggest that something goes on besides waiting. Many feel that the nonconscious takes an active role in the creative process, although there is much disagreement as to what happens or indeed as to what the nonconscious is.

Various hypotheses have been offered to avoid using the concept of the nonconscious to explain the increased level of performance after a period of rest. One is that the problem solver gets tired and the period of incubation gives him a rest, after which his level of performance is naturally higher. A second hypothesis is that taking up the problem after a period of rest offers the problem solver an opportunity for a fresh start, and so permits him to try new directions more easily.

Some investigators who do accept the role of the nonconscious maintain that the new information interacts in some unknown fashion over time with elements already in memory storage. Eventually, the elements are rearranged to give a solution. Motivation, as Bernard Weiner has pointed out, may play a part in this process. The fact that the stored bits of information may change just because of the passage of time, and that in addition the interaction between them may be altered by other factors such as motivation, raises many exciting questions for researcher and retail executive alike. To what extent does the conscious interact with the nonconscious? Can the conscious program the nonconscious? What factors other than motivation can influence the interaction in the nonconscious? And of course, how are we to use the nonconscious to improve the effectiveness of our decision making?

**Stage four: illumination or insight** The insight is the answer to the problem. For most individuals, such insights will usually come after they have begun to look for an answer again. A person works on a problem over some period of time and arrives at some solution. Many creative alternatives, however, come "out of the blue." There is a sudden increment of progress toward a solution without effort at that time by the individual. To the recipient the insight is new. Sudden increments of this type most often occur in periods of rest and relaxation or of dispersed attention. Although a number of experiments can be offered on the problem of insight, we are still very dependent upon anecdotal information. Many individuals have testified to the fact that they were thinking about something else and all of a sudden the solution was in front of them. Indeed most students will have already had this experience themselves, many times. Most observers of creativity agree, then, that insight, or sudden increments of progress toward solutions, do in fact occur.

**Stage five: verification** There is little reason to feel that solutions obtained from sudden flashes of insight are necessarily correct. Indeed, one would perhaps automatically suspect solutions generated in this way. Thus the insights derived from the crea-

tive process must be verified by the judgment, intellect, or research of the creator and as many others as have an interest in establishing their validity.

### Increasing Individual Creativity

An executive or student can do a great deal to increase his creativity. Naturally some executives will benefit more from certain techniques and some from others. Some of these techniques are as follows:

1. *Awareness of stages.* An executive might try to increase his facility with the individual stages of creativity outlined in the previous sections. Presumably, if one could increase one's productivity at even one stage, one's entire performance would improve. Preparation and incubation would appear to be the stages in which the greatest individual improvement is possible. Thus Eugene J. Koprowski has suggested that creative people tend to spend more time on the early stages than the later ones.

At the preparation stage an individual should work extremely hard to become familiar with all the facets of a problem. Insight, however dazzling, still depends on learning. It is true that chance has a lot to do with creativity and indeed with success of most types, but "chance favors the prepared mind." This would suggest that a merchant should become immersed in his problems. In addition, since the executive will be influenced by what he knows, and since merchandise is what most top store executives know best, executives would be expected to be most creative with regard to merchandise and least creative with regard to everything else. In this author's opinion, that is an accurate description of most retail executives. Department stores, for example, have done a poor job in such nonmerchandise areas as sensing the opportunities in the various related fields, understanding the movement to the suburbs (especially in its incipient stages), and developing of computer systems and analytical techniques.

2. *Making the familiar strange.* Many feel that the essence of becoming more creative is to make the familiar strange. We can deliberately rearrange what

we know in order to find out what we do not know. Analogies are useful here. For example, someone trying to design a new chair might pretend that he is one. Presumably he will become more aware of the key aspect of chairs and will be forced to examine them in a new context. This is known as *personal analogy,* as opposed to *direct analogy,* in which there is no personal involvement. Thus ideas for women's dresses may be obtained by direct analogy with military uniforms, or new ideas about stores may come from comparing the store with a human body.

Checklists of various types may be useful in stimulating creativity. Indeed, checklists have been devised for almost all types of retail activity, from holding a sale to opening a new store. There are also creativity checklists that call for the decision maker to consider the problem from a number of viewpoints. A general checklist to aid in creativity might as Carl Gregory has shown, induce the decision maker to adapt, magnify, duplicate, multiply, exaggerate, add to, maximize, minimize, substitute, revise, invert, combine, turn inside out, omit, take apart, or synthesize.

A checklist might also describe the attributes of a given product. This technique involves listing the attributes of the object and then modifying them in a search for the combination that will improve the object's performance in the desired respects. As Philip Kotler suggests, a problem often used to illustrate attribute listing is that of inventing a better screwdriver. First, one lists the attributes that completely define the existing type of screwdriver; a round, steel shank; a wooden handle; a wedge-shaped end for engaging a particular size and type of screw; manual operation; and torque provided by a twisting action. The next step might be to imagine one or more changes in these attributes that might improve the tool's value to its users. The round shank could be changed to a hexagonal shank so that a wrench might be applied easily to increase the torque; the wooden handle might be replaced by a composition handle in order to cut down on breakage, decrease the chance of electrical shock, and increase the attractiveness; the end of the screwdriver might be altered to fit different types of screw heads; alternative types of power such as electrical might

replace the manual power; or the torque could be supplied by pushing.

Attribute checklists can be combined with the general checklist. One might further combine these two types of list with a "key question" list including such questions as how, what, why, when, where, and who to form a three-dimensional matrix. Such a matrix is shown in Figure 21.1.

3. *Inviting the nonconscious.* It can also be argued that one of the main contributions an individual can make to his creativity is to prepare himself so that the nonconscious can do the maximum job during the period of incubation when there is maximum probability of a useful insight occurring. If indeed there is a nonconscious, the following steps might be taken by a merchant to activate it. First, he might identify and define his problems as soon as possible, so that the nonconscious might be given maximum exposure to them. A store management might encourage this by requiring written reports from each merchandise executive immediately after an important season or event. Second, he might establish a system for bringing the most important problems periodically to the attention of his conscious mind, perhaps by establishing some special type of checklist. This, of course will succeed only to the extent that the conscious can tell the nonconscious what to do.

Mood and environment are important here. Insights are often thought to come at relaxed, relatively carefree times. Both Indian Yoga and Japanese Zen have developed rigorous methods of physical and mental release. The purpose of these seems to be more or less one of releasing the conscious mind so that the nonconscious can bring its creative acts to the threshold. The merchant, however, will doubtless prefer to try the more conventional methods first. Many actions and environments have been credited with inducing insights, even such mundane tasks as shaving or taking a bath. Merchants should be aware of the possibilities of using such relaxed occasions to foster insights into important problems. It would appear that the probability of having insights is increased if one "lives his job," because business matters would then be in the foreground of the nonconscious during periods of relaxation.

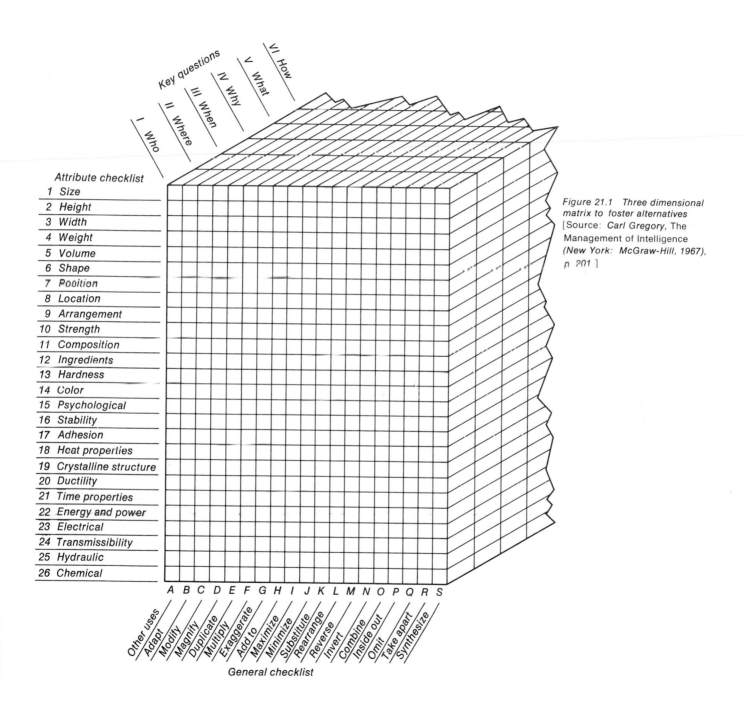

**Key questions**

I Who
II Where
III When
IV Why
V What
VI How

**Attribute checklist**

1 Size
2 Height
3 Width
4 Weight
5 Volume
6 Shape
7 Position
8 Location
9 Arrangement
10 Strength
11 Composition
12 Ingredients
13 Hardness
14 Color
15 Psychological
16 Stability
17 Adhesion
18 Heat properties
19 Crystalline structure
20 Ductility
21 Time properties
22 Energy and power
23 Electrical
24 Transmissibility
25 Hydraulic
26 Chemical

A B C D E F G H I J K L M N O P Q R S

Other uses
Adapt
Modify
Magnify
Duplicate
Multiply
Exaggerate
Add to
Maximize
Minimize
Substitute
Rearrange
Reverse
Invert
Combine
Inside out
Omit
Take apart
Synthesize

**General checklist**

*Figure 21.1  Three dimensional matrix to foster alternatives* [Source: *Carl Gregory*, The Management of Intelligence *(New York: McGraw-Hill, 1967), p. 201.*]

No effort will be made here to explore the non-conscious as such, or to differentiate systematically between the various terms used for nonconscious processes and functions. The executive will just have to decide for himself whether exploring this particular aspect of creativity is worth his while.

4. *Job experience.* Many techniques that foster creativity involve combining the known in order to discover the unknown. It would appear obvious, then, that if the number of different experiences an executive is exposed to is increased, he should become more creative. It follows that it would be in the best interest of many retail organizations to broaden their executives' experience by retraining them and even getting them to switch jobs periodically, conceivably to the point of locating merchants in non-merchandising positions. It may also follow that the general practice of promoting from within the firm decreases creativity. Executives who have had experience with several firms would appear to bring a wider repertoire of solutions to bear on the firm's problems, everything else remaining equal. This is not to say that promoting from within is not in the firm's best interests. However, one of the costs of such a policy may be having to put up with the lower creativity of the executives.

It also seems rather likely that if a newcomer to a field has the necessary information, he is more likely to achieve creative solutions than a person who has been working in the area for a long time. This would tend to support the view that outside consultants are especially valuable to a company in helping it to attack direct line decisions, such as merchandise problems. However, store executives appear to use consultants mainly in areas where they themselves lack expertise, on the apparent assumption that if they already know the area, then their own judgment is superior.

5. *Relevance of combinations.* Other things being equal, the more relevant elements a person is capable of combining, the higher the probability that he will find a creative solution. In particular, the more relevant the dimensions of a merchandising analysis, the more relevant should be the alternatives developed. For instance, an executive in a women's fash-ion store will benefit if she can identify the major dimensions in the customers' thinking about sweaters. Do they think in terms of collars, fabric, color, types of button, or what?

6. *Deferred judgment.* Suspension of judgment during the preparation period may also contribute to creativity, despite the need for relevance. It is often argued that deferred judgment produces both a greater quantity and a better quality of ideas. Thus the executive is caught in a bind. He wants to keep the dimensions of his thought as relevant as possible, because the more relevant the dimensions he is considering, the more relevant the final product. However, if he judges too rapidly, he may thwart some exciting ideas and concepts that could have improved the final product. Accordingly, he must develop some type of balance between these two aspects of creativity.

7. *Extended effort.* The longer the decision maker considers the subject matter, the more likely he is to come up with some original ideas. Such extended new effort may improve creativity because: (a) the subject will react at first in terms of established behavior patterns, and will tend toward originality only after he has gotten these off his chest; (b) the subject will list his safest, least original ideas first—the ones that he is certain will be well accepted.

8. *Group techniques.* There has been continuous debate as to the use of groups in inducing creativity. Some believe that appropriate group creativity is superior to individual creativity, others that it reduces the creative individual to the common level of the group. Regardless of which view is right, clearly some group techniques can aid some individuals to be more creative. One group technique that has received particular attention in the literature is that of *brainstorming.* Here, criticism is ruled out in the early stages, while unusual ideas are encouraged. A quantity of ideas are sought and combined in an effort to create superior creative alternatives. The interactions of the group members are supposed to induce more divergent thought on the part of each. Thomas J. Bouchard has pointed out that the basics of brainstorming appear to be enhanced by having each person in the group asked to speak in sequence,

so that no one member dominates. Also groups that use the method of personal analogy appear to get superior results.

### Other Important Aspects

A creative person may need a substantial degree of independence. Dependence of any kind would appear to be conducive to conformity rather than creativity. It is often suggested that the creative person should be able to take or leave other people, and this may well be so. Substantial dependence on others inhibits, perhaps consciously, perhaps not, the number of alternatives that one can consider. On the other hand, a person who can hold himself aloof from the psychological punishment of the rejection by others is freer to come up with unusual ideas. David Ogilvy, one of this country's most successful advertising men, has suggested that great leaders do not suffer from the crippling need to be loved. This viewpoint appears at odds with the standard requirement that retailers must like people. If a store hires potential executives who like people and perhaps are dependent on others, they may be low in creativity. Indeed, a store may have to develop a tradeoff among such characteristics, since they tend to exclude each other. To some extent, of course, all individuals present a set of strengths and weaknesses. The selection of individuals therefore requires numerous tradeoffs.

Another important aspect is that a creative person is considered able to live with complexity and contradiction. Indeed, it has been suggested that he both needs and welcomes them.

There is also some agreement that creativity requires a certain amount of adventuresomeness, including the willingness to take risks. Store managements may desire to both select and encourage individuals with these qualities. One way of doing so might be to not be literal in interpreting such constraints as open to buy (p. 109). Unfortunately, identifying creative people is difficult. Business, after all, looks to the end product. While individuals may be creative in many ways, and can be encouraged to be so, evaluating an individual's total creative potential in a business environment is at best a risky procedure. It is clear that since creativity is very different from intelligence, intelligence tests should not be outstanding predictors of creative behavior. The best predictor is probably some indication of creative performance in a person's past history.

Finally, it should be emphasized that creativity is not independent of the atmosphere in which the individual exists. Thus if a store or manager is desirous of fostering creativity, he must provide a creative atmosphere.

### Summary

1. Creativity can be of value to a retail executive in many ways. He can be creative in laying out the floor; in setting up displays; in the way he negotiates for concessions from suppliers. Indeed, creativity can make a contribution to most elements of retail decision making.

2. A most important aspect of creativity for many in retailing relates to the creation of new products. Changing the physical product can bring many advantages to the retailer, including a lower price from suppliers; the ability to more exactly cater to the needs and desires of customers; some competitive insulation from other retailers; and the excitement of creating something new.

3. Serious investigators of the creative process have postulated specific stages in it. Five recognizable stages might be: (a) identification and formulation of the problem or set of problems; (b) preparation; (c) incubation; (d) illumination or insight; (e) verification.

4. A key problem for many executives is how to induce more divergent thought within themselves.

A. It is one of the paradoxes of creativity that before the individual can create something new, he or she must become extremely familiar with the work of others in the same field of endeavor. This requires hard work.

B. After becoming familiar with the work of others, the individual can adopt many artificial methods of inducing creative alternatives. Many of these emphasize making the familiar strange. Key devices for achieving this are checklists, forced relations, and analogies.

C. The nonconscious is a most interesting dimension of creativity. Some observers feel that it prods and programs the conscious mind, urging it to contribute new insights. If an executive accepts the creative role of the nonconscious, he has the problem of how to use it.

5. Other methods of improving individual creativity are offered, including broadened job experiences; keeping creative thought relevant; deferred judgment; extended effort; and group techniques.

6. Various practical aspects of creativity are outlined. The creative decision maker may also need a certain degree of independence and be capable and perhaps desirous of existing with complexity and contradiction. An executive may be more creative if he or she is more adventuresome and is willing to take risks.

### Discussion Questions

1. Define creativity.

2. Do you agree that it is important for a retailer to change the physical offerings of suppliers? Why?

3. What are the stages of the creative process?

4. What are some key ways of making the familiar strange?

5. What does the saying "Chance favors the prepared mind" have to do with creativity?

6. Indicate several kinds of checklist that might be used to induce creativity.

7. What are some ways of making the strange familiar?

8. What has your nonconscious mind meant to your decision making in nonbusiness matters? If it has meant something, can ways be developed to make it aid in business decision making?

9. Do you think that liking people aids or inhibits the creative process?

### References

Gregory, Carl, *The Management of Intelligence* (New York: McGraw-Hill, 1967), p. 201.

Guilford, J. P., "Creativity, Yesterday, Today, and Tomorrow," *Journal of Creative Behavior*, Winter, 1967.

———, "Creativity: Retrospect and Prospect," *Journal of Creative Behavior*, Summer, 1970.

Haefele, John W., *Creativity and Innovation* (New York: Reinhold, 1962), p. 5.

Koprowski, Eugene J., "Creativity, Men, and Organizations," *Journal of Creative Behavior*, Spring, 1972, pp. 49–54.

Kotler, Philip, *Marketing Management, Analysis, Planning, and Control* (Englewood Cliffs, N.J.: Prentice-Hall, 1967), p. 255.

Ogilvy, David, in *New York Times*, June 11, 1972, section 3, p. 17.

Roe, Anne, "Psychological Approaches to Creativity in Science," in Myron A. Coler (ed.), *Essays on Creativity in the Sciences* (New York: New York University Press, 1963).

Weiner, Bernard, "Effects of Motivation on the Availability and Retrieval of Memory Traces," *Psychological Bulletin*, January 1966, pp. 124–137.

### Further Reading

Alamshah, William H., "The Conditions of Creativity," *Journal of Creative Behavior*, July 1967.

Bouchard, Thomas J., "Whatever Happened to Brainstorming?" *Journal of Creative Behavior*, Fall, 1971.

Dickinson, Roger A., "Creativity in Retailing," *Journal of Retailing*, Winter, 1969–70, pp. 3–18.

Fouraker, Lawrence, and Siegel, Sidney, *Bargaining Behavior* (New York: McGraw-Hill, 1963).

Gordon, William J. J., *Synectics: The Development of Creative Capacity* (New York: Harper and Row, 1961).

———, "On Being Explicit About the Creative Process," *Journal of Creative Behavior*, Winter, 1972, pp. 295–300.

Guilford, J. P., *The Nature of Human Intelligence* (New York: McGraw-Hill, 1967).

———, "Some Misconceptions Regarding Measurement of Creative Talents," *Journal of Creative Behavior*, Summer, 1971, pp. 77–87.

Harrison, H. G., and Gough, C., "Imagination—Underdeveloped Resource," in Sidney Parnes and Harold Harding (eds.), *A Source Book of Creative Thinking* (New York: Scribner, 1962).

Kneller, George F., *The Art and Science of Creativity* (New York: Holt, Rinehart, and Winston, 1966).

Koestler, Arthur, *The Act of Creation* (New York: Macmillan, 1964).

McDermid, Charles D., "Some Correlates of Creativity in Engineering Personnel," *Journal of Applied Psychology*, February 1965, pp. 14–19.

Parnes, Sidney, J., "The Literature of Creativity (Part II)," *Journal of Creative Behavior*, Spring, 1967.

Rugg, Harold, *Imagination* (New York: Harper and Row, 1963).

# 22

*People in Retailing*

The importance of people to most facets of retailing was discussed earlier. They receive and mark the merchandise; people write the advertising copy; people buy, display, and price the merchandise; people sell the merchandise; people stock the merchandise. Suppliers, purchasing agents, and customers are all people. Thus managing and understanding people are two activities that are critical to the success of the retail operation. Indeed, it is difficult to get ahead in most forms of retailing without constantly interacting with people.

While people are important to all corporations, many observers feel that they are more important in retailing than in other types of business for the following reasons:

1. *Payroll costs.* For most kinds of retailing payroll costs represent the largest nonmerchandise expense. Thus according to a Cornell University study, payroll in self-service discount department stores was 12.45 percent of owned sales in 1971–72 for chains with an annual volume of $20 million to $100 million, and 13.22 percent for chains with an annual volume of over $100 million, in the same period ("owned sales" are sales from departments not leased by the store to other retailers). Drugstore chains were reported by a trade source in 1973 as having a 1972 labor cost of 16.9 percent of sales. Total payroll for all department stores with annual volumes over $1 million has been similarly reported as 18.3 percent of sales, also in 1972. Any expense that is this large deserves the attention of top management.

2. *Personal service.* The performance of a retail firm's salespeople and other employees is a key element in differentiating it from its competition. The consumer usually deals directly with the employees of the retailer, and the treatment she receives from them can be a key element in whether or not she comes back.

3. *Quality of labor.* There was a time when employees were thankful that they had a job at all. Today if employees are thankful for their jobs, many observers feel that they hide it rather well. Indeed, the independence, arrogance, and thoughtlessness of employees in retailing is thought to be increasing substantially. David Schwartzman has presented evidence that the quality of labor at the retail level is decreasing over time. The average

hourly earnings of nonsupervisory personnel in retailing were only $2.44 in 1971, hardly a wage to inspire a professional level of service. All of this adds up to a rather significant problem for the retail manager, who would like to increase the attractiveness of his store by having effective interaction with the customer at the point of sale, during adjustment of a bill, the return of merchandise, and so on.

4. *Seasonal sales patterns.* Employment in retailing is further complicated by the highly seasonal sales patterns. On one occasion, the skirt department in a leading department store did about three and one-half times the first quarter's business in the month of December. For women's retractable umbrellas, the same store did over four times the first quarter's business in December. It is not uncommon for discount catalog showrooms to do 50 percent of their business in the November-December period. These increases create great problems in merchandising as well as in personnel: imagine going from four salespeople to 25 during the key weeks in December. The store's problems in this respect leave most customers cold. Nor will they always differentiate between regular employees and the Christmas employees.

5. *Use of part-time employees.* Another key aspect of retailing is that many of the firm's employees are part-time, particularly in sales. Since customers do not come in at a rate to accommodate the number of salespeople, the store must accommodate the customers coming in. For example, in central business districts the lunchtimes are very busy.

Thus people are important to the retail manager, probably more important than they are in most other occupations. The retail manager must therefore be intimately concerned with all facets of personnel work, including training, compensation, and working conditions.

## Human Problems of Retailing

There are many ways that a manager can approach the management of the people who are under him. He can try to bring out the talent in each employee, to match the potential of this employee with positions in the firm or even outside it. The focus here is on the employee. The logic of this approach is that employees really want to work hard, but must be given tasks that are meaningful to them and that they can perform well. It is argued that if the manager approaches her subordinates in this manner, not only will each employee perform well because his abilities have been matched to his job, but also the employee will probably get the impression that the manager really cares about him as a person. Proponents of this approach would recognize that it would not work equally well at all levels of management. Indeed, certain nonexecutive personnel just want a job; they are putting their kids through school, or need the money for some other pressing reason, and they neither need or desire someone to develop their talents other than through a pay check. Clearly, a manager must be flexible if he is to use what might be termed an employee-centered approach to management.

A second approach that might be used in the managing of employees is to aim at making each one's performance the optimum that can be achieved from the firm's, not the employee's point of view. Presumably such a manager would approach each subordinate as an individual and try to motivate him to perform his assigned task as effectively as possible. Such a manager would be conscious of the fact that employees tend to form groups and that group standards may have to be considered in maximizing individual performance. Texts in personnel management usually emphasize the advantages of positive rewards to employees, but empirical support for their assertions is often lacking.

While managers in most retail firms tend to emphasize positive rewards, there appears to be a greater amount of deviant managerial behavior in large retail firms than in firms of most other types. This may be because most retail firms create strong profit centers and hold executives to a certain level of performance in those centers. Unusual behavior may be tolerated from an executive who has excelled at this task. In addition, it can be argued that many executives in retailing are not college graduates, and have therefore not acquired the standard college manners and attitudes. Further, retailers tend to be tight with their training dollars. Finally, some management techniques that would be inappropriate elsewhere may have value in retailing.

One example of such an "inappropriate" technique might be worth examining. Assume that a department manager of a large discount store has a sloppy-looking selling floor. The store's general manager comes to this selling floor and starts screaming at the department manager in front of the customers and all the other salespeople. The net effect of this technique is difficult to evaluate. The general manager, according to some theories, may have found an emotional outlet that will increase his performance level for the rest of the day. The manager being screamed at is probably not pleased, although in some firms this type of behavior may be so common that he may not really mind. Whether he minds or not, he will probably take a greater interest in the appearance of the selling floor than he did previously. The salespeople will in most instances feel sorry for the manager and work harder for him than they would have otherwise. Other decision makers in the firm—the head of the marking department, for instance, may empathize with the lower-level manager and give his department better service in the future. The customers' reaction is more difficult to evaluate. While some may be impressed with the manager's interest in the store's appearance, most will probably feel embarrassed. Whether they or those to whom they might speak will buy more or less at the store is difficult to say. However, the lower-level retail manager may come to consider *not* being screamed at as a type of reward. A manager in such an environment always knows where he stands with the higher-ups. Of course, such negative approaches to behavior require a lot more thought. Much depends on the options of the subordinate. Can he easily leave his job? Can he unionize? Most executive subordinates cannot. If the subordinate has few other opportunities, my guess is that he will react rather quickly and well to negative techniques applied by top management. Perhaps the biggest loser will be the society, which will have a greater number of embittered people.

Alternatively, a retail manager might take an objective approach. Proponents of this approach would suggest the one reason a manager is hired or promoted is that he has displayed an ability to relate to people in a reasonable manner. If he can do this, so the argument goes, he will have more time and energy to worry about the other aspects of his job. Presumably he will also treat people objectively and fairly. He may not be as flexible as other managers, but flexibility usually comes at a cost. And employees may react very well to a no-nonsense, let's-get-the-job-done attitude.

### Interaction Upward

Most management texts emphasize how a manager can get the most out of his employees. This, however, is probably not the key question for most executives in retailing. What they want to know is how they can make the kind of impression on top management that will get them promoted. And indeed the support of top managers is critical for advancement in most enterprises. Seldom can an executive's immediate boss promote him unless he, too, is being promoted. A much belabored rule of thumb for any executive is to make every effort to get one's boss promoted, regardless of his competence. Someone above the boss must take a liking to him for some reason, whether it is high praise from his boss, the praise of others in the firm, or personal acquaintance. This problem can become complex. For example, an executive may not praise a competent subordinate because promoting that person will only force him to retrain someone else and the replacement, even after training, may be inferior. Further, the new subordinate may be a political risk to the boss because his loyalty is unknown.

A young executive might start to differentiate himself by doing a brilliant job in the position to which he has been assigned. This is far easier to say than to do. Usually, doing a brilliant job will be easier if the person who had the position before you did not do one. In addition, even if an executive were to do a brilliant job that was recognized as such by top management, there would be little reason to suppose that his talents at level $x$ are transferable to level $x + 1$. For example, let us suppose that you buy merchandise for a store. The level above this will probably have little to do with merchandise and everything to do with managing the people who are buying the merchandise.

Most young retail executives try to make themselves noticed by working an 80-hour week. They hope, of course, that this effort will be appreciated by whoever counts in the organization. However, students should be aware that quality of work output is probably not the main criterion for executive advancement. What matters is that the work output should be favorably perceived by top management. Hopefully, superior quality is related to the perception of it. In any case, it is the job of the junior executive to indicate by any means available to him that he is qualified to handle more responsibility, and can handle this better than others at a similar level in the organization. This conclusion may seem highly debatable, but judging from personal experience and that of my students, I would say that it is correct.

One way to look better is to make others look worse in the eyes of whoever matters. This is an extremely difficult technique to use, but one that, it seems, is often used in a discrete manner by many young executives. The usefulness of this technique, as well as its morality, is left for the reader to determine.

Winning credit for ideas is a key problem for a young executive, particularly if he is shrewd enough to get other people to believe they thought up the ideas he is putting over on them. It is commonplace to suggest that executives react more positively to their own ideas than to the ideas of others. A young executive trying to institute change might effectively take advantage of this. For example, let us assume that an assistant buyer went to the branch stores on a given day to examine the departments for which he is responsible. Looking at the unit controls in one store, he might see that it obviously needs a new price line. He could draw this to the attention of the department manager and even, under certain merchandise philosophies, order the merchandise into the branch store himself. He might, however, go to some lengths to see that this rather obvious idea

"occurred" to the department manager. Assume that he succeeds in this lengthy procedure. How is he going to get credit? If getting credit is difficult in this case, won't it be still more difficult if he has to do the same thing with his superior? While this example may be somewhat artificial, the tradeoff between improving the performance of the enterprise and getting the credit one wants for it poses a very real dilemma for many positions in and out of retailing.

In general, it should be noted that most executives interact with many others who are on more or less the same plane. How is an executive to get the most out of the advertising department, the receiving department, branch managers, and so forth? It is difficult to forget that most executives are not only competitors but collaborators, otherwise the firm could not function. The key problem, then, is to get support from these executives so that a better job can be done for one's own area, while getting promoted oneself.

Another group that is very important to the retail executive consists of the store's suppliers. These can be particularly important to him because the supplying firms represent alternative career routes for many merchandise executives. The whole problem of relationships with suppliers, as we saw in Chapters 3 and 14, is of critical interest to the retailing community.

## Selected Problems

This section discusses some problems that an executive may face in getting things done through others and in having others get things done through him. No effort is made to discuss any of the questions in depth, nor are any of the answers intended as definitive.

### Authority and Responsibility

A common management concept is that a manager's authority should be commensurate with his responsibility. This seldom happens. Indeed, seldom is the nature of a position's authority or responsibility made entirely clear. And yet the concept that authority should equal responsibility appears quite logical. How can an executive be held responsible for something that he does not control in all its key aspects? The answer is that he will be held responsible for it in any case. Thus lines of authority and responsibility are commonly blurred at all levels.

The relationships among people in a retail enterprise or indeed most other kinds of enterprise are not usually prescribed down to the last detail, and indeed from many perspectives should not be. A person who feels that he has six bosses may behave very differently from a person who feels that he has only one. Indeed, the demands of getting along with six people may be very different from the demands of getting along with one. Perhaps an executive ought to be capable of thriving in this atmosphere of uncertainty and contradiction. There is even a certain kind of security in reporting to six bosses, particularly for an executive who changes jobs rather frequently within an organization.

### Chain of Command

When an executive hires a subordinate Y, according to a rigid interpretation of the chain of command, he normally cuts himself off from most kinds of relationship with Y's subordinates. In other words, there is supposed to be a clear chain of command. Obviously, if the chain-of-command approach to a retail organization is accepted the person at level $x + 2$ does not interact with those at level $x$, except on the most formal basis. If a manager at level $x + 2$ interacts with someone at level $x$, then he is seen as undercutting the authority of the manager beneath him at level $x + 1$. However, if the managers at both levels are both intelligent about the subject and understand exactly what is happening, there is no reason to assume an unfavorable outcome. Indeed, the outcome might be rather favorable. For example, the manager at level $x + 2$ may be more skilled at activity $z$ and far more able to communicate this skill to the individual at level $x$ than the manager at that level

$x + 1$. Indeed, the two managers working together may be able to do a better job of training the individual at level $x$ than either separately. It is true that the intervention of the senior manager brings uncertainty into the situation, and unless there is harmony between the two managers, trouble is likely to result. The benefits, however, may be large. Look at what the executive at level $x$ is getting: exposure to an executive who can promote him; help with his job; and a feeling that higher management really cares. If he does not get along with his immediate boss, doing a great job in the eyes of the executive at level $x + 2$ will not hurt him at all. Thus the possible benefits of breaking the chain of command may be well worth the costs.

Two cases will illustrate this. First, let us consider a merchandise vice-president of a large department or discount chain who is wondering if he should have monthly meetings with the buyers, two levels below him in the organizational structure? Clearly, meetings of this type can cause trouble, but the organization was not created with the sole idea of minimizing trouble. The lines of authority are clearly blurred in this situation. Nevertheless, with qualified managers at all levels, the benefits would appear to be highly worthwhile. The buyers will receive some expert guidance in the presence of their bosses. This will give them a type of involvement in the goals of top management that is critical. They will also get to know how the top management feels about key issues. My guess would even be that effective intermediate managers—intermediate that is, between buyer and vice-president—could use such meetings to their advantage.

Second, consider the friendly president of a large store. He is so friendly that he has gotten to know 750 out of the 1,000 people in the store on a first-name basis. He frequently stops to speak to the salespeople on the floor. Not only does he know them by their first names, but they call him by his first name. And they proceed to tell him about all the department's problems. What a catastrophe! The chain of command is in great trouble. Yet look at what happens. The salespeople feel a sense of participation in the store that would be hard to duplicate by other means (salespeople do not tend to get ahead in other than sales activities, but the fact that the president does not support them for higher positions need not be known). The managers at all levels know that this is happening and prepare for it. Many of them want what happens in their departments to be broadcast all over the store. If a manager works 80 hours a week preparing for a sale, he wants this fact to be known to top management.

A word of caution. Each manager at every level should understand what he is doing to the individuals under him. An executive should not bypass people in a chain of command without understanding the ramifications of his actions.

### Committees

Business executives use committees in many ways. Key executives for instance, may come to a meeting in order to decide what to do. It can be argued, however, that this approach will inevitably result in the most undesirable sort of compromise. Men under great pressure and stress will rarely take a venturesome course collectively. What is needed for really important decisions is leadership. It is not that the leader should refuse to consult with the top executives concerned. Reaching the actual decision however, is difficult in a committee environment. Or, to put it another way, perhaps key decisions have to be individual decisions. One might note that the military once used committees to make decisions, but gave it up, according to General James M. Gavin, after receiving evidence that it did not work. It is interesting to speculate on how committees with diffused responsibilities have affected the fortunes of large corporations. The Japanese, for instance, appear to have used committees very effectively.

### Organizational Structure

As a store grows in size, the need for formal organization becomes greater and greater. There are a great number of organizational structures that one might adopt. In Chapter 9 we discussed the merits of centralized versus decentralized forms of organization and the possible effects of each on various research endeavors. Clearly, the purpose of organizing is to foster the prosperity of the enterprise. One key to the future of the enterprise is the quality of personnel at the higher levels. Thus organization charts should not be created unless their impact on specific key personnel is considered. Moreover, as the personnel situation changes, the organization of the store may also have to be changed.

For example, let us assume that the merchandise vice-president has four merchandise managers that report to him. Let us further assume that a particular buyer is considered an excellent prospect to be president of the store at some time in the future. A competitive offer, or top management's desire to forestall such an offer, may make it essential to appoint this buyer the fifth merchandise manager, although the store has no need of one. Many such examples could be offered where firms have successfully changed organization charts to adapt to specific personnel requirements.

### Social Distance

A problem that most executives face is how close can one or should one be to those above and below them in the organization. Some management philosophies suggest that everyone should be part of the team. Others suggest that managers should keep some distance from subordinates. Much may depend on the approach to the chain of command. It is difficult, however, for an executive to be both judge and participant in all phases of an operation. The best balance for a given executive would appear to vary with such factors as his personality, the personalities of the other executives involved, the situation, and so forth.

### Executive Rivalries

It is a fact of executive life that many executives within a firm develop rather strong rivalries, particularly as they progress toward the top. These rivalries are generally known to the various other executives of approximately the same level on the organization chart. Many executives have to decide how they fit into the battle. A common recommendation is to avoid any involvement: just do the best job that you can under the circumstances, and avoid alliances that could be held against you in the future. Unfortunately, this course of action runs the risk of appealing to no one. Each of the alternatives involves some risk, and each party must select his own course of action after considering all the relevant factors.

### Other Key Issues

**Training**  Most large retail organizations have training departments. For nonexecutives, the training programs tend to be job-oriented. The training department tries to impart as much information and technical expertise as possible in the short time allotted. Hopefully, the trainees will then become a credit to the store and feel more at home in their positions. Some large organizations have executive training programs. These programs offer college graduates and other potential executives an introduction to retail management and the policies of the firm.

**Group interaction**  There is such a thing as a group influence. Individuals interact in a manner that affects the behavior of all members of the group. For example, many salespeople have books that they run indicating how much they sell each day: one will sell $200 a day, another $300, and so forth. There are mechanisms at work within most work groups to insure that nobody works too hard. Thus in the example just given, a salesperson who started selling $600 a day would probably be brought in line by the others. Group norms, then, are to be expected and are operative under many conditions.

**Women's liberation**  A most fascinating problem is that of equal pay for equal work. While most would agree with the general principle that women should be paid the same as men if they do the same work,

putting this principle into practice is another matter. For example, let us suppose that a store management feels that it must have male salespeople to sell men's clothing. In order to attract the men it needs for this, this store may have to offer $7,500 or so a year in some form. Then the question comes up, Is selling men's clothing the same as selling women's clothing? And if it is similar in some sense, then shouldn't the pay be the same for women and men? And what about back pay over the years?

**Job enrichment**  Many years ago it was a truism of business that jobs were organized in an economically efficient manner. For example, if it appeared most efficient to completely divide the work of the salesperson and the stock person, this was done. Today it is becoming more and more important in many industrial jobs to consider how the employee perceives the job. For example, the assembly-line production techniques of many firms are being questioned—by the firms. The rates of absenteeism and other costs of mass production are large. And there are human costs, to the firm as well as the individual, in having someone with talents work on a job requiring little talent. Automobile manufacturers and other firms are therefore changing the concept of the assembly line to include other kinds of cost. Not that we will ever get back to the point where each employee makes his own car. But substantial compromises are being made with the old-fashioned ideal of complete mechanical efficiency. Retailing, too, must try to develop means of matching the talents of the individual to the demands of a position. Perhaps an employee will find it more interesting to combine work in sales, stock supervision, and stock than to do any of them separately. Managers should consider all the relevant factors in creating positions.

**Compensation**  A key question in many types of retailing is how to compensate the various kinds of worker. While money is not all of the job, it is certainly an important element. People have to meet their obligations, and most of us want to live better.

Not only do people want more money than they have, but they often are very interested in how they fare relative to other employees. Are they being treated fairly? Sales employees are frequently offered various types of incentive. A common one is to offer the sales person some type of commission in addition to a base salary. Others are offered base salary only but the amount of that base salary may be directly related to the level of sales or other production. Still others may be on a straight commission basis, perhaps with a base draw against commission. Other managements may offer so-called spiffs or PM's (prize money or push money) for the sale of certain merchandise or perhaps for meeting certain sales targets. See Chapter 23.

**Unions**    Unions are becoming increasingly important in retailing, although many large retail firms have managed to avoid unionization over the years. The influence of unions is felt far beyond the firms in which they exist. Many firms go to great lengths to stay nonunion. In order to do so, such firms must pay satisfactory wages and create reasonable working conditions.

## Summary

1. People are very important to retailing.

  A. People are the largest nonmerchandise expense.

  B. The consumer tends to deal directly with the employees of the firm.

  C. The quality of labor in retailing is apparently declining.

  D. Seasonal sales patterns make the employment of many extra salespeople necessary.

  E. Many employees are part-time.

2. There are many organizational problems related to retailing.

  A. Authority seldom equals responsibility.

  B. The chain of command is frequently (and perhaps constructively) abridged.

  C. Committees are used in various ways.

  D. The impact of key personnel on the organizational structure should be considered.

  E. The closeness of superior to subordinate is a key problem.

  F. Executive rivalries should be considered.

3. Other key issues are:

  A. Training;

  B. Group interaction;

  C. Women's liberation;

  D. Job enrichment;

  E. Compensation;

  F. Unions.

## Discussion Questions

1. Why are people so important to a retail operation?

2. What can a trainee do to look better in the eyes of his superior?

3. Do you think that a manager ought to receive authority commensurate with his responsibility? Give your reasons.

4. Should an executive have considerable contact with employees two levels below him? If not, would occasional contact be useful?

5. How can an executive make a stockman's job more interesting?

6. List three ways a manager might approach the problem of managing people under him.

7. Why is there considerable deviant behavior among retail executives?

8. What are some of the problems that the women's liberation movement presents to retail firms and vice

versa? Do you think these problems can be resolved by legislation?

9. Should a store's management try to discourage its employees from becoming unionized?

## References

Gavin, James M., interviewed in *TIMS Bulletin*, February 1971, pp. 1–10.

Mass Retailing Institute, *Operating Results of Self-Service Discount Department Stores 1971–72*.

Schwartzman, David, *The Decline of Service in Retail Trade* (Pullman, Wash.: Washington State University Press, 1971).

## Further Reading

Bingham, Wheelock H., and Yurich, David L., "Retail Organization," *Harvard Business Review*, July–August, 1963, pp. 129–146.

Maslow, Abraham H., *Eupsychian Management* (Homewood, Ill.: Irwin/Dorsey, 1965).

Michman, Ronald D., "Union Impact on Retail Management," *Business Horizons*, Spring 1967, pp. 79–84.

## Case History: *A Spiff Revealed*

Roger Tannenbaum had been the only buyer for a major appliance store for over one year. He believed quite firmly that in order to have a profitable department one had to be able to control what was sold. Therefore he exercised great control over the sales force. About four times a day, either Roger or his assistant Julie checked a list of what had been sold to see the pattern of sales. If a salesman had started to sell too many low-markup items, he was censured rather mildly. If the practice continued, a sterner approach was taken. In Roger's organization, the salesmen reported mainly to the buyers. While words of a less-than-pleasant nature were occasionally exchanged between the buying force and sales personnel, by and large the relationship that developed over time was good. Indeed, Roger and Julie were very careful to compliment exceptional effort on the part of salesmen to move the merchandise that was the most profitable for the store.

Roger thought that he had to have control over the sales of his items in order to buy in great quantities. He was a vicious bargainer with suppliers, but because of the quantity in which he bought he had to offer some of this saving to the customer. Clearly, if Roger bought 1,000 washing machines either as a special price of an existing model or as a closeout, he had to pass some of these savings onto the customer, and the salesmen had to sell them. Therefore in Roger's mind much of the directing of salespeople really aided the customer, because the store had to offer better value.

Roger could negotiate his best values from two of the five suppliers with whom he did business. While the profits were slim, the two suppliers doing the volume were basically pleased with the business. The three other suppliers, however, did not like to deal in large quantities at special prices, and therefore found their business slipping in both absolute and relative terms.

Faced with this situation, the sales manager of company X, one of the three firms doing a small business with the store decided to develop a spiff or PM program. (See discussion on page 327.) PMs had been offered for years in industries such as furniture, television, high fidelity equipment, appliances, men's clothing, and bedding. PMs were generally given by the manufacturer or supplier directly to the salesman for selling particular elements of the supplier line, particularly at the higher-priced end. Generally, if the item spiffed was a high-margin item to the retailer, the latter would not object to the extra compensation being given to the salesman. Perhaps the retailer should give higher compensation to the salesman on high-profit items anyway, in the store's own interest.

The big problem with PMs came when suppliers were desirous of selling more low-markup merchandise. The store was not in favor of this because management preferred the salesman to sell the high-margin merchandise. The sales manager of company X knew all this. But what did he really have to lose by a spiff program? He felt that he could approach the salesmen over the buyer's head. The salesmen would understand the situation and, since there was no ban on spiffs, might not regard the offer as a direct violation of the rules. And even if the supplier were caught, the store needed his line of merchandise. Therefore, most stores in such circumstances might well call the sales manager in for a soul-searching, screaming session. Stores, however, like most elements of society, scream morals but act according to the best interests of their pocketbook. Furthermore, he was not doing that much business with the store, and his losses would not be large if he were cut off.

The sales manager of company X did approach a key salesman at lunch one day. The deal was set up: the key elements of the washer line would be spiffed $5 per unit. Payment would be made personally by the sales manager, once a month, to the one salesman.

Roger and Julie kept up their tactics of controlling the selling floor. After a month they saw the sales of line X increasing. Finally, Roger suspected something and confronted the salesman. He told Roger the complete details of the deal.

### Discussion Questions

1. Are Roger's sales policies in need of revision?

2. Should the store cut off the supplier?

# 23

## Personal Selling

Until World War II, personal salesmanship was the essential ingredient in effective retailing. Then came the dramatic rise of self-service. Not only discount stores, which emphasized self-service, but many department stores were caught up in the new trend, though to a lesser extent. Supermarkets greatly increased their share of the food industry; drugstores and other retail outlets began to aggressively merchandise self-service displays. Thus personal selling in many cases has become a far less important part of the retail merchandising mix.

Many observers feel that the level of personal selling in retail outlets has deteriorated markedly. Salesmen are not supposed to take care of customers the way they used to do, but instead have developed an air of independence that impresses many customers as being close to arrogance. Not unrelatedly, the prestige of retail selling has decreased.

But the salesman is nowhere near gone. Nor does he appear to be disappearing. Most cars are sold by salesmen: so are most appliances, furniture, and men's clothing. Most fashion outlets rely heavily on personal selling. Indeed, more retail volume passes through retail salesmen than is sold through what might be termed self-service. In fact, it is difficult to see at this time how personal selling will decrease much more in relative importance unless great innovations are introduced in such major areas as the automobile industry.

The fact that there is a retail salesman who approaches the customer may mean a great deal to marketing firms, retail firms, and society. At one level, the salesman is another channel member whose needs, aspirations, and desires must be taken into account by retailer and manufacturer alike. The salesman is often his own profit center and will therefore do his best under most conditions to sell the items that make the most money for him. While there are both long-run and short-run aspects of a salesman's approach to the future, compensation plans with differing compensation per item can be quite effective in changing the pattern of sales. Thus salesmen are a force that must be considered in the merchandising of items to the consumer.

On another level, the salesman is a force in the battle between retailer and supplier for control over what is to be sold at the retail store. In Chapter 3 it was suggested that a retailer might well make an effort to sell just a few brands when customers come in asking for many. A salesman can act in some sense as a distorting influence in changing the wishes of the customer to approximate the wishes of the retailer and/or the supplier. Or, from the retailer's point of view, the salesman can counteract the propaganda offered the consumer by national advertising. Thus the salesman becomes a force in many merchandise areas by selling the consumer more of the retailer's brands.

On another level, the salesman is an employee of the retailer and as such can be motivated to be helpful in many ways; for instance he may help the retailer dispose of merchandise that would otherwise be unsalable.

Another way of looking at the salesman is as the communications link between consumer and store, or perhaps between consumer and marketing channel. Some observers would even call him the communications link between the consumer and the core of the business system. Many salesmen are very proud of the influence they can have over consumers, and of the fact that they sell them merchandise that will meet their needs.

A final dimension of personal selling at the retail level is that it is often the younger person's first exposure to the marketing system as a worker, and apparently increasingly so. Many become soured on certain aspects of our competitive system by this initial exposure. Personal selling, then, is an activity that is important to society in more than a strictly economic sense.

## The Retail Selling Job

As a job, retail selling presents many aspects. In some types of retail outlet, in addition to selling, the salesmen or saleswomen are supposed to maintain the appearance of merchandise on the selling floor; take counts of the merchandise in the selling and stock areas for input into the unit control systems; maintain the condition of the back stock area; communicate the desires of the consumers to the store decision makers; and prevent consumer and other employee theft—among other things. The amount of stock keeping, and so on, that a salesperson will do will vary with many factors, including the store, the merchandise area, and the state of labor relations. Unions, in fact, are extremely influential in this area, as Ronald D. Michman has pointed out.

A study by Robert J. Paul and Robert W. Bell, which they conducted in a midwestern department store, indicated that a saleswoman spent her time as follows: selling, about 30 percent; stock work, about 10 percent; no required activity, about 20 percent; away from selling floor, about 20 percent; and the remainder performing miscellaneous activities. In short, there are retail selling positions of many kinds. Even a service station attendant does a certain amount of selling, although the retail oil companies would question this. In a department store there is often a hierarchy of selling positions. There are the positions in which beginners are placed—for example, selling men's shirts. At some point in time the successful salesperson progresses to the *commission departments*. There also tends to be a hierarchy among these departments. One hierarchy, from low to high, might be: shoes, television, major appliances, rugs, and furniture. The compensation in the departments that belong to the upper levels of such a hierarchy can be quite high and provide incentives for all the salespeople in the store.

Another type of retail salesman is the store representative that goes to the customer's home. In certain areas such as heating and air conditioning, storm windows, draperies, rugs, and kitchen cabinets, there is a particular need to send representatives of the retailer to the house where the merchandise is to be installed. Even if there is no legitimate need to do this, a higher percentage of closings will generally take place in the home than in the store. Thus there is both the need of the customer to have a representative of the company understand his problems and a desire on the part of the retailer to have a salesman service the customer in the home. Clearly, this type of selling job is very different from selling in the store—different, too, many claim, from selling door-to-door.

## The Importance of Selling

Most salespeople have heard executives tell them how important salespeople are to the store—even if they are not paid high salaries. They are told that the merchandise of the various stores is largely the same; that their prices, at least in that geographic area, are about the same; that their fixtures and displays are about the same; and that their credit policies, delivery schedules, and so forth are about the same. The real difference between stores, they are told, lies in the attitude of their respective salespeople. Thus it is up to the salespeople the executives continue, to be so effective that the consumer will think of their store as a really different kind of place and rush back to it.

From management's point of view, the problem is: How do we mold these poorly paid people into an effective team that can accomplish the above job, particularly in an environment in which individualism is running rampant, the prestige of the retail employee is decreasing, and the desire for hard work seems to be at an all-time low. Thus while improving someone's personal selling performance is not easy, stores do make a great effort in this area.

It is interesting to note that, in general, the smaller the store, the larger the proportion of the customers that will be dealt with by each salesperson. Thus if only two salespeople meet all the customers, it is they who will be chiefly responsible for the firm's image. This gives them substantial importance. Retail selling is probably what most types of retail enterprises do most of, and if the enterprise is successful one of the owners is usually quite skilled in personal selling.

## Successful Personal Selling

Since retail salespeople have many duties, it is not always easy to identify the ones who are good at selling. The retail sales volume for each employee is usually known, but in the other areas of a salesperson's job performance evaluation is highly subjective. And even the sales figures are biased by such factors as the amount of work spent on activities other than selling, the degree to which a salesperson will sell the low-priced items, and the amount of time a salesperson will spend on selling both merchandise and customers that are harder to sell. For example, in a toy store a salesperson might stand next to the 20-inch bicycle section during the Christmas season. If she can bully her way to controlling the bicycle section, she is bound to run a high book. Not only are such games played in most stores in which management wants a high sales volume, but the salespeople are aware of them and know who the players are. Thus identifying the best-qualified salesperson is no easy task. Each manager will generally be ready enough to say who are the most valuable contributors to the sales of his merchandise classification, but there is practically no way of telling whether he knows what he is talking about.

It is obviously in the retailer's interest to identify the characteristics of an effective salesperson. If he can do so, he should be better able to select individuals who will be successful, and will presumably be able to train both new and old salespeople in a manner that will lead to a better effort for the store. Among the ways in which he might set about identifying effective salespeople are the following:

1. *Outline the requirements.* Clearly, selling furniture is different from selling candy; likewise, selling outside the store is different from selling inside it. The manager, then, might outline the specific characteristics that, he thinks, are required for the position. To these he might add some characteristics that on both deductive and empirical grounds seem to be associated with almost all successful selling. Thus a key element of most successful selling would appear to be the ability to do intelligent, conscientious work including some idea of the management of time. Another key element is that the salesperson must have a thorough understanding of the importance of the customer to the store. This must be more than an intellectual understanding. For most retail operators, the salesperson's actions and thoughts must be that the customer is king. A salesperson who has empathy, that is, the ability to feel what others are feeling, should be able to develop an appropriate attitude toward customers, though perhaps empathy, as Lewis H. Woolman has argued, is not essential.

2. *Examine performance.* Effective salespeople can also be identified on the job. Top management can either have the manager of the salesperson's department make a special evaluation or proceed to the assumption that the higher volume salesmen are effective and the lower-volume ones are not. Paul and Bell, in the study already cited, examined whether high-volume and low-volume salespeople differed in their use of time. They concluded that the ones with the highest dollar volume spent more time selling, and worked at a faster pace. Unfortunately, top management's perception and the dollar-volume performance need not be related. Numerous studies could be undertaken to see how the more effective salespeople spend their time. If it were desirable, other salespeople might be encouraged to emulate them.

3. *Administer personality tests.* A popular way of determining the key characteristics of effective salespeople is to give various personality and other tests to people already identified as effective and ineffective and then look for differences in the scores of the two groups. We might examine them for such aspects as intelligence, sales aptitude, personality, social intelligence, empathy, and personal life history. James C. Cotham, in a study of major appliance salesmen, found little relationship among most of the traits and characteristics generally assumed to be related to sales success, although his "sales aptitude" variable was correlated significantly with most of his performance measures. Indeed, there was little evidence that any of the personality dimensions he studied, including empathy, affected selling performance. The older and less educated the salesman, and the more varied his selling experience, the more likely he was to be seen as successful by his boss, but none of these factors appeared significantly related to his sales performance measured in terms of sales volume and commission earnings. Moreover, there was very little relationship between job satisfaction and job performance. In the Paul and Bell study, the highest-volume salespeople were older, more experienced in selling, and slightly better educated. Clearly identifying the characteristics of successful or unsuccessful salespeople is not easy, especially when these characteristics can be expected

to change. Among the possible sources of change are: changes in the basic customer population; variation in the role of personal salesmanship from store to store, from one merchandise area to another within a store, and from store type to store type; and change in any of these over time.

## Consumer Approaches

Many customers freely criticize both stores and their salespeople. Customers, it is assumed, are good, and salesmen, if not exactly bad, are at least not as good. It never occurs to these critics that there may be such a thing as customer responsibility. How many customers feel a responsibility for the profits of the retailer? How many would have pangs of conscience at having bought merchandise at under the dealer's cost? How many would give a second thought to misrepresenting the competitive price at which an automobile can be purchased from another dealer? Pursuing this line of thought, Alfred R. Oxenfeldt has divided customers for television sets into three groups:

1. *The enemy.* This substantial and apparently growing group of consumers is aggressive and well-informed. Its members consider a major purchase such as a television set or a car as a challenge to outsmart the retailer. They place a very high value on small savings because it is a matter of pride to them to purchase such merchandise at the lowest possible price—preferably one better than their friends can get. The enemy have little store loyalty and no friendships with salesmen or retailers. Not surprisingly, they tend not to purchase their major appliances and televisions in department stores. Salesmen develop methods of dealing with such customers. Initially they withhold their fire, until they have made an estimate of their intentions and capabilities. But after they have identified an enemy, most appliance salesmen enter into what is considered an intense struggle. Any behavior by the salesmen is considered fair, indeed, more than justified, in matching the behavior of the customer. Such tactics are necessary for survival. Oxenfeldt states that "it is impos-

sible to explain the low ethical standards one finds among metropolitan salesmen of appliances unless one recognizes the aggressiveness and unscrupulousness of many consumers. Consumer avarice certainly reinforces seller deceitfulness."

2. *The gentleman.* These customers manifest a genuine concern for the interest of the retailer. He makes no effort to beat the retailer down in price even if he feels that he would be successful. Gentlemen regard retailers as basically honest and as a general rule believe their statements and advice. They patronize mainly local shops and become acquainted with the proprietors or salesmen there.

3. *The lamb.* Lambs are uninformed and unsophisticated purchasers who also tend to be both gullible and malleable. They are so anxious to own the items for which they are shopping that they welcome sales arguments that make the purchase easier. This group does not have the respect of the appliance salesman. Lambs are generally attracted to stores that claim to offer bargains.

It is not clear how appliance salesmen modify their behavior when they meet a lamb or a gentleman. Some undoubtedly would be motivated only by short-run considerations, that is, how to get the customer to sign a profitable contract. Others will apparently match the customer's consideration for them if they do not suffer a meaningful financial loss by so doing.

The reader should be cautioned against generalizing from television sales in large metropolitan areas to other merchandise situations. Nevertheless, certain product categories seem to be quite amenable to this type of activity on the part of customer and dealer. And as the educational level of consumers increases, the number falling into the "enemy" group will also increase. Unfortunately, there does not appear to be any ready solution to the problem. The enemy want to deal with reputable dealers of all types, but they do not want to pay the retail price that these dealers require, often just to stay alive in business. Thus the enemy have to purchase from the type of dealer who is willing to play their game. And the best retail players of this game find that honesty is a luxury that few can afford. Further, the enemy usually have to keep coming back to the same dealers because the alternatives are more offensive to them.

### The Selling Process

It is useful, as Duncan and Phillips have said, to think of the selling process as composed of seven steps, as follows: (a) the approach; (b) determining the customer's needs; (c) presenting the merchandise as effectively as possible; (d) meeting various objections; (e) closing the sale; (f) suggesting additional items; (g) developing good will after the sale. Clearly there is nothing sacred about these steps or the order in which they appear here: under certain conditions, some will be skipped. However, they do provide a basis on which to discuss personal selling.

#### The Approach

Nationally known sales trainers have been heard to remark that the first 20 seconds of a salesman's interaction with a customer are the most important. If he cannot make an impact in this period of time, the whole selling presentation will be jeopardized. While the context of this opinion is that of nonretail selling, the approach is important in retail selling. It is surprising, then, that so little research has been done on the customer approach.

A standard form of welcome is "May I help you?" It can be argued, however, that this approach begs for a negative answer and that it cuts off valuable communication. Customers have become so used to saying no to this question that they do so quite automatically. A more sophisticated argument is that the opening should vary according to the nature of the product, the number of customers in the vicinity of the salesman, the particular type of customer, the salesman's personality, and other such factors. Thus when a car drives up to a gas pump, a "May I help you?" or "May I be of service?" would not appear to cut off conversation. It might be even better to ask "Would you like the tank filled?" In a men's clothing department, on the other hand, a salesman might approach the customer with a choice of positives in an effort to force a response other than no. Thus he may ask "Do you take a 42 or 44?" While the salesman may still receive an answer such as "I am only looking," the question does usually bring some answer other than a plain no. If the department is crowded, it may be useful to classify customers by their intention to buy. In such an instance, "May I help you?" can be desirable because customers who are not interested or only mildly interested will readily answer no. Thus the customer does not feel left alone by the salesperson but also does not take up valuable time. All this should be a major concern of top management.

### Determining the Customer's Needs

An advertisement can seldom be tailored to the needs and desires of one individual. However, almost all sales communications should be tailored to the apparent needs of the individual to whom the sales presentation is directed. Thus skilled saleswomen will typically ask the customer questions about her needs, desires, prejudices, and so forth, but in a discrete manner. The time that can be devoted to this kind of activity depends on many factors: whether the customer is in a hurry, the number of other customers waiting in line, the dollar potential of the sale, and so forth.

### Presenting the Merchandise

A key part of retail selling is presenting the merchandise. The better the job that the salesperson has done in determining the customer's needs, the easier it will be for her to select the merchandise to present to the customer. This merchandise will usually represent some type of compromise among the needs of the store, the needs of the customer, and the needs of the salesperson. The store may want certain merchandise pushed because it carries a higher margin; because it is old; because it is the store's private brand and may lead to repeat sales; because it is a better value—and so on. The managers will usually have made their desires clear to the salesperson.

But the salesperson has her own needs. She may make more money on higher dollar unit sales. If she is paid 1 percent of sales, the higher the dollar level of sales the higher will be her commissions. Even if she is not on commission, her raises may be directly related to her sales volume or she may perceive this to be so. It should be emphasized that a customer's choice of merchandise can be influenced in many ways other than by salespeople. Displays, signs, lighting, location of merchandise, and so forth can be used quite effectively to change the pattern of consumer sales in the desired directions. For example, if only 12 out of 30 television antennas work well in a store, the sets at the 12 antennas will tend to sell better than they would otherwise.

Three principles of merchandise presentation have particular merit:

1. *A salesperson should always talk in terms of benefits to the customer, not in terms of facts related to the product.* The customer is primarily interested in what the feature will do for her and only secondarily in the feature itself. An effective salesman will adjust the supposed benefits to the customer's inferred needs. There are, of course, instances where a feature may have value when presented just as a feature. For example, a salesperson might indicate to the customer that the bowling ball is coated with "nepotite." This is a differentiating feature that may have value even if the customer does not know and is not told what this special coating is for. However, under most sets of conditions the saleswoman will do better to tell the customer the benefits of having this special coating; it is longer-lasting, or whatever.

2. *The customer should be offered a viable assortment.* In particular, if a customer is offered no alternatives, she may be offended and think that the store has nothing to offer. On the other hand, if she is shown an extremely large selection, she may get so confused that she buys nothing. That is why a well-managed department will often give the impression of huge assortment but have the display, fixtures, salespeople, advertising, and so forth focus the consumer's interest on a few key items from which most will choose.

3. *Salespeople can deviate only so much from the needs and desires of the customer.* There are few salesmen who can sell customers items that they really

do not want or like. And the salesman will close a lot more sales if he strongly considers the needs and desires of his customers in presenting the merchandise. If a customer expresses a strong interest in one brand of television set, it will be a foolish salesman who has that brand in stock and does not try to sell it. These aspects are discussed below.

### Meeting Objections

An integral part of all personal selling is the meeting of the customer's objections. It is naturally very difficult to differentiate between sincere objections and excuses for not buying, but the salesperson must be capable of resolving serious difficulties in his customer's mind.

### The Close

Many sales are lost because of the salesperson's inability to close. The salesperson can always ask the customer directly if he or she wants the item, but this action violates most of the canons of personal selling. It does Ask For The Order (AFTO in personal selling manuals), but it also invites the answer no. Instead, most observers would suggest that the customer be offered a choice of positives. For example: Would you like delivery Monday or Friday? Would you like the item delivered or will you take it with you? Cash or charge? Would you like me to send the gray tie or the brown one?

The above were all low-pressure closes. However, for some stores, especially furniture and appliance stores, a high-pressure close might be more appropriate. The customer may be told that the price will go up $10 at 9:30 A.M. tomorrow. A customer might well appreciate being informed of such a price increase, if it is really going to happen. Naturally merchandise mixes can be created that will make it happen; indeed, they can be created for the very purpose of easing the closing problem of the personal salesman. All other elements of the sale may be relatively unimportant compared with this one. This can be particularly true of house-to-house sell-

ing. The justification for the hardsell close is usually that, since customers who do not make up their minds today will very seldom purchase at all, all the stops must be pulled out so that the customer who wants the item will buy it here and now.

### Suggestion Selling

A person who purchases a shirt may be an ideal customer for a tie. A customer for gas may also be a customer for gas and oil additives. The customer is often open to suggestions of all types and indeed may welcome these suggestions. She may be particularly interested in items at special prices or in new items that just came into the department. Salesmen should particularly emphasize additional items that do not have a high probability of unselling what has been sold. For example, if a man has just decided to purchase a $6 shirt, the salesman may lose the sale if he tries to sell him another shirt of the same type at $4. In any case, suggestion selling is a way that the retailer can substantially increase the volume in his specific merchandise area.

### Developing Goodwill After the Sale

The sale does not end with the order: in retailing, the elements that come after the sale may be more important than those that come before. The customer must get what she ordered, when she expects it, in an appropriate package, correctly billed. In addition, if the customer believes that the store is responsible for her purchase of the item, the item had better live up to her expectations, particularly during the period that she vividly associates it with the store.

### Other Aspects of Selling

Certain practices, while not necessarily essential to the process of personal selling, have traditionally been part of it.

### Trading Up

If a customer comes in for a $2.98 tie, it is generally both appropriate and desirable from management's point of view to show the $3.98 and perhaps the $4.98 tie. Great increases in business can occur if more customers are traded up to a higher price level, provided that (a) the salesman does not lose a great many customers in the process; (b) the cost in salesman's time and in terms of lost sales is not too great.

To trade up is to switch a customer from one price line to a higher one. In many types of merchandise, the percentage markup to the retailer increases as the price line increases. The retailer, then, is generally all for selling merchandise at the higher price. Trading up is considered by many to be an appropriate activity of the retailer—even, perhaps, a responsibility to the consumer. It can be argued effectively that the best mattress buy for the consumer is the highest-priced mattress in the store. Such merchandise generally offers the store the highest percentage margin and therefore the highest dollar margin. The manufacturer also makes his highest dollar margin on this item. However, the satisfaction per dollar invested may still be the highest for the customer. The fact that something is highly profitable to a retailer does not necessarily mean that it is not the customer's best buy. Similarly, the fact that something is unprofitable for a store does not make it profitable for the consumer. Indeed, in certain instances the salesman may have a moral responsibility to show the higher-priced merchandise to the customer and give a complete description of the extra value that it offers.

### Trading Away

"Bait and switch," as trading away is often called, is a frequent retail practice. It occurs when a retailer advertises or displays an item that he does not want to sell and even may not sell to anyone. The advertised item is usually offered at a price low enough to make it instantly recognizable as an outstanding value and so bring customers running to the store.

It is the job of the salesperson not only to switch these customers to another item but to make them like both him and the store because he was so considerate as to point out the features of the "better" merchandise. Some "bait" items are virtually nailed to the floor in that selling them is almost prohibited. Others are just "Scotch-taped" to the floor, that is, selling them is discouraged. While it is widely assumed by most that nailing something to the floor is both immoral and illegal, Scotch-taping an item is common practice and more difficult to evaluate. Scotch-taping cannot easily be differentiated from normal trading up; the difference exists only in the degree to which the salesperson recommends the alternative item. Moreover, a nailed item is often difficult for a customer to spot because he has to be fairly obnoxious just to find out if it has been nailed. Many salesmen are effective switchers, and the customer would have to say, in effect, "I do not care what you say, I want that machine." Only then would the customer know if it was nailed and possibly not then, as the following story shows. About 14 years ago a buyer asked his store shopper to purchase a washing machine and have it sent to his home. The salesman for the competitor would not sell the machine even though there was no reason to suppose that he had recognized the shopper. The buyer asked the shopper to go back and insist on buying it. The salesman referred the shopper to the manager. Eventually the order was accepted. Later, a representative of the store called and stated that they did not have any of the machines but would deliver a better one at the same price. One was delivered to the buyer's house.

Trading away has no necessary connection with price and often results in trading down as well as trading up. A recognized value with a brand name will be advertised at a low price for that item. When the customer comes in, he is traded away to another brand at a higher margin, or perhaps to a so-called closeout of the same brand, at a lower price. In some instances the value traded to will offer more satisfaction per dollar to the consumer than the item advertised. The dollar value to the customer may actually be better. The better value may not have been advertised in the newspaper because the store did not feel that it would have the same drawing power with the relevant customer segments. Or, in some instances, the supplier might not permit the other item to be advertised at that price, perhaps because it will create problems with other retailers.

Trading up and switching have substantial economic importance for our society. Indeed, they present very real problems and opportunities to marketers. Oxenfeldt has suggested that retail salesmen in the television industry succeed in trading up or switching over 65 percent of their customers. Clearly, the power of some retailers and salesmen in many industries is very large. Their moral responsibility is correspondingly high.

### PM's

Manufacturers in many industries have offered PM's (push money or prize money) to retail salesmen for years, sometimes with the retailer's approval and sometimes without. The PM, or spiff as it is sometimes called, is usually offered to the retail salespeople for selling highest-priced merchandise in the supplier's line. This practice is usual in major appliances, television, furniture, and rugs. Prestigious firms such as Eastman Kodak, SONY, and Panasonic have had spiff programs.

In many instances the retail management will go along with almost any push money provided that the profits of the store are thought to be enhanced. If, for example, the manufacturer offers incentives to the salesmen to sell the highest-priced items in the manufacturer's line and the store not only makes a higher dollar margin but also a higher percentage margin, then the store may have little reason to complain. On the other hand, perhaps the store management should have offered its own extra incentives to the salespeople. The store might also regard these extra moneys as compensation to the employee and pay them so much less for their services. Salespeople often appoint one salesperson to be in charge of getting PM's. Thus in the above instance the store, the supplier, and the salespeople perceive themselves as better off through the use of PM's.

In December 1970, the Consumer's Union petitioned the FTC to outlaw the PM's on the grounds that they are inherently harmful and deceptive to the public. However, the FTC did not rule in favor of the Consumer's Union. Interestingly, the customer may not suffer from PM's. As we have seen, it may not be in his best interests to buy the less expensive merchandise. And the salesman may need the extra compensation before he will take the extra time to push an item that will usually not sell that easily. Otherwise, he may just sell what is easiest to sell, which may not be in the consumer's best interests at all. Thus a salary system has a bias in favor of easy sales that may be detrimental to the consumer. Self-service also has this bias. A straight commission system (e.g., 2 percent of sales) gives higher income to the salesperson for selling higher-priced merchandise. A PM system is therefore an additional incentive for salaried or commission salespeople to sell higher-priced, higher-profit merchandise.

At certain points the interests of the supplier and the retailer may clash through the use of PM's. Let us suppose that a supplier has a high-budget consumer advertising program. This advertising program is so effective that the store is forced to carry the items advertised even though they offer only a low percentage and a low absolute margin. In most instances, the manager of the profit center in question will use numerous techniques in an effort to have the salesmen trade the customers to the higher-margin merchandise. Usually the display, the advertising, and other factors will be developed so that it will be easy to trade the customer away to more profitable merchandise. The manufacturer who is traded away from will lose a great many sales under these conditions and knows it. He may try to introduce some type of PM program, which can be in the form of vacation trips and so forth, in order to start the sales coming his way again. This, of course, is against the store's desires. For this reason, if the manufacturer is not too worried about losing the account completely, or if he feels that the store would never dare throw a supplier out, he may offer PM's or other incentives to the retail salesmen without the retailer's knowledge.

PM's, often, are introduced to change the flow of merchandise from what it would have been otherwise. A manufacturer has good reason to influence the flow on behalf of his brand. A store has its own brands, and will in many cases try to do the same on behalf of them by offering incentives. Store managers also have an interest in getting rid of old merchandise that has somehow resisted the clutches of customers. It may be in their interest to offer incentives to the salesmen selling these and other unattractive items. These incentives may be: (a) in addition to a price markdown; (b) as a replacement for a price markdown; (c) as a complement to a price markdown.

### TO's

Some salesmen make a practice of turning difficult customers over to other salesmen. Thus if salesman A feels that he cannot close with a given customer, he may make a turnover (TO). This other salesman may be called the manager, assistant manager, senior salesman, or the like, and may indeed be a manager. Under certain conditions a TO system may be a method of systematic price discrimination in that the second person may have more price latitude than the first. In other words, if a manager is on straight salary, or a lower commission than the salesman who turned over the customer, the store can make the same profit per unit at a lower retail price. There is also no reason why a commission could not be split between the two salesmen. While TO's tend to be associated with customers who are being difficult, often over price, there may be many reasons why customers are turned over to other salesmen. One salesman may have specialized knowledge that he can bring to bear on a difficult problem raised by the customer, while two of the salesmen, perhaps called the assistant manager and manager, may be far more knowledgeable than the others. A retailer might even brag about the "team approach" that is evident in his salespeople's use of TO's.

### Sales Management at Retail

A manager of retail salesmen is concerned with many complex issues. He participates in the selection, training, motivation, firing, and compensation of salespeople. He tries to achieve the objectives of the store while fostering a psychologically healthy environment in which the various salespeople can thrive. He is responsible for scheduling their work so that the customer can be served while the employee lives an almost human life.

A major dimension of the sales management job in certain retail outlets is to direct the merchandise effort in a pattern that is reasonably consistent with the store's profit interest. As a general rule, the merchandise that is bought in the largest quantities must be sold. Of course, the merchant who buys the merchandise thinks that the customer will want it, and it is certainly easier to sell if he is right. The problem of integrating the sale and the purchase of merchandise is of great importance for most types of retailing. Some retailers put the buying and selling of merchandise under one executive, in order to minimize the problems of integrating these two functions.

### Summary

1. The retail salesperson is important to both retail and supply firms.

2. The retail selling job varies from industry to industry and from firm to firm.

3. By any standards, the selling position is important. But evaluating successful salespeople is not easy. Part of the problem is to identify the characteristics of successful salespeople. This may be done in the following ways.

    A. One may deductively outline the requirements of an effective salesperson for a specific job.

    B. One can examine the performance of successful salespeople.

    C. One can statistically analyze the characteristics of successful salespeople.

4. The attitude of the salesperson is influenced by the attitude of the customer. Three types of customers have been identified.

    A. The *enemy* regards a major purchase as a challenge to outsmart the retailer.

B. The *gentleman* manifests a genuine concern for the interests of the retailer.

C. The *lamb* is an uninformed and unsophisticated purchaser.

5. The selling process may be broken down as follows:

A. The approach;

B. Determining the customer's needs;

C. Presenting the merchandise;

D. Meeting objections;

E. The close;

F. Suggestion selling;

G. Developing goodwill after the sale.

6. Other important aspects of selling are:

A. Trading up customers to a higher price line;

B. Trading customers away from a low-profit item to a more profitable item, up or down in price;

C. PM's, or spiffs, which are incentives paid by the retailer or supplier to the retail salesperson as an incentive to sell specific merchandise;

D. TO's, or turnovers, in which a salesperson turns over a customer to another salesperson when the first salesperson feels that he or she cannot make a sale.

## Discussion Questions

1. Is the salesman a member of the channel of distribution?

2. Create a close for the selling of men's shirts.

3. What are some ways a salesperson might approach a customer?

4. Outline the selling process.

5. How would you ascertain the characteristics of a successful salesperson?

6. What is the attitude of the public toward salespeople? Why?

7. Consumer's Union petitioned the Federal Trade Commission in 1970 to eliminate PM's. What do you think of PM's? Or of payment by commission?

8. What is trading up?

9. How does trading up differ from trading away?

10. What are the pro's and con's of TO's?

## References

Michman, Ronald D., "Union Impact on Retail Management," *Business Horizons*, Spring 1967, pp. 79–84.

Oxenfeldt, Alfred R., "Customer Types and Salesman Tactics in Appliance Selling," *Journal of Retailing*, Winter 1963–64, pp. 9–15, 55–56.

Paul, Robert J., and Bell, Robert W., "Evaluating the Retail Salesman," *Journal of Retailing*, Summer, 1968, pp. 17–26.

Woolman, Lewis H., *Salesmanship Concepts and Strategies* (Belmont, Ca.: Wadsworth, 1970), p. 28.

## Further Reading

Cotham, James C., "The Case for Personal Selling," *Business Horizons*, April 1968, pp. 75–80.

Duncan, Delbert J., and Phillips, Charles F., *Retailing Principles and Methods* (Homewood, Ill.: Irwin, 1967).

Mayer, D., and Greenberg, H. M., "What Makes a Good Salesman?" *Harvard Business Review*, July–August, 1964, pp. 119–125.

Wingate, John B., "Personal Selling for the Years Ahead," in John B. Wingate and Arnold Corbin (eds.), *Changing Patterns in Retailing* (Homewood, Ill.: Irwin, 1956), pp. 243–249.

## Case History: *What Price Morality?*

Ken Chapman was the merchandise manager and principal purchasing agent for a leading major appliance chain. Ken regarded himself as basically a moral man, and indeed he was regarded as such by everyone in his organization. When Ken said something, you could count on it; he lived by his word—no small accomplishment in a business world permeated by politics. Although Ken was tough on suppliers, they tended to like him. He drove a hard bargain with them, but was personable and scrupulously lived up to his word.

One day Ken explained his merchandising philosophy to an assistant. First, you had to get customers into the store in some fashion. Second, you had to sell them something that was profitable for the store.

To get customers into the store Ken thought that you had to give them the illusion of great value. It had to be an illusion because no firm could consistently give substantially better value than another and stay in business—not, that is, unless he had developed a very unique business. Ken emphasized two ways of creating this illusion.

First, Ken developed comparative values: "Gigantic Washer Value, Formerly $239.99, Now $199.99!" To create comparative values, prices were put up and down regularly. Thus a week before special events, the prices were raised on the relevant items, if they were not at the higher price already. In addition, comparative values were established months in advance, so that items could be artificially priced in anticipation of future promotions.

The other way that Ken introduced the illusion of value was by promoting well-known brands at prices that would be perceived as low by the customers. Then it was the job of the salesman to sell most of the customers something more profitable to the store. Ken would buy other merchandise that would retail at about the same price and be profitable to the store. It was the salesman's job to sell the customer this other merchandise. And the customer might be perceived as better off as the result of the other purchase. For example, Ken would bring in closeouts of last year's models and sell these at about $20 under the advertised price of the current model but with a substantially large profit to the store.

The assistant replied that some people might find these policies dishonest. Ken replied that he knew they were dishonest by biblical standards, but most things in this world were. He also believed that most larger operations worked with these basic principles, and quite successfully so. He also felt that the principles had the following arguments in their favor.

"First," Ken said, "let us look at the consumer. Most consumers who come to the store need the item they're looking for. Washers and dryers aren't usually status symbols. Giving the customer a reason to buy simply induces customers to buy when they should. And my prices are competitive, I can promise you."

Ken went on to explain that comparison shopping indicated there were few differences among the aggressive chains in the prices at which these appliances were sold. Therefore, what harm was done by this little misrepresentation? The assistant shook his head and confessed he didn't know.

But Ken had not finished. Some customers, he said, liked to feel they are smarter than others; it was a kind of game. Few customers paid list prices for tires and other items, and nearly all of them realized it. If everyone were to get a sale price, then no one would get a sale price. However, if everyone felt better as a result of the sale price, then why not make them feel better?

The same, Ken argued, was true of someone who bought a bait-and-switch item. He might be getting an even better value than the advertised one, and presumably he feels he is or he would not buy the item. The job of the salesmen in Ken's stores was to make the customer feel that he was getting a much better buy by buying the more profitable item.

Thus Ken felt that the customer was probably better off being misled; he felt better, and he got as good or (probably) better value than he would otherwise. If Ken were asked why he did not advertise closeouts, he might offer several answers depending on the situation. First, the customer would not perceive the value to be as good as the closeouts in the advertisement. Many features are difficult to offer in an advertisement and have to be demonstrated on the floor. Second, the supplier might not pay for the advertising of last year's model. Third, the supplier might not permit the advertising of the closeout items. Moreover, by forcing his salesmen to sell into profitable patterns Ken could buy great values on closeouts from suppliers. Part of this value was passed on to the customer in the form of lower prices. The customers were sold these closeouts, and then Ken assaulted the market for new closeout values.

What Ken did not point out on this occasion (there were too many other employees within earshot) was that the store was also a party to the deception. The store was not only important to Ken; he really felt that it was important to the community. Who offered better service? Who stood behind the product better? Also, the store employed 35 salesmen, and they were well paid. In fact, it was the selling into a profitable pattern established by Ken that permitted them to be well paid. If they were only taking customers' orders, they would be worth almost nothing. Indeed, in stores that survived with an order-taking philosophy, just about nothing was what the salesmen got paid.

And what about the community? Wasn't it a party to the deception too? Ken felt that his actions raised the consumption function in that individual consumers in his area bought more than they would otherwise. Total consumption was therefore probably higher—an advantage from some interpretations of Keynesian economics. The main negative to the community was that some of the selling procedures were dishonest and might therefore damage it. But in Ken's perception the community itself was so dishonest that his absolute dishonesty was above the average level of honesty for the community and therefore had an improving effect. Furthermore, if he were completely honest, he would be out of a job and the firm would be out of business. Or so Ken thought, as he hurried out to lunch with a supplier.

### Discussion Questions

1. Is the dishonesty of Ken to the advantage of the community?

2. What would you do if you were in Ken's position? Could you establish selling patterns that would be both profitable and moral?

At a conference in January 1973, a group of speakers released the findings of a study of the future of general merchandising and retailing. The study, sponsored by the newspaper industry, used the so-called Delphi technique, named after the Delphic oracle of ancient Greece.

In the Delphi technique, experts in different places are asked to make guesses as to the likelihood that certain events will occur. They are then given a chance to compare their first guesses with those of their fellow experts, so that they can modify their opinions after reflection. As this process is repeated, the experts' judgments tend to move toward a consensus. At no stage do the participants meet.

During the first stage of the study, a dozen retail leaders were assembled at a conference center for a day and a half of questioning, discussion, and balloting on the issues and trends likely to affect retailing in the rest of this century. Out of this came a questionnaire to which another 105 top retailing executives responded. Seventy-three went on to complete two more questionnaires.

There was remarkably little change in their forecasts as they modified their initial judgments. In general, they exhibited a fairly high degree of confidence in their own predictions. The highlights of the forecast were as follows:

# Afterword — the Future of Retailing

## I. Economic Forces

*Event*   U.S. population will stop growing in size.

*Forecast*   No. The market will keep growing in actual numbers despite the decline in the birth rate.

*Event*   Sixty percent of U.S. households will have incomes of $15,000 or more (in 1972 dollars) compared to 25 percent today.

*Forecast*   Four out of five say yes, by 1987.

Reprinted, in slightly adapted form, by permission of the Newspaper Advertising Bureau, Inc.

*Event*  Poverty eliminated by negative income tax or other federal programs.

*Forecast*  Two-thirds say yes, within the coming decade.

*Event*  Fifty percent of men aged 30–34 will have some college education, compared to 33 percent today.

*Forecast*  Seventy-five percent say yes — and predict considerable impact on retailing.

*Event*  Pricing to include cost of disposing of goods and other effects on environment.

*Forecast*  Yes, by the 1980s, say 75 percent of panel, but with little effect on retailing.

## II. Social Forces

*Event*  Solution to be found for teenage unemployment in urban ghettos.

*Forecast*  Seventy-five percent say yes, but they lack confidence in their optimistic judgment.

*Event*  Massive government aid will revive central cities, to which the white middle class will then return.

*Forecast*  Half the panel think it may happen in this century. If it does, the consequences for retailing will be considerable.

*Event*  Percentage of population moving per year to rise to 25 percent (from 18 in 1972).

*Forecast*  Yes, by 1985 (actually, there was no recent trend in this direction).

## III. Employment
## Patterns and Store Hours

*Event*  Four-day work week.

*Forecast*  Eighty percent say yes, by the late 1980s, and predict considerable impact on store hours and personnel.

*Event*  Work week of 32 hours, down from 38.2 hours in 1972.

*Forecast*  Yes, by a large majority (87%), but with less impact on retailing than the four-day week.

*Event*  Sixty-five percent of woman aged 18–64 to be employed (52 percent in 1972).

*Forecast*  Eighty percent say yes, by 1987. This could upgrade women's fashions and encourage longer store hours, among other effects.

*Event*  Sunday openings legal in 95 percent of the country.

*Forecast*  Yes, by 1983, nearly all think.

*Event*  Twenty-four-hour, seven-day openings, at least in substores.

*Forecast*  Few think so.

*Event*  Department store labor costs down to 15 percent of operating expenses (19 percent in 1972).

*Forecast*  No, despite new techniques and new technology.

*Event*  Employee turnover down 20 percent.

*Forecast*  No — but many feel that sweeping changes must occur here if stores are to remain profitable.

## IV. Technological Innovations

*Event*  Fifty percent of U.S. households will be linked to cable television (8 percent in 1972).

*Forecast*  Yes, with two-way television communication by the early 1990s and revolutionary impact on merchandising and sales methods.

*Event*  Better use of computerized information to reverse centralized tactical decisions in chain operations.

*Forecast*  Yes, within 10 years. A substantial number (43 percent) believe this to be an area for immediate attention.

*Event*  Improvement of in-store man-machine systems will reduce both sales transaction time and customers' anxiety.

*Forecast*  Yes. Eighty percent say by 1985, and many say a start should be made now.

*Event*  Individual credit accounts will be eliminated and replaced by a national credit and banking system.

*Forecast*  Two out of three panelists say yes, by 1989. One result may be some erosion of store loyalty, but the reduction in store operating costs will be considerable.

*Event*  Central buying offices and facilities to grow.

*Forecast*  Yes. A majority say they will account for three-quarters of general merchandise bought by 1986.

## V. Store Operations

*Event*  Number of items carried per store will go down by 20 percent.

*Forecast*  No. But the panel believes this matter deserves action.

*Event*  Sales per net square foot 20 percent higher.

*Forecast*  Yes. Projected date is 1985.

*Event*  Self-service racks will double their present volume.

*Forecast*  Three of four panelists say yes, by 1990. The impact on shrinkage controls, store layouts, and fixtures will be considerable. There will be a 50 percent increase in sales of items sold in standardized packaging.

*Event*  Less floor space for high fashion.

*Forecast*  No, but more floor space set aside for free and flexible "swing areas."

*Event*  Branches to be specialty stores, rather than full-line.

*Forecast*  Two of three panelists say yes, while seven of 10 say it is a major development, and most believe it calls for immediate planning.

*Event*  Profit margins on most utilitarian items will shrink.

*Forecast*  Yes. Three of five panelists say this trend already has made considerable impact.

*Event*  No free home delivery.

*Forecast*  Yes, say 75 percent, by as early as 1981.

*Event*  Same volume of business handled by 25 percent fewer store units.

*Forecast*  No.

## VI. The Competitive Picture

*Event*  One-third of all general merchandise sales done outside the store.

*Forecast*  A significant minority (44 percent) see this by 1984, while many believe that sweeping changes are called for now.

*Event*  Furniture warehouse selling will increase its share of the market fourfold.

*Forecast*  Yes, according to three out of four. Eighty-two percent see a considerable impact, and seven of 10 feel department stores must respond.

*Event*  Discounters will do 25 percent of general merchandise business (15 percent in 1972).

*Forecast*  Sixty-two percent say yes, by 1986, but less than half see an immediate need for action by department stores.

*Event*  Emphasis on boutiques, specialty shops, in large stores to be increased.

*Forecast*  Yes, and quite soon, say 80 percent.

*Event*  Specialty stores to expand market share by 20 percent.

*Forecast*  Yes, say 3 of 5, because the big stores will seek shopping excitement at new suburban locations.

## VII. Service, Merchandise, Promotion

*Event*  Leasing of consumer durables up 50 percent.

*Forecast*  Three-quarters say yes, by 1986.

*Event*  Fifty percent of general merchandise sold will be under private labels.

*Forecast*  Only two of five panelists think this might happen.

*Event*  Further individualization of store images to appeal to distinct market segments.

*Forecast*  Yes. Three of four say this tendency will be evident by 1980.

*Event*  One-third of advertising to be pinpointed to specific consumer targets.

*Forecast*  Yes, say most on panel, and by 1982. But no increase was foreseen in the advertising-sales ratio.

*Event*  Services to represent 40 percent of all personal consumption expenditures.

*Forecast*  Eighty-seven percent say yes, by 1990. This trend is seen as very important.

*Event*   Consumers will pay higher markup for more personal service.

*Forecast*   Yes, according to three-quarters.

### Highlights and Conclusions

A substantial number of the retailers in this project felt that some immediate action should be taken in the following areas:

Shrinking profits should be revived through improvement in man-machine systems;

Retailers should take advantage of the steady trend toward a service-oriented society by offering more new and profitable services, by expanding the boutique concept to personalize customer service, and by developing branch stores as specialty shops. The department store concept of "one-stop shopping" might well give way to the "one-stop shopping center";

Retailers would have to face up to a steady increase in competition, and with it a reshuffling of the merchandise mix. Stores might eventually classify themselves more by what they sold than by how they bought, marked up, or sold it.

It seems fair to conclude that retailing is a business that shows great confidence as it faces the future. Retailers expect change but are also rather sure of their ability to live with it successfully. They will be dealing in years to come with a customer who is better disposed to trade up, more strongly oriented to high fashion and good taste, more inclined to pick and choose, more sophisticated and skeptical, and more deeply concerned to get information about the merchandise he or she buys. They expect to be selling to these customers in a more selective fashion, to sharpen the image of their stores, and to appeal to specific kinds of consumers—specific as to where they live and specific as to how they live.

### Case History:
### Who Are the Innovators?

After the results of the newspaper industry study had been presented, a group of friends got together.

Almost immediately the conversation got around to the presentation. The reactions of some (fictitious) members of the group were as follows:

Professor Lloyd Rucklin suggested that he did not really understand why analysts would go to department store retailers to estimate the future of the department store. Most observers believed that department stores were *anything* but innovators. Indeed, the noted merchandiser E. B. Weiss was on record as saying that he had as yet to discover any important retail innovation that had first been introduced by department stores during the past 50 years. Furthermore, the wheel of retailing and other theories suggested that key innovations were not likely to be introduced by the large, establishment-oriented companies. Indeed, most institutional innovations had been introduced by low-margin entrepreneurs. Leading retailers did not appear capable of innovating and therefore would probably miss the truly important innovations.

George Everett was a very successful investment advisor who specialized in the retail field. He had long since given up on the established retailers. The real action was with the new areas such as fabric houses, warehouse outlets, and most of all, George's real "baby"—the discount catalog showrooms. George had been following discount catalog showrooms for about four years. Indeed, about three years ago he had tried in vain to talk a leading hard goods manager into creating a discount catalog showroom. George observed that in the report they had just heard no mention was even made of this form, although its sales were estimated to be over $1 billion in 1972 and were projected at $3 billion in 1975. George was not sure that the omission made any difference anyway. After all, department stores would not know what to do with the innovation! One giant retailer had been considering this innovation for several years, but still was not sure that profits could be made with it. And this at a time when Wall Street was evaluating some of these new enterprises at more than 70 times earnings. The managements of traditional department stores, George mused, knew about the existence of the discount store back in 1948. However, none was capable of taking advantage of this information because the department store managements could not run discount stores, for whatever reason. However, George was really happy that the existing retailers were so inept in meeting competition. This had been a key factor in making him the millionaire that he was.

Morgan Cohen was the planning vice-president for a leading retail chain. Morgan stated that the newspaper industry study was truly outstanding. He believed the admonitions of his professor in college: the greatest benefits of planning were achieved by the *act* of planning, not by its results. Here, the key executives of various retail firms had gotten together and analyzed the future in some detail. The process itself would contribute substantially to the performance of these executives. Thus, while Morgan did not feel that the results of the study indicated brilliance, he believed that the executives who had participated in the study would benefit substantially.

George Olsen, the vice-president for marketing for a large discount chain, indicated that all projections, let alone the Delphi type, are so hazardous as to be almost worthless anyway. If one had started in 1910 and tried to predict the next 10 years, would one have predicted World War I? What good was the long-term projection if one could not predict such events? In 1920, would one have been capable of predicting the stock market crash of 1929? If not, why bother with long-term projections at all? In 1929, could one have projected the long economic depression, followed by another world war? Or the full employment after that war? Or the Korean War? Or Vietnam? Or Watergate? Furthermore, it is generally felt that no sages accurately predicted the civil rights movement, the war on poverty, women's liberation, and so forth. Therefore, long-term predictions of any

type were highly suspect. Therefore the predictions they had just heard were as good—and as bad—as any.

Mark Green was president of a leading department store. He did not offer his opinions, but several members of the group urged him on. Mark found the results very interesting and provocative. He felt that the background provided by the study would impart a greater depth to the decision making of his key executives. At least they would be asking more of the right questions. He could not be more appreciative towards the individuals who had made the study possible. Furthermore, he got all the information for nothing. What a bargain!

Mike Blaine was a sales promotion agent. He felt that the study was a great success, if only because apparently every leading retailer who had been asked to participate did participate. Therefore, no matter what the conclusions, they had to be accepted by the industry. It was an obvious psychological truth that if you repeat an individual's opinion back to him in different words, he will tend to accept them. Thus from a promotional point of view the study had to be well received.

### Discussion Questions

1. Which of these opinions of the study is closest to yours? Why?

2. Do you think the Delphi technique of prediction makes sense in an industry like retailing?

# Appendix A

## Suburban Movement and Suburban Stores

Two key changes in our society have been the movement to the suburbs by many who live in the city and the migration to the city of many who live in the country. For years these forces almost balanced out. Recently, however, migration to cities has declined, while the exodus to the suburbs has continued. As a result, there has been an absolute decline in the population of some of our cities.

Stores follow people and their purchasing power. One would therefore expect stores to emulate the migration of people to the suburbs. This has happened, although certain types of store have been affected more directly than others, and small cities have been affected differently than large cities. Such differences are examined in this appendix, for which the chief source has been the Census of Business data for 1958, 1963, and 1967 (the most recent Census of Business at the time this book was written). It should be noted that the data for these periods are not strictly comparable. One problem, as previously mentioned, is that stores change with time. Are the newer stores that carry drugs sufficiently like the old drugstores to permit meaningful comparison? For example, many drugstores have added different types of merchandise. To take another example, in recent years variety stores have raised the price lines that they carry so significantly that many customers may no longer recognize them as being the same type of store. Thus the changing character of retail institutions often makes meaningful comparisons problematic.

The geographic units also change. The unit for most of these analyses was the Standard Metropolitan Statistical Area (see Chapter 10). The number of SMSAs is increased over time as the areas change and as smaller areas grow in population. In the 1967 Census of Business the boundaries of many SMSAs had been changed from 1963, usually to add adjacent counties as demographic and economic considerations warranted. City boundaries also change over time.

The proportion of metropolitan area retail sales accounted for in the suburbs, i.e., outside the political boundaries of cities, in 1958, 1963, and 1967 were as follows:

|  | 1958 | 1963 | 1967 |
|---|---|---|---|
| All SMSAs | 36.0% | 42.8% | 45.0% |
| Sample SMSAs | 41.9% | 49.5% | 52.8% |

Source: The Suburbanization of Retail Trade (New York: Columbia Broadcasting System, 1970).

The trend toward the suburbs is clear, although the rate of increase between the respective periods has slowed even when allowance is made for the irregular intervals at which the Census of Business is conducted. In one study of 28 SMSAs from 1958 to 1963, the rate of increase in retail sales was 4 percent overall, 1.2 percent for the central cities, and 7.5 percent for the suburbs. In this sample, the annual increment in the suburbs was over six times the rate of the central city. During the years from 1963 to 1967, the overall retail sales for the same 28 SMSAs rose at an average annual rate of 6.2 percent—4.5 percent for the central cities and 7.9 percent for the suburbs. The rate of growth has declined for the suburbs. However, in the entire nine-year period the suburbs accounted for about 85 percent of the total growth, and in the 1963–67 period the suburbs claimed 65 percent of the growth.

The rate of suburbanization differed with the size of the metropolitan area. In the period from 1958 to 1967, the number of retail outlets located in the central cities of the "large" SMSAs, i.e., New York, Chicago, and Los Angeles, declined by about 19 percent while the number in the suburbs increased by 10 percent. In the "small" areas during the same period, the number of urban units declined by about 12 percent, while the number of stores doing business in the suburban communities increased by about 32 percent.*

The above analysis appears accurate for describing what happened from 1958 to 1967 and, probably, through 1970. The key question is what is going to happen in the coming years. It would appear that despite these trends, our society still has a great stake in the central city, and that substantial government efforts will be forthcoming to revive it.

### Suburbanization by Store Type

Overall statistics for a trend often mask basic changes that are occurring in the components of that trend. Here, a key element that bears separate examination is the variation among the different store categories—different, that is, mainly in terms of the type of product sold. Study of this variation will indicate if the trend to the suburbs is universal or dependent on the specific products involved.

**Department stores**    In the sample areas of the CBS study, the suburbs by 1958 accounted for 27 percent of the retail sales for department stores (including discount stores). By 1967, however, they had reached equality with the cities. Department store sales in the suburbs had increased 343 percent during the nine-year period but only 58 percent in the central cities. The central-city outlet had average sales of three times its suburban counterpart in 1958, but only one-and-one-half times its suburban counterpart in 1967. Over the nine-year period in the sample areas, the department store increased its share of the relevant market for general merchandise, apparel, home furnishings, and appliances from 40 percent in 1958 to 53 percent in 1967. The increase in the central cities was from

* The "small" areas, with populations of from 1 to 2 million, were Baltimore, Houston, Minneapolis–St. Paul, Dallas, Cincinnati, Milwaukee, Seattle, Atlanta, Buffalo, Anaheim–Santa Ana–Garden Grove, Kansas City, San Diego, Miami, Denver, San Bernardino–Riverside–Ontario, New Orleans, and Indianapolis. The study also covered "medium-sized" areas with populations of 2 to 5 million. These were Philadelphia, Detroit, Boston, San Francisco, Washington, Pittsburgh, St. Louis, and Cleveland.

Table A.1
Department store sales, by place, 1958–1967

| Size of met. area | Percent increase 1958–67 | | | Suburban sales as percent of total SMSA | |
| | Total SMSA | Central cities | Suburbs | 1958 | 1967 |
|---|---|---|---|---|---|
| All sample areas | 134% | 58% | 343% | 27% | 50% |
| Large areas | 142 | 71 | 307 | 30 | 51 |
| Medium-sized areas | 117 | 23 | 301 | 34 | 62 |
| Small areas | 146 | 78 | 552 | 14 | 38 |

Source: CBS, op. cit., p. 33.

42 percent to 50 percent, but from 33 to 55 percent in the suburban areas. Table A.1 offers some perspective on the sales changes.

**Food stores**    Over the years food stores have been growing larger in size but fewer in number. During the 1958–67 period, the total number of food stores in the sample area declined by over 20 percent. Most of this decline was experienced in the central city, where the store count declined by about one-third. Average sales per outlet increased by almost 80 percent.

The suburban food store is substantially larger than the one in the central city, although the percentage discrepancy did not change over the nine-year period. Sales of the suburban food store averaged about 60 percent higher. One might anticipate this because the central-city residents are on the whole less mobile and have lower incomes. In addition, the central-city areas are older and therefore offer fewer large lots for development. Table A.2 shows the sales changes for food stores.

Table A.2
Food store sales, by place, 1958–1967

| Size of met. area | Percent increase 1958–67 | | | Suburban sales as percent of total SMSA | |
| | Total SMSA | Central cities | Suburbs | 1958 | 1967 |
|---|---|---|---|---|---|
| All sample areas | 39% | 16% | 66% | 47% | 56% |
| Large areas | 33 | 16 | 58 | 42 | 50 |
| Medium-sized areas | 38 | 7 | 60 | 58 | 68 |
| Small areas | 51 | 22 | 92 | 41 | 52 |

Source: Ibid., p. 36.

Table A.3
Furniture store sales, by place, 1958–1967

| Size of met. area | Total SMSA | Percent increase 1958–67 | | | Suburban sales as percent of total SMSA | |
|---|---|---|---|---|---|---|
| | | Central cities | Suburbs | | 1958 | 1967 |
| All sample areas | 32% | 12% | 69% | | 35% | 44% |
| Large areas | 31 | 17 | 59 | | 34 | 42 |
| Medium-sized areas | 24 | −5 | 63 | | 42 | 56 |
| Small areas | 42 | 21 | 101 | | 26 | 37 |

Source: *Ibid., p. 39.*

Table A.5
Men's apparel store sales, by place, 1958–1967

| Size of met. area | Total SMSA | Percent increase 1958–67 | | | Suburban sales as percent of total SMSA | |
|---|---|---|---|---|---|---|
| | | Central cities | Suburbs | | 1958 | 1967 |
| All sample areas | 38% | 14% | 100% | | 28% | 40% |
| Large areas | 33 | 11 | 102 | | 25 | 37 |
| Medium-sized areas | 42 | 12 | 97 | | 36 | 50 |
| Small areas | 44 | 26 | 101 | | 24 | 34 |

Source: *Ibid., p. 45.*

**Furniture stores** The number of furniture stores decreased by about 10 percent between 1958 and 1967. In the central-city area there were about 25 percent fewer outlets in the latter year than in the earlier one. In the suburbs, however, the number of outlets increased by about 13 percent. By 1967 both areas had approximately the same number of furniture stores. Still, 56 percent of the furniture sales in the sample area in 1967 were accounted for by the inner city because these stores had larger sales per store.

Table A.3 indicates the sales change in furniture, although these figures are particularly biased because department store sales are not included. I say "particularly" because the problem of classification is present in most of the tables in this appendix.

**Women's apparel** There were somewhat fewer women's specialty stores in 1967 than in 1958. In 1967, about 55 percent of all women's specialty stores were located in the central city. This 55 percent of the outlets did 60 percent of the business. The sales changes are shown in Table A.4.

**Men's apparel** The city still dominates the market for men's clothing, accounting for 60 percent of the sales volume in 1967. Nevertheless, this represents a decline of 12 percent since 1958. The dominance of the central city in this category is probably due to the large number of men who work there. However, the number of men's clothing stores in the sample cities declined by about 40 percent, while the decrease in the suburbs was slightly over 10 percent. In 1967, 59 percent of the retail outlets in the central city were doing 60 percent of the business. This suggests that the average size differential in terms of volume per store was not large. The sales changes in men's apparel are shown in Table A.5.

**Shoe stores** Between 1958 and 1967, the number of specialty shoe stores conducting business in the city declined by about 30 percent. However, the number of outlets in suburban areas increased by about 5 percent. In 1958, about three out of five stores were operating in the city, but by 1967 the figures were about even. The average sales volume for the city store was higher than for the suburban store. The sales changes are shown in Table A.6.

Table A.4
Women's apparel stores sales, by place, 1958–1967

| Size of met. area | Total SMSA | Percent increase 1958–67 | | | Suburban sales as percent of total SMSA | |
|---|---|---|---|---|---|---|
| | | Central cities | Suburbs | | 1958 | 1967 |
| All sample areas | 29% | 12% | 67% | | 31% | 40% |
| Large areas | 25 | 15 | 49 | | 30 | 36 |
| Medium-sized areas | 30 | 2 | 74 | | 39 | 53 |
| Small areas | 37 | 16 | 106 | | 22 | 34 |

Source: *Ibid., p. 42.*

Table A.6
Shoe store sales, by place, 1958–1967

| Size of met. area | Total SMSA | Percent increase 1958–67 | | | Suburban sales as percent of total SMSA | |
|---|---|---|---|---|---|---|
| | | Central cities | Suburbs | | 1958 | 1967 |
| All sample areas | 38% | 14% | 82% | | 35% | 46% |
| Large areas | 32 | 17 | 61 | | 34 | 42 |
| Medium-sized areas | 42 | 1 | 95 | | 44 | 60 |
| Small areas | 46 | 22 | 116 | | 25 | 37 |

Source: *Ibid., p. 48.*

### Table A.7
#### Automotive dealer sales, by place, 1958–1967

| Size of met. area | Total SMSA | Percent increase 1958–67 Central cities | Suburbs | Suburban sales as percent of total SMSA 1958 | 1967 |
|---|---|---|---|---|---|
| All sample areas | 79% | 44% | 118% | 48% | 58% |
| Large areas | 71 | 43 | 97 | 52 | 60 |
| Medium-sized areas | 79 | 33 | 113 | 58 | 69 |
| Small areas | 90 | 53 | 170 | 32 | 46 |

Source: *Ibid., p. 51.*

### Table A.9
#### Restaurant sales, by place, 1958–1967

| Size of met. area | Total SMSA | Percent increase 1958–67 Central cities | Suburbs | Suburban sales as percent of total SMSA 1958 | 1967 |
|---|---|---|---|---|---|
| All sample areas | 53% | 33% | 91% | 34% | 43% |
| Large areas | 45 | 28 | 82 | 31 | 39 |
| Medium-sized areas | 50 | 25 | 84 | 41 | 51 |
| Small areas | 71 | 49 | 119 | 32 | 41 |

Source: *Ibid., p. 57.*

**Automotive dealers**   A higher proportion of the automotive business is done in suburban areas than of most other types of retailing. Fifty-eight percent of the sample areas' automotive dealers were located in the suburbs. The total number of automotive dealers in the sample communities rose by roughly 9.5 percent between 1958 and 1967, while the number located in the related central cities declined by more than 10 percent. The average dealer in the suburbs did a bit smaller volume of sales than did his counterpart located in the city. The sales changes of automotive dealers are shown in Table A.7.

**Drugstores**   The number of drugstores in the sample cities declined by about 25 percent over the nine-year period. In the same period, the drugstore count increased by about 25 percent in the suburban areas. The net result was a decline of 7 percent in the total number of units. The average sales of the suburban stores were about 12 percent

higher than those of the central-city stores. The sales changes are shown in Table A.8.

**Restaurants**   Restaurants located in the city declined about 10 percent in number. They increased in the suburbs by some 18 percent. City restaurants do slightly more volume than suburban ones. The sales changes of restaurants are shown in Table A.9.

**Building materials**   This branch of retailing consists mainly of hardware, lumber, and building materials. The number of outlets in these areas declined about 37 percent in the city and by about half that in the suburbs, to produce an overall decline of about 27 percent. The sales changes of building materials retailers are shown in Table A.10.

### Table A.8
#### Drug store sales, by place, 1958–1967

| Size of met. area | Total SMSA | Percent increase 1958–67 Central cities | Suburbs | Suburban sales as percent of total SMSA 1958 | 1967 |
|---|---|---|---|---|---|
| All sample areas | 58% | 27% | 100% | 42% | 53% |
| Large areas | 56 | 29 | 97 | 39 | 50 |
| Medium-sized areas | 56 | 19 | 92 | 51 | 63 |
| Small areas | 62 | 31 | 119 | 35 | 47 |

Source: *Ibid., p. 54.*

### Table A.10
#### Building materials sales, by place, 1958–1967

| Size of met. area | Total SMSA | Percent increase 1958–67 Central cities | Suburbs | Suburban sales as percent of total SMSA 1958 | 1967 |
|---|---|---|---|---|---|
| All sample areas | 5% | −14% | 20% | 56% | 64% |
| Large areas | −1 | −17 | 12 | 55 | 63 |
| Medium-sized areas | 8 | −14 | 19 | 67 | 74 |
| Small areas | 9 | −10 | 30 | 47 | 57 |

Source: *Ibid., p. 60.*

Table A.11
Appliance store sales, by place, 1958–1967

| Size of met. area | Total SMSA | Central cities | Suburbs | Suburban sales as percent of total SMSA 1958 | 1967 |
|---|---|---|---|---|---|
| | | Percent increase 1958–67 | | | |
| All sample areas | 42% | 13% | 90% | 38% | 50% |
| Large areas | 19 | −2 | 54 | 38 | 49 |
| Medium-sized areas | 62 | 13 | 118 | 47 | 63 |
| Small areas | 64 | 38 | 133 | 27 | 39 |

Source: *Ibid.*, p. 62.

**Appliance stores**   The number of appliance dealers in the city was down by more than 25 percent during the study period. In the suburbs there was a 6 percent increase in the number of units, which balanced out to a decline in the overall number of about 10 percent. The sales changes of appliance stores are shown in Table A.11.

## References

Columbia Broadcasting System, *The Suburbanization of Retail Trade* (New York: CBS, Inc., 1970).

# *Appendix B*

## *Some Retail Economic Variables in Perspective*

This section, developed from a study by David Schwartzman,* offers some historical perspective on a number of key variables related to retailing.

**Constant-dollar sales per man-hour of labor**  This figure grew 84 percent from 1929 to 1963. The average rate of increase in output per man-hour for the period was 1.7 percent.

**Quality of labor**  Over the period from 1929 to 1963, the quality of labor in retail trade declined by 0.6 percent per year. The index of quality of labor combines an estimate of the change in retail trade earnings relative to earnings in the economy as a whole, and a measure of the change in the quality of employed persons in all industries combined. The latter is based on age, sex, and education. Schwartzman's observations indicate that the female fraction of the retail labor force increased more than in other industries, and that the teen-age fraction increased in retailing while it in fact declined in other industries. Table B.1 shows the annual rate of decline by retail sector.

**Capital growth**  From 1929 to 1963 the annual rate of capital growth was 1.8 percent. Capital is here defined to include cash, notes and accounts receivable, inventory, and depreciable assets gross of depreciation allowance. Table B.2 outlines the growth of capital by store type. It will be seen that the rate of growth in capital per man-

---

* Schwartzman, David, *The Decline of Service in Retail Trade* (Pullman, Wash.: Washington State University Press, 1971).

Table B.1
*Average annual rates of change of quality of labor and sales per man-hour in retail trade and eight types of store, 1929–63*

|  | Quality of labor (% p.a.) | Sales per man-hour (% p.a.) |
|---|---|---|
| Retail trade | −.6 | 1.7 |
| General merchandise stores | −.4 | 1.9 |
| Food stores | .1 | 2.6 |
| Automotive dealers | −.3 | 2.0 |
| Gasoline stations | −.6 | 3.1 |
| Apparel stores | −1.2 | .9 |
| Furniture stores | −.9 | 2.3 |
| Eating and drinking places | −.3 | 1.0 |
| Drug stores | −.3 | 2.0 |

Source: *Adapted from Schwartzman, op. cit., p. 54.*

Table B.2
*Average annual rate of growth of capital, man-hours, and capital per man-hour in retail trade and ten types of store, 1929–63*

|  | Capital (% p.a.) | Man-hours (% p.a.) | Capital per man-hour (% p.a.) |
|---|---|---|---|
| Retail trade | 1.8 | 1.1 | .7 |
| Lumber, building materials, hardware, farm equipment dealers | 1.5 | .2 | 1.3 |
| General merchandise group stores | 1.2 | .4 | .8 |
| Food stores | 1.8 | .4 | 1.4 |
| Automotive dealers | 2.0 | 1.5 | .6 |
| Gasoline service stations | 3.7 | 2.6 | 1.1 |
| Apparel, accessory stores | .6 | .7 | −.1 |
| Furniture, home furnishings, equipment stores | 1.4 | .7 | .6 |
| Eating, drinking places | 3.4 | 2.8 | .6 |
| Drug stores, proprietary stores | 1.3 | .8 | .5 |
| Other retail stores | 1.9 | .8 | 1.1 |

Source: *Ibid., p. 67.*

hour was positive for every type of store with the exception of apparel stores. A large part of the growth of capital per unit of labor took the form of an increase in inventory.

**Transaction size**    As income rises; as price increases for whatever reason; as the mobility of the customer increases; it may be anticipated that the consumer will spend more dollars per transaction. This increase in transaction size can be considered a key element in the development of such retail institutions as the supermarket. An index of transaction size, deflated for price increases, is presented in Table B.3.

Table B.3
*Transaction size for seven types of store, 1929–63*

| Store-Type | Index of transaction (size 1963 on base 1929) |
|---|---|
| General merchandise stores | 106 |
| Automotive dealers | 145 |
| Gasoline stations | 223 |
| Apparel stores | 83 |
| Furniture stores | 170 |
| Eating, drinking places | 100 |
| Drug stores | 224 |

Source: *Ibid., p. 151.*

# *Appendix C*

## *Channel Control as a Two-Party Problem*

This discussion, essentially a supplement to Chapter 3, focuses on the large retailer's relationship to the channel, although some nonretailing aspects are also involved. The discussion is further limited to consideration of a single channel in which there are only two important members. Those other than the two important members, whether wholesaler or manufacturer, may be regarded for the purposes of this discussion as being facilitating members. Thus control of the channel is envisioned as a two-party problem, although the second party may be relatively powerless.

The topic of interest is, of course, the potential economic power of the various participants in the channel struggle. The models specify variables that affect the relationships among other variables. Other problems, including those of measurement and verification, are not resolved. A member of a channel is defined as having potential economic control when its potential economic power with regard to the other important unit exceeds a specified level. The net potential economic power (NPEP) is the result of the interaction between the potential economic power of the store with regard to the vendor (PEPR) and the potential economic power of the vendor with regard to the store (PEPV). Whether net potential economic power ever becomes control by one member of a channel depends on the degree of the difference between PEPR and PEPV as well as on various noneconomic factors.

### PEPV

One of the more difficult aspects of quantifying the potential economic power of the store in relation to the supplier or other member of the channel is deciding on the range of the relevant product relationships. With regard to the nonretail channel member, should the relevant unit be item, product line, entire brand, corporation, or what? With regard to the store, should the relevant unit be mer-

chandise subclassification, buyer, department, store, or corporation? All occasions will not call for the same type of division. Here, the relevant supplier unit would appear to be brand within a subclassification — for example, General Electric television sets.

$$PEPV \text{ is defined as: } \frac{CB - CA}{TCR}$$

All these terms are defined in the glossary. In practice, they would be estimates of the decision maker.

One might well ask why there should be any substantial difference between the contribution of one accepted supplier and the alternatives. After all, such a supplier can reduce his contribution to the store in a variety of ways. He can increase his price to the retailer, reduce the number of specials or deals per period of time, and so on. Suppliers, however, are more interested in maximizing their long-term profits than in maximizing control. In addition, the following obstacles may arise:

1. Suppliers may be forced by operational and legal requirements to use the same marketing mix (more or less) for a brand in many stores rather than to raise and lower selectively each element of the mix in order to accommodate a particular retailing situation.

2. Becoming of no essential short-term worth to the retailer, a condition that exists if the contribution difference $(CB - CA)$ is zero, does not appear to be the most advantageous long-term position for a supplier of a brand. Since the smaller the contribution difference, the greater the risk of losing the account, suppliers may be willing to pay for a lower risk level.

3. If a store has substantial economic power with regard to a supplier, the supplier may be seeking to increase the contribution difference in order to achieve a balance or perhaps influence certain other factors within the channel.

4. Control may be something that is worth paying for. A large difference between contribution to overhead of the retailer in the allocated space and contribution of items replacing the brand may be the price that the nonretailer must pay for the benefits of control. One such benefit might be lower costs through the remainder of the channel.

5. Power at the margin may be useful for adding items to a product line or adopting a unique package shape, and power at the margin is usually possible only if an average difference exists.

### CDM

The contribution difference $(CB - CA)$ of the smallest unit of space that might reasonably be eliminated for a given brand in a subclassification is the contribution difference at the margin, $(CDM)$. If the $CDM$ is negative, the store will make additional short-term profit by dropping some or all of the supplier's line. If the $CDM$ is positive and has been always diminishing with additional space, the supplier has a positive contribution difference for all aspects of the product line. A large $CDM$ would tend to (but need not) indicate that a related new product might be introduced, that a larger or more awkward container might be tolerated by the retailer, or that more space might be allocated to the line.

For example, suppose that a manager of a food store decided that half a foot was the smallest reasonable amount by which the space allocated to a specific brand of catsup could be reduced. Suppose, too, that he estimated the additional contribution to overhead for one week of that last half a foot for the specific brand was, all factors considered, $25. Thus $CB$ in this example would be $25. In this instance, let us say the manager estimated that the largest contribution increment, all factors considered, could be attained by allocating this footage to increasing the space of canned peas. If the estimated contribution of the extra half a foot given to canned peas for the week $(CA)$ was $15, the specific brand of catsup would have a contribution difference at the margin $(CDM)$ of $10, with the attendant advantages described above.

### PEPR

$PEPR$ is defined as $\dfrac{CVW - CVWO}{TCV}$

The above terms are described in the glossary. $CVW$ and $CVWO$ are developed by considering the following factors:

1. The merchandise sold to the retailer in the brand subclassification contributes to the overhead of the supplier.

2. Certain other stores (not part of the chain) select items or lines because another store has purchased them. If a store influences the selection of merchandise by other stores, and the bargaining parties perceive this as so, the influencing store will receive what might be called bargaining credit for the purchases made by these stores. One such relationship might be termed *satellite*, another *parasitic*. A satellite store selects merchandise purchased by another store and anticipates maintaining approximately the same price for it. A store may follow a more prestigious store because when the latter selects a product line, the line may thereby achieve legitimation in the eyes of the consumer. In addition to legitimizing the brand, a prestigious store may increase acceptance of the prices charged for that brand. The probability of substantial advertising by a large store may also induce a buyer to "buy with" a more prestigious store. Further, prestigious retail units often have buyers whose talents are respected and followed by other retailers. In the parasitic relationship, on the other hand, one store may simply trade off the prices of another. Certain stores—discount stores, for instance—may select particular items because they are carried at higher prices by other outlets. If the major store or stores drop a supplier line, parasitic outlets may also drop it. Where a discernible relationship exists, the store's $PEPR$ will be increased.

### Combining PEPR and PEPV to Create NPEP

Each individual computation in the development of $PEPR$ and $PEPV$ appears feasible in the sense that subjective estimates may be made. However, the problem of selecting the range of product and time relationships of the two must be satisfactorily resolved before any meaningful statement can be made on the relative economic power of each.

The following flow chart indicates the relationships in question:

$$\frac{CB - CA}{TCR} = PEPV \rightarrow NPEP \leftarrow PEPR = \frac{CVW - CVWO}{TCV}$$

# *Appendix D*

## *Some Aspects of the Retail Method*

### Markdowns

The retail method has evolved in many different ways over the years. One of its more controversial aspects is the taking of markdowns. For example, if a men's store reduces the price of a suit from $70 to $60, a markdown of $10 must be taken so that the retail book value of the inventory will reflect the decision. In the three-part method of developing the gross margin, explained in Chapter 8, markdowns were not considered in the determination of the markup and therefore in the determination of the cost percentage. This resulted in a higher initial markup and a correspondingly lower cost percentage. The ending inventory was therefore valued lower than it would have been with a lower initial markup and a higher cost percentage. If most markdowns relate to merchandise that has already been sold, this method of creating the cost percentage brings the remaining inventory back to an approximate cost value.

The practice of not including markdowns but including additional markups in the creation of the cost percentage has led to use of the term "markup cancellation," as distinct from "markdown." The logic of including additional markups in the compilation of initial markup is clear. A merchant might raise the price of an item that cost him $18 from $30 to $40. If one used a cost complement of 60 percent for the higher retail price, this particular item would be listed in the inventory as having cost $24. In other words, one could increase the cost value of the inventory by marking merchandise up *after* it had been brought into the system at its cost and retail prices.

The effect of not including the markdown in the creation of the cost complement may be seen in the following example. If our $30 item is marked down to $25, the new cost reflected in the inventory would be $15, with a cost complement of 60 percent. Thus the cost of the item for valuation purposes is reduced. Since goods are usually marked down because they are not what the customer wants, the cost base probably ought to be lowered when a markdown is taken.

Some observers would dispute the omission of markdowns from the creation of the cost percentage. If markdowns are used for this purpose, inventory costs are not reduced when retail prices are marked down; rather the effect of the markdowns is felt as the goods are sold, because the markdown merchandise is considered in stock. If markdowns do not enter into the cost percentages, the cost of all markdowns is charged to the month in which they are taken. In many cases, of course, this is when markdowns are sold. The following simplified example will illustrate the difference between the two methods.

Table D.1
*Effect on inventory costs, etc., when markdowns are/are not included in creation of cost percentage (in dollars)*

| | Markdown not not included in cost percentage | | Markdown included in cost percentage | |
| --- | --- | --- | --- | --- |
| | Cost | Retail | Cost | Retail |
| Beginning inventory | 600.00 | 1,000.00 | 600.00 | 1,000.00 |
| Purchases | 1,570.00 | 2,616.60 | 1,570.00 | 2,616.60 |
| Merchandise available for sale | 2,170.00 | 3,616.60 | 2,170.00 | 3,616.60 |
| Less markdowns | | — | | 175.00 |
| Retail relevant to cost percentage | | 3,616.60 | | 3,441.60 |
| Initial markup | 40% | | 36.95% | |
| Cost percentage | 60% | | 63.05% | |
| Sales | | 670.00 | | 670.00 |
| Markdowns | | 175.00 | | — |
| Ending inventory at retail | | 2,771.60 | | 2,771.60 |
| | 3,616.60 − 670.00 − 175.00 | | 3,441.60 − 670.00 | |
| Ending inventory at cost | | 1,662.96 | | 1,747.49 |
| | 2,771.60 × 60% | | 2,771.60 × 63.05% | |
| Cost of sales | | 507.04 | | 442.51 |
| | 2,170.00 − 1,662.96 | | 2,170.00 − 1,747.49 | |
| Gross profit | | 162.96 | | 247.49 |
| | 670.00 − 507.04 | | 670.00 − 422.51 | |

It is obvious from Table D.1 that profits for the first year are higher when the markdowns are included in the cost complement. After the first year, however, the difference in profits would not be large because the beginning inventory value for the second and subsequent years would reflect this condition. Indeed, the differences in inventory value would continue over the years.

### Discounts

Most stores do not deduct cash discount offered by suppliers to arrive at a net cost for a given merchandise shipment. Rather, they periodically include cash discounts in the departmental profit-and-loss statements, as a part of gross margin. Part of the problem is that one is never sure that cash discounts will in fact be earned. The effect of taking cash discounts in this manner is to value the inventory on a gross cost basis.

### Averaging

The cost value inventory is needed for the preparation of financial gross margin and related reports. The closing retail value of the inventory is converted to cost by means of an average relationship between the cost and retail of all the merchandise handled within the relevant classification. In the retail method, it is assumed that the final inventory is divided in the same manner as the purchases plus the initial inventory. There is no problem if the markup for the merchandise within the department or classification is the same or close to the same. However, where variations in markup exist, substantial misstatements of inventory value are likely.

Other things remaining the same, when the ending inventory comprises a higher proportion of higher markup goods than the figures from which the cost complement is developed, the retail method will tend to overstate the closing value of the inventory. Because in most retail operations lower markup merchandise can be expected to sell faster in relation to stock than higher markup merchandise, the retail method will tend to overvalue the cost of the inventory. First-year profits under the retail method should therefore be overstated, as the cost value of the beginning inventory will be created by the cost method, and the cost value of the ending inventory will be created by the retail method. In subsequent years, however, the retailer will be dealing with two inflated inventories, so that he will find the effect on profits more difficult to evaluate. Clearly, however, the effect is adverse when a firm is taxed on the value of its inventories, as in the state of California. It also follows that merchandise areas in which the price of selected items has been lowered as part of an aggressive price policy will show higher profits in the beginning period because the value of the inventory has been overstated. These elements of the retail method will be made clearer by the following examples.[*]

### Example: *Department A*

Imagine a department that sells only two items. Item L (for low markup) has a markup of 30 percent and sells three times its inventory level for the period. Item H (for high markup) has a markup of 40 percent and sells twice its inventory level for the period. This situation can be analyzed as follows:

| Opening inventory | Cost | Retail | Cost percentage |
|---|---|---|---|
| Item L | $ 70 | $100 | 70% |
| Item H | $ 60 | $100 | 60% |
| Total: | $130 | $200 | 65% |
| | | | |
| Purchases | | | |
| Item L—(3 times) | $210 | $300 | |
| Item H—(2 times) | $120 | $200 | |
| Total: | $330 | $500 | 66% |
| | | | |
| Total goods available for sale | $460 | $700 | 65.7% |
| Less: Sales | | $500 | |
| Ending inventory at retail | | $200 | |
| Cost   $131.40 | | | |

Thus while we know that the actual cost of the inventory in the above example should be $130.00, the retail method has given a cost of $131.40. It is interesting to note that if this procedure is continued in exactly the same manner for subsequent years, the value of the inventory varies thus:

| | |
|---|---|
| End year 2 | $131.82 |
| End year 3 | $131.94 |
| End year 4 | $131.98 |
| End year 5 | $131.99 |

---

[*] Adapted from a presentation by Robert Kahn, CMC, to the Society of Auditor-Appraisers, June 28, 1969.

Thus the bias increases, but at a substantially reduced rate. As the procedure is repeated, the cost value of the inventory will be nearly $132. But it will never reach $200 × .66, or the value of the cost percentage of the purchases times the retail dollar value of the ending inventory.

## Example: *Department B*

Department B is just like Department A except that the manager is very alert and accepts one special order for item S. Since he incurs no extra cost in processing this special order, he sells the item at a relatively low margin. This leads to the following results:

| Opening inventory | | Cost | Retail | Cost percentage |
|---|---|---|---|---|
| Item L | | $ 70 | $100 | 70% |
| Item H | | $ 60 | $100 | 60% |
| | Total: | $130 | $200 | 65% |
| | | | | |
| Purchases | | | | |
| Item L | | $210 | $300 | |
| Item H | | $120 | $200 | |
| Item S | | $150 | $200 | |
| | Total: | $480 | $700 | 68.6% |
| | | | | |
| Total goods available for sale | $610 | $900 | 67.8% | |
| Less: Sales | | | $700 | |
| Ending inventory at retail | | | $200 | |
| Cost   $135.60 | | | | |

Thus while we know that the inventory in this case would be $130.00 in actual cost, the retail method has given a value of $135.60 because of a low-markup extra that is not proportionately represented in the ending inventory.

## Example: *Department C*

Department C is like Department B except that the manager has decided to promote a special item, item P (for promotion). He buys $80 worth of this item and sells it out in two days at $100, that is, at a markup of 20 percent.

Since he does not incur extra costs because of this sale, he feels that the store is better off. The results look as follows:

| Opening inventory | | Cost | Retail | Cost percentage |
|---|---|---|---|---|
| Item I | | $ 70 | $ 100 | 70% |
| Item H | | $ 60 | $ 100 | 60% |
| | Total: | $130 | $ 200 | 65% |
| | | | | |
| Purchases | | | | |
| Item L | | $210 | $ 300 | |
| Item H | | $120 | $ 200 | |
| Item S | | $150 | $ 200 | |
| Item P | | $ 80 | $ 100 | |
| | Total: | $560 | $ 800 | 70% |
| | | | | |
| Total goods available for sale | $690 | $1,000 | 69% | |
| Less: sales | | | 800 | |
| Ending inventory at retail | | | $ 200 | |
| Cost   $138 | | | | |

Thus while we know that the inventory in this case should be $130 in actual cost, the retail method develops a value of $138 to give an overstatement of 5.8 percent. The reason for such overstatements is clear: the retail method assumes that the mixture of the markups in the ending inventory is the same as in the purchases plus the opening inventory. When this assumption is not correct, the value of the ending inventory will only approach the cost version in unusual cases.

Many other averages are used in the retail method; they have all the usual disadvantages of averages plus the risk of bias. A good example is *maintained markup* (that is, dollar sales minus the cost of goods sold, divided by dollar sales): if used as a percentage, it will be biased because of the incorrect inventory figure. The initial markup is not biased in this way, but it, too, has all the limitations of an average and has been blamed for many of the inadequacies of the retail method. Thus merchants seeking a higher initial markup have been accused of setting high markup as a goal in and of itself, and forgetting that it can be far more profitable to sell a great deal of merchandise at a lower price. In any case, the various averages referred to here are provided very rapidly in most large retail systems, so that top management gets rapid feedback from operations and can watch trends over time.

# Glossary

*Belly sizes* — The sizes that one sells most of (from "bell-shaped curve," i.e., the normal distribution).

*CA* — The contribution of the items that would, in the last of a sequence of possible chain reactions, replace the deleted element of the brand.

*CB* — The brand contribution to retailer overhead in the allocated space for a specific time period.

*CDM* — The contribution difference *(CB − CA)* of the smallest reasonable unit of space that might be eliminated for a given brand in a subclassification for the time period utilized in the creation of *CB* and *CA*.

*Central place* — That area in which the most types of goods are sold.

*Commission departments* — Those departments of a retail enterprise in which the salesperson derives the major part of his or her income from commissions on sales.

*Consumer panel* — A specific group of people whose behavior as consumers is examined over time by a researcher.

*Customer segmentation* — The act of classifying customers in various ways, instead of regarding them as homogeneous.

*CVW* — The contribution to overhead of the supplying firm if the large retailer purchases the merchandise of the brand subclassification utilized in the construction of *PEPV* during the same time period as *CA*.

*CVWO* — The contribution to overhead of the supplying firm if the large retailer does not purchase the merchandise of the brand subclassification utilized in the construction of *PEPV* in the same time period as *CA*.

*Differential pricing* — A method of pricing by which the decision maker takes an established point on a given demand curve for a successful item, and then asks what is the difference between the item to be priced and the established item.

*Direct profit* — Profit that excludes fixed costs.

*Discount rate* — The percentage by which the value of an asset is reduced, over time on a yearly basis.

*Disposable income* — Income that actually gets into the hands of consumers and is left there for them to dispose of.

*Economies of scale* — Economies that result from variations in the size of the enterprise. Costs per unit of sale may well decrease as the size of the enterprise increases. In retailing, two aspects of size are of particular interest: size of store and buying power.

*Equity* — The stockholders' dollar interest in the firm.

*Expected value* — The product of each value, $x$, and the probability that $x$ will assume that value, summed for all variables, e.g., for both $x$ and $y$.

*Facing* — A stock shelf unit extending the width of the unit and to the top and back of the display case. Thus a facing for a can of nuts, for instance, might be four cans high and four cans deep.

*Gross national product (GNP)* — The sum of all a nation's final products, such as consumption goods and gross investment.

*Horizontal competition* — Competition on the same level of the channel of distribution, as when one retail organization competes with another.

*Imputed interest* — The rates charged to departments for assets used, whether money is borrowed to obtain the assets or not. The idea is to make decision makers aware that assets cost something.

*Joint profits* — In the sense used in this text, the combined profits of the buyer and seller.

*Judgment sampling* — The selection of a sample or samples without giving each element of the population a known probability of being selected. Thus if the population consists of people, they will be sampled primarily in accordance with the judgment of the research, not the laws of probability.

*Loss leader*—An item that is priced at, near, or below cost in order to induce customers to come into the store.

*Mathematical model*—A simplification of reality based on mathematical relationships.

*Mean*—The sum of the individual values divided by the number of elements to which the values are attributed. Also known as the *arithmetic mean.*

*Median*—The value of the middle item in any array of data containing an odd number of items; also the value of a variable that both exceeds half the observations and is exceeded by half.

*Mod look*—An informal but elegant style of clothing for young adults, both male and female, that was introduced into the United States from Great Britain in the mid-1960s.

*Mode*—The value in a set of data that occurs with the greatest frequency.

*Moving average*—An average that is constantly recalculated as new readings are obtained. For example, a six-month moving average adds the new period and drops the old as time passes, always keeping an average based on the last six months.

*NPEP*—The net potential economic power that results from the interaction between the economic power of the retailer and the economic power of the supplier.

*Oligopoly*—A market is represented as an oligopoly when there are few sellers.

*Opportunity costs*—The costs of not doing something else, i.e., of the opportunities foregone.

*Out-of-pocket expenses*—Money actually paid out for some purpose.

*Perfect competition*—A state of the market in which no participant controls a big enough part of the market to have an influence on the market price.

*PEPR*—The potential economic power of the retailer with regard to the supplier. It is expressed by: $\dfrac{CVW - CVWO}{TCV}$.

*PEPV*—The potential economic power of the vendor or supplier with regard to the store. It is expressed by: $\dfrac{CB - CA}{TCR}$.

*Private brand*—Essentially, any brand that is not advertised heavily by its manufacturer, but often applied to brands that are "private" to (i.e., exclusively manufactured for and sold by) large retailers. Although such retail brands are often extensively advertised by the retailer, most observers would classify them as private.

*Proxy variable*—A variable used in place of another. This is done usually because the variable not used cannot be accurately estimated, although its relationship to the proxy variable is known at least to a degree thought useful in dealing with the problem.

*Psychographics*—The study of the effects of nondemographic variables, such as attitudes and values, on consumer behavior.

*Rack jobbers*—Wholesalers who operate the merchandise aspects of small areas (usually goods displayed on racks) for retailers.

*Retail price maintenance*—The maintenance of prices at the retail level by the suppliers. This can be done in some states under fair trade laws. It may be done in any state by selecting a compatible retailer, i.e., one who will maintain prices.

*Scrambled merchandising*—A term used to refer to the disregard shown by some retailers for traditional store classifications, e.g., drugstores that also sell housewares, liquor, and other merchandise not traditionally sold in drugstores.

*Sequential sampling*—Taking samples in stages (see W. Edwards Deming, *Sample Design in Business Research,* New York: Wiley, 1960, pp. 270–271).

*Standard deviation*—The positive square root of the variance.

*Stock outs*—Instances of being out of stock.

*TCR*—The total contribution to overhead of the merchandise subclassification of the store, including *CB.*

*TCV*—The total contribution to overhead of the brand subclassification for the supplying firm, including the contribution relating to *CVW.*

*Trickle-down theory*—In retailing, a theory suggesting that fashion is disseminated from the upper to the lower classes.

*Value added*—In the value-added approach, when calculating the contribution of a firm or industry to society, the analyst excludes purchases of materials and services from other firms. Thus, in the creation of various economic measures, it is possible to avoid counting the same materials and services twice.

*Variance*—The squared deviations of the individual values from their mean. The variance is the standard deviation squared.

# Index